OXFORD WORL

GEORGE BERN.

Major Cultural Essays

Edited with an Introduction and Notes by
DAVID KORNHABER

OXFORD
UNIVERSITY PRESS

OXFORD

UNIVERSITY PRESS

Great Clarendon Street, Oxford, OX2 6DP,
United Kingdom

Oxford University Press is a department of the University of Oxford.
It furthers the University's objective of excellence in research, scholarship,
and education by publishing worldwide. Oxford is a registered trade mark of
Oxford University Press in the UK and in certain other countries

First published as an Oxford World's Classics paperback 2021

Impression: 1

British Library Cataloguing in Publication Data

Data available

ISBN 978-0-19-881772-7

Printed and bound in Great Britain by
Clays Ltd, Elcograf S.p.A.

OXFORD WORLD'S CLASSICS

THE OXFORD GEORGE BERNARD SHAW

General Editor: BRAD KENT

MAJOR CULTURAL ESSAYS

GEORGE BERNARD SHAW was born in Dublin in 1856 into a family of Ireland's well-established Protestant Ascendancy. His father's alcoholism and business ineptitude caused the family's fortunes to decline, and Shaw left school at 15 to work as a clerk in a land agent's office. In 1876, he moved to London, where he attended public lectures, joined political and cultural organizations, and, on most days, furthered his learning in the Reading Room of the British Museum. In 1884, he became a member of the newly founded Fabian Society, which was devoted to political reform along socialist principles, and remained one of their leading pamphleteers and campaigners for much of his life. Starting in the mid-1880s, Shaw worked variously as a book, music, art, and theatre reviewer, and this cultural criticism formed the basis of his important studies *The Quintessence of Ibsenism* (1891) and *The Perfect Wagnerite* (1898). He began playwrighting in earnest with *Widowers' Houses* (1892), but his early plays were largely unperformed as they did not conform with the commercial theatre's demands for musicals, farces, and melodramas. Shaw finally found success in New York in 1898 with *The Devil's Disciple* (1897). With the windfall from the production, he retired from journalism and married Irish heiress Charlotte Payne-Townshend. In the new century, Shaw embarked on forging a theatre of the future, transforming the problem and discussion play into a theatre of ideas with *Man and Superman* (1903), *John Bull's Other Island* (1904), and *Major Barbara* (1905). The popular writer of *Fanny's First Play* (1911) and *Pygmalion* (1912) became a pariah following his condemnation of jingoistic patriotism at the outset of the First World War. His comeback was slow but he achieved worldwide acclaim as the writer of *Saint Joan* (1923) and was awarded the 1925 Nobel Prize for Literature. He continued to write plays, including *The Apple Cart* (1928) and *Geneva* (1936), but his output dropped off significantly in the 1940s. Shaw died at his home in Ayot St Lawrence in 1950.

DAVID KORNHABER is Associate Professor of English and Comparative Literature at the University of Texas at Austin. He is the author of *Theatre & Knowledge* (Palgrave, 2019) and *The Birth of Theater from the Spirit of Philosophy: Nietzsche and the Modern Drama* (Northwestern University Press, 2016), and he is, with Lawrence Switzky, the editor of the journal *Modern Drama*.

OXFORD WORLD'S CLASSICS

*For over 100 years Oxford World's Classics have brought
readers closer to the world's great literature. Now with over 700
titles—from the 4,000-year-old myths of Mesopotamia to the
twentieth century's greatest novels—the series makes available
lesser-known as well as celebrated writing.*

*The pocket-sized hardbacks of the early years contained
introductions by Virginia Woolf, T. S. Eliot, Graham Greene,
and other literary figures which enriched the experience of reading.
Today the series is recognized for its fine scholarship and
reliability in texts that span world literature, drama and poetry,
religion, philosophy and politics. Each edition includes perceptive
commentary and essential background information to meet the
changing needs of readers.*

ACKNOWLEDGEMENTS

ALL unpublished quotations in this volume are used by the kind permission of The Society of Authors, on behalf of the Bernard Shaw Estate.

CONTENTS

Introduction   ix

Note on the Text   xxxvii

Select Bibliography   xxxix

A Chronology of George Bernard Shaw   xliii

I. SUBSTANTIAL ESSAYS

The Quintessence of Ibsenism (1891–1922)   3

The Perfect Wagnerite (1898–1922)   127

II. AN OPEN LETTER AND A PREFACE

The Sanity of Art (1895–1908)   227

Preface to Three Plays by Brieux (1909)   244

III. SHORTER ESSAYS AND REVIEWS

11 October 1893   261

1 August 1894   265

8 August 1894   270

The Case for the Critic-Dramatist (1895)   274

The Late Censor (1895)   279

Church and Stage (1896)   285

Nietzsche in English (1896)   291

Madox Brown, Watts, and Ibsen (1897)   295

The Board School (1897)   300

Henry Irving and Ellen Terry (1905)   304

Edgar Allan Poe (1909)   313

Rodin (1912–17)   318

Mr Arnold Bennett Thinks Play-Writing Easier than
Novel Writing (1916)   322

Oscar Wilde (1918)   330

Ruskin's Politics (1919–21)   341

Keats (1921)   349

Tolstoy: Tragedian or Comedian? (1921)   353

Beethoven's Centenary (1927)   357

My First Talkie (1931)   361

Am I an Educated Person? (1947)   363

The Play of Ideas (1950)   367

Explanatory Notes   373

INTRODUCTION

HAD George Bernard Shaw never written a single play, he would still be remembered as a pivotal figure of the late nineteenth-century British stage, and of turn-of-the-century culture more generally, due to the impact of his voluminous criticism. Before he was Bernard Shaw, dramatist, he was Bernard Shaw, drama critic. And before that, music critic. And before that still, art critic. In one sense, Shaw left behind these appointments relatively early in his career. His last day as a drama critic was on 21 May 1898—more than fifty-one years before the premiere of his last completed play, *Shakes versus Shav*, in August 1949. In another sense, he never left behind these early roles at all. Forty-nine years after departing from his perch at the *Saturday Review*, the prominent London weekly, Shaw, age 92, would reflect on the importance of that early journalistic work to the trajectory of his career: 'It was this equipment that saved me from being starved out of literature . . . as a critic I came to the top irresistibly' (p. 364).

The critic's eye would always remain with him. 'These years of criticism', he later observed, 'advanced my mental education by compelling me to deliver carefully considered judgments, and to discriminate between the brilliant talents . . . and the genius that is not for an age but for all time' (p. 365). And so too would the journalistic impulse remain, the intellectual pugilist's need to hash out ideas in print as he had so frequently done in the rowdy world of London newspaper publishing in the 1890s. One of Shaw's very last pieces of writing would be an article in the *New Statesman and Nation* defending his plays against an attack by Terence Rattigan, published in the same paper two months earlier. That article, titled simply 'The Play of Ideas' and published in May 1950, appeared just months before Shaw passed away in November. It was as vibrant and combative as ever. 'The difference between [Rattigan's] practice and mine', he writes, 'is that I reason out every sentence I write to the utmost of my capacity before I commit it to print, whereas he slams down everything that comes into his head without reasoning about it at all' (p. 367). He was a drama critic still.

Cultural criticism was Shaw's entry point into the life of letters he so desperately sought as a young man. Moving to London at the age of 19, following his mother who had relocated there from Dublin, Shaw originally thought he might be a novelist. When not working in the London offices of the Edison Telephone Company, he took a desk at the

reading room of the British Museum—the precursor to the British
Library and the same locale where Karl Marx had written *Das Kapital*
barely ten years earlier—and set to work. He penned five novels there,
all of them summarily rejected by publishers (though they would eventually be published in serialized versions by various socialist periodic-
als). But his time at the British Museum was hardly wasted. It was there
that he struck up a friendship with the critic William Archer, who mar-
velled at the young Irishman's eccentric reading habits. 'I saw him, day
after day, poring over Karl Marx's *Das Kapital* and an orchestral score
of Wagner's *Tristan und Isolde*.'[1] Archer was then just beginning in the
world of London journalism but had at least a toehold in the business—he had started as a drama critic for the *London Figaro*,
a leading arts paper of the period, some three years prior and had
moved to *The World*, a prominent weekly known especially for its society pages, by the time he met Shaw. When Archer was offered an
appointment as the art critic for *The World*, a post for which he felt he
was entirely unqualified, he recommended that it be given to Shaw
instead. Shaw saw his first art column published on 10 February 1886.
    Shaw had no training whatsoever in art criticism beyond that which
he had given to himself. As an adolescent, he had stalked the hallways
of the National Gallery of Ireland obsessively, finding there both relief
from a tumultuous home life and a gateway to a wider world beyond
Dublin. He would come to take his amateur qualifications as a point of
pride, arguing that for the critic the only truly necessary training 'is to
look at pictures until you have acquired the power of seeing them. If
you look at several thousand good pictures every year, and form some
sort of practical judgment about every one of them . . . then at the end
of five years or so you will, if you have a wise eye, be able to see what is
actually in a picture' (p. 291). Shaw never went to university, and he
derided those who thought that they understood art by virtue of their
formal schooling. He once argued that the elite education of his literary
colleague and fellow Dubliner, Oscar Wilde, entirely prevented him
from properly appreciating art: 'The notion that a Portora [i.e., Portora
Royal School] boy, passed on to T.C.D. [Trinity College Dublin] and
thence to Oxford and spending his vacations in Dublin, could without
special circumstances have any genuine intimacy with music and painting, is to me ridiculous' (p. 335).

[1] Charles Archer, *William Archer: Life, Work, and Friendships* (London: George Allen
& Unwin, 1931), 119.

Shaw's artistic populism shows in every review. He could be brash, associative, dismissive, digressive (sometimes excessively digressive), but he was never uninteresting and never at all concerned with catering to elite sensibilities even as he wrote about the world of elite art. He was already, as T. S. Eliot later called him, 'the gadfly of the commonwealth'.[2] Shaw soon brought this same approach to music criticism, taking a new role writing concert reviews at *The Star*, a smaller daily paper, in 1888 and then subsequently at *The World*. Here Shaw was on somewhat firmer ground than in the world of fine art. He had grown up in a musical household and was himself a proficient musician, having taught himself to play piano as a young man using the score to Mozart's *Don Giovanni*.[3] His mother, Bessie, was an active and respected amateur singer and for many years had a close relationship with the esteemed Dublin music teacher George John Vandeleur Lee, who lived with the Shaw family for a time before he and Bessie decamped for musical opportunities in London, leaving Shaw's father behind. In fact, Shaw's very first professional writing job, years before he became a proper critic, came in ghost-writing occasional music columns published by Lee in a weekly called *The Hornet*.

Shaw's music criticism was vast. Though he worked as a music critic for only six years, his articles numbered in the hundreds, running to over 2,000 pages in one edition.[4] Most of this work was semi-anonymous, published first under the pseudonym Corno di Bassetto and then later with the initials 'G.B.S.'. This was part of a shift in journalistic practices, as such newspaper criticism was wholly anonymous at the time, both by tradition and to allow for a certain free exchange of opinions and ideas.[5] That Shaw's articles were signed at all was an assertion of his voice as a critic. Shaw did not hold back on his opinions, paying no heed to feelings or fashions. He was a vocal supporter of Wagner at a time when the composer's reputation in England was still forming, and a vocal critic of certain composers then very much in fashion, including Johannes Brahms and Felix Mendelssohn. Though he could delve into the finer points of technical musical terminology with the best of them—and occasionally would do so as a rhetorical flourish, as

[2] T. S. Eliot, 'London Letter', *The Dial*, 71/4 (October 1921), 453.

[3] See T. L. Southgate, 'Salvation through the Piano', *Musical News*, 6/155 (17 February 1894), 153–5.

[4] See *Shaw's Music: The Complete Musical Criticism in Three Volumes*, ed. Dan H. Laurence (London: Bodley Head, 1981).

[5] See Nelson O'Ceallaigh Ritschel, *Bernard Shaw, W. T. Stead, and the New Journalism: Whitechapel, Parnell, Titanic, and the Great War* (London: Palgrave-Macmillan, 2017).

if to remind his readers that he did actually know from whence he spoke—his copy was eminently readable even to non-experts, the voice of an impassioned enthusiast rather than a condescending maestro. As Shaw himself remarked later in life, 'I could make deaf stockbrokers read my two pages on music, the alleged joke being that I knew nothing about it. The real joke was that I knew all about it' (p. 336).

That Shaw would eventually turn to drama criticism was by no means a foregone conclusion. Shaw had already made some tentative steps towards establishing himself as a playwright during the later years of his tenure as a music critic—receiving private productions of *Widowers' Houses* in 1892 and *Arms and the Man* in 1894 while also writing *The Philanderer* and *Mrs Warren's Profession* in 1893 and *Candida* in 1894. But his transition to drama criticism was driven more by editorial personalities than artistic professions. Shaw was drawn to taking a position at the *Saturday Review* largely due to his admiration for its owner, Frank Harris, and he later recalled that the drama critic post was 'fairly forced on me by Harris'.[6] Shaw in fact worried that he might prove more successful as a critic than a playwright and speculated as to 'whether it is quite decent for a dramatic author to be also a dramatic critic'.[7]

Yet if Shaw was hesitant about embarking on a new path as a drama critic, he nevertheless threw himself into the role with his usual gusto. He could hardly have started his tenure at a more momentous time. By his own estimation, the current London stage was overwhelmingly moribund, a sorry collection of plays based on 'vulgar attachments, rapacities, generosities, resentments, ambitions, misunderstandings, oddities and so forth as to which no moral question is raised' (p. 116). The French stage was not much better in Shaw's view: he had no end of vitriol for the so-called well-made plays of Eugène Scribe and Victorien Sardou that then dominated the Parisian boulevard theatres. Cosseted by the licensing restrictions imposed by the Lord Chamberlain's Office, which since 1737 had exerted an explicit censoring function on the British stage that had no parallel in other domains of British arts and letters, most London theatres seemed to Shaw specifically calculated to be inoffensive.

Yet changes on the British stage had begun to emerge, and Shaw came to play an important role in helping them take hold. The work of the radical playwright Henrik Ibsen—by then a well-established figure

⁶ Quoted in Stanley Weintraub, *Shaw's People: Victoria to Churchill* (University Park, PA: Pennsylvania State University Press, 1996), 144.

⁷ Quoted in Weintraub, *Shaw's People*, 144–5.

in Europe and even the recipient of a knighthood from the king in his native Norway—was only just beginning to be performed in London, the first true staging of one of his plays in English, *A Doll's House*, having occurred in a limited three-week production in 1889, six years before Shaw joined the *Saturday Review* in 1895. Before then, there had been only an extremely loose adaptation of the play called *Breaking a Butterfly* staged in 1884 and a private reading of Ibsen's text at the home of Eleanor Marx, daughter of Karl Marx, in 1886—in which Shaw himself had read the part of Krogstad. Shaw was not quite at the vanguard of bringing Ibsen to England—that credit belongs more to figures like Marx and to Shaw's friend Archer, who took it upon himself to translate Ibsen's works into English and seek out productions for them, as with *A Doll's House*. But Shaw was an extremely influential advocate for Ibsen and for other new playwrights of the era. Though Shaw would not have a name for it yet, he was witnessing the development of what scholars would later term modern drama, a loose transnational affiliation of dramatists and dramatic movements of the late nineteenth and early twentieth centuries linked by their shared opposition to prevailing commercial theatre practices of the age. From his perch at the *Saturday Review*, Shaw played an active role in championing this nascent movement and advocating for its adoption in England.

And he would, of course, famously join that movement himself as a playwright. It cannot be forgotten how much Shaw's turn to theatre was intertwined with his position as a journalist and drama critic. Shaw's first attempt at professional playwriting came by way of the suggestion of another critic: Archer again, who in 1884 proposed that Shaw try his hand at dramatizing a prose scenario he was developing. Both critics eventually abandoned the effort, but in 1892, Shaw returned to the project at the urging of J. T. Grein, a visionary young theatre producer who knew of Shaw primarily through his work as a critic. Shaw developed the material into *Widowers' Houses*, his first completed play, and became a vocal advocate of Grein and his Independent Theatre Society. Inspired by new producers like Grein and new playwrights like Ibsen and the dramatic possibilities they represented, Shaw wrote several more plays during his theatre critic years, including *The Man of Destiny*, *You Never Can Tell*, and *The Devil's Disciple*. Shaw still had only intermittent success with securing productions—*The Philanderer*, *Mrs Warren's Profession*, and *You Never Can Tell* all remained unproduced through most of the 1890s, and to that point only *The Devil's Disciple* had seen any real commercial success. Yet the acclaim and notoriety that his plays brought was no small matter: 'My reputation as a dramatist grows with every play of mine that is *not* performed,' he joked in one inter-view.[8] By 1898, he was established enough in his theatrical career and secure enough in his upcoming marriage to the wealthy Charlotte Payne-Townshend that he finally left theatre criticism behind.

Or, rather, he found a way to continue that theatre criticism by other means. For if ever there was a theatre critic's playwright, it was Shaw. It is not just that he could never help but write reviews for his own plays and publish them as prefaces and afterwords, essentially transposing the digressive, political, ponderous, and intellectually combative prose he once wrote about other people's plays into essays focused instead on his own dramatic works. It is also that he could never stop being an advocate and champion for a new kind of art and theatre in England. 'I am always electioneering,' he once observed of his work as a critic. 'I desire certain reforms, and in order to get them, I make every notable per-formance an example of the want of them.'[9] Shaw's entire playwriting career might be viewed as a continued extrapolation of that impulse, offering his own examples of the new style of play-craft he had always professed in his columns at the *Saturday Review* rather than simply imploring others to follow his dictums.

Ultimately, Shaw saw little difference between the artist and the critic—at most it was a difference of degree or emphasis rather than kind. Hence the spirited defence he offered of his dual roles as play-wright and critic during the years he was both writing plays and review-ing them: 'On the whole there is only as much validity in the theory that a critic should not be a dramatist, as in the theory that a judge should not be a lawyer nor a general nor a soldier. You cannot have qualifica-tions without experience' (p. 278). Shaw's position was different from that of his contemporary Wilde, who famously enjoined that we see 'the critic as artist' in his 1891 essay of the same name.[10] For Shaw, the real truth was actually something like the reverse: the artist as critic. Criticism was for Shaw always ultimately a chance to advocate and debate ideas, with his reviews sometimes having little obvious connection to the artwork at hand. Art, and theatre especially, was for him the same. 'There is, flatly, no future now for any drama without music except the drama of thought,' he declared in the 'Author's Apology' to

---

  [8] 'The Man of Destiny', *Daily Mail*, 15 May 1897.
  [9] *The World*, 6 July 1892.
  [10] See Oscar Wilde, 'The Critic as Artist Part I' and 'The Critic as Artist Part II', in *Oscar Wilde: The Major Works*, ed. Isobel Murray (Oxford: Oxford University Press, 1989), 241–66 and 266–98.

Mrs Warren's Profession.[11] All great art, Shaw claimed, was an attempt at communication, the work of 'one for whom poetry is only a means to an end, the end being to deliver a message which clamors to be revealed through him' (p. 350). All great criticism was the same. Shaw had switched roles, but he had never switched perspectives.

It is in this light that we can best understand the works collected here, prose works that were not just precursors to or supplements of a prominent dramatic career but part and parcel of that career itself. Shaw's outlook and style as a dramatist and polemicist were shaped by his years in the London newspaper world, and his plays form a continuum with the essays he wrote throughout his life. Even in interpreting artworks of others, Shaw is always also interpreting his own. And in both he is always also interpreting the world. As he writes, '[T]he great dramatist has something better to do than to amuse either himself or his audience. He has to interpret life' (p. 255).

The Quintessence of Ibsenism

The most complete and in many ways most profound work of critical interpretation that Shaw ever put forward was his *Quintessence of Ibsenism*, first published in 1891 and later reprinted and expanded in 1913 and 1922. The origins of this tome—one of the longest works of Shaw's career—were decidedly humble. Shaw was an active and influential member of London's Fabian Society, a socialist organization whose members were committed to spreading radical ideas and social reforms not through revolution or direct political action but through intellectual debate and cultural dissemination. In 1890, as Shaw recounts within *The Quintessence* itself, it was suggested that the members make a series of presentations to one another on socialism in contemporary literature. Shaw volunteered to deliver a presentation on Ibsen, which he did on 18 July 1890 at the St James's Restaurant, reading his (then much shorter) essay to a small assemblage of fellow Fabians and believing the matter finished.

At the time, Ibsen was still relatively unknown even among the cultural elites of the Fabian Society, with only a few of his works translated into English (and still unpublished) and only *A Doll's House* having been performed in London. All of that changed in 1891 when London saw a sudden rush of Ibsen productions: *Rosmersholm*, directed by and

---

[11] Bernard Shaw, 'The Author's Apology', *Mrs. Warren's Profession* (London: Constable, 1905), p. xxii.

starring Florence Farr, in March at the Vaudeville Theatre; *Ghosts* at the Independent Theatre Society that same month; and *Hedda Gabler* at the Vaudeville Theatre in April. The productions caused a scandal in the London papers, with numerous critics denouncing both playwright and producers as degenerate. The production of *Ghosts* was particularly contentious: the play was sure to be denied a licence by the Lord Chamberlain's Office due to its scandalous subject matter, which includes venereal disease and incest, and was put on in a private subscription performance as a means of circumventing that decree. Shaw in fact devotes several pages of the published version of *The Quintessence* to quoting from the intemperate reviews occasioned by these plays, and he is not exaggerating the sense of cultural alarm when he calls the response 'bedlamite' (p. 59). Ibsen had few defenders in the press, Shaw and Archer being almost the lone voices of support, and most members of the British public had little idea who this controversial new playwright was beyond the vituperation devoted to his latest plays. Shaw saw it as his mission to offer an explanation and defence of Ibsen's work, being legitimately one of the few figures in the country who had actually read all of it. He feverishly reshaped his address to the Fabians into a book in a matter of weeks, working passionately and unceasingly for days on end. 'Finished the Ibsen MS in great excitement. Sat working at it all the evening,' he recorded in his diary.[12]

This context around the publication of *The Quintessence* is important to understanding the structure and approach that Shaw deploys. Though often regarded as a book of criticism—Shaw himself described it as 'contributing to the literature of philosophy' (p. 292)—it is as much a primer and introduction to Ibsen as it is an interpretation of his works. Shaw follows Ibsen's career chronologically and devotes pages upon pages of each section of the book to summarizing the plots of his various plays as most of them were entirely unknown to English audiences. His purpose was in large part to provide a greater context for the newspaper debate over Ibsen that originally prompted the book's publication.

At heart, Shaw urges the English theatre-going public to understand Ibsen not as an insolent iconoclast seeking scandal for its own sake, as many in the press had intimated, but as a systemic thinker who had been putting forward a sustained critique of contemporary morals across the breadth of his career. Shaw made no effort to soften that

---

[12] *Bernard Shaw: The Diaries, 1885–1897*, ed. Stanley Weintraub (University Park, PA: Pennsylvania State University Press, 1986), ii. 713.

critique for delicate Victorian sensibilities; he sought only to assert its cogency and urgency. He wanted the English to understand Ibsen not as a firebrand but as a philosopher. That the philosopher Shaw constructed in his summaries and evaluations of Ibsen's plays looked a lot like Friedrich Nietzsche, a contemporary of both playwrights, is attested to by the anecdote Shaw relays in the 1913 edition of *The Quintessence* in which a German audience member listening to Shaw deliver remarks from the book assumes that it is based explicitly on Nietzsche's *Beyond Good and Evil*, which Shaw then claimed not to have read (p. 29). This is probably true in its specifics, as *Beyond Good and Evil* was not yet widely available in England and had not yet been translated into English, though Shaw's remarks elsewhere indicate that he was already familiar with some of Nietzsche's work before writing *The Quintessence*. However, in truth, the philosopher who is best explicated in *The Quintessence* is neither Nietzsche nor Ibsen but rather Shaw himself, with the book reading in parts like a blueprint for Shaw's later career. The tome has not infrequently been called *The Quintessence of Shavianism* for this very reason, with Eric Bentley going so far as to suggest that one substitute the name 'Shaw' for every appearance of 'Ibsen' in the book.[13]

It is not that Shaw's analysis of Ibsen is inaccurate. For years, the book was uncharitably dismissed by many scholars as manifesting an overly politicized and largely inaccurate picture of Ibsen's work. Thus, Keith May's influential judgement that *The Quintessence* represents 'a mixture of accurate exposition and progressionist misrepresentation'.[14] Though some continue to find the book's polemicism less than useful as a means of understanding Ibsen's subtleties, others, like Joan Templeton, have more recently seen much merit in Shaw's readings of the plays and have sought to contextualize its role in responding to the vituperative reaction to Ibsen in the British press.[15] In fact, contra its early critics, the book is not especially focused on the social problem plays of Ibsen's middle period that would seem to be the nearest precursor to Shaw, plays like *A Doll's House* or *An Enemy of the People* where specific social issues like marriage and public health are at question. Shaw devotes the greatest number of pages to *Emperor and Galilean*, a classical fantasia about the Roman emperor Julian and the origins of Christianity, and he continually alludes to Ibsen's mordant

---

[13] Eric Bentley, *Bernard Shaw* (1947; New York: Applause Books, 2002), 139.

[14] Keith M. May, *Ibsen and Shaw* (New York: St Martin's Press, 1985), 121.

[15] Joan Templeton, *Shaw's Ibsen: A Re-appraisal* (London: Palgrave-Macmillan, 2018).

psychological drama *Rosmersholm*. The book's true limitation is actually one and the same as its greatest strength: that in devising a formula
for approaching Ibsen's work, Shaw seems to have inadvertently provided a decoder key for his own.

Shaw cheekily declares near the end of his book that the actual quintessence of Ibsenism is that 'there is no formula' (p. 104). But most of
his analysis follows from a structure he establishes early in the work,
a thought experiment wherein he contends that any group of 1,000
individuals can be divided into a 'community of 700 Philistines, 299
idealists, and 1 realist' (p. 26). The philistines—a term that Shaw
derives from Matthew Arnold's coinage in *Culture and Anarchy*
(1869)—mindlessly accept whatever social norms are then prevalent.
The idealists secretly understand the limitations of these norms but
uphold them out of a combination of cowardice and self-deception.
Meanwhile, the realist recognizes those limitations and refuses to conform. For Shaw, the greatest social conflict comes between the idealists
and the realist:

the idealists will be terrified beyond measure at the proclamation of their
hidden thought—at the presence of the traitor among the conspirators of
silence—at the rending of the beautiful veil they and their poets have
woven to hide the unbearable face of the truth. They will crucify him, burn
him, violate their own ideals of family affection by taking his children away
from him, ostracize him, brand him as immoral, profligate, filthy, and
appeal against him to the despised Philistines, specially idealized for the
occasion as Society. (p. 24)

As a rubric, this approach can only get one so far with Ibsen. It roughly
suits a play like *A Doll's House*, wherein Nora graduates into the realist
position through her disillusionment with her husband Torvald, or
a play like *An Enemy of the People*, where Dr Stockmann is openly persecuted for his commitment to scientific truth. But it does little to help
unravel the dark psychological complexity of a play like *Hedda Gabler*
or the epic nihilism of *The Master Builder*. As a codex to Shaw's own
future work, however, it does much to illuminate the thread that binds
together plays as different in style and subject matter as *Mrs Warren's
Profession*, *Man and Superman*, *Major Barbara*, *Pygmalion*, and many
more. Shaw's drama returns obsessively to the conflict between the
realist and idealist, using Shaw's own quixotic definitions of those
terms—the sharp debate between the most intelligent and original
defenders of the status quo and its most incisive critics. Shaw had not
yet written any of these plays, making it all the more surprising how

closely they track to this framework crafted in his journalism days. Or maybe not so surprising: like all of Shaw's art, they grew out of his perceptions as a critic.

The Perfect Wagnerite

In many ways, *The Perfect Wagnerite* is a companion piece to *The Quintessence of Ibsenism*, offering an echo of that work's structure and purpose. Like any echo, it is also somewhat diminished as compared to the original. That is to say, *The Perfect Wagnerite* is not nearly so comprehensive in the treatment of its subject, nor was the occasion of its publication as urgent. Shaw does not attempt an excavation of Richard Wagner's entire career, as he does with Ibsen, nor was the publication of the book an attempt to intervene in a particularly explosive debate. By 1898, when the book first appeared, Wagner already had a devoted following in England—Shaw himself had been sent to Bayreuth as a music critic by *The World* years before he began the book, and performances of Wagner's work were a common and uncontroversial occurrence at Covent Garden and Drury Lane in London. By the time the book was reprinted and slightly expanded in 1901, 1913, and 1922, Wagner was among the most famous composers in the world. If Ibsen's work had been a scandal when Shaw first took to defending it, Wagner's work was already becoming commonplace.

This difference helps to account for the major distinction in content and approach between the two works. *The Perfect Wagnerite* is neither an introduction to Wagner nor a defence of his art but rather a reassessment. To Shaw's mind, the scandal to which the book was responding was not one of outraged newspaper notices but one of gross and complacent miscomprehension. Shaw saw among Wagner's supporters and detractors alike a profound underestimation of the composer's art. The former were too convinced of that work's mythic aloofness and epic escapism, the latter too obsessed with its departures from the conventions of classical opera. Shaw set out to prove both camps wrong, arguing for a contemporary political purpose behind Wagner's mythic tales and severing them entirely from the tradition of opera, proclaiming them to be a new genre of music-drama as Wagner himself had explained.

The immediate occasion for Shaw's publication of the treatise was in fact the publication of a different set of essays on Wagner, William Ashton Ellis's 1892 English translation of Wagner's prose works, Wagner being almost as much the polemicist as Shaw himself in explicating his own

art. Wagner's essays convinced Shaw that his long-standing views on
the composer were correct and that the English public needed education in Wagner's new form of music-drama—a form particularly suited
to Shaw's critical talents as both a drama critic and a music critic. In
fact, the ideas put forward in *The Perfect Wagnerite* probably started to
form years before the book's publication and may have been some of
Shaw's earliest sustained critical insights into music and drama. If
Archer is correct in remembering a young Shaw vigorously turning
from Marx's *Das Kapital* to *Tristan und Isolde* in the reading room at the
British Museum, then the connections being forged in Shaw's mind at
that time are in substance no different from those put forward in *The
Perfect Wagnerite*, making the work a latter-day exposition of Shaw's
youthful observations.

At its heart, *The Perfect Wagnerite* offers a reading of the first three
operas in *Der Ring des Nibelungen*, or the Ring cycle—*Das Rhinegold,
Die Walküre*, and *Siegfried*—as Marxist allegories of capitalist exploitation and aristocratic decline. This might seem like a far-fetched
imposition of Shaw's own political peccadillos were it not for the fact
that Wagner himself was a one-time radical who was actively involved
as both a pamphleteer and combatant in the Dresden Uprising of May
1849, which sought democratic reforms in the German state of Saxony
and took place barely a year after the publication of *The Communist
Manifesto*. Wagner's reflections on the uprising in Ellis's translation
helped provide the impetus for Shaw's book, and Shaw makes much of
reading the legacy of Dresden into Wagner's work. Shaw also focuses
attention on Wagner's transition away from radicalism towards
a nationalist conservatism, as seen in the composer's mocking response
to the Paris Commune of 1871, which drew inspiration from Dresden,
and his turn away from the music drama of the first three parts of the
Ring cycle towards what Shaw sees as the grand opera of its fourth
instalment, *Götterdämmerung*.

In its persistent focus on the connections between radical politics
and seemingly unrelated cultural forms, *The Perfect Wagnerite* offers
a kind of blunt anticipation of the Marxist cultural criticism put forward by the critics of the Frankfurt School just a few decades later,
beginning around 1930. Shaw's reading of the Ring cycle is largely
allegorical; in this way, it specifically anticipates aspects of Walter
Benjamin's 1928 *The Origin of German Tragic Drama*, with its pivotal
distinctions between allegory and symbolism. As a consequence, the
book separates its considerations of dramatic content and musical
form rather than treating them in tandem. The result is sometimes

awkward—Shaw's rhetorical cadenza of music terminology towards the end of the book after eschewing such language for nearly the entire work is particularly jarring—but its insights can be substantial. 'There is not a single bar of "classical music" in The Ring—not a note in it that has any other point than the single direct point of giving musical expression to the drama' (p. 137), Shaw declares, acknowledging Wagner's musical innovations and recognizing their connections to the new form of dramatic storytelling he was trying to develop.

As with *The Quintessence*, scholarly reaction to *The Perfect Wagnerite* has been mixed, and the work has yet to receive as thoroughgoing a reappraisal as Templeton has offered of Shaw's work on Ibsen. Writing in the journal *Opera*, the English music writer John Warrack sums up the response of many music scholars to the treatise, writing that 'Whatever Shaw's brilliance, *The Perfect Wagnerite* is, in both senses of the word, a partial account; and it becomes increasingly so as the power-political manoeuvrings of *Das Rheingold* recede behind a very different kind of world view.'[16] Just as *The Quintessence of Ibsenism* has been jokingly retitled *The Quintessence of Shavianism* on occasion, so too has *The Perfect Wagnerite* not infrequently become *The Imperfect Wagnerite* in critical appraisals. In practice, though, Shaw's allegorical approach to Wagner has been occasionally adopted, inspiring extreme consternation and extreme praise alike. Both were directed at Patrice Chéreau's controversial centenary production of the Ring Cycle at Bayreuth in 1976, which updated the mythic operas to the industrial age and drew in part from Shaw's political readings.[17]

Yet regardless of Shaw's impact on Wagner's legacy, Wagner's mode of music-drama would have a substantial effect on the development of Shaw's own dramatic art. For one, Wagner's self-institutionalization through the creation of the Bayreuth Festspielhaus, founded in 1876 and dedicated to performing only his works according to his exact specifications, inspired Shaw's own emphasis on building new institutional structures for English theatre. This manifested both in his campaign to help establish an endowed National Theatre in England and in the early twentieth-century rise of dedicated theatre festivals outside London, as with the annual Malvern Festival, which ran from 1929 to 1939 and primarily produced Shaw's plays. Even more potently, Shaw recognized an opportunity to invert Wagner's artistic equation—rather than

[16] John Warrack, 'A "Ring" Master', *Opera*, 30/7–12 (1979), 1043–5.
[17] See Lawrence Switzky, 'Allegory and Its Limits in the *Ring*: Bernard Shaw and Patrice Chéreau on Wagner', *Opera Quarterly*, 30/2–3 (Spring–Summer 2014), 172–87.

making opera more like drama, he would come to make drama more like opera. Hence Shaw's explanation decades later that his own plays have always functioned like verbal operas. 'Opera taught me to shape my plays into recitatives, arias, duets, trios, ensemble finales, and bravura pieces to display the technical accomplishments of the executants' (p. 370), he observed at the end of his career. Likewise, he recognized that the emotional impact of Wagner's music-drama form was potentially greater than that which drama itself could ever hope to achieve. Shaw's influential statement in the Author's Apology to *Mrs Warren's Profession* that 'there is, flatly, no future now for any drama without music except the drama of thought', is not just about the importance of the drama of ideas but also the importance of the music-drama, the drama *with* music, as a new emotional force on the stage. Shaw does not in the end pay Wagner the same honour he paid to Ibsen, of making him out to be a philosopher himself. Rather, Wagner's philosophy, such as Shaw sees it, is all borrowed second-hand from Marx and other radical thinkers, until Wagner eschews such politics, at which point, in Shaw's view, he has nothing of interest left to say. The music-drama is, for Shaw, merely a vehicle, albeit a powerful one. The drama of ideas that Shaw first saw in Ibsen, however, is an actual 'factory of thought'.[18] Though Shaw admired Wagner, he ultimately saw his work as a counterpoint and challenge to his own dramatic mission.

The Sanity of Art *and* Preface to Three Plays by Brieux

Shaw always regarded *The Quintessence of Ibsenism* and *The Perfect Wagnerite* as his major works of cultural criticism, but they were not his only long-form treatises on art and culture. Sandwiched between them lay *The Sanity of Art*, first published in 1895 (four years after *The Quintessence* and three years before *The Perfect Wagnerite*), which offers a useful addendum to them both. In its full version, *The Sanity of Art* shows Shaw at his most polemical. The piece was originally written as an open letter to the American anarchist Benjamin Tucker to be published in his bi-weekly journal *Liberty* in aggrieved response to a recent book called *Degeneration* by Max Nordau, a Parisian social critic of German-Hungarian origin and later a prominent Zionist. The set-up was almost too perfect. For Shaw, Nordau was a prime example of what he called in *The Quintessence* an idealist: an upholder of social norms

---

[18] Bernard Shaw, 'The Author's Apology', *Our Theatres in the Nineties* (London, Archibald Constable & Co. Ltd, 1932), vol. i, p. vii.

and mores who was actually intelligent enough to know better but who could not accept the truth. In crafting his response, Shaw got to play the realist deftly cutting the idealist down to size like a character out of one of his own dramas. Given the notoriety of Nordau's book at the time, it was for Shaw a pressing mission—one that he felt compelled to repeat with his reissue of the book in 1908, as he grew concerned that Nordau's ideas on modern profligacy were not only achieving lasting prominence but generally entering the lexicon of informed opinion on contemporary art and letters.[19]

At issue was the supposed degeneracy of modern art, Nordau fashioning example after example of artists and artistic works that in his view dangerously undercut traditional values and thereby showed signs of neurosis. Shaw takes up Nordau nearly point for point in places, especially in a long section titled 'Echolalia' (named after a medical condition where one repeats what one hears unthinkingly); this becomes a verbal duel that can at times be nearly impenetrable for anyone not steeped in the finer cultural details of the later nineteenth century. But Shaw also steps back from such sparring to take a wider view, and it is these sections, excerpted here, that remain the most interesting. In dedicated sections on Ibsen and on Wagner, Shaw offers a useful recapitulation of his views from *The Quintessence* and a masterful account of Wagner's place in the history of classical music before his Marxist reading of *The Ring*; in many ways his attempt to communicate those ideas pithily here was yet another prompt to write a more elaborate book on Wagner not long after. In a section on the impressionists, Shaw reminds us of the scandal behind this now-hallowed movement, which still had its detractors in England and elsewhere in the 1890s.

Perhaps most interesting is the theory put forward in sections on law, religion, and art within the book. Shaw's explanation here of art's role in society is largely unique from those he offered elsewhere at other points in his career, though one can see his thinking in this work undergirding his later statements. Shaw's later estimations of art's socio-religious role often tend toward the grandiose, as in his claim that true artists 'are prophets rather than poets' (p. 350). Here, though, he offers a practical and largely pragmatic argument for art's utility, almost a kind of aesthetic positivism. Accepting that most individuals, even the most radical and iconoclastic by disposition, have neither the time nor the inclination to challenge accepted standards and mores in every aspect

---

[19] William Greenslade, *Degeneration, Culture and the Novel, 1880–1940* (Cambridge: Cambridge University Press, 1994).

of their lives, Shaw puts forward a case for art's role in proposing and testing out revisions to established custom. It is a functionary view of art, to be sure, and not radically different from his theory of the realist as put forward in *The Quintessence*, but it offers a mechanism for assessing art's social value absent the individualist (and implicitly masculinist) framework of the lone, revolutionary iconoclast. Art itself becomes the engine of social change—the change of ongoing maintenance and improvement rather than the radical break of individualist revolt—and takes its place alongside the law and the Church as an institutional pillar of society. It is an especially Fabian view, based on the premise that social change can and should be an eminently reasonable affair—not neurotic but perfectly sane.

If Nordau, the subject of Shaw's critique in *The Sanity of Art*, is rarely remembered today, the subject of his advocacy in his *Preface to Three Plays by Brieux* has become even more obscure. Eugène Brieux was a prominent but controversial French dramatist of the later nineteenth century, known for his social problem plays and for his frank treatment of scandalous subjects from syphilis to birth control. Although associated with the Théâtre Libre, a prominent home for naturalist and other early avant-garde works in Paris, his plays were banned from performance in England and were occasionally censored in France as well, available to be seen only in private performances. Shaw praises him excessively in his long introduction to a 1914 English translation of his plays, painting him as second to Ibsen in importance on the modern stage and as a giant in French literary history after Molière. Neither Brieux's plays nor Shaw's praise has aged especially well, but the sections excerpted here on French naturalist drama, Molière and Shakespeare, and the rise of the well-made play in the Parisian boulevard theatres offer a fascinating Gallic complement to Shaw's extensive criticism of the English stage from earlier in his career. Ultimately, Shaw takes issue with all three aspects of the French theatrical tradition: the naturalist, the classical, and the popular. His antipathy towards the well-made plays of Scribe and Sardou was well known to any reader of his London theatre criticism, where both figures come in for regular vituperation. More surprising is his caution against the excesses of naturalism, which though it shares a political purpose with much of Shaw's work is for Shaw's taste too lacking in poetry. Shaw extends to Molière many of the same criticisms he makes elsewhere of Shakespeare, epitomized in his remark that 'the reason why Shakespear and Molière are always well spoken of and recommended to the young is that their quarrel is really a quarrel with God for not making men better' (p. 250). In contrast, he writes, 'If they had quarrelled with a specified class of persons with incomes of four figures for not doing their work better, or for doing no work at all, they would be denounced as seditious, impious, and profligate corruptors of morality' (p. 250). That is the drama he seeks, a drama of social concern, but also one, as he writes elsewhere, wherein the artist 'secures a hearing for it by clothing it with word-garments of such beauty, authority, and eternal memorableness, that the world must needs listen to it' (p. 350). As Shaw explains here in the section titled 'The Interpreter of Life', one of his most complete and cogent articulations of the special purpose he saw for the stage, it is always the job of the great dramatist to 'pick out the significant incidents from the chaos of daily happenings, and arrange them so that their relation to one another becomes significant, thus changing us from bewildered spectators of a monstrous confusion to men intelligently conscious of the world and its destinies' (p. 256).

SELECTED SHORTER ESSAYS AND REVIEWS

Shaw's great set-piece essays, *The Quintessence* and *The Perfect Wagnerite* especially and *The Sanity of Art* and *Preface to Brieux* to a lesser extent, paint a certain picture of the playwright as a cultural critic: lengthy and considered, they push inexorably towards a master thesis of their subjects. But to get a true sense of Shaw's journalistic verve and the roiling cauldron of ideas from which these masterworks arose, one needs to turn to the shorter essays and reviews that started his career and that he continued to periodically undertake throughout his life. Assertive and digressive, funny and occasionally profound, they evince most of all a mind and spirit deeply invested not just in appreciating art but also in vigorously debating it.

The selections collected here are meant to offer a variety of views into Shaw's journalistic work, demonstrating both the range of his cultural interests and the evolution of his artistic views. The earliest of these writings are drawn from Shaw's years as a music critic. An untitled review from 11 October 1893 presents Shaw's reaction to Gilbert and Sullivan's *Utopia, Limited*, their first work together in many years and a particularly Shavian entry into their comic-opera canon. The paired reviews from 1 August 1894 and 8 August 1894—Shaw's last two professional music reviews—chart the author's experiences on his visit to the Bayreuth Festspielhaus and form a vivid prologue to *The Perfect Wagnerite*.

The next set of essays and reviews are drawn from Shaw's years as a professional theatre critic. Shaw himself was often circumspect about

the lasting value of these works, even as he kept them in public circulation through multiple collections and reprintings. 'In justice to many
well-known public persons who are handled rather recklessly in the
following pages, I beg my readers not to mistake my journalistic utterances for final estimates of their worth and achievements as dramatic
artists and authors,' he writes on the opening page of one such volume.[20] Later commentators, however, have come to value Shaw's criticism precisely for its discursive and opinionated nature. As Sally Peters
observes, 'His pieces are so interlaced with provocative commentary on
social, moral, and artistic issues that they offer a lens into the very fabric of his society . . . Outfitted with sound judgment, discriminating
taste, and an unfailing wit, Shaw produced the finest body of dramatic
criticism since William Hazlitt.'[21] As with *The Quintessence*, much of
the value of that criticism lies in its explication of Shaw's own views and
techniques, anticipating his later play-craft as much as it responded to
that of his peers. Shaw himself admitted as much, conceding later in
life that his body of early reviews 'contain something like a body of
doctrine, because when I criticized I really did know definitely what
I wanted'. Or, as he puts it elsewhere in his retrospective account, 'I
postulated as desirable a certain kind of play in which I was destined
ten years later to make my mark (as I very well fore-knew in the depth
of my own unconsciousness).'[22]

The selections included here give a taste of that foreknowledge. 'The
Case for the Critic-Dramatist' (1895) presents a spirited defence of
Shaw's dual roles as playwright and critic, enumerating the ways that
both professions interlace in his work. 'The Late Censor' (1895) finds
Shaw pining for the dissolution of the censorship functions of the Lord
Chamberlain's Office and decrying its effects on the English stage.
'Church and Stage' (1896) begins with a description of a recent controversy over religious matters in a West End play and from there launches
into a wider discussion of the separate but overlapping roles of religion
and art in exploring morality and metaphysics. 'Nietzsche in English'
(1896) represents Shaw's first published writing on the German philosopher who would have such an outsized influence on his playwriting,
especially in plays like *Man and Superman* and *Major Barbara*. 'Madox
Brown, Watts, and Ibsen' (1897) represents an example of Shaw's visual

---

[20] Shaw, 'The Author's Apology', p. v.
[21] Sally Peters, 'Shaw's Life: A Feminist in Spite of Himself', in Christopher Innes
(ed.), *The Cambridge Companion to George Bernard Shaw* (Cambridge: Cambridge
University Press, 1998), 7.
[22] Shaw, 'The Author's Apology', p. vii.

arts criticism, examining recent exhibitions of the painters Ford Madox Brown and G. F. Watts and considering their role in the project of social transformation alongside playwrights like Ibsen. 'The Board School' (1897) offers Shaw's views on education and his belief in the primacy of art in proper schooling.

The remaining essays span the breadth of Shaw's twentieth-century prose writings. 'Henry Irving and Ellen Terry' (1905) represents a pair of notices that Shaw wrote for the actor and actress who together dominated the London theatre scene of the late nineteenth century, comparing their respective artistries and their impacts on the theatre world. 'Edgar Allan Poe' (1909) presents Shaw's views on the poet and short-story writer in particular and on the state of American literature more generally. 'Rodin' (1912/1917) returns to the realm of visual arts and relates Shaw's experiences sitting for the famous sculptor—one whom Shaw admired immensely, claiming that in the future he himself might most be remembered as someone who once sat for Rodin. 'Mr Arnold Bennett Thinks Play-Writing Easier than Novel Writing' (1916) is a raucous piece in which Shaw, incensed at a recent book arguing for the primacy of prose fiction over drama, rewrites a famous scene from *Macbeth* in the style of a nineteenth-century realist novel, producing one of the most entertaining of all of Shaw's prose works. On a more personal level, 'Oscar Wilde' (1918) details Shaw's complicated relationship with his contemporary and sometime artistic rival both before and after Wilde's infamous trial and imprisonment for gross indecency, a time through which Shaw continued to support and defend Wilde. A selection from *Ruskin's Politics*, first delivered as a speech to the Royal Academy in 1919 and subsequently published as a standalone volume in 1921, finds Shaw drawing links between the visual arts, the novel, and socialism. 'Keats' (1921) puts forward Shaw's views on the legendary poet and the relationship between aesthetics and politics more generally. 'Tolstoy: Tragedian or Comedian?' (1921) juggles a triumvirate of topics: Tolstoy's plays, the history of tragedy, and the place of comedy in society. 'Beethoven's Centenary' (1927) represents Shaw's most extended treatise on the composer, whom he ranks alongside his beloved idols Wagner and Mozart; the piece was one of the last of his major writings on music. 'My First Talkie' (1931) serves as a brief introduction to Shaw's semi-successful foray into film with the 1931 adaptation of his short play *How He Lied to Her Husband*.

The final two selections date from the last years of Shaw's life. 'Am I an Educated Person?' (1947) finds Shaw reflecting on his self-education, on the importance of art in a young person's maturation, and on the relationship between his youthful work as a critic and his dramas. 'The Play of Ideas' (1950) is both one of Shaw's very last published pieces and one of the most trenchant explanations of his landmark concept of the 'play of ideas', placing his view of the concept's role in theatre history against the form's many detractors.

G.B.S., Artist-Critic

Shaw always attested that his career as a dramatist would not have been the same without the training of his prior career as a critic, but it is still remarkable the degree to which this indebtedness manifested within his plays even decades after he had put criticism aside. It is not just the rhetorical and intellectual practice of his journalistic years that informed his later art. It is also, in many ways, the substance of that criticism itself. In the Epistle Dedicatory to *Man and Superman*, Shaw famously argued that intellectual artists—what he calls the 'artist-philosopher'—'are the only sort of artists I take quite seriously'.[23] But what exactly Shaw meant by the term 'philosopher' in this formulation is very much up for debate.[24] The only actual philosopher that Shaw includes in his list of 'writers whose peculiar sense of the world I recognize as more or less akin to my own' is Friedrich Nietzsche—and even here the case is suspect.[25] As Shaw himself was at pains to point out in his writings on Nietzsche, the famous German thinker was a philosophical aspirant only. He was, by profession, a German professor of classical philology, or as Shaw once called him 'a German professor like any other German professor'.[26] Where Nietzsche was most valuable, according to Shaw, was not as a programmatic thinker but as a pithy aphorist and unrivalled stylist. 'Nietzsche does not write in chapters or treatises: he writes leading articles, leaderettes, occasional notes, and epigrams,' Shaw observed. 'He recognizes that humanity, having tasted the art of the journalist, will no longer suffer men to inflict books on it' (pp. 293–4). That is to say, Nietzsche was most valuable to Shaw as a critic. What we might say,

[23] Bernard Shaw, 'Epistle Dedicatory to Arthur Bingham Walkley', in *The Bodley Head Bernard Shaw: Collected Plays with Their Prefaces*, ed. Dan H. Laurence (London: Bodley Head, 1970–4), ii. 519.

[24] See David Kornhaber, 'Philosophy', in Brad Kent (ed.), *George Bernard Shaw in Context* (Cambridge: Cambridge University Press, 2015), 306–13.

[25] Bernard Shaw, 'Epistle Dedicatory to Arthur Bingham Walkley', in *The Bodley Head Bernard Shaw: Collected Plays with Their Prefaces*, ed. Laurence, ii. 520.

[26] Bernard Shaw, 'Our Book-Shelf: "Friedrich Nietzsche: The Dionysian Spirit of the Age" ', in Brian Tyson (ed.), *Bernard Shaw's Book Reviews*, 2 vols (University Park, PA: The Pennsylvania State University Press, 1991), ii. 227.

then, is that Shaw was not so much interested in the artist-philosopher bent on offering fully developed intellectual systems communicated through art as on something more like the artist-critic whose work is infused with aesthetic and intellectual concerns in equal measure. As Shaw himself said, intellectual systems were decidedly overrated, whereas an ever-curious intellectualism was eternally valuable. 'All the assertions get disproved sooner or later,' he writes in the 'Epistle Dedicatory'. 'And so we find the world full of a magnificent debris of artistic fossils, with the matter-of-fact credibility gone clean out of them.'[27]

Ultimately, there would be no more exemplary artist-critic than Shaw himself: the traces of his journalistic days are everywhere apparent in his plays. At the most basic level, there is the matter of topics and opinions from his newspaper work filtering into the plays themselves, forming an obvious continuum between the work of Bernard Shaw, critic, and Bernard Shaw, playwright. Take, for example, Shaw's life-long affection for Mozart's *Don Giovanni*, the score by which he taught himself to play the piano in his youth. Even just in the selection of essays collected here, the opera is mentioned nearly a dozen times, showing up repeatedly in discussions of Wagner, Beethoven, and even Nietzsche. That the opera would become a point of inspiration for Shaw's *Man and Superman* seems almost inevitable. Shaw described the work as his 'Don Juan play', just as *Don Giovanni* was an adaptation of that legend.[28] And true to form, the actual strains of Mozart's beloved music appear within the play itself, in the self-contained 'Don Juan in Hell' sequence that reimagines Mozart's opera. In Shaw's less well-known play *The Six of Calais*, from 1934, the connection between his playwriting and his critical interests is even more apparent. The inspiration for the play came directly from Rodin's famous sculpture *The Burghers of Calais* (1889), based on the siege of Calais during the Hundred Years War. Shaw imagined a dramatic scenario wherein those same Burghers became the central characters of his story, as King Edward III decides their fate after seizing control of the town.

This connection between music, art, and drama was common for Shaw. His 1923 drama *Saint Joan* was inspired not so much by the historical figure of Joan of Arc as various artistic representations of her, the painting *Joan of Arc* (1879) by Jules Bastien-Lepage especially.[29]

---

[27] Shaw, 'Epistle Dedicatory to Arthur Bingham Walkley', 527.

[28] Shaw, 'Epistle Dedicatory to Arthur Bingham Walkley', 493.

[29] See Stanley Weintraub, 'Exploiting Art: The Pictures in Bernard Shaw's Plays', *Modern Drama*, 18/3 (Fall 1975), 215–38.

Likewise, drama scholar Martin Meisel notes a distinct lineage running from Luc-Olivier Merson's painting *Le Repos pendant la fuite en Egypte* (1880), which depicts the Virgin Mary sleeping in the lap of the Sphinx in Egypt, and a similar Egyptian vista evoked in Shaw's *Caesar and Cleopatra*.[30] There a sentinel describes how the moon 'rises full over the desert; and a vast horizon comes into relief, broken by a huge shape which soon reveals itself in the spreading radiance as a Sphinx pedestaled on the sands'—as though again Shaw were taking an artistic work of special interest to him and finding a way to intellectually inhabit it and translate it into dramatic form.[31] In *Candida* (1894), he takes such allusions another step forward, placing a print of Titian's *Assumption of the Virgin* (1518) on the mantelpiece of his set and eventually having his main character assume a pose that echoes the painting itself during the play's climactic discussion.[32] Shaw referred to the play as his 'modern Pre-Raphaelite play', evoking the British literary and visual arts movement that showed a similar interest in the arts of the early Renaissance, and called upon Titian's work to draw a contrast between the social idealization of womanhood and the lived reality of modern women.[33] In so doing, he makes through his dramatic practice a point he made in prose in *The Quintessence*: 'that there is no such species in creation as "Woman, lovely woman," the woman being simply the female of the human species, and that to have one conception of humanity for the woman and another for the man, or one law for the woman and another for the man, or one artistic convention for woman and another for man' is 'unnatural' and ultimately and inevitably 'unworkable' (p. 108). Time and again, art proved a natural part of Shaw's dramatic vocabulary. Here, his love of painting would be expressed not in the pages of *The World* or *The Star* or *Truth*, where he published art criticism in his youth, but on the stage boards of the Open Air Theatre in Regent's Park in London, the Garrick Theatre in New York City, the Theatre Royal in Newcastle upon Tyne, and the Theatre Royal in South Shields, where *The Six of Calais*, *Saint Joan*, *Caesar and Cleopatra*, and *Candida* each premiered—the journeyman critic now having matured into the

[30] See Martin Meisel, 'Cleopatra and "The Flight into Egypt"', *Shaw Review*, 7 (1964), 62–3.
[31] Bernard Shaw, *Caesar and Cleopatra*, in *The Bodley Head Bernard Shaw: Collected Plays with Their Prefaces*, ed. Laurence, ii. 493.
[32] See Charles A. Berst, 'The Action of Shaw's Settings and Props', *SHAW* 3 (1983), 41–65.
[33] Quoted in Weintraub, 'Exploiting Art: The Pictures in Bernard Shaw's Plays', 216.

accomplished dramatist with a far larger platform at his disposal to express those interests and ideas.

Yet nothing would be so direct as the way that Shaw occasionally brought his experience in drama criticism onto the stage. The Sphinx in *Caesar and Cleopatra* has a dramatic as well as an artistic antecedent, with Peer Gynt's confrontation—and apparent conversation—with the monument being a significant moment in Ibsen's eponymous play, which Shaw discusses at length in *The Quintessence* (p. 39). Ibsen himself was not just an artistic inspiration for Shaw but a point of discussion in his own plays: Act II of *The Philanderer* (1893), written just two years after *The Quintessence*, takes place in 'the Library of the Ibsen Club', while in *Misalliance* (1910) one character dourly commands another to 'read Ibsen', and by the time of *Back to Methuselah* (1922) the Norwegian playwright is literally canonized as a saint. What we might call this metacritical trend in Shaw's play-craft comes to a head in the most metatheatrical of his works, *Fanny's First Play* (1911). Serving primarily to showcase a play-within-a-play composed by an imagined fledgling playwright, Fanny O'Dowda—whose talent and instinct for showcasing uncomfortable truths in her works echoes Shaw's statement in the 1913 edition of *The Quintessence* that by the early 1900s 'women were writing better plays than men' (p. 116)—Shaw's play ends in a remarkable cadenza of drama criticism put on stage. Baffled by who could have written this play-within-the-play, the coterie of drama critics who make up the dramatis personae put forward a torrent of epigraphs critically describing the main dramatic talents of the day, statements that would have been entirely at home in Shaw's own youthful columns: 'It's intensely disagreeable. Therefore it's not by [J. M.] Barrie', or Arthur Wing Pinero has a 'habit of saying silly things that have no real sense in them', and even 'Shaw doesn't write his plays as plays. All he wants to do is to insult everybody all round and set us talking about him'.[34] Here, the two main periods of Shaw's career in letters, first as a drama critic and then as an actual dramatist, seem to have entirely folded in on themselves: the biting back-and-forth of drama criticism has at last become the actual substance of his playwriting.

The epilogue of *Fanny's First Play* is tongue-in-cheek, to be sure: much of the joke depended on Shaw's withholding of his name from the initial productions of the play so that the audience might guess along with the characters on stage as to whose play it was. But the intellectual

---

[34] Bernard Shaw, *Fanny's First Play*, in *Misalliance, The Dark Lady of the Sonnets, and Fanny's First Play* (New York: Brentano's, 1914), 242, 243.

inheritance of those years as a critic was also deeply serious for Shaw, an origin point for some of his most profound theatrical innovation. Reading Shaw's play-craft against his criticism can highlight some remarkable connections, instances where Shaw uses his drama to further develop or complete ideas first expressed in his early prose. In this vein, the drama scholar Alfred Turco Jr notes a powerful parallel between Shaw's *Major Barbara* and ideas originally put forward in *The Perfect Wagnerite*.[35] There, Shaw criticizes the opera composer for not following through on the potent dramatic premise of an aristocratic daughter fulfilling her father's world vision specifically by rebelling against him. As Shaw writes of *Die Walküre*, 'This daughter, the Valkyrie Brynhild, is [her father Wotan's] true will, his real self' and represents her father's 'aspiration from the high life to the higher life that is its divine element'; she is inevitably forced to rebel when pursuit of 'temporal power has made it false to itself' (pp. 156, 158). By contrast, *Die Götterdämmerung*, the final opera in the cycle, shatters the potential of the earlier operas in Shaw's view, offering only trite platitudes about love. Yet in *Major Barbara*, the dramatic situation of the Ring Cycle is recapitulated in a contemporary vein. Undershaft and Barbara inadvertently collaborate in a social revolution, marked first by Barbara's rejection of the values of her munitioner father by devoting her life to the Salvation Army and then by her accepting the challenge to bring those salvationist values to Undershaft's industrial village, at once both undoing and fulfilling his life's vision. Here Cusins, the mild-mannered professor of Greek who is Barbara's betrothed, becomes a latter-day Siegfried, entirely unencumbered at the play's end by contemporary morality and values.

If *Major Barbara* owes a debt to the ideas first put forward in *The Perfect Wagnerite*, even more of Shaw's oeuvre draws from *The Quintessence*. That early critical text lays out a set of particular interests within Ibsen's work that Shaw will return to repeatedly in his play-craft. Take, for example, *The Quintessence*'s unusual focus on Ibsen's *Rosmersholm*, seemingly among the least proto-Shavian of the Norwegian's works. Shaw returns to the play some eight times within *The Quintessence* beyond the six pages he devotes to discussing it directly. More than almost any other Ibsen play, Shaw seems haunted by that work and its nihilistic dance between love and suicide, its philosophy expressed in the sentiment that '"There is no judge over us: therefore we must do justice upon ourselves"' (p. 69). Might it not have eventually become a model for Shaw's own *Heartbreak House* (1919) some twenty-eight

[35] See Alfred Turco Jr, 'Music', in Kent (ed.), *George Bernard Shaw in Context*, 160–7.

years later? Shaw openly attributes that play—one of the least Shavian of Shavian dramas by the standards of effusive political and social debate—to Anton Chekhov, subtitling it 'A Fantasia in the Russian Manner on English Themes'. Yet the mordant atmosphere of regret and the existential dread that marks that play in general and the welcoming of death in the play's final scenes in particular seem as much borrowed from Ibsen as Chekhov. Nearly three decades after marvelling at Ibsen's study of self-destruction, Shaw returned to the theme within his own dramaturgy in his maturity.

One sees these echoes within *The Quintessence* again and again, as though Shaw had almost purposefully been staking out the main thematic points of his own future dramatic career. The notion of duty, for instance, is incessantly on Shaw's mind in that text: the subject comes up nearly sixty times in the book. At issue in Ibsen's work, Shaw argues, is the idea that 'every step of progress means a duty repudiated, and a scripture torn up' (p. 15). As a core insight into Ibsen's work this is debatable, but as a key to Shaw's own plays it is indisputable: from *Mrs Warren's Profession* and *Arms and the Man* to *Man and Superman* and *Major Barbara*, the repudiation of one's perceived social duty is a theme Shaw would continue to work through in his plays. It extends even to the realm of personal duty in the most domestic of matters. In a sense, the original ending of *Pygmalion* on which Shaw was so insistent—that Liza should not become romantically attached to Professor Higgins, as Shaw was at pains to emphasize in later revisions of the play against the impulses of London actors and Hollywood producers alike—might be seen as an inheritance from the ending of *A Doll's House*. 'She sweeps out,' the final stage direction for Liza in Shaw's play, is one of the few consistent elements across the play's three main revisions; the phrase offers an echo of Shaw's exultation in *The Quintessence* of 'the wives who slammed the front door like Nora' (p. 7).[36] Of Ibsen's ending, Shaw observes in *The Quintessence*: 'she leaves him then and there and goes out into the real world to find out its reality for herself, and to gain some position not fundamentally false' (p. 56). Though in substance *Pygmalion* is far removed from the strictly bourgeois concerns of Ibsen's masterwork—by design, Ibsen was working just a few steps away from the dictates of the well-made plays of Eugène Scribe or Victorien

---

[36] Bernard Shaw, *Pygmalion*, in *The Bodley Head Bernard Shaw: Collected Plays with Their Prefaces*, ed. Laurence, iv. 782. On the revisions to *Pygmalion*, see Derek McGovern, 'From Stage Play to Hybrid: Shaw's Three Editions of *Pygmalion*', *SHAW* 31/1 (2011), 9–30.

Sardou that Shaw so detested, save for his play's explosive ending—the greater shape of Shaw's drama about a woman objectified and turned into a plaything by a powerful man who cares for her dignity not at all seems very much indebted to Ibsen. Shaw's insistence that Liza end the play by rejecting Higgins seems perhaps not so far removed from his explication of the importance of Ibsen's prior rejection of an agreeable conclusion. 'To gain some position not fundamentally false', as Shaw describes Nora's motive, seems like an apt description of Liza's imperative as well.

Arguably, the culmination of Shaw's work as an artist-critic comes in his 1921 play *Back to Methuselah*, an epic five-part rumination on humanity's past, present, and future. According to Shaw's vision, it is the critics who will one day inherit the earth, eventually even severing their connection to art as an obsolete vehicle of thought. In the final section of the play titled *As Far as Thought Can Reach: A.D. 31,920*, an artistic competition is held by the younger members of a society defined by extreme longevity. Yet the winner of the contest is a sculptor who utterly rejects art, claiming that he destroyed all his creations as being inferior to life itself. 'In the end,' he says, 'the intellectual conscience that tore you away from the fleeting in art to the eternal must tear you away from art altogether, because art is false and life alone is true.'[37] Instead, he brings forward a scientist who has created an artificial man and woman, declaring that scientist to be the true artist. The beings malfunction, however, and have to be destroyed by the elder members of the society, who in turn teach the younger generation a lesson on the relationship between art, life, and thought. 'You use a glass mirror to see your face: you use works of art to see your soul,' they explain. 'But we who are older use neither glass mirrors nor works of art. We have a direct sense of life.'[38] Even their bodies will one day be discarded as unnecessary, just as they have discarded art. 'The day will come when there will be no people, only thought,' they intone.[39] Art is but a step in humankind's development, a means of better understanding life. But even life as it is currently understood is just a step in that same development, the ultimate object of existence being contemplation itself absent the constraints of matter, time, and space. Art and thought are again indelibly intertwined for Shaw: here the very point of the former is as a vehicle of the latter. Eventually art will be needed no longer, he

---

[37] Bernard Shaw, *Back to Methuselah*, in *The Bodley Head Bernard Shaw: Collected Plays with Their Prefaces*, ed. Laurence, v. 589.
[38] Shaw, *Back to Methuselah*, 595.   [39] Shaw, *Back to Methuselah*, 621.

speculates. The artist-philosophers—or, really, the artist-critics—will become not pure artists but pure thinkers, exercising their critical faculties absent any object of contemplation. The very point of art is to lead to thought. The artist must always give way to the critic.

The Legacy of Shaw's Cultural Essays

To read Shaw as a cultural critic is thus to discover him and his art anew. It is also to discover his era and his age anew. Aside from the framework they provide for Shaw's dramatic works, part of the pleasure and insight of these essays is simply the window they provide into the lived experience of a period of artistic and cultural ferment. Ever the playwright, Shaw brings us inside Rodin's studio so that we can see the sculptor at work, shaping and reshaping Shaw's bust relentlessly while the restless subject tries to look on patiently. Ever the critic, Shaw shows us the other side of Henry Irving's theatrical legacy that other more hagiographic accounts of the period tended to ignore: the arrogance and presumption that went along with his unique status in the London theatre world and the way his tastes and viewpoints shaped the wider direction of the commercial drama of his era. And ever the Dubliner, Shaw is at his most humane when discussing his complicated relationship to Wilde—the status rivalries behind their very different Dublin social strata and very different schooling, the wicked anecdote about the time they both improbably discovered one another at a formal naval review, and the sense of sadness and helplessness around Wilde's trials and suffering.

Across these various works, one sees faintly or in flickers the making of a master theory of art and culture, one distinct from yet influential on the views Shaw put forward in the prefaces to his own plays. Not just his own work, but all cultural products of consequence have in his mind a social purpose at their core. Shaw proved almost as dismissive of British aestheticism and its 'art for art's sake' sloganeering as he did of the well-made play and empty melodrama, yet he never questioned the value of their art itself. William Morris, Edward Burne-Jones, Algernon Swinburne, even Wilde all receive high praise at various points in Shaw's writing, their art holding for him a value beyond sheer aesthetics whether or not they wanted to admit as much. Art was for Shaw a site of not only political but also moral and even metaphysical questioning. He rejects utterly those who criticize him for never coming to any definitive answers to the social and philosophical problems that he once so urgently posed, dismissing those who claim 'I should have solved the riddle of the universe, as every criticaster complains I have never done. Of course not. Nobody knows' (p. 369). The point is to wonder and to probe, to challenge and to debate—to offer critique, always. As much as Shaw liked to speak of a philosophical purpose to art, he never sought to make art the servant of any established philosophy or merely a vehicle for communication. Art *was* the philosophy. Art and critique were always one.

NOTE ON THE TEXT

THE works collected in this volume were published in multiple editions across Shaw's lifetime, sometimes re-edited and reworked and sometimes simply reprinted. The versions published here are derived from the last published editions over which Shaw had editorial input, though many of these pieces continued to be reissued or republished after his death. *The Quintessence of Ibsenism*, *The Perfect Wagnerite*, and *The Sanity of Art* are taken from Shaw's *Major Critical Essays* (London: Constable & Co. Ltd, 1932). The Preface to *Three Plays by Brieux* is taken from *Three Plays by Brieux* (London: A. C. Fifield, 1914). Shaw's works of music criticism, '11 October 1893', '1 August 1894', and '8 August 1894' are taken from *Music in London, 1890–1894*, 3 vols (London: Constable & Co. Ltd, 1932). His essays 'The Case for the Critic-Dramatist', 'The Late Censor', 'Church and Stage', 'Nietzsche in English', 'Madox Brown, Watts, and Ibsen', and 'The Board School' are taken from *Our Theatres in the Nineties*, 3 vols (London: Constable & Co. Ltd, 1932). The profile pieces 'Henry Irving and Ellen Terry', 'Edgar Allan Poe', 'Rodin', 'Mr Arnold Bennett Thinks Play-Writing Easier than Novel Writing', 'Oscar Wilde', 'Keats', 'Tolstoy: Tragedian or Comedian?', and 'Beethoven's Centenary' are taken from the 1949 reprint of *Pen Portraits and Reviews* (London: Constable & Co. Ltd, 1932). The remaining essays are taken from a variety of sources: 'My First Talkie' comes from the Malvern Festival Program, 1931; 'Am I an Educated Person?' is taken from *Sixteen Self Sketches* (London: Constable & Co. Ltd, 1949); 'Ruskin's Politics' is excerpted from *Ruskin's Politics* (London: The Ruskin Centenary Council, 1921); and 'The Play of Ideas' appeared in *New Statesman and Nation*, 39 (6 May 1950). Throughout, matters of spelling and punctuation—often eclectic in Shaw's writings—are kept as they appeared in these editions. Important variants or changes between editions are marked in the notes. All footnotes are Shaw's own, while explanatory notes, marked with an asterisk (*) are the editor's. For those texts not included in full, abridgements are indicated by three centred asterisks (***).

SELECT BIBLIOGRAPHY

Works by George Bernard Shaw

Bernard Shaw on the London Art Scene, 1885–1950, ed. Stanley Weintraub (University Park, PA: Pennsylvania State University Press, 1989).
Bernard Shaw: The Drama Observed, 4 vols, ed. Bernard Dukore (University Park, PA: Pennsylvania State University Press, 1993).
Major Critical Essays (London: Constable & Co. Ltd, 1932).
Music in London, 1890–1894, 3 vols (London: Constable & Co. Ltd, 1932).
Our Theatres in the Nineties, 3 vols (London: Constable & Co. Ltd, 1932).
Pen Portraits and Reviews (London: Constable & Co. Ltd, 1932).
Preface to *Three Plays by Brieux* (London: A. C. Fifield, 1914).
Shaw's Music: The Complete Musical Criticism in Three Volumes, ed. Dan H. Laurence (London: Bodley Head, 1981).
Sixteen Self Sketches (London: Constable & Co. Ltd, 1949).

Shaw and Ibsen

Bullock, Philip Ross, 'Ibsen on the London Stage: Independent Theatre as Transnational Space', *Forum for Modern Language Studies*, 53/3 (July 2017), 360–70.
Decker, C. R., 'Ibsen's Literary Reputation and Victorian Taste', *Studies in Philology*, 32/4 (October 1935), 632–45.
Dukore, Bernard F., 'Karl Marx's Youngest Daughter and *A Doll's House*', *Theatre Journal*, 42/3 (October 1990), 308–21.
Gerould, Daniel Charles, 'George Bernard Shaw's Criticism of Ibsen', *Comparative Literature*, 15/2 (Spring 1963), 130–45.
Ibsen, Henrik, *A Doll's House*, trans. William Archer (London: T. Fischer Unwin, 1939).
May, Keith M., *Ibsen and Shaw* (New York: St Martin's Press, 1985).
Templeton, Joan, *Shaw's Ibsen: A Re-appraisal* (London: Palgrave-Macmillan, 2018).

Shaw and Music

Gates, Eugene, 'The Music Criticism and Aesthetics of George Bernard Shaw', *Journal of Aesthetic Education*, 35/3 (Autumn, 2001), 63–71.
Henson, Janice, 'Bernard Shaw's Contribution to the Wagner Controversy in England', *Shaw Review*, 4/1 (January 1961), 21–6.
Sessa, Anne Dzamba, *Richard Wagner and the English* (Teaneck, NJ: Fairleigh Dickinson University Press, 1978).
Turco Jr, Alfred, 'Music', in Brad Kent (ed.), *George Bernard Shaw in Context* (Cambridge: Cambridge University Press, 2015), 160–7.

Turco Jr, Alfred, 'Nobody's Perfect: George Bernard Shaw as Wagnerite', *Leitmotive: The Journal of the Wagner Society of Northern California*, 19/2 (2005): 1, 3–6; 19/3 (2005), 2–5, 16.

Wagner, Richard, *Opera and Drama*, trans. William Ashton Ellis (1851; Lincoln, NE: University of Nebraska Press: 1995).

Weiner, Marc A., *Richard Wagner and the Anti-Semitic Imagination* (Lincoln, NE: University of Nebraska Press, 1997).

General Shaw Criticism

Albert, Sidney P., *Shaw, Plato, and Euripides: Classical Currents in 'Major Barbara'* (Gainesville, FL: University Press of Florida, 2012).

Conolly, L. W., 'Shaw as a Critic: Paper for the American Theatre Critics Association Meeting (Shaw Festival, 15 June 2006)', *Pittsburgh Post-Gazette*, 19 July 2006.

Eliot, T. S., 'London Letter', *The Dial*, 71/4 (October 1921), 452–5.

Fromm, Harold, *Bernard Shaw and the Theater of the Nineties* (Lawrence, KA: University of Kansas Press, 1967).

Hale, Piers J., 'The Search for Purpose in a Post-Darwinian Universe: George Bernard Shaw, "Creative Evolution," and Shavian Eugenics: "The Dark Side of the Force"', *History and Philosophy of the Life Sciences*, 28/2 (2006), 191–213.

Kakutani, Michiko, 'G. B. Shaw and the Women in His Life', *New York Times*, 27 September 1981.

Kornhaber, David, 'Philosophy', in Brad Kent (ed.), *George Bernard Shaw in Context* (Cambridge: Cambridge University Press, 2015), 306–13.

Meisel, Martin, 'Visual Arts', in Brad Kent (ed.), *George Bernard Shaw in Context* (Cambridge: Cambridge University Press, 2015), 183–96.

Miller, Elizabeth, 'Journalism', in Brad Kent (ed.), *Bernard Shaw in Context* (Cambridge: Cambridge University Press, 2015), 127–34.

Mills, Carl Henry, 'Shaw's Theory of Creative Evolution', *Shaw Review*, 16/3 (September 1973), 123–32.

Nethercot, Arthur H., 'Bernard Shaw, Philosopher', *PMLA* 69/1 (March 1954), 57–75.

Ritschel, Nelson O'Ceallaigh, *Bernard Shaw, W. T. Stead, and the New Journalism: Whitechapel, Parnell, Titanic, and the Great War* (London: Palgrave-Macmillan, 2017).

Rodenbeck, John von B., 'Shaw's Revolt Against Rationalism', *Victorian Studies*, 15/4 (June 1972), 409–37.

Ruskino, Susan, 'Rattigan Versus Shaw: The "Drama of Ideas" Debate', *SHAW* 2 (1982), 171–8.

Weintraub, Stanley, 'Exploiting Art: The Pictures in Bernard Shaw's Plays', *Modern Drama*, 18/3 (Fall 1975), 215–38.

Weintraub, Stanley, *Shaw's People: Victoria to Churchill* (University Park, PA: Pennsylvania State University Press, 1996).

West, E. J., 'The Critic as Analyst: Bernard Shaw as Example', *Educational Theatre Journal* 4/3 (October 1952), 200–5.

Yde, Matthew, *Bernard Shaw and Totalitarianism: Longing for Utopia* (London: Palgrave-Macmillan, 2013).

Cultural and Historical Context

Archer, Charles, *William Archer: Life, Work, and Friendships* (London: George Allen & Unwin, 1931).

Mayhall, Laura E. Nym, *The Militant Suffrage Movement: Citizenship and Resistance in Britain, 1860–1930* (Oxford: Oxford University Press, 2003).

Newey, Katherine, *Women's Theatre Writing in Victorian Britain* (London: Palgrave-Macmillan, 2005).

Nietzsche, Friedrich, *The Gay Science*, ed. Bernard Williams (Cambridge: Cambridge University Press, 2001).

Nietzsche, Friedrich, *On the Genealogy of Morality*, in *On the Genealogy of Morality and Other Writings*, ed. Keith Ansell-Pearson, trans. Carol Diethe (Cambridge: Cambridge University Press, 1994).

Powell, Frank. *Censorship in England* (London: Frank Palmer, 1913).

Further Reading in Oxford World's Classics

Shaw, George Bernard, *The Apple Cart, Too True to Be Good, On the Rocks, and The Millionairess*, ed. Matthew Yde.

Shaw, George Bernard, *Arms and the Man, The Devil's Disciple, Caesar and Cleopatra*, ed. Lawrence Switzky.

Shaw, George Bernard, *Major Political Writings*, ed. Elizabeth Miller.

Shaw, George Bernard, *Man and Superman, John Bull's Other Island, Major Barbara*, ed. Brad Kent.

Shaw, George Bernard, *Mrs Warren's Profession, Candida, You Never Can Tell*, ed. Sos Eltis.

Shaw, George Bernard, *Playlets*, ed. James Moran.

Shaw, George Bernard, *Pygmalion, Heartbreak House, and Saint Joan*, ed. Brad Kent.

A CHRONOLOGY OF
GEORGE BERNARD SHAW

Plays and novels are listed according to the dates on which their composition was completed. The parenthetical information provides the date and place of the play's first performance, not including specially arranged copyright performances, as well as the subtitle in some instances; in the case of novels, the date on which each was first published as a book—as opposed to serialized in a journal—is indicated. Other major writings are listed according to their date of publication.

1856 Born in Dublin on 26 July.

1871 Leaves school for good in October; begins work as an office boy for a Dublin land agent in November.

1873 Promoted to cashier in February.

1876 Leaves job with Dublin land agent in March; moves to London on 1 April.

1878 *Passion Play* (unfinished).

1879 *Immaturity* (1930).

1880 *The Irrational Knot* (1905).

1882 *Love Among the Artists* (1900).

1883 *Cashel Byron's Profession* (1886); *An Unsocial Socialist* (1887).

1884 The Fabian Society is founded on 4 January; GBS attends his first meeting on 16 May and formally joins on 5 September; publishes his first pamphlet for them, 'A Manifesto', in October.

1886 Begins as art critic for *The World*, a position he will keep until January 1890.

1889 Begins as music critic for *The Star* under the pseudonym 'Corno di Bassetto' in February; *Fabian Essays in Socialism*.

1890 Resigns as music critic for *The Star* and begins as music critic for *The World* in May under the name G.B.S.

1891 *The Quintessence of Ibsenism*.

1892 *Widowers' Houses* (9 December 1892, Royalty Theatre, London).

1893 *The Philanderer: A Topical Comedy* (20 February 1905, Cripplegate Institute, London); *Mrs Warren's Profession* (5 January 1902, New Lyric Club, London).

1894   *Arms and the Man: An Anti-Romantic Comedy* (21 April 1894, Avenue Theatre, London); *Candida: A Mystery* (30 July 1897, Her Majesty's Theatre, Aberdeen); writes last article for *The World* in August.

1895   Begins as theatre critic at the *Saturday Review* in January; *The Man of Destiny: A Fictitious Paragraph of History* (1 July 1897, Grand Theatre, Croydon).

1896   *You Never Can Tell: A Comedy* (26 November 1899, Royalty Theatre, London).

1897   *The Devil's Disciple: A Melodrama* (1 October 1897, Harmanus Bleecker Hall, Albany, NY); elected as a member of the Vestry of the Parish of St Pancras, 18 May 1897.

1898   Resigns as theatre critic at the *Saturday Review* in May; marries Charlotte Frances Payne-Townshend at the Registry Office, Henrietta Street, Covent Garden, on 1 June; *The Perfect Wagnerite*; *Caesar and Cleopatra: A History* (1 May 1901, Anna Morgan Studios for Art and Expression at the Fine Arts Building, Chicago).

1899   *Captain Brassbound's Conversion: An Adventure* (16 December 1900, Strand Theatre, London).

1900   Re-elected for a second (and final) three-year term as a member of the St Pancras Borough Council (reconfigured since the prior election of 1897); *Fabianism and the Empire*.

1901   *The Admirable Bashville: or, Constancy Unrewarded* (14 December 1902, Pharos Club, London).

1903   *Man and Superman: A Comedy and a Philosophy* (21 May 1905, Court Theatre, London, though without Act III; *Don Juan in Hell* is first performed on 4 June 1907, Court Theatre, London; the entire play is first performed on 11 June 1915, Lyceum Theatre, Edinburgh).

1904   *How He Lied to Her Husband* (26 September 1904, Berkeley Lyceum, New York); *John Bull's Other Island* (1 November 1904, Court Theatre, London).

1905   *Passion, Poison, and Petrifaction: or the Fatal Gazogene* (A Brief Tragedy for Barns and Booths) (14 July 1905, Theatrical Garden Party, Regent's Park, London); *Major Barbara* (A Discussion) (28 November 1905, Court Theatre, London).

1906   *The Doctor's Dilemma: A Tragedy* (20 November 1906, Court Theatre, London).

1908   *The Sanity of Art* (First published as 'A Degenerate's View of Nordau', in *Liberty* (New York), 27 July 1895); *Getting Married: A Disquisitory Play* (12 May 1908, Haymarket Theatre, London).

1909 *The Shewing-up of Blanco Posnet: A Sermon in Crude Melodrama* (25 August 1909, Abbey Theatre, Dublin); *Press Cuttings* (A Topical Sketch Compiled from the Editorial and Correspondence Columns of the Daily Papers during the Women's War in 1909) (9 July 1909, Court Theatre, London); *The Fascinating Foundling* (A Disgrace to the Author) (28 January 1928, Arts Theatre Club, London); *Misalliance* (A Debate in One Sitting) (23 February 1910, Duke of York's Theatre, London).

1910 *The Dark Lady of the Sonnets: An Interlude* (24 November 1910, Haymarket Theatre, London); *The Glimpse of Reality: A Tragedietta* (8 October 1927, Fellowship Hall, Glasgow).

1911 *Fanny's First Play: An Easy Play for a Little Theatre* (19 April 1911, Little Theatre, London).

1912 *Androcles and the Lion: A Fable Play* (1 September 1913, St James's Theatre, London); *Pygmalion* (A Romance) (16 October 1913, Hofburg Theater, Vienna); *Overruled: A Demonstration* (14 October 1912, Duke of York's Theatre, London).

1913 *Great Catherine (Whom Glory Still Adores)* (A Thumbnail Sketch of Russian Court Life in the XVIII Century) (18 November 1913, Vaudeville Theatre, London).

1914 *The Music-Cure: A Piece of Utter Nonsense* (28 January 1914, Little Theatre, London); outbreak of the First World War on 28 July—Britain enters on 4 August; *Common Sense About the War* (supplement to *The New Statesman*, 14 November).

1915 *The Inca of Perusalem: An Almost Historical Comedietta* (7 October 1916, Repertory Theatre, Birmingham); *O'Flaherty V.C.: A Recruiting Pamphlet* (17 February 1917, Western Front, Treizennes, Belgium).

1916 *Augustus Does His Bit: A True-to-Life Farce* (An Unofficial Dramatic Tract on War Saving and Cognate Topics) (21 January 1917, Court Theatre, London).

1917 *Annajanska, The Bolshevik Empress: A Revolutionary Romancelet* (21 January 1918, Coliseum Theatre, London); *Heartbreak House: A Fantasia in the Russian Manner on English Themes* (10 November 1920, Garrick Theatre, New York).

1918 First World War ends, 11 November.

1920 *Back to Methuselah: A Metabiological Pentateuch* (A Play Cycle) (Parts I and II, 27 February 1922; Parts III and IV, 6 March 1922; Part V, 13 March 1922, Garrick Theatre, New York).

1921 *Jitta's Atonement*, by Siegfried Trebitsch, translated by Shaw (8 January 1923, Shubert-Garrick Theatre, Washington, DC).

1923 *Saint Joan: A Chronicle Play in Six Scenes and an Epilogue* (28 December 1923, Garrick Theatre, New York).

1926 *Translations and Tomfooleries*; the Swedish Academy announces that Shaw has won the 1925 Nobel Prize for Literature, 12 November.

1927 Accepts the Nobel Prize in February.

1928 *The Intelligent Woman's Guide to Socialism and Capitalism*; *The Apple Cart: A Political Extravaganza* (14 June 1929, Teatr Polski, Warsaw).

1931 *Music in London 1890–94: Criticisms contributed Week by Week to the World*; *Our Theatres in the Nineties*; *Too True To Be Good: A Political Extravaganza* (29 February 1932, Colonial Theatre, Boston, MA).

1932 *The Adventures of the Black Girl in Her Search for God.*

1933 *Village Wooing: A Comedietta for Two Voices* (16 April 1934, Little Theatre, Dallas, TX); *On the Rocks: A Political Comedy* (25 November 1933, Winter Garden Theatre, London).

1934 *The Simpleton of the Unexpected Isles: A Vision of Judgment* (18 February 1935, Guild Theatre, New York); *The Six of Calais: A Medieval War Story* (17 July 1934, Open Air Theatre, Regent's Park, London).

1935 *The Millionairess* (A Jonsonian Comedy) (4 January 1936, Akademie Theater, Vienna).

1936 *Geneva: Another Political Extravaganza* (25 July 1938, Teatr Polski, Warsaw).

1937 *Cymbeline Refinished: A Variation on Shakespear's Ending* (16 November 1937, Embassy Theatre, London).

1939 Wins the Academy Award for the best screenplay for the cinematic adaptation of *Pygmalion*; *'In Good King Charles's Golden Days': A True History that Never Happened* (12 August 1939, Festival Theatre, Malvern); outbreak of the Second World War: Britain and France declare war on Germany on 3 September.

1944 *Everybody's Political What's What.*

1945 Second World War ends.

1947 *Buoyant Billions: A Comedy of No Manners* (21 October 1948, Schauspielhaus, Zurich, Switzerland).

1949 *Sixteen Self Sketches*; *Shakes Versus Shav: A Puppet Play* (9 August 1949, Lyttelton Hall, Malvern).

1950 *Farfetched Fables* (6 September 1950, Watergate Theatre, London). Dies in Ayot St Lawrence on 2 November.

I

SUBSTANTIAL ESSAYS

THE QUINTESSENCE OF IBSENISM

PREFACE TO THE THIRD EDITION

SINCE the last edition of this book was printed, war, pestilence and famine have wrecked civilization and killed a number of people of whom the first batch is calculated as not less than fifteen millions.* Had the gospel of Ibsen been understood and heeded, these fifteen millions might have been alive now; for the war was a war of ideals. Liberal ideals, Feudal ideals, National ideals, Dynastic ideals, Republican ideals, Church ideals, State ideals, and Class ideals, bourgeois and proletarian, all heaped up into a gigantic pile of spiritual high explosive,* and then shovelled daily into every house with the morning milk by the newspapers, needed only a bomb thrown at Serajevo by a handful of regicide idealists to blow the centre out of Europe.* Men with empty phrases in their mouths and foolish fables in their heads have seen each other, not as fellow-creatures, but as dragons and devils, and have slaughtered each other accordingly. Now that our frenzies are forgotten, our commissariats disbanded, and the soldiers they fed demobilized to starve when they cannot get employment in mending what we broke, even the iron-mouthed Ibsen, were he still alive, would perhaps spare us, disillusioned wretches as we are, the well-deserved 'I told you so.'

Not that there is any sign of the lesson being taken to heart. Our reactions from Militarist idealism into Pacifist idealism will not put an end to war: they are only a practical form of the *reculer pour mieux sauter*.* We still cannot bring ourselves to criticize our ideals, because that would be a form of self-criticism. The vital force that drives men to throw away their lives and those of others in the pursuit of an imaginative impulse, reckless of its apparent effect on human welfare, is, like all natural forces, given to us in enormous excess to provide against an enormous waste. Therefore men, instead of economizing it by consecrating it to the service of their highest impulses, grasp at a phrase in a newspaper article, or in the speech of a politician on a vote-catching expedition, as an excuse for exercising it violently, just as a horse turned out to grass will gallop and kick merely to let off steam. The shallowness of the ideals of men ignorant of history is their destruction.

But I cannot spend the rest of my life drawing the moral of the war. It must suffice to say here that as war throws back civilization inevitably, leaving everything worse than it was, from razors and scissors to the characters of the men that make and sell and buy them, old abuses revive eagerly in a world that dreamed it had got rid of them for ever; old books on morals become new and topical again; and old prophets stir in their graves and are read with a new sense of the importance of their message.* That is perhaps why a new edition of this book is demanded.

In spite of the temptation to illustrate it afresh by the moral collapse of the last ten years, I have left the book untouched. To change a pre-war book into a post-war book would in this case mean interpreting Ibsen in the light of a catastrophe of which he was unaware. Nobody can pretend to say what view he would have taken of it. He might have thought the demolition of three monstrous idealist empires cheap at the cost of fifteen million idealists' lives. Or he might have seen in the bourgeois republics which have superseded them a more deeply entrenched fortification of idealism at its suburban worst. So I have refrained from tampering with what I wrote when I, too, was as pre-war as Ibsen.

1922.   G.B.S.

In the pages which follow I have made no attempt to tamper with the work of the bygone man of thirty-five who wrote them. I have never admitted the right of an elderly author to alter the work of a young author, even when the young author happens to be his former self.* In the case of a work which is a mere exhibition of skill in conventional art, there may be some excuse for the delusion that the longer the artist works on it the nearer he will bring it to perfection. Yet even the victims of this delusion must see that there is an age limit to the process, and that though a man of forty-five may improve the workmanship of a man of thirty-five, it does not follow that a man of fifty-five can do the same.

When we come to creative art, to the living word of a man delivering a message to his own time, it is clear that any attempt to alter this later on is simply fraud and forgery. As I read the old Quintessence of Ibsenism I may find things that I see now at a different angle, or correlate with so many things then unnoted by me that they take on a different aspect. But though this may be a reason for writing another book, it is not a reason for altering an existing one. What I have written I have written,* said Pilate, thinking (rightly, as it turned out) that his blunder might prove truer than its revision by the elders; and what he said after a lapse of twenty-one seconds I may very well say after a lapse of twenty-one years.

However, I should not hesitate to criticize my earlier work if I thought it likely to do any mischief that criticism can avert. But on reading it through I have no doubt that it is as much needed in its old form as ever it was. Now that Ibsen is no longer frantically abused, and is safe in the Pantheon, his message is in worse danger of being forgotten or ignored than when he was in the pillory.* Nobody now dreams of calling me a 'muck ferretting dog' because I think Ibsen a great teacher. I will not go so far as to say I wish they did; but I do say that the most effective way of shutting our minds against a great man's ideas is to take them for granted and admit he was great and have done with him. It really matters very little whether Ibsen was a great man or not: what does matter is his message and the need of it.

That people are still interested in the message is proved by the history of this book. It has long been out of print in England; but it has never been out of demand. In spite of the smuggling of unauthorized American editions, which I have winked at because the absence of an

English reprint was my own fault (if it be a fault not to be able to do more than a dozen things at a time), the average price of copies of the original edition stood at twenty-four shillings* some years ago, and is no doubt higher now. But it was not possible to reprint it without additions. When it was issued in 1891 Ibsen was still alive, and had not yet produced The Master Builder, or Little Eyolf, or John Gabriel Borkman, or When We Dead Awaken. Without an account of these four final masterpieces, a book entitled The Quintessence of Ibsenism would have been a fraud on its purchasers; and it was the difficulty of finding time to write the additional chapters on these plays, and review Ibsen's position from the point of view reached when his work ended with his death and his canonization as an admitted grand master of European literature, that has prevented me for twenty years from complying with the demand for a second edition. Also, perhaps, some relics of my old, or rather my young conscience, which revolted against hasty work. Now that my own stream is nearer the sea, I am more inclined to encourage myself in haste and recklessness by reminding myself that *le mieux est l'ennemi du bien,** and that I had better cobble up a new edition as best I can than not supply it at all.

I have taken all possible precautions to keep the reader's mind free from verbal confusion in following Ibsen's attack on ideals and idealism, a confusion that might have been avoided could his plays, without losing the naturalness of their dialogue, have been translated into the language of the English Bible. It is not too much to say that the works of Ibsen furnish one of the best modern keys to the prophecies of Scripture. Read the prophets, major and minor, from Isaiah to Malachi, without such a key, and you will be puzzled and bored by the almost continuous protest against and denunciation of idolatry and prostitution. Simpletons read all this passionate invective with sleepy unconcern, concluding thoughtlessly that idolatry means praying to stocks and stones instead of to brass lectern eagles and the new reredos* presented by the local distiller in search of a title; and as to prostitution, they think of it as 'the social evil,' and regret that the translators of the Bible used a much blunter word. But nobody who has ever heard real live men talking about graven images and traders in sex can for a moment suppose them to be the things the prophets denounced so earnestly. For idols and idolatry read ideals and idealism; for the prostitution of Piccadilly Circus* read not only the prostitution of the journalist, the political lawyer, the parson selling his soul to the squire, the ambitious politician selling his soul for office, but the much more intimate and widespread idolatries and prostitutions of the private snob, the domestic tyrant and voluptuary, and the industrial adventurer. At once the prophetic warnings and curses take on meaning and proportion, and lose that air of exaggerated righteousness and tiresome conventional rant which repels readers who do not possess Ibsen's clue. I have sometimes thought of reversing the operation, and substituting in this book the words idol and idolatry for ideal and idealism; but it would be impossible without spoiling the actuality of Ibsen's criticism of society. If you call a man a rascally idealist, he is not only shocked and indignant but puzzled: in which condition you can rely on his attention. If you call him a rascally idolater, he concludes calmly that you do not know that he is a member of the Church of England. I have therefore left the old wording. Save for certain adaptations made necessary by the lapse of time and the hand of death, the book stands as it did, with a few elucidations which I might have made in 1891 had I given the text a couple of extra revisions. Also, of course, the section dealing with the last four plays. The two concluding chapters are new. There is no fundamental change: above all, no dilution.

Whether this edition will change people's minds to the extent to which the first did (to my own great astonishment) I do not know. In the eighteen-nineties one jested about the revolt of the daughters, and of the wives who slammed the front door like Nora. At present the revolt has become so general that even the feeblest and oldest after-dinner jesters dare no longer keep Votes for Women* on their list of stale pleasantries about mothers-in-law, rational dress, and mixed bathing. Men are waking up to the perception that in killing women's souls they have killed their own. Mr Granville-Barker's worthy father of six unmarriageable daughters in The Madras House,* ruefully exclaiming, 'It seems to me Ive been made a convenience of all my life,' has taken away the excited attention that Nora once commanded when she said, 'I have been living all these years with a strange man.' When she meets Helmer's 'No man sacrifices his honor for a woman' with her 'Thousands of women have done that for men,' there is no longer the old impressed assent: men fiercely protest that it is not true; that, on the contrary, for every woman who has sacrificed her honor for a man's sake, ten men have sacrificed their honor for a woman's. In the plays of Gorki and Tchekov, against which all the imbecilities and outrages of the old anti-Ibsen campaign are being revived (for the Press never learns anything by experience), the men appear as more tragically sacrificed by evil social conditions and their romantic and idealistic disguises than the women. Now it may be that into this new atmosphere my book will come with quite an old-fashioned air. As I write these

lines the terrible play with which Strindberg wreaked the revenge of the
male for A Doll's House has just been performed for the first time in
London under the title of Creditors. In that, as in Brieux's Les
Hannetons,* it is the man who is the victim of domesticity, and the
woman who is the tyrant and soul destroyer. Thus A Doll's House did
not dispose of the question: it only brought on the stage the endless
recriminations of idealistic marriage. And how has Strindberg, Ibsen's
twin giant, been received? With an even idler stupidity than Ibsen himself, because Ibsen appealed to the rising energy of the revolt of women
against idealism; but Strindberg attacks women ruthlessly, trying to
rouse men from the sloth and sensuality of their idealized addiction to
them; and as the men, unlike the women, do not want to be roused,
whilst the women do not like to be attacked, there is no conscious
Strindberg movement to relieve the indifference, the dull belittlement,
the spiteful hostility against which the devotees of Ibsen fought so
slashingly in the nineties. But the unconscious movement is violent
enough. As I write, it is only two days since an eminent bacteriologist
filled three columns of The Times with a wild Strindbergian letter* in
which he declared that women must be politically and professionally
secluded and indeed excluded, because their presence and influence
inflict on men an obsession so disabling and dangerous that men and
women can work together or legislate together only on the same conditions as horses and mares: that is, by the surgical destruction of the
male's sex. The Times and The Pall Mall Gazette gravely accept this
outburst as 'scientific,' and heartily endorse it; though only a few weeks
have elapsed since The Times dismissed Strindberg's play and
Strindberg himself with curt superciliousness as uninteresting and
negligible. Not many years ago, a performance of a play by myself,* the
action of which was placed in an imaginary Ibsen Club, in which the
comedy of the bewilderment of conventional people when brought
suddenly into contact with the Ibsenist movement (both understood
and misunderstood) formed the atmosphere of the piece, was criticized
in terms which shewed that our critics are just as hopelessly in the rear
of Ibsen as they were in 1891. The only difference was that whereas in
1891 they would have insulted Ibsen, they now accept him as a classic.
But understanding of the change of mind produced by Ibsen, or notion
that they live in a world which is seething with the reaction of Ibsen's
ideas against the ideas of Sardou and Tom Taylor,* they have none.
They stare with equal unintelligence at the sieges and stormings of
separate homesteads by Ibsen or Strindberg, and at the attack all along
the front of refined society into which these sieges and stormings have

now developed. Whether the attack is exquisite, touching, delicate, as in Tchekov's Cherry Orchard, Galsworthy's Silver Box, and Granville-Barker's Anne Leete,* or ruthless, with every trick of intellectual ruffianism and ribaldry, and every engine of dramatic controversy, there is the same pettish disappointment at the absence of the old conventions, the same gaping unconsciousness of the meaning and purpose of the warfare in which each play is a battle, as in the days when this book was new.

Our political journalists are even blinder than our artistic ones in this matter. The credit of our domestic ideals having been shaken to their foundations, as through a couple of earthquake shocks, by Ibsen and Strindberg (the Arch-Individualists of the nineteenth century) whilst the Socialists have been idealizing, sentimentalizing, denouncing Capitalism for sacrificing Love and Home and Domestic Happiness and Children and Duty to money greed and ambition, yet it remains a commonplace of political journalism to assume that Socialism is the deadliest enemy of the domestic ideals and Unsocialism their only hope and refuge. In the same breath the world-grasping commercial synthesis we call Capitalism, built up by generations of Scotch Rationalists and English Utilitarians, Atheists, Agnostics and Natural-Selectionists, with Malthus* as the one churchman among all its prophets, is proclaimed the bulwark of the Christian Churches. We used to be told that the people that walked in darkness have seen a great light. When our people see the heavens blazing with suns, they simply keep their eyes shut, and walk on in darkness until they have led us into the pit. No matter: I am not a domestic idealist; and it pleases me to think that the Life Force may have providential aims in thus keeping my opponents off the trail.

But for all that I must not darken counsel. I therefore, without further apology, launch my old torpedo with the old charge in it, leaving to the new chapters at the end what I have to say about the change in the theatre since Ibsen set his potent leaven to work there.

AYOT ST LAWRENCE, 1912–13.

PREFACE TO THE FIRST EDITION

IN the spring of 1890, the Fabian Society,* finding itself at a loss for a course of lectures to occupy its summer meetings, was compelled to make shift with a series of papers put forward under the general heading of Socialism in Contemporary Literature. The Fabian Essayists, strongly pressed to do 'something or other,' for the most part shook their heads; but in the end Sydney Olivier consented to 'take Zola'; I consented to 'take Ibsen'; and Hubert Bland undertook to read all the Socialist novels of the day, an enterprise the desperate failure of which resulted in the most amusing paper of the series. William Morris, asked to read a paper on himself, flatly declined, but gave us one on Gothic Architecture. Stepniak also came to the rescue with a lecture on modern Russian fiction; and so the Society tided over the summer without having to close its doors, but also without having added anything whatever to the general stock of information on Socialism in Contemporary Literature.* After this I cannot claim that my paper on Ibsen, which was duly read at the St James's Restaurant on the 18th July 1890, under the presidency of Mrs Annie Besant, and which was the first form of this little book, is an original work in the sense of being the result of a spontaneous internal impulse on my part. Having purposely couched it in the most provocative terms (of which traces may be found by the curious in its present state), I did not attach much importance to the somewhat lively debate that arose upon it; and I had laid it aside as a *pièce d'occasion** which had served its turn, when the production of Rosmersholm at the Vaudeville Theatre by Florence Farr, the inauguration of the Independent Theatre by Mr J. T. Grein with a performance of Ghosts, and the sensation created by the experiment of Elizabeth Robins and Marion Lea with Hedda Gabler,* started a frantic newspaper controversy, in which I could see no sign of any of the disputants having ever been forced by circumstances, as I had, to make up his mind definitely as to what Ibsen's plays meant, and to defend his view face to face with some of the keenest debaters in London. I allow due weight to the fact that Ibsen himself has not enjoyed this Fabian advantage; but I have also shewn that the existence of a discoverable and perfectly definite thesis in a poet's work by no means depends on the completeness of his own intellectual consciousness of it. At any rate, the controversialists, whether in the abusive stage, or the apologetic stage, or the hero-worshipping stage, by no means made clear what they were abusing, or apologizing for, or going into ecstasies about; and I came to the conclusion that my explanation might as well be placed in the field until a better could be found.

With this account of the origin of the book, and a reminder that it is not a critical essay on the poetic beauties of Ibsen, but simply an exposition of Ibsenism, I offer it to my readers to make what they can of.

LONDON, June 1891.

THE QUINTESSENCE OF IBSENISM

THE TWO PIONEERS

THAT is, pioneers of the march to the plains of heaven (so to speak).

The second, whose eyes are in the back of his head, is the man who declares that it is wrong to do something that no one has hitherto seen any harm in.

The first, whose eyes are very longsighted and in the usual place, is the man who declares that it is right to do something hitherto regarded as infamous.

The second is treated with great respect by the army. They give him testimonials; name him the Good Man; and hate him like the devil.

The first is stoned and shrieked at by the whole army. They call him all manner of opprobrious names; grudge him his bare bread and water; and secretly adore him as their savior from utter despair.

Let me take an example from life of my pioneers. Shelley* was a pioneer and nothing else: he did both first and second pioneer's work.

Now compare the effect produced by Shelley as abstinence preacher or second pioneer with that which he produced as indulgence preacher or first pioneer. For example:

SECOND PIONEER PROPOSITION: It is wrong to kill animals and eat them.

FIRST PIONEER PROPOSITION: It is not wrong to take your sister as your wife.[1]*

[1] The curious persistence of this proposition in the higher poetry of the nineteenth century is not easy to account for now that it sounds both unimportant and old-fashioned. It is as if one said 'It is not wrong to stand on one's head.' The reply is 'You may be very right; but as nobody wants to, why bother about it?' Yet I think this sensible way of treating the matter—obviously more healthy than the old morbid horror—has been produced largely by the refusal of poets like Shelley and Wagner to accept the theory of natural antipathy as the basis of the tables of Consanguinity,* and by the subsequent publication of masses of evidence by sociologists, from Herbert Spencer to Westermarck,* shewing that such tables are entirely conventional and that all our prohibitions have been either ignored or actually turned into positive obligations at one time or another without any shock to human instincts. The consequence is that our eyes are now opened to the practical social reasons for barring marriage between Laon and Cythna, Siegmund and Sieglinda;* and the preaching of incest as something poetic in itself has lost all its morbid interest and ceased. Also we are beginning to recognize the important fact that the absence of romantic illusion as between persons brought up together, which undoubtedly

Here the second pioneer appears as a gentle humanitarian, and the first as an unnatural corrupter of public morals and family life. So much easier is it to declare the right wrong than the wrong right in a society with a guilty conscience, to which, as to Dickens's detective, 'Any possible move is a probable move provided it's in a wrong direction.'* Just as the liar's punishment is, not in the least that he is not believed, but that he cannot believe any one else; so a guilty society can more easily be persuaded that any apparently innocent act is guilty than that any apparently guilty act is innocent.

The English newspaper which best represented the guilty conscience of the middle class, was, when Ibsen's plays reached England, The Daily Telegraph. If we can find that The Daily Telegraph attacked Ibsen as *The Quarterly Review used to attack Shelley,** it will occur to us at once that there must be something of the first pioneer about Ibsen.

The late Clement Scott,* at that time dramatic critic to The Daily Telegraph, was a sentimentally goodnatured gentleman, not then a pioneer, though he had in his time fought hard for the advance in British drama represented by the plays of Robertson.* He was also an emotional, impressionable, zealous, and sincere Roman Catholic. He accused Ibsen of dramatic impotence, ludicrous amateurishness, nastiness, vulgarity, egotism, coarseness, absurdity, uninteresting verbosity, and 'suburbanity,' declaring that he has taken ideas that would have inspired a great tragic poet, and vulgarized and debased them in dull, hateful, loathsome, horrible plays. This criticism, which occurs in a notice of the first performance of Ghosts in England, is to be found in The Daily Telegraph for the 14th March 1891, and is supplemented by a leading article which compares the play to an open drain, a loathsome sore unbandaged, a dirty act done publicly, or a lazar house with all its doors and windows open. Bestial, cynical, disgusting, poisonous, sickly, delirious, indecent, loathsome, fetid, literary carrion, crapulous stuff, clinical confessions: all these epithets are used in the article as descriptive of Ibsen's work. 'Realism,' said the writer, 'is one thing; but the nostrils of the audience must not be visibly held before a play can be stamped as true to nature. It is difficult to expose in decorous words the gross and almost putrid indecorum of this play.' As the performance of

exists, and which used to be mistaken for natural antipathy, cannot be depended on as between strangers, however close their consanguinity, and that any domestic or educational system which segregates the sexes produces romantic illusion, no matter how undesirable it may be. It will be seen later on in the chapter dealing with the play called Ghosts, that Ibsen took this modern view that consanguinity does not count between strangers. I have accepted it myself in my play Mrs Warren's Profession. (1912.)

Ghosts took place on the evening of the 13th March, and the criticism appeared next morning, it is evident that Clement Scott must have gone straight from the theatre to the newspaper office, and there, in an almost hysterical condition, penned his share of this extraordinary protest. The literary workmanship bears marks of haste and disorder, which, however, only heighten the expression of the passionate horror produced in the writer by seeing Ghosts on the stage. He calls on the authorities to cancel the license of the theatre, and declares that he has been exhorted to laugh at honor, to disbelieve in love, to mock at virtue, to distrust friendship, and to deride fidelity.

If this document were at all singular, it would rank as one of the curiosities of criticism, exhibiting, as it does, the most seasoned playgoer in London thrown into convulsions by a performance which was witnessed with approval, and even with enthusiasm, by many persons of approved moral and artistic conscientiousness. But Clement Scott's criticism was hardly distinguishable in tone from dozens of others which appeared simultaneously. His opinion was the vulgar opinion. Mr Alfred Watson,* critic to The Standard, the leading Tory daily paper, proposed that proceedings should be taken against the theatre under Lord Campbell's Act* for the suppression of disorderly houses. Clearly Clement Scott and his editor Sir Edwin Arnold,* with whom rested the final responsibility for the article which accompanied the criticism, represented a considerable party.

How then is it that Ibsen, a Norwegian playwright of European celebrity, attracted one section of the English people so strongly that they hailed him as the greatest living dramatic poet and moral teacher, whilst another section was so revolted by his works that they described him in terms which they themselves admitted to be, by the necessities of the case, all but obscene? This phenomenon, which has occurred throughout Europe whenever Ibsen's plays have been acted, as well as in America and Australia, must be exhaustively explained before the plays can be described without danger of reproducing the same confusion in the reader's own mind. Such an explanation, therefore, must be my first business.

Understand, at the outset, that the explanation will not be an explaining away. Clement Scott's judgment did not mislead him in the least as to Ibsen's meaning. Ibsen means all that most revolted his critic. For example, in Ghosts, the play in question, a clergyman and a married woman fall in love with one another. The woman proposes to abandon her husband and live with the clergyman. He recalls her to her duty, and makes her behave as a virtuous woman. She afterwards tells him that this was a crime on his part. Ibsen agrees with her, and has written the play to bring you round to his opinion. Clement Scott did not agree with her, and believed that when you are brought round to her opinion you have been morally corrupted. By this conviction he was impelled to denounce Ibsen as he did, Ibsen being equally impelled to propagate the convictions which provoked the attack. Which of the two is right cannot be decided until it is ascertained whether a society of persons holding Ibsen's opinions would be higher or lower than a society holding Clement Scott's.

There are many people who cannot conceive this as an open question. To them a denunciation of any recognized practices is an incitement to unsocial conduct; and every utterance in which an assumption of the eternal validity of these practices is not implicit is a paradox. Yet all progress involves the beating of them from that position. By way of illustration, one may rake up the case of Proudhon,* who in the year 1840 carefully defined property as theft. This was thought the very maddest paradox that ever man hazarded: it seemed obvious that a society which countenanced such a proposition must speedily be reduced to the condition of a sacked city. Today schemes for the confiscation by taxation and supertaxation of mining royalties and ground rents are commonplaces of social reform; and the honesty of the relation of our big property holders to the rest of the community is challenged on all hands. It would be easy to multiply instances, though the most complete are now ineffective through the triumph of the original paradox having obliterated all memory of the opposition it first had to encounter. The point to seize is that social progress takes effect through the replacement of old institutions by new ones; and since every institution involves the recognition of the duty of conforming to it, progress must involve the repudiation of an established duty at every step. If the Englishman had not repudiated the duty of absolute obedience to his king, his political progress would have been impossible. If women had not repudiated the duty of absolute submission to their husbands, and defied public opinion as to the limits set by modesty to their education, they would never have gained the protection of the Married Women's Property Act, the municipal vote, or the power to qualify themselves as medical practitioners.* If Luther had not trampled on his duty to the head of his Church and on his vow of chastity, our clergy would still have to choose between celibacy and profligacy. There is nothing new, then, in the defiance of duty by the reformer: every step of progress means a duty repudiated, and a scripture torn up. And every reformer is denounced accordingly: Luther as an apostate, Cromwell as a traitor,

Mary Wollstonecraft* as an unwomanly virago, Shelley as a libertine, and Ibsen as all the things enumerated in The Daily Telegraph.

This crablike progress of social evolution, in which the individual advances by seeming to go backward, continues to illude us in spite of all the lessons of history. To the pious man the newly made freethinker, suddenly renouncing supernatural revelation, and denying all obligation to believe the Bible and obey the commandments as such, appears to be claiming the right to rob and murder at large. But the freethinker soon finds reasons for not doing what he does not want to do; and these reasons seem to him to be far more binding on our conscience than the precepts of a book of which the infallibility cannot be rationally proved. The pious man is at last forced to admit—as he was in the case of the late Charles Bradlaugh,* for instance—that the disciples of Voltaire and Tom Paine* do not pick pockets or cut throats oftener than your even Christian: he actually is driven to doubt whether Voltaire himself (poor Voltaire, who built a church, and was the greatest philanthropist of his time!) really screamed and saw the devil on his deathbed.

This experience by no means saves the rationalist[1]* from falling into the same conservatism when the time comes for his own belief to be questioned. No sooner has he triumphed over the theologian than he forthwith sets up as binding on all men the duty of acting logically with the object of securing the greatest good of the greatest number, with the result that he is presently landed in vivisection, Contagious Diseases Acts,* dynamite conspiracies, and other grotesque but strictly reasonable abominations. Reason becomes Dagon, Moloch, and Jehovah* rolled into one. Its devotees exult in having freed themselves from the old slavery to a collection of books written by Jewish men of letters. To worship such books was, they can prove, as absurd as to worship sonatas composed by German musicians, as was done by the hero of Wagner's novelette, who sat up on his death-bed to say his creed, beginning, 'I believe in God, Mozart, and Beethoven.' The Voltairean freethinker despises such a piece of sentiment; but is it not much more sensible to worship a sonata constructed by a musician than to worship a syllogism constructed by a logician, since the sonata may encourage heroism, or at least inspire feelings of awe and devotion? This does not occur to the votary of reason; and the rationalist's freethinking soon comes to mean syllogism worship with rites of human sacrifice; for just as the rationalist's pious predecessor thought that the man who scoffed

---

[1] I had better here warn students of philosophy that I am speaking of rationalism, not as classified in the books, but as apparent in men.

at baptism and the Bible must infallibly yield without resistance to all his criminal propensities, so the rationalist in turn becomes convinced that when a man once loses his faith in vaccination and in Herbert Spencer's Data of Ethics,* he is no longer to be trusted to keep his hands off his neighbor's person, purse, or wife.

In process of time the age of reason had to go its way after the age of faith. In actual experience, the first shock to rationalism comes from the observation that though nothing can persuade women to adopt it, their impatience of reasoning no more prevents them from arriving at right conclusions than the masculine belief in it (never a very deeply rooted faith in England, by the way, whatever it may have been in France or Greece) saves men from arriving at wrong ones. When this generalization has to be modified in view of the fact that some women are beginning to try their skill at ratiocination, reason is not re-established on the throne; because the result of Woman's reasoning is that she begins to fall into all the errors which men are just learning to mistrust. The moment she sets about doing things for reasons instead of merely finding reasons for what she wants to do, there is no saying what mischief she will be at next: there being just as good reasons for burning a heretic at the stake as for rescuing a shipwrecked crew from drowning: in fact, there are better.

One of the first and most famous utterances of rationalism would have condemned it without further hearing had its full significance been seen at the time. Voltaire, taking exception to the trash of some poetaster, was met with the plea 'One must live.' 'I dont see the necessity,' replied Voltaire.* The evasion was worthy of the Father of Lies* himself; for Voltaire was face to face with the very necessity he was denying; must have known, consciously or not, that it is the universal postulate; would have understood, if he had lived today, that since all valid human institutions are constructed to fulfil man's will, and his will is to live even when his reason teaches him to die, logical necessity, which was the sort Voltaire meant (the other sort being visible enough) can never be a motor in human action, and is, in short, not necessity at all. But that was not brought to light in Voltaire's time; and he died impenitent, bequeathing to his disciples that most logical of agents, the guillotine, which also 'did not see the necessity.'

In our own century the recognition of the will as distinct from the reasoning machinery began to spread. Schopenhauer* was the first among the moderns[1] to appreciate the enormous practical importance

---

[1] I say the moderns, because the will is our old friend the soul or spirit of man; and the doctrine of justification, not by works, but by faith, clearly derives its validity from the

of the distinction, and to make it clear to amateur metaphysicians by concrete instances. Out of his teaching came the formulation of the dilemma Voltaire had shut his eyes to. Here it is. Rationally considered, life is only worth living when its pleasures are greater than its pains. Now to a generation which has ceased to believe in heaven, and has not yet learned that the degradation by poverty of four out of every five of its number is artificial and remediable, the fact that life is not rationally worth living is obvious. It is useless to pretend that the pessimism of Koheleth, Shakespear, Dryden, and Swift* can be refuted if the world progresses solely by the destruction of the unfit, and yet can only maintain its civilization by manufacturing the unfit in swarms of which that appalling proportion of four to one represents but the comparatively fit survivors. Plainly then, the reasonable thing for the rationalists to do is to refuse to live. But as none of them will commit suicide in obedience to this demonstration of 'the necessity' for it, there is an end of the notion that we live for reasons instead of in fulfilment of our will to live. Thus we are landed afresh in mystery; for positive science gives no account whatever of this will to live. Positive science has dazzled us for nearly a century with its analyses of the machinery of sensation. Its researches into the nature of sound and the construction of the ear, the nature of light and the construction of the eye, its measurement of the speed of sensation, its localization of the functions of the brain, and its hints as to the possibility of producing a homunculus presently as the fruit of its chemical investigation of protoplasm have satisfied the souls of our atheists as completely as belief in divine omniscience and scriptural revelation satisfied the souls of their pious fathers. The fact remains that when Young, Helmholtz, Darwin, Haeckel, and the rest, popularized here among the literate classes by Tyndall and Huxley,* and among the proletariat by the lectures of the National Secular Society, have taught you all they know, you are still as utterly at a loss to explain the fact of consciousness as you would have been in the days when you were instructed from The Child's Guide to Knowledge.*

consideration that no action, taken apart from the will behind it, has any moral character: for example, the acts which make the murderer and incendiary infamous are exactly similar to those which make the patriotic hero famous. 'Original sin' is the will doing mischief. 'Divine grace' is the will doing good. Our fathers, unversed in the Hegelian dialectic,* could not conceive that these two, each the negation of the other, were the same. Schopenhauer's philosophy, like that of all pessimists, is really based on the old view of the will as original sin, and on the 1750–1850 view that the intellect is the divine grace that is to save us from it. It is as well to warn those who fancy that Schopenhauerism is one and indivisible, that acceptance of its metaphysics by no means involves endorsement of its philosophy.

Materialism, in short, only isolated the great mystery of consciousness
by clearing away several petty mysteries with which we had confused it;
just as Rationalism isolated the great mystery of the will to live.* The
isolation made both more conspicuous than before. We thought we had
escaped for ever from the cloudy region of metaphysics; and we were
only carried further into the heart of them.[1]

We have not yet worn off the strangeness of the position to which we
have now been led. Only the other day our highest boast was that we
were reasonable human beings. Today we laugh at that conceit, and see
ourselves as wilful creatures. Ability to reason accurately is as desirable
as ever; for by accurate reasoning only can we calculate our actions so
as to do what we intend to do: that is, to fulfil our will; but faith in reason as a prime motor is no longer the criterion of the sound mind, any
more than faith in the Bible is the criterion of righteous intention.

At this point, accordingly, the illusion as to the retrogressive movement of progress recurs as strongly as ever. Just as the beneficent step
from theology to rationalism seems to the theologist a growth of impi-
ety, does the step from rationalism to the recognition of the will as the
prime motor strike the rationalist as a lapse of common sanity; so that
to both theologist and rationalist progress at last appears alarming,
threatening, hideous, because it seems to tend towards chaos. The
deists Voltaire and Tom Paine were, to the divines of their day, predestined devils, tempting mankind hellward.[2] To deists and divines alike
Ferdinand Lassalle,* the godless self-worshipper and man-worshipper,
would have been a monster. Yet many who today echo Lassalle's demand
that economic and political institutions should be adapted to the poor
man's will to eat and drink his fill out of the product of the labor he
shares, are revolted by Ibsen's acceptance of the impulse towards greater
freedom as sufficient ground for the repudiation of any customary

[1] The correlation between Rationalism and Materialism in this process has some
immediate practical importance. Those who give up Materialism whilst clinging to
Rationalism generally either relapse into abject submission to the most paternal of the
Churches, or are caught by the attempts, constantly renewed, of mystics to found a new
faith by rationalizing on the hollowness of materialism. The hollowness has nothing in it;
and if you have come to grief as a materialist by reasoning about something, you are not
likely, as a mystic, to improve matters by reasoning about nothing.

[2] This is not precisely true. Voltaire was what we should now call an advanced
Congregationalist: in fact, modern Dissent, on its educated side, is sound Voltaireanism.
Voltaire was for some time on very friendly terms with the Genevese pastors. But what
with his jests at the expense of Bible worship, and the fact that he could not formally cut
himself off from the Established Church of France without placing himself in its power,
the pastors had finally to conceal their agreement with him. (1912.)

duty, however sacred, that conflicts with it. Society, were it even as free as Lassalle's Social-Democratic republic, *must*, it seems to them, go to pieces when conduct is no longer regulated by inviolable covenants.

For what, during all these overthrowings of things sacred and things infallible, has been happening to that pre-eminently sanctified thing, Duty? Evidently it cannot have come off scatheless. First there was man's duty to God, with the priest as assessor. That was repudiated; and then came Man's duty to his neighbor, with Society as the assessor. Will this too be repudiated, and be succeeded by Man's duty to himself, assessed by himself?* And if so, what will be the effect on the conception of Duty in the abstract? Let us see.

I have just called Lassalle a self-worshipper. In doing so I cast no reproach on him; for this is the last step in the evolution of the conception of duty. Duty arises at first, a gloomy tyranny, out of man's helplessness, his self-mistrust, in a word, his abstract fear. He personifies all that he abstractly fears as God, and straightway becomes the slave of his duty to God. He imposes that slavery fiercely on his children, threatening them with hell, and punishing them for their attempts to be happy. When, becoming bolder, he ceases to fear everything, and dares to love something, this duty of his to what he fears evolves into a sense of duty to what he loves. Sometimes he again personifies what he loves as God; and the God of Wrath becomes the God of Love: sometimes he at once becomes a humanitarian, an altruist, acknowledging only his duty to his neighbor. This stage is correlative to the rationalist stage in the evolution of philosophy and the capitalist phase in the evolution of industry. But in it the emancipated slave of God falls under the dominion of Society, which, having just reached a phase in which all the love is ground out of it by the competitive struggle for money, remorselessly crushes him until, in due course of the further growth of his courage, a sense at last arises in him of his duty to himself. And when this sense is fully grown the tyranny of duty perishes; for now the man's God is his own humanity; and he, self-satisfied at last, ceases to be selfish. The evangelist of this last step must therefore preach the repudiation of duty. This, to the unprepared of his generation, is indeed the wanton masterpiece of paradox. What! after all that has been said by men of noble life as to the secret of all right conduct being only Duty, Duty, Duty, is he to be told now that duty is the primal curse from which we must redeem ourselves before we can advance another step on the road along which, as we imagine (having forgotten the repudiations made by our fathers) duty and duty alone has brought us thus far? But why not? God Almighty was once the most sacred of our conceptions; and he had to be denied. Then Reason became the Infallible Pope,* only to be deposed in turn. Is Duty more sacred than God or Reason?

Having now arrived at the prospect of the repudiation of duty by Man, I shall make a digression on the subject of ideals and idealists, as treated by Ibsen. I shall go round in a loop, and come back to the same point by way of the repudiation of duty by Woman; and then at last I shall be in a position to describe Ibsen's plays without risk of misunderstanding.

IDEALS AND IDEALISTS

WE have seen that as Man grows through the ages, he finds himself bolder by the growth of his courage: that is, of his spirit (for so the common people name it), and dares more and more to love and trust instead of to fear and fight. But his courage has other effects: he also raises himself from mere consciousness to knowledge by daring more and more to face facts and tell himself the truth. For in his infancy of helplessness and terror he could not face the inexorable; and facts being of all things the most inexorable, he masked all the threatening ones as fast as he discovered them; so that now every mask requires a hero to tear it off. The king of terrors, Death, was the Arch-Inexorable: Man could not bear the dread of that. He must persuade himself that Death can be propitiated, circumvented, abolished. How he fixed the mask of personal immortality on the face of Death for this purpose we all know. And he did the like with all disagreeables as long as they remained inevitable. Otherwise he must have gone mad with terror of the grim shapes around him, headed by the skeleton with the scythe and hourglass. The masks were his ideals, as he called them; and what, he would ask, would life be without ideals? Thus he became an idealist, and remained so until he dared to begin pulling the masks off and looking the spectres in the face—dared, that is, to be more and more a realist.* But all men are not equally brave; and the greatest terror prevailed whenever some realist bolder than the rest laid hands on a mask which they did not yet dare to do without.

We have plenty of these masks around us still: some of them more fantastic than any of the Sandwich islanders' masks in the British Museum.* In our novels and romances especially we see the most beautiful of all the masks: those devised to disguise the brutalities of the sexual instinct in the earlier stages of its development, and to soften the rigorous aspect of the iron laws by which Society regulates its gratification. When the social organism becomes bent on civilization, it has to force marriage and family life on the individual, because it can perpetuate itself in no other way whilst love is still known only by fitful glimpses, the basis of sexual relationship being in the main mere physical appetite. Under these circumstances men try to graft pleasure on necessity by desperately pretending that the institution forced upon them is a congenial one, making it a point of public decency to assume always that men spontaneously love their kindred better than their chance acquaintances, and that the woman once desired is always desired: also that the family is woman's proper sphere, and that no really womanly woman ever forms an attachment, or even knows what it means, until she is requested to do so by a man. Now if anyone's childhood has been embittered by the dislike of his mother and the ill-temper of his father; if his wife has ceased to care for him and he is heartily tired of his wife; if his brother is going to law with him over the division of the family property, and his son acting in studied defiance of his plans and wishes, it is hard for him to persuade himself that passion is eternal and that blood is thicker than water. Yet if he tells himself the truth, all his life seems a waste and a failure by the light of it. It comes then to this, that his neighbors must either agree with him that the whole system is a mistake, and discard it for a new one, which cannot possibly happen until social organization so far outgrows the institution that Society can perpetuate itself without it; or else they must keep him in countenance by resolutely making believe that all the illusions with which it has been masked are realities.

For the sake of precision, let us imagine a community of a thousand persons, organized for the perpetuation of the species on the basis of the British family as we know it at present. Seven hundred of them, we will suppose, find the British family arrangement quite good enough for them. Two hundred and ninety-nine find it a failure, but must put up with it since they are in a minority. The remaining person occupies a position to be explained presently. The 299 failures will not have the courage to face the fact that they are irremediable failures, since they cannot prevent the 700 satisfied ones from coercing them into conformity with the marriage law. They will accordingly try to persuade themselves that, whatever their own particular domestic arrangements may be, the family is a beautiful and holy natural institution. For the fox not only declares that the grapes he cannot get are sour: he also insists that the sloes he *can* get are sweet.* Now observe what has happened. The family as it really is is a conventional arrangement, legally enforced, which the majority, because it happens to suit them, think good enough for the minority, whom it happens not to suit at all. The family as a beautiful and holy natural institution is only a fancy picture of what every family would have to be if everybody was to be suited, invented by the minority as a mask for the reality, which in its nakedness is intolerable to them. We call this sort of fancy picture an Ideal; and the policy of forcing individuals to act on the assumption that all ideals are real, and to recognize and accept such action as standard moral conduct, absolutely valid under all circumstances, contrary conduct or any advocacy of it being discountenanced and punished as immoral, may therefore be described as the policy of Idealism. Our 299 domestic failures are therefore become idealists as to marriage; and in proclaiming the ideal in fiction, poetry, pulpit and platform oratory, and serious private conversation, they will far outdo the 700 who comfortably accept marriage as a matter of course, never dreaming of calling it an 'institution,' much less a holy and beautiful one, and being pretty plainly of opinion that Idealism is a crackbrained fuss about nothing. The idealists, hurt by this, will retort by calling them Philistines. We then have our society classified as 700 Philistines and 299 idealists, leaving one man unclassified: the man strong enough to face the truth the idealists are shirking.

Such a man says of marriage, 'This thing is a failure for many of us. It is insufferable that two human beings, having entered into relations which only warm affection can render tolerable, should be forced to maintain them after such affections have ceased to exist, or in spite of the fact that they have never arisen. The alleged natural attractions and repulsions upon which the family ideal is based do not exist; and it is historically false that the family was founded for the purpose of satisfying them. Let us provide otherwise for the social ends which the family subserves, and then abolish its compulsory character altogether.' What will be the attitude of the rest to this outspoken man? The Philistines will simply think him mad. But the idealists will be terrified beyond measure at the proclamation of their hidden thought—at the presence of the traitor among the conspirators of silence—at the rending of the beautiful veil they and their poets have woven to hide the unbearable face of the truth. They will crucify him, burn him, violate their own ideals of family affection by taking his children away from him, ostracize him, brand him as immoral, profligate, filthy, and appeal against him to the despised Philistines, specially idealized for the occasion as Society. How far they will proceed against him depends on how far his courage exceeds theirs. At his worst, they call him cynic and paradoxer: at his best they do their utmost to ruin him if not to take his life. Thus, purblindly courageous moralists like Mandeville and Larochefoucauld,* who merely state unpleasant facts without denying the validity of current ideals, and who indeed depend on those ideals to make their statements piquant, get off with nothing worse than this name of cynic, the free use of which is a familiar mark of the zealous idealist. But take the case of the man who has already served us as an example: Shelley. The idealists did not call Shelley a cynic: they called him a fiend until they invented a new illusion to enable them to enjoy the beauty of his lyrics, this illusion being nothing less than the pretence that since he was at bottom an idealist himself, his ideals must be identical with those of Tennyson and Longfellow,* neither of whom ever wrote a line in which some highly respectable ideal was not implicit.[1]

Here the admission that Shelley, the realist, was an idealist too, seems to spoil the whole argument. And it certainly spoils its verbal consistency. For we unfortunately use this word ideal indifferently to denote both the institution which the ideal masks and the mask itself, thereby producing desperate confusion of thought, since the institution may be an effete and poisonous one, whilst the mask may be, and indeed generally is, an image of what we would fain have in its place. If the existing facts, with their masks on, are to be called ideals, and the future possibilities which the masks depict are also to be called ideals—if, again, the man who is defending existing institutions by maintaining their identity with their masks is to be confounded under one name with the man who is striving to realize the future possibilities by tearing the mask and the thing masked asunder, then the position cannot he intelligibly described by mortal pen: you and I, reader, will be at cross purposes at every sentence unless you allow me to distinguish pioneers like Shelley and Ibsen as realists from the idealists of my imaginary community of one thousand. If you ask why I have not allotted the terms the other way, and called Shelley and Ibsen idealists and the conventionalists realists, I reply that Ibsen himself, though he has not formally made the distinction, has so repeatedly harped on conventions and conventionalists as ideals and idealists that if I were now perversely to call them realities and realists, I should confuse readers of The Wild Duck and Rosmersholm more than I should help them. Doubtless I shall be reproached for puzzling people by thus limiting the meaning

---

[1] The following are examples of the two stages of Shelley criticism:

'We feel as if one of the darkest of the fiends had been clothed with a human body to enable him to gratify his enmity against the human race, and as if the supernatural atrocity of his hate were only heightened by his power to do injury. So strongly has this impression dwelt upon our minds that we absolutely asked a friend, who had seen this individual, to describe him to us—as if a cloven hoof, or horn, or flames from the mouth, must have marked the external appearance of so bitter an enemy of mankind.' (Literary Gazette, 19th May 1821.)

'A beautiful and ineffectual angel, beating in the void his luminous wings in vain.' (MATTHEW ARNOLD, in the preface to his selection of poems by Byron, dated 1881.)

The 1881 opinion is much sillier than the 1821 opinion. Further samples will be found in the articles of Henry Salt,* one of the few writers on Shelley who understand his true position as a social pioneer.

of the term ideal. But what, I ask, is that inevitable passing perplexity compared to the inextricable tangle I must produce if I follow the custom, and use the word indiscriminately in its two violently incompatible senses? If the term realist is objected to on account of some of its modern associations, I can only recommend you, if you must associate it with something else than my own description of its meaning (I do not deal in definitions), to associate it, not with Zola and Maupassant, but with Plato.*

Now let us return to our community of 700 Philistines, 299 idealists, and 1 realist. The mere verbal ambiguity against which I have just provided is as nothing beside that which comes of any attempt to express the relations of these three sections, simple as they are, in terms of the ordinary systems of reason and duty. The idealist, higher in the ascent of evolution than the Philistine, yet hates the highest and strikes at him with a dread and rancor of which the easy-going Philistine is guiltless. The man who has risen above the danger and the fear that his acquisitiveness will lead him to theft, his temper to murder, and his affections to debauchery: this is he who is denounced as an arch-scoundrel and libertine, and thus confounded with the lowest because he is the highest. And it is not the ignorant and stupid who maintain this error, but the literate and the cultured. When the true prophet speaks, he is proved to be both rascal and idiot, not by those who have never read of how foolishly such learned demonstrations have come off in the past, but by those who have themselves written volumes on the crucifixions, the burnings, the stonings, the headings and hangings, the Siberia transportations, the calumny and ostracism which have been the lot of the pioneer as well as of the camp follower. It is from men of established literary reputation that we learn that William Blake was mad, that Shelley was spoiled by living in a low set, that Robert Owen was a man who did not know the world, that Ruskin* was incapable of comprehending political economy, that Zola was a mere blackguard, and that Ibsen was 'a Zola with a wooden leg.'* The great musician, accepted by the unskilled listener, is vilified by his fellow-musicians: it was the musical culture of Europe that pronounced Wagner the inferior of Mendelssohn and Meyerbeer.* The great artist finds his foes among the painters, and not among the men in the street: it was the Royal Academy which placed forgotten nobodies above Burne Jones.* It is not rational that it should be so; but it is so, for all that.

The realist at last loses patience with ideals altogether, and sees in them only something to blind us, something to numb us, something to murder self in us, something whereby, instead of resisting death, we can disarm it by committing suicide. The idealist, who has taken refuge with the ideals because he hates himself and is ashamed of himself, thinks that all this is so much the better. The realist, who has come to have a deep respect for himself and faith in the validity of his own will, thinks it so much the worse. To the one, human nature, naturally corrupt, is held back from ruinous excesses only by self-denying conformity to the ideals. To the other these ideals are only swaddling clothes which man has outgrown, and which insufferably impede his movements. No wonder the two cannot agree. The idealist says, 'Realism means egotism; and egotism means depravity.' The realist declares that when a man abnegates the will to live and be free in a world of the living and free, seeking only to conform to ideals for the sake of being, not himself, but 'a good man,' then he is morally dead and rotten, and must be left unheeded to abide his resurrection, if that by good luck arrive before his bodily death.[1] Unfortunately, this is the sort of speech that nobody but a realist understands. It will be more amusing as well as more convincing to take an actual example of an idealist criticizing a realist.

---

[1] The above was written in 1890, ten years before Ibsen, in When We Dead Awaken, fully adopted its metaphor without, as far as I know, having any knowledge of my essay. Such an anticipation is a better proof than any mere argument that I found the right track of Ibsen's thought. (1912.)

THE WOMANLY WOMAN

IN 1890 the literary sensation of the day was the Diary of Marie Bashkirtseff.* An outline of it, with a running commentary, was given in The Review of Reviews (June 1890) by the editor, the late William Stead,* who, having gained an immense following by a public service in rendering which he had to simulate a felony and suffer imprisonment for it in order to prove that it was possible, was engaged in a campaign with the object of establishing the ideal of sexual 'purity' as a condition of public life. He had certain Ibsenist qualities: faith in himself, wilfulness, conscientious unscrupulousness, and could always make himself heard. Prominent among his ideals was an ideal of womanliness. In support of that ideal he would, like all idealists, make and believe any statement, however obviously and grotesquely unreal. When he found Marie Bashkirtseff's account of herself utterly incompatible with the picture of a woman's mind presented to him by his ideal, he was confronted with the dilemma that either Marie was not a woman or else his ideal was false to nature. He actually accepted the former alternative. 'Of the distinctively womanly,' he says, 'there is in her but little trace. She was the very antithesis of a true woman.'* William's next difficulty was, that self-control, being a leading quality in his ideal, could not have been possessed by Marie: otherwise she would have been more like his ideal. Nevertheless he had to record that she, without any compulsion from circumstances, made herself a highly skilled artist by working ten hours a day for six years. Let anyone who thinks that this is no evidence of self-control just try it for six months. William's verdict nevertheless was 'No self-control.' However, his fundamental quarrel with Marie came out in the following lines. 'Marie,' he said, 'was artist, musician, wit, philosopher, student, anything you like but a natural woman with a heart to love, and a soul to find its supreme satisfaction in sacrifice for lover or for child.' Now of all the idealist abominations that make society pestiferous, I doubt if there be any so mean as that of forcing self-sacrifice on a woman under pretence that she likes it; and, if she ventures to contradict the pretence, declaring her no true woman. In India they carried this piece of idealism to the length of declaring that a wife could not bear to survive her husband, but would be prompted by her own faithful, loving, beautiful nature to offer up her life on the pyre which consumed his dead body. The astonishing thing is that women, sooner than be branded as unsexed wretches, allowed themselves to be stupefied with drink, and in that unwomanly condition burnt alive. British Philistinism put down widow idealizing with the strong hand; and suttee is abolished in India.* The English form of it still flourishes; and Stead, the rescuer of the children,[1] was one of its high priests. Imagine his feelings on coming across this entry in a woman's diary: 'I love myself.' Or this, 'I swear solemnly—by the Gospels, by the passion of Christ, by MYSELF—that in four years I will be famous.' The young woman was positively proposing to exercise for her own sake all the powers that were given to her, in Stead's opinion, solely that she might sacrifice them for her lover or child! No wonder he was driven to exclaim again, 'She was very clever, no doubt; but woman she was not.'

Now observe this notable result. Marie Bashkirtseff, instead of being a less agreeable person than the ordinary female conformer to the ideal of womanliness, was most conspicuously the reverse. Stead himself wrote as one infatuated with her mere diary, and pleased himself by representing her as a person who fascinated everybody, and was a source of delight to all about her by the mere exhilaration and hope-giving atmosphere of her wilfulness. The truth is, that in real life a self-sacrificing woman, or, as Stead would have put it, a womanly woman, is not only taken advantage of, but disliked as well for her pains. No man pretends that his soul finds its supreme satisfaction in self-sacrifice: such an affectation would stamp him as coward and weakling: the manly man is he who takes the Bashkirtseff view of himself. But men are not the less loved on this account. No one ever feels helpless by the side of the self-helper; whilst the self-sacrificer is always a drag, a responsibility, a reproach, an everlasting and unnatural trouble with whom no really strong soul can live. Only those who have helped themselves know how to help others, and to respect their right to help themselves.[2]

Although romantic idealists generally insist on self-surrender as an indispensable element in true womanly love, its repulsive effect is well

[1] It was to force the Government to take steps to suppress child prostitution that Stead resorted to the desperate expedient already alluded to. He succeeded.

[2] Shortly after the publication of this passage, a German lady told me that she knew 'where I had got it from,' evidently not meaning from Ibsen. She added 'You have been reading Nietzsche's Through Good and Evil and Out at the other Side.' That was the first I ever heard of Nietzsche.* I mention this fact, not with the ridiculous object of vindicating my 'originality' in nineteenth century fashion, but because I attach great importance to the evidence that the movement voiced by Schopenhauer, Wagner, Ibsen, Nietzsche, and Strindberg, was a world movement, and would have found expression if every one of these writers had perished in his cradle. I have dealt with this question in the preface to my play Major Barbara. The movement is alive today in the philosophy of Bergson and the plays of Gorki, Tchekov, and the post-Ibsen English drama. (1912.)

known and feared in practice by both sexes. The extreme instance is the reckless self-abandonment seen in the infatuation of passionate sexual desire. Everyone who becomes the object of that infatuation shrinks from it instinctively. Love loses its charm when it is not free; and whether the compulsion is that of custom and law, or of infatuation, the effect is the same: it becomes valueless and even abhorrent, like the caresses of a maniac. The desire to give inspires no affection unless there is also the power to withhold; and the successful wooer, in both sexes alike, is the one who can stand out for honorable conditions, and, failing them, go without. Such conditions are evidently not offered to either sex by the legal marriage of today; for it is the intense repugnance inspired by the compulsory character of the legalized conjugal relation that leads, first to the idealization of marriage whilst it remains indispensable as a means of perpetuating society; then to its modification by divorce and by the abolition of penalties for refusal to comply with judicial orders for restitution of conjugal rights; and finally to its disuse and disappearance as the responsibility for the maintenance and education of the rising generation is shifted from the parent to the community.[1]

Although the growing repugnance to face the Church of England marriage service has led many celebrants to omit those passages which frankly explain the object of the institution, we are not likely to dispense with legal ties and obligations, and trust wholly to the permanence of love, until the continuity of society no longer depends on the private nursery. Love, as a practical factor in society, is still a mere

---

[1] A dissertation on the anomalies and impossibilities of the marriage law at its present stage would be too far out of the main course of my argument to be introduced in the text above; but it may be well to point out in passing to those who regard marriage as an inviolable and inviolate institution, that necessity has already forced us to tamper with it to such an extent that at this moment (1891) the highest court in the kingdom is face to face with a husband and wife, the one demanding whether a woman may saddle him with all the responsibilities of a husband and then refuse to live with him, and the other asking whether the law allows her husband to commit abduction, imprisonment, and rape upon her. If the court says Yes to the husband, indissoluble marriage is made intolerable for men; if it says Yes to the wife, the position is made intolerable for women; and as this exhausts the possible alternatives, it is clear that provision must be made for the dissolution of such marriages if the institution is to be maintained at all, which it must be until its social function is otherwise provided for. Marriage is thus, by force of circumstances, compelled to buy extension of life by extension of divorce, much as if a fugitive should try to delay a pursuing wolf by throwing portions of his own heart to it. [The court decided against the man; but England still lags behind the rest of Protestant Europe in the necessary readjustment of the law of divorce. See the preface to my play Getting Married, which supplies the dissertation crowded out of the foregoing note. (1912.)]

appetite. That higher development of it which Ibsen shews us occurring in the case of Rebecca West in Rosmersholm is only known to most of us by the descriptions of great poets, who themselves, as their biographies prove, have known it, not by sustained experience, but only by brief glimpses. Dante loved Beatrice* with the higher love; but neither during her life nor after her death was he 'faithful' to her or to the woman he actually married. And he would be a bold bourgeois who would pretend to a higher mind than Dante. Tannhäuser may die in the conviction* that one moment of the emotion he felt with St Elizabeth was fuller and happier than all the hours of passion he spent with Venus; but that does not alter the fact that love began for him with Venus, and that its earlier tentatives towards the final goal were attended with relapses. Now Tannhäuser's passion for Venus is a development of the humdrum fondness of the bourgeois Jack for his Jill, a development at once higher and more dangerous, just as idealism is at once higher and more dangerous than Philistinism. The fondness is the germ of the passion: the passion is the germ of the more perfect love. When Blake told men that through excess they would learn moderation* he knew that the way for the present lay through the Venusberg,* and that the race would assuredly not perish there as some individuals have, and as the Puritan fears we all shall unless we find a way round. Also he no doubt foresaw the time when our children would be born on the other side of it, and so be spared that fiery purgation.

But the very facts that Blake is still commonly regarded as a crazy visionary, and that the current criticism of Rosmersholm entirely fails even to notice the evolution of Rebecca's passion for Rosmer into her love for him, much more to credit the moral transfiguration which accompanies it, shew how absurd it would be to pretend, for the sake of edification, that the ordinary marriage of today is a union between a William Blake and a Rebecca West, or that it would be possible, even if it were enlightened policy, to deny the satisfaction of the sexual appetite to persons who have not reached that stage. An overwhelming majority of such marriages as are not purely *de convenance** are entered into for the gratification of that appetite either in its crudest form or veiled only by those idealistic illusions which the youthful imagination weaves so wonderfully under the stimulus of desire, and which older people indulgently laugh at.

This being so, it is not surprising that our society, being directly dominated by men, comes to regard Woman, not as an end in herself like Man, but solely as a means of ministering to his appetite. The ideal wife is one who does everything that the ideal husband likes, and nothing

else. Now to treat a person as a means instead of an end is to deny
that person's right to live. And to be treated as a means to such an end
as sexual intercourse with those who deny one's right to live is insufferable to any human being. Woman, if she dares face the fact that she is
being so treated, must either loathe herself or else rebel. As a rule, when
circumstances enable her to rebel successfully—for instance, when the
accident of genius enables her to 'lose her character' without losing her
employment or cutting herself off from the society she values—she
does rebel; but circumstances seldom do. Does she then loathe herself?
By no means: she deceives herself in the idealist fashion by denying
that the love which her suitor offers her is tainted with sexual appetite
at all. It is, she declares, a beautiful, disinterested, pure, sublime devotion to another by which a man's life is exalted and purified, and a woman's rendered blest. And of all the cynics, the filthiest to her mind is the
one who sees, in the man making honorable proposals to his future
wife, nothing but the human male seeking his female. The man himself
keeps her confirmed in her illusion; for the truth is unbearable to him
too: he wants to form an affectionate tie, and not to drive a degrading
bargain. After all, the germ of the highest love is in them both; though
as yet it is no more than the appetite they are disguising so carefully
from themselves. Consequently every stockbroker who has just brought
his business up to marrying point woos in terms of the romantic illusion; and it is agreed between the two that their marriage shall realize
the romantic ideal. Then comes the breakdown of the plan. The young
wife finds that her husband is neglecting her for his business; that his
interests, his activities, his whole life except that one part of it to which
only a cynic ever referred before her marriage, lies away from home;
and that her business is to sit there and mope until she is wanted. Then
what can she do? If she complains, he, the self-helper, can do without
her; whilst she is dependent on him for her position, her livelihood, her
place in society, her home, her name, her very bread.[1] All this is brought
home to her by the first burst of displeasure her complaints provoke.
Fortunately, things do not remain for ever at this point: perhaps the
most wretched in a woman's life. The self-respect she has lost as a wife
she regains as a mother, in which capacity her use and importance to

---

[1] I should have warned my male readers to be very careful how they presume on this
position. In actual practice marriage reduces the man to a greater dependence on the
woman than is good for either party. But the woman can tyrannize only by misconduct or
threats of misconduct, whilst the man can tyrannize legally, though it must be added that
a good deal of the makeshift law that has been set up to restrain this tyranny is very unfair
to the man. The writings of Belfort Bax* are instructive on this point. (1912.)

the community compare favorably with those of most men of business. She is wanted in the house, wanted in the market, wanted by the children; and now, instead of weeping because her husband is away in the city, thinking of stocks and shares instead of his ideal woman, she would regard his presence in the house all day as an intolerable nuisance. And so, though she is completely disillusioned on the subject of ideal love, yet, since it has not turned out so badly after all, she countenances the illusion still from the point of view that it is a useful and harmless means of getting boys and girls to marry and settle down. And this conviction is the stronger in her because she feels that if she had known as much about marriage the day before her wedding as she did six months after, it would have been extremely hard to induce her to get married at all.*

This prosaic solution is satisfactory only within certain limits. It depends altogether upon the accident of the woman having some natural vocation for domestic management and the care of children, as well as on the husband being fairly good-natured and livable-with. Hence arises the idealist illusion that a vocation for domestic management and the care of children is natural to women, and that women who lack them are not women at all, but members of the third, or Bashkirtseff sex. Even if this were true, it is obvious that if the Bashkirtseffs are to be allowed to live, they have a right to suitable institutions just as much as men and women. But it is not true. The domestic career is no more natural to all women than the military career is natural to all men; and although in a population emergency it might become necessary for every ablebodied woman to risk her life in childbed just as it might become necessary in a military emergency for every man to risk his life in the battlefield, yet even then it would by no means follow that the child-bearing would endow the mother with domestic aptitudes and capacities as it would endow her with milk. It is of course quite true that the majority of women are kind to children and prefer their own to other people's. But exactly the same thing is true of the majority of men, who nevertheless do not consider that their proper sphere is the nursery. The case may be illustrated more grotesquely by the fact that the majority of women who have dogs are kind to them, and prefer their own dogs to other people's; yet it is not proposed that women should restrict their activities to the rearing of puppies. If we have come to think that the nursery and the kitchen are the natural sphere of a woman, we have done so exactly as English children come to think that a cage is the natural sphere of a parrot: because they have never seen one anywhere else. No doubt there are Philistine parrots who agree with their owners that it is better to be in a cage than out, so long as there is plenty of hempseed and Indian corn there. There may even be idealist parrots who persuade themselves that the mission of a parrot is to minister to the happiness of a private family by whistling and saying Pretty Polly, and that it is in the sacrifice of its liberty to this altruistic pursuit that a true parrot finds the supreme satisfaction of its soul. I will not go so far as to affirm that there are theological parrots who are convinced that imprisonment is the will of God because it is unpleasant; but I am confident that there are rationalist parrots who can demonstrate that it would be a cruel kindness to let a parrot out to fall a prey to cats, or at least to forget its accomplishments and coarsen its naturally delicate fibres in an unprotected struggle for existence. Still, the only parrot a free-souled person can sympathize with is the one that insists on being let out as the first condition of making itself agreeable. A selfish bird, you may say: one that puts its own gratification before that of the family which is so fond of it—before even the greatest happiness of the greatest number: one that, in aping the independent spirit of a man, has unparroted itself and become a creature that has neither the home-loving nature of a bird nor the strength and enterprise of a mastiff. All the same, you respect that parrot in spite of your conclusive reasoning; and if it persists, you will have either to let it out or kill it.

The sum of the matter is that unless Woman repudiates her womanliness, her duty to her husband, to her children, to society, to the law, and to everyone but herself, she cannot emancipate herself. But her duty to herself is no duty at all, since a debt is cancelled when the debtor and creditor are the same person. Its payment is simply a fulfilment of the individual will, upon which all duty is a restriction, founded on the conception of the will as naturally malign and devilish. Therefore Woman has to repudiate duty altogether. In that repudiation lies her freedom; for it is false to say that Woman is now directly the slave of Man: she is the immediate slave of duty; and as man's path to freedom is strewn with the wreckage of the duties and ideals he has trampled on, so must hers be. She may indeed mask her iconoclasm by proving in rationalist fashion, as Man has often done for the sake of a quiet life, that all these discarded idealist conceptions will be fortified instead of shattered by her emancipation. To a person with a turn for logic, such proofs are as easy as playing the piano is to Paderewski.* But it will not be true. A whole basketful of ideals of the most sacred quality will be smashed by the achievement of equality for women and men. Those who shrink from such a clatter and breakage may comfort themselves with the reflection that the replacement of the broken goods will be prompt and certain. It is always a case of 'The ideal is dead: long live the ideal!' And the advantage of the work of destruction is that every new ideal is less of an illusion than the one it has supplanted; so that the destroyer of ideals, though denounced as an enemy of society, is in fact sweeping the world clear of lies.

My digression is now over. Having traversed my loop as I promised, and come back to Man's repudiation of duty by way of Woman's, I may at last proceed to give some more particular account of Ibsen's work without further preoccupation with Clement Scott's protest, or the many others of which it is the type. For we now see that the pioneer must necessarily provoke such outcry as he repudiates duties, tramples on ideals, profanes what was sacred, sanctifies what was infamous, always driving his plough through gardens of pretty weeds in spite of the laws made against trespassers for the protection of the worms which feed on the roots, always letting in light and air to hasten the putrefaction of decaying matter, and everywhere proclaiming that 'the old beauty is no longer beautiful, the new truth no longer true.'* He can do no less; and what more and what else he does it is not given to all of his generation to understand. And if any man does not understand, and cannot foresee the harvest, what can he do but cry out in all sincerity against such destruction, until at last we come to know the cry of the blind like any other street cry, and to bear with it as an honest cry, albeit a false alarm?

THE PLAYS

Brand, 1866

WE are now prepared to learn without misgiving that a typical Ibsen play is one in which the leading lady is an unwomanly woman, and the villain an idealist. It follows that the leading lady is not a heroine of the Drury Lane type;* nor does the villain forge or assassinate, since he is a villain by virtue of his determination to do nothing wrong. Therefore readers of Ibsen—not playgoers—have sometimes so far misconceived him as to suppose that his villains are examples rather than warnings, and that the mischief and ruin which attend their actions are but the tribulations from which the soul comes out purified as gold from the furnace. In fact, the beginning of Ibsen's European reputation was the edification with which the pious received his great dramatic poem Brand. Brand is not his first play: indeed it is his seventh;* and of its six forerunners all are notable and some splendid; but it is in Brand that he definitely, if not yet quite consciously, takes the field against idealism and, like another Luther, nails his thesis to the door of the Temple of Morality.* With Brand therefore we must begin, lest we should be swept into an eddy of mere literary criticism, a matter altogether beside the purpose of this book, which is to distil the quintessence of Ibsen's message to his age.

Brand the priest is an idealist of heroic earnestness, strength, and courage. Conventional, comfortable, sentimental church-going withers into selfish snobbery and cowardly weakness before his terrible word. 'Your God,' he cries, 'is an old man: mine is young'; and all Europe, hearing him, suddenly realizes that it has so far forgotten God as to worship an image of an elderly gentleman with a well-trimmed beard, an imposing forehead, and the expression of a headmaster. Brand, turning from such idolatrous follies with fierce scorn, declares himself the champion, not of things as they are, nor of things as they can be made, but of things as they ought to be. Things as they ought to be mean for him things as ordered by men conformed to his ideal of the perfect Adam, who, again, is not man as he is or can be, but man conformed to all the ideals: man as it is his duty to be. In insisting on this conformity, Brand spares neither himself nor anyone else. Life is nothing: self is nothing: the perfect Adam is everything. The imperfect Adam does not fall in with these views. A peasant whom he urges to cross a glacier in a fog because it is his duty to visit his dying daughter, not only flatly declines, but endeavors forcibly to prevent Brand from risking his own life. Brand knocks him down, and sermonizes him with fierce earnestness and scorn. Presently Brand has to cross a fiord in a storm to reach a dying man who, having committed a series of murders, wants 'consolation' from a priest. Brand cannot go alone: someone must hold the rudder of his boat whilst he manages the sail. The fisher folk, in whom the old Adam is strong, do not adopt his estimate of the gravity of the situation, and refuse to go. A woman, fascinated by his heroism and idealism, goes. That ends in their marriage, and in the birth of a child to which they become deeply attached. Then Brand, aspiring from height to height of devotion to his ideal, plunges from depth to depth of murderous cruelty. First the child must die from the severity of the climate because Brand must not flinch from the post of duty and leave his congregation exposed to the peril of getting an inferior preacher in his place. Then he forces his wife to give the clothes of the dead child to a gipsy whose baby needs them. The bereaved mother does not grudge the gift; but she wants to hold back only one little garment as a relic of her darling. But Brand sees in this reservation the imperfection of the imperfect Eve. He forces her to regard the situation as a choice between the relic and his ideal. She sacrifices the relic to the ideal, and then dies, broken-hearted. Having killed her, and thereby placed himself beyond ever daring to doubt the idealism upon whose altar he has immolated her; having also refused to go to his mother's death-bed because she compromises with his principles in disposing of her property, he is hailed by the people as a saint, and finds his newly built church too small for his congregation. So he calls upon them to follow him to worship God in His own temple, the mountains. After a brief practical experience of this arrangement, they change their minds, and stone him. The very mountains themselves stone him, indeed; for he is killed by an avalanche.*

Peer Gynt, 1867

Brand dies a saint, having caused more intense suffering by his saintliness than the most talented sinner could possibly have done with twice his opportunities. Ibsen does not leave this to be inferred. In another dramatic poem he gives us a rapscallion named Peer Gynt, an idealist who avoids Brand's errors by setting up as his ideal the realization of himself through the utter satisfaction of his own will. In this he would seem to be on the path to which Ibsen himself points; and indeed all

who know the two plays will agree that whether or no it was better to be
Peer Gynt than Brand, it was beyond all question better to be the
mother or the sweetheart of Peer, scapegrace and liar as he was, than
mother or wife to the saintly Brand. Brand would force his ideal on all
men and women: Peer Gynt keeps his ideal for himself alone: it is
indeed implicit in the ideal itself that it should be unique—that he
alone should have the force to realize it. For Peer's first boyish notion
of the self-realized man is not the saint, but the demigod whose indomitable will is stronger than destiny, the fighter, the master, the man
whom no woman can resist, the mighty hunter, the knight of a thousand adventures, the model, in short, of the lover in a lady's novel, or
the hero in a boy's romance. Now, no such person exists, or ever did
exist, or ever can exist. The man who cultivates an indomitable will and
refuses to make way for anything or anybody, soon finds that he cannot
hold a street crossing against a tram car, much less a world against the
whole human race. Only by plunging into illusions to which every fact
gives the lie can he persuade himself that his will is a force that can
overcome all other forces, or that it is less conditioned by circumstances
than a wheelbarrow is. However, Peer Gynt, being imaginative enough
to conceive his ideal, is also imaginative enough to find illusions to hide
its unreality, and to persuade himself that Peer Gynt, the shabby countryside loafer, is Peer Gynt, Emperor of Himself, as he writes over the
door of his hut in the mountains. His hunting feats are invented; his
military genius has no solider foundation than a street fight with
a smith; and his reputation as an adventurous daredevil he has to gain
by the bravado of carrying off the bride from a wedding at which the
guests snub him. Only in the mountains can he enjoy his illusions
undisturbed by ridicule; yet even in the mountains he finds obstacles he
cannot force his way through, obstacles which withstand him as spirits
with voices, telling him that he must go round. But he will not: he will
go forward: he will cut his path sword in hand, in spite of fate. All the
same, he has to go round; for the world-will is outside Peer Gynt as well
as inside him.

Then he tries the supernatural, only to find that it means nothing
more than the transmogrifying of squalid realities by lies and pretences.
Still, like our amateurs of thaumaturgy,* he is willing to enter into
a conspiracy of make-believe up to a certain point. When the Trold
king's daughter* appears as a repulsive ragged creature riding on a pig,
he is ready to accept her as a beautiful princess on a noble steed, on
condition that she accepts his mother's tumble-down farmhouse, with
the broken window panes stopped up with old clouts, as a splendid

castle. He will go with her among the Trolds, and pretend that the gruesome ravine in which they hold their orgies is a glorious palace; he will partake of their filthy food and declare it nectar and ambrosia; he will applaud their obscene antics as exquisite dancing, and their discordant din as divine music; but when they finally propose to slit his eyes so that he may see and hear these things, not as they are, but as he has been pretending to see and hear them, he draws back, resolved to be himself even in self-deception. He leaves the mountains and becomes a prosperous man of business in America, highly respectable and ready for any profitable speculation: slave trade, Bible trade, whisky trade, missionary trade, anything! His commercial success in this phase persuades him that he is under the special care of God; but he is shaken in his opinion by an adventure in which he is marooned on the African coast, and does not recover his faith until the treacherous friends who marooned him are destroyed before his eyes by the blowing-up of the steam yacht they have just stolen from him, when he utters his celebrated exclamation, 'Ah, God is a Father to me after all; but economical he certainly is not.' He finds a white horse in the desert, and is accepted on its account as the Messiah by an Arab tribe,* a success which moves him to declare that now at last he is really worshipped for himself, whereas in America people only respected his breast-pin, the symbol of his money. In commerce, too, he reflects, his eminence was a mere matter of chance, whilst as a prophet he is eminent by pure natural fitness for the post. This is ended by his falling in love with a dancing-girl, who, after leading him into every sort of undignified and ludicrous extravagance, ranging from his hailing her as the Eternal-Feminine of Goethe* to the more practical folly of giving her his white horse and all his prophetic finery, runs away with the spoil, and leaves him once more helpless and alone in the desert. He wanders until he comes to the Great Sphinx, beside which he finds a German gentleman in great perplexity as to who the Sphinx is. Peer Gynt, seeing in that impassive, immovable, majestic figure, a symbol of his own ideal, is able to tell the German gentleman at once that the Sphinx is itself.* This explanation dazzles the German, who, after some further discussion of the philosophy of self-realization, invites Peer Gynt to accompany him to a club of learned men in Cairo, who are ripe for enlightenment on this very question. Peer, delighted, accompanies the German to the club, which turns out to be a madhouse in which the lunatics have broken loose and locked up their keepers. It is in this madhouse, and by these madmen, that Peer Gynt is at last crowned Emperor of Himself. He receives their homage as he lies in the dust fainting with terror.

As an old man, Peer Gynt, returning to the scenes of his early adventures, is troubled with the prospect of meeting a certain button moulder
who threatens to make short work of his realized self by melting it down
in his crucible with a heap of other button-material. Immediately the
old exaltation of the self realizer is changed into an unspeakable dread
of the button moulder Death, to avoid whom Peer Gynt has already
pushed a drowning man from the spar he is clinging to in a shipwreck
lest it should not suffice to support two. At last he finds a deserted
sweetheart of his youth still waiting for him and still believing in him.
In the imagination of this old woman he finds the ideal Peer Gynt;
whilst in himself, the loafer, the braggart, the confederate of sham
magicians, the Charleston speculator, the false prophet, the dancing-
girl's dupe, the bedlam emperor, the thruster of the drowning man into
the waves, there is nothing heroic: nothing but commonplace self-
seeking and shirking, cowardice and sensuality, veiled only by the
romantic fancies of the born liar. With this crowningly unreal realization he is left to face the button moulder as best he can.[1]

Peer Gynt has puzzled a good many people by Ibsen's fantastic and
subtle treatment of its metaphysical thesis. It is so far a difficult play,
that the ideal of unconditional self-realization, however familiar its
suggestions may be to the ambitious reader, is not understood by him.
When it is stated to him by some one who does understand it, he
unhesitatingly dismisses it as idiotic; and because he is perfectly right
in doing so—because it is idiotic in the most accurate sense of the
term—he does not easily recognize it as the common ideal of his own
prototype, the pushing, competitive, success-craving man who is the
hero of the modern world.

There is nothing novel in Ibsen's dramatic method of reducing these
ideals to absurdity. Exactly as Cervantes took the old ideal of chivalry,
and shewed what came of a man attempting to act as if it were real, so

[1] Miss Pagan,* who has produced scenes from Peer Gynt in Edinburgh and London
(which, to its shame, has not yet seen a complete public performance of Peer Gynt),
regards the death of Peer as occurring in the scene where all the wasted possibilities of his
life drift about him as withered leaves and fluffs of bog-cotton. He picks up an onion,
and, playing with the idea that it is himself, and that its skins are the phases of his own
career wrapped round the kernel of his real self, strips them off one after another, only to
discover that there is no kernel. 'Nature is ironical,' says Peer bitterly; and that discovery
of his own nothingness is taken by Miss Pagan as his death, the subsequent adventures
being those of his soul. It is impossible to demur to so poetic an interpretation; though it
assumes, in spite of the onion, that Peer had not wholly destroyed his soul. Still, as the
button moulder (who might be Brand's ghost) does respite Peer 'until the next cross
roads,' it cannot be said that Ibsen leaves Peer definitely scrapped. (1912.)

Ibsen takes the ideals of Brand and Peer Gynt, and subjects them to the same test. Don Quixote acts as if he were a perfect knight in a world of giants and distressed damsels instead of a country gentleman in a land of innkeepers and farm wenches;* Brand acts as if he were the perfect Adam in a world where, by resolute rejection of all compromise with imperfection, it was immediately possible to change the rainbow 'bridge between flesh and spirit' into as enduring a structure as the tower of Babel* was intended to be, thereby restoring man to the condition in which he walked with God in the garden; and Peer Gynt tries to act as if he had in him a special force that could be concentrated so as to prevail over all other forces. They ignore the real—ignore what they are and where they are, not only, like Nelson,* shutting their eyes to the signals a brave man may disregard, but insanely steering straight on rocks no man's resolution can move or resist. Observe that neither Cervantes nor Ibsen is incredulous, in the Philistine way, as to the power of ideals over men. Don Quixote, Brand, and Peer Gynt are, all three, men of action seeking to realize their ideals in deeds. However ridiculous Don Quixote makes himself, you cannot dislike or despise him, much less think that it would have been better for him to have been a Philistine like Sancho;* and Peer Gynt, selfish rascal as he is, is not unlovable. Brand, made terrible by the consequences of his idealism to others, is heroic. Their castles in the air are more beautiful than castles of brick and mortar; but one cannot live in them; and they seduce men into pretending that every hovel is such a castle, just as Peer Gynt pretended that the Trold king's den was a palace.

Emperor and Galilean, 1873

When Ibsen, by merely giving the rein to the creative impulse of his poetic nature, had produced Brand and Peer Gynt, he was nearly forty. His will, in setting his imagination to work, had produced a tough puzzle for his intellect. In no case does the difference between the will and the intellect come out more clearly than in that of the poet, save only that of the lover. Had Ibsen died in 1867, he, like many another great poet, would have gone to his grave without having ever rationally understood his own meaning. Nay, if in that year an intellectual expert—a commentator, as we call him—having read Brand, had put forward the explanation which Ibsen himself must have arrived at before he constructed Ghosts and The Wild Duck, he would perhaps have repudiated it with as much disgust as a maiden would feel if anyone were prosaic enough to give her the physiological explanation of

her dreams of meeting a fairy prince. Only simpletons go to the creative
artist presuming that he must be able to answer their 'What does this
obscure passage mean?' That is the very question the poet's own intellect, which had no part in the conception of the poem, may be asking
him. And this curiosity of the intellect, this restless life in it which dif-
ferentiates it from dead machinery, and troubles our lesser artists but
little, is one of the marks of the greater sort. Shakespear, in Hamlet,
made a drama of the self-questioning that came upon him when his
intellect rose up in alarm, as well it might, against the vulgar optimism
of his Henry V, and yet could mend it to no better purpose than by the
equally vulgar pessimism of Troilus and Cressida.* Dante took pains to
understand himself: so did Goethe. Richard Wagner, one of the greatest poets of our own day, has left us as many volumes of criticism of art
and life as he has left musical scores; and he has expressly described
how the keen intellectual activity he brought to the analysis of his music
dramas was in abeyance during their creation. Just so do we find Ibsen,
after composing his two great dramatic poems, entering on a struggle
to become intellectually conscious of what he had done.

We have seen that with Shakespear such an effort became itself creative and produced a drama of questioning. With Ibsen the same thing
occurred: he harked back to an abandoned project of his, and wrote two
huge dramas on the subject of the apostasy of the Emperor Julian.* In
this work we find him at first preoccupied with a piece of old-fashioned
freethinking: the dilemma that moral responsibility presupposes free-
will, and that free-will sets man above God. Cain, who slew because he
willed,* willed because he must, and must have willed to slay because
he was himself, comes upon the stage to claim that murder is fertile,
and death the ground of life, though, not having read Weismann* on
death as a method of evolution, he cannot say what is the ground of
death. Judas asks whether, when the Master chose him, he chose foreknowingly.* This part of the drama has no very deep significance. It is
easy to invent conundrums which dogmatic evangelicalism cannot
answer; and no doubt, whilst it was still a nine days' wonder that evangelicalism could not solve all enigmas, such invention seemed something much deeper than the mere intellectual chess-play which it is
seen to be now that the nine days are past. In his occasional weakness
for such conundrums, and later on in his harping on the hereditary
transmission of disease, we see Ibsen's active intellect busy, not only
with the problems peculiar to his own plays, but with the fatalism and
pessimism of the middle of the nineteenth century, when the typical
advanced culture was attainable by reading Strauss's Leben Jesu,* the

popularizations of Helmholtz and Darwin by Tyndall and Huxley, and George Eliot's novels, vainly protested against by Ruskin* as peopled with 'the sweepings of a Pentonville omnibus.' The traces of this period in Ibsen's writings shew how well he knew the crushing weight with which the sordid cares of the ordinary struggle for money and respectability fell on the world when the romance of the creeds was discredited, and progress seemed for the moment to mean, not the growth of the spirit of man, but an effect of the survival of the fittest brought about by the destruction of the unfit, all the most frightful examples of this systematic destruction being thrust into the utmost prominence by those who were fighting the Church with Mill's favorite dialectical weapon,* the incompatibility of divine omnipotence with divine benevolence. His plays are full of an overwhelming sense of the necessity for rousing ourselves into self-assertion against this numbing fatalism; and yet he certainly had not at this time freed his intellect from an acceptance of its scientific validity as our Samuel Butler did,* though Butler was more like Ibsen than any man in Europe, having the same grim hoaxing humor, the same grip of spiritual realities behind material facts, the same toughness of character holding him unshaken against the world.

Butler revelled in Darwinism for six weeks, and then, grasping the whole scope and the whole horror of it, warned us (we did not listen until we had revelled for half a century) that Darwin had 'banished mind from the universe,' meaning from Evolution. Ibsen, belonging to an earlier generation, and intellectually nursed on northern romance and mysticism rather than on the merely industrious and prosaic science of the interval between the discovery of Evolution at the end of the eighteenth century and the discovery and overrating of Natural Selection* as a method of evolution in the middle of the nineteenth, was, when Darwin arrived, past the age at which Natural Selection could have swept him away as it swept Butler and his contemporaries. But, like them, he seems to have welcomed it for the mortal blow it dealt to the current travesties of Christianity, which were really only reductions of the relations between man and God to the basis of the prevalent Commercialism, shewing how God may be cheated, and how salvation can be got for nothing through the blood of Christ by sweaters, adulterators, quacks, sharks, and hypocrites; also how God, though the most dangerously capricious and short-tempered of Anarchists, is also the most sentimental of dupes. It is against this conception of God as a sentimental dupe that Brand rages. Ibsen evidently regarded the brimstone conception, 'the Almighty Fiend' of Shelley,* as not worth his powder and shot, partly, no doubt, because he knew that the Almighty Fiend's votaries would never read or understand his works, and partly because the class he addressed, the cultured class, had thrown off that superstition, and were busy with the sentimental religion of love in which we are still wallowing, and which only substitutes twaddle for terror.

At first sight this may seem an improvement; but it is no defence against that fear of man which is so much more mischievous than the fear of God. The cruelty of Natural Selection was a powerful antidote to such sentimentalism; and Ibsen, who was perhaps no expert in recent theories of evolution, was quite ready to rub it in uncritically for the sake of its value as a tonic. Indeed, as a fearless observer of the cruelty of Nature, he was quite independent of Darwin: what we find in his works is an unmistakeable Darwinian atmosphere, but not the actual Darwinian discoveries and technical theory. If Natural Selection, the gloomiest and most formidable of the castles of Giant Despair, had stopped him, he would no doubt, like Butler, have set himself deliberately to play Greatheart and reduce it;* but his genius pushed him past it and left it to be demolished philosophically by Butler, and practically by the mere march of the working class, which, by its freedom from the economic bias of the middle classes, has escaped their characteristic illusions, and solved many of the enigmas they found insoluble because they did not wish to have them solved. For instance, according to the theory of Natural Selection, progress can take place only through an increase in the severity of the material conditions of existence; and as the working classes were quite determined that progress should consist of just the opposite, they had no difficulty in seeing that it generally does occur in that way, whereas the middle class wished, on the contrary, to be convinced that the poverty of the working classes and all the hideous evils attending it were inevitable conditions of progress, and that every penny in the pound on the rates spent in social amelioration, and every attempt on the part of the workers to raise their wages by Trade Unionism or otherwise, were vain defiances of biologic and economic science.

How far Ibsen was definitely conscious of all this is doubtful; but one of his most famous utterances pointed to the working class and the women as the great emancipators. His prophetic belief in the spontaneous growth of the will made him a meliorist without reference to the operation of Natural Selection; but his impression of the light thrown by physical and biological science on the facts of life seems to have been the gloomy one of the middle of the nineteenth century. External nature often plays her most ruthless and destructive part in his works, which have an extraordinary fascination for the pessimists of that period, in spite of the incompatibility of his individualism with that mechanical utilitarian ethic of theirs which treats Man as the sport of every circumstance, and ignores his will altogether.

Another inessential but very prominent feature in Ibsen's dramas will be understood easily by anyone who has observed how a change of religious faith intensifies our concern about our own salvation. An ideal, pious or secular, is practically used as a standard of conduct; and whilst it remains unquestioned, the simple rule of right is to conform to it. In the theological stage, when the Bible is accepted as the revelation of God's will, the pious man, when in doubt as to whether he is acting rightly or wrongly, quiets his misgivings by searching the Scripture until he finds a text which endorses his action.[1] The rationalist, for whom the Bible has no authority, brings his conduct to such tests as asking himself, after Kant, how it would be if everyone did as he proposes to do; only calculating the effect of his action on the greatest happiness of the greatest number; or by judging whether the liberty of action he is claiming infringes the equal liberty of others, etc. etc.* Most men are ingenious enough to pass examinations of this kind successfully in respect to everything they really want to do. But in periods of transition, as, for instance, when faith in the infallibility of the Bible is shattered, and faith in that of reason not yet perfected, men's uncertainty as to the rightness and wrongness of their actions keeps them in a continual perplexity, amid which casuistry seems the most important branch of intellectual activity. Life, as depicted by Ibsen, is very full of it. We find the great double drama of Emperor and Galilean occupied at first with Julian's case regarded as a case of conscience. It is compared, in the manner already described, with the cases of Cain and Judas, the three men being introduced as 'corner stones under the wrath of necessity,' 'great freedmen under necessity,' and so forth. The qualms of Julian are theatrically effective in producing the most exciting suspense as to whether he will dare to choose between Christ and the imperial purple;* but the mere exhibition of a man struggling between his ambition and his creed belongs to a phase of intellectual interest which Ibsen had passed even before the production of Brand, when he wrote his Kongs Emnerne (The Pretenders). Emperor and Galilean might have been appropriately, if prosaically, named The

---

[1] As such misgivings seldom arise except when the conscience revolts against the contemplated action, an appeal to Scripture to justify a point of conduct is generally found in practice to be an attempt to excuse a crime.

Mistake of Maximus the Mystic. It is Maximus who forces the choice
on Julian, not as between ambition and principle; between Paganism
and Christianity; between 'the old beauty that is no longer beautiful
and the new truth that is no longer true,' but between Christ and Julian
himself. Maximus knows that there is no going back to 'the first empire'
of pagan sensualism. 'The second empire,' Christian or self-abnegatory
idealism, is already rotten at heart. 'The third empire' is what he looks
for: the empire of Man asserting the eternal validity of his own will. He
who can see that not on Olympus, not nailed to the cross, but in himself
is God: he is the man to build Brand's bridge between the flesh and the
spirit, establishing this third empire in which the spirit shall not be
unknown, nor the flesh starved, nor the will tortured and baffled. Thus
throughout the first part of the double drama we have Julian prompted
step by step to the stupendous conviction that he no less than the
Galilean is God. His final resolution to seize the throne is expressed in
his interruption of the Lord's prayer, which he hears intoned by worshippers in church as he wrestles in the gloom of the catacombs with
his own fears and the entreaties and threats of his soldiers urging him
to take the final decisive step. At the cue 'Lead us not into temptation;
but deliver us from evil' he rushes to the church with his soldiers,
exclaiming 'For mine is the kingdom.' Yet he halts on the threshold,
dazzled by the light, as his follower Sallust points the declaration by
adding, 'and the power, and the glory.'*

Once on the throne Julian becomes a mere pedant-tyrant, trying to
revive Paganism mechanically by cruel enforcement of external conformity to its rites. In his moments of exaltation he half grasps the
meaning of Maximus, only to relapse presently and pervert it into
a grotesque mixture of superstition and monstrous vanity. We have him
making such speeches as this, worthy of Peer Gynt at his most ludicrous: 'Has not Plato long ago enunciated the truth that only a god can
rule over men? What did he mean by that saying? Answer me: what did
he mean? Far be it from me to assert that Plato, incomparable sage
though he was, had any individual, even the greatest, in his prophetic
eye,' etc. In this frame of mind Christ appears to him, not as the prototype of himself, as Maximus would have him feel, but as a rival god over
whom he must prevail at all costs. It galls him to think that the Galilean
still reigns in the hearts of men whilst the emperor can only extort lip
honor from them by brute force; for in his wildest excesses of egotism
he never so loses his saving sense of the realities of things as to mistake
the trophies of persecution for the fruit of faith. 'Tell me who shall
conquer,' he demands of Maximus: 'the emperor or the Galilean?'

'Both the emperor and the Galilean shall succumb,' says Maximus.
'Whether in our time or in hundreds of years I know not; but so it shall
be when the right man comes.'

'Who is the right man?' says Julian.

'He who shall swallow up both emperor and Galilean,'[1] replies the
seer. 'Both shall succumb; but you shall not therefore perish. Does not
the child succumb in the youth and the youth in the man: yet neither
child nor youth perishes. You know I have never approved of your policy as emperor. You have tried to make the youth a child again. The
empire of the flesh is fallen a prey to the empire of the spirit. But the
empire of the spirit is not final, any more than the youth is. You have
tried to hinder the youth from growing: from becoming a man. Oh fool,
who have drawn your sword against that which is to be: against the
third empire, in which the twin-natured shall reign. For him the Jews
have a name. They call him Messiah, and are waiting for him.'

Still Julian stumbles on the threshold of the idea without entering
into it. He is galled out of all comprehension by the rivalry of the
Galilean, and asks despairingly who shall break his power. Then
Maximus drives the lesson home.

MAXIMUS. Is it not written, 'Thou shalt have none other gods but
   me?'

JULIAN. Yes—yes—yes.

MAXIMUS. The seer of Nazareth* did not preach this god or that: he
   said 'God is I: I am God.'

JULIAN. And that is what makes the emperor powerless? The third
   empire? The Messiah? Not the Jews' Messiah, but the Messiah of
   the two empires, the spirit and the world?

MAXIMUS. The God-Emperor.

JULIAN. The Emperor-God.

MAXIMUS. Logos in Pan, Pan in Logos.*

JULIAN. How is he begotten?

MAXIMUS. He is self-begotten in the man who wills.*

But it is of no use. Maximus's idea is a synthesis of relations in which
not only is Christ God in exactly the same sense as that in which Julian

---

[1] Or, as we should now say, the Superman. (1912.)

is God, but Julian is Christ as well. The persistence of Julian's jealousy
of the Galilean shews that he has not comprehended the synthesis at
all, but only seized on that part of it which flatters his own egotism.
And since this part is only valid as a constituent of the synthesis, and
has no reality when isolated from it, it cannot by itself convince Julian.
In vain does Maximus repeat his lesson in every sort of parable, and in
such pregnant questions as 'How do you know, Julian, that you were not
in him whom you now persecute?' He can only wreak him to utter commands to the winds, and to exclaim, in the excitement of burning his
fleet on the borders of Persia, 'The third empire is here, Maximus.
I feel that the Messiah of the earth lives within me. The spirit has
become flesh and the flesh spirit. All creation lies within my will and
power. More than the fleet is burning. In that glowing, swirling pyre the
crucified Galilean is burning to ashes; and the earthly emperor is burning with the Galilean. But from the ashes shall arise, phœnix-like, the
God of earth and the Emperor of the spirit in one, in one, in one.' At
which point he is informed that a Persian refugee, whose information
has emboldened him to burn his ships, has fled from the camp and is
a manifest spy. From that moment he is a broken man. In his next and
last emergency, when the Persians fall upon his camp, his first desperate exclamation is a vow to sacrifice to the gods. 'To what gods, oh fool?'
cries Maximus. 'Where are they; and what are they?' 'I will sacrifice to
this god and that god: I will sacrifice to many,' he answers desperately.
'One or other must surely hear me. *I must call on something without me
and above me*.' A flash of lightning seems to him a response from above;
and with this encouragement he throws himself into the fight, clinging,
like Macbeth, to an ambiguous oracle* which leads him to suppose that
only in the Phrygian regions need he fear defeat. He imagines he sees
the Nazarene in the ranks of the enemy; and in fighting madly to reach
him he is struck down, in the name of Christ, by one of his own soldiers. Then his one Christian General, Jovian, calls on his 'believing
brethren' to give Cæsar what is Cæsar's.* Declaring that the heavens
are open and the angels coming to the rescue with their swords of fire,
he rallies the Galileans of whom Julian has made slave-soldiers. The
pagan free legions, crying out that the god of the Galileans is on the
Roman side, and that he is the strongest, follow Jovian as he charges the
enemy, who fly in all directions whilst Julian, sinking back from a vain
effort to rise, exclaims, 'Thou hast conquered, O Galilean.'

Julian dies quietly in his tent, averring, in reply to a Christian friend's
inquiry, that he has nothing to repent of. 'The power which circumstances placed in my hands,' he says, 'and which is an emanation of

divinity, I am conscious of having used to the best of my skill. I have never wittingly wronged anyone. If some should think that I have not fulfilled all expectations, they should in justice reflect that there is a mysterious power outside us, which in a great measure governs the issue of human undertakings.' He still does not see eye to eye with Maximus, though there is a flash of insight in his remark to him, when he learns that the village where he fell is called the Phrygian region, that 'the world-will has laid an ambush for him.' It was something for Julian to have seen that the power which he found stronger than his individual will was itself will; but inasmuch as he conceived it, not as the whole of which his will was but a part, but as a rival will, he was not the man to found the third empire. He had felt the godhead in himself, but not in others. Being only able to say, with half conviction, 'The kingdom of heaven is within ME,' he had been utterly vanquished by the Galilean who had been able to say, 'The kingdom of heaven is within YOU.' But he was on the way to that full truth. A man cannot believe in others until he believes in himself; for his conviction of the equal worth of his fellows must be filled by the overflow of his conviction of his own worth. Against the spurious Christianity of asceticism, starving that indispensable prior conviction, Julian rightly rebelled: and Maximus rightly incited him to rebel. But Maximus could not fill the prior conviction even to fulness, much less to overflowing; for the third empire was not yet, and is not yet.

However, the tyrant dies with a peaceful conscience; and Maximus is able to tell the priest at the bedside that the world-will will answer for Julian's soul. What troubles the mystic is his having misled Julian by encouraging him to bring upon himself the fate of Cain and Judas. As water can be boiled by fire, man can be prompted and stimulated from without to assert his individuality; but just as no boiling can fill a half-empty well, no external stimulus can enlarge the spirit of man to the point at which he can self-beget the Emperor-God in himself by willing. At that point 'to will is to have to will'; and it is with these words on his lips that Maximus leaves the stage, still sure that the third empire is to come.

It is not necessary to translate the scheme of Emperor and Galilean into terms of the antithesis between idealism and realism. Julian, in this respect, is a reincarnation of Peer Gynt. All the difference is that the subject which was instinctively projected in the earlier poem, is intellectually constructed in the later history, Julian plus Maximus the Mystic being Peer plus one who understands him better than Ibsen did when he created him.

The interest for us of Ibsen's interpretation of original Christianity is obvious. The deepest sayings recorded in the gospels are now nothing but eccentric paradoxes to most of those who reject the supernatural view of Christ's divinity. Those who accept that view often consider that such acceptance absolves them from attaching any sensible meaning to his words at all, and so might as well pin their faith to a stock or stone. Of these attitudes the first is superficial, and the second stupid. Ibsen's interpretation, whatever may be its validity, will certainly hold the field long after the current 'Crosstianity,'* as it has been aptly called, becomes unthinkable.

THE OBJECTIVE ANTI-IDEALIST PLAYS

IBSEN had now written three immense dramas, all dealing with the effect of idealism on individual egotists of exceptional imaginative excitability. This he was able to do whilst his intellectual consciousness of his theme was yet incomplete, by simply portraying sides of himself. He has put himself into the skin of Brand and Peer Gynt. He has divided himself between Maximus and Julian. These figures have accordingly a certain direct vitality which we shall find in none of his later male figures until it reappears under the shadow of death, less as vitality than as mortality putting on immortality, in the four great plays with which he closed and crowned his life's work. There are flashes of it in Relling, in Lövborg, in Ellida's stranger from the sea;* but they are only flashes: henceforth for many years, indeed until his warfare against vulgar idealism is accomplished and a new phase entered upon in The Master Builder, all his really vivid and solar figures are women. For, having at last completed his intellectual analysis of idealism, he could now construct methodical illustrations of its social working, instead of, as before, blindly projecting imaginary personal experiences which he himself had not yet succeeded in interpreting. Further, now that he understood the matter, he could see plainly the effect of idealism as a social force on people quite unlike himself: that is to say, on everyday people in everyday life: on shipbuilders, bank managers, parsons, and doctors, as well as on saints, romantic adventurers, and emperors.

With his eyes thus opened, instances of the mischief of idealism crowded upon him so rapidly that he began deliberately to inculcate their lesson by writing realistic prose plays of modern life, abandoning all production of art for art's sake.* His skill as a playwright and his genius as an artist were thenceforth used only to secure attention and effectiveness for his detailed attack on idealism. No more verse, no more tragedy for the sake of tears or comedy for the sake of laughter, no more seeking to produce specimens of art forms in order that literary critics might fill the public belly with the east wind. The critics, it is true, soon declared that he had ceased to be an artist; but he, having something else to do with his talent than to fulfil critics' definitions, took no notice of them, not thinking their ideal sufficiently important to write a play about.

The League of Youth, 1869

The first of the series of realistic prose plays is called Pillars of Society; but before describing this, a word must be said about a previous work which seems to have determined the form the later series took. Between Peer Gynt and Emperor and Galilean, Ibsen had let fall an amusing comedy called The League of Youth (*De Unges Forbund*) in which the imaginative egotist reappears farcically as an ambitious young lawyer-politician who, smarting under a snub from a local landowner and county magnate, relieves his feelings with such a passionate explosion of Radical eloquence that he is cheered to the echo by the progressive party. Intoxicated with this success, he imagines himself a great leader of the people and a wielder of the mighty engine of democracy. He narrates to a friend a dream in which he saw kings swept helplessly over the surface of the earth by a mighty wind. He has hardly achieved this impromptu when he receives an invitation to dine with the local magnate, whose friends, to spare his feelings, have misled him as to the person aimed at in the new demagogue's speech. The invitation sets the egotist's imagination on the opposite tack: he is presently pouring forth his soul in the magnate's drawing-room to the very friend to whom he related the great dream.

'My goal is this: in the course of time I shall get into Parliament, perhaps into the Ministry, and marry happily into a rich and honorable family. I intend to reach it by my own exertions. I must and shall reach it without help from anyone. Meanwhile I shall enjoy life here, drinking in beauty and sunshine. Here there are fine manners: life moves gracefully here: the very floors seem laid to be trodden only by lacquered shoes: the arm-chairs are deep; and the ladies sink exquisitely into them. Here the conversation goes lightly and elegantly, like a game at battledore; and no blunders come plumping in to make an awkward silence. Here I feel for the first time what distinction means. Yes: we have indeed an aristocracy of culture; and to it I will belong. Dont you yourself feel the refining influence of the place,' etc., etc.

For the rest, the play is an ingenious comedy of intrigue, clever enough in its mechanical construction to entitle the French to claim that Ibsen owes something to his technical education as a playwright in the school of Scribe.* One or two episodes are germs of later plays; and the suitability of the realistic prose comedy form to these episodes no doubt confirmed Ibsen in his choice of it.

Pillars of Society, 1877

Pillars of Society is the history of one Karsten Bernick, a 'pillar of society' who, in pursuance of the duty of maintaining the respectability of his father's firm of shipbuilders, has averted a disgraceful exposure by allowing another man to bear the discredit not only of a love affair in which he himself had been the sinner, but of a theft which was never committed at all, having been merely alleged as an excuse for the firm being out of funds at a critical period. Bernick is an abject slave to the idealizings of one Rörlund, a schoolmaster, about respectability, duty to society, good example, social influence, health of the community, and so on. When Bernick falls in love with a married actress, he feels that no man has a right to shock the feelings of Rörlund and the community for his own selfish gratification. However, a clandestine intrigue will shock nobody, since nobody need know of it. He accordingly adopts this method of satisfying himself and preserving the moral tone of the community at the same time. Unluckily, the intrigue is all but discovered; and Bernick has either to see the moral security of the community shaken to its foundations by the terrible scandal of his exposure, or else to deny what he did and put it on another man. As the other man happens to be going to America, where he can easily conceal his imputed shame, Bernick's conscience tells him that it would be little short of a crime against society to neglect such an opportunity; and he accordingly lies his way back into the good opinion of Rörlund and Company at the emigrant's expense.

There are three women in the play for whom the schoolmaster's ideals have no attractions. First, there is the actress's daughter, who wants to get to America because she hears that people there are not good; for she is heartily tired of good people, since it is part of their goodness to look down on her because of her mother's disgrace. The schoolmaster, to whom she is engaged, condescends to her for the same reason. The second has already sacrificed her happiness and wasted her life in conforming to the Rörlund ideal of womanliness; and she earnestly advises the younger woman not to commit that folly, but to break her engagement with the schoolmaster, and elope promptly with the man she loves. The third is a naturally free woman who has snapped her fingers at the current ideals all her life; and it is her presence that at last encourages the liar to break with the ideals by publicly telling the truth about himself.

The comic personage of the piece is a useless hypochondriac whose function in life, as described by himself, is 'to hold up the banner of the ideal.' This he does by sneering at everything and everybody for not resembling the heroic incidents and characters he reads about in novels and tales of adventure. But his obvious peevishness and folly make him much less dangerous than the pious idealist, the earnest and respectable Rörlund. The play concludes with Bernick's admission that the spirits of Truth and Freedom are the true pillars of society, a phrase which sounds so like an idealistic commonplace that it is necessary to add that Truth in this passage does not mean the nursery convention of truth-telling satirized by Ibsen himself in a later play, as well as by Labiche* and other comic dramatists. It means the unflinching recognition of facts, and the abandonment of the conspiracy to ignore such of them as do not bolster up the ideals. The idealist rule as to truth dictates the recognition only of those facts or idealistic masks of facts which have a respectable air, and the mentioning of these on all occasions and at all hazards. Ibsen urges the recognition of all facts; but as to mentioning them, he wrote a whole play, as we shall see presently, to shew that you must do that at your own peril, and that a truth-teller who cannot hold his tongue on occasion may do as much mischief as a whole university-ful of trained liars. The word Freedom means freedom from the tyranny of the Rörlund ideals.

A Doll's House, 1879

Unfortunately, Pillars of Society, as a propagandist play, is disabled by the circumstance that the hero, being a fraudulent hypocrite in the ordinary police-court sense of the phrase, would hardly be accepted as a typical pillar of society by the class he represents. Accordingly, Ibsen took care next time to make his idealist irreproachable from the stand-point of the ordinary idealist morality. In the famous Doll's House,* the pillar of society who owns the doll is a model husband, father, and citizen. In his little household, with the three darling children and the affectionate little wife, all on the most loving terms with one another, we have the sweet home, the womanly woman, the happy family life of the idealist's dream. Mrs Nora Helmer is happy in the belief that she has attained a valid realization of all these illusions; that she is an ideal wife and mother; and that Helmer is an ideal husband who would, if the necessity arose, give his life to save her reputation. A few simply contrived incidents disabuse her effectually on all these points. One of her earliest acts of devotion to her husband has been the secret raising of a sum of money to enable him to make a tour which was necessary to restore his health. As he would have broken down sooner than go into debt, she has had to persuade him that the money was a gift from her father. It was really obtained from a moneylender, who refused to make her the loan unless she induced her father to endorse the promissory note.* This being impossible, as her father was dying at the time, she took the shortest way out of the difficulty by writing the name herself, to the entire satisfaction of the moneylender, who, though not at all duped, knew that forged bills are often the surest to be paid. Since then she has slaved in secret at scrivener's work until she has nearly paid off the debt.

At this point Helmer is made manager of the bank in which he is employed; and the moneylender, wishing to obtain a post there, uses the forged bill to force Nora to exert her influence with Helmer on his behalf. But she, having a hearty contempt for the man, cannot be persuaded by him that there was any harm in putting her father's name on the bill, and ridicules the suggestion that the law would not recognize that she was right under the circumstances. It is her husband's own contemptuous denunciation of a forgery formerly committed by the moneylender himself that destroys her self-satisfaction and opens her eyes to her ignorance of the serious business of the world to which her husband belongs: the world outside the home he shares with her. When he goes on to tell her that commercial dishonesty is generally to be traced to the influence of bad mothers, she begins to perceive that the happy way in which she plays with the children, and the care she takes to dress them nicely, are not sufficient to constitute her a fit person to train them. To redeem the forged bill, she resolves to borrow the balance due upon it from an intimate friend of the family. She has learnt to coax her husband into giving her what she asks by appealing to his affection for her: that is, by playing all sorts of pretty tricks until he is wheedled into an amorous humor. This plan she has adopted without thinking about it, instinctively taking the line of least resistance with him. And now she naturally takes the same line with her husband's friend. An unexpected declaration of love from him is the result; and it at once explains to her the real nature of the domestic influence she has been so proud of.

All her illusions about herself are now shattered. She sees herself as an ignorant and silly woman, a dangerous mother, and a wife kept for her husband's pleasure merely; but she clings all the harder to her illusion about him: he is still the ideal husband who would make any sacrifice to rescue her from ruin. She resolves to kill herself rather than allow him to destroy his own career by taking the forgery on himself to save her reputation. The final disillusion comes when he, instead of at once proposing to pursue this ideal line of conduct when he hears of the forgery, naturally enough flies into a vulgar rage and heaps invective on her for disgracing him. Then she sees that their whole family life has been a fiction: their home a mere doll's house in which they have been playing at ideal husband and father, wife and mother. So she leaves him then and there and goes out into the real world to find out its reality for herself, and to gain some position not fundamentally false, refusing to see her children again until she is fit to be in charge of them, or to live with him until she and he become capable of a more honorable relation to one another. He at first cannot understand what has happened, and flourishes the shattered ideals over her as if they were as potent as ever. He presents the course most agreeable to him—that of her staying at home and avoiding a scandal—as her duty to her husband, to her children, and to her religion; but the magic of these disguises is gone; and at last even he understands what has really happened, and sits down alone to wonder whether that more honorable relation can ever come to pass between them.*

Ghosts, 1881

In his next play, Ibsen returned to the charge with such an uncompromising and outspoken attack on marriage as a useless sacrifice of human beings to an ideal, that his meaning was obscured by its very obviousness. Ghosts, as it is called, is the story of a woman who has faithfully acted as a model wife and mother, sacrificing herself at every point with selfless thoroughness. Her husband is a man with a huge capacity and appetite for sensuous enjoyment. Society, prescribing ideal duties and not enjoyment for him, drives him to enjoy himself in underhand and illicit ways. When he marries his model wife, her devotion to duty only makes life harder for him; and he at last takes refuge in the caresses of an undutiful but pleasure-loving housemaid, and leaves his wife to satisfy her conscience by managing his business affairs whilst he satisfies his cravings as best he can by reading novels, drinking, and flirting, as aforesaid, with the servants. At this point even those who are most indignant with Nora Helmer for walking out of the doll's house must admit that Mrs Alving would be justified in walking out of *her* house. But Ibsen is determined to shew you what comes of the scrupulous line of conduct you were so angry with Nora for not pursuing. Mrs Alving feels that her place is by her husband for better for worse, and by her child. Now the ideal of wifely and womanly duty which demands this from her also demands that she shall regard herself as an outraged wife, and her husband as a scoundrel. And the family ideal calls upon her to suffer in silence lest she shatter her innocent son's faith in the purity of home life by letting him know the disreputable truth about his father. It is her duty to conceal that truth from the world and from him. In this she falters for one moment only. Her marriage has not been a love match: she has, in pursuance of her duty as a daughter, contracted it for the sake of her family, although her heart inclined to a highly respectable clergyman, a professor of her own idealism, named Manders. In the humiliation of her first discovery of her husband's infidelity, she leaves the house and takes refuge with Manders; but he at once leads her back to the path of duty, from which she does not again swerve. With the utmost devotion she now carries out an elaborate scheme of lying and imposture. She so manages her husband's affairs and so shields his good name that everybody believes him to be a public-spirited citizen of the strictest conformity to current ideals of respectability and family life. She sits up of nights listening to his lewd and silly conversation, and even drinking with him, to keep him from going into the streets and being detected by the neighbors in what she considers his vices. She provides for the servant he has seduced, and brings up his illegitimate daughter as a maid in her own household. And, as a crowning sacrifice, she sends her son away to Paris to be educated there, knowing that if he stays at home the shattering of his ideals must come sooner or later.

Her work is crowned with success. She gains the esteem of her old love the clergyman, who is never tired of holding up her household as a beautiful realization of the Christian ideal of marriage. Her own martyrdom is brought to an end at last by the death of her husband in the odor of a most sanctified reputation, leaving her free to recall her son from Paris and enjoy his society, and his love and gratitude, in the flower of his early manhood.

But when her son comes home, the facts refuse as obstinately as ever to correspond to her ideals. Oswald has inherited his father's love of enjoyment; and when, in dull rainy weather, he returns from Paris to the solemn strictly ordered house where virtue and duty have had their temple for so many years, his mother sees him shew the unmistakable signs of boredom with which she is so miserably familiar from of old; then sit after dinner killing time over the bottle; and finally—the climax of anguish—begin to flirt with the maid who, as his mother alone knows, is his own father's daughter. But there is this worldwide difference in her insight to the cases of the father and the son. She did not love the father: she loves the son with the intensity of a heart-starved

woman who has nothing else left to love. Instead of recoiling from him
with pious disgust and Pharisaical consciousness of moral superiority,
she sees at once that he has a right to be happy in his own way, and that
she has no right to force him to be dutiful and wretched in hers. She
sees, too, her injustice to the unfortunate father, and the cowardice of
the monstrous fabric of lies and false appearances she has wasted her
life in manufacturing. She resolves that the son's life shall not be sacrificed to ideals which are to him joyless and unnatural. But she finds that
the work of the ideals is not to be undone quite so easily. In driving the
father to steal his pleasures in secrecy and squalor, they had brought
upon him the diseases bred by such conditions; and her son now tells
her that those diseases have left their mark on him, and that he carries
poison in his pocket against the time, foretold to him by a Parisian surgeon, when general paralysis of the insane may destroy his faculties. In
desperation she undertakes to rescue him from this horrible apprehension by making his life happy. The house shall be made as bright as
Paris for him: he shall have as much champagne as he wishes until he is
no longer driven to that dangerous resource by the dulness of his life
with her: if he loves the girl he shall marry her if she were fifty times his
half-sister. But the half-sister, on learning the state of his health, leaves
the house; for she, too, is her father's daughter, and is not going to sacrifice her life in devotion to an invalid. When the mother and son are
left alone in their dreary home, with the rain still falling outside, all she
can do for him is to promise that if his doom overtakes him before he
can poison himself, she will make a final sacrifice of her natural feelings
by performing that dreadful duty, the first of all her duties that has any
real basis. Then the weather clears up at last; and the sun, which the
young man has so longed to see, appears. He asks her to give it to him
to play with; and a glance at him shews her that the ideals have claimed
their victim, and that the time has come for her to save him from a real
horror by sending him from her out of the world, just as she saved him
from an imaginary one years before by sending him out of Norway.

   This last scene of Ghosts is so appallingly tragic that the emotions it
excites prevent the meaning of the play from being seized and discussed like that of A Doll's House. In England nobody, as far as I know,
seems to have perceived that Ghosts is to A Doll's House what the late
Sir Walter Besant intended his own sequel[1]* to that play to be. Besant

---

[1] A forgotten production, published in the English Illustrated Magazine for January
1890. Besant makes the moneylender, as a reformed man, and a pattern of all the virtues,
hold a forged bill *in terrorem* over Nora's grown-up daughter, engaged to his son. The bill

attempted to shew what might come of Nora's repudiation of that idealism of which he was one of the most popular professors. But the effect made on Besant by A Doll's House was very faint compared to that produced on the English critics by the first performance of Ghosts in this country. In the earlier part of this essay I have shewn that since Mrs Alving's early conceptions of duty are as valid to ordinary critics as to Pastor Manders, who must appear to them as an admirable man, endowed with Helmer's good sense without Helmer's selfishness, a pretty general disapproval of the moral of the play was inevitable. Fortunately, the newspaper press went to such bedlamite lengths on this occasion that Mr William Archer, the well-known dramatic critic and translator of Ibsen, was able to put the whole body of hostile criticism out of court by simply quoting its excesses in an article entitled Ghosts and Gibberings, which appeared in The Pall Mall Gazette of the 8th of April 1891. Mr Archer's extracts, which he offers as a nucleus for a Dictionary of Abuse modelled upon the Wagner *Schimpf-Lexicon,** are worth reprinting here as samples of contemporary idealist criticism of the drama.

DESCRIPTIONS OF THE PLAY

'Ibsen's positively abominable play entitled Ghosts...This disgusting representation...Reprobation due to such as aim at infecting the modern theatre with poison after desperately inoculating themselves and others...An open drain; a loathsome sore unbandaged; a dirty act done publicly; a lazar-house with all its doors and windows open...Candid foulness...Kotzebue turned bestial and cynical. Offensive cynicism... Ibsen's melancholy and malodorous world...Absolutely loathsome and fetid...Gross, almost putrid indecorum...Literary carrion... Crapulous stuff...Novel and perilous nuisance.' *Daily Telegraph* [leading article]. 'This mass of vulgarity, egotism, coarseness, and absurdity.' *Daily Telegraph* [criticism]. 'Unutterably offensive...Prosecution under Lord Campbell's Act...Abominable piece...Scandalous.' *Standard*.

---

has been forged by her brother, who has inherited a tendency to forge from his mother. Helmer having taken to drink after the departure of his wife, and forfeited his social position, the moneylender tells the girl that if she persists in disgracing him by marrying his son, he will send her brother to gaol. She evades the dilemma by drowning herself. The moral is that if Nora had never run away from her husband her daughter would never have drowned herself. Note that the moneylender does over again what he did in Ibsen's play, with the difference that, having become eminently respectable, he has also become a remorseless scoundrel. Ibsen shews him as a good-natured fellow at bottom. I wrote a sequel to this sequel. Another sequel was written by Eleanor, the youngest daughter of Karl Marx. I forget where they appeared.

'Naked loathsomeness...Most dismal and repulsive production.' *Daily News*. 'Revoltingly suggestive and blasphemous...Characters either contradictory in themselves, uninteresting or abhorrent.' *Daily Chronicle*. 'A repulsive and degrading work.' *Queen*. 'Morbid, unhealthy, unwholesome and disgusting story...A piece to bring the stage into disrepute and dishonour with every right-thinking man and woman.' *Lloyd's*. 'Merely dull dirt long drawn out.' *Hawk*. 'Morbid horrors of the hideous tale...Ponderous dulness of the didactic talk...If any repetition of this outrage be attempted, the authorities will doubtless wake from their lethargy.' *Sporting and Dramatic News*. 'Just a wicked nightmare.' *The Gentlewoman*. 'Lugubrious diagnosis of sordid impropriety... Characters are prigs, pedants, and profligates...Morbid caricatures... Maunderings of nookshotten* Norwegians...It is no more of a play than an average Gaiety burlesque.' *Black and White*. 'Most loathsome of all Ibsen's plays...Garbage and offal.' *Truth*. 'Ibsen's putrid play called Ghosts...So loathsome an enterprise.' *Academy*. 'As foul and filthy a concoction as has ever been allowed to disgrace the boards of an English theatre...Dull and disgusting...Nastiness and malodorousness laid on thickly as with a trowel.' *Era*. 'Noisome corruption.' *Stage*.

DESCRIPTIONS OF IBSEN

'An egotist and a bungler.' *Daily Telegraph*. 'A crazy fanatic...A crazy, cranky being...Not only consistently dirty but deplorably dull.' *Truth*. 'The Norwegian pessimist *in petto*'* [*sic*]. *Black and White*. 'Ugly, nasty, discordant, and downright dull...A gloomy sort of ghoul, bent on groping for horrors by night, and blinking like a stupid old owl when the warm sunlight of the best of life dances into his wrinkled eyes.' *Gentlewoman*. 'A teacher of the æstheticism of the Lock Hospital.'* *Saturday Review*.

DESCRIPTIONS OF IBSEN'S ADMIRERS

'Lovers of prurience and dabblers in impropriety who are eager to gratify their illicit tastes under the pretence of art.' *Evening Standard*. 'Ninety-seven per cent of the people who go to see Ghosts are nasty-minded people who find the discussion of nasty subjects to their taste in exact proportion to their nastiness.' *Sporting and Dramatic News*. 'The sexless...The unwomanly woman, the unsexed females, the whole army of unprepossessing cranks in petticoats...Educated and muck-ferreting dogs...Effeminate men and male women...They all of them—men and women alike—know that they are doing not only a nasty but an illegal thing...The Lord Chamberlain* left them alone to wallow in Ghosts...Outside a silly clique, there is not the slightest interest in the Scandinavian humbug or all his works...A wave of human folly.' *Truth*.[1]

An Enemy of the People, 1882

After this, the reader will understand the temper in which Ibsen set about his next play, An Enemy of the People, in which, having done sufficient execution among the ordinary middle-class domestic and social ideals, he puts his finger for a moment on commercial political ideals. The play deals with a local majority of middle-class people who are pecuniarily interested in concealing the fact that the famous baths which attract visitors to their town and customers to their shops and hotels are contaminated by sewage. When an honest doctor insists on exposing this danger, the towns-people immediately disguise them-selves ideally. Feeling the disadvantage of appearing in their true char-acter as a conspiracy of interested rogues against an honest man, they pose as Society, as The People, as Democracy, as the solid Liberal Majority, and other imposing abstractions, the doctor, in attacking them, of course being thereby made an enemy of The People, a danger to Society, a traitor to Democracy, an apostate from the great Liberal party, and so on. Only those who take an active part in politics can

---

[1] Outrageous as the above extracts now seem, I could make them appear quite moder-ate by setting beside them the hue and cry raised in New York in 1905 against a play of my own entitled Mrs Warren's Profession.* But there was a commercial reason for that. My play exposed what has since become known as the White Slave Traffic: that is, the organization of prostitution as a regular commercial industry yielding huge profits to capital invested in it, directly or indirectly, by 'pillars of society.' The attack on the play was so corrupt that the newspaper that took the lead in it was heavily fined shortly after-wards for trading in advertisements of the traffic. But the attack on Ghosts was, I believe, really disinterested and sincere on its moral side. No doubt Ibsen was virulently hated by some of the writers quoted, as all great and original artists are hated by contemporary mediocrity, which needs must hate the highest when it sees it. Our own mediocrities would abuse Ibsen as heartily as their fathers did if they were not young enough to have started with an entirely inculcated and unintelligent assumption that he is a classic, like Shakespear and Goethe, and therefore must not be abused and need not be understood. But we have only to compare the frantic and indecent vituperation quoted above with the mere disparagement and dislike expressed towards Ibsen's other plays at the same period to perceive that here Ibsen struck at something much deeper than the fancies of critics as to the proper way to write plays. An ordinary farcical comedy ridiculing Pastor Manders and making Alving out to be a good fellow would have enlisted their sympathy at once, as their tradition was distinctly 'Bohemian.' Their horror at Ghosts is a striking proof of the worthlessness of mere Bohemianism, which has all the idle sentimentality and idolatry of conventionality without any of its backbone of contract and law. (1912.)

appreciate the grim fun of the situation, which, though it has an intensely local Norwegian air, will be at once recognized as typical in England, not, perhaps, by the professional literary critics, who are for the most part *fainéants** as far as political life is concerned, but certainly by everyone who has got as far as a seat on the committee of the most obscure Ratepayers' Association.*

As An Enemy of the People contains one or two references to Democracy which are anything but respectful, it is necessary to examine Ibsen's criticism of it with precision. Democracy is really only an arrangement by which the governed are allowed to choose (as far as any choice is possible, which in capitalistic society is not saying much) the members of the representative bodies which control the executive. It has never been proved that this is the best arrangement; and it has been made effective only to the very limited extent short of which the dissatisfaction which it appeases might take the form of actual violence. Now when men had to submit to kings, they consoled themselves by making it an article of faith that the king was always right, idealizing him as a Pope, in fact. In the same way we who have to submit to majorities set up Voltaire's pope, *Monsieur Tout-le-monde*,* and make it blasphemy against Democracy to deny that the majority is always right, although that, as Ibsen says, is a lie. It is a scientific fact that the majority, however eager it may be for the reform of old abuses, is always wrong in its opinion of new developments, or rather is always unfit for them (for it can hardly be said to be wrong in opposing developments for which it is not yet fit). The pioneer is a tiny minority of the force he heads; and so, though it is easy to be in a minority and yet be wrong, it is absolutely impossible to be in the majority and yet be right as to the newest social prospects. We should never progress at all if it were possible for each of us to stand still on democratic principles until we saw whither all the rest were moving, as our statesmen declare themselves bound to do when they are called upon to lead. Whatever clatter we may make for a time with our filing through feudal serf collars and kicking off old mercantilist fetters, we shall never march a step forward except at the heels of 'the strongest man, he who is able to stand alone' and to turn his back on 'the damned compact Liberal majority.' All of which is no disparagement of parliaments and adult suffrage, but simply a wholesome reduction of them to their real place in the social economy as pure machinery: machinery which has absolutely no principles except the principles of mechanics, and no motive power in itself whatsoever. The idealization of public organizations is as dangerous as that of kings or priests. We need to be reminded that though there is in the world a vast number of buildings in which a certain ritual is conducted before crowds called congregations by a functionary called a priest, who is subject to a central council controlling all such functionaries on a few points, there is not therefore any such thing in the concrete as the ideal Catholic Church, nor ever was, nor ever will be. There may, too, be a highly elaborate organization of public affairs; but there is no such thing as the ideal State. There may be a combination of persons living by the practice of medicine, surgery, or physical or biological research; or by drawing up wills and leases, and preparing, pleading, or judging cases at law; or by painting pictures, writing books, and acting plays; or by serving in regiments and battle ships; or by manual labor or industrial service. But when any of these combinations, through its organizers or leaders, claims to deliver the Verdict of Science, or to act with the Authority of the Law, or to be as sacred as the Mission of Art, or to revenge criticisms of themselves as outrages on the Honor of His Majesty's Services, or to utter the Voice of Labor, there is urgent need for the guillotine,* or whatever may be the mode in vogue of putting presumptuous persons in their proper place. All abstractions invested with collective consciousness or collective authority, set above the individual, and exacting duty from him on pretence of acting or thinking with greater validity than he, are man-eating idols red with human sacrifices.

This position must not be confounded with Anarchism, or the idealization of the repudiation of Governments. Ibsen did not refuse to pay the tax collector, but may be supposed to have regarded him, not as the vicar of an abstraction called THE STATE, but simply as the man sent round by a committee of citizens (mostly fools as far as Maximus the Mystic's Third Empire is concerned)* to collect the money for the police or the paving and lighting of the streets.

The Wild Duck, 1884

After An Enemy of the People, Ibsen, as I have said, left the vulgar ideals for dead, and set about the exposure of those of the choicer spirits, beginning with the incorrigible idealists who had idealized his very self, and were becoming known as Ibsenites. His first move in this direction was such a tragi-comic slaughtering of sham Ibsenism that his astonished victims plaintively declared that The Wild Duck, as the new play was called, was a satire on his former works; whilst the pious, whom he had disappointed so severely by his interpretation of Brand, began to hope that he was coming back repentant to the fold. The household to which we are introduced in The Wild Duck is not, like

Mrs Alving's, a handsome one made miserable by superstitious illusions, but a shabby one made happy by romantic illusions. The only member of it who sees it as it really is *is* the wife, a good-natured Philistine who desires nothing better. The husband, a vain, petted, spoilt dawdler, believes that he is a delicate and high-souled man, devoting his life to redeeming his old father's name from the disgrace brought on it by imprisonment for breach of the forest laws. This redemption he proposes to effect by making himself famous as a great inventor some day when he has the necessary inspiration. Their daughter, a girl in her teens, believes intensely in her father and in the promised invention. The disgraced grandfather cheers himself by drink whenever he can get it; but his chief resource is a wonderful garret full of rabbits and pigeons. The old man has procured a number of second-hand Christmas trees; and with these he has turned the garret into a sort of toy forest, in which he can play at bear hunting, which was one of the sports of his youth and prosperity. The weapons employed in the hunting expeditions are a gun which will not go off, and a pistol which occasionally brings down a rabbit or a pigeon. A crowning touch is given to the illusion by a wild duck, which, however, must not be shot, as it is the special property of the girl, who reads and dreams whilst her mother cooks, washes, sweeps and carries on the photographic work which is supposed to be the business of her husband. Mrs Ekdal does not appreciate Hjalmar's highly strung sensitiveness of character, which is constantly suffering agonizing jars from her vulgarity; but then she does not appreciate that other fact that he is a lazy and idle impostor. Downstairs there is a disgraceful clergyman named Molvik, a hopeless drunkard; but even he respects himself and is tolerated because of a special illusion invented for him by another lodger, Dr Relling, upon whom the lesson of the household above has not been thrown away. Molvik, says the doctor, must break out into drinking fits because he is daimonic, an imposing explanation which completely relieves the reverend gentleman from the imputation of vulgar tippling.

Into this domestic circle there comes a new lodger, an idealist of the most advanced type. He greedily swallows the daimonic theory of the clergyman's drunkenness, and enthusiastically accepts the photographer as the high-souled hero he supposes himself to be; but he is troubled because the relations of the man and his wife do not constitute an ideal marriage. He happens to know that the woman, before her marriage, was the cast-off mistress of his own father; and because she has not told her husband this, he conceives her life as founded on a lie, like that of Bernick in Pillars of Society. He accordingly sets himself to work out the woman's salvation for her, and establish ideally frank relations between the pair, by simply blurting out the truth, and then asking them, with fatuous self-satisfaction, whether they do not feel much the better for it. This wanton piece of mischief has more serious results than a mere domestic scene. The husband is too weak to act on his bluster about outraged honor and the impossibility of his ever living with his wife again; and the woman is merely annoyed with the idealist for telling on her; but the girl takes the matter to heart and shoots herself. The doubt cast on her parentage, with her father's theatrical repudiation of her, destroy her ideal place in the home, and make her a source of discord there; so she sacrifices herself, thereby carrying out the teaching of the idealist mischief-maker, who has talked a good deal to her about the duty and beauty of self-sacrifice, without foreseeing that he might be taken in mortal earnest. The busybody thus finds that people cannot be freed from their failings from without. They must free themselves. When Nora is strong enough to live out of the doll's house, she will go out of it of her own accord if the door stands open; but if before that period you take her by the scruff of the neck and thrust her out, she will only take refuge in the next establishment of the kind that offers to receive her. Woman has thus two enemies to deal with: the old-fashioned one who wants to keep the door locked, and the new-fashioned one who wants to thrust her into the street before she is ready to go. In the cognate case of a hypocrite and liar like Bernick, exposing him is a mere police measure: he is none the less a liar and hypocrite when you have exposed him. If you want to make a sincere and truthful man of him, all you can wisely do is to remove what you can of the external obstacles to his exposing himself, and then wait for the operation of his internal impulse to confess. If he has no such impulse, then you must put up with him as he is. It is useless to make claims on him which he is not yet prepared to meet. Whether, like Brand, we make such claims because to refrain would be to compromise with evil, or, like Gregers Werle, because we think their moral beauty must recommend them at sight to every one, we shall alike incur Relling's impatient assurance that 'life would be quite tolerable if we could only get rid of the confounded duns that keep on pestering us in our poverty with the claims of the ideal.'

Rosmersholm, *1886*

Ibsen did not in The Wild Duck exhaust the subject of the danger of forming ideals for other people, and interfering in their lives with a view to enabling them to realize those ideals. Cases far more typical than that of the meddlesome lodger are those of the priest who regards the ennobling of mankind as a sort of trade process of which his cloth gives him a monopoly, and the clever woman who pictures a noble career for the man she loves, and devotes herself to helping him to achieve it. In Rosmersholm, the play with which Ibsen followed up The Wild Duck, there is an unpractical country parson, a gentleman of ancient stock, whose family has been for many years a centre of social influence. The tradition of that influence reinforces his priestly tendency to regard the ennoblement of the world as an external operation to be performed by himself; and the need of such ennoblement is very evident to him; for his nature is a fine one: he looks at the world with some dim previ- sion of 'the third empire.' He is married to a woman of passionately affectionate nature, who is very fond of him, but does not regard him as a regenerator of the human race. Indeed she does not share any of his dreams, and only acts as an extinguisher on the sacred fire of his ideal- ism. He, she, her brother Kroll the headmaster, Kroll's wife, and their set, form a select circle of the best people in the place, comfortably orbited in our social system, and quite planetary in ascertained position and unimpeachable respectability. Into the orbit comes presently a wandering star, one Rebecca Gamvik, an unpropertied orphan, who has been allowed to read advanced books, and is a Freethinker and a Radical: things that disqualify a poor woman for admission to the Rosmer world. However, one must live somewhere; and as the Rosmer world is the only one in which an ambitious and cultivated woman can find powerful allies and educated companions, Rebecca, being both ambitious and cultivated, makes herself agreeable to the Rosmer circle with such success that the affectionate and impulsive but unintelligent Mrs Rosmer becomes wildly fond of her, and is not content until she has persuaded her to come and live with them. Rebecca, then a mere adventuress fighting for a foothold in polite society (which has hitherto shewn itself highly indignant at her thrusting herself in where nobody has thought of providing room for her), accepts the offer all the more readily because she has taken the measure of Parson Rosmer, and formed the idea of playing upon his aspirations, and making herself a leader in politics and society by using him as a figurehead.

But now two difficulties arise. First, there is Mrs Rosmer's extin- guishing effect on her husband: an effect which convinces Rebecca that nothing can be done with him whilst his wife is in the way. Second—a contingency quite unallowed for in her provident calculations—she finds herself passionately enamored of him. The poor parson, too, falls in love with her; but he does not know it. He turns to the woman who understands him like a sunflower to the sun, and makes her his real friend and companion. The wife feels this soon enough; and he quite unconscious of it, begins to think that her mind must be affected, since she has become so intensely miserable and hysterical about nothing—nothing that he can see. The truth is that she has come under the curse of Rebecca's ideal: she sees herself standing, a useless obstacle, between her husband and the woman he really loves, the woman who can help him to a glorious career. She cannot even be the mother in the household; for she is childless. Then comes Rebecca, fortified with a finely reasoned theory that Rosmer's future is staked against his wife's life, and says that it is better for all their sakes that she should quit Rosmersholm. She even hints that she must go at once if a grave scandal is to be avoided. Mrs Rosmer, regarding a scandal in Rosmersholm as the most terrible thing that can happen, and seeing that it could be averted by the marriage of Rebecca and Rosmer if she were out of the way, writes a letter secretly to Rosmer's bitterest enemy, the editor of the local Radical paper, a man who has forfeited his moral reputation by an intrigue which Rosmer has pitilessly denounced. In this letter she implores him not to believe or publish any stories that he may hear about Rosmer, to the effect that he is in any way to blame for anything that may happen to her. Then she sets Rosmer free to marry Rebecca, and to realize his ideals, by going out into the garden and throwing herself into the millstream that runs there.

Now follows a period of quiet mourning at Rosmersholm. Everybody except Rosmer suspects that Mrs Rosmer was not mad, and guesses why she committed suicide. Only it would not do to compromise the aristocratic party by treating Rosmer as the Radical editor was treated. So the neighbors shut their eyes and condole with the bereaved clergyman; and the Radical editor holds his tongue because Radicalism is growing respectable, and he hopes, with Rebecca's help, to get Rosmer over to his side presently. Meanwhile the unexpected has again happened to Rebecca. Her passion is worn out; but in the long days of mourning she has found the higher love; and it is now for Rosmer's own sake that she urges him to become a man of action, and brood no more over the dead. When his friends start a Conservative paper and ask him to become editor, she induces him to reply by declaring himself a Radical and Freethinker. To his utter amazement, the result is, not an animated discussion of his views, but just such an attack on his home life and private conduct as he had formerly made on those of the Radical editor. His friends tell him plainly that the compact of silence

is broken by his defection, and that there will be no mercy for the traitor to the party. Even the Radical editor not only refuses to publish the
fact that his new ally is a Freethinker (which would destroy all his social
weight as a Radical recruit), but brings up the dead woman's letter as
a proof that the attack is sufficiently well-founded to make it unwise to
go too far. Rosmer, who at first had been simply shocked that men
whom he had always honored as gentlemen should descend to such
hideous calumny, now sees that he really did love Rebecca, and is indeed
guilty of his wife's death. His first impulse is to shake off the spectre of
the dead woman by marrying Rebecca; but she, knowing that the guilt
is hers, puts that temptation behind her and refuses. Then, as he thinks
it all over, his dream of ennabling the world slips away from him: such
work can only be done by a man conscious of his own innocence. To
save him from despair, Rebecca makes a great sacrifice. She 'gives him
back his innocence' by confessing how she drove his wife to kill herself;
and, as the confession is made in the presence of Kroll, she ascribes the
whole plot to her ambition, and says not a word of her passion. Rosmer,
confounded as he realizes what helpless puppets they have all been in
the hands of this clever woman, for the moment misses the point that
unscrupulous ambition, though it explains her crime, does not account
for her confession. He turns his back on her and leaves the house with
Kroll. She quietly packs up her trunk, and is about to vanish from
Rosmersholm without another word when he comes back alone to ask
why she confessed. She tells him why, offering him her self-sacrifice as
a proof that his power of ennobling others was no vain dream, since it is
his companionship that has changed her from the selfish adventuress
she was to the devoted woman she has just proved herself to be. But he
has lost his faith in himself, and cannot believe her. The proof seems to
him subtle, artful: he cannot forget that she duped him by flattering
this very weakness of his before. Besides, he knows now that it is not
true: people are not ennobled from without. She has no more to say; for
she can think of no further proof. But he has thought of an unanswerable one. Dare she make all doubt impossible by sacrificing her share in
his future in the only absolutely final way: that is, by doing for his sake
what his wife did? She asks what would happen if she had the heart and
the will to do it. 'Then,' he replies, 'I should have to believe in you.
I should recover my faith in my mission. Faith in my power to ennoble
human souls. Faith in the human soul's power to attain nobility.' 'You
shall have your faith again,' she answers. At this pass the inner truth of
the situation comes out; and the thin veil of a demand for proof, with its
monstrous sequel of asking the woman to kill herself in order to restore

the man's good opinion of himself, falls away. What is really driving Rosmer is the superstition of expiation by sacrifice. He sees that when Rebecca goes into the millstream he must go too. And he speaks his real mind in the words, 'There is no judge over us: therefore we must do justice upon ourselves.' But the woman's soul is free of this to the end; for when she says, 'I am under the power of the Rosmersholm view of life *now*. What I have sinned it is fit I should expiate,' we feel in that speech a protest against the Rosmersholm view of life: the view that denied her right to live and be happy from the first, and now at the end, even in denying its God, exacts her life as a vain blood-offering for its own blindness. The woman has the higher light: she goes to her death out of fellowship with the man who is driven thither by the superstition which has destroyed his will. The story ends with his taking her solemnly as his wife, and casting himself with her into the millstream.

It is unnecessary to repeat here what is said on page [74] as to the vital part played in this drama by the evolution of the lower into the higher love. Peer Gynt, during the prophetic episode in his career, shocks the dancing girl Anitra into a remonstrance by comparing himself to a cat. He replies, with his wisest air, that from the standpoint of love there is perhaps not so much difference between a tomcat and a prophet as she may imagine. The number of critics who have entirely missed the point of Rebecca's transfiguration seems to indicate that the majority of men, even among critics of dramatic poetry, have not got beyond Peer Gynt's opinion in this matter. No doubt they would not endorse it as a definitely stated proposition, aware, as they are, that there is a poetic convention to the contrary. But if they fail to recognize the only possible alternative proposition when it is not only stated in so many words by Rebecca West, but when without it her conduct dramatically contradicts her character—when they even complain of the contradiction as a blemish on the play, I am afraid there can be no further doubt that the extreme perplexity into which the first performance of Rosmersholm in England* plunged the Press was due entirely to the prevalence of Peer Gynt's view of love among the dramatic critics.

The Lady from the Sea, 1888

Ibsen's next play, though it deals with the old theme, does not insist on the power of ideals to kill, as the two previous plays do. It rather deals with the origin of ideals in unhappiness, in dissatisfaction with the real. The subject of The Lady from the Sea is the most poetic fancy imaginable. A young woman, brought up on the sea-coast, marries a respectable doctor, a widower, who idolizes her and places her in his household with nothing to do but dream and be made much of by everybody. Even the housekeeping is done by her stepdaughter: she has no responsibility, no care, and no trouble. In other words, she is an idle, helpless, utterly dependent article of luxury. A man turns red at the thought of being such a thing; but he thoughtlessly accepts a pretty and fragile-looking woman in the same position as a charming natural picture. The lady from the sea feels an indefinite want in her life. She reads her want into all other lives, and comes to the conclusion that man once had to choose whether he would be a land animal or a creature of the sea; and that having chosen the land, he has carried about with him ever since a secret sorrow for the element he has forsaken. The dissatisfaction that gnaws her is, as she interprets it, this desperate longing for the sea. When her only child dies and leaves her without the work of a mother to give her a valid place in the world, she yields wholly to her longing, and no longer cares for her husband, who, like Rosmer, begins to fear that she is going mad.

At last a seaman appears and claims her as his wife on the ground that they went years before through a rite which consisted of their marrying the sea by throwing their rings into it. This man, who had to fly from her in the old time because he killed his captain, and who fills her with a sense of dread and mystery, seems to her to embody the mystic attraction the sea has for her. She tells her husband that she must go away with the seaman. Naturally the doctor expostulates—declares that he cannot for her own sake let her do so mad a thing. She replies that he can only prevent her by locking her up, and asks him what satisfaction it will be to him to have her body under lock and key whilst her heart is with the other man. In vain he urges that he will only keep her under restraint until the seaman goes—that he must not, dare not, allow her to ruin herself. Her argument remains unanswerable. The seaman openly declares that she will come; so that the distracted husband asks him does he suppose he can force her from her home. To this the seaman replies that, on the contrary, unless she comes of her own free will there is no satisfaction to him in her coming at all: the unanswerable argument again. She echoes it by demanding her freedom to choose. Her husband must cry off his law-made and Church-made bargain; renounce his claim to the fulfilment of her vows; and leave her free to go back to the sea with her old lover. Then the doctor, with a heavy heart, drops his prate about his heavy responsibility for her actions, and throws the responsibility on her by crying off as she demands. The moment she feels herself a free and responsible woman, all her childish fancies vanish: the seaman becomes simply an old acquaintance whom she no longer cares for; and the doctor's affection produces its natural effect. In short, she says No to the seaman, and takes over the housekeeping keys from her stepdaughter without any further maunderings over that secret sorrow for the abandoned sea.

It should be noted here that Ellida [call her Eleeda], the Lady from the Sea, seems more fantastic to English readers than to Norwegian ones. The same thing is true of many other characters drawn by Ibsen, notably Peer Gynt, who, if born in England, would certainly not have been a poet and metaphysician as well as a blackguard and a speculator. The extreme type of Norwegian, as depicted by Ibsen, imagines himself doing wonderful things, but does nothing. He dreams as no Englishman dreams, and drinks to make himself dream the more, until his effective will is destroyed, and he becomes a broken-down, disreputable sot, carrying about the tradition that he is a hero, and discussing himself on that assumption. Although the number of persons who dawdle their life away over fiction in England must be frightful, and is probably increasing, yet their talk is not the talk of Ulric Brendel,* Rosmer, Ellida, or Peer Gynt; and it is for this reason that Rosmersholm and the Lady from the Sea strike English audiences as more fantastic and less literal than A Doll's House and the plays in which the leading figures are men and women of action, though to a Norwegian there is probably no difference in this respect.

Hedda Gabler, 1890*

Hedda Gabler has no ethical ideals at all, only romantic ones. She is a typical nineteenth-century figure, falling into the abyss between the ideals which do not impose on her and the realities she has not yet discovered. The result is that though she has imagination, and an intense appetite for beauty, she has no conscience, no conviction: with plenty of cleverness, energy, and personal fascination she remains mean, envious, insolent, cruel in protest against others' happiness, fiendish in her dislike of inartistic people and things, a bully in reaction from her own cowardice. Hedda's father, a general, is a widower. She has the traditions of the military caste about her; and these narrow her activities to the customary hunt for a socially and pecuniarily eligible husband. She makes the acquaintance of a young man of genius who, prohibited by an ideal-ridden society from taking his pleasures except where there is nothing to restrain him from excess, is going to the bad in search of his good, with the usual consequences. Hedda is intensely curious about the side of life which is forbidden to her, and in which powerful instincts, absolutely ignored and condemned in her circle, steal their satisfaction. An odd intimacy springs up between the inquisitive girl and the rake. Whilst the general reads the paper in the afternoon, Lövborg and Hedda have long conversations in which he describes to her all his disreputable adventures. Although she is the questioner, she never dares to trust him: all the questions are indirect; and the responsibility for his interpretations rests on him alone. Hedda has no conviction whatever that these conversations are disgraceful; but she will not risk a fight with society on the point: it is easier to practise hypocrisy, the homage that truth pays to falsehood, than to endure ostracism. When he proceeds to make advances to her, Hedda has again no conviction that it would be wrong for her to gratify his instinct and her own; so that she is confronted with the alternative of sinning against herself and him, or sinning against social ideals in which she has no faith. Making the coward's choice, she carries it out with the utmost bravado, threatening Lövborg with one of her father's pistols, and driving him out of the house with all that ostentation of outraged purity which is the instinctive defence of women to whom chastity is not natural, much as libel actions are mostly brought by persons concerning whom libels are virtually, if not technically, justifiable.

Hedda, deprived of her lover, now finds that a life of conformity without faith involves something more terrible than the utmost ostracism: to wit, boredom. This scourge, unknown among revolutionists, is the curse which makes the security of respectability as dust in the balance against the unflagging interest of rebellion, and which forces society to eke out its harmless resources for killing time by licensing gambling, gluttony, hunting, shooting, coursing, and other vicious distractions for which even idealism has no disguise. These licenses, being expensive, are available only for people who have more than enough money to keep up appearances; and as Hedda's father, being in the army instead of in commerce, is too poor to leave her much more than the pistols, her boredom is only mitigated by dancing, at which she gains much admiration, but no substantial offers of marriage.

At last she has to find somebody to support her. A good-natured mediocrity of a professor is the best that is to be had; and though she regards him as a member of an inferior class, and despises almost to loathing his family circle of two affectionate old aunts and the inevitable general servant who has helped to bring him up, she marries him *faute de mieux*,* and immediately proceeds to wreck this prudent provision for her livelihood by accommodating his income to her expenditure instead of accommodating her expenditure to his income. Her nature so rebels against the whole sordid transaction that the prospect of bearing a child to her husband drives her almost frantic, since it will not only expose her to the intimate solicitude of his aunts in the course of a derangement of her health in which she can see nothing that is not repulsive and humiliating, but will make her one of his family in earnest.

To amuse herself in these galling circumstances, she forms an underhand alliance with a visitor who belongs to her old set, an elderly gallant who quite understands how little she cares for her husband, and proposes a *ménage à trois* to her. She consents to his coming there and talking to her as he pleases behind her husband's back; but she keeps her pistols in reserve in case he becomes seriously importunate. He, on the other hand, tries to get some hold over her by placing her husband under pecuniary obligations, as far as he can do it without being out of pocket.

Meanwhile Lövborg is drifting to disgrace by the nearest way: drink. In due time he descends from lecturing at the university on the history of civilization to taking a job in an out-of-the-way place as tutor to the little children of Sheriff Elvsted. This functionary, on being left a widower with a number of children, marries their governess, finding that she will cost him less and be bound to do more for him as his wife. As for her, she is too poor to dream of refusing such a settlement in life. When Lövborg comes, his society is heaven to her. He does not dare tell her about his dissipations; but he tells her about his unwritten books, which he never discussed with Hedda. She does not dare to remonstrate with him for drinking; but he gives it up as soon as he sees that it shocks her. Just as Mr Fearing, in Bunyan's story, was in a way the bravest of the pilgrims, so this timid and unfortunate Mrs Elvsted trembles her way to a point at which Lövborg, quite reformed, publishes one book which makes him celebrated for the moment, and completes another, fair-copied in her handwriting, to which he looks for a solid position as an original thinker. But he cannot now stay tutoring Elvsted's children; so off he goes to town with his pockets full of the money the published book has brought him. Left once more in her old lonely plight, knowing that without her Lövborg will probably relapse into dissipation, and that without him her life will not be worth living, Mrs Elvsted must either sin against herself and him or against the institution of marriage under which Elvsted purchased his housekeeper. It never occurs to her that she has any choice. She knows that her action will count as 'a dreadful thing'; but she sees that she must go; and accordingly Elvsted finds himself without a wife and his children without a governess, and so disappears unpitied from the story.

Now it happens that Hedda's husband, Jörgen Tesman, is an old friend and competitor (for academic honors) of Lövborg, and also that Hedda was a schoolfellow of Mrs Elvsted, or Thea, as she had better now be called. Thea's first business is to find out where Lövborg is; for hers is no preconcerted elopement: she has hurried to town to keep Lövborg away from the bottle, a design she dare not hint at to himself. Accordingly, the first thing she does in town is to call on the Tesmans, who have just returned from their honeymoon, to beg them to invite Lövborg to their house so as to keep him in good company. They consent, with the result that the two pairs are brought together under the same roof, and the tragedy begins to work itself out.

Hedda's attitude now demands a careful analysis. Lövborg's experience with Thea has enlightened his judgment of Hedda; and as he is, in his gifted way, an arrant *poseur* and male coquet,* he immediately tries to get on romantic terms with her (for have they not 'a past'?) by impressing her with the penetrating criticism that she is and always was a coward. She admits that the virtuous heroics with the pistol were pure cowardice; but she is still so void of any other standard of conduct than conformity to the conventional ideals, that she thinks her cowardice consisted in not daring to be wicked. That is, she thinks that what she actually did was the right thing; and since she despises herself for doing it, and feels that he also rightly despises her for doing it, she gets a passionate feeling that what is wanted is the courage to do wrong. This unlooked-for reaction of idealism, this monstrous but very common setting-up of wrong-doing as an ideal, and of the wrongdoer as hero or heroine *qua* wrongdoer, leads Hedda to conceive that when Lövborg tried to seduce her he was a hero, and that in allowing Thea to reform him he has played the recreant. In acting on this misconception she is restrained by no consideration for any of the rest. Like all people whose lives are valueless, she has no more sense of the value of Lövborg's or Tesman's or Thea's lives than a railway shareholder has of the value of a shunter's.* She gratifies her intense jealousy of Thea by deliberately taunting Lövborg into breaking loose from her influence by joining a carouse at which he not only loses his manuscript, but finally gets into the hands of the police through behaving outrageously in the house of a disreputable woman whom he accuses of stealing it, not knowing that it has been picked up by Tesman and handed to Hedda for safe keeping. Now Hedda's jealousy of Thea is not jealousy of her bodily fascination: at that Hedda can beat her. It is jealousy of her power of making a man of Lövborg, of her part in his life as a man of genius.* The manuscript which Tesman gives to Hedda to lock up safely is in Thea's handwriting.

It is the fruit of Lövborg's union with Thea: he himself speaks of it as 'their child.' So when he turns his despair to romantic account by coming to the two women and making a tragic scene, telling Thea that he has cast the manuscript, torn into a thousand pieces, out upon the fiord; and then, when she is gone, telling Hedda that he has brought 'the child' to a house of ill-fame and lost it there, she, deceived by his posing, and thirsting to gain faith in the beauty of her own influence over him from a heroic deed of some sort, makes him a present of one of her pistols, only begging him to 'do it beautifully,' by which she means that he is to kill himself in some manner that will make his suicide a romantic memory and an imaginative luxury to her for ever. He takes it unblushingly, and leaves her with the air of a man who is looking his last on earth. But the moment he is out of sight of his audience, he goes back to the house where he still supposes the manuscript to lie stolen, and there renews the wrangle of the night before, using the pistol to threaten the woman, with the result that he gets shot in the abdomen, leaving the weapon to fall into the hands of the police. Meanwhile Hedda deliberately burns 'the child.' Then comes her elderly gallant to disgust her with the unromantically ugly details of the deed which Lövborg promised her to do so beautifully, and to make her understand that he himself has now got her into his power by his ability to identify the pistol. She must either be the slave of this man, or else face the scandal of the connection of her name at the inquest with a squalid debauch ending in a murder. Thea, too, is not crushed by Lövborg's death. Ten minutes after she has received the news with a cry of heart-felt loss, she sits down with Tesman to reconstruct 'the child' from the old notes she has piously preserved. Over the congenial task of collecting and arranging another man's ideas Tesman is perfectly happy, and forgets his beautiful Hedda for the first time. Thea the trembler is still mistress of the situation, holding the dead Lövborg, gaining Tesman, and leaving Hedda to her elderly admirer, who smoothly remarks that he will answer for Mrs Tesman not being bored whilst her husband is occupied with Thea in putting the pieces of the book together. However, he has again reckoned without General Gabler's second pistol. She shoots herself then and there; and so the story ends.*

THE LAST FOUR PLAYS*

Down Among the Dead Men

IBSEN now lays down the completed task of warning the world against
its idols and anti-idols, and passes into the shadow of death, or rather
into the splendor of his sunset glory; for his magic is extraordinarily
potent in these four plays, and his purpose more powerful. And yet the
shadow of death is here; for all four, except Little Eyolf, are tragedies
of the dead, deserted and mocked by the young who are still full of life.
The Master Builder is a dead man before the curtain rises: the breaking of his body to pieces in the last act by its fall from the tower is
rather the impatient destruction of a ghost of whose delirious whisper-
ings Nature is tired than of one who still counts among the living.
Borkman and the two women, his wife and her sister, are not merely
dead: they are buried; and the creatures we hear and see are only their
spirits in torment. 'Never dream of life again,' says Mrs Borkman to
her husband: 'lie quiet where you are.' And the last play of all is frankly
called When We Dead Awaken. Here the quintessence of Ibsenism
reaches its final distillation; morality and reformation give place to
mortality and resurrection; and the next event is the death of Ibsen
himself: he, too, creeping ghost-like through the blackening mental
darkness until he reaches his actual grave, and can no longer make
Europe cry with pity by sitting at a copybook, like a child, trying to
learn again how to write, only to find that divine power gone for ever
from his dead hand. He, the crustiest, grimmest hero since Beethoven,
could not die like him, shaking his fist at the thunder and alive to the
last: he must follow the path he had traced for Solness* and Borkman,
and survive himself. But as these two were dreamers to the last, and
never so luminous in their dreams as when they could no longer put
the least of them into action; so we may believe that when Ibsen could
no longer remember the alphabet, or use a dictionary, his soul may
have been fuller than ever before of the unspeakable. Do not snivel,
reader, over the contrast he himself drew between the man who was
once the greatest writer in the world, and the child of seventy-six trying to begin again at pothooks and hangers. Depend on it, whilst there
was anything left of him at all there was enough of his iron humor to
grin as widely as the skeleton with the hour-glass who was touching
him on the shoulder.

The Master Builder, *1892*

Halvard Solness is a dead man who has been a brilliantly successful builder, and, like the greatest builders, his own architect. He is sometimes in the sublime delirium that precedes bodily death, and sometimes in the horror that varies the splendors of delirium. He is mortally afraid of young rivals; of the younger generation knocking at the door. He has built churches with high towers (much as Ibsen built great historical dramas in verse). He has come to the end of that and built 'homes for human beings' (much as Ibsen took to writing prose plays of modern life). He has come to the end of that too, as men do at the end of their lives; and now he must take to dead men's architecture, the building of castles in the air. Castles in the air are the residences not only of those who have finished their lives, but of those who have not yet begun them. Another peculiarity of castles in the air is that they are so beautiful and so wonderful that human beings are not good enough to live in them: therefore when you look round you for somebody to live with you in your castle in the air, you find nobody glorious enough for that sanctuary. So you resort to the most dangerous of all the varieties of idolization: the idolization of the person you are most in love with; and you take him or her to live with you in your castle. And as imaginative young people, because they are young, have no illusions about youth, whilst old people, because they are old, have no illusions about age, elderly gentlemen very often idolize adolescent girls, and adolescent girls idolize elderly gentlemen.* When the idolization is not reciprocal, the idolizer runs terrible risks if the idol is selfish and unscrupulous. Cases of girls enslaved by elderly gentlemen whose scrupulous respect for their maiden purity is nothing but an excuse for getting a quantity of secretarial or domestic service out of them that is limited only by their physical endurance, without giving them anything in return, are not at all so rare as they would be if the theft of a woman's youth and devotion were as severely condemned by public opinion as the comparatively amiable and negligible theft of a few silver spoons and forks. On the other hand doting old gentlemen are duped and ruined by designing young women who care no more for them than a Cornish fisherman cares for a conger eel. But sometimes, when the two natures are poetic, we have scenes of Bettina and Goethe,* which are perhaps wholesome as well as pleasant for both parties when they are good enough and sensible enough to face the inexorable on the side of age and to recognize the impossible on the side of youth. On these conditions, old gentlemen are indulged in fancies for poetic little girls;

and the poetic little girls have their emotions and imaginations satisfied harmlessly until they find a suitable mate.

But the master builder, though he gets into just such a situation, does not get out of it so cheaply, because he is not outwardly an old, or even a very elderly gentleman. 'He is a man no longer young, but healthy and vigorous, with closely cut curly hair, dark moustache, and dark thick eyebrows.' Also he is daimonic, not sham daimonic like Molvik in The Wild Duck, but really daimonic, with luck, a star, and mystic 'helpers and servers' who find the way through the maze of life for him. In short, a very fascinating man, whom nobody, himself least of all, could suspect of having shot his bolt and being already dead. Therefore a man for whom a girl's castle in the air is a very dangerous place, as she may easily thrust upon him adventures that would tax the prime of an unexhausted man, and are mere delirious madness for a spent one.

Grasp this situation and you will be able to follow a performance of The Master Builder without being puzzled; though to the unprepared theatregoer it is a bewildering business. You see Solness in his office, ruthlessly exploiting the devotion of the girl secretary Kaia, who idolizes him, and giving her nothing in return but a mesmerizing word occasionally. You see him with equal ruthlessness apparently, but really with the secret terror of 'the priest who slew the slayer and shall himself be slain,' trying to suppress a young rival who is as yet only a draughtsman in his employment. To keep the door shut against the younger generation already knocking at it: that is all he can do now, except build castles in the air; for, as I have said, the effective part of the man is dead. Then there is his wife, who, knowing that he is failing in body and mind, can do nothing but look on in helpless terror. She cannot make a happy home for Solness, because her own happiness has been sacrificed to his genius. Or rather, her own genius, which is for 'building up the souls of little children,' has been sacrificed to his. For they began their family life in an old house that was part of her property: the sort of house that may be hallowed by old family associations and memories of childhood, but that it pays the speculative builder to pull down and replace by rows of villas. Now the ambitious Solness knows this but dares not propose such a thing to his wife, who cherishes all the hallowing associations, and even keeps her dolls: nine lovely dolls, feeling them 'under her heart, like little unborn children.' Everything in the house is precious to her: the old silk dresses, the lace, the portraits. Solness knows that to touch these would be tearing her heart up by the roots. So he says nothing; does nothing; only notes a crack in the old chimney which should be repaired if the house is to be safe against fire, and does not repair it. Instead, he pictures to himself a fire, with his wife out in the sledge with his two children, and nothing but charred ruins facing her when she returns; but what matter, since the children have escaped and are still with her? He even calls upon his helpers and servers to consider whether this vision might not become a reality. And it does. The house is burnt; the villas rise on its site and cover the park; and Halvard Solness becomes rich and successful.

But the helpers and servers have not stuck to the program for all that. The fire did not come from the crack in the chimney when all the domestic fires were blazing. It came at night when the fires were low, and began in a cupboard quite away from the chimney. It came when Mrs Solness and the children were in bed. It shattered the mother's health; it killed the children she was nursing; it devoured the portraits and the silk dresses and the old lace; it burnt the nine lovely dolls; and it broke the heart under which the dolls had lain like little unborn children. That was the price of the master builder's success. He is married to a dead woman; and he is trying to atone by building her a new villa: a new tomb to replace the old home; for he is gnawed with remorse.

But the fire was not only a good building speculation: it also led to his obtaining commissions to build churches. And one triumphant day, when he was celebrating the completion of the giant tower he had added to the old church at Lysanger, it suddenly flashed on him that his house had been burnt, his wife's life laid waste, and his own happiness destroyed, so that he might become a builder of churches. Now it happens that one of his difficulties as a builder is that he has a bad head for heights, and cannot venture even on a second floor balcony. Yet in the fury of that thought he mounts to the pinnacle of his tower, and there, face to face with God, who has, he feels, wasted the wife's gift of building up the souls of little children to make the husband a builder of steeples, he declares that he will never set hand to church-building again, and will henceforth build nothing but homes for happier men than he. Which vow he keeps, only to find that the home, too, is a devouring idol, and that men and women have no longer any use for it.

In spite of his excitement, he very nearly breaks his neck after all; for among the crowd below there is a little devil of a girl who waves a white scarf and makes his head swim. This tiny animal is no other than the younger stepdaughter of Ellida, The Lady from the Sea, Hilda Wangel, of whose taste for 'thrilling' sensations we had a glimpse in that play. On the same evening Solness is entertained at a club banquet, in consequence of which he is not in the most responsible condition when he returns to sup at the house of Dr Wangel, who is putting him up for the night. He meets the imp there; thinks her like a little princess in her white dress; kisses her; and promises her to come back in ten years and carry her off to the kingdom of Orangia. Perhaps it is only just to mention that he stoutly denies these indiscretions afterwards; though he admits that when he wishes something to happen between himself and somebody else, the somebody else always imagines it actually has happened.

The play begins ten years after the climbing of the tower. The younger generation knocks at the door with a vengeance. Hilda, now a vigorous young woman, and a great builder of castles in the air, bursts in on him and demands her kingdom; and very soon she sends him up a tower again (the tower of the new house) and waves her scarf to him as madly as ever. This time he really does break his neck; and so the story ends.

Little Eyolf, 1894

Though the most mischievous ideals are social ideals which have become institutions, laws, and creeds, yet their evil must come to a personal point before they can strike down the individual. Jones is not struck down by an ideal in the abstract, but by Smith making monstrous claims or inflicting monstrous injuries on him in the name of an ideal. And it is fair to add that the ideals are sometimes beneficent, and their repudiation sometimes cruel. For ideals are in practice not so much matters of conscience as excuses for doing what we like; and thus it happens that of two people worshipping the same ideals, one will be a detestable tyrant and the other a kindly and helpful friend of mankind. What makes the bad side of idealism so dangerous is that wicked people are allowed to commit crimes in the name of the ideal that would not be tolerated for a moment as open devilment. Perhaps the worst, because the commonest and most intimate cases, are to be found in family life. Even during the Reign of Terror,* the chances of any particular Frenchman or French-woman being guillotined were so small as to be negligible. Under Nero a Christian was far safer from being smeared with pitch and set on fire than he was from domestic trouble. If the private lives that have been wasted by idealistic persecution could be recorded and set against the public martyrdoms and slaughterings and torturings and imprisonments, our millions of private Neros and Torquemadas and Calvins, Bloody Maries and Cleopatras and Semiramises,* would eclipse the few who have come to the surface of history by the accident of political or ecclesiastical conspicuousness.

Thus Ibsen, at the beginning of his greatness, shewed us Brand sacrificing his wife; and this was only the first of a series of similar exhibitions, ending, so far, in Solness sacrificing his wife and being himself sacrificed to a girl's enthusiasm. And he brings Solness to the point of rebelling furiously against the tyranny of his wife's ideal of home, and declaring that 'building homes for happy human beings is not worth a rap: men are not happy in these homes: I should not have been happy in such a home if I had had one.' It is not surprising to find that Little Eyolf is about such a home.

This home clearly cannot be a working-class home. And here let it be said that the comparative indifference of the working class to Ibsen's plays is neither Ibsen's fault nor that of the working class. To the man who works for his living in modern society home is not the place where he lives, nor his wife the woman he lives with. Home is the roof under which he sleeps and eats; and his wife is the woman who makes his bed, cooks his meals, and looks after their children when they are neither in school nor in the streets, or who at least sees that the servants do these things. The man's work keeps him from home from eight to twelve hours a day. He is unconscious through sleep for another eight hours. Then there is the public house and the club. There is eating, washing, dressing, playing with the children or the dog, entertaining or visiting friends, reading, and pursuing hobbies such as gardening and the like. Obviously the home ideal cannot be tested fully under these conditions, which enable a married pair to see less and know less of one another than they do of those who work side by side with them. It is in the propertied class only that two people can really live together and devote themselves to one another if they want to. There are certain businesses which men and women can conduct jointly, and certain professions which men can pursue at home; and in these the strain of idealism on marriage is more severe than when the two work separately. But the full strain comes on with the modern unearned income from investments, which does not involve even the management of an estate. And it is under this full strain that Ibsen tests it in Little Eyolf.

Shakespear, in a flash of insight which has puzzled many commentators, and even set them proposing alterations of a passage which they found unthinkable, has described one of his characters as 'a fellow almost damned in a fair wife.'* There is no difficulty or obscurity about this phrase at all: you have only to look round at the men who have ventured to marry very fascinating women to see that most of them are not merely 'almost damned' but wholly damned. Allmers, in Little Eyolf, is a fellow almost damned in a fair wife. She, Rita Allmers, has brought him 'gold and green forests' (a reminiscence from an early play called The Feast at Solhoug), and not only troubles and uncentres him as only a woman can trouble and uncentre a man who is susceptible to her bodily attraction, but is herself furiously and jealously in love with him. In short, they form the ideal home of romance; and it would be hard to find a compacter or more effective formula for a small private hell. The 'almost damned' are commonly saved by the fact that the devotion is usually on one side only, and that the lovely lady (or gentleman; for a woman almost damned in a fair husband is also a common object in domestic civilization), if she has only one husband, relieves the boredom of his devotion by having fifty courtiers. But Rita will neither share Allmers with anyone else nor be shared. He must be wholly and exclusively hers; and she must be wholly and exclusively his. By her gold and green forests she snatches him from his work as a schoolmaster and imprisons him in their house, where the poor wretch pretends to occupy himself by writing a book on Human Responsibility, and forming the character of their son, little Eyolf. For your male sultana takes himself very seriously indeed, as do most sultanas and others who are so closely shut up with their own vanities and appetites that they think the world a little thing to be moulded and arranged at their silly pleasure like a lump of plasticine. Rita is jealous of the book, and hates it not only because Allmers occupies himself with it instead of with her, but talks about it to his half-sister Asta, of whom she is of course also jealous. She is jealous of little Eyolf, and hates him too, because he comes between her and her prey.

One day, when the baby child is lying on the table, they have an amorous fit and forget all about him. He falls off the table and is crippled for life. He and his crutch become thenceforth a standing reproach to them. They hate themselves; they hate each other; they hate him; their atmosphere of ideal conjugal love breeds hate at every turn: hatred masquerading as a loving bond that has been drawn closer and sanctified by their common misfortune. After ten years of this hideous slavery the man breaks loose: actually insists on going for a short trip into the mountains by himself. It is true that he reassures Rita by coming back before his time; but her conclusion that this was because he could not abstain from her society is rudely shattered by his conduct on his return. She dresses herself beautifully to receive him, and makes the seraglio* as delightful as possible for their reunion; but he purposely arrives tired out, and takes refuge in the sleep of exhaustion, without a caress. As she says, quoting a popular poem when reproaching him for this afterwards, 'There stood your champagne and you

tasted it not.'* It soon appears that he has come to loathe his champagne, and that the escape into the mountains has helped him to loathe
his situation to some extent, even to discovering the absurdity of his
book on Human Responsibility, and the cruelty of his educational
experiments on Eyolf. In future he is going to make Eyolf 'an open air
little boy,' which of course involves being a good deal in the open air
with him, and out of the seraglio. Then the woman's hatred of the child
unveils itself; and she openly declares what she really feels as to this
little creature, with its 'evil eyes,' that has come between them.

At this point, very opportunely, comes the Rat Wife, who, like the
Pied Piper, clears away rats for a consideration. Has Rita any little
gnawing things she wants to get rid of? Here, it seems, is a helper and
server for Rita. The Rat Wife's method is to bewitch the rats so that
when she rows out to sea they follow her and are drowned. She describes
this with a heart-breaking poetry that frightens Rita, who makes
Allmers send her away. But a helper and server is not so easily exor-
cized. Rita's little gnawing thing, Eyolf, has come under the spell; and
when the Rat Wife rows out to sea, he follows her and is drowned.

The family takes the event in a very proper spirit. Horror, lamenta-
tion, shrieks and tears, and all the customary homages to death and
attestations of bereavement are duly and even sincerely gone through;
for the shock of such an accident makes us all human for a moment.
But next morning Allmers finds some difficulty in keeping it up, miserable as he is. He finds himself forgetting about Eyolf for several minutes, and thinking about other things, even about his breakfast; and in
his idealistic self-devotion to artificial attitudes he reproaches himself
and tries to force himself to keep thinking of Eyolf and being over-
whelmed with grief about him. Besides, it is an excuse for avoiding his
wife. The revulsion against his slavery to her has made her presence
unbearable to him. He can bear nobody but his half-sister Asta, whose
relation to him is a most blessed comfort and relief because their blood
kinship excludes from it all the torment and slavery of his relation to
Rita. But this consolation is presently withdrawn; for Asta has just discovered, in some old correspondence, convincing proofs that she is not
related to him at all; and the effect of the discovery has been to remove
the inhibition which has hitherto limited her strong affection for him;
so that she now perceives that she must leave him. Hitherto, she has
refused, for his sake, the offers of Borgheim, an engineer who wants to
marry her, but who, like Rita, wants to take her away and make her
exclusively his own; for he, too, cannot share with anyone. And though
both Allmers and Rita implore her to stay, dreading now nothing so

much as being left alone with one another, she knows that she cannot stay innocently, and accepts the engineer and vanishes lest a worse thing should befall.

And now Rita has her man all to herself. Eyolf dead, Asta gone, the Book on Human Responsibility thrown into the waste paper basket: there are no more rivals now, no more distractions: the field is clear for the ideal union of 'two souls with but a single thought, two hearts that beat as one.' The result may be imagined.

The situation is insufferable from the beginning. Allmers' attempts to avoid seeing or speaking to Rita are of course impracticable. Equally impracticable are their efforts to behave kindly to one another. They are presently at it hammer and tongs, each tearing the mask from the other's grief for the child, and leaving it exposed as their remorse: hers for having jealously hated Eyolf: his for having sacrificed him to his passion for Rita, and to the schoolmasterly vanity and folly which sees in the child nothing more than the vivisector sees in a guinea-pig: something to experiment on with a view to rearranging the world to suit his own little ideas. If ever two cultivated souls of the propertied middle class were stripped naked and left bankrupt, these two are. They cannot bear to live; and yet they are forced to confess that they dare not kill themselves.

The solution of their problem, as far as it is solved, is, as coming from Ibsen, very remarkable. It is not, as might have been expected after his long propaganda of Individualism, that they should break up the seraglio and go out into the world until they have learnt to stand alone, and through that to accept companionship on honorable conditions only. Ibsen here explicitly insists for the first time that 'we are members one of another,' and that though the strongest man is he who stands alone, the man who is standing alone for his own sake solely is literally an idiot. It is indeed a staring fact in history and contemporary life that nothing is so gregarious as selfishness, and nothing so solitary as the selflessness that loathes the word Altruism because to it there are no 'others': it sees and feels in every man's case the image of its own. 'Inasmuch as ye have done it unto one of the least of these my brethren ye have done it unto me'* is not Altruism or Othersism. It is an explicit repudiation of the patronizing notion that 'the least of these' is *another* to whom you are invited to be very nice and kind: in short, it accepts entire identification of 'me' with 'the least of these.' The fashionably sentimental version, which runs, in effect, 'If you subscribe eighteen-pence to give this little dear a day in the country I shall regard it as a loan of one-and-sixpence to myself' is really more conceitedly remote from the spirit of the famous Christian saying than even the sham political economy that took in Mr Gradgrind.* Accordingly, if you would see industrial sweating at its vilest, you must go, not to the sempstresses who work for commercial firms, but to the victims of pious Altruistic Ladies' Work Guilds and the like, in which ladies with gold and green forests offer to 'others' their blouses to be stitched at prices that the most sordid East End slave-driver would recoil from offering.

Thus we see that in Ibsen's mind, as in the actual history of the nineteenth century, the way to Communism lies through the most resolute and uncompromising Individualism. James Mill,* with an inhuman conceit and pedantry which leaves the fable of Allmers and Eyolf far behind, educated John Stuart Mill to be the arch Individualist of his time, with the result that John Stuart Mill became a Socialist quarter of a century before the rest of his set moved in that direction. Herbert Spencer lived to write despairing pamphlets against the Socialism of his ablest pupils.* There is no hope in Individualism for egotism. When a man is at last brought face to face with himself by a brave Individualism, he finds himself face to face, not with an individual, but with a species, and knows that to save himself, he must save the race. He can have no life except a share in the life of the community; and if that life is unhappy and squalid, nothing that he can do to paint and paper and upholster and shut off his little corner of it can really rescue him from it.

It happens so to that bold Individualist Mrs Rita Allmers. The Allmers are, of course, snobs, and have always been very determined that the common little children down at the pier should be taught their place as Eyolf's inferiors. They even go the length of discussing whether these dirty little wretches should not be punished for their cowardice in not rescuing Eyolf. Thereby they raise the terrible question whether they themselves, who are afraid to commit suicide in their misery, would have been any braver. There is nobody to comfort them; for the income from the gold and green forests, by enabling them to cut themselves off from all industry of the place, has led them into something like total isolation. They hate their neighbors as themselves. They are alone together with nothing to do but wear each other out and drive each other mad to an extent impossible under any other conditions. And Rita's plight is the more desperate of the two, because as she has been the more unscrupulous, the more exacting, she has left him something to look forward to: freedom from her. He is bent on that, at least: he will not live with her on any terms, not stay anywhere within reach of her: the one thing he craves is that he may never see her or speak to her again. That is the end of the 'two souls with but a single thought,' &c. But to her his release is only a supreme privation, the end of everything that gave life any meaning for her. She has not even egotism to fall back on.

At this pass, an annoyance of which she has often complained occurs again. The children down at the pier make a noise, playing and yelling as if Eyolf had never existed. It suddenly occurs to her that these are children too, just like Eyolf, and that they are suffering a good deal from neglect. After all, they too are little Eyolfs. Inasmuch as she can do it unto one of the least of these his brethren she can do it unto him. She determines to take the dirty little wretches in hand and look after them. It is at all events a more respectable plan than that of the day before, which was to throw herself away on the first man she met if Allmers dared to think of anybody but her. And it has the domestic advantage that Allmers has nothing to fear from a woman who has something else to do than torment him with passions that devour and jealousies that enslave him. The world and the home suddenly take on their natural aspect. Allmers offers to stay and help her. And so they are delivered from their evil dream, and, let us hope, live happily ever after.

John Gabriel Borkman, 1896

In Little Eyolf the shadow of death lifted for a moment; but now we enter it again. Here the persons of the drama are not only dead but buried. Borkman is a Napoleon of finance. He has the root of finance in him in a born love of money in its final reality: a love, that is, of precious metals. He does not dream of beautiful ladies calling to him for knightly rescue from dragons and tyrants, but of metals imprisoned in undiscovered mines, calling to him to release them and send them out into all lands fertilizing, encouraging, creating. Music to him means the ring of the miner's pick and hammer: the eternal night underground is as magical to him as the moonlit starlit night of the upper air to the romantic poet. This love of metal is common enough: no man feels towards a cheque for £20 as he does towards twenty gold sovereigns: he will part from the paper with less of a pang than from the coins. There are misers whose fingers tremble when they touch gold, but close steadily on banknotes. True love of money is, in fact, a passion based on a physical appetite for precious metals. It is not greed: you cannot call a man who starves himself sooner than part with one sovereign* from his sack of sovereigns, greedy. If he did the same for the love of God, you would call him a saint: if for the love of a woman, a perfect gentle knight. Men

grow rich according to the strength of their obsession by this passion:
its great libertines become Napoleons of finance: its narrow debauch-
ees become misers, petty moneylenders, and the like. It must not be
looked for in all our millionaires, because most of these are rich by pure
accident (our abandonment of industry to the haphazard scrambles of
private adventurers necessarily produces occasional windfalls which
enrich the man who happens to be on the spot), as may be seen when
the lucky ones are invited to display their supposed Napoleonic powers
in spending their windfalls, when they reveal themselves as quite ordinary mortals, if not indeed sometimes as exceptionally resourceless ones.
Besides, finance is one business, and industrial organization another:
the man with a passion for altering the map by digging isthmuses never
thinks of money save as a means to his end. But those who as financiers
have passionately 'made' money instead of merely holding their hats
under an accidental shower of it will be found to have a genuine disinterested love of it. It is not easy to say how common this passion is.
Poverty is general, which would seem to indicate a general lack of it; but
poverty is mainly the result of organized robbery and oppression (politely
called Capitalism) starving the passion for gold as it starves all the passions. The evidence is further confused by the decorative instinct: some
men will load their fingers and shirt-fronts with rings and studs, whilst
others of equal means are ringless and fasten their shirts with sixpen-
north of mother-of-pearl. But it is significant that Plato, and, following
him, Sir Thomas More, saw with Ibsen, and made complete indifference to the precious metals, minted or not, a necessary qualification for
aristocracy.* This indifference is, as a matter of fact, so characteristic of
our greatest non-industrial men that when they do not happen to inherit
property they are generally poor and in difficulties. Therefore we who
have never cared for money enough to do more than keep our heads
above water, and are therefore tempted to regard ourselves as others
regard us (that is, as failures, or, at best, as persons of no account) may
console ourselves with the reflection that money-hunger is no more
respectable than gluttony, and that unless its absence or feebleness is
only a symptom of a general want of power to care for anything at all, it
usually means that the soul has risen above it to higher concerns.

   All this is necessary to the appreciation of Ibsen's presentment of the
Napoleon of finance. Ibsen does not take him superficially: he goes to
the poetic basis of the type: the love of gold—actual metallic gold—and
the idealization of gold through that love.

   Borkman meets the Misses Rentheim: two sisters: the elder richer
than the younger. He falls in love with the younger; and she falls in love

with him; but the love of gold is the master passion: he marries the elder. Yet he respects his secondary passion in the younger. When he speculates with other people's securities he spares hers. On the point of bringing off a great stroke of finance, the other securities are missed; and he is imprisoned for embezzlement. That is the end of him. He comes out of prison a ruined man and a dead man, and would not have even a tomb to sleep in but for the charity of Ella Rentheim, whose securities he spared when he broke her heart. She maintains his old home for him.

He now enters on the grimmest lying in state ever exposed to public view by mortal dramatist. His wife, a proud woman, must live in the same house with the convicted thief who has disgraced her, because she has nowhere else to lay her head; but she will not see him nor speak to him. She sits downstairs in the drawing-room eating the bitter bread of her sister's charity, and listening with loathing to her husband's steps as he paces to and fro in the long gallery upstairs 'like a sick wolf.' She listens not for days but for years. And her one hope is that her son Erhart will rehabilitate the family name; repay the embezzled money; and lead her from her tomb up again into honor and prosperity. To this task she has devoted *his* life.

Borkman has quite another plan. He is still Napoleon, and will return from his Elba to scatter his enemies and complete the stroke that ill-luck and the meddlesomeness of the law frustrated. But he is proud: prouder than Napoleon. He will not come back to the financial world until it finds out that it cannot do without him and comes to ask him to resume his place at the head of the board. He keeps himself in readiness for that deputation. He is always dressed for it; and when he hears steps on the threshold he stands up by the table; puts one hand into the breast of his coat; and assumes the attitude of a conqueror receiving suppliants. And this also goes on not for days but for years, long after the world has forgotten him, and there is nobody likely to come for him except Peer Gynt's button moulder.

Borkman, like all madmen, cannot nourish his delusion without some response from without. One of the victims of his downfall is a clerk who once wrote a tragedy, and has lived ever since in his own imagination as a poet. His family ridicules his tragedy and his pretensions; and as he is a poor ineffectual little creature who has never lived enough to feel dignified among the dead, like Borkman, he too finds it hard to keep his illusion alive without help. Fortunately he has admired Borkman, the great financier; and Borkman, when he has ruined him and ruined himself, is quite willing to be admired by this humble victim, and even to reward him by a pretence of believing in his poetic genius. Thus the two form one of those Mutual Admiration Societies on which the world so largely subsists, and make the years in the long gallery tolerable by flattering each other. There are even moments when Borkman is nerved to the point of starting for his second advent as a great financial redeemer. On such occasions the woman downstairs hears the footsteps of the sick wolf on the stairs approaching the hat-stand where his hat and stick have waited unused all the years of his entombment; but they never reach that first stage of the journey. They always turn back into the gallery again.

This melancholy household of the dead crumbles to dust at the knock of the younger generation at the door. Erhart, dedicated by his mother to the task of paying his father's debts and retrieving his ruin, and by his aunt to the task of sweetening her last days with his grateful love, has dedicated himself to his own affairs—for the moment mostly love affairs—and has not the faintest intention of concerning himself with the bygone career of the crazy ex-felon upstairs or the sentimen-talities of the old maid downstairs. He detests the house and the atmos-phere, and associates his aunt's broken heart with nothing more important than the scent of stale lavender, which he dislikes. He spends his time happily in the house of a pretty lady in the neighborhood, who has been married and divorced, and knows how to form an adolescent youth. And as to the unpardonable enemy of the family, one Hinkel, who betrayed Borkman to the police and rose on his ruins, Erhart cares so little for that old story that he goes to Hinkel's parties and enjoys himself there very much. And when at last the pretty lady raises his standard of happiness to a point at which the old house and the old people become impossible, unthinkable, unbearable, he goes off with her to Italy and leaves the dead to bury their dead.*

The details of this catastrophe make the play. The fresh air and the light of day break into the tomb; and its inhabitants crumble into dust. Foldal, the poet clerk, lets slip the fact that he has not the slightest belief in Borkman's triumphant return to the world; and Borkman retorts by telling him he is no poet. After this comedy comes the tra-gedy of the son's defection; and amid the recriminations of the broken heart, the baffled pride, and the shattered dreams, the castles in the air vanish and reveal the open grave they have hidden. Poor Foldal, limp-ing home after being run over by a sledge in which his daughter is run-ning away to act as 'second string' and chaperone for Erhart and the pretty lady, is the only one who is wanted in the world, since he must still work for his derisive family. But Borkman returns to his dream, and ventures out of doors at last, not this time to resume his place as governor of the bank, but to release the imprisoned metal that rings and sings to him from the earth. In other words, to die in the open, mad but happy, whilst the two sisters, 'we two shadows,' end their strife over his body.

When We Dead Awaken, 1900

This play, the last work of Ibsen, and at first the least esteemed, has had its prophecy so startlingly fulfilled in England that nobody will now question the intensity of its inspiration. With us the dead have awakened in the very manner prefigured in the play. The simplicity and brevity of the story is so obvious, and the enormous scope of the conception so difficult to comprehend, that many of Ibsen's most devoted admirers failed to do it justice. They knew that he was a man of seventy, and were prepossessed with the belief that at such an age his powers must be falling off. It certainly was easier at that time to give the play up as a bad job than to explain it. Now that the great awakening of women which we call the Militant Suffrage Movement* is upon us, and you may hear our women publicly and passionately paraphrasing Ibsen's heroine without having read a word of the play, the matter is simpler. There is no falling-off here in Ibsen. It may be said that this is physically impossible; but those who say so forget that the natural decay of a writer's powers may shew itself in two ways. The inferiority of the work produced is only one way. The other is the production of equally good or even better work with much greater effort than it would have cost its author ten years earlier. Ibsen produced this play with great difficulty in twice as long a period as had before sufficed; and even at that the struggle left his mind a wreck; for he not only never wrote another play, but, like an overstrained athlete, lost even the normal mental capacity of an ordinary man. Yet it would be hard to say that the play was not worth the sacrifice. It shews no decay of Ibsen's highest qualities: his magic is nowhere more potent. It is shorter than usual: that is all. The extraordinarily elaborate private history, family and individual, of the personages, which lies behind the action of the other plays, is replaced by a much simpler history of a few people in their general human relations without any family history at all. And the characteristically conscientious fitting of the play to the mechanical conditions of old-fashioned stages has given way to demands that even the best equipped and largest modern stages cannot easily comply with; for the second act takes place in a valley; and though it is easy to represent a valley by a painted scene when the action is confined to one spot in the foreground, it is a different matter when the whole valley has to be practicable, and the movements of the figures cover distances which do not exist on the stage, and cannot, as far as my experience goes, be satisfactorily simulated by the stage carpenter, though they are easy enough for the painter. I should attach no importance at all to this in a writer less mindful of technical limitations and less ingenious in circumventing them than Ibsen, who was for some years a professional stage manager; but in his case it is clear that in calling on the theatre to expand to his requirements instead of, as his custom was, limiting his scene of action to the possibilities of a modest provincial theatre, he knew quite well what he was doing. Here then, we have three differences, from the earlier plays. None of them are inferiorities. They are proper to the difference of subject, and in fact increased the difficulty of the playwright's task by throwing him back on sheer dramatic power, unaided by the cheaper interest that can be gained on the stage by mere ingenuity of construction. Ibsen, who has always before played on the spectator by a most elaborate gradual development which would have satisfied Dumas,* here throws all his cards on the table as rapidly as possible, and proceeds to deal intensively with a situation that never alters.

This situation is simple enough in its general statement, though it is so complex in its content that it raises the whole question of domestic civilization. Take a man and a woman at the highest pitch of natural ability and charm yet attained, and enjoying all the culture that modern art and literature can offer them; and what does it all come to? Contrast them with an essentially uncivilized pair, with a man who lives for hunting and eating and ravishing, and whose morals are those of the bully with the strong hand: in short, a man from the stone age as we conceive it (such men are still common enough in the classes that can afford the huntsman's life); and couple him with a woman who has no interest or ambition in life except to be captured by such a man (and of these we have certainly no lack). Then face this question. What is there to choose between these two pairs? Is the cultured gifted man less hardened, less selfish towards the women, than the paleolithic man? Is the woman less sacrificed, less enslaved, less dead spiritually in the one case than in the other? Modern culture, except when it has rotted into mere cynicism, shrieks that the question is an insult. The stone age, anticipating Ibsen's reply, guffaws heartily and says, 'Bravo, Ibsen!' Ibsen's reply is that the sacrifice of the woman of the stone age to fruitful passions which she herself shares is as nothing compared to the wasting of the modern woman's soul to gratify the imagination and stimulate the genius of the modern artist, poet, and philosopher. He shews us that no degradation ever devized or permitted is as disastrous as this degradation; that through it women die into luxuries for men, and yet can kill them; that men and women are becoming conscious of this; and that what remains to be seen as perhaps the most interesting of all imminent social developments is what will happen 'when we dead awaken.'

Ibsen's greatest contemporary outside his own art was Rodin the French sculptor. Whether Ibsen knew this, or whether he was inspired to make his hero a sculptor just as Dickens was inspired to make Pecksniff* an architect, is not known. At all events, having to take a type of the highest and ablest masculine genius, he made him a sculptor, and called his name, not Rodin, but Rubeck: a curious assonance, if it was not intentional. Rubeck is as able an individual as our civilization can produce. The difficulty of presenting such an individual in fiction is that it can be done only by a writer who occupies that position himself; for a dramatist cannot conceive anything higher than himself. No doubt he can invest an imaginary figure with all sorts of imaginary gifts. A drunken author may make his hero sober; an ugly, weak, puny, timid one may make him a Hyperion or a Hercules;* a deaf mute may write novels in which the lover is an orator and his mistress a prima donna; but whatever ornaments and accomplishments he may pile up on his personages, he cannot give them greater souls than his own. Defoe* could invent wilder adventures for Robinson Crusoe than Shakespear for Hamlet; but he could not make that mean adventurer, with his dull eulogies of the virtues of 'the middle station of life'* anything even remotely like Shakespear's prince.

For Ibsen this difficulty did not exist. He knew quite well that he was one of the greatest men living; so he simply said 'Suppose ME to be a sculptor instead of a playwright,' and the thing was done. Thus he came forward himself to plead to his own worst indictment of modern culture. One of the touches by which he identifies himself has all the irony of his earliest work. Rubeck has to make money out of human vanity, as all sculptors must nowadays, by portrait busts; but he revenges himself by studying and bringing out in his sitters 'the respectable pompous horse faces, and self-opinionated donkey-muzzles, and lop-eared low-browed dog-skulls, and fatted swine-snouts, and dull brutal bull fronts' that lurk in so many human faces. All artists who deal with humanity do this, more or less. Leonardo da Vinci ruled his notebook in columns headed fox, wolf, etc., and made notes of faces by ticking them off in these columns, finding this, apparently, as satisfactory a memorandum as a drawing. Domestic animals, terriers, pugs, poultry, parrots, and cockatoos, are specially valuable to the caricaturist, as giving the original types which explain many faces. Ibsen must have classified his acquaintances a good deal in this way, not without an occasional chuckle; and his attribution of the practice to Rubeck is a confession of it.

Rubeck makes his reputation, as sculptors often do, by a statue of a woman. Not, be it observed, of a dress and a pair of boots, with a head protruding from them, but of a woman from the hand of Nature. It is worth noting here that we have hardly any portraits, either painted or carved, of our famous men and women or even of our nearest and dearest friends. Charles Dickens is known to us as a guy with a human head and face on top. Shakespear is a laundry advertisement of a huge starched collar with his head sticking out of it. Dr Johnson* is a face looking through a wig perched on a snuffy suit of old clothes. All the great women of history are fashion plates of their period. Bereaved parents, orphans, and widows weep fondly over photographs of uniforms, frock coats, gowns, and hats, for the sake of the little scrap of humanity that is allowed to peep through these trappings. Women with noble figures and plain or elderly faces are outdressed and outfaced by rivals who, if revealed as they really are, would be hardly human. Carlyle staggers humanity by inviting the House of Commons to sit unclothed, so that we, and they themselves, shall know them for what they really are.*

Hence it is that the artist who adores mankind as his highest subject always comes back to the reality beneath the clothes. His claim to be allowed to do this is so irresistible that in every considerable city in England you will find, supported by the rates of prudish chapel goers, and even managed and inspected by committees of them, an art school where, in the 'life class' (significant term!) young women posed in ridiculous and painful attitudes by a drawing master, and mostly under the ugliest circumstances of light, color, and surroundings, earn a laborious wage by allowing a crowd of art students to draw their undraped figures. It is a joylessly grotesque spectacle: one wonders whether anything can really be learnt from it; for never have I seen one of these school models in an attitude which any human being would, unless the alternative were starvation, voluntarily sustain for thirty seconds, or assume on any natural occasion or provocation whatever. Male models are somewhat less slavish; and the stalwart laborer or olive-skinned young Italian who poses before a crowd of easels with ludicrously earnest young ladies in blue or vermilion gowns and embroidered pinafores drawing away at him for dear life is usually much more comfortably and possibly posed. But Life will not yield up her more intimate secrets for eighteenpence an hour; and these earnest young ladies and artsome young men, when they have filled portfolios with such sordid life studies, know less about living humanity than they did before, and very much less about even the mechanism of the body and the shape of its muscles than they could learn less inhumanly from a series of modern kinematographs* of figures in motion.

Rubeck does not make his statues in a class at a municipal art school by looking at a weary girl in a tortured attitude with a background of match-boarding, under a roof of girders, and with the ghastly light of a foggy, smoky manufacturing town making the light side of her flesh dirty yellow and the shadowed side putrid purple. He knows better than that. He finds a beautiful woman, and tells her his vision of a statue of The Resurrection Day in the form of a woman 'filled with a sacred joy at finding herself unchanged in the higher, freer, happier region after the long dreamless sleep of death.' And the woman, immediately seizing his inspiration and sharing it, devotes herself to the work, not merely as his model, but as his friend, his helper, fellow worker, comrade, all things, save one, that may be humanly natural and necessary between them for an unreserved co-operation in the great work. The one exception is that they are not lovers; for the sculptor's ideal is a virgin, or, as he calls it, a pure woman.

And her reward is that when the work is finished and the statue achieved, he says 'Thank you for a priceless EPISODE,' at which significant word, revealing as it does that she has, after all, been nothing to him but a means to his end, she leaves him and drops out of his life. To earn her living she must then pose, not to him, but before crowds in Variety Theatres in living pictures,* gaining much money by her beauty, winning rich husbands, and driving them all to madness or to death by 'a fine sharp dagger which she always has with her in bed,' much as Rita Allmers nearly killed her husband. And she calls the statue her child and Rubeck's, as the book in Hedda Gabler was the child of Thea and Eilert Lövberg. But finally she too goes mad under the strain.

Rubeck presently meets a pretty Stone Age woman, and marries her. And as he is not a Stone Age man, and she is bored to distraction by his cultured interests, he disappoints her as thoroughly as she disgusts and wearies him: the symptoms being that though he builds her a splendid villa, full of works of art and so forth, neither he nor she can settle down quietly; and they take trips here, trips there, trips anywhere to escape being alone and at home together.

But the retribution for his egotism takes a much subtler form, and strikes at a much more vital place in him: namely, his artistic inspiration.

Working with Irene, the lost model, he had achieved a perfect work of art; and, having achieved it, had supposed that he was done with her. But art is not so simple as that. The moment she forsakes him and leaves him to the Stone Age woman and to his egotism, he no longer sees the perfection of his work. He becomes dissatisfied with it. He sees that it can be improved: for instance, why should it consist of a figure of Irene alone? Why should he not be in it himself? Is he not a far more important factor in the conception? He changes the single figure design to a group. He adds a figure of himself. He finds that the woman's figure, with its wonderful expression of gladness, puts his own image out of countenance. He rearranges the group so as to give himself more prominence. Even so the gladness outshines him; and at last he 'tones it down,' striking the gladness out with his chisel, and making his own expression the main interest of the group. But he cannot stop there. Having destroyed the thing that was superior to him, he now wants to introduce things that are inferior. He carves clefts in the earth at the feet of his figure, and from these clefts he makes emerge the folk with the horse faces and the swine snouts that are nearer the beast than his own fine face. Then he is satisfied with his work; and it is in this form that it makes him famous and is finally placed in a public museum. In his days with Irene, they used to call these museums the prisons of works of art. Precisely what the Italian Futurist painters of today are calling them.*

And now the play begins. Irene comes from her madhouse to a 'health resort.' Thither also comes Rubeck, wandering about with the Stone Age woman to avoid being left at home with her. Thither also comes the man of the Stone Age with his dogs and guns, and carries off the Stone Age woman, to her husband's great relief. Rubeck and Irene meet; and as they talk over old times, she learns, bit by bit, what has happened to the statue, and is about to kill him when she realizes, also bit by bit, that the history of its destruction is the history of his own, and that as he used her up and left her dead, so with her death the life went out of him. But, like Nora in A Doll's House, she sees the possibility of a miracle. The dead may awaken if only they can find an honest and natural relation in which they shall no longer sacrifice and slay one another. She asks him to climb to the top of a mountain with her and see that promised land. Half way up, they meet the Stone Age pair hunting. There is a storm coming. It is death to go up and danger to climb down. The Stone Age man faces the danger and carries his willing prey down. The others are beyond the fear of death, and go up. And that is the end of them and of the plays of Henrik Ibsen.

The end, too, let us hope, of the idols, domestic, moral, religious and political, in whose name we have been twaddled into misery and confusion and hypocrisy unspeakable. For Ibsen's dead hand still keeps the grip he laid on their masks when he first tore them off; and whilst that grip holds, all the King's horses and all the King's men will find it hard to set those Humpty-Dumpties up again.

THE LESSON OF THE PLAYS

IN following this sketch of the plays written by Ibsen to illustrate his thesis that the real slavery of today is slavery to ideals of goodness, it may be that readers who have conned Ibsen through idealist spectacles have wondered that I could so pervert the utterances of a great poet. Indeed I know already that many of those who are most fascinated by the poetry of the plays will plead for any explanation of them rather than that given by Ibsen himself in the plainest terms through the mouths of Mrs Alving, Relling, and the rest. No great writer uses his skill to conceal his meaning. There is a tale by a famous Scotch story-teller which would have suited Ibsen exactly if he had hit on it first. Jeanie Deans* sacrificing her sister's life on the scaffold to ideal truthfulness is far more horrible than the sacrifice in Rosmersholm; and the *deus ex machina* expedient by which Scott makes the end of his story agreeable* is no solution of the ethical problem raised, but only a puerile evasion of it. He dared not, when it came to the point, allow Effie to be hanged for the sake of Jeanie's ideals.[1] Nevertheless, if I were to pretend that Scott wrote The Heart of Midlothian to shew that people are led to do as mischievous, as unnatural, as murderous thing, by their religious and moral ideals as by their envy and ambition, it would be easy to confute me from the pages of the book itself. And Ibsen, like Scott, has made his opinion plain. If any one attempts to maintain that Ghosts is a polemic in favor of indissoluble monogamic marriage, or that The Wild Duck was written to inculcate that truth should be told for its own sake, they must burn the text of the plays if their contention is to stand. The reason that Scott's story is tolerated by those who shrink from Ghosts is not that it is less terrible, but that Scott's views are familiar to all well-brought-up ladies and gentlemen, whereas Ibsen's are for the moment so strange to them as to be unthinkable. He is so great a poet that the idealist finds himself in the dilemma of being

---

[1] The common-sense solution of the ethical problem has often been delivered by acclamation in the theatre. Many years ago I witnessed a performance of a melodrama founded on this story.* After the painful trial scene, in which Jeanie Deans condemns her sister to death by refusing to swear to a perfectly innocent fiction, came a scene in the prison. 'If it had been me,' said the jailor, 'I wad ha sworn a hole through an iron pot.' The roar of applause which burst from the pit and gallery was thoroughly Ibsenist in sentiment. The speech, by the way, must have been a gag of the actor's: at all events I cannot find it in the acting edition of the play.

unable to conceive that such a genius should have an ignoble meaning, and yet equally unable to conceive his real meaning otherwise than as ignoble. Consequently he misses the meaning altogether in spite of Ibsen's explicit and circumstantial insistence on it, and proceeds to substitute a meaning congenial to his own ideal of nobility.

Ibsen's deep sympathy with his idealist figures seems to countenance this confusion. Since it is on the weaknesses of the higher types of character that idealism seizes, his most tragic examples of vanity, self-ishness, folly, and failure are not vulgar villains, but men who in an ordinary novel or melodrama would be heroes. Brand and Rosmer, who drive those they love to death, do so with all the fine airs of the Sophoclean or Shakespearean good man persecuted by Destiny.* Hilda Wangel, who kills the Master Builder literally to amuse herself, is the most fascinating of sympathetic girl-heroines. The ordinary Philistine commits no such atrocities: he marries the woman he likes and lives with her more or less happily ever after; but that is not because he is greater than Brand or Rosmer: he is less. The idealist is a more danger-ous animal than the Philistine just as a man is a more dangerous animal than a sheep. Though Brand virtually murdered his wife, I can under-stand many a woman, comfortably married to an amiable Philistine, reading the play and envying the victim her husband. For when Brand's wife, having made the sacrifice he has exacted, tells him that he was right; that she is happy now; that she sees God face to face; and then reminds him that 'whoso sees Jehovah dies,' he instinctively clasps his hands over her eyes; and that action raises him at once far above the criticism that sneers at idealism from beneath, instead of surveying it from the clear ether above, which can only be reached through its mists.

If, in my account of the plays, I have myself suggested false judg-ments by describing the errors of the idealists in the terms of the life they have risen above rather than in those of the life they fall short of, I can only plead, with but moderate disrespect for the general reader, that if I had done otherwise I should have failed wholly to make my exposition intelligible. Indeed accurate terms for realist morality, though they are to be found in the Bible, are so out of fashion and forgotten that in this very distinction between idealism and realism, I am forced to insist on a sense of the words which, had not Ibsen forced my hand, I should perhaps have conveyed otherwise, to avoid the conflict of many of its applications with the vernacular use of the words.

This, however, was a trifle compared to the difficulty which arose from our inveterate habit of labelling men with the abstract names of their qualities without the slightest reference to the underlying will which sets these qualities in action. At an anniversary celebration of the Paris Commune of 1871, I was struck by the fact that no speaker could find a eulogy for the Federals which would not have been equally appropriate to the peasants of La Vendée who fought for their tyrants against the French revolutionists, or to the Irishmen and Highlanders who fought for the Stuarts at the Boyne or Culloden.* The statements that the slain members of the Commune were heroes who died for a noble ideal would have left a stranger quite as much in the dark about them as the counter statements, once common enough in our newspapers, that they were incendiaries and assassins. Our obituary notices are examples of the same ambiguity. Of all the public men lately deceased when Ibsenism was first discussed in England, none was made more interesting by strongly marked personal characteristics than the famous atheist orator Charles Bradlaugh. He was not in the least like any other notable member of the House of Commons. Yet when the obituary notices appeared, with the usual string of qualities: eloquence, determination, integrity, strong common-sense, and so on, it would have been possible, by merely expunging all names and other external details from these notices, to leave the reader entirely unable to say whether the subject of them was Gladstone, Lord Morley, William Stead, or any one else no more like Bradlaugh than Garibaldi or the late Cardinal Newman,* whose obituary certificates of morality might nevertheless have been reprinted almost verbatim for the occasion without any gross incongruity. Bradlaugh had been the subject of many sorts of newspaper notices in his time. Thirty years ago, when the middle classes supposed him to be a revolutionist, the string of qualities which the press hung upon him were all evil ones, great stress being laid on the fact that as he was an atheist it would be an insult to God to admit him to Parliament. When it became apparent that he was an anti-socialist force in politics, he, without any recantation of his atheism, at once had the string of evil qualities exchanged for a rosary of good ones; but it is hardly necessary to add that neither the old badge nor the new could ever give any inquirer the least clue to the sort of man he actually was: he might have been Oliver Cromwell or Wat Tyler or Jack Cade, Penn or Wilberforce or Wellington, the late Mr Hampden of flat-earth-theory notoriety or Proudhon or the Archbishop of Canterbury,* for all the distinction such labels could give him one way or the other. The worthlessness of these abstract descriptions is recognized in practice every day. Tax a stranger before a crowd with being a thief, a coward, and a liar; and the crowd will suspend its judgment until you answer the question, 'What's he done?' Attempt to take up a collection for him on the ground that he is an upright, fearless, high-principled hero; and the same question must be answered before a penny goes into the hat.

The reader must therefore discount those partialities which I have permitted myself to express in telling the stories of the plays. They are as much beside the mark as any other example of the sort of criticism which seeks to create an impression favorable or otherwise to Ibsen by simply pasting his characters all over with good or bad conduct marks. If any person cares to describe Hedda Gabler as a modern Lucretia* who preferred death to dishonor, and Thea Elvsted as an abandoned, perjured strumpet who deserted the man she had sworn before her God to love, honor, and obey until her death, the play contains conclusive evidence establishing both points. If the critic goes on to argue that as Ibsen manifestly means to recommend Thea's conduct above Hedda's by making the end happier for her, the moral of the play is a vicious one, that, again, cannot be gainsaid. If, on the other hand, Ghosts be defended, as the dramatic critic of Piccadilly did defend it,* because it throws into divine relief the beautiful figure of the simple and pious Pastor Manders, the fatal compliment cannot be parried. When you have called Mrs Alving an emancipated woman or an unprincipled one, Alving a debauchee or a victim of society, Nora a fearless and noble-hearted woman or a shocking little liar and an unnatural mother, Helmer a selfish hound or a model husband and father, according to your bias, you have said something which is at once true and false, and in both cases perfectly idle.

The statement that Ibsen's plays have an immoral tendency, is, in the sense in which it is used, quite true. Immorality does not necessarily imply mischievous conduct: it implies conduct, mischievous or not, which does not conform to current ideals. All religions begin with a revolt against morality, and perish when morality conquers them and stamps out such words as grace and sin, substituting for them morality and immorality. Bunyan places the town of Morality, with its respectable leading citizens Mr Legality and Mr Civility, close to the City of Destruction.* In the United States today he would be imprisoned for this. Born as I was in the seventeenth century atmosphere of mid-nineteenth century Ireland, I can remember when men who talked about morality were suspected of reading Tom Paine, if not of being downright atheists. Ibsen's attack on morality is a symptom of the revival of religion, not of its extinction. He is on the side of the prophets in having devoted himself to shewing that the spirit or will of Man is constantly outgrowing the ideals, and that therefore thoughtless conformity to them is constantly producing results no less tragic than those which follow thoughtless violation of them. Thus the main effect of his plays is to keep before the public the importance of being always prepared to act immorally. He reminds men that they ought to be as careful how they yield to a temptation to tell the truth as to a temptation to hold their tongues, and he urges upon women who either cannot or will not marry that the inducements held out to them by society to preserve their virginity and refrain from motherhood may be called temptations as logically as the inducements to the contrary held out by individuals and by their own temperaments, the practical decision depending on circumstances just as much as a decision between walking and taking a cab, however less trivial both the action and the circumstances may be. He protests against the ordinary assumption that there are certain moral institutions which justify all means used to maintain them, and insists that the supreme end shall be the inspired, eternal, ever growing one, not the external unchanging, artificial one; not the letter but the spirit; not the contract but the object of the contract; not the abstract law but the living will. And because the will to change our habits and thus defy morality arises before the intellect can reason out any racially beneficent purpose in the change, there is always an interval during which the individual can say no more than that he wants to behave immorally because he likes, and because he will feel constrained and unhappy if he acts otherwise. For this reason it is enormously important that we should 'mind our own business' and let other people do as they like unless we can prove some damage beyond the shock to our feelings and prejudices. It is easy to put revolutionary cases in which it is so impossible to draw the line that they will always be decided in practice more or less by physical force; but for all ordinary purposes of government and social conduct the distinction is a commonsense one. The plain working truth is that it is not only good for people to be shocked occasionally, but absolutely necessary to the progress of society that they should be shocked pretty often. But it is not good for people to be garotted* occasionally, or at all. That is why it is a mistake to treat an atheist as you treat a garotter, or to put 'bad taste' on the footing of theft and murder. The need for freedom of evolution is the sole basis of toleration, the sole valid argument against Inquisitions and Censorships, the sole reason for not burning heretics and sending every eccentric person to the madhouse.

In short, our ideals, like the gods of old, are constantly demanding human sacrifices. Let none of them, says Ibsen, be placed above the obligation to prove itself worth the sacrifices it demands; and let everyone religiously refuse to sacrifice himself and others from the moment he loses his faith in the validity of the ideal. Of course it will be said here by incorrigibly slipshod readers that this, far from being immoral, is the highest morality; but I really will not waste further definition on those who will neither mean one thing or another by a word nor allow me to do so. Suffice it that among those who are not ridden by current ideals no question as to the ethical soundness of Ibsen's plays will ever arise; and among those who are so ridden his plays will be denounced as immoral, and cannot be defended against the accusation.

There can be no question as to the effect likely to be produced on an individual by his conversion from the ordinary acceptance of current ideals as safe standards of conduct, to the vigilant open-mindedness of Ibsen. It must at once greatly deepen the sense of moral responsibility. Before conversion the individual anticipates nothing worse in the way of examination at the judgment bar of his conscience than such questions as, Have you kept the commandments? Have you obeyed the law? Have you attended church regularly? paid your rates and taxes to Cæsar? and contributed, in reason, to charitable institutions? It may be hard to do all these things; but it is still harder not to do them, as our ninety-nine moral cowards in the hundred well know. And even a scoundrel can do them all and yet live a worse life than the smuggler or prostitute who must answer No all through the catechism.* Substitute for such a technical examination one in which the whole point to be settled is, Guilty or Not Guilty? one in which there is no more and no less respect for virginity than for incontinence, for subordination than for rebellion, for legality than for illegality, for piety than for blasphemy: in short, for the standard qualities than for the standard faults, and immediately, instead of lowering the ethical standard by relaxing the tests of worth, you raise it by increasing their stringency to a point at which no mere Pharisaism or moral cowardice can pass them.

Naturally this does not please the Pharisee.* The respectable lady of the strictest Church principles, who has brought up her children with such relentless regard to their ideal morality that if they have any spirit left in them by the time they arrive at years of independence they use their liberty to rush deliriously to the devil: this unimpeachable woman has always felt it unjust that the respect she wins should be accompanied by deep-seated detestation, whilst the latest spiritual heiress of Nell Gwynne,* whom no respectable person dare bow to in the street, is a popular idol. The reason is—though the idealist lady does not know it—that Nell Gwynne is a better woman than she; and the abolition of the idealist test which brings her out a worse one, and its replacement by the realist test which would shew the true relation between them, would be a most desirable step forward in public morals, especially as it would act impartially, and set the good side of the Pharisee above the bad side of the Bohemian as ruthlessly as it would set the good side of the Bohemian above the bad side of the Pharisee.[1] For as long as convention goes counter to reality in these matters, people will be led into Hedda Gabler's error of making an ideal of vice. If we maintain the convention that the distinction between Catherine of Russia* and Queen Victoria, between Nell Gwynne and Mrs Proudie,* is the distinction between a bad woman and a good woman, we need not be surprised when those who sympathize with Catherine and Nell conclude that it is better to be a loose woman than a strict one, and go on recklessly to conceive a prejudice against teetotalism and monogamy, and a prepossession in favor of alcoholic excitement and promiscuous amours. Ibsen himself is kinder to the man who has gone his own way as a rake and a drunkard than to the man who is respectable because he dare not be otherwise. We find that the franker and healthier a boy is, the more certain is he to prefer pirates and highwaymen, or Dumas musketeers,* to 'pillars of society' as his favorite heroes of romance. We have already seen both Ibsenites and anti-Ibsenites who seem to think that the cases of Nora and Mrs Elvsted are meant to establish a golden rule for women who wish to be 'emancipated': the said golden rule being simply, Run away from your husband. But in Ibsen's view of life, that would come under the same condemnation as the ecclesiastical rule, Cleave to your husband until death do you part. Most people know of a case or two in which it would be wise for a wife to follow the example of Nora or even of Mrs Elvsted. But they must also know cases in which the results of such a course would be as tragi-comic as those of Gregers Werle's attempt in The Wild Duck to do for the Ekdal household what Lona Hessel did for the Bernick household. What Ibsen insists on is that there is no golden rule; that conduct must justify itself by its effect upon life and not by its conformity to any rule or ideal. And since life consists in the fulfilment of the will, which is constantly growing, and cannot be fulfilment today under the conditions which secured its fulfilment yesterday, he claims afresh the old Protestant right of

[1] The warning implied in this sentence is less needed now than it was twenty years ago. The association of Bohemianism with the artistic professions and with revolutionary political views has been weakened by the revolt of the children of the Bohemians against its domestic squalor and social outlawry. Bohemianism is now rather one of the stigmata of the highly conservative 'smart sets' of the idle rich than of the studio, the stage, and the Socialist organizations. (1912.)

private judgment in questions of conduct as against all institutions, the so-called Protestant Churches themselves included.

Here I must leave the matter, merely reminding those who may think that I have forgotten to reduce Ibsenism to a formula for them, that its quintessence is that there is no formula.

I NOW come to the question: Why, since neither human nature nor the specific talent of the playwright has changed since the days of Charles Dickens and Dumas *père*, are the works of Ibsen, of Strindberg, of Tolstoy, of Gorki, of Tchekov, of Brieux, so different from those of the great fictionists of the first half of the nineteenth century? Tolstoy actually imitated Dickens. Ibsen was not Dickens's superior as an observer, nor is Strindberg, nor Gorki, nor Tchekov, nor Brieux. Tolstoy and Ibsen together, gifted as they were, were not otherwise gifted or more gifted than Shakespear and Molière. Yet a generation which could read all Shakespear and Molière, Dickens and Dumas, from end to end without the smallest intellectual or ethical perturbation, was unable to get through a play by Ibsen or a novel by Tolstoy without having its intellectual and moral complacency upset, its religious faith shattered, and its notions of right and wrong conduct thrown into confusion and sometimes even reversed. It is as if these modern men had a spiritual force that was lacking in even the greatest of their forerunners. And yet, what evidence is there in the lives of Wagner, Ibsen, Tolstoy, Strindberg, Gorki, Tchekov, and Brieux, that they were or are better men in any sense than Shakespear, Molière, Dickens, and Dumas?

I myself have been told by people that the reading of a single book of mine or the witnessing of a single play has changed their whole lives; and among these are some who tell me that they cannot read Dickens at all, whilst all of them have read books and seen plays by authors obviously quite as gifted as I am, without finding anything more in them than pastime.

The explanation is to be found in what I believe to be a general law of the evolution of ideas. 'Every jest is an earnest in the womb of time' says Peter Keegan in John Bull's Other Island. 'There's many a true word spoken in jest' says the first villager you engage in philosophic discussion. All very serious revolutionary propositions begin as huge jokes. Otherwise they would be stamped out by the lynching of their first exponents. Even these exponents themselves have their revelations broken to them mysteriously through their sense of humor. Two friends of mine, travelling in remote parts of Spain, were asked by the shepherds what their religion was.* 'Our religion,' replied one of them, a very highly cultivated author and traveller, with a sardonic turn, 'is that there is no God.' This reckless remark, taken seriously, might have provided nineteenth century scepticism with a martyr. As it was, the countryside rang with laughter for days afterwards as the stupendous joke was handed round. But it was just by tolerating the blasphemy as a joke that the shepherds began to build it into the fabric of their minds. Being now safely lodged there, it will in due time develop its earnestness; and at last travellers will come who will be taken quite seriously when they say that the imaginary hidalgo* in the sky whom the shepherds call God does indeed not exist. And they will remain godless, and call their streets Avenue Paul Bert* and so forth, until in due time another joker will arrive with sidesplitting intimations that Shakespear's 'There's a divinity that shapes our ends, rough hew them how we will'* was a strictly scientific statement of fact, and that 'neo-Darwinism' consists for the most part of grossly unscientific statements of superstitious nonsense. Which jest will in its due time come to its own as very solid earnest.

The same phenomenon may be noticed in our attitude towards matters of fact so obvious that no dispute can arise as to their existence. And here the power of laughter is astonishing. It is not enough to say merely that men enable themselves to endure the unbearablest nuisances and the deadliest scourges by setting up a merry convention that they are amusing. We must go further and face the fact that they actually are amused by them—that they are not laughing with the wrong side of the mouth. If you doubt it, read the popular fiction of the pre-Dickensian age, from the novels of Smollett to Tom Cringle's Log.* Poverty in rags is a joke, yellow fever is a joke, drunkenness is a joke, dysentery is a joke, kickings, floggings, falls, frights, humiliations, and painful accidents of all sorts are jokes. Henpecked husbands and termagant mothers-in-law are prime jokes. The infirmities of age and the inexperience and shyness of youth are jokes; and it is first-rate fun to insult and torment those that suffer from them.

We take some of these jokes seriously enough now. Humphrey Clinker* may not have become absolutely unreadable (I have not tried him for more than forty years); but there is certainly a good deal in the book that is now simply disgusting to the class of reader that in its own day found it uproariously amusing. Much of Tom Cringle has become mere savagery: its humors are those of a donkey race. Also, the fun is forced: one sees beneath the determination of the old sea dog to put a hearty smiling English face on pain and discomfort, that he has not merely looked on at it, and that he did not really like it. The mask of laughter wears slowly off the shames and the evils; but men finally see them as they really are.

Sometimes the change occurs, not between two generations, but actually in the course of a single work by one author. Don Quixote and Mr Pickwick are recognized examples of characters introduced in pure ridicule, and presently gaining the affection and finally the respect of their authors. To them may be added Shakespear's Falstaff.* Falstaff is introduced as a subordinate stage figure with no other function than to be robbed by the Prince and Poins, who was originally meant to be the *raisonneur* of the piece,* and the chief figure among the prince's dissolute associates. But Poins soon fades into nothing, like several characters in Dickens's early works; whilst Falstaff develops into an enormous joke and an exquisitely mimicked human type. Only in the end the joke withers. The question comes to Shakespear: *Is* this really a laughing matter? Of course there can be only one answer; and Shakespear gives it as best he can by the mouth of the prince become king, who might, one thinks, have the decency to wait until he has redeemed his own character before assuming the right to lecture his boon companion. Falstaff, rebuked and humiliated, dies miserably. His followers are hanged, except Pistol, whose exclamation 'Old do I wax; and from my weary limbs honor is cudgelled'* is a melancholy exordium to an old age of beggary and imposture.

But suppose Shakespear had begun where he left off! Suppose he had been born at a time when, as the result of a long propaganda of health and temperance, sack had come to be called alcohol, alcohol had come to be called poison, corpulence had come to be regarded as either a disease or a breach of good manners, and a conviction had spread throughout society that the practice of consuming 'a half-pennyworth of bread to an intolerable deal of sack'* was the cause of so much misery, crime, and racial degeneration that whole States prohibited the sale of potable spirits altogether, and even moderate drinking was more and more regarded as a regrettable weakness! Suppose (to drive the change well home) the women in the great theatrical centres had completely lost that amused indulgence for the drunken man which still exists in some out-of-the-way places, and felt nothing but disgust and anger at the conduct and habits of Falstaff and Sir Toby Belch!* Instead of Henry IV and The Merry Wives of Windsor, we should have had something like Zola's L'Assommoir.* Indeed, we actually have Cassio,* the last of Shakespear's gentleman-drunkards, talking like a temperance reformer, a fact which suggests that Shakespear had been roundly lectured for the offensive vulgarity of Sir Toby by some woman of refinement who refused to see the smallest fun in giving a knight such a name as Belch, with characteristics to correspond to it. Suppose, again, that

the first performance of The Taming of the Shrew had led to a modern
Feminist demonstration in the theatre,* and forced upon Shakespear's
consideration a whole century of agitatresses, from Mary Wollstonecraft
to Mrs Fawcett and Mrs Pankhurst,* is it not likely that the jest of
Katharine and Petruchio* would have become the earnest of Nora and
Torvald Helmer?

In this light the difference between Dickens and Strindberg becomes
intelligible. Strindberg simply refuses to regard the cases of Mrs Raddle
and Mrs Macstinger and Mrs Jo Gargery* as laughing matters. He
insists on taking them seriously as cases of a tyranny which effects more
degradation and causes more misery than all the political and sectarian
oppressions known to history. Yet it cannot be said that Strindberg,
even at his fiercest, is harder on women than Dickens. No doubt his
case against them is far more complete, because he does not shirk the
specifically sexual factors in it. But this really softens it. If Dickens had
allowed us, were it but for an instant, to see Jo Gargery and Mrs Jo as
husband and wife, he would perhaps have been accused by fools of
immodesty; but we should have at least some more human impression
than the one left by an unredeemed shrew married to a grown-up terrified child. It was George Gissing,* a modern realist, who first pointed
out the power and truth to nature of Dickens's women, and the fact
that, funny as they are, they are mostly detestable. Even the amiable
ones are silly and sometimes disastrous. When the few good ones are
agreeable they are not specifically feminine: they are the Dickensian
good man in petticoats; yet they lack that strength which they would
have had if Dickens had seen clearly that there is no such species in
creation as 'Woman, lovely woman,'* the woman being simply the
female of the human species, and that to have one conception of
humanity for the woman and another for the man, or one law for the
woman and another for the man, or one artistic convention for woman
and another for man, or, for the matter of that, a skirt for the woman
and a pair of breeches for the man, is as unnatural, and in the long run
as unworkable, as one law for the mare and another for the horse.
Roughly it may be said that all Dickens's studies from life of the differ-
entiated creatures our artificial sex institutions have made of women
are, for all their truth, either vile or ridiculous or both. Betsy Trotwood
is a dear because she is an old bachelor in petticoats: a manly woman,
like all good women: good men being equally all womanly men. Miss
Havisham, an insanely womanly woman, is a horror, a monster, though
a Chinese monster: that is, not a natural one, but one produced by
deliberate perversion of her humanity.* In comparison, Strindberg's

women are positively amiable and attractive. The general impression that Strindberg's women are the revenge of a furious woman-hater for his domestic failures, whilst Dickens is a genial idealist (he had little better luck domestically, by the way), is produced solely by Dickens either making fun of the affair or believing that women are born so and must be admitted to the fellowship of the Holy Ghost on a feminine instead of a human basis; whilst Strindberg takes womanliness with deadly seriousness as an evil not to be submitted to for a moment without vehement protest and demand for quite practicable reform. The nurse in his play who wheedles her old nursling and then slips a strait waistcoat on him revolts us;* but she is really ten times more lovable and sympathetic than Sairey Gamp,* an abominable creature whose very soul is putrid, and who is yet true to life. It is very noteworthy that none of the modern writers who take life as seriously as Ibsen have ever been able to bring themselves to depict depraved people so pitilessly as Dickens and Thackeray and even the genial Dumas *père*. Ibsen was grim enough in all conscience: no man has said more terrible things both privately and publicly; and yet there is not one of Ibsen's characters who is not, in the old phrase, the temple of the Holy Ghost, and who does not move you at moments by the sense of that mystery. The Dickens-Thackeray spirit is, in comparison, that of a Punch and Judy showman,* who is never restrained from whacking his little figures unmercifully by the sense that they, too, are images of God, and, 'but for the grace of God,'* very like himself. Dickens does deepen very markedly towards this as he grows older, though it is impossible to pretend that Mrs Wilfer is treated with less levity than Mrs Nickleby;* but to Ibsen, from beginning to end, every human being is a sacrifice, whilst to Dickens he is a farce. And there you have the whole difference. No character drawn by Dickens is more ridiculous than Hjalmar Ekdal in The Wild Duck, or more eccentric than old Ekdal, whose toy game-preserve in the garret is more fantastic than the house of Miss Havisham; and yet these Ekdals wring the heart whilst Micawber and Chivery* (who sits between the lines of clothes hung out to dry because 'it reminds him of groves' as Hjalmar's garret reminds old Ekdal of bear forests) only shake the sides.

It may be that if Dickens could read these lines he would say that the defect was not in him but in his readers; and that if we will return to his books now that Ibsen has opened our eyes we will have to admit that he also saw more in the soul of Micawber than mere laughing gas. And indeed one cannot forget the touches of kindliness and gallantry which ennoble his mirth. Still, between the man who occasionally remembered and the man who never forgot, between Dick Swiveller and Ulrik Brendel,* there is a mighty difference. The most that can be said to minimize it is that some of the difference is certainly due to the difference in the attitude of the reader. When an author's works produce violent controversy, and are new, people are apt to read them with that sort of seriousness which is very appropriately called deadly: that is, with a sort of solemn paralysis of every sense except a quite abstract and baseless momentousness which has no more to do with the contents of the author's works than the horrors of a man in delirium tremens have to do with real rats and snakes. The Bible is a sealed literature to most of us because we cannot read it naturally and unsophisticatedly: we are like the old lady who was edified by the word Mesopotamia,* or Samuel Butler's Chowbok, who was converted to Christianity by the effect on his imagination of the prayer for Queen Adelaide.* Many years elapsed before those who were impressed with Beethoven's music ventured to enjoy it sufficiently to discover what a large part of it is a riot of whimsical fun. As to Ibsen, I remember a performance of The Wild Duck, at which the late Clement Scott* pointed out triumphantly that the play was so absurd that even the champions of Ibsen could not help laughing at it. It had not occurred to him that Ibsen could laugh like other men. Not until an author has become so familiar that we are quite at our ease with him, and are up to his tricks of manner, do we cease to imagine that he is, relatively to older writers, terribly serious.

Still, the utmost allowance we can make for this difference does not persuade us that Dickens took the improvidence and futility of Micawber as Ibsen took the improvidence and futility of Hjalmar Ekdal. The difference is plain in the works of Dickens himself; for the Dickens of the second half of the nineteenth century (the Ibsen half) is a different man from the Dickens of the first half. From Hard Times and Little Dorrit to Our Mutual Friend every one of Dickens's books lays a heavy burden on our conscience without flattering us with any hopes of a happy ending. But from The Pickwick Papers to Bleak House* you can read and laugh and cry and go happy to bed after forgetting yourself in a jolly book. I have pointed out elsewhere how Charles Lever*, after producing a series of books in which the old manner of rollicking through life as if all its follies and failures were splendid jokes, and all its conventional enjoyments and attachments delightful and sincere, suddenly supplied the highly appreciative Dickens (as editor of All the Year Round*) with a quite new sort of novel, called A Day's Ride: A Life's Romance,* which affected both Dickens and the public very unpleasantly by the bitter but tonic flavor we now know as Ibsenism; for the hero began as that uproarious old joke, the boaster who, being a coward, is led into all sorts of dangerous situations, like Bob Acres and Mr Winkle,* and then unexpectedly made them laugh very much on the wrong side of their mouths, exactly as if he were a hero by Ibsen, Strindberg, Turgenieff,* Tolstoy, Gorki, Tchekov, or Brieux. And here there was no question of the author being taken too gloomily. His readers, full of Charles O'Malley and Mickey Free,* were approaching the work with the most unsuspicious confidence in its entire jollity. The shock to the security of their senseless laughter caught them utterly unprepared; and they resented it accordingly.

Now that a reaction against realism has set in, and the old jolly ways are coming into fashion again, it is perhaps not so easy as it once was to conceive the extraordinary fascination of this mirthless comedy, this tragedy that stripped the soul naked instead of bedizening it in heroic trappings. But if you have not experienced this fascination yourself, and cannot conceive it, you may take my word for it that it exists, and operates with such power that it puts Shakespear himself out of countenance. And even for those who are in full reaction against it, it can hardly be possible to go back from the death of Hedwig Ekdal to the death of Little Nell* otherwise than as a grown man goes down on all fours and pretends to be a bear for the amusement of his children. Nor need we regret this: there are noble compensations for our increase of wisdom and sorrow. After Hedwig you may not be able to cry over Little Nell, but at least you can read Little Dorrit without calling it twaddle, as some of its first critics did. The jests do not become poorer as they mature into earnest. It was not through joyless poverty of soul that Shelley never laughed, but through an enormous apprehension and realization of the gravity of things that seemed mere fun to other men. If there is no Swiveller and no Trabbs's boy* in The Pilgrim's Progress, and if Mr Badman* is drawn as Ibsen would have drawn him and not as Sheridan* would have seen him, it does not follow that there is less strength (and joy is a quality of strength) in Bunyan than in Sheridan and Dickens. After all, the salvation of the world depends on the men who will not take evil good-humoredly, and whose laughter destroys the fool instead of encouraging him. 'Rightly to be great,' said Shakespear when he had come to the end of mere buffoonery, 'is greatly to find quarrel in a straw.'* The English cry of 'Amuse us: take things easily: dress up the world prettily for us' seems mere cowardice to the strong souls that dare look facts in the face; and just so far as people cast off levity and idolatry they find themselves able to bear the company of Bunyan and Shelley, of Ibsen and Strindberg and the great Russian realists, and unable to tolerate the sort of laughter that African tribes cannot restrain when a man is flogged or an animal trapped and wounded.* They are gaining strength and wisdom: gaining, in short, that sort of life which we call the life everlasting, a sense of which is worth, for pure well-being alone, all the brutish jollities of Tom Cringle and Humphrey Clinker, and even of Falstaff, Pecksniff, and Micawber.

THE TECHNICAL NOVELTY
IN IBSEN'S PLAYS*

IT is a striking and melancholy example of the preoccupation of critics with phrases and formulas to which they have given life by taking them into the tissue of their own living minds, and which therefore seem and feel vital and important to them whilst they are to everybody else the deadest and dreariest rubbish (this is the great secret of academic dryasdust), that to this day they remain blind to a new technical factor in the art of popular stage-play making which every considerable playwright has been thrusting under their noses night after night for a whole generation. This technical factor in the play is the discussion. Formerly you had in what was called a well made play an exposition in the first act, a situation in the second, and unravelling in the third. Now you have exposition, situation, and discussion; and the discussion is the test of the playwright. The critics protest in vain. They declare that discussions are not dramatic, and that art should not be didactic. Neither the playwrights nor the public take the smallest notice of them. The discussion conquered Europe in Ibsen's Doll's House; and now the serious playwright recognizes in the discussion not only the main test of his highest powers, but also the real centre of his play's interest. Sometimes he even takes every possible step to assure the public beforehand that his play will be fitted with that newest improvement.

This was inevitable if the drama was ever again to be raised above the childish demand for fables without morals. Children have a settled arbitrary morality: therefore to them moralizing is nothing but an intolerable platitudinizing. The morality of the grown-up is also very largely a settled morality, either purely conventional and of no ethical significance, like the rule of the road or the rule that when you ask for a yard of ribbon the shopkeeper shall give you thirty-six inches and not interpret the word yard as he pleases, or else too obvious in its ethics to leave any room for discussion: for instance, that if the boots keeps you waiting too long for your shaving water you must not plunge your razor into his throat in your irritation, no matter how great an effort of self-control your forbearance may cost you.

Now when a play is only a story of how a villain tries to separate an honest young pair of betrothed lovers; to gain the hand of the woman by calumny; and to ruin the man by forgery, murder, false witness, and other commonplaces of the Newgate Calendar,* the introduction of

a discussion would clearly be ridiculous. There is nothing for sane
people to discuss; and any attempt to Chadbandize* on the wickedness
of such crimes is at once resented as, in Milton's phrase, 'moral
babble.'*

But this sort of drama is soon exhausted by people who go often to
the theatre. In twenty visits one can see every possible change rung on
all the available plots and incidents out of which plays of this kind can
be manufactured. The illusion of reality is soon lost: in fact it may be
doubted whether any adult ever entertains it: it is only to very young
children that the fairy queen is anything but an actress. But at the age
when we cease to mistake the figures on the stage for *dramatis personae*,*
and know that they are actors and actresses, the charm of the performer
begins to assert itself; and the child who would have been cruelly hurt
by being told that the Fairy Queen was only Miss Smith dressed up to
look like one, becomes the man who goes to the theatre expressly to see
Miss Smith, and is fascinated by her skill or beauty to the point of
delighting in plays which would be unendurable to him without her.
Thus we get plays 'written round' popular performers, and popular
performers who give value to otherwise useless plays by investing them
with their own attractiveness. But all these enterprises are, commercially speaking, desperately precarious. To begin with, the supply of
performers whose attraction is so far independent of the play that their
inclusion in the cast sometimes makes the difference between success
and failure is too small to enable all our theatres, or even many of them,
to depend on their actors rather than on their plays. And to finish with,
no actor can make bricks entirely without straw. From Grimaldi to
Sothern, Jefferson, and Henry Irving* (not to mention living actors) we
have had players succeeding once in a lifetime in grafting on to a play
which would have perished without them some figure imagined wholly
by themselves; but none of them has been able to repeat the feat, nor to
save many of the plays in which he has appeared from failure. In the
long run nothing can retain the interest of the playgoer after the theatre
has lost its illusion for his childhood, and its glamor for his adolescence,
but a constant supply of interesting plays; and this is specially true in
London, where the expense and trouble of theatregoing have been
raised to a point at which it is surprising that sensible people of middle
age go to the theatre at all. As a matter of fact, they mostly stay at home.

Now an interesting play cannot in the nature of things mean anything but a play in which problems of conduct and character of personal importance to the audience are raised and suggestively discussed.
People have a thrifty sense of taking away something from such plays:

they not only have had something for their money, but they retain that something as a permanent possession. Consequently none of the commonplaces of the box office hold good of such plays. In vain does the experienced acting manager declare that people want to be amused and not preached at in the theatre; that they will not stand long speeches; that a play must not contain more than 18,000 words; that it must not begin before nine nor last beyond eleven; that there must be no politics and no religion in it; that breath of these golden rules will drive people to the variety theatres;* that there must be a woman of bad character, played by a very attractive actress, in the piece; and so on and so forth. All these counsels are valid for plays in which there is nothing to discuss. They may be disregarded by the playwright who is a moralist and a debater as well as a dramatist. From him, within the inevitable limits set by the clock and by the physical endurance of the human frame, people will stand anything as soon as they are matured enough and cultivated enough to be susceptible to the appeal of his particular form of art. The difficulty at present is that mature and cultivated people do not go to the theatre, just as they do not read penny novelets; and when an attempt is made to cater for them they do not respond to it in time, partly because they have not the habit of playgoing, and partly because it takes too long for them to find out that the new theatre is not like all the other theatres. But when they do at last find their way there, the attraction is not the firing of blank cartridges at one another by actors, nor the pretence of falling down dead that ends the stage combat, nor the simulation of erotic thrills by a pair of stage lovers, nor any of the other tomfooleries called action, but the exhibition and discussion of the character and conduct of stage figures who are made to appear real by the art of the playwright and the performers.

This, then, is the extension of the old dramatic form effected by Ibsen. Up to a certain point in the last act, A Doll's House is a play that might be turned into a very ordinary French drama by the excision of a few lines,* and the substitution of a sentimental happy ending for the famous last scene: indeed the very first thing the theatrical wiseacres did with it was to effect exactly this transformation, with the result that the play thus pithed had no success and attracted no notice worth mentioning. But at just that point in the last act, the heroine very unexpectedly (by the wiseacres) stops her emotional acting and says: 'We must sit down and discuss all this that has been happening between us.' And it was by this new technical feature: this addition of a new movement, as musicians would say, to the dramatic form, that A Doll's House conquered Europe and founded a new school of dramatic art.

Since that time the discussion has expanded far beyond the limits of the last ten minutes of an otherwise 'well made' play. The disadvantage of putting the discussion at the end was not only that it came when the audience was fatigued, but that it was necessary to see the play over again, so as to follow the earlier acts in the light of the final discussion, before it became fully intelligible. The practical utility of this book is due to the fact that unless the spectator at an Ibsen play has read the pages referring to it beforehand, it is hardly possible for him to get its bearings at a first hearing if he approaches it, as most spectators still do, with conventional idealist prepossessions. Accordingly, we now have plays, including some of my own, which begin with discussion and end with action, and others in which the discussion interpenetrates the action from beginning to end. When Ibsen invaded England discussion had vanished from the stage; and women could not write plays. Within twenty years women were writing better plays than men;* and these plays were passionate arguments from beginning to end. The action of such plays consists of a case to be argued. If the case is uninteresting or stale or badly conducted or obviously trumped up, the play is a bad one. If it is important and novel and convincing, or at least disturbing, the play is a good one. But anyhow the play in which there is no argument and no case no longer counts as serious drama. It may still please the child in us as Punch and Judy does; but nobody nowadays pretends to regard the well made play as anything more than a commercial product which is not in question when modern schools of serious drama are under discussion. Indeed within ten years of the production of A Doll's House in London, audiences had become so derisive of the more obvious and hackneyed features of the methods of Sardou that it became dangerous to resort to them; and playwrights who persisted in 'constructing' plays in the old French manner lost ground not for lack of ideas, but because their technique was unbearably out of fashion.

In the new plays, the drama arises through a conflict of unsettled ideals rather than through vulgar attachments, rapacities, generosities, resentments, ambitions, misunderstandings, oddities and so forth as to which no moral question is raised.* The conflict is not between clear right and wrong: the villain is as conscientious as the hero, if not more so: in fact, the question which makes the play interesting (when it *is* interesting) is which is the villain and which the hero. Or, to put it another way, there are no villains and no heroes. This strikes the critics mainly as a departure from dramatic art; but it is really the inevitable return to nature which ends all the merely technical fashions. Now the natural is mainly the everyday; and its climaxes must be, if not everyday, at least everylife, if they are to have any importance for the spectator. Crimes, fights, big legacies, fires, shipwrecks, battles, and thunderbolts are mistakes in a play, even when they can be effectively simulated. No doubt they may acquire dramatic interest by putting a character through the test of an emergency; but the test is likely to be too obviously theatrical, because, as the playwright cannot in the nature of things have much experience of such catastrophes, he is forced to substitute a set of conventions or conjectures for the feelings they really produce.

In short, pure accidents are not dramatic: they are only anecdotic. They may be sensational, impressive, provocative, ruinous, curious, or a dozen other things; but they have no specifically dramatic interest. There is no drama in being knocked down or run over. The catastrophe in Hamlet would not be in the least dramatic had Polonius fallen downstairs and broken his neck, Claudius succumbed to delirium tremens, Hamlet forgotten to breathe in the intensity of his philosophic speculation, Ophelia died of Danish measles, Laertes been shot by the palace sentry, and Rosencrantz and Guildenstern drowned in the North Sea. Even as it is, the Queen, who poisons herself by accident, has an air of being polished off to get her out of the way: her death is the one dramatic failure of the piece. Bushels of good paper have been inked in vain by writers who imagined they could produce a tragedy by killing everyone in the last act accidentally. As a matter of fact no accident, however sanguinary, can produce a moment of real drama, though a difference of opinion between husband and wife as to living in town or country might be the beginning of an appalling tragedy or a capital comedy.

It may be said that everything is an accident: that Othello's character is an accident, Iago's character another accident, and the fact that they happened to come together in the Venetian service an even more accidental accident. Also that Torvald Helmer might just as likely have married Mrs Nickleby as Nora. Granting this trifling for what it is worth, the fact remains that marriage is no more an accident than birth or death: that is, it is expected to happen to everybody. And if every man has a good deal of Torvald Helmer in him, and every woman a good deal of Nora, neither their characters nor their meeting and marrying are accidents. Othello, though entertaining, pitiful, and resonant with the thrills a master of language can produce by mere artistic sonority is certainly much more accidental than A Doll's House; but it is correspondingly less important and interesting to us. It has been kept alive, not by its manufactured misunderstandings and stolen handkerchiefs and the like, nor even by its orchestral verse, but by its exhibition and discussion of human nature, marriage, and jealousy; and it would be a prodigiously better play if it were a serious discussion of the highly interesting problem of how a simple Moorish soldier would get on with a 'supersubtle' Venetian lady of fashion* if he married her. As it is, the play turns on a mistake; and though a mistake can produce a murder, which is the vulgar substitute for a tragedy, it cannot produce a real tragedy in the modern sense. Reflective people are not more interested in the Chamber of Horrors than in their own homes, nor in murderers, victims, and villains than in themselves; and the moment a man has acquired sufficient reflective power to cease gaping at waxworks, he is on his way to losing interest in Othello, Desdemona, and Iago exactly to the extent to which they become interesting to the police. Cassio's weakness for drink comes much nearer home to most of us than Othello's strangling and throat cutting, or Iago's theatrical confidence trick. The proof is that Shakespear's professional colleagues, who exploited all his sensational devices, and piled up torture on murder and incest on adultery until they had far out-Heroded Herod,* are now unmemorable and unplayable. Shakespear survives because he coolly treated the sensational horrors of his borrowed plots as inorganic theatrical accessories, using them simply as pretexts for dramatizing human character as it exists in the normal world. In enjoying and discussing his plays we unconsciously discount the combats and murders: commentators are never so astray (and consequently so ingenious) as when they take Hamlet seriously as a madman, Macbeth as a homicidal Highlander, and impish humorists like Richard and Iago as lurid villains of the Renascence. The plays in which these figures appear could be changed into comedies without altering a hair of their beards. Shakespear, had anyone been intelligent enough to tax him with this, would perhaps have said that most crimes are accidents that happen to people exactly like ourselves, and that Macbeth, under propitious circumstances, would have made an exemplary rector of Stratford,* a real criminal being a defective monster, a human accident, useful on the stage only for minor parts such as Don Johns, second murderers, and the like. Anyhow, the fact remains that Shakespear survives by what he has in common with Ibsen, and not by what he has in common with Webster* and the rest. Hamlet's surprise at finding that he 'lacks gall' to behave in the idealistically conventional manner, and that no extremity of rhetoric about the duty of revenging 'a dear father slain' and exterminating the 'bloody bawdy villain' who murdered him seems to make any difference in their domestic relations in the palace in Elsinore, still keeps us talking about him and going to the theatre to listen to him, whilst the older Hamlets, who never had any Ibsenist hesitations, and shammed madness, and entangled the courtiers in the arras and burnt them, and stuck hard to the theatrical school of the fat boy in Pickwick ('I wants to make your flesh creep'),* are as dead as John Shakespear's mutton.*

We have progressed so rapidly on this point under the impulse given to the drama by Ibsen that it seems strange now to contrast him favorably with Shakespear on the ground that he avoided the old catastrophes which left the stage strewn with the dead at the end of an Elizabethan tragedy. For perhaps the most plausible reproach levelled at Ibsen by modern critics of his own school is just that survival of the old school in him which makes the death rate so high in his last acts. Do Oswald Alving, Hedvig Ekdal, Rosmer and Rebecca, Hedda Gabler, Solness, Eyolf, Borkman, Rubeck and Irene die dramatically natural deaths, or are they slaughtered in the classic and Shakespearean manner, partly because the audience expects blood for its money, partly because it is difficult to make people attend seriously to anything except by startling them with some violent calamity? It is so easy to make out a case for either view that I shall not argue the point. The post-Ibsen playwrights apparently think that Ibsen's homicides and suicides were forced. In Tchekov's Cherry Orchard,* for example, where the sentimental ideals of our amiable, cultured, Schumann playing propertied class are reduced to dust and ashes by a hand not less deadly than Ibsen's because it is so much more caressing, nothing more violent happens than that the family cannot afford to keep up its old house. In Granville-Barker's plays, the campaign against our society is carried on with all Ibsen's implacability; but the one suicide (in Waste) is unhistorical; for neither Parnell nor Dilke, who were the actual cases in point of the waste which was the subject of the play,* killed himself. I myself have been reproached because the characters in my plays 'talk but do nothing', meaning that they do not commit felonies. As a matter of fact we have come to see that it is no true *dénouement** to cut the Gordian knot as Alexander did with a stroke of the sword.* If people's souls are tied up by law and public opinion it is much more tragic to leave them to wither in these bonds than to end their misery and relieve the salutary compunction of the audience by outbreaks of violence. Judge Brack was, on the whole, right when he said that people dont do such things.* If they did, the idealists would be brought to their senses very quickly indeed.

But in Ibsen's plays the catastrophe, even when it seems forced, and when the ending of the play would be more tragic without it, is never an accident; and the play never exists for its sake. His nearest to an

accident is the death of little Eyolf, who falls off a pier and is drowned.
But this instance only reminds us that there is one good dramatic use
for an accident: it can awaken people. When England wept over the
deaths of little Nell and Paul Dombey,* the strong soul of Ruskin was
moved to scorn: to novelists who were at a loss to make their books sell
he offered the formula: When at a loss, kill a child.* But Ibsen did not
kill little Eyolf to manufacture pathos. The surest way to achieve a thoroughly bad performance of Little Eyolf is to conceive it as a sentimental tale of a drowned darling. Its drama lies in the awakening of Allmers
and his wife to the despicable quality and detestable rancors of the life
they have been idealizing as blissful and poetic. They are so sunk in
their dream that the awakening can be effected only by a violent shock.
And that is just the one dramatically useful thing an accident can do. It
can shock. Hence the accident that befalls Eyolf.

As to the deaths in Ibsen's last acts, they are a sweeping up of the
remains of dramatically finished people. Solness's fall from the tower is
as obviously symbolic as Phaeton's fall from the chariot of the sun.*
Ibsen's dead bodies are those of the exhausted or destroyed: he does not
kill Hilda, for instance, as Shakespear killed Juliet.* He is ruthless
enough with Hedvig and Eyolf because he wants to use their deaths to
expose their parents; but if he had written Hamlet nobody would have
been killed in the last act except perhaps Horatio, whose correct nullity
might have provoked Fortinbras* to let some of the moral sawdust out
of him with his sword. For Shakespearean deaths in Ibsen you must go
back to Lady Inger* and the plays of his nonage, with which this book
is not concerned.

The drama was born of old from the union of two desires: the desire
to have a dance and the desire to hear a story. The dance became a rant:
the story became a situation. When Ibsen began to make plays, the art
of the dramatist had shrunk into the art of contriving a situation. And
it was held that the stranger the situation, the better the play. Ibsen saw
that, on the contrary, the more familiar the situation, the more interesting the play. Shakespear had put ourselves on the stage but not our
situations. Our uncles seldom murder our fathers, and cannot legally
marry our mothers;* we do not meet witches; our kings are not as a rule
stabbed and succeeded by their stabbers; and when we raise money by
bills we do not promise to pay pounds of our flesh. Ibsen supplies the
want left by Shakespear. He gives us not only ourselves, but ourselves
in our own situations. The things that happen to his stage figures are
things that happen to us. One consequence is that his plays are much
more important to us than Shakespear's. Another is that they are

capable both of hurting us cruelly and of filling us with excited hopes of escape from idealistic tyrannies, and with visions of intenser life in the future.

Changes in technique follow inevitably from these changes in the subject matter of the play. When a dramatic poet can give you hopes and visions, such old maxims as that stage-craft is the art of preparation become boyish, and may be left to those unfortunate playwrights who, being unable to make anything really interesting happen on the stage, have to acquire the art of continually persuading the audience that it is going to happen presently. When he can stab people to the heart by shewing them the meanness or cruelty of something they did yesterday and intend to do tomorrow, all the old tricks to catch and hold their attention become the silliest of superfluities. The play called The Murder of Gonzago, which Hamlet makes the players act before his uncle, is artlessly constructed; but it produces a greater effect on Claudius than the Œdipus of Sophocles, because it is about himself. The writer who practises the art of Ibsen therefore discards all the old tricks of preparation, catastrophe, *dénouement*, and so forth without thinking about it, just as a modern rifleman never dreams of providing himself with powder horns, percussion caps, and wads: indeed he does not know the use of them. Ibsen substituted a terrible art of sharp-shooting at the audience, trapping them, fencing with them, aiming always at the sorest spot in their consciences. Never mislead an audience, was an old rule. But the new school will trick the spectator into forming a meanly false judgment, and then convict him of it in the next act, often to his grievous mortification. When you despise something you ought to take off your hat to, or admire and imitate something you ought to loathe, you cannot resist the dramatist who knows how to touch these morbid spots in you and make you see that they are morbid. The dramatist knows that as long as he is teaching and saving his audience, he is as sure of their strained attention as a dentist is, or the Angel of the Annunciation.* And though he may use all the magic of art to make you forget the pain he causes you or to enhance the joy of the hope and courage he awakens, he is never occupied in the old work of manufacturing interest and expectation with materials that have neither novelty, significance, nor relevance to the experience or prospects of the spectators.

Hence a cry has arisen that the post-Ibsen play is not a play, and that its technique, not being the technique described by Aristotle, is not a technique at all. I will not enlarge on this: the fun poked at my friend Mr A. B. Walkley in the prologue of Fanny's First Play* need not be repeated here. But I may remind him that the new technique is new only on the modern stage. It has been used by preachers and orators ever since speech was invented. It is the technique of playing upon the human conscience; and it has been practised by the playwright whenever the playwright has been capable of it. Rhetoric, irony, argument, paradox, epigram, parable, the rearrangement of haphazard facts into orderly and intelligent situations: these are both the oldest and the newest arts of the drama; and your plot construction and art of preparation are only the tricks of theatrical talent and the shifts of moral sterility, not the weapons of dramatic genius. In the theatre of Ibsen we are not flattered spectators killing an idle hour with an ingenious and amusing entertainment: we are 'guilty creatures sitting at a play';* and the technique of pastime is no more applicable than at a murder trial.

The technical novelties of the Ibsen and post-Ibsen plays are, then: first the introduction of the discussion and its development until it so overspreads and interpenetrates the action that it finally assimilates it, making play and discussion practically identical; and, second, as a consequence of making the spectators themselves the persons of the drama, and the incidents of their own lives its incidents, the disuse of the old stage tricks by which audiences had to be induced to take an interest in unreal people and improbable circumstances, and the substitution of a forensic technique of recrimination, disillusion, and penetration through ideals to the truth, with a free use of all the rhetorical and lyrical arts of the orator, the preacher, the pleader, and the rhapsodist.

NEEDED: AN IBSEN THEATRE*

IT must now be plain to my readers that the doctrine taught by Ibsen can never be driven home from the stage whilst his plays are presented to us in haphazard order at the commercial theatres. Indeed our commercial theatres are so well aware of this that they have from the first regarded Ibsen as hopelessly uncommercial: he might as well never have lived as far as they are concerned. Even the new advanced theatres which now deal freely with what I have called post-Ibsenist plays hardly meddle with him. Had it not been for the great national service disinterestedly rendered by Mr William Archer in giving us a complete translation of Ibsen's plays (a virtually unremunerated public service which I hope the State will recognize fitly), Ibsen would be less known in England than Swedenborg.* By losing his vital contribution to modern thought we are losing ground relatively to the countries which, like Germany, have made his works familiar to their playgoers. But even in Germany Ibsen's meaning is seen only by glimpses. What we need is a theatre devoted primarily to Ibsen as the Bayreuth Festspielhaus is devoted to Wagner. I have shewn how the plays, as they succeed one another, are parts of a continuous discussion; how the difficulty left by one is dealt with in the next; how Mrs Alving is a reply to your hasty remark that Nora Helmer ought to be ashamed of herself for leaving her husband; how Gregers Werle warns you not to be as great a fool in your admiration of Lona Hessel as of Patient Grisel. The plays should, like Wagner's Ring, be performed in cycles; so that Ibsen may hunt you down from position to position until you are finally cornered.

The larger truth of the matter is that modern European literature and music now form a Bible far surpassing in importance to us the ancient Hebrew Bible that has served us so long. The notion that inspiration is something that happened thousands of years ago, and was then finished and done with, never to occur again: in other words, the theory that God retired from business at that period and has not since been heard from, is as silly as it is blasphemous. He who does not believe that revelation is continuous does not believe in revelation at all, however familiar his parrot's tongue and pewsleepy ear may be with the word. There comes a time when the formula 'Also sprach Zarathustra'* succeeds to the formula 'Thus saith the Lord', and when the parable of the doll's house is more to our purpose than the parable of the prodigal son. When Bunyan published The Pilgrim's Progress, his first difficulty was with the literal people who said, 'There is no such individual in the directory as Christian, and no such place in the gazetteer as the City of Destruction: therefore you are a liar'. Bunyan replied by citing the parables: asking, in effect, whether the story of the wise and foolish virgins* is also a lie. A couple of centuries or so later, when I myself wrote a play for the Salvation Army* to shew them that the dramatic method might be used for their gospel as effectively as the lyric or orchestral method, I was told that unless I could guarantee that the persons in my play actually existed, and the incidents had actually occurred, I, like Bunyan, would be regarded by the elderly soldiers in the army as no better than Ananias*. As it was useless for me to try to make these simple souls understand that in real life truth is revealed by parables and falsehood supported by facts, I had to leave the army to its oratorical metaphors and to its popular songs about heartbroken women waiting for the footsteps of their drunken husbands, and hearing instead the joyous step of the converted man whose newly found salvation will dry all their tears. I had not the heart to suggest that these happy pairs were as little authentic as The Second Mrs Tanqueray;* for I spied behind the army's confusion of truth with mere fact the old doubt whether anything good can come out of the theatre, a doubt as inveterate and neither more nor less justifiable than the doubt of our Secularists whether anything good can come out of the gospels.

But I think Ibsen has proved the right of the drama to take scriptural rank, and his own right to canonical rank as one of the major prophets of the modern Bible. The sooner we recognize that rank and give up the idea of trying to make a fashionable entertainment of his plays the better. It ends in our not performing them at all, and remaining in barbarous and dangerous ignorance of the case against idealism. We want a frankly doctrinal theatre. There is no more reason for making a doctrinal theatre inartistic than for putting a cathedral organ out of tune: indeed all experience shews that doctrine alone nerves us to the effort called for by the greatest art. I therefore suggest that even the sciolists* and voluptuaries who care for nothing in art but its luxuries and its executive feats are as strongly interested in the establishment of such a theatre as those for whom the What is always more important than the How, if only because the How cannot become really magical until such magic is indispensable to the revelation of an all-important What.

I do not suggest that the Ibsen theatre should confine itself to Ibsen any more than the Established Church confines itself to Jeremiah.* The post-Ibsenists could also be expounded there; and Strindberg should have his place, were it only as Devil's Advocate. But performances should be in the order of academic courses, designed so as to take audiences over the whole ground as Ibsen and his successors took them; so that the exposition may be consecutive. Otherwise the doctrine will not be interesting, and the audiences will not come regularly. The efforts now being made to regenerate the drama are often wasted through lack of doctrinal conviction and consequent want of system, the net result being an irresolute halting between the doctrinal and the merely entertaining.

For this sort of enterprise an endowment is necessary,* because commercial capital is not content in a theatre with reasonable interest: it demands great gains even at the cost of great hazards. Besides, nobody will endow mere pleasure, whereas doctrine can always command endowment. It is the foolish disclaiming of doctrine that keeps dramatic art unendowed. When we ask for an endowed theatre we always take the greatest pains to assure everybody that we do not mean anything unpleasantly serious, and that our endowed theatre will be as bright and cheery (meaning as low and common) as the commercial theatres. As a result of which we get no endowment. When we have the sense to profit by this lesson and promise that our endowed theatre will be an important place, and that it will make people of low tastes and tribal or commercial ideas horribly uncomfortable by its efforts to bring conviction of sin to them, we shall get endowment as easily as the religious people who are not foolishly ashamed to ask for what they want.

THE PERFECT WAGNERITE

A COMMENTARY ON THE NIBLUNG'S RING

PREFACE TO THE FOURTH EDITION

MUCH water, some of it deeply stained with blood, has passed under the bridges since this book was first published twenty-four years ago.* Musically Wagner is now more old-fashioned than Handel and Bach, Mozart and Beethoven,* whose fashions have perished though their music remains; whilst his own fashion has been worn to rags by young composers in their first efforts to draw the bow of Ulysses.* Finally, it has been discarded as Homerically impossible; and England, after two centuries of imitative negligibility, has suddenly flung into the field a cohort of composers whose methods have made a technical revolution in musical composition so complete that the conductor does not dare to correct the most cacophonous errors in band parts lest the composer should have intended them, and looks in vain for key signatures because young men no longer write in keys but just mark their notes flat or sharp as they come. One can imagine Wagner trying to conduct the latest British tone poem,* and exclaiming in desperation, 'Is this music?' just as his own contemporaries did when they were confronted with the 'false relations' in the score of Tristan.* It is true that most of the modern developments, as far as they are really developments and not merely experimental eccentricities, are implicit in Parsifal. Indeed, for that matter, they are implicit in Bach: still, the first man to be scandalized by a new departure is usually he that found the path for it; and I cannot feel sure that Wagner would have encouraged Messrs Bax, Ireland, Cyril Scott, Holst, Goossens, Vaughan Williams, Frank Bridge, Boughton, Holbrooke, Howells* and the rest (imagine being able to remember offhand so many names of British composers turning out serious music in native styles of their own!!!) any more than Haydn* encouraged Beethoven. Wagner, after his 1855 London season as conductor of the Philharmonic, would not have believed that such a thing could happen in England. Had he been told that within two years a British baby Elgar* would arrive who would attain classic rank as a European composer, he would hardly have kept his temper. Yet all this has happened very much as it happened before in Shakespear's time; and the English people at large are just as unconcerned about it, and indeed unconscious of it, as they were then.

Also the English have taken, as I said in this book they might, to Wagner singing and acting; and there is now no question of going to Bayreuth or importing German singers when we wish to hear The Ring or Parsifal;* for much better performances of both can be heard now from English companies in England than Wagner ever heard at Bayreuth; and even a transpontine theatre like the Old Vic.* thinks no more of doing Tannhäuser than it would have thought of doing Black-Eyed Susan* half a century ago.

Another change has outmoded my description of the Bayreuth Festival Playhouse as an ultra modern theatre. Bayreuth has a pictorial stage framed by a proscenium, and the framed picture stage is not now in the latest fashion. When the monarchy and the theatre were restored in England simultaneously on the accession of Charles II,* the representation of Shakespear's plays as he planned them was made impossible* by the introduction of pictorial scenery and of the proscenium with its two curtains, the act drop and the final green baize, to divide the plays into acts and hide the stage for intervals during which elaborate scenes were built up on it. His plays had to be chopped into fragments; divided into acts; re-written and provided with new endings to make effective 'curtains', in which condition they were intolerably tedious except as mere pedestals for irresistibly attractive actors and actresses.

Thus the pictorial stage not only murdered Shakespear, and buried the old Athenian drama, but dictated the form of opera (which grew up with it) and changed the form of the spoken drama. Wagner submitted to it as inevitable; but when he conceived the performances of The Ring, and planned a theatre for them, he made a desperate effort to elaborate its machinery so as to enable complete changes of scene to be made without stopping the performance and keeping the audience staring idly for fifteen minutes at a dropped curtain, or scrambling to and from their seats to fill up the time by smoking cigarets and drinking.* One of his devices was to envelop the stage in mists produced by what was called a steam curtain, which looked exactly like what it really was, and made the theatre smell like a laundry. By its aid The Rhine Gold was performed without a break instead of in three acts with long intervals between each.

One had to admit at Bayreuth that here was the utmost perfection of the pictorial stage, and that its machinery could go no further. Nevertheless, having seen it at its best, fresh from Wagner's own influence, I must also admit that my favorite way of enjoying a performance of The Ring is to sit at the back of a box, comfortable on two chairs, feet up, and listen without looking. The truth is, a man whose imagination cannot serve him better than the most costly devices of the imitative scenepainter, should not go to the theatre, and as a matter of fact does not. In planning his Bayreuth theatre, Wagner was elaborating what he had better have scrapped altogether.

But as this did not occur to him, he allowed his technical plan of The Ring to be so governed by pictorial visions that it is as unreasonable to ask Bayreuth to scrap the Wagner tradition as it would be to ask the Théâtre Français to scrap the Molière tradition.* Only, I must now treat that tradition as old-fashioned, whereas when this book was first published it was the latest development. What has happened since in England is that an Englishman, Mr Harley Granville-Barker, developing certain experiments made from time to time by Mr William Poel,* another Englishman, inaugurated twentieth century Shakespear by a series of performances in which the plays were given with unprecedented artistic splendor without the omission of a single decently presentable line, undivided into acts, without the old pictorial scenery, and with, as a result, a blessed revelation of Shakespear as the Prince of Entertainers instead of the most dreaded of bores, and a degree of illusion which the pictorial theatre had not only failed to attain, but had sedulously destroyed, nowhere more effectively than (save only in certain scenes of pure ritual in Parsifal) at Bayreuth.

Almost simultaneously with Mr Granville-Barker's revolutionary restoration of Shakespear, the pictorial stage triumphantly announced that at the English Bayreuth, which is the Shakespear Memorial Theatre at Stratford-on-Avon,* the play of Coriolanus* had been, by a climax of Procrustean adaptation, cut down to a performance lasting only one hour, in which state it was humbly hoped that the public would steel itself to bear it just once or twice for the sake of our national playwright. That was too much. Mr Bridges Adams,* who had started with Mr Granville-Barker, took the new method to Stratford, where the former victims of the pictorial stage now find to their amazement that three hours of unabbreviated Shakespear fly faster than one hour of Procrusty Coriolanus. And at the Old Vic. in London, where the reform was adopted by Mr Atkins,* Shakespear now draws better than would-be popular melodrama.

Thus have Englishmen left Wagner behind as to methods, and made obsolete all that part of this book which presents him as a pioneer. I must add that nobody who knows the snobbish contempt in which most Englishmen hold one another will be surprised when I mention that in England the exploits of Poel, Granville-Barker, Bridges Adams, Atkins, and the English designers and painters who have worked for

them, are modestly attributed to Herr Reinhardt,* their eminent
German contemporary. The only Englishman who is given any credit
by his countrymen is Mr Gordon Craig,* a fascinating propagandist
who still loves the stage picture better than the stage play, and, living in
the glamor of the Continent, seldom meddles with the actual theatre
except to wipe his boots on it and on all the art that grows on its boards.

As to the sociological aspect of The Ring, which is unaffected by the
rapid ageing of its technical aspect as a musical composition and a theatrical spectacle, it seems to challenge the so-called Great War to invalidate
it if it can. Gross as the catastrophe has been, it has not shaken Bayreuth.
But post-war contemplation of The Ring must not make us forget that all
the progress Wagner saw was from the revolutions of 1848, when he was
with the barricaders, to the Imperialist climax of 1871,* when he sang:

> Hail, hail, our Cæsar!
> Royal William!*
> Rock and ward of German freedom!

What would he have said had he lived to see 1917 in Russia and 1918 in
Germany, with England singing 'Hang, hang that Kaiser!' and Germany
sympathizing to such an extent that the grandson of Wagner's William
had to seek safety in Holland?* Rhine maidens walking out with British
Tommies, Senegalese negroes in Goethe's house, Marx enthroned in
Russia, pistolled Romanoffs, fugitive Hapsburgs, exiled Hohenzollerns
marking the ruins of empires* with no more chance of restoration than
the Stuarts and Bourbons:* such a Götterdämmerung,* in short, as in
its craziness can be fitted into no allegory until its upshot becomes
plainer than it now is: all this has so changed the political atmosphere
in which Wagner lived, and in which this book was written, that it says
much for the comprehensiveness of his grasp of things that his allegory
should still be valid and important. Indeed the war was more a great
tearing off of masks than a change of face: the main difference is that
Alberic is richer, and his slaves hungrier and harder worked when they
are so lucky as to have any work to do. The Ring ends with everybody
dead except three mermaids; and though the war went far enough in
that conclusive direction to suggest that the next war may possibly kill
even the mermaids with 'depth charges', the curtain is not yet down on
our drama, and we have to carry on as best we can. If we succeed, this
book may have to pass into yet another edition: if not, the world itself
will have to be re-edited.

AYOT ST LAWRENCE, 1922.

PREFACE TO THE THIRD EDITION

IN 1907 The Perfect Wagnerite was translated into German by my friend Siegfried Trebitsch.* On reading through his version in manuscript I was struck by the inadequacy of the merely negative explanation given by me of the irrelevance of Night Falls on The Gods (Die Götterdämmerung) to the general philosophic scheme of The Ring. That explanation was correct as far as it went; but, put as I had put it, it seemed to me to suggest that the operatic character of Night Falls on The Gods was the result of indifference or forgetfulness produced by the lapse of twenty-five years between the first projection of The Ring and its completion. Now it is clear that in whatever other ways Wagner may have changed, he never became careless and never became indifferent. I therefore inserted in the first German edition a new section in which I shewed how the revolutionary history of Western Europe from the Liberal explosion of 1848 to the confused attempt at a popular and *quasi* Socialist military and municipal administration by the Commune of Paris in 1871 (that is to say, from the literary beginning of The Niblung's Ring by Wagner to the long-delayed musical completion of Night Falls on The Gods) had demonstrated practically that the passing away of the present capitalistic order was going to be a much more complicated business than it appears in Wagner's dramatization.

Since 1907, then, the German edition has been more complete than the English one. I now, after six years' pure procrastination, for which I have no excuse except preoccupation with other work, add the German extension to the English text. It begins on page [p. 192], and ends on page [p. 198]. Otherwise the book remains as it was.

I have sometimes been asked why anyone should read a philosophic treatise merely to find out the story of The Ring. I take this opportunity to reply publicly that there is, as far as I know, no reason why anyone should take any trouble in the matter at all unless they want to, and that the degree of trouble must be determined by the degree of want, which, again, will be determined by the wanter's capacity. But this I will say. Even for the purposes of the idlest Bayreuth tourist the story of The Ring must be told as Wagner's score tells it if it is to be of any real use to the visitor who cannot understand what the singers are saying. Anyone can, without knowing a bar of the score, string the events narrated in The Ring together in the order of their occurrence on the stage, add the names of the *dramatis personae* and a description of the scenes, and offer the result as a guide to The Ring. But such a mechanical account of the affair will hinder more than it will help. It will pass over as trivial, or even omit altogether, points to which Wagner has given immense weight and consequence, either by the length or intensity of his direct musical treatment or by the recurrence of themes connected with them; and it will rhetorically emphasize or spread itself descriptively over the more obvious matters which speak for themselves to the spectator and occupy little space and less depth in the musical fabric. People primed with such accounts sit waiting to see the bear or the dragon or the rainbow, or the transformation of Alberic into a snake and a toad, or the magic fire or the swimming feats of the Rhine daughters, and are bored because these exciting spectacles are so unconscionably delayed whilst Wotan, Fricka, Brynhild, Erda, Alberic, and Loki discuss things of which the 'synopsis' gives no hint.

Now the story as it is told in this book has its centres of gravity placed exactly where Wagner has placed them in his score. What Wagner has made much of, I have made much of; and I have explained why he made much of it. What he passed lightly over, I have passed lightly over. There is a good deal in The Ring which is on the surface of the score: nobody with ears and eyes can miss its significance at the performance. But there is also a good deal that was at the back of Wagner's mind, and that determined what I have called the centres of gravity; and this, which is neither in the score nor in the stage action, being assumed by Wagner to be part of the common consciousness of mankind, is what I have chiefly attended to. For this, obvious as it was to Wagner, and as it is to anyone who has reflected on human history and destiny in the light of a competent knowledge of modern capitalistic civilization, is an absolute blank to many persons who are highly susceptible to the musical qualities of Wagner's music and poetry, but have never reflected on human destiny at all, and have been brought up in polite ignorance of the infernal depths our human society descended to in the nineteenth century. Clearly none of your synopses or popular guides or lists of musical themes would be of the slightest use here. That, I take it, is why this little book remains, after some fifteen years, still in demand, and why I have found it necessary to complete it in this edition by a chapter dealing neither with music nor poetry, but with European history. For it was in that massive material, and not in mere crotchets and quavers,* that Wagner found the stuff for his masterpiece.

AYOT ST LAWRENCE, 1913.   G.B.S.

THE preparation of a Second Edition of this booklet is quite the most unexpected literary task that has ever been set me. When it first appeared I was ungrateful enough to remonstrate with its publisher for printing, as I thought, more copies than the most sanguine Wagnerite could ever hope to sell. But the result proved that exactly one person buys a copy on every day in the year, including Sundays; and so, in the process of the suns, a reprint has become necessary.

Save a few verbal slips of no importance, I have found nothing to alter in this edition. As usual, the only protests the book has elicited are protests, not against the opinions it expresses, but against the facts it records. There are people who cannot bear to be told that their hero was associated with a famous Anarchist in a rebellion; that he was proclaimed as 'wanted' by the police; that he wrote revolutionary pamphlets; and that his picture of Niblunghome under the reign of Alberic is a poetic vision of unregulated industrial capitalism as it was made known in Germany in the middle of the nineteenth century by Engels's Condition of the Laboring Classes in England.* They frantically deny these facts, and then declare that I have connected them with Wagner in a paroxysm of senseless perversity. I am sorry I have hurt them; and I appeal to charitable publishers to bring out a new life of Wagner, which shall describe him as a court musician of unquestioned fashion and orthodoxy, and a pillar of the most exclusive Dresden circles.* Such a work would, I believe, have a large sale, and be read with satisfaction and reassurance by many lovers of Wagner's music.

As to my much demurred-to relegation of Night Falls on The Gods to the category of grand opera,* I have nothing to add or withdraw. Such a classification is to me as much a matter of fact as the Dresden rising or the police proclamation; but I shall not pretend that it is a matter of such fact as everybody's judgment can grapple with. People who prefer grand opera to serious music-drama* naturally resent my placing a very grand opera below a very serious music-drama. The ordinary lover of Shakespear would equally demur to my placing his popular catchpenny plays, of which As You Like It is an avowed type, below true Shakespearean plays like Measure for Measure.* I cannot help that. Popular dramas and operas may have overwhelming merits as enchanting make-believes; but a poet's sincerest vision of the world must always take precedence of his prettiest fool's paradise.

As many English Wagnerites seem to be still under the impression that Wagner composed Rienzi in his youth, Tannhäuser and Lohengrin in his middle age, and The Ring in his later years, may I again remind them that The Ring was the result of a political convulsion which occurred when Wagner was only thirty-six, and that the poem was completed when he was forty, with thirty more years of work before him? It is as much a first essay in political philosophy as Die Feen is a first essay in romantic opera.* The attempt to recover its spirit twenty years later, when the music of Night Falls on the Gods was added, was an attempt to revive the barricades of Dresden in the Temple of the Grail.* Only those who have never had any political enthusiasms to survive can believe that such an attempt could succeed.

LONDON, 1901.   G.B.S.

PREFACE TO THE FIRST EDITION

THIS book is a commentary on The Niblung's Ring, Richard Wagner's chief work. I offer it to those enthusiastic admirers of Wagner who are unable to follow his ideas, and do not in the least understand the dilemma of Wotan,* though they are filled with indignation at the irreverence of the Philistines who frankly avow that they find the remarks of the god too often tedious and nonsensical. Now to be devoted to Wagner merely as a dog is devoted to his master, sharing a few elementary ideas, appetites and emotions with him, and, for the rest, reverencing his superiority without understanding it, is no true Wagnerism. Yet nothing better is possible without a stock of ideas common to master and disciple. Unfortunately, the ideas of the revolutionary Wagner of 1848 are taught neither by the education nor the experience of English and American gentleman-amateurs, who are almost always political mugwumps,* and hardly ever associate with revolutionists. The earlier attempts to translate his numerous pamphlets and essays into English resulted in ludicrous mixtures of pure nonsense with the absurdest distortions of his ideas into the ideas of the translators. We now have a translation which is a masterpiece of interpretation and an eminent addition to our literature;* but that is not because its author, Mr Ashton Ellis, knows the German dictionary better than his predecessors. He is simply in possession of Wagner's ideas, which were to them inconceivable.

All I pretend to do in this book is to impart the ideas which are most likely to be lacking in the conventional Englishman's equipment. I came by them myself much as Wagner did, having learnt more about music than about anything else in my youth,* and sown my political wild oats subsequently in the revolutionary school. This combination is not common in England; and as I seem, so far, to be the only publicly articulate result of it, I venture to add my commentary to what has already been written by musicians who are no revolutionists, and revolutionists who are no musicians.

PITFOLD, HINDHEAD, 1898.   G.B.S.

THE PERFECT WAGNERITE

PRELIMINARY ENCOURAGEMENTS

A FEW of these will be welcome to the ordinary citizen visiting the theatre to satisfy his curiosity, or his desire to be in the fashion, by witnessing a representation of Richard Wagner's famous tetralogy: The Niblung's Ring.

First, The Ring, with all its gods and giants and dwarfs, its watermaidens and Valkyries, its wishing-cap, magic ring, enchanted sword, and miraculous treasure, is a drama of today, and not of a remote and fabulous antiquity. It could not have been written before the second half of the nineteenth century, because it deals with events which were only then consummating themselves. Unless the spectator recognizes in it an image of the life he is himself fighting his way through, it must needs appear to him a monstrous development of the Christmas pantomimes,* spun out here and there into intolerable lengths of dull conversation by the principal baritone. Fortunately, even from this point of view, The Ring is full of extraordinarily attractive episodes, both orchestral and dramatic. The nature music alone—music of river and rainbow, fire and forest—is enough to bribe people with any love of the country in them to endure the passages of political philosophy in the sure hope of a prettier page to come. Everybody, too, can enjoy the love music, the hammer and anvil music, the clumping of the giants, the tune of the young woodsman's horn, the trilling of the bird, the dragon music and nightmare music and thunder and lightning music, the profusion of simple melody, the sensuous charm of the orchestration: in short, the vast extent of common ground between The Ring and the ordinary music we use for play and pleasure. Hence it is that the four separate music-plays of which it is built have become popular throughout Europe as operas. We shall presently see that one of them, Night Falls on The Gods, actually is an opera.

It is generally understood, however, that there is an inner ring of superior persons to whom the whole work has a most urgent and searching philosophic and social significance. I profess to be such a superior person; and I write this pamphlet for the assistance of those who wish to be introduced to the work on equal terms with that inner circle of adepts.

My second encouragement is addressed to modest citizens who may suppose themselves to be disqualified from enjoying The Ring by their technical ignorance of music. They may dismiss all such misgivings speedily and confidently. If the sound of music has any power to move them, they will find that Wagner exacts nothing further. There is not a single bar of 'classical music' in The Ring—not a note in it that has any other point than the single direct point of giving musical expression to the drama.* In classical music there are, as the analytical programs tell us, first subjects and second subjects, free fantasias, recapitulations, and codas; there are fugues, with counter-subjects, strettos, and pedal points; there are passacaglias on ground basses, canons ad hypodia-pente,* and other ingenuities, which have, after all, stood or fallen by their prettiness as much as the simplest folk-tune. Wagner is never driving at anything of this sort any more than Shakespear in his plays is driving at such ingenuities of verse-making as sonnets, triolets,* and the like. And this is why he is so easy for the natural musician who has had no academic teaching. The professors, when Wagner's music is played to them, exclaim at once 'What is this? Is it aria, or recitative? Is there no cabaletta to it—not even a full close?* Why was that discord not prepared; and why does he not resolve it correctly? How dare he indulge in those scandalous and illicit transitions into a key that has not one note in common with the key he has just left? Listen to those false relations! What does he want with six drums and eight horns when Mozart worked miracles with two of each? The man is no musician.' The layman neither knows nor cares about any of these things. If Wagner were to turn aside from his straightforward dramatic purpose to propitiate the professors with correct exercises in sonata form, his music would at once become unintelligible to the unsophisticated spectator, upon whom the familiar and dreaded 'classical' sensation would descend like the influenza. Nothing of the kind need be dreaded. The unskilled, untaught musician may approach Wagner boldly; for there is no possibility of a misunderstanding between them: the Ring music is perfectly single and simple. It is the adept musician of the old school who has everything to unlearn; and him I leave, unpitied, to his fate.

THE NIBLUNG'S RING

THE Ring consists of four plays, intended to be performed on four successive evenings, entitled The Rhine Gold (a prologue to the other three), The Valkyrie, Siegfried, and Night Falls on The Gods; or, in the original German, Das Rheingold, Die Walküre, Siegfried, and Die Götterdämmerung.

THE RHINE GOLD

LET me assume for a moment that you are a young and good-looking woman. Try to imagine yourself in that character at Klondyke five years ago.* The place is teeming with gold. If you are content to leave the gold alone, as the wise leave flowers without plucking them, enjoying with perfect naïveté its color and glitter and preciousness, no human being will ever be the worse for your knowledge of it; and whilst you remain in that frame of mind the golden age will endure.

Now suppose a man comes along: a man who has no sense of the golden age, nor any power of living in the present: a man with common desires, cupidities, ambitions, just like most of the men you know. Suppose you reveal to that man the fact that if he will only pluck this gold up, and turn it into money, millions of men, driven by the invisible whip of hunger, will toil underground and overground night and day to pile up more and more gold for him until he is master of the world! You will find that the prospect will not tempt him so much as you might imagine, because it involves some distasteful trouble to himself to start with, and because there is something else within his reach involving no distasteful toil, which he desires more passionately; and that is yourself. So long as he is preoccupied with love of you, the gold, and all that it implies, will escape him: the golden age will endure. Not until he forswears love will he stretch out his hand to the gold, and found the Plutonic empire* for himself. But the choice between love and gold may not rest altogether with him. He may be an ugly, ungracious, unamiable person, whose affections may seem merely ludicrous and despicable to you. In that case, you may repulse him, and most bitterly humiliate and disappoint him. What is left to him then but to curse the love he can never win, and turn remorselessly to the gold? With that, he will make short work of your golden age, and leave you lamenting its lost thoughtlessness and sweetness.

In due time the gold of Klondyke will find its way to the great cities of the world. But the old dilemma will keep continually reproducing itself. The man who will turn his back on love, and upon all the fruitful, creative, life-pursuing activities into which the loftiest human energy can develop it, and will set himself single-heartedly to gather gold in an exultant dream of wielding its Plutonic powers, will find the treasure yielding quickly to his touch. But few men will make this sacrifice voluntarily. Not until the Plutonic power is so strongly set up that the higher human impulses are suppressed as rebellious, and even the mere appetites are denied, starved, and insulted when they cannot purchase their satisfaction with gold, are the energetic spirits driven to build their lives upon riches. How inevitable that course has become to us is plain enough to those who have the power of understanding what they see as they look at the plutocratic societies of our modern capitals.

First Scene

Here, then, is the subject of the first scene of The Rhine Gold. As you sit waiting for the curtain to rise, you suddenly catch the booming ground-tone of a mighty river. It becomes plainer, clearer: you get nearer to the surface, and catch the green light and the flights of bubbles. Then the curtain goes up and you see what you heard—the depths of the Rhine,* with three strange fairy fishes, half water-maidens, singing and enjoying themselves exuberantly. They are not singing barcarolles or ballads about the Lorely and her fated lovers,* but simply trolling any nonsense that comes into their heads in time to the dancing of the water and the rhythm of their swimming. It is the golden age; and the attraction of this spot for the Rhine maidens is a lump of the Rhine gold, which they value, in an entirely uncommercial way, for its bodily beauty and splendor. Just at present it is eclipsed, because the sun is not striking down through the water.

Presently there comes a poor devil of a dwarf stealing along the slippery rocks of the river bed, a creature with energy enough to make him strong of body and fierce of passion, but with a brutish narrowness of intelligence and selfishness of imagination: too stupid to see that his own welfare can only be compassed as part of the welfare of the world, too full of brute force not to grab vigorously at his own gain. Such dwarfs are quite common in London. He comes now with a fruitful impulse in him, in search of what he lacks in himself, beauty, lightness of heart, imagination, music. The Rhine maidens, representing all these to him, fill him with hope and longing; and he never considers that he has nothing to offer that they could possibly desire, being by natural limitation incapable of seeing anything from anyone else's point of view. With perfect simplicity, he offers himself as a sweetheart to them. But they are thoughtless, elemental, only half real things, much like modern young ladies. That the poor dwarf is repulsive to their sense of physical beauty and their romantic conception of heroism, that he is ugly and awkward, greedy and ridiculous, disposes for them of his claim to live and love. They mock him atrociously, pretending to fall in love with him at first sight, and then slipping away and making game of him, heaping ridicule and disgust on the poor wretch until he is beside himself with mortification and rage. They forget him when the water begins to glitter in the sun, and the gold to reflect its glory. They break into ecstatic worship of their treasure; and though they know the parable of Klondyke quite well, they have no fear that the gold will be wrenched away by the dwarf, since it will yield to no one who has not forsworn love for it, and it is in pursuit of love that he has come to them. They forget that they have poisoned that desire in him by their mockery and denial of it, and that he now knows that life will give him nothing that he cannot wrest from it by the Plutonic power. It is just as if some poor, rough, vulgar, coarse fellow were to offer to take his part in aristocratic society, and be snubbed into the knowledge that only as a millionaire could he ever hope to bring that society to his feet and buy himself a beautiful and refined wife. His choice is forced on him. He forswears love as thousands of us forswear it everyday; and in a moment the gold is in his grasp, and he disappears in the depths, leaving the water-fairies vainly screaming 'Stop thief!' whilst the river seems to plunge into darkness and sink from us as we rise to the cloud regions above.

And now, what forces are there in the world to resist Alberic, our dwarf, in his new character of sworn plutocrat? He is soon at work wielding the power of the gold. For his gain, hordes of his fellow-creatures are thenceforth condemned to slave miserably, overground and underground, lashed to their work by the invisible whip of starvation. They never see him, any more than the victims of our 'dangerous trades' ever see the shareholders whose power is nevertheless every-where, driving them to destruction. The very wealth they create with their labor becomes an additional force to impoverish them; for as fast as they make it it slips from their hands into the hands of their master, and makes him mightier than ever. You can see the process for yourself in every civilized country today, where millions of people toil in want and disease to heap up more wealth for our Alberics, laying up nothing for themselves, except sometimes horrible and agonizing disease and the certainty of premature death. All this part of the story is frightfully real, frightfully present, frightfully modern; and its effects on our social life are so ghastly and ruinous that we no longer know enough of happiness to be discomposed by it. It is only the poet, with his vision of what life might be, to whom these things are unendurable. If we were a race of poets we would make an end of them before the end of this miserable century. Being a race of moral dwarfs instead, we think them highly respectable, comfortable and proper, and allow them to breed and multiply their evil in all directions. If there were no higher power in the world to work against Alberic, the end of it would be utter destruction.

Such a force there is, however; and it is called Godhead.* The mysterious thing we call life organizes itself into all living shapes, bird, beast, beetle and fish, rising to the human marvel in cunning dwarfs and in laborious muscular giants, capable, these last, of enduring toil, willing to buy love and life, not with suicidal curses and renunciations, but with patient manual drudgery in the service of higher powers. And these higher powers are called into existence by the same self-organization of life still more wonderfully into rare persons who may by comparison be called gods, creatures capable of thought, whose aims extend far beyond the satisfaction of their bodily appetites and personal affections, since they perceive that it is only by the establishment of a social order founded on common bonds of moral faith that the world can rise from mere savagery. But how is this order to be set up by Godhead in a world of stupid giants, since these thoughtless ones pursue only their narrower personal ends and can by no means understand the aims of a god? Godhead, face to face with Stupidity, must compromise. Unable to enforce on the world the pure law of thought, it must resort to a mechanical law of commandments to be enforced by brute punishments and the destruction of the disobedient. And however carefully these laws are framed to represent the highest thoughts of the framers at the moment of their promulgation, before a day has elapsed that thought has grown and widened by the ceaseless evolution of life; and lo! yesterday's law already fallen out with today's thought. Yet if the high givers of that law themselves set the example of breaking it before it is a week old, they destroy all its authority with their subjects, and so break the weapon they have forged to rule them for their own good. They must therefore maintain at all costs the sanctity of the law, even when it has ceased to represent their thought; so that at last they get entangled in a network of ordinances which they no longer believe in, and yet have made so sacred by custom and so terrible by punishment, that they cannot themselves escape from them. Thus Godhead's resort to law finally costs it half its integrity—as if a spiritual king, to gain temporal power, had plucked out one of his eyes—and it finally begins secretly to long for the advent of some power higher than itself which will destroy its artificial empire of law, and establish a true republic of free thought.

This is by no means the only difficulty in the dominion of Law. The brute force for its execution must be purchased; and the mass of its subjects must be persuaded to respect the authority which employs this force. But how is such respect to be implanted in them if they are unable to comprehend the thought of the lawgiver? Clearly, only by associating the legislative power with such displays of splendor and majesty as will impress their senses and awe their imaginations. The god turned lawgiver, in short, must be crowned Pontiff and King. Since he cannot be known to the common folk as their superior in wisdom, he must be known to them as their superior in riches, as the dweller in castles, the wearer of gold and purple, the eater of mighty feasts, the commander of armies, and the wielder of powers of life and death, of salvation and damnation after death. Something may be done in this way without corruption whilst the golden age still endures. Your gods may not prevail with the dwarf's; but they may go to these honest giants who will give a day's work for a day's pay, and induce them to build for Godhead a mighty fortress, complete with hall and chapel, tower and bell, for the sake of the homesteads that will grow up in security round that church-castle. This only, however, whilst the golden age lasts. The moment the Plutonic power is let loose, and the loveless Alberic comes into the field with his corrupting millions, the gods are face to face with destruction; since Alberic, able with invisible hunger-whip to force the labor of the dwarfs and to buy the services of the giants, can outshine all the temporal shows and splendors of the golden age, and make himself master of the world, unless the gods, with their bigger brains, can capture his gold. This, the dilemma of the Church today, is the situation created by the exploit of Alberic in the depths of the Rhine.

Second Scene

From the bed of the river we rise into cloudy regions, and finally come out into the clear in a meadow, where Wotan, the god of gods, and his consort Fricka lie sleeping. Wotan, you will observe, has lost one eye;

and you will presently learn that he plucked it out voluntarily as the price to be paid for his alliance with Fricka, who in return has brought to him as her dowry all the powers of Law. The meadow is on the brink of a ravine, beyond which, towering on distant heights, stands Godhome, a mighty castle, newly built as a house of state for the one-eyed god and his all-ruling wife. Wotan has not yet seen this castle except in his dreams: two giants have just built it for him whilst he slept; and the reality is before him for the first time when Fricka wakes him. In that majestic burg he is to rule with her and through her over the humble giants, who have eyes to gape at the glorious castles their own hands have built from his design, but no brains to design castles for themselves, or to comprehend divinity. As a god, he is to be great, secure, and mighty; but he is also to be passionless, affectionless, wholly impartial; for Godhead, if it is to live with Law, must have no weaknesses, no respect for persons. All such sweet littlenesses must be left to the humble stupid giants to make their toil sweet to them; and the god must, after all, pay for Olympian power the same price the dwarf has paid for Plutonic power.

Wotan has forgotten this in his dreams of greatness. Not so Fricka. What she is thinking of is this price that Wotan has consented to pay, in token whereof he has promised this day to hand over to the giants Fricka's sister, the goddess Freia, with her golden love-apples. When Fricka reproaches Wotan with having selfishly forgotten this, she finds that he, like herself, is not prepared to go through with his bargain, and that he is trusting to another great world-force, the Lie (a European Power, as Lassalle said*), to help him to trick the giants out of their reward. But this force does not dwell in Wotan himself, but in another, a god over whom he has triumphed, one Loki, the god of Intellect, Argument, Imagination, Illusion, and Reason. Loki has promised to deliver him from his contract, and to cheat the giants for him; but he has not arrived to keep his word: indeed, as Fricka bitterly points out, why should not the Lie fail Wotan, since such failure is the very essence of him?

The giants come soon enough; and Freia flies to Wotan for protection against them. Their purposes are quite honest; and they have no doubt of the god's faith. There stands their part of the contract fulfilled, stone on stone, port and pinnacle all faithfully finished from Wotan's design by their mighty labor. They have come undoubtingly for their agreed wage. Then there happens what is to them an incredible, inconceivable thing. The god begins to shuffle. There are no moments in life more tragic than those in which the humble common man, the manual worker, leaving with implicit trust all high affairs to his betters, and reverencing them wholly as worthy of that trust, even to the extent of accepting as his rightful function the saving of them from all roughening and coarsening drudgeries, first discovers that they are corrupt, greedy, unjust and treacherous. The shock drives a ray of prophetic light into one giant's mind, and gives him a momentary eloquence. In that moment he rises above his stupid gianthood, and earnestly warns the Son of Light that all his power and eminence of priesthood, godhood, and kingship must stand or fall with the unbearable cold greatness of the incorruptible lawgiver. But Wotan, whose assumed character of lawgiver is altogether false to his real passionate nature, despises the rebuke; and the giant's ray of insight is lost in the murk of his virtuous indignation.

In the midst of the wrangle, Loki comes at last, excusing himself for being late on the ground that he has been detained by a matter of importance which he has promised to lay before Wotan. When pressed to give his mind to the business immediately in hand, and to extricate Wotan from his dilemma, he has nothing to say except that the giants are evidently altogether in the right. The castle has been duly built: he has tried every stone of it, and found the work first-rate: there is nothing to be done but pay the price agreed upon by handing over Freia to the giants. The gods are furious; and Wotan passionately declares that he only consented to the bargain on Loki's promise to find a way for him out of it. But Loki says no: he has promised to find a way out if any such way exist, but not to make a way if there is no way. He has wandered over the whole earth in search of some treasure great enough to buy Freia back from the giants; but in all the world he has found nothing for which Man will give up Woman. And this, by the way, reminds him of the matter he had promised to lay before Wotan. The Rhine maidens have complained to him of Alberic's theft of their gold; and he mentions it as a curious exception to his universal law of the unpurchasable preciousness of love, that this gold-robber has forsworn love for the sake of the fabulous riches of the Plutonic empire and the mastery of the world through its power.

No sooner is the tale told than the giants stoop lower than the dwarf. Alberic forswore love only when it was denied to him and made the instrument for cruelly murdering his self-respect. But the giants, with love within their reach, with Freia and her golden apples in their hands, offer to give her up for the treasure of Alberic. Observe, it is the treasure alone that they desire. They have no fierce dreams of dominion over their superiors, or of moulding the world to any conceptions of their own. They are neither clever nor ambitious: they simply covet money.

Alberic's gold: that is their demand, or else Freia, as agreed upon, whom they now carry off as hostage, leaving Wotan to consider their ultimatum.

Freia gone, the gods begin to wither and age: her golden apples, which they so lightly bargained away, they now find to be a matter of life and death to them; for not even the gods can live on Law and Godhead alone, be their castles ever so splendid. Loki alone is unaffected: the Lie, with all its cunning wonders, its glistenings and shiftings and mirages, is a mere appearance: it has no body and needs no food. What is Wotan to do? Loki sees the answer clearly enough: he must bluntly rob Alberic. There is nothing to prevent him except moral scruple; for Alberic, after all, is a poor, dim, dwarfed, credulous creature whom a god can outsee and a lie can outwit. Down, then, Wotan and Loki plunge into the mine where Alberic's slaves are piling up wealth for him under the invisible whip.

Third Scene

This glooomy place need not be a mine: it might just as well be a matchfactory, with yellow phosphorus, phossy jaw, a large dividend, and plenty of clergymen shareholders. Or it might be a whitelead factory, or a chemical works, or a pottery, or a railway shunting yard, or a tailoring shop, or a little gin-sodden laundry, or a bakehouse, or a big shop, or any other of the places where human life and welfare are daily sacrificed in order that some greedy foolish creature may be able to hymn exultantly to his Plutonic idol:

> Thou mak'st me eat whilst others starve,
> And sing while others do lament:
> Such unto me Thy blessings are,
> As if I were Thine only care.*

In the mine, which resounds with the clinking anvils of the dwarfs toiling miserably to heap up treasure for their master. Alberic has set his brother Mime—more familiarly, Mimmy—to make him a helmet. Mimmy dimly sees that there is some magic in this helmet, and tries to keep it; but Alberic wrests it from him, and shews him, to his cost, that it is the veil of the invisible whip, and that he who wears it can appear in what shape he will, or disappear from view altogether. This helmet is a very common article in our streets, where it generally takes the form of a tall hat. It makes a man invisible as a shareholder, and changes him into various shapes, such as a pious Christian, a subscriber to hospitals, a benefactor of the poor, a model husband and father, a shrewd, practical, independent Englishman, and what not, when he is really a pitiful parasite on the commonwealth, consuming a great deal, and producing nothing, feeling nothing, knowing nothing, believing nothing, and doing nothing except what all the rest do, and that only because he is afraid not to do it, or at least pretend to do it.

When Wotan and Loki arrive, Loki claims Alberic as an old acquaintance. But the dwarf has no faith in these civil strangers: Greed instinctively mistrusts Intellect, even in the garb of Poetry and the company of Godhead, whilst envying the brilliancy of the one and the dignity of the other. Alberic breaks out at them with a terrible boast of the power now within his grasp. He paints for them the world as it will be when his dominion over it is complete, when the soft airs and green mosses of its valleys shall be changed into smoke, slag, and filth; when slavery, disease, and squalor, soothed by drunkenness and mastered by the policeman's baton, shall become the foundation of society; and when nothing shall escape ruin except such pretty places and pretty women as he may like to buy for the slaking of his own lusts. In that kingdom of evil he sees that there will be no power but his own. These gods, with their moralities and legalities and intellectual subtlety, will go under and be starved out of existence. He bids Wotan and Loki beware of it; and his 'Hab' Acht!'* is hoarse, horrible, and sinister. Wotan is revolted to the very depths of his being: he cannot stifle the execration that bursts from him. But Loki is unaffected: he has no moral passion: indignation is as absurd to him as enthusiasm. He finds it exquisitely amusing—having a touch of the comic spirit in him—that the dwarf, in stirring up the moral fervor of Wotan, has removed his last moral scruple about becoming a thief. Wotan will now rob the dwarf without remorse; for is it not positively his highest duty to take this power out of such evil hands and use it himself in the interests of Godhead? On the loftiest moral grounds, he lets Loki do his worst.

A little cunningly disguised flattery makes short work of Alberic. Loki pretends to be afraid of him; and he swallows that bait unhesitatingly. But how, inquires Loki, is he to guard against the hatred of his million slaves? Will they not steal from him, whilst he sleeps, the magic ring, the symbol of his power, which he has forged from the gold of the Rhine? 'You think yourself very clever', sneers Alberic, and then begins to boast of the enchantments of the magic helmet. Loki refuses to believe in such marvels without witnessing them. Alberic, only too glad to shew off his powers, puts on the helmet and transforms himself into a monstrous serpent. Loki gratifies him by pretending to be frightened out of his wits, but ventures to remark that it would be better still if the helmet could transform its owner into some tiny creature that could hide and spy in the smallest cranny. Alberic promptly transforms himself into a toad. In an instant Wotan's foot is on him; Loki tears away the helmet; they pinion him, and drag him away a prisoner up through the earth to the meadow by the castle.

Fourth Scene

There, to pay for his freedom, he has to summon his slaves from the depths to place all the treasure they have heaped up for him at the feet of Wotan. Then he demands his liberty; but Wotan must have the ring as well. And here the dwarf, like the giant before him, feels the very foundations of the world shake beneath him at the discovery of his own base cupidity in a higher power. That evil should, in its loveless desperation, create malign powers which Godhead could not create, seems but natural justice to him. But that Godhead should steal those malign powers from evil, and wield them itself, is a monstrous perversion; and his appeal to Wotan to forego it is almost terrible in its conviction of wrong. It is of no avail. Wotan falls back again on virtuous indignation. He reminds Alberic that he stole the gold from the Rhine daughters, and takes the attitude of the just judge compelling a restitution of stolen goods. Alberic, knowing perfectly well that the judge is taking the goods to put them in his own pocket, has the ring torn from his finger, and is once more as poor as he was when he came slipping and stumbling among the slimy rocks in the bed of the Rhine.

This is the way of the world. In older times, when the Christian laborer was drained dry by the knightly spendthrift, and the spendthrift was drained by the Jewish usurer, Church and State, religion and law, seized on the Jew and drained him as a Christian duty.* When the forces of lovelessness and greed had built up our own sordid capitalist systems, driven by invisible proprietorship, robbing the poor, defacing the earth, and forcing themselves as a universal curse even on the generous and humane, then religion and law and intellect, which would never themselves have discovered such systems, their natural bent being towards welfare, economy, and life instead of towards corruption, waste, and death, nevertheless did not scruple to seize by fraud and force these powers of evil on pretence of using them for good. And it inevitably happens that when the Church, the Law, and all the Talents have made common cause to rob the people, the Church is far more vitally harmed by that unfaithfulness to itself than its more mechanical confederates; so that finally they turn on their discredited ally and rob the Church, with the cheerful co-operation of Loki, as in France and Italy for instance.*

The twin giants come back with their hostage, in whose presence Godhead blooms again. The gold is ready for them; but now that the moment has come for parting with Freia the gold does not seem so tempting; and they are sorely loth to let her go. Not unless there is gold enough to utterly hide her from them—not until the heap has grown so that they can see nothing but gold—until money has come between them and every human feeling, will they part with her. There is not gold enough to accomplish this: however cunningly Loki spreads it, the glint of Freia's hair is still visible to Giant Fafnir, and the magic helmet must go on the heap to shut it out. Even then Fafnir's brother, Fasolt, can catch a beam from her eye through a chink, and is rendered incapable thereby of forswearing her. There is nothing to stop that chink but the ring; and Wotan is as greedily bent on keeping that as Alberic himself was; nor can the other gods persuade him that Freia is worth it, since for the highest god, love is not the highest good, but only the universal delight that bribes all living things to travail with renewed life. Life itself, with its accomplished marvels and its infinite potentialities, is the only force that Godhead can worship. Wotan does not yield until he is reached by the voice of the fruitful earth, that before he or the dwarfs or the giants or the Law or the Lie or any of these things were, had the seed of them all in her bosom, and the seed perhaps of something higher even than himself, that shall one day supersede him and cut the tangles and alliances and compromises that already have cost him one of his eyes. When Erda, the First Mother of life, rises from her sleeping-place in the heart of the earth, and warns him to yield the ring, he obeys her; the ring is added to the heap of gold; and all sense of Freia is cut off from the giants.

But now what Law is left to these two poor stupid laborers whereby one shall yield to the other any of the treasure for which they have each paid the whole price in surrendering Freia? They look by mere habit to the god to judge for them; but he, with his heart stirring towards higher forces than himself, turns with disgust from these lower forces. They settle it as two wolves might; and Fafnir batters his brother dead with his staff. It is a horrible thing to see and hear, to anyone who knows how much blood has been shed in the world in just that way by its brutalized toilers, honest fellows enough until their betters betrayed them. Fafnir goes off with his booty. It is quite useless to him. He has neither the cunning nor the ambition to establish the Plutonic empire with it.

Merely to prevent others from getting it is the only purpose it brings him. He piles it in a cave; transforms himself into a dragon by the helmet; and devotes his life to guarding it, as much a slave to it as a jailor is to his prisoner. He had much better have thrown it all back into the Rhine and transformed himself into the shortest-lived animal that enjoys at least a brief run in the sunshine. His case, however, is far too common to be surprising. The world is overstocked with persons who sacrifice all their affections, and madly trample and batter down their fellows to obtain riches of which, when they get them, they are unable to make the smallest use, and to which they become the most miserable slaves.

The gods soon forget Fafnir in their rejoicing over Freia. Donner, the Thunder god, springs to a rocky summit and calls the clouds as a shepherd calls his flocks. They come at his summons; and he and the castle are hidden by their black legions. Froh, the Rainbow god, hastens to his side. At the stroke of Donner's hammer the black murk is riven in all directions by darting ribbons of lightning; and as the air clears, the castle is seen in its fullest splendor, accessible now by the rainbow bridge which Froh has cast across the ravine. In the glory of this moment Wotan has a great thought. With all his aspirations to establish a reign of noble thought, of righteousness, order, and justice, he has found that day that there is no race yet in the world that quite spontaneously, naturally, and unconsciously realizes his ideal. He himself has found how far short Godhead falls of the thing it conceives. He, the greatest of gods, has been unable to control his fate: he has been forced against his will to choose between evils, to make disgraceful bargains, to break them still more disgracefully, and even then to see the price of his disgrace slip through his fingers. His consort has cost him half his vision; his castle has cost him his affections; and the attempt to retain both has cost him his honor. On every side he is shackled and bound, dependent on the laws of Fricka and on the lies of Loki, forced to traffic with dwarfs for handicraft and with giants for strength, and to pay them both in false coin. After all, a god is a pitiful thing. But the fertility of the First Mother is not yet exhausted. The life that came from her has ever climbed up to a higher and higher organization. From toad and serpent to dwarf, from bear and elephant to giant, from dwarf and giant to a god with thoughts, with comprehension of the world, with ideals. Why should it stop there? Why should it not rise from the god to the Hero? to the creature in whom the god's unavailing thought shall have become effective will and life, who shall make his way straight to truth and reality over the laws of Fricka and the lies of Loki with a strength that overcomes giants and a cunning that outwits dwarfs? Yes: Erda, the First Mother, must travail again, and breed him a race of heroes to deliver the world and himself from his limited powers and disgraceful bargains. This is the vision that flashes on him as he turns to the rainbow bridge and calls his wife to come and dwell with him in Valhalla, the home of the gods.

They are all overcome with Valhalla's glory except Loki. He is behind the scenes of this joint reign of the Divine and the Legal. He despises these gods with their ideals and their golden apples. 'I am ashamed,' he says, 'to have dealings with these futile creatures.' And so he follows them to the rainbow bridge. But as they set foot on it, from the river below rises the wailing of the Rhine daughters for their lost gold. 'You down there in the water,' cries Loki with brutal irony: 'you used to bask in the glitter of your gold: henceforth you shall bask in the splendor of the gods.' And they reply that the truth is in the depths and the darkness, and that what blazes on high there is falsehood. And with that the gods pass into their glorious stronghold.

Wagner as Revolutionist

Before leaving this explanation of The Rhine Gold, I must have a word or two about it with the reader.

It is the least popular of the sections of The Ring. The reason is that its dramatic moments lie quite outside the consciousness of people whose joys and sorrows are all domestic and personal, and whose religions and political ideas are purely conventional and superstitious. To them it is a struggle between half a dozen fairytale personages for a ring, involving hours of scolding and cheating, and one long scene in a dark, gruesome mine, with gloomy, ugly music, and not a glimpse of a handsome young man or pretty woman. Only those of wider consciousness can follow it breathlessly, seeing in it the whole tragedy of human history and the whole horror of the dilemmas from which the world is shrinking today. At Bayreuth I have seen a party of English tourists, after enduring agonies of boredom from Alberic, rise in the middle of the third scene, and almost force their way out of the dark theatre into the sunlit pinewood without. And I have seen people who were deeply affected by the scene driven almost beside themselves by this disturbance. But it was a very natural thing for the unfortunate tourists to do, since in this Rhine Gold prologue there is no interval between the acts for escape. Roughly speaking, people who have no general ideas, no touch of the concern of the philosopher and statesman for the race, cannot enjoy The Rhine Gold as a drama. They may find compensations in some exceedingly pretty music, at times even grand and glorious, which will enable them to escape occasionally from the struggle between Alberic and Wotan; but if their capacity for music should be as limited as their comprehension of the world, they had better stay away.

And now, attentive Reader, we have reached the point at which some foolish person is sure to interrupt us by declaring that The Rhine Gold is what they call 'a work of art' pure and simple, and that Wagner never dreamt of shareholders, tall hats, whitelead factories, and industrial and political questions looked at from the socialistic and humanitarian points of view. We need not discuss these impertinences: it is easier to silence them with the facts of Wagner's life. In 1843 he obtained the position of conductor of the Opera at Dresden at a salary of £225 a year, with a pension. This was a first-rate permanent appointment in the service of the Saxon State, carrying an assured professional position and livelihood with it. In 1848, the year of revolutions, the discontented middle class, unable to rouse the Church-and-State governments of the day from their bondage to custom, caste, and law by appeals to morality or constitutional agitation for Liberal reforms, made common cause with the starving wage-working class, and resorted to armed rebellion, which reached Dresden in 1849. Had Wagner been the mere musical epicure and political mugwump that the term 'artist' seems to suggest to so many critics and amateurs—that is, a creature in their own lazy likeness—he need have taken no more part in the political struggles of his day than Bishop took in the English Reform agitation of 1832, or Sterndale Bennett in the Chartist or Free Trade movements.* What he did do was first to make a desperate appeal to the King to cast off his bonds and answer the need of the time by taking true kingship on himself and leading his people to the redress of their intolerable wrongs (fancy the poor monarch's feelings!), and then, when the crash came, to take his side with the right and the poor against the rich and the wrong. When the insurrection was defeated, three leaders of it were especially marked down for vengeance: August Roeckel,* an old friend of Wagner's to whom he wrote a well-known series of letters; Michael Bakoonin, afterwards a famous apostle of revolutionary Anarchism;* and Wagner himself. Wagner escaped to Switzerland: Roeckel and Bakoonin suffered long terms of imprisonment. Wagner was of course utterly ruined, pecuniarily and socially (to his own intense relief and satisfaction); and his exile lasted twelve years. His first idea was to get his Tannhäuser produced in Paris. With the notion of explaining himself to the Parisians he wrote a pamphlet entitled Art and Revolution, a glance through which will shew how thoroughly the socialistic side of the revolution had his sympathy, and how completely he had got free from the influence of the established Churches of his day. For three years he kept pouring forth pamphlets—some of them elaborate treatises in size and intellectual rank, but still essentially the pamphlets and manifestoes of a born agitator—on social evolution, religion, life, art, and the influence of riches. In 1853 the poem of The Ring was privately printed; and in 1854, five years after the Dresden insurrection, The Rhine Gold score was completed to the last drum tap.

These facts are on official record in Germany, where the proclamation summing up Wagner as 'a politically dangerous person' may be consulted to this day. The pamphlets are now accessible to English readers in the translation of Mr Ashton Ellis. This being so, any person who, having perhaps heard that I am a Socialist, attempts to persuade you that my interpretation of The Rhine Gold is only 'my socialism' read into the works of a dilettantist who borrowed an idle tale from an old saga to make an opera book with, may safely be dismissed from your consideration as an ignoramus.

If you are now satisfied that The Rhine Gold is an allegory, do not forget that an allegory is never quite consistent except when it is written by someone without dramatic faculty, in which case it is unreadable. There is only one way of dramatizing an idea; and that is by putting on the stage a human being possessed by that idea, yet none the less a human being with all the human impulses which make him akin and therefore interesting to us. Bunyan, in his Pilgrim's Progress, does not, like his unread imitators, attempt to personify Christianity and Valour: he dramatizes for you the life of the Christian and the Valiant Man. Just so, though I have shewn that Wotan is Godhead and Kingship, and Loki Logic and Imagination without living Will (Brain without Heart, to put it vulgarly); yet in the drama Wotan is a religiously moral man, and Loki a witty, ingenious, imaginative and cynical one. As to Fricka, who stands for State Law, she does not assume her allegorical character in The Rhine Gold at all, but is simply Wotan's wife and Freia's sister: nay, she contradicts her allegorical self by conniving at all Wotan's rogueries. That, of course, is just what State Law would do; but we must not save the credit of the allegory by a quip. Not until she reappears in the next play (The Valkyries) does her function in the allegorical scheme become plain.

One preconception will bewilder the spectator hopelessly unless he has been warned against it or is naturally free from it. In the old-fashioned orders of creation, the supernatural personages are invariably conceived as greater than man, for good or evil. In the modern humanitarian order as adopted by Wagner, Man is the highest. In The Rhine Gold, it is pretended that there are as yet no men on the earth. There are dwarfs, giants, and gods. The danger is that you will jump to the conclusion that the gods, at least, are a higher order than the human order. On the contrary, the world is waiting for Man to redeem it from the lame and cramped government of the gods. Once grasp that, and the allegory becomes simple enough. Really, of course, the dwarfs, giants, and gods are dramatizations of the three main orders of men: to wit, the instinctive, predatory, lustful, greedy people; the patient, toiling, stupid, respectful, money-worshipping people; and the intellectual, moral, talented people who devise and administer States and Churches. History shews us only one order higher than the highest of these: namely, the order of Heroes.

Now it is quite clear—though you have perhaps never thought of it—that if the next generation of Englishmen consisted wholly of Julius Cæsars, all our political, ecclesiastical, and moral institutions would vanish, and the less perishable of their appurtenances be classed with Stonehenge and the cromlechs and round towers* as inexplicable relics of a bygone social order. Julius Cæsars would no more trouble themselves about such contrivances as our codes and churches than a Fellow of the Royal Society* will touch his hat to the squire and listen to the village curate's sermons. This is precisely what must happen some day if life continues thrusting towards higher and higher organization as it has hitherto done.* As most of our English professional men are to Australian bushmen, so, we must suppose, will the average man of some future day be to Julius Cæsar. Let any man of middle age, pondering this prospect, consider what has happened within a single generation to the articles of faith his father regarded as eternal, nay, to the very scepticisms and blasphemies of his youth (Bishop Colenso's criticism of the Pentateuch,* for example!); and he will begin to realize how much of our barbarous Theology and Law the man of the future will do without. Bakoonin, the Dresden revolutionary leader with whom Wagner went out in 1849, put forward later on a program, often quoted with foolish horror, for the abolition of all institutions, religious, political, juridical, financial, legal, academic, and so on, so as to leave the will of man free to find its own way.* All the loftiest spirits of that time were burning to raise Man up, to give him self-respect, to shake him out of his habit of grovelling before the ideals created by his own imagination, of attributing the good that sprang from the ceaseless energy of the life within himself to some superior power in the clouds, and of making a fetish of self-sacrifice to justify his own cowardice.

Farther on in The Ring we shall see the Hero arrive and make an end of dwarfs, giants, and gods. Meanwhile, let us not forget that godhood means to Wagner infirmity and compromise, and manhood strength and integrity. Above all, we must understand—for it is the key to much that we are to see—that the god, since his desire is toward a higher and fuller life, must long in his inmost soul for the advent of that greater power whose first work, though this he does not see as yet, must be his own undoing.

In the midst of all these far-reaching ideas, it is amusing to find Wagner still full of his ingrained theatrical professionalism, and introducing effects which now seem old-fashioned and stagey with as much energy and earnestness as if they were his loftiest inspirations. When Wotan wrests the ring from Alberic, the dwarf delivers a lurid and blood-curdling stage curse, calling down on its every future possessor care, fear, and death. The musical phrase accompanying this outburst was a veritable harmonic and melodic bogey to mid-century ears, though time has now robbed it of its terrors. It sounds again when Fafnir slays Fasolt, and on every subsequent occasion when the ring brings death to its holder. This episode must justify itself purely as a piece of stage sensationalism. On deeper ground it is superfluous and confusing, as the ruin to which the pursuit of riches leads needs no curse to explain it; nor is there any sense in investing Alberic with providential powers in the matter.

THE VALKYRIE

BEFORE the curtain rises on the Valkyrie, let us see what has happened since it fell on The Rhine Gold. The persons of the drama will tell us presently; but as we probably do not understand German, that may not help us.

Wotan is still ruling the world in glory from his giant-built castle with his wife Fricka. But he has no security for the continuance of his reign, since Alberic may at any moment contrive to recover the ring, the full power of which he can wield because he has forsworn love. Such forswearing is not possible to Wotan: love, though not his highest need, is a higher than gold: otherwise he would be no god. Besides, as we have seen, his power has been established in the world by and as a system of laws enforced by penalties. These he must consent to be bound by himself; for a god who broke his own laws would betray the fact that legality and conformity are not the highest rule of conduct—a discovery fatal to his supremacy as Pontiff and Lawgiver. Hence he may not wrest the ring unlawfully from Fafnir, even if he could bring himself to forswear love.

In this insecurity he has hit on the idea of forming a heroic body-guard. He has trained his love children as war-maidens (Valkyries) whose duty it is to sweep through battle-fields and bear away to Valhalla the souls of the bravest who fall there. Thus reinforced by a host of warriors, he has thoroughly indoctrinated them, Loki helping him as dialectician-in-chief, with the conventional system of law and duty, supernatural religion and self-sacrificing idealism, which they believe to be the essence of his godhood, but which is really only the machinery of the love of necessary power which is his mortal weakness. This process secures their fanatical devotion to his system of government; but he knows perfectly well that such systems, in spite of their moral pretensions, serve selfish and ambitious tyrants better than benevolent despots, and that, if once Alberic gets the ring back, he will easily out-Valhalla Valhalla, if not buy it over as a going concern. The only chance of permanent security, then, is the appearance in the world of a hero who, without any illicit prompting from Wotan, will destroy Alberic and wrest the ring from Fafnir. There will then, he believes, be no further cause for anxiety, since he does not yet conceive Heroism as a force hostile to Godhead. In his longing for a rescuer, it does not occur to him that when the Hero comes, his first exploit must be to sweep the gods and their ordinances from the path of the heroic will.

Indeed, he feels that in his own Godhead is the germ of such Heroism, and that from himself the Hero must spring. He takes to wandering, mostly in search of love, from Fricka and Valhalla. He seeks the First Mother; and through her womb, eternally fertile, the inner true thought that made him first a god is reborn as his daughter, uncorrupted by his ambition, unfettered by his machinery of powder and his alliances with Fricka and Loki. This daughter, the Valkyrie Brynhild, is his true will, his real self (as he thinks): to her he may say what he must not say to anyone, since in speaking to her he but speaks to himself. 'Was keinem in Worten ich künde' he says to her 'unausgesprochen bleib es ewig: mit mir nur rath' ich, red' ich zu dir.'*

But from Brynhild no hero can spring until there is a man of Wotan's race to breed with her. Wotan wanders further; and a mortal woman bears him twins: a son and a daughter. He separates them by letting the girl fall into the hands of a forest tribe which in due time gives her as wife to a fierce chief, one Hunding. With the son he himself leads the life of a wolf, and teaches him the only power a god can teach, the power of doing without happiness. When he has given him this terrible training, he abandons him, and goes to the bridal feast of his daughter Sieglinda and Hunding. In the blue cloak of the wanderer, wearing the broad hat that flaps over the socket of his forfeited eye, he appears in Hunding's house, the middle pillar of which is a mighty tree. Into that tree, without a word, he strikes a sword up to the hilt, so that only the might of a hero can withdraw it. Then he goes out as silently as he came, blind to the truth that no weapon from the armory of Godhead can serve the turn of the true Human Hero. Neither Hunding nor any of his guests can move the sword; and there it stays awaiting the destined hand. That is the history of the generations between The Rhine Gold and The Valkyries.

The First Act

This time, as we sit looking expectantly at the curtain, we hear, not the deep booming of the Rhine, but the patter of a forest downpour, accompanied by the mutter of a storm which soon gathers into a roar and culminates in crashing thunderbolts. As it passes off, the curtain rises; and there is no mistaking whose forest habitation we are in; for the central pillar is a mighty tree, and the place fit for the dwelling of a fierce chief. The door opens; and an exhausted man reels in: an adept from the school of unhappiness. Sieglinda finds him lying on the hearth. He explains that he has been in a fight; that his weapons, not being as strong as his arms, were broken; and that he had to fly. He desires some drink and a moment's rest; then he will go; for he is an unlucky person, and does not want to bring his ill-luck on the woman who is succoring him. But she, it appears, is also unhappy; and a strong sympathy springs up between them. When her husband arrives, he observes not only this sympathy, but a resemblance between them, a gleam of the snake in their eyes. They sit down to table; and the stranger tells them his unlucky story. He is the son of Wotan, who is known to him only as Wolfing, of the race of the Volsungs. The earliest thing he remembers is returning from a hunt with his father to find their home destroyed, his mother murdered, and his twin-sister carried off. This was the work of a tribe called the Neidings, upon whom he and Wolfing thenceforth waged implacable war until the day when his father disappeared, leaving no trace of himself but an empty wolfskin. The young Volsung was thus cast alone upon the world, finding most hands against him, and bringing no good luck even to his friends. His latest exploit has been the slaying of certain brothers who were forcing their sister to wed against her will. The result has been the slaughter of the woman by her brothers' clansmen, and his own narrow escape by flight.

His luck on this occasion is even worse than he supposes; for Hunding, by whose hearth he has taken refuge, is clansman to the slain brothers and is bound to avenge them. He tells the Volsung that in the morning, weapons or no weapons, he must fight for his life. Then he orders the woman to bed, and follows her himself, taking his spear with him.

The unlucky stranger, left brooding by the hearth, has nothing to console himself with but an old promise of his father's that he shall find a weapon to his hand when he most needs one. The last flicker of the dying fire strikes on the golden hilt of the sword that sticks in the tree; but he does not see it; and the embers sink into blackness. Then the woman returns. Hunding is safely asleep: she has drugged him. She tells the story of the one-eyed man who appeared at her forced marriage, and of the sword. She has always felt, she says, that her miseries will end in the arms of the hero who shall succeed in drawing it forth. The stranger, diffident as he is about his luck, has no misgivings as to his strength and destiny. He gives her his affection at once, and abandons himself to the charm of the night and the season; for it is the beginning of Spring. They soon learn from their confidences that she is his stolen twin-sister. He is transported to find that the heroic race of the Volsungs need neither perish nor be corrupted by a lower strain. Hailing the sword by the name of Nothung (or Needed), he plucks it from the tree as her bride-gift, and then, crying 'Both bride and sister

be of thy brother; and blossom the blood of the Volsungs!' clasps her as
the mate the Spring has brought him.

The Second Act

So far, Wotan's plan seems prospering. In the mountains he calls his
war-maiden Brynhild, the child borne to him by the First Mother, and
bids her see to it that Hunding shall fall in the approaching combat.
But he is reckoning without his consort, Fricka. What will she, the Law,
say to the lawless pair who have heaped incest on adultery? A hero may
have defied the law, and put his own will in its place; but can a god hold
him guiltless, when the whole power of the gods can enforce itself only
by law? Fricka, shuddering with horror, outraged in every instinct,
comes clamoring for punishment. Wotan pleads the general necessity of
encouraging heroism in order to keep up the Valhalla bodyguard; but his
remonstrances only bring upon him torrents of reproaches for his own
unfaithfulness to the law in roaming through the world and begetting
war-maidens, 'wolf-cubs,' and the like. He is hopelessly beaten in the
argument. Fricka is absolutely right when she declares that the ending of
the gods began when he brought this wolf-hero into the world; and now,
to save their very existence, she pitilessly demands his destruction.
Wotan has no power to refuse: it is Fricka's mechanical force, and not his
thought, that really rules the world. He has to recall Brynhild; take back
his former instructions; and ordain that Hunding shall slay the Volsung.

But now comes another difficulty. Brynhild is the inner thought and
will of Godhead, the aspiration from the high life to the higher that is
its divine element, and only becomes separated from it when its resort
to kingship and priestcraft for the sake of temporal power has made it
false to itself. Hitherto, Brynhild, as Valkyrie or hero chooser, has
obeyed Wotan implicitly, taking her work as the holiest and bravest in
his kingdom; and now he tells her what he could not tell Fricka—what
indeed he could not tell to Brynhild, were she not, as she says, his own
will—the whole story of Alberic and of that inspiration about the raising up of a hero. She thoroughly approves of the inspiration; but when
the story ends in the assumption that she too must obey Fricka, and
help Fricka's vassal, Hunding, to undo the great work and strike the
hero down, she for the first time hesitates to accept his command. In his
fury and despair he overawes her by the most terrible threats of his
anger; and she submits.

Then comes the Volsung Siegmund, following his sister bride, who
has fled into the mountains in a revulsion of horror at having allowed

herself to bring her hero to shame. Whilst she is lying exhausted and senseless in his arms, Brynhild appears to him and solemnly warns him that he must presently leave the earth with her. He asks whither he must follow her. To Valhalla, to take his place there among the heroes. He asks, shall he find his father there? Yes. Shall he find a wife there? Yes: he will be waited on by beautiful wish-maidens. Shall he meet his sister there? No. Then, says Siegmund, I will not come with you. She tries to make him understand that he cannot help himself. Being a hero, he will not be so persuaded: he has his father's sword, and does not fear Hunding. But when she tells him that she comes from his father, and that the sword of a god will not avail in the hands of a hero, he accepts his fate, but will shape it with his own hand, both for himself and his sister, by slaying her, and then killing himself with the last stroke of the sword. And thereafter he will go to Hell, rather than to Valhalla.

How now can Brynhild, being what she is, choose her side freely in a conflict between this hero and the vassal of Fricka? By instinct she at once throws Wotan's command to the winds, and bids Siegmund nerve himself for the combat with Hunding, in which she pledges him the protection of her shield. The horn of Hunding is soon heard; and Siegmund's spirits rise to fighting pitch at once. The two meet; and the Valkyrie's shield is held before the hero. But when he delivers his sword-stroke at his foe, the weapon shivers on the spear of Wotan, who suddenly appears between them and the first of the race of heroes falls with the weapon of the Law's vassal through his breast. Brynhild snatches the fragments of the broken sword, and flies, carrying off the woman with her on her war-horse; and Wotan, in terrible wrath, slays Hunding with a wave of his hand, and starts in pursuit of his disobedient daughter.

The Third Act

On a rocky peak, four of the Valkyries are waiting for the rest. The absent ones soon arrive, galloping through the air with slain heroes, gathered from the battle-field, hanging over their saddles. Only, Brynhild, who comes last, has for her spoil a live woman. When her eight sisters learn that she has defied Wotan, they dare not help her; and Brynhild has to rouse Sieglinda to make an effort to save herself, by reminding her that she bears in her the seed of a hero, and must face everything, endure anything, sooner than let that seed miscarry. Sieglinda, in a transport of exaltation, takes the fragments of the sword and flies into the forest. Then Wotan comes; the sisters fly in terror at his command; and he is left alone with Brynhild.

Here, then, we have the first of the inevitable moments which Wotan did not foresee. Godhead has now established its dominion over the world by a mighty Church, compelling obedience through its ally the Law, with its formidable State organization of force of arms and cunning of brain. It has submitted to this alliance to keep the Plutonic power in check—built it up primarily for the sake of that soul in itself which cares only to make the highest better and the best higher; and now here is that very soul separated from it and working for the destruction of its indispensable ally, the lawgiving State. How is the rebel to be disarmed? Slain it cannot be by Godhead, since it is still Godhead's own very dearest soul. But hidden, stifled, silenced it must be; or it will wreck the State and leave the Church defenceless. Not until it passes completely away from Godhead, and is reborn as the soul of the hero, can it work anything but the confusion and destruction of the existing order. How is the world to be protected against it in the meantime? Clearly Loki's help is needed here: it is the Lie that must, on the highest principles, hide the Truth. Let Loki surround this mountain top with the appearance of a consuming fire; and who will dare penetrate to Brynhild? It is true that if any man will walk boldly into that fire, he will discover it at once to be a lie, an illusion, a mirage through which he might carry a sack of gunpowder without being a penny the worse. Therefore let the fire seem so terrible that only the hero, when in the fulness of time he appears upon earth, will venture through it; and the problem is solved. Wotan, with a breaking heart, takes leave of Brynhild; throws her into a deep sleep; covers her with her long warshield; summons Loki, who comes in the shape of a wall of fire surrounding the mountain peak; and turns his back on Brynhild for ever.

The allegory here is happily not so glaringly obvious to the younger generations of our educated classes as it was forty years ago. In those days, any child who expressed a doubt as to the absolute truth of the Church's teaching, even to the extent of asking why Joshua told the sun to stand still* instead of telling the earth to cease turning, or of pointing out that a whale's throat would hardly have been large enough to swallow Jonah,* was unhesitatingly told that if it harbored such doubts it would spend all eternity after its death in horrible torments in a lake of burning brimstone. It is difficult to write or read this nowadays without laughing; yet no doubt millions of ignorant and credulous people are still teaching their children that. When Wagner himself was a little child, the fact that hell was a fiction devised for the intimidation and subjection of the masses was a well-kept secret of the thinking and governing classes. At that time the fires of Loki were a very real terror to all except persons of exceptional force of character and intrepidity of thought. Even thirty years after Wagner had printed the verses of The Ring for private circulation, we find him excusing himself from perfectly explicit denial of current superstitions, by reminding his readers that it would expose him to prosecution. In England, so many of our respectable voters are still grovelling in a gloomy devil worship, of which the fires of Loki are the main bulwark, that no Government has yet had the conscience or the courage to repeal our monstrous laws against 'blasphemy.'*

SIEGFRIED

SIEGLINDA, when she flies into the forest with the hero's son unborn in her womb, and the broken pieces of his sword in her hand, finds shelter in the smithy of a dwarf, where she brings forth her child and dies. This dwarf is no other than Mimmy, the brother of Alberic, the same who made for him the magic helmet. His aim in life is to gain possession of the helmet, the ring, and the treasure, and through them to obtain that Plutonic mastery of the world under the beginnings of which he himself writhed during Alberic's brief reign. Mimmy is a blinking, shambling, ancient creature, too weak and timid to dream of taking arms himself to despoil Fafnir, who still, transformed to a monstrous serpent, broods on the gold in a hole in the rocks. Mimmy needs the help of a hero for that; and he has craft enough to know that it is quite possible, and indeed much in the ordinary way of the world, for senile avarice and craft to set youth and bravery to work to win empire for it. He knows the pedigree of the child left on his hands, and nurses it to manhood with great care.

His pains are too well rewarded for his comfort. The boy Siegfried, having no god to instruct him in the art of unhappiness, inherits none of his father's ill luck, and all his father's hardihood. The fear against which Siegmund set his face like flint, and the woe which he wore down, are unknown to the son. The father was faithful and grateful: the son knows no law but his own humor; detests the ugly dwarf who has nursed him; chafes furiously under his claims for some return for his tender care; and is, in short, a totally unmoral person, a born anarchist, the ideal of Bakoonin, an anticipation of the 'overman' of Nietzsche.* He is enormously strong, full of life and fun, dangerous and destructive to what he dislikes, and affectionate to what he likes; so that it is fortunate that his likes and dislikes are sane and healthy. Altogether an inspiriting young forester, a son of the morning, in whom the heroic race has come out into the sunshine from the clouds of his grandfather's majestic entanglements with law, and the night of his father's tragic struggle with it.

The First Act

Mimmy's smithy is a cave, in which he hides from the light like the eyeless fish of the American caverns.* Before the curtain rises the music already tells us that we are groping in darkness. When it does rise Mimmy is in difficulties. He is trying to make a sword for his nursling, who is now big enough to take the field against Fafnir. Mimmy can make mischievous swords; but it is not with dwarfmade weapons that heroic man will hew the way of his own will through religions and governments and plutocracies and all the other devices of the kingdom of the fears of the unheroic. As fast as Mimmy makes swords, Siegfried Bakoonin smashes them, and then takes the poor old swordsmith by the scruff of the neck and chastises him wrathfully. The particular day on which the curtain rises begins with one of these trying domestic incidents. Mimmy has just done his best with a new sword of surpassing excellence. Siegfried returns home in rare spirits with a wild bear, to the extreme terror of the wretched dwarf. When the bear is dismissed, the new sword is produced. It is promptly smashed, as usual, with, also, the usual effects on the temper of Siegfried, who is quite boundless in his criticisms of the smith's boasted skill, and declares that he would smash the sword's maker too if he were not too disgusting to be handled.

Mimmy falls back on his stock defence: a string of maudlin reminders of the care with which he has nursed the little boy into manhood. Siegfried replies candidly that the strangest thing about all this care is that instead of making him grateful, it inspires him with a lively desire to wring the dwarf's neck. Only, he admits that he always comes back to his Mimmy, though he loathes him more than any living thing in the forest. On this admission the dwarf attempts to build a theory of filial instinct. He explains that he is Siegfried's father, and that this is why Siegfried cannot do without him. But Siegfried has learned from his forest companions, the birds and foxes and wolves, that mothers as well as fathers go to the making of children. Mimmy, on the desperate ground that man is neither bird nor fox, declares that he is Siegfried's father and mother both. He is promptly denounced as a filthy liar, because the birds and foxes are exactly like their parents, whereas Siegfried, having often watched his own image in the water, can testify that he is no more like Mimmy than a toad is like a trout. Then, to place the conversation on a plane of entire frankness, he throttles Mimmy until he is speechless. When the dwarf recovers, he is so daunted that he tells Siegfried the truth about his birth, and for testimony thereof produces the pieces of the sword that broke upon Wotan's spear. Siegfried instantly orders him to repair the sword on pain of an unmerciful thrashing, and rushes off into the forest, rejoicing in the discovery that he is no kin of Mimmy's, and need have no more to do with him when the sword is mended.

Poor Mimmy is now in a worse plight than ever; for he has long ago found that the sword utterly defies his skill: the steel will yield neither to his hammer nor to his furnace. Just then there walks into his cave a Wanderer, in a blue mantle, spear in hand, with one eye concealed by the brim of his wide hat. Mimmy, not by nature hospitable, tries to drive him away; but the Wanderer announces himself as a wise man, who can tell his host, in emergency, what it most concerns him to know. Mimmy, taking this offer in high dudgeon, because it implies that his visitor's wits are better than his own, offers to tell the wise one something that *he* does not know: to wit, the way to the door. The imperturbable Wanderer's reply is to sit down and challenge the dwarf to a trial of wit. He wagers his head against Mimmy's that he will answer any three questions the dwarf can put to him.

Now here were Mimmy's opportunity, had he only the wit to ask what he wants to know, instead of pretending to know everything already. It is above all things needful to him at this moment to find out how that sword can be mended; and there has just dropped in upon him in his need the one person who can tell him. In such circumstances a wise man would hasten to shew to his visitor his three deepest ignorances, and ask him to dispel them. The dwarf, being a crafty fool, desiring only to detect ignorance in his guest, asks him for information on the three points on which he is proudest of being thoroughly well instructed himself. His three questions are, Who dwell under the earth? Who dwell on the earth? and Who dwell in the cloudy heights above? The Wanderer, in reply, tells him of the dwarfs and of Alberic; of the earth, and the giants Fasolt and Fafnir; of the gods and of Wotan: himself, as Mimmy now recognizes with awe.

Next, it is Mimmy's turn to face three questions. What is that race, dearest to Wotan, against which Wotan has nevertheless done his worst? Mimmy can answer that: he knows the Volsungs, the race of heroes born of Wotan's infidelities to Fricka, and can tell the Wanderer the whole story of the twins and their son Siegfried. Wotan compliments him on his knowledge, and asks further with what sword Siegfried will slay Fafnir? Mimmy can answer that too: he has the whole history of the sword at his fingers' ends. Wotan hails him as the knowingest of the knowing, and then hurls at him the question he should himself have asked: Who will mend the sword? Mimmy, his head forfeited, confesses with loud lamentations that he cannot answer. The Wanderer reads him an appropriate little lecture on the folly of being too clever to ask what he wants to know, and informs him that a smith to whom fear is unknown will mend Nothung. To this smith he leaves the forfeited head of his host, and wanders off into the forest. Then Mimmy's nerves give way completely. He shakes like a man in delirium tremens, and has a horrible nightmare, in the supreme convulsion of which Siegfried, returning from the forest, presently finds him.

A curious and amusing conversation follows. Siegfried himself does not know fear, and is impatient to acquire it as an accomplishment. Mimmy is all fear: the world for him is a phantasmagoria of terrors. It is not that he is afraid of being eaten by bears in the forest, or of burning his fingers in the forge fire. A lively objection to being destroyed or maimed does not make a man a coward: on the contrary, it is the beginning of a brave man's wisdom. But in Mimmy, fear is not the effect of danger: it is a natural quality of him which no security can allay. He is like many a poor newspaper editor, who dares not print the truth, however simple, even when it is obvious to himself and all his readers. Not that anything unpleasant would happen to him if he did—not, indeed, that he could fail to become a distinguished and influential leader of opinion by fearlessly pursuing such a course, but solely because he lives in a world of imaginary terrors, rooted in a modest and gentlemanly mistrust of his own strength and worth, and consequently of the value of his opinion. Just so is Mimmy afraid of anything that can do him any good, especially of the light and the fresh air. He is also convinced that anybody who is not sufficiently steeped in fear to be constantly on his guard must perish immediately on his first sally into the world. To preserve Siegfried for the enterprise to which he has destined him he makes a grotesque attempt to teach him fear. He appeals to his experience of the terrors of the forest, of its dark places, of its threatening noises, its stealthy ambushes, its sinister flickering lights, its heart-tightening ecstasies of dread.

All this has no other effect than to fill Siegfried with wonder and curiosity; for the forest is a place of delight for him. He is as eager to experience Mimmy's terrors as a schoolboy to feel what an electric shock is like. Then Mimmy has the happy idea of describing Fafnir to him as a likely person to give him an exemplary fright. Siegfried jumps at the idea, and, since Mimmy cannot mend the sword for him, proposes to set to work then and there to mend it for himself. Mimmy shakes his head, and bids him see now how his youthful laziness and frowardness have found him out—how he would not learn the smith's craft from Professor Mimmy, and therefore does not know how even to begin mending the sword. Siegfried Bakoonin's retort is simple and crushing. He points out that the net result of Mimmy's academic skill is that he can neither make a decent sword himself nor even set one to rights when it is damaged. Reckless of the remonstrances of the scandalized professor, he seizes a file, and in a few moments utterly destroys the fragments of the sword by rasping them into a heap of steel filings. Then he puts the filings into a crucible; buries it in the coals; and sets to at the bellows with the shouting exultation of the anarchist who destroys only to clear the ground for creation. When the steel is melted he runs it into a mould; and lo! a sword-blade in the rough. Mimmy, amazed at the success of this violation of all the rules of his craft, hails Siegfried as the mightiest of smiths, professing himself barely worthy to be his cook and scullion; and forthwith proceeds to poison some soup for him so that he may murder him safely when Fafnir is slain. Meanwhile Siegfried forges and tempers and hammers and rivets, uproariously singing the while as nonsensically as the Rhine daughters themselves. Finally he assails the anvil on which Mimmy's swords have been shattered, and cleaves it with a mighty stroke of the newly forged Nothung.

The Second Act

In the darkest hour before the dawn of that night, we find ourselves before the cave of Fafnir; and there we find Alberic, who can find nothing better to do with himself than to watch the haunt of the dragon, and eat his heart out in vain longing for the gold and the ring. The wretched Fafnir, once an honest giant, can only make himself terrible enough to keep his gold by remaining a venomous reptile. Why he should not become an honest giant again, and clear out of his cavern, leaving the gold and the ring and the rest of it for anyone fool enough to take them at such a price, is the first question that would occur to anyone except a civilized man, who would be too accustomed to that sort of mania to be at all surprised at it.

To Alberic in the night comes the Wanderer, whom the dwarf, recognizing his despoiler of old, abuses as a shameless thief, taunting him with the helpless way in which all his boasted power is tied up with the laws and bargains recorded on the haft of his spear, which, says Alberic truly, would crumble like chaff in his hands if he dared use it for his own real ends. Wotan, having already had to kill his own son with it, knows that very well; but it troubles him no more; for he is now at last rising to abhorrence of his own artificial power, and looking to the coming hero, not for its consolidation but its destruction. When Alberic breaks out again with his still unquenched hope of one day destroying the gods and ruling the world through the ring, Wotan is no longer shocked. He tells Alberic that Brother Mime approaches with a hero whom Godhead can neither help nor hinder. Alberic may try his luck against him without disturbance from Valhalla. Perhaps, he suggests, if Alberic warns Fafnir, and offers to deal with the hero for him, Fafnir may give him the ring. They accordingly wake up the dragon, who condescends to enter into bellowing conversation, but is proof against their proposition, strong in the magic of property. 'I have and hold,' he says: 'leave me to sleep.' Wotan, with a wise laugh, turns to Alberic. 'That shot missed,' he says: 'no use abusing me for it. And now let me tell you one thing. All things happen according to their nature; and *you* cant alter them.' And so he leaves him. Alberic, raging with the sense that his old enemy has been laughing at him, and yet prophetically convinced that the last word will not be with the god, hides himself as the day breaks, and his brother approaches with Siegfried.

Mimmy makes a final attempt to frighten Siegfried by discoursing of the dragon's terrible jaws, poisonous breath, corrosive spittle, and deadly, stinging tail. Siegfried is not interested in the tail: he wants to know whether the dragon has a heart, being confident of his ability to stick Nothung into it if it exists. Reassured on this point, he drives Mimmy away, and stretches himself under the trees, listening to the morning chatter of the birds. One of them has a great deal to say to him; but he cannot understand it; and after vainly trying to carry on the conversation with a reed which he cuts, he takes to entertaining the bird with tunes on his horn, asking it to send him a loving mate such as all the other creatures of the forest have. His tunes wake up the dragon; and Siegfried makes merry over the grim mate the bird has sent him. Fafnir is highly scandalized by the irreverence of the young Bakoonin. He loses his temper; fights; and is forthwith slain, to his own great astonishment.

In such conflicts one learns to interpret the messages of Nature a little. When Siegfried, stung by the dragon's vitriolic blood, pops his finger into his mouth and tastes it, he understands what the bird is saying to him, and, instructed by it concerning the treasures within his reach, goes into the cave to secure the gold, the ring and the wishing cap. Then Mimmy returns, and is confronted by Alberic. The two quarrel furiously over the sharing of the booty they have not yet secured, until Siegfried comes from the cave with the ring and the helmet, not much impressed by the heap of gold, and disappointed because he has not yet learned to fear.

He has, however, learnt to read the thoughts of such a creature as poor Mimmy, who, intending to overwhelm him with flattery and

fondness, only succeeds in making such a self-revelation of murderous
envy that Siegfried smites him with Nothung and slays him, to the keen
satisfaction of the hidden Alberic. Caring nothing for the gold, which
he leaves to the care of the slain; disappointed in his fancy for learning
fear; and longing for a mate, he casts himself wearily down, and again
appeals to his friend the bird, who tells him of a woman sleeping on
a mountain peak within a fortress of fire that only the fearless can penetrate. Siegfried is up in a moment with all the tumult of spring in his
veins, and follows the flight of the bird as it pilots him to the fiery
mountain.

The Third Act

To the foot of the mountain comes also the Wanderer, now nearing his
doom. He calls up the First Mother from the depths of the earth, and
begs counsel from her. She bids him confer with the Norns (the Fates).
But they are of no use to him: what he seeks is some foreknowledge of
the way of the Will in its perpetual strife with these helpless Fates who
can only spin the net of circumstance and environment round the feet
of men. Why not, says Erda then, go to the daughter I bore you, and
take counsel with her? He has to explain how he has cut himself off
from her, and sets the fires of Loki between the world and her counsel.
In that case the First Mother cannot help him: such a separation is part
of the bewilderment that is ever the first outcome of her eternal work of
thrusting the life energy of the world to higher and higher organization. She can shew him no way of escape from the destruction he fore-
sees. Then from the innermost of him breaks the confession that he
rejoices in his doom, and now himself exults in passing away with all his
ordinances and alliances, with the spear-sceptre which he has only
wielded on condition of slaying his dearest children with it, with the
kingdom, the power and the glory which will never again boast themselves as 'world without end.' And so he dismisses Erda to her sleep in
the heart of the earth as the forest bird draws near, piloting the slain
son's son to his goal.

Now it is an excellent thing to triumph in the victory of the new
order and the passing away of the old; but if you happen to be part of
the old order yourself, you must none the less fight for your life. It
seems hardly possible that the British army at the battle of Waterloo did
not include at least one Englishman intelligent enough to hope, for the
sake of his country and humanity, that Napoleon might defeat the allied
sovereigns;* but such an Englishman would kill a French cuirassier

rather than be killed by him just as energetically as the silliest soldier ever encouraged, by people who ought to know better, to call his ignorance, ferocity and folly, patriotism and duty. Outworn life may have become mere error; but it still claims the right to die a natural death, and will raise its hand against the millennium itself in self defence if it tries to come by the short cut of murder. Wotan finds this out when he comes face to face with Siegfried, who is brought to a standstill at the foot of the mountain by the disappearance of the bird. Meeting the Wanderer there, he asks him the way to the mountain where a woman sleeps surrounded by fire. The Wanderer questions him, and extracts his story from him, breaking into fatherly delight when Siegfried, describing the mending of the sword, remarks that all he knew about the business was that the broken bits of Nothung would be of no use to him unless he made a new sword out of them right over again from the beginning. But the Wanderer's interest is by no means reciprocated by Siegfried. His majesty and elderly dignity are thrown away on the young anarchist, who, unwilling to waste time talking, bluntly bids him either shew him the way to the mountain, or else 'shut his muzzle.' Wotan is a little hurt. 'Patience, my lad,' he says: 'if you were an old man I should treat you with respect.' 'That would be a precious notion,' says Siegfried. 'All my life long I was bothered and hampered by an old man until I swept him out of my way. I will sweep you in the same fashion if you dont let me pass. Why do you wear such a big hat; and what has happened to one of your eyes? was it knocked out by somebody whose way you obstructed?' To which Wotan replies allegorically that the eye that is gone—the eye that his marriage with Fricka cost him—is now looking at him out of Siegfried's head. At this, Siegfried gives up the Wanderer as a lunatic, and renews his threats of personal violence. Then Wotan throws off the mask of the Wanderer; uplifts the world-governing spear; and puts forth all his divine awe and grandeur as the guardian of the mountain, round the crest of which the fires of Loki now break into a red background for the majesty of the god. But all this is lost on Siegfried Bakoonin. 'Aha!' he cries, as the spear is levelled against his breast: 'I have found my father's foe'; and the spear falls in two pieces under the stroke of Nothung. 'Up then,' says Wotan: 'I cannot withhold you,' and disappears forever from the eye of man. The fires roll down the mountain; but Siegfried goes at them as exultantly as he went at the forging of the sword or the heart of the dragon, and shoulders his way through them, joyously sounding his horn to the accompaniment of their crackling and seething. And never a hair of his head is singed. Those frightful flames which have scared mankind for centuries from the Truth have not heat enough in them to make a child shut its eyes. They are mere phantasmagoria, highly creditable to Loki's imaginative stage-management; but nothing ever has perished or will perish eternally in them except the Churches which have been so poor and faithless as to trade for their power on the lies of a romancer.

Back to Opera Again

And now, O Nibelungen Spectator, pluck up; for all allegories come to an end somewhere; and the hour of your release from these explanations is at hand. The rest of what you are going to see is opera, and nothing but opera. Before many bars have been played, Siegfried and the wakened Brynhild, newly become tenor and soprano, will sing a concerted cadenza; plunge on from that to a magnificent love duet; and end with a precipitous *allegro a capella*, driven headlong to its end by the impetuous semiquaver triplets of the famous finales to the first act of Don Giovanni or the coda to the Leonore overture, with a specifically contrapuntal theme, *points d' orgue*, and a high C for the soprano all complete.*

What is more, the work which follows, entitled Night Falls on The Gods, is a thorough grand opera. In it you shall see what you have so far missed, the opera chorus in full parade on the stage, not presuming to interfere with the prima donna as she sings her death song over the footlights. Nay, that chorus will have its own chance when it first appears, with a good roaring strain in C major, not, after all, so very different from, or at all less absurd than the choruses of courtiers in La Favorita or 'Per te immenso giubilo' in Lucia.* The harmony is no doubt a little developed, Wagner augmenting his fifths with a G sharp where Donizetti would have put his fingers in his ears and screamed for G natural. But it is an opera chorus all the same; and along with it we have theatrical grandiosites that recall Meyerbeer and Verdi:* *pezzi d' insieme* for all the principals in a row, vengeful conjurations for trios of them, romantic death song for the tenor: in short, all manner of operatic conventions.

Now it is probable that some of us will have been so talked by the more superstitious Bayreuth pilgrims into regarding Die Götterdämmerung as the mighty climax to a mighty epic, more Wagnerian than all the other three sections put together, as not to dare notice this startling atavism, especially if we find the trio-conjurations more exhilarating than the metaphysical discourses of Wotan in the three true music dramas of The Ring. There is, however, no real atavism involved. Die

Götterdämmerung, though the last of The Ring dramas in order of performance, was the first in order of conception, and was indeed the root from which all the others sprang.

The history of the matter is as follows. All Wagner's works prior to The Ring are operas. The last of them, Lohengrin, is perhaps the best known of modern operas. As performed in its entirety at Bayreuth, it is even more operatic than it appears at Covent Garden,* because it happens that its most old-fashioned features, notably some of the big set concerted pieces for principals and chorus (*pezzi d' insieme* as I have called them above), are harder to perform than the more modern and characteristically Wagnerian sections, and for that reason were cut out in preparing the abbreviated fashionable version. Thus Lohengrin came upon the ordinary operatic stage as a more advanced departure from current operatic models than its composer had made it. Still, it is unmistakably an opera, with chorus, concerted pieces, grand finales, and a heroine who, if she does not sing florid variations with flute obbligato, is none the less a very perceptible prima donna.* In everything but musical technique the change from Lohengrin to The Rhine Gold is quite revolutionary.

The explanation is that Night Falls on The Gods came in between them, although its music was not finished until twenty years after that of The Rhine Gold, and thus belongs to a later and more masterful phase of Wagner's harmonic style. It first came into Wagner's head as an opera to be entitled Siegfried's Death, founded on the old Niblung Sagas, which offered to Wagner the same material for an effective theatrical tragedy as they did to Ibsen. Ibsen's Vikings in Helgeland* is, in kind, what Siegfried's Death was originally intended to be: that is, a heroic piece for the theatre, without the metaphysical or allegorical complications of The Ring. Indeed, the ultimate catastrophe of the Saga cannot by any perversion of ingenuity be adapted to the perfectly clear allegorical design of The Rhine Gold, The Valkyries, and Siegfried.

SIEGFRIED AS PROTESTANT

THE philosophically fertile element in the original project of Siegfried's Death was the conception of Siegfried himself as a type of the healthy man raised to perfect confidence in his own impulses by an intense and joyous vitality which is above fear, sickliness of conscience, malice, and the makeshifts and moral crutches of law and order which accompany them. Such a character appears extraordinarily fascinating and exhilarating to our guilty and conscience-ridden generations, however little they may understand him. The world has always delighted in the man who is delivered from conscience. From Punch and Don Juan down to Robert Macaire, Jeremy Diddler and the pantomime clown,* he has always drawn large audiences; but hitherto he has been decorously given to the devil at the end. Indeed eternal punishment is sometimes deemed too high a compliment to his nature. When the late Lord Lytton, in his Strange Story,* introduced a character personifying the joyousness of intense vitality, he felt bound to deny him the immortal soul which was at that time conceded even to the humblest characters in fiction, and to accept mischievousness, cruelty, and utter incapacity for sympathy as the inevitable consequence of his magnificent bodily and mental health.

In short, though men felt all the charm of abounding life and abandonment to its impulses, they dared not, in their deep self-mistrust, conceive it otherwise than as a force making for evil—one which must lead to universal ruin unless checked and literally mortified by self-renunciation in obedience to superhuman guidance, or at least to some reasoned system of morals. When it became apparent to the cleverest of them that no such superhuman guidance existed, and that their secularist systems had all the fictitiousness of 'revelation' without its poetry, there was no escaping the conclusion that all the good that man had done must be put down to his arbitrary will as well as all the evil he had done; and it was also obvious that if progress were a reality, his beneficent impulses must be gaining on his destructive ones. It was under the influence of these ideas that we began to hear about the joy of life where we had formerly heard about the grace of God or the Age of Reason, and that the boldest spirits began to raise the question whether churches and laws and the like were not doing a great deal more harm than good by their action in limiting the freedom of the human will. Four hundred years ago, when belief in God and in revelation was general throughout Europe, a similar wave of thought led the strongest-hearted peoples to affirm that every man's private judgment was a more trustworthy interpreter of God and revelation than the Church. This was called Protestantism; and though the Protestants were not strong enough for their creed, and soon set up a Church of their own, yet the movement, on the whole, has justified the direction it took. Nowadays the supernatural element in Protestantism has perished; and if every man's private judgment is still to be justified as the most trustworthy interpreter of the will of Humanity (which is not a more extreme proposition than the old one about the will of God) Protestantism must take a fresh step in advance, and become Anarchism. Which it has accordingly done, Anarchism being one of the notable new creeds of the eighteenth and nineteenth centuries.

The weak place which experience finds out in the Anarchist theory is its reliance on the progress already achieved by 'Man.' There is no such thing as Man in the world: what we have to deal with is a multitude of men, some of them great rascals, some of them great statesmen, others both, with a vast majority capable of managing their personal affairs, but not of comprehending social organization, or grappling with the problems created by their association in enormous numbers. If 'Man' means this majority, then 'Man' has made no progress: he has, on the contrary, resisted it. He will not even pay the cost of existing institutions: the requisite money has to be filched from him by 'indirect taxation.'* Such people, like Wagner's giants, must be governed by laws; and their assent to such government must be secured by deliberately filling them with prejudices and practising on their imaginations by pageantry and artificial eminences and dignities. The government is of course established by the few who are capable of government, though, its mechanism once complete, it may be, and generally is, carried on unintelligently by people who are incapable of it, the capable people repairing it from time to time when it gets too far behind the continuous advance or decay of civilization. All these capable people are thus in the position of Wotan, forced to maintain as sacred, and themselves submit to, laws which they privately know to be obsolescent makeshifts, and to affect the deepest veneration for creeds and ideals which they ridicule among themselves with cynical scepticism. No individual Siegfried can rescue them from this bondage and hypocrisy; in fact, the individual Siegfried has come often enough, only to find himself confronted with the alternative of governing those who are not Siegfrieds or risking destruction at their hands. And this dilemma will persist until Wotan's inspiration comes to our governors, and they see that

their business is not the devising of laws and institutions to prop up the
weaknesses of mobs and secure the survival of the unfittest, but the
breeding of men whose wills and intelligences may be depended on to
produce spontaneously the social wellbeing our clumsy laws now aim at
and miss. The majority of men at present in Europe have no business
to be alive;* and no serious progress will be made until we address ourselves earnestly and scientifically to the task of producing trustworthy
human material for society.* In short, it is necessary to breed a race of
men in whom the life-giving impulses predominate, before the New
Protestantism becomes politically practicable.[1]

The most inevitable dramatic conception, then, of the nineteenth
century is that of a perfectly naïve hero upsetting religion, law and
order in all directions, and establishing in their place the unfettered
action of Humanity doing exactly what it likes, and producing order
instead of confusion thereby because it likes to do what is necessary for
the good of the race. This conception, already incipient in Adam
Smith's Wealth of Nations, was certain at last to reach some great artist, and be embodied by him in a masterpiece. It was also certain that if
that master happened to be a German, he should take delight in describing his hero as the Freewiller of Necessity,* thereby beyond measure
exasperating Englishmen with a congenital incapacity for metaphysics.

Panacea Quackery, otherwise Idealism

Unfortunately, human enlightenment does not progress by nicer and
nicer adjustments, but by violent corrective reactions which invariably
send us clean over our saddle and would bring us to the ground on the
other side if the next reaction did not send us back again with equally
excessive zeal. Ecclesiasticism and Constitutionalism sends us one way,
Protestantism and Anarchism the other; Order rescues us from confusion and lands us in Tyranny; Liberty then saves the situation and is
presently found to be as great a nuisance as Despotism. A scientifically
balanced application of these forces, theoretically possible, is practically incompatible with human passion. Besides, we have the same weakness in morals as in medicine: we cannot be cured of running after

---

[1] The necessity for breeding the governing class from a selected stock has always been
recognized by Aristocrats, however erroneous their methods of selection. We have
changed our system from Aristocracy to Democracy without considering that we were at
the same time changing, as regards our governing class, from Selection to Promiscuity.
Those who have taken a practical part in modern politics best know how farcical the
result is.

panaceas, or, as they are called in the sphere of morals, ideals. One generation sets up duty, renunciation, self-sacrifice as a panacea. The next generation, especially the women, wake up at the age of forty or thereabouts to the fact that their lives have been wasted in the worship of this ideal, and, what is still more aggravating, that the elders who imposed it on them did so in a fit of satiety with their own experiments in the other direction. Then that defrauded generation foams at the mouth at the very mention of duty, and sets up the alternative panacea of love, their deprivation of which seems to them to have been the most cruel and mischievous feature of their slavery to duty. It is useless to warn them that this reaction, if prescribed as a panacea, will prove as great a failure as all the other reactions have done; for they do not recognize its identity with any reaction that ever occurred before. Take for instance the hackneyed historic example of the austerity of the Commonwealth being followed by the licence of the Restoration.* You cannot persuade any moral enthusiast to accept this as a pure oscillation from action to reaction. If he is a Puritan he looks upon the Restoration as a national disaster: if he is an artist he regards it as the salvation of the country from gloom, devil worship, and starvation of the affections. The Puritan is ready to try the Commonwealth again with a few modern improvements: the Amateur is equally ready to try the Restoration with modern enlightenments. And so for the present we must be content to proceed by reactions, hoping that each will establish some permanently practical and beneficial reform or moral habit that will survive the correction of its excesses by the next reaction.*

Dramatic Origin of Wotan

We can now see how a single drama in which Wotan does not appear, and of which Siegfried is the hero, expanded itself into a great fourfold drama of which Wotan is the hero. You cannot dramatize a reaction by personifying the reacting force only, any more than Archimedes could lift the world without a fulcrum for his lever. You must also personify the established power against which the new force is reacting; and in the conflict between them you get your drama, conflict being the essential ingredient in all drama. Siegfried, as the hero of Die Götterdämmerung, is only the *primo tenore robusto** of an opera book, deferring his death, after he has been stabbed in the last act, to sing rapturous love strains to the heroine exactly like Edgardo in Donizetti's Lucia. In order to make him intelligible in the wider significance which his joyous, fearless, conscienceless heroism soon assumed in Wagner's imagination, it was necessary to provide him with a much vaster dramatic antagonist than the operatic villain Hagen. Hence Wagner had to create Wotan as the anvil for Siegfried's hammer; and since there was no room for Wotan in the original opera book, Wagner had to work back to a preliminary drama reaching primarily to the very beginnings of human society. And since, on this world-embracing scale, it was clear that Siegfried must come into conflict with many baser and stupider forces than those lofty ones of supernatural religion and political constitutionalism typified by Wotan and his wife Fricka, these minor antagonists had to be dramatized also in the persons of Alberic, Mime, Fafnir, Loki, and the rest. None of these appear in Night Falls on The Gods save Alberic, whose weird dream-colloquy with Hagen, effective as it is, is as purely theatrical as the scene of the Ghost in Hamlet, or the statue in Don Giovanni.* Cut the conference of the Norns and the visit of Valtrauta to Brynhild out of Night Falls on The Gods, and the drama remains coherent and complete without them. Retain them, and the play becomes connected by conversational references with the three music dramas; but the connection establishes no philosophic coherence, no real identity between the operatic Brynhild of the Gibichung episode (presently to be related) and the daughter of Wotan and the First Mother.

The Love Panacea

We shall now find that at the point where The Ring changes from music drama into opera, it also ceases to be philosophic, and becomes didactic. The philosophic part is a dramatic symbol of the world as Wagner observed it. In the didactic part the philosophy degenerates into the prescription of a romantic nostrum for all human ills. Wagner, only mortal after all, succumbed to the panacea mania when his philosophy was exhausted, like any of the rest of us.

The panacea is by no means an original one. Wagner was anticipated in the year 1819 by a young country gentleman from Sussex named Shelley, in a work of extraordinary artistic power and splendor. Prometheus Unbound* is an English attempt at a Ring; and when it is taken into account that the author was only 27, whereas Wagner was 40 when he completed the poem of The Ring, our vulgar patriotism may find an envious satisfaction in insisting upon the comparison. Both works set forth the same conflict between humanity and its gods and governments, issuing in the redemption of man from their tyranny by the growth of his will into perfect strength and self-confidence; and

both finish by a lapse into panacea-mongering didacticism by the holding up of Love as the remedy for all evils and the solvent of all social
difficulties.

The differences between Prometheus Unbound and The Ring are as
interesting as the likenesses. Shelley, caught in the pugnacity of his
youth and the first impetuosity of his prodigious artistic power by the
first fierce attack of the New Reformation, gave no quarter to the antagonist of his hero. His Wotan, whom he calls Jupiter, is the almighty
fiend into whom the Englishman's God had degenerated during two
centuries of ignorant Bible worship and shameless commercialism. He
is Alberic, Fafnir, Loki and the ambitious side of Wotan all rolled into
one melodramatic demon who is finally torn from his throne and hurled
shrieking into the abyss by a spirit representing that conception of
Eternal Law which has been replaced since by the conception of
Evolution. Wagner, an older, more experienced man than the Shelley
of 1819, understood Wotan and pardoned him, separating him tenderly
from all the compromising alliances to which Shelley fiercely held him;
making the truth and heroism which overthrow him the children of his
inmost heart; and representing him as finally acquiescing in and working for his own supersession and annihilation. Shelley, in his later
works, is seen progressing towards the same tolerance, justice, and
humility of spirit, as he advanced towards the middle age he never
reached. But there is no progress from Shelley to Wagner as regards the
panacea, except that in Wagner there is a certain shadow of night and
death come on it: nay, even a clear opinion that the supreme good of
love is that it so completely satisfies the desire for life that after it the
Will to Live ceases to trouble us, and we are at last content to achieve
the highest happiness of death.

This reduction of the panacea to absurdity was not forced upon
Shelley, because the love which acts as a universal solvent in his
Prometheus Unbound is a sentiment of affectionate benevolence which
has nothing to do with sexual passion. It might, and in fact does, exist
in the absence of any sexual interest whatever. The words mercy and
kindness connote it less ambiguously than the word love. But Wagner
sought always for some point of contact between his ideas and the
physical senses, so that people might not only think or imagine them in
the eighteenth century fashion, but see them on the stage, hear them
from the orchestra, and feel them through the infection of passionate
emotion. Dr Johnson kicking the stone to confute Berkeley* is not
more bent on common-sense concreteness than Wagner: on all occasions he insists on the need for sensuous apprehension to give reality to

abstract comprehension, maintaining, in fact, that reality has no other meaning. Now he could apply this process to poetic love only by follow-ing it back to its alleged origin in sexual passion, the emotional phe-nomena of which he has expressed in music with a frankness and forcible naturalism which would possibly have scandalized Shelley. The love duet in the first act of The Valkyries is brought to a point at which the conventions of our society demand the precipitate fall of the curtain; whilst the prelude to Tristan and Isolde is such an astonish-ingly intense and faithful translation into music of the emotions which accompany the union of a pair of lovers that it is questionable whether the great popularity of this piece at our orchestral concerts really means that our audiences are entirely catholic in their respect for life in all its beneficently creative functions, or whether they simply enjoy the music without understanding it.

But however offensive and inhuman may be the superstition which brands such exaltations of natural passion as shameful and indecorous, there is at least as much common sense in disparaging love as in setting it up as a panacea. Even the mercy and loving-kindness of Shelley do not hold good as a universal law of conduct: Shelley himself makes extremely short work of Jupiter, just as Siegfried does of Fafnir, Mime, and Wotan; and the fact that Prometheus is saved from doing the destructive part of his work by the intervention of that very nebulous personification of Eternity called Demogorgon does not in the least save the situation, because, flatly, there is no such person as Demogorgon, and if Prometheus does not pull down Jupiter himself, no one else will. It would be exasper-ating, if it were not so funny, to see these poets leading their heroes through blood and destruction to the conclusion that, as Browning's David puts it (David of all people!), 'All's Love; yet all's Law.'*

Certainly it is clear enough that such love as that implied by Siegfried's first taste of fear as he cuts through the mailed coat of the sleeping figure on the mountain, and discovers that it is a woman; by her fierce revolt against being touched by him when his terror gives way to ardor; by his manly transports of victory; and by the womanly mix-ture of rapture and horror with which she abandons herself to the pas-sion which has seized on them both, is an experience which it is much better, like the vast majority of us, never to have passed through, than to allow it to play more than a recreative holiday part in our lives. It did not play a very large part in Wagner's own laborious life, and does not occupy more than two scenes of The Ring. Tristan and Isolde,* wholly devoted to it, is a poem of destruction and death. The Mastersingers, a work full of health, fun, and happiness, contains not a single bar of love music that can be described as passionate: the hero of it is a widower who cobbles shoes, writes verses, and contents himself with looking on at the sweetheartings of his customers. Parsifal makes an end of it altogether. The truth is that the love panacea in Night Falls on The Gods and in the last act of Siegfried is a survival of the first crude operatic conception of the story, modified by an anticipation of Wagner's later, though not latest, conception of love as the fulfiller of our Will to Live and consequently our reconciler to night and death.

Not Love, but Life

The only faith which any reasonable disciple can gain from The Ring is not in love, but in life itself as a tireless power which is continually driving onward and upward—not, please observe, being beckoned or drawn by *Das ewig Weibliche** or any other external sentimentality, but growing from within, by its own inexplicable energy, into ever higher and higher forms of organization, the strengths and the needs of which are continually superseding the institutions which were made to fit our former requirements. When your Bakoonins call out for the demolition of all these venerable institutions, there is no need to fly into a panic and lock them up in prison whilst your parliament is bit by bit doing exactly what they advised you to do. When your Siegfrieds melt down the old weapons into new ones, and with disrespectful words chop in twain the antiquated constable's staves in the hands of their elders, the end of the world is no nearer than it was before. If human nature, which is the highest organization of life reached on this planet, is really degenerating, then human society will decay; and no panic-begotten penal measures can possibly save it: we must, like Prometheus, set to work to make new men instead of vainly torturing old ones. On the other hand, if the energy of life is still carrying human nature to higher and higher levels, then the more young people shock their elders and deride and discard their pet institutions the better for the hopes of the world, since the apparent growth of anarchy is only the measure of the rate of improvement. History, as far as we are capable of history (which is not saying much as yet), shews that all changes from crudity of social organization to complexity, and from mechanical agencies in government to living ones, seems anarchic at first sight. No doubt it is natural to a snail to think that any evolution which threatens to do away with shells will result in general death from exposure. Nevertheless, the most elaborately housed beings today are born not only without houses on their backs but without even fur or feathers to clothe them.

Anarchism no Panacea

One word of warning to those who may find themselves attracted by Siegfried's Anarchism, or, if they prefer a term with more respectable associations, his neo-Protestantism. Anarchism, as a panacea, is just as hopeless as any other panacea, and will still be so even if we breed a race of perfectly benevolent men. It is true that in the sphere of thought, Anarchism is an inevitable condition of progressive evolution. A nation without Freethinkers—that is, without intellectual Anarchists—will share the fate of China.* It is also true that our criminal law, based on a conception of crime and punishment which is nothing but our vindictiveness and cruelty in a virtuous disguise, is an unmitigated and abominable nuisance, bound to be beaten out of us finally by the mere weight of our experience of its evil and uselessness. But it will not be replaced by anarchy. Applied to the industrial or political machinery of modern society, anarchy must always reduce itself speedily to absurdity. Even the modified form of anarchy on which modern civilization is based: that is, the abandonment of industry, in the name of individual liberty, to the upshot of competition for personal gain between private capitalists, is a disastrous failure, and is, by the mere necessities of the case, giving way to ordered Socialism. For the economic rationale of this, I must refer disciples of Siegfried to a tract from my hand published by the Fabian Society and entitled The Impossibilities of Anarchism,* which explains why, owing to the physical constitution of our globe, society cannot effectively organize the production of its food, clothes, and housing, nor distribute them fairly and economically on any anarchic plan: nay, that without concerting our social action to a much higher degree than we do at present we can never get rid of the wasteful and iniquitous welter of a little riches and a great deal of poverty which current political humbug calls our prosperity and civilization. Liberty is an excellent thing: but it cannot begin until society has paid its daily debt to Nature by first earning its living. There is no liberty before that except the liberty to live at somebody else's expense, a liberty much sought after nowadays, since it is the criterion of gentility, but not wholesome from the point of view of the common weal.

Siegfried Concluded

In returning now to the adventures of Siegfried there is little more to be described except the finale of an opera. Siegfried, having passed unharmed through the fire, wakes Brynhild and goes through all the fancies and ecstasies of love at first sight in a duet which ends with an apostrophe to 'leuchtende Liebe, lachender Tod!', which has been romantically translated into 'Love that illumines, laughing at death,' whereas it really identifies enlightening love and laughing death as involving each other so closely as to be virtually one and the same thing.

NIGHT FALLS ON THE GODS

Prologue

DIE GÖTTERDÄMMERUNG begins with an elaborate prologue. The three Norns sit in the night on Brynhild's mountain top spinning their thread of destiny, and telling the story of Wotan's sacrifice of his eye, and of his breaking off a bough from the World Ash to make a haft for his spear, also how the tree withered after suffering that violence. They have also some fresher news to discuss. Wotan, on the breaking of his spear by Siegfried, has called all his heroes to cut down the withered World Ash and stack its faggots in a mighty pyre about Valhalla. Then, with his broken spear in his hand, he has seated himself in state in the great hall, with the Gods and Heroes assembled about him as if in council, solemnly waiting for the end. All this belongs to the old legendary materials with which Wagner began The Ring.

The tale is broken by the thread snapping in the hands of the third Norn; for the hour has arrived when man has taken his destiny in his own hands to shape it for himself, and no longer bows to circumstance, environment, necessity (which he now freely wills), and all the rest of the inevitables. So the Norns recognize that the world has no further use for them, and sink into the earth to return to the First Mother. Then the day dawns; and Siegfried and Brynhild come, and have another duet. He gives her his ring; and she gives him her horse. Away then he goes in search of more adventures; and she watches him from her crag until he disappears. The curtain falls; but we can still hear the trolling of his horn, and the merry clatter of his horse's shoes trotting gaily down the valley. The sound is lost in the grander rhythm of the Rhine as he reaches its banks. We hear again an echo of the lament of the Rhine maidens for the ravished gold; and then, finally, a new strain, which does not surge like the mighty flood of the river, but has an unmistakable tramp of hardy men and a strong land flavor about it. And on this the opera curtain at last goes up—for please remember that all that has gone before is only the overture.

The First Act

We now understand the new tramping strain. We are in the Rhineside hall of the Gibichungs, in the presence of King Gunther, his sister

Gutruna, and Gunther's grim half brother Hagen, the villain of the piece. Gunther is a fool, and has for Hagen's intelligence the respect a fool always has for the brains of a scoundrel. Feebly fishing for compliments, he appeals to Hagen to pronounce him a fine fellow and a glory to the race of Gibich. Hagen declares that it is impossible to contemplate him without envy, but thinks it a pity that he has not yet found a wife glorious enough for him. Gunther doubts whether so extraordinary a person can possibly exist. Hagen then tells him of Brynhild and her rampart of fire; also of Siegfried. Gunther takes this rather in bad part, since not only is he afraid of the fire, but Siegfried, according to Hagen, is not, and will therefore achieve this desirable match himself. But Hagen points out that since Siegfried is riding about in quest of adventures, he will certainly pay an early visit to the renowned chief of the Gibichungs. They can then give him a philtre which will make him fall in love with Gutruna and forget every other woman he has yet seen.

Gunther is transported with admiration of Hagen's cunning when he takes in this plan; and he has hardly assented to it when Siegfried, with operatic opportuneness, drops in just as Hagen expected, and is duly drugged into the heartiest love for Gutruna and total oblivion of Brynhild and his own past. When Gunther declares his longing for the bride who lies inaccessible within a palisade of flame, Siegfried at once offers to undertake the adventure for him. Hagen then explains to both of them that Siegfried can, after braving the fire, appear to Brynhild in the semblance of Gunther through the magic of the wishing cap (or Tarnhelm, as it is called throughout The Ring), the use of which Siegfried now learns for the first time. It is of course part of the bargain that Gunther shall give his sister to Siegfried in marriage. On that they swear blood-brotherhood; and at this opportunity the old operatic leaven breaks out amusingly in Wagner. With tremendous exordium of brass, the tenor and baritone go at it with a will, showing off the power of their voices, following each other in canonic imitation, singing together in thirds and sixths, and finishing with a lurid unison, quite in the manner of Ruy Gomez and Ernani, or Othello and Iago.* Then without further ado Siegfried departs on his expedition, taking Gunther with him to the foot of the mountain, and leaving Hagen to guard the hall and sing a very fine solo which has often figured in the programs of the Richter concerts,* explaining that his interest in the affair is that Siegfried will bring back the Ring, and that he, Hagen, will presently contrive to possess himself of that Ring and become Plutonic master of the world.

And now it will be asked how does Hagen know all about the Plutonic empire; and why was he able to tell Gunther about Brynhild and

Siegfried, and to explain to Siegfried the trick of the Tarnhelm. The explanation is that though Hagen's mother was the mother of Gunther, his father was not the illustrious Gibich, but no less a person than our old friend Alberic, who, like Wotan, has begotten a son to do for him what he cannot do for himself.

In the above incidents, those gentle moralizers who find the serious philosophy of the music dramas too terrifying for them, may allegorize pleasingly on the philtre as the maddening chalice of passion which, once tasted, causes the respectable man to forget his lawfully wedded wife and plunge into adventures which eventually lead him headlong to destruction.

We now come upon a last relic of the tragedy of Wotan. Returning to Brynhild's mountain, we find her visited by her sister Valkyrie Valtrauta, who has witnessed Wotan's solemn preparations with terror. She repeats to Brynhild the account already given by the Norns. Clinging in anguish to Wotan's knees, she has heard him mutter that were the ring returned to the daughters of the deep Rhine, both Gods and world would be redeemed from that stage curse of Alberic's in The Rhine Gold. On this she has rushed on her warhorse through the air to beg Brynhild to give the Rhine back its ring. But this is asking Woman to give up love for the sake of Church and State. She declares that she will see them both perish first; and Valtrauta returns to Valhalla in despair. Whilst Brynhild is watching the course of the black thundercloud that marks her sister's flight, the fires of Loki again flame high round the mountain; and the horn of Siegfried is heard as he makes his way through them. But the man who now appears wears the Tarnhelm: his voice is a strange voice: his figure is the unknown one of the king of the Gibichungs. He tears the ring from her finger, and, claiming her as his wife, drives her into the cave without pity for her agony of horror, and sets Nothung between them in token of his loyalty to the friend he is impersonating. No explanation of this highway robbery of the ring is offered. Clearly, this Siegfried is not the Siegfried of the previous drama.

The Second Act

In the second act we return to the hall of Gibich, where Hagen, in the last hours of that night, still sits, his spear in his hand, and his shield beside him. At his knees crouches a dwarfish spectre, his father Alberic, still full of his old grievances against Wotan, and urging his son in his dreams to win back the ring for him. This Hagen swears to do; and as the apparition of his father vanishes, the sun rises and Siegfried suddenly comes from the river bank tucking into his belt the Tarnhelm, which has transported him from the mountain like the enchanted carpet of the Arabian tales. He describes his adventures to Gutruna until Gunther's boat is seen approaching, when Hagen seizes a cow-horn and calls the tribesmen to welcome their chief and his bride. It is most exhilarating, this colloquy with the startled and hastily armed clan, ending with a thunderous chorus, the drums marking the time with mighty pulses from dominant to tonic, much as Rossini* would have made them do if he had been a pupil of Beethoven's.

A terrible scene follows. Gunther leads his captive bride straight into the presence of Siegfried, whom she claims as her husband by the ring, which she is astonished to see on his finger: Gunther, as she supposes, having torn it from her the night before. Turning on Gunther, she says, 'Since you took that ring from me, and married me with it, tell him of your right to it; and make him give it back to you.' Gunther stammers, 'The ring! I gave him no ring—er—do you know him?' The rejoinder is obvious. 'Then where are you hiding the ring that you had from me?' Gunther's confusion enlightens her; and she calls Siegfried trickster and thief to his face. In vain he declares that he got the ring from no woman, but from a dragon whom he slew; for he is manifestly puzzled; and she, seizing her opportunity, accuses him before the clan of having played Gunther false with her.

Hereupon we have another grandiose operatic oath, Siegfried attesting his innocence on Hagen's spear, and Brynhild rushing to the footlights and thrusting him aside to attest his guilt, whilst the clansmen call upon their gods to send down lightnings and silence the perjured. The gods do not respond; and Siegfried, after whispering to Gunther that the Tarnhelm seems to have been only half effectual after all, laughs his way out of the general embarrassment and goes off merrily to prepare for his wedding, with his arm round Gutruna's waist, followed by the clan. Gunther, Hagen, and Brynhild are left together to plot operatic vengeance. Brynhild, it appears, has enchanted Siegfried in such a fashion that no weapon can hurt him. She has, however, omitted to protect his back, since it is impossible that he should ever turn that to a foe. They agree accordingly that on the morrow a great hunt shall take place, at which Hagen shall thrust his spear into the hero's vulnerable back. The blame is to be laid on the tusk of a wild boar. Gunther, being a fool, is remorseful about his oath of blood-brotherhood and about his sister's bereavement, without having the strength of mind to prevent the murder. The three burst into a herculean trio, similar in conception to that of the three conspirators in Un Ballo in

Maschera;* and the act concludes with a joyous strain heralding the appearance of Siegfried's wedding procession, with strewing of flowers, sacrificing to the gods, and carrying bride and bridegroom in triumph.

It will be seen that in this act we have lost all connection with the earlier drama. Brynhild is not only not the Brynhild of The Valkyries, she is the Hiordis of Ibsen,* a majestically savage woman, in whom jealousy and revenge are intensified to heroic proportions. That is the inevitable theatrical treatment of the murderous heroine of the Saga. Ibsen's aim in The Vikings was purely theatrical, and not, as in his later dramas, also philosophically symbolic. Wagner's aim in Siegfried's Death was equally theatrical, and not, as it afterwards became in the dramas of which Siegfried's antagonist Wotan is the hero, likewise philosophically symbolic. The two master-dramatists therefore produce practically the same version of Brynhild. Thus on the second evening of The Ring we see Brynhild in the character of the truth-divining instinct in religion, cast into an enchanted slumber and surrounded by the fires of hell lest she should overthrow a Church corrupted by its alliance with government. On the fourth evening, we find her swearing a malicious lie to gratify her personal jealousy, and then plotting a treacherous murder with a fool and a scoundrel. In the original draft of Siegfried's Death, the incongruity is carried still further by the conclusion, at which the dead Brynhild, restored to her godhead by Wotan, and again a Valkyrie, carries the slain Siegfried to Valhalla to live there happily ever after with its pious heroes.

As to Siegfried himself, he talks of women, both in this second act and the next, with the air of a man of the world. 'Their tantrums,' he says, 'are soon over.' Such speeches do not belong to the novice of the preceding drama, but to the original Siegfried's Tod, with its leading characters sketched on the ordinary romantic lines from the old Sagas, and not yet reminted as the original creations of Wagner's genius whose acquaintance we have made on the two previous evenings. The very title 'Siegfried's Death' survives as a strong theatrical point in the following passage. Gunther, in his rage and despair, cries, 'Save me, Hagen: save my honor and thy mother's who bore us both.' 'Nothing can save thee,' replies Hagen: 'neither brain nor hand, but *Siegfried's Death.*' And Gunther echoes with a shudder, '*Siegfried's Death!*'

A Wagnerian Newspaper Controversy

The devotion which Wagner's work inspires has been illustrated lately in a public correspondence on this very point. A writer in The Daily

Telegraph having commented on the falsehood uttered by Brynhild in accusing Siegfried of having betrayed Gunther with her, a correspondence in defence of the beloved heroine was opened in The Daily Chronicle.* The imputation of falsehood to Brynhild was strongly resented and combated, in spite of the unanswerable evidence of the text. It was contended that Brynhild's statement must be taken as establishing the fact that she actually was ravished by somebody whom she believed to be Siegfried, and that since this somebody cannot have been Siegfried, he being as incapable of treachery to Gunther as she of falsehood, it must have been Gunther himself after a second exchange of personalities not mentioned in the text. The reply to this—if so obviously desperate a hypothesis needs a reply—is that the text is perfectly explicit as to Siegfried, disguised as Gunther, passing the night with Brynhild with Nothung dividing them, and in the morning bringing her down the mountain *through the fire* (an impassable obstacle to Gunther) and there transporting himself in a single breath, by the Tarnhelm's magic, back to the hall of the Gibichungs, leaving the real Gunther to bring Brynhild down the river after him. One controversialist actually pleaded for the expedition occupying two nights, on the second of which the alleged outrage might have taken place. But the time is accounted for to the last minute: it all takes place during the single night watch of Hagen. There is no possible way out of the plain fact that Brynhild's accusation is to her own knowledge false; and the impossible ways just cited are only interesting as examples of the fanatical worship which Wagner and his creations have been able to inspire in minds of exceptional power and culture.

More plausible was the line taken by those who admitted the falsehood. Their contention was that when Wotan deprived Brynhild of her Godhead, he also deprived her of her former high moral attributes; so that Siegfried's kiss awakened an ordinary mortal jealous woman. But a goddess can become mortal and jealous without plunging at once into perjury and murder. Besides, this explanation involves the sacrifice of the whole significance of the allegory, and the reduction of The Ring to the plane of a child's conception of The Sleeping Beauty. Whoever does not understand that, in terms of The Ring philosophy, a change from godhead to humanity is a step higher and not a degradation, misses the whole point of The Ring. It is precisely because the truthfulness of Brynhild is proof against Wotan's spells that he has to contrive the fire palisade with Loki, to protect the fictions and conventions of Valhalla against her.

The only tolerable view is the one supported by the known history of The Ring, and also, for musicians of sufficiently fine judgment, by the evidence of the scores; of which more anon. As a matter of fact Wagner began, as I have said, with Siegfried's Death. Then, wanting to develop the idea of Siegfried as neo-Protestant, he went on to The Young Siegfried. As a Protestant cannot be dramatically projected without a pontifical antagonist, The Young Siegfried led to The Valkyries, and that again to its preface The Rhine Gold (the preface is always written after the book is finished). Finally, of course, the whole was revised. The revision, if carried out strictly, would have involved the cutting out of Siegfried's Death, now become inconsistent and superfluous; and that would have involved, in turn, the facing of the fact that The Ring was no longer a Niblung epic, and really demanded modern costumes, tall hats for Tarnhelms, factories for Nibelheims, villas for Valhallas, and so on—in short, a complete confession of the extent to which the old Niblung epic had become the merest pretext and name directory in the course of Wagner's travail. But, as Wagner's most eminent English interpreter* once put it to me at Bayreuth between the acts of Night Falls on The Gods, the master wanted to 'Lohengrinize' again after his long abstention from opera; and Siegfried's Death (first sketched in 1848, the year before the rising in Dresden and the subsequent events which so deepened Wagner's sense of life and the seriousness of art) gave him exactly the libretto he required for that outbreak of the old operatic Adam in him. So he changed it into Die Götterdämmerung, retaining the traditional plot of murder and jealousy, and with it, necessarily, his original second act, in spite of the incongruity of its Siegfried and Brynhild with the Siegfried and Brynhild of the allegory. As to the legendary matter about the world-ash and the destruction of Valhalla by Loki, it fitted in well enough; for though, allegorically, the blow by which Siegfried breaks the god's spear is the end of Wotan and of Valhalla, those who do not see the allegory, and take the story literally, like children, are sure to ask what becomes of Wotan after Siegfried gets past him up the mountain; and to this question the old tale told in Night Falls on The Gods is as good an answer as another. The very senselessness of the scenes of the Norns and of Valtrauta in relation to the three foregoing dramas, gives them a highly effective air of mystery; and no one ventures to challenge their consequentiality, because we are all more apt to pretend to understand great works of art than to confess that the meaning (if any) has escaped us. Valtrauta, however, betrays her irrelevance by explaining that the gods can be saved by the restoration of the ring to the Rhine daughters. This, considered as part of the previous allegory, is nonsense; so that even this scene, which has a more plausible air of organic connection with The Valkyries than any other in

Night Falls on The Gods, is as clearly part of a different and earlier conception as the episode which concludes it, in which Siegfried actually robs Brynhild of her ring, though he has no recollection of having given it to her. Night Falls on The Gods, in fact, was not even revised into any real coherence with the world-poem which sprang from it; and that is the authentic solution of all the controversies which have arisen over it.

The Third Act

The hunting party comes off duly. Siegfried strays from it and meets the Rhine maidens, who almost succeed in coaxing the ring from him. He pretends to be afraid of his wife; and they chaff him as to her beating him and so forth; but when they add that the ring is accursed and will bring death upon him, he discloses to them, as unconsciously as Julius Cæsar disclosed it long ago,* that secret of heroism, never to let your life be shaped by fear of its end.[1] So he keeps the ring; and they leave him to his fate. The hunting party now finds him; and they all sit down together to make a meal by the river side, Siegfried telling them meanwhile the story of his adventures. When he approaches the subject of Brynhild, as to whom his memory is a blank, Hagen pours an antidote to the love philtre into his drinking horn, whereupon, his memory returning, he proceeds to narrate the incident of the fiery mountain, to Gunther's intense mortification. Hagen then plunges his spear into the back of Siegfried, who falls dead on his shield, but gets up again, after the old operatic custom, to sing about thirty bars to his love before allowing himself to be finally carried off to the strains of the famous Trauermarsch.*

The scene then changes to the hall of the Gibichungs by the Rhine. It is night; and Gutruna, unable to sleep, and haunted by all sorts of vague terrors, is waiting for the return of her husband, and wondering whether a ghostly figure she has seen gliding down to the river bank is Brynhild, whose room is empty. Then comes the cry of Hagen, returning with the hunting party to announce the death of Siegfried by the tusk of a wild boar. But Gutruna divines the truth; and Hagen does not

---

[1] 'We must learn to die, and to die in the fullest sense of the word. The fear of the end is the source of all lovelessness; and this fear is generated only when love begins to wane. How came it that this love, the highest blessedness to all things living, was so far lost sight of by the human race that at last it came to this: all that mankind did, ordered, and established, was conceived only in fear of the end? My poem sets this forth.'—Wagner to Roeckel, 25th Jan. 1854.

deny it. Siegfried's body is brought in; Gunther claims the ring; Hagen
will not suffer him to take it; they fight; and Gunther is slain. Hagen
then attempts to take it; but the dead man's hand closes on it and raises
itself threateningly. Then Brynhild comes; and a funeral pyre is raised
whilst she declaims a prolonged scena, extremely moving and imposing, but yielding nothing to resolute intellectual criticism except a very
powerful and elevated exploitation of theatrical pathos, psychologically
identical with the scene of Cleopatra and the dead Antony in
Shakespear's tragedy. Finally she flings a torch into the pyre, and rides
her warhorse into the flames. The hall of the Gibichungs catches fire, as
most halls would were a cremation attempted in the middle of the floor
(I permit myself this gibe purposely to emphasize the excessive artifici-
ality of the scene); but the Rhine overflows its banks to allow the three
Rhine maidens to take the ring from Siegfried's finger, incidentally
extinguishing the conflagration as it does so. Hagen attempts to snatch
the ring from the maidens, who promptly drown him; and in the distant
heavens the Gods and their castle are seen perishing in the fires of Loki
as the curtain falls.

Collapse of the Allegory

In all this, it will be observed, there is nothing new. The musical fabric
is enormously elaborate and gorgeous; but you cannot say, as you must
in witnessing the Rhine Gold, The Valkyries, and the first two acts of
Siegfried, that you have never seen anything like it before, and that the
inspiration is entirely original. Not only the action, but most of the
poetry, might conceivably belong to an Elizabethan drama. The situation of Cleopatra and Antony* is unconsciously reproduced without
being bettered, or even equalled in point of majesty and musical expression. The loss of all simplicity and dignity, the impossibility of any
credible scenic presentation of the incidents, and the extreme staginess
of the conventions by which these impossibilities are got over, are no
doubt covered from the popular eye by the overwhelming prestige of
Die Götterdämmerung as part of so great a work as The Ring, and by
the extraordinary storm of emotion and excitement which the music
keeps up. But the very qualities that intoxicate the novice in music
enlighten the adept. In spite of the fulness of the composer's technical
accomplishment, the finished style and effortless mastery of harmony
and instrumentation displayed, there is not a bar in the work which
moves us as the same themes moved us in The Valkyries, nor is anything
but external splendor added to the life and humor of Siegfried.

In the original poem, Brynhild delays her self-immolation on the pyre of Siegfried to read the assembled choristers a homily on the efficacy of the Love panacea. 'My holiest wisdom's hoard,' she says, 'now I make known to the world. I believe not in property, nor money, nor godliness, nor hearth and high place, nor pomp and peerage, nor contract and custom, but in Love. Let that only prevail; and ye shall be blest in weal or woe.' Here the repudiations still smack of Bakoonin; but the saviour is no longer the volition of the full-grown spirit of Man, the Free Willer of Necessity, sword in hand, but simply Love, and not even Shelleyan love, but vehement sexual passion. It is highly significant of the extent to which this uxorious commonplace lost its hold of Wagner (after disturbing his conscience, as he confesses to Roeckel, for years) that it disappears in the full score of Night Falls on The Gods, which was not completed until he was on the verge of producing Parsifal, twenty years after the publication of the poem. He cut the homily out, and composed the music of the final scene with a flagrant recklessness of the old intention. The rigorous logic with which representative musical themes are employed in the earlier dramas is here abandoned without scruple; and for the main theme at the conclusion he selects a rapturous passage sung by Sieglinda in the third act of The Valkyries (p. 189, *ante*) when Brynhild inspires her with a sense of her high destiny as the mother of the unborn hero. There is no dramatic logic whatever in the recurrence of this theme to express the transport in which Brynhild immolates herself. There is of course an excuse for it, inasmuch as both women have an impulse of self-sacrifice for the sake of Siegfried; but this is really hardly more than an excuse; since the Valhalla theme might be attached to Alberic on the no worse ground that both he and Wotan are inspired by ambition, and that the ambition has the same object, the possession of the ring. The common sense of the matter is that the only themes which had fully retained their old hold on Wagner's intellectual conscience when he composed Night Falls on The Gods are those which are mere labels of external features, such as the Dragon, the Fire, the Water and so on. This particular theme of Sieglinda's is, in truth, of no great musical merit: it might easily be the pet climax of a popular sentimental ballad: in fact, the gushing effect which is its sole valuable quality is so cheaply attained that it is hardly going too far to call it the most trumpery phrase in the entire tetralogy. Yet, since it undoubtedly does gush very emphatically, Wagner chose, for convenience' sake, to work up this final scene with it rather than with the more distinguished, elaborate and beautiful themes connected with the love of Brynhild and Siegfried.

He would certainly not have thought this a matter of no consequence had he finished the whole work ten years earlier. It must always be borne in mind that the poem of The Ring was complete and printed in 1853, and represents the sociological ideas which, after germinating in the European atmosphere for many years, had been brought home to Wagner, who was intensely susceptible to such ideas, by the crash of 1849 at Dresden.* Now no man whose mind is alive and active, as Wagner's was to the day of his death, can keep his political and spiritual opinions, much less his philosophic consciousness, at a standstill for quarter of a century until he finishes an orchestral score. When Wagner first sketched Night Falls on The Gods he was 35. When he finished the score for the first Bayreuth festival in 1876* he had turned 60. No wonder he had lost his old grip of it and left it behind him. He even tampered with The Rhine Gold for the sake of theatrical effect when stage-managing it, making Wotan pick up and brandish a sword to give visible point to his sudden inspiration as to the raising up of a hero. The sword had first to be discovered by Fafnir among the Niblung treasures and thrown away by him as useless. There is no sense in this device; and its adoption shews the same recklessness as to the original intention which we find in the music of the last act of The Dusk of the Gods.[1]

Why He Changed His Mind*

Wagner, however, was not the man to allow his grip of a great philosophic theme to slacken, even in twenty-five years, had the theme stood the test of the world's experience. If the history of Germany from 1849 to 1876* had been the history of Siegfried and Wotan transposed into the key of actual life, Night Falls on The Gods would have been the logical consummation of The Rhine Gold and The Valkyrie instead of the operatic anachronism it actually is.

But, as a matter of fact, Siegfried did not arrive and Bismarck* did. Roeckel faded into a prisoner whose imprisonment made no difference. Bakoonin broke up, not Valhalla, but The International, which petered out in an undignified quarrel between him and Karl Marx.* The Siegfrieds of 1848 were hopeless political failures, whereas the Wotans and Alberics and Lokis were conspicuous political successes. Even the Mimes held their own as against Siegfried. With the single exception of

[1] Die Götterdämmerung means literally Godsgloaming. The English versions of the opera are usually called The Dusk of the Gods, or The Twilight of the Gods. I have purposely introduced the ordinary title in the sentence above for the reader's information.

Ferdinand Lassalle, there was no revolutionary leader who was not an obvious Impossibilist in practical politics; and Lassalle got himself killed in a romantic and quite indefensible duel after wrecking his health in a titanic oratorical campaign which convinced him that the great majority of the working classes were not ready to join him, and that the minority who were ready did not understand him. The International, founded in 1864 by Karl Marx in London, and mistaken for several years by nervous newspapers for a red spectre, was really only a turnip ghost. It achieved some beginnings of international Trade Unionism by inducing English workmen to send money to support strikes on the continent, and recalling English workers who had been taken across the North Sea to defeat such strikes; but on its revolutionary socialistic side it was a romantic figment. The suppression of the Paris Commune,* one of the most tragic examples in history of the pitilessness with which capable practical administrators and soldiers are forced by the pressure of facts to destroy romantic amateurs and theatrical dreamers, made an end of melodramatic Socialism. It was as easy for Marx, with his literary talent, to hold up Thiers as the most execrable of living scoundrels, and to put upon Gallifet a brand indelible enough to ostracize him politically for ever, as it was for Victor Hugo to bombard Napoleon III from his paper battery in Jersey. It was also easy to hold up Félix Pyat and Delescluze* as men of much loftier ideals than Thiers and Gallifet; but the one fact that could not be denied was that when it came to actual shooting, it was Gallifet who got Delescluze shot and not Delescluze who got Gallifet shot, and that when it came to administering the affairs of France, Thiers could in one way or another get it done, whilst Pyat could neither do it nor stop talking and allow somebody else to do it. True, the penalty of following Thiers was to be exploited by the landlord and capitalist; but then the penalty of following Pyat was to be shot like a mad dog, or at best sent to New Caledonia,* quite unnecessarily and uselessly.

To put it in terms of Wagner's allegory, Alberic had got the ring back again, and was marrying into the best Valhalla families with it. He had thought better of his old threat to dethrone Wotan and Loki. He had found that Nibelheim was a very gloomy place, and that if he wanted to live handsomely and safely, he must not only allow Wotan and Loki to organize society for him, but pay them very handsomely for doing it. He needed splendor, military glory, loyalty, enthusiasm, and patriotism; and his greed and gluttony were wholly unable to create them, whereas Wotan and Loki carried them all to their most triumphant climax in Germany in 1871, when Wagner himself celebrated the event with his Kaisermarsch,* which sounded much more convincing than the Marseillaise or the Carmagnole.*

How, after the Kaisermarsch, could Wagner go back to his idealization of Siegfried in 1853? How could he believe seriously in Siegfried slaying the dragon and charging through the mountain fire, when the immediate foreground was occupied by the Hôtel de Ville* with Félix Pyat endlessly discussing the principles of Socialism whilst the shells of Thiers were already battering the Arc de Triomphe and ripping up the pavement of the Champs Elysées?* Is it not clear that things had taken an altogether unexpected turn; that although The Ring may, like the famous Communist Manifesto of Marx and Engels, be an inspired guess at the historic laws and predestined end of our capitalistic-theocratic epoch, yet Wagner, like Marx, was too inexperienced in technical government and administration and too melodramatic in his hero-contra-villain conception of the class struggle, to foresee the actual process by which his generalization would work out, or the part to be played in it by the classes involved.

Let us go back for a moment to the point at which the Niblung legend first becomes irreconcilable with Wagner's allegory. Fafnir in the real world becomes a capitalist; but Fafnir in the allegory is a mere hoarder. His gold does not bring him in any revenue. It does not even support him: he has to go out and forage for food and drink. In fact, he is on the way to his drinking-pool when Siegfried kills him. And Siegfried himself has no more use for the gold than Fafnir: the only difference between them in this respect is that Siegfried does not waste his time watching a barren treasure that is useless to him, whereas Fafnir sacrifices his humanity and his life merely to prevent anybody else getting it. This contrast, true to human nature, is not true to modern economic development. The real Fafnir is not a miser: he seeks dividends, a comfortable life, and admission to the circles of Wotan and Loki. His only means of procuring these is to restore the gold to Alberic in exchange for scrip in Alberic's enterprises. Thus fortified with capital, Alberic exploits his fellow dwarfs as before, and also exploits Fafnir's fellow giants who have no capital. What is more, the competitive strategy and large-scaled enterprise the exploitation involves, and the self-respect and social esteem its success wins, effect a development in Alberic's own character which neither Marx nor Wagner appears to have foreseen. He discovers that to be a dull, greedy, narrow-minded moneygrubber is not the way to make money on the modern scale; for though greed may suffice to turn tens into hundreds and even hundreds into thousands, to turn thousands into hundreds of thousands

requires economic magnanimity and a will to power as well as to pelf.*
And to turn hundreds of thousands into millions, Alberic must make
himself an earthly Providence for masses of workmen, creating towns,
and governing markets. In the meantime, Fafnir, wallowing in the dividends he has done nothing to earn, may rot, intellectually and morally,
from mere disuse of his energies and lack of incentive to excel; but the
more impotent he becomes, the more dependent he is upon Alberic for
his income, on Loki for his politics, and on Wotan for his respectability
and safety from rebellion: Alberic, as the purse-bearer, being, under
Destiny, the real master of the situation. Consequently, though Alberic
in 1850 may have been merely the vulgar Manchester factory-owner
portrayed in Friedrich Engels' Condition of the Working Classes, in
1876 he was well on the way towards becoming exoterically a model
philanthropic employer and esoterically a financier.*

Now, without exaggerating the virtues of such gentlemen, it will be
conceded by everybody except perhaps those veteran Social-Democrats
who have made a cult of obsolescence under the name of Marxism, that
the dominant sort of modern employer is not to be displaced and dismissed so lightly as Alberic in The Ring. Wotan is hardly less dependent
on him than Fafnir: the War-Lord visits his works, acclaims them in
stirring speeches, and imprisons his enemies; whilst Loki does his
political jobs in Parliament, making wars and commercial treaties for
him at command. And he owns and controls a new god, called The
Press, which manufactures public opinion on his side,* and organizes
the persecution and suppression of Siegfried.

The end cannot come until Siegfried learns Alberic's trade and
shoulders Alberic's burden. Not having as yet done so, he is still completely mastered by Alberic. He does not even rebel against him except
when he is too stupid and ignorant, or too romantically impracticable,
to see that Alberic's work, like Wotan's work and Loki's work, is necessary work, and that therefore Alberic can never be superseded by a war-
rior, but only by a capable man of business who is prepared to continue
his work without a day's intermission. Even though the proletarians of
all lands were to become 'class-conscious,' and obey the call of Marx
by uniting to rush the class struggle to a proletarian victory in which
all capital should become common property, and all Monarchs,
Millionaires, Landlords, and Capitalists become common citizens, the
triumphant proletarians would have either to starve in anarchy next day
or else do the political and industrial work which now gets itself done
somehow under limited monarchs, despotic presidents, irresponsible
financiers, and bourgeois parliaments. And in the meantime these mag-

nates must defend their power and property with all their might against
the revolutionary forces until these forces become positive, executive,
administrative forces, instead of the conspiracies of protesting, moralizing, virtuously indignant amateurs who mistook Marx for a man of
affairs and Thiers for a stage villain.

Now all this represents a development of which one gathers no fore-
cast from Wagner or Marx. Both of them prophesied the end of our
epoch; and, though in 1913 that epoch seemed so prosperous that the
prophecy seemed ridiculously negligible, within ten years the centre
had fallen out of Europe; and humane men could only shake their
heads and shrug their shoulders when they were asked for another half-
crown to help to save another ten million children from starvation.
Alberic had prospered so greatly that he had come to believe himself
immortal; and his alliances with Wotan had brought his sons and
daughters under the influences, dangerous to commerce, of feudal
militarist ideals. The abyss in his path had been pointed out to him not
only by Wagner and Marx, but by men who, instead of vainly consulting the oracle in the pages of Das Kapital, had sought new and safe
paths by the light of contemporary history and practical administrative
experience. But Alberic would neither believe that the old path led to
the abyss nor explore the new paths; and the masses knew nothing of
paths and much of poverty. So he went faster and faster, at last march-
ing sword in hand with his feudal sons-in-law, blasting his way with
cyclopean explosives, at which point he crashed into the abyss he
had not believed in, bringing down the civilization of Central and
Eastern Europe along with him, and leaving the Bolshevists (ci-devant*
Marxists), Social-Democrats, Republicans and amorphous revolution-
aries generally to extricate it as best they could, and to learn in the
process the truth of these last few pages.

But Wagner did not live to see this reduction of Alberic to absurdity.
What he did see was the reduction of Siegfried to absurdity. Siegfried
had done nothing that promised success in his struggle with Alberic;
and Alberic had not yet outdone Siegfried in ineptitude by committing
suicide. Now Wagner was compelled by his profession to be, compared
with Siegfried, a practical man. It is possible to learn more of the world
by producing a single opera, or even conducting a single orchestral
rehearsal, than by ten years reading in the library of the British
Museum.* Wagner must have learnt between The Rhine Gold and the
Kaisermarsch that there are yet several dramas to be interpolated in
The Ring after The Valkyrie before the allegory can tell the whole story.
If anyone doubts the extent to which Wagner's eyes had been opened to

the administrative childishness and romantic conceit of the heroes of the revolutionary generation that served its apprenticeship on the barricades of 1848–49, and perished on those of 1871 under Thiers' mitrailleuses,* let him read Eine Kapitulation,* that scandalous burlesque in which the poet and composer of Siegfried, with the levity of a schoolboy, mocked the French republicans who were doing in 1871 what he himself was exiled for doing in 1849. He had set the enthusiasm of the Dresden revolution to his own greatest music; but he set the enthusiasm of twenty years later in derision to the music of Rossini. There is no mistaking the tune he meant to suggest by his doggerel of Republik, Republik, Republik-lik-lik. The Overture to William Tell* is there as plainly as if it were noted down in full score.

In the case of such a man as Wagner, you cannot explain this *volte-face** as mere jingoism produced by Germany's overwhelming victory in the Franco-Prussian war, nor as personal spite against the Parisians for the Tannhäuser fiasco.* Wagner had more cause for personal spite against his own countrymen than he ever had against the Parisians: he was ten times bitterer against his respectable prosperity in Dresden than against his starvation in Paris. No doubt his outburst gratified the pettier feelings which great men have in common with small ones; but he was not a man to indulge in such gratifications or indeed to feel them as gratifications, if he had not become convinced of the administrative impotence of the agitators who were crying to wield Nothung, and who had done less for Wagner's own art than a single German king, and he, too, a mad one. Wagner had by that time done too much himself not to know that the world is ruled by deeds, not by good intentions, and that one efficient sinner is worth ten futile saints and martyrs.

I need not elaborate the point further in these pages. Like all men of genius, Wagner had exceptional sincerity, exceptional respect for facts, exceptional freedom from the hypnotic influence of sentimental popular movements, exceptional sense of the realities of political power as distinguished from the pretences and idolatries behind which the real masters of modern States pull their wires and train their guns.* When he scored Night Falls on The Gods, he had accepted the failure of Siegfried and the triumph of the Wotan-Loki-Alberic trinity as a fact. He had given up dreaming of heroes, heroines, and final solutions, and had conceived a new protagonist in Parsifal, whom he announced, not as a hero, but as a fool, armed, not with a sword which cut irresistibly, but with a spear which he held only on condition that he did not use it: one who, instead of exulting in the slaughter of a dragon, was ashamed of having shot a swan. The change in the conception of the Deliverer could hardly be more complete. It reflects the change which took place in Wagner's mind between the composition of The Rhine Gold and Night Falls on The Gods; and it explains why he found it so easy to drop the Ring allegory and fall back on Lohengrinizing.

WAGNER'S OWN EXPLANATION

AND now, having given my explanation of The Ring, can I give Wagner's explanation of it? If I could (and I can) I should not by any means accept it as conclusive. Nearly half a century has passed since the tetralogy was written; and in that time the purposes of many half instinctive acts of genius have become clearer to the common man than they were to the doers. Some years ago, in the course of an explanation of Ibsen's plays, I pointed out that it was by no means certain or even likely that Ibsen was as definitely conscious of his thesis as I. All the stupid people, and some critics who, though not stupid, had not themselves written what the Germans call 'tendency' works, saw nothing in this but a fantastic affectation of the extravagant self-conceit of knowing more about Ibsen than Ibsen himself. Fortunately, in taking exactly the same position now with regard to Wagner, I can claim his own authority to support me. 'How,' he wrote to Roeckel on the 23rd August 1856, 'can an artist expect that what he has felt intuitively should be perfectly realized by others, seeing that he himself feels in the presence of his work, if it is true Art, that he is confronted by a riddle, about which he, too, might have illusions, just as another might?'

The truth is, we are apt to deify men of genius, exactly as we deify the creative force of the universe, by attributing to logical design what is the result of blind instinct. What Wagner meant by 'true Art' is the operation of the artist's instinct, which is just as blind as any other instinct. Mozart, asked for an explanation of his works, said frankly 'How do I know?' Wagner, being a philosopher and critic as well as a composer, was always looking for moral explanations of what he had created; and he hit on several very striking ones, all different. In the same way one can conceive Henry the Eighth* speculating very brilliantly about the circulation of his own blood without getting as near the truth as Harvey* did long after his death.

None the less, Wagner's own explanations are of exceptional interest. To begin with, there is a considerable portion of The Ring, especially the portraiture of our capitalistic industrial system from the socialist's point of view in the slavery of the Niblungs and the tyranny of Alberic, which is unmistakeable, as it dramatizes that portion of human activity which lies well within the territory covered by our intellectual consciousness. All this is concrete Home Office* business, so to speak: its meaning was as clear to Wagner as it is to us. Not so that part of the work which deals with the destiny of Wotan. And here, as it happened, Wagner's recollection of what he had been driving at was completely upset by his discovery, soon after the completion of The Ring poem, of Schopenhauer's famous treatise 'The World as Will and Representation.'* So obsessed did he become with this masterpiece of philosophic art that he declared that it contained the intellectual demonstration of the conflict of human forces which he himself had demonstrated artistically in his great poem. 'I must confess,' he writes to Roeckel, 'to having arrived at a clear understanding of my own works of art through the help of another, who has provided me with the reasoned conceptions corresponding to my intuitive principles.'

Schopenhauer, however, had done nothing of the sort. Wagner's determination to prove that he had been a Schopenhauerite all along without knowing it only shews how completely the fascination of the great treatise on The Will had run away with his memory. It is easy to see how this happened. Wagner says of himself that 'seldom has there taken place in the soul of one and the same man so profound a division and estrangement between the intuitive or impulsive part of his nature and his consciously or reasonably formed ideas.'* And since Schopenhauer's great contribution to modern thought was to educate us into clear consciousness of this distinction—a distinction familiar, in a fanciful way, to the Ages of Faith and Art before the Renascence, but afterwards swamped in the Rationalism of that movement—it was inevitable that Wagner should jump at Schopenhauer's metaphysiology (I use a word less likely to be mistaken than metaphysics) as the very thing for him. But metaphysiology is one thing, political philosophy another. The political philosophy of Siegfried is exactly contrary to the political philosophy of Schopenhauer, although the same clear metaphysiological distinction between the instinctive part of man (his Will) and his reasoning faculty (dramatized in The Ring as Loki) is insisted on in both. The difference is that to Schopenhauer the Will is the universal tormentor of man, the author of that great evil, Life; whilst reason is the divine gift that is finally to overcome this life-creating will and lead, through its abnegation, to cessation and peace, annihilation and Nirvana.* This is the doctrine of Pessimism. Now Wagner was, when he wrote The Ring, a most sanguine revolutionary Meliorist,* contemptuous of the reasoning faculty, which he typified in the shifty, unreal, delusive Loki, and full of faith in the life-giving Will, which he typified in the glorious Siegfried. Not until he read Schopenhauer did he become bent on proving that he had always been a Pessimist at heart, and that Loki was the most sensible and worthy adviser of Wotan in The Rhine Gold.

Sometimes he faces the change in his opinions frankly enough. 'My Niblung drama,' he writes to Roeckel, 'had taken form at a time when I had built up with my reason an optimistic world on Hellenic principles, believing that nothing was necessary for the realization of such a world but that men should wish it. I ingeniously set aside the problem why they did not wish it. I remember that it was with this definite creative purpose that I conceived the personality of Siegfried, with the intention of representing an existence free from pain.'* But he appeals to his earlier works to shew that behind all these artificial optimistic ideas there was always with him an intuition of 'the sublime tragedy of renunciation, the negation of the will.' In trying to explain this, he is full of ideas philosophically, and full of the most amusing contradictions personally. Optimism, as an accidental excursion into the barren paths of reason on his own part, he calls 'Hellenic.'* In others he denounces it as rank Judaism, the Jew having at that time become for him the whipping boy for all modern humanity.* In a letter from London he expounds Schopenhauer to Roeckel with enthusiasm, preaching the renunciation of the Will to Live as the redemption from all error and vain pursuits: in the next letter he resumes the subject with unabated interest, and finishes by mentioning that on leaving London he went to Geneva and underwent 'a most beneficial course of hydropathy.' Seven months before this he had written as follows: 'Believe me, I too was once possessed by the idea of a country life. In order to become a radically healthy human being, I went two years ago to a Hydropathic Establishment, prepared to give up Art and everything if I could once more become a child of Nature. But, my good friend, I was obliged to laugh at my own naïveté when I found myself almost going mad. None of us will reach the promised land: we shall all die in the wilderness. Intellect is, as some one has said, a sort of disease: it is incurable.'

Roeckel knew his man of old, and evidently pressed him for explanations of the inconsistencies of The Ring with Night Falls on The Gods. Wagner defended himself with unfailing cleverness and occasional petulances, ranging from such pleas as 'I believe a true instinct has kept me from a too great definiteness; for it has been borne in on me that an absolute disclosure of the intention disturbs true insight,' to a volley of explanations and commentaries on the explanations. He gets excited and annoyed because Roeckel will not admire the Brynhild of Night Falls on The Gods; reinvents the Tarnhelm scene; and finally, the case being desperate, exclaims, 'It is wrong of you to challenge me to explain it in words: you must feel that something is being enacted that is not to be expressed in mere words.'

The Pessimist as Amorist

Sometimes he gets very far away from Pessimism indeed, and recommends Roeckel to solace his captivity, not by conquering the will to live
at liberty, but by 'the inspiring influences of the Beautiful.' The next
moment he throws over even Art for Life. 'Where life ends,' he says,
very wittily, 'Art begins. In youth we turn to Art, we know not why; and
only when we have gone through with Art and come out on the other
side, we learn to our cost that we have missed Life itself.' His only comfort is that he is beloved. And on the subject of love he lets himself loose
in a manner that would have roused the bitterest scorn in Schopenhauer,
though, as we have seen (p. 178), it is highly characteristic of Wagner.
'Love in its most perfect reality,' he says, 'is only possible between the
sexes: it is only as man and woman that human beings can truly love.
Every other manifestation of love can be traced back to that one absorbingly real feeling, of which all other affections are but an emanation,
a connection, or an imitation. It is an error to look on this as only one
of the forms in which love is revealed, as if there were other forms
coequal with it, or even superior to it. He who after the manner of
metaphysicians prefers *unreality* to *reality*, and derives the concrete
from the abstract—in short, puts the word before the fact—may be
right in esteeming the idea of love as higher than the expression of love,
and may affirm that actual love made manifest in feeling is nothing but
the outward and visible sign of a preexistent, non-sensuous, abstract
love; and he will do well to despise that sensuous function in general. In
any case it were safe to bet that such a man had never loved or been
loved as human beings can love, or he would have understood that in
despising this feeling, what he condemned was its sensual expression,
the outcome of man's animal nature, and not true human love. The
highest satisfaction and expression of the individual is only to be found
in his complete absorption, and that is only possible through love. Now
a human being is both *man* and *woman*: it is only when these two are
united that the real human being exists; and thus it is only by love that
man and woman attain to the full measure of humanity. But when nowadays we talk of a human being, such heartless blockheads are we that
quite involuntarily we only think of man. It is only in the union of man
and woman by love (sensuous and supersensuous) that the human
being exists; and as the human being cannot rise to the conception
of anything higher than his own existence—his own being—so the
transcendent act of his life is this consummation of his humanity
through love.'

It is clear after this utterance from the would-be Schopenhauerian, that Wagner's explanations of his works for the most part explain nothing but the mood in which he happened to be on the day he advanced them, or the train of thought suggested to his very susceptible imagination and active mind by the points raised by his questioner. Especially in his private letters, where his outpourings are modified by his dramatic consciousness of the personality of his correspondent, do we find him taking all manner of positions, and putting forward all sorts of cases which must be taken as clever and suggestive special pleadings, and not as serious and permanent expositions of his works. These works must speak for themselves: if The Ring says one thing, and a letter written afterwards says that it said something else, The Ring must be taken to confute the letter just as conclusively as if the two had been written by different hands. However, nobody fairly well acquainted with Wagner's utterances as a whole will find any unaccountable contradictions in them. As in all men of his type, our manifold nature was so marked in him that he was like several different men rolled into one. When he had exhausted himself in the character of the most pugnacious, aggressive, and sanguine of reformers, he rested himself as a Pessimist and Nirvanist. In The Ring the quietism of Brynhild's 'Rest, rest, thou God' is sublime in its deep conviction; but you have only to turn back the pages to find the irrepressible bustle of Siegfried and the revelry of the clansmen expressed with equal zest. Wagner was not a Schopenhauerite every day in the week, nor even a Wagnerite. His mind changes as often as his mood. On Monday nothing will ever induce him to return to quill-driving: on Tuesday he begins a new pamphlet. On Wednesday he is impatient of the misapprehensions of people who cannot see how impossible it is for him to preside as a conductor over platform performances of fragments of his works, which can only be understood when presented strictly according to his intention on the stage: on Thursday he gets up a concert of Wagnerian selections, and when it is over writes to his friends describing how profoundly both bandsmen and audience were impressed. On Friday he exults in the self-assertion of Siegfried's will against all moral ordinances, and is full of a revolutionary sense of 'the universal law of change and renewal': on Saturday he has an attack of holiness, and asks, 'Can you conceive a moral action of which the root idea is not renunciation?' In short, Wagner can be quoted against himself almost without limit, much as Beethoven's adagios could be quoted against his scherzos if a dispute arose between two fools as to whether he was a melancholy man or a merry one.*

THE MUSIC OF THE RING

The Representative Themes

To be able to follow the music of The Ring, all that is necessary is to become familiar enough with the brief musical phrases out of which it is built to recognize them and attach a certain definite significance to them, exactly as any ordinary Englishman recognizes and attaches a definite significance to the opening bars of God Save the Queen.* There is no difficulty here: every soldier is expected to learn and distinguish between different bugle calls and trumpet calls; and anyone who can do this can learn and distinguish between the representative themes or 'leading motives' (Leitmotifs)* of The Ring. They are the easier to learn because they are repeated again and again; and the main ones are so emphatically impressed on the ear whilst the spectator is looking for the first time at the objects, or witnessing the first strong dramatic expression of the ideas they denote, that the requisite association is formed unconsciously. The themes are neither long, nor complicated, nor difficult. Whoever can pick up the flourish of a coach-horn, the note of a bird, the rhythm of the postman's knock or of a horse's gallop, will be at no loss in picking up the themes of The Ring. No doubt, when it comes to forming the necessary mental association with the theme, it may happen that the spectator may find his ear conquering the tune more easily than his mind conquers the thought. But for the most part the themes do not denote thoughts at all, but either emotions of a quite simple universal kind, or the sights, sounds and fancies common enough to be familiar to children. Indeed some of them are as frankly childish as any of the funny little orchestral interludes which, in Haydn's Creation,* introduce the horse, the deer, or the worm. We have both the horse and the worm in The Ring, treated exactly in Haydn's manner, and with an effect not a whit less ridiculous to superior people who decline to take it good-humoredly. Even the complaisance of good Wagnerites is occasionally rather overstrained by the way in which Brynhild's allusions to her charger Grani elicit from the band a little rum-ti-tum triplet which by itself is in no way suggestive of a horse, although a continuous rush of such triplets makes a very exciting musical gallop.

Other themes denote objects which cannot be imitatively suggested by music: for instance, music cannot suggest a ring, and cannot suggest gold; yet each of these has a representative theme which pervades the

score in all directions. In the case of the gold the association is established by the very salient way in which the orchestra breaks into the
pretty theme in the first act of The Rhine Gold at the moment when the
sunrays strike down through the water and light up the glittering treasure, thitherto invisible. The reference of the strange little theme of the
wishing cap is equally manifest from the first, since the spectator's
attention is wholly taken up with the Tarnhelm and its magic when the
theme is first pointedly uttered by the orchestra. The sword theme is
introduced at the end of The Rhine Gold to express Wotan's hero
inspiration; and I have already mentioned that Wagner, unable, when it
came to practical stage management, to forego the appeal to the eye as
well as to the thought, here made Wotan pick up a sword and brandish
it, though no such instruction appears in the printed score. When this
sacrifice to Wagner's scepticism as to the reality of any appeal to an
audience that is not made through their bodily sense is omitted, the
association of the theme with the sword is not formed until that point
in the first act of The Valkyries at which Siegmund is left alone by
Hunding's hearth, weaponless, with the assurance that he will have to
fight for his life at dawn with his host. He recalls then how his father
promised him a sword for his hour of need; and as he does so, a flicker
from the dying fire is caught by the golden hilt of the sword in the tree,
when the theme immediately begins to gleam through the quiver of
sound from the orchestra, and only dies out as the fire sinks and the
sword is once more hidden by the darkness. Later on, this theme, which
is never silent whilst Sieglinda is dwelling on the story of the sword,
leaps out into the most dazzling splendor the band can give it when
Siegmund triumphantly draws the weapon from the tree. As it consists
of seven notes only, with a very marked measure, and a melody like
a simple flourish on a trumpet or post horn, nobody capable of catching
a tune can easily miss it.

The Valhalla theme, sounded with solemn grandeur as the home of
the gods first appears to us and to Wotan at the beginning of the second
scene of The Rhine Gold, also cannot be mistaken. It, too, has a mem-
orable rhythm; and its majestic harmonies, far from presenting those
novel or curious problems in polyphony of which Wagner still stands
suspected by superstitious people, are just those three simple chords
which festive students who vamp accompaniments to comic songs 'by
ear' soon find sufficient for nearly all the popular tunes in the world.

On the other hand, the ring theme, when it begins to hurtle through
the third scene of The Rhine Gold, cannot possibly be referred to any
special feature in the general gloom and turmoil of the den of the

dwarfs. It is not a melody, but merely the displaced metric accent which musicians call syncopation, rung on the notes of the familiar chord formed by piling three minor thirds on top of one another (technically, the chord of the minor ninth, *ci-devant* diminished seventh).* One soon picks it up and identifies it; but it does not get introduced in the unequivocally clear fashion of the themes described above, or of that malignant monstrosity, the theme which denotes the curse on the gold. Consequently it cannot be said that the musical design of the work is perfectly clear at the first hearing as regards all the themes; but it is so as regards most of them, the main lines being laid down as emphatically and intelligibly as the dramatic motives in a Shakespearean play. As to the coyer subtleties of the score, their discovery provides fresh interest for repeated hearings, giving The Ring a Beethovenian inexhaustibility and toughness of wear.

The themes associated with the individual characters get stamped on the memory easily by the simple association of the sound of the theme with the appearance of the person indicated. Its appropriateness is generally pretty obvious. Thus, the entry of the giants is made to a vigorous stumping, tramping measure. Mimmy, being a quaint, weird old creature, has a quaint, weird theme of two thin chords that creep down eerily one to the other. Gutruna's theme is pretty and caressing: Gunther's bold, rough, and commonplace. It is a favorite trick of Wagner's, when one of his characters is killed on the stage, to make the theme attached to that character weaken, fail, and fade away with a broken echo into silence.

The Characterization

All this, however, is the mere child's play of theme work. The more complex characters, instead of having a simple musical label attached to them, have their characteristic ideas and aspirations identified with special representative themes as they come into play in the drama; and the chief merit of the thematic structure of The Ring is the mastery with which the dramatic play of the ideas is reflected in the contrapuntal play of the themes. We do not find Wotan, like the dragon or the horse, or, for the matter of that, like the stage demon in Weber's Freischütz or Meyerbeer's Robert the Devil,* with one fixed theme attached to him like a name plate to an umbrella, blaring unaltered from the orchestra whenever he steps on the stage. Sometimes we have the Valhalla theme used to express the greatness of the gods as an idea of Wotan's. Again, we have his spear, the symbol of his power, identified with another theme, on which Wagner finally exercises his favorite device by making it break and fail, cut through, as it were, by the tearing sound of the theme identified with the sword, when Siegfried shivers the spear with the stroke of Nothung. Yet another theme connected with Wotan is the Wanderer music which breaks with such a majestic reassurance on the nightmare terror of Mimmy when Wotan appears at the mouth of his cave in the scene of the three riddles. Thus not only are there several Wotan themes, but each varies in its inflexions and shades of tone color according to its dramatic circumstances. So, too, the merry horn tune of the young Siegfried changes its measure, loads itself with massive harmonies, and becomes an exordium of the most imposing splendor when it heralds his entry as full-fledged hero in the prologue to Night Falls on The Gods. Even Mimmy has his two or three themes: the weird one already described; the little one in triple measure imitating the tap of his hammer, and fiercely mocked in the savage laugh of Alberic at his death; and finally the crooning tune in which he details all his motherly kindnesses to the little foundling Siegfried. Besides this there are all manner of little musical blinkings and shamblings and whinings, the least hint of which from the orchestra at any moment instantly brings Mimmy to mind, whether he is on the stage at the time or not.

In truth, dramatic characterization in music cannot be carried very far by the use of representative themes. Mozart, the greatest of all masters of this art, never dreamt of employing them; and, extensively as they are used in The Ring, they do not enable Wagner to dispense with the Mozartian method. Apart from the themes, Siegfried and Mimmy are still as sharply distinguished from one another by the character of their music as Don Giovanni from Leporello, Wotan from Gutruna as Sarastro from Papagena.* It is true that the themes attached to the characters have the same musical appropriateness as the rest of the music: for example, neither the Valhalla nor the spear themes could, without the most ludicrous incongruity, be used for the forest bird or the unstable, delusive Loki; but for all that the musical characterization must be regarded as independent of the specific themes, since the entire elimination of the thematic system from the score would leave the characters as well distinguished musically as they are at present.

One more illustration of the way in which the thematic system is worked. There are two themes connected with Loki. One is a rapid, sinuous, twisting, shifty semiquaver figure suggested by the unsubstantial, elusive logic-spinning of the clever one's braincraft. The other is the fire theme. In the first act of Siegfried, Mimmy makes his unavailing attempt to explain fear to Siegfried. With the horror fresh upon him of the sort of nightmare into which he has fallen after the departure of the Wanderer, and which has taken the form, at once fanciful and symbolic, of a delirious dread of light, he asks Siegfried whether he has never, whilst wandering in the forest, had his heart set hammering in frantic dread by the mysterious lights of the gloaming. To this, Siegfried, greatly astonished, replies that on such occasions his heart is altogether healthy and his sensations perfectly normal. Here Mimmy's question is accompanied by the tremulous sounding of the fire theme with its harmonies most oppressively disturbed and troubled; whereas with Siegfried's reply they become quite clear and straightforward, making the theme sound bold, brilliant, and serene. This is a typical instance of the way in which the themes are used.

The thematic system gives symphonic interest, reasonableness and unity to the music, enabling the composer to exhaust every aspect and quality of his melodic material, and, in Beethoven's manner, to work miracles of beauty, expression and significance with the briefest phrases. As a set-off against this, it has led Wagner to indulge in repetitions that would be intolerable in a purely dramatic work. Almost the first thing that a dramatist has to learn in constructing a play is that the persons must not come on the stage in the second act and tell one another at great length what the audience has already seen pass before its eyes in the first act. The extent to which Wagner has been seduced into violating this rule by his affection for his themes is startling to a practised playwright. Siegfried inherits from Wotan a mania for autobiography which leads him to inflict on everyone he meets the story of Mimmy and the dragon, although the audience have spent a whole evening witnessing the events he is narrating. Hagen tells the story to Gunther; and that same night Alberic's ghost tells it over again to Hagen, who knows it already as well as the audience. Siegfried tells the Rhine maidens as much of it as they will listen to, and then keeps telling it to his hunting companions until they kill him. Wotan's autobiography on the second evening becomes his biography in the mouths of the Norns on the fourth. The little that the Norns add to it is repeated an hour later by Valtrauta. How far all this repetition is tolerable is a matter of individual taste. A good story will bear repetition; and if it has woven into it such pretty tunes as the Rhine maidens' yodel, Mimmy's tinkling anvil beat, the note of the forest bird, the call of Siegfried's horn, and so on, it will bear a good deal of rehearsing. Those who have but newly learnt their way through The Ring will not readily admit that there is a bar too much repetition.

But how if you find some anti-Wagnerite raising the question whether the thematic system does not enable the composer to produce a music drama with much less musical fertility than was required from his predecessors for the composition of operas under the old system!

Such discussions are not within the scope of this little book. But as the book is now finished (for really nothing more need be said about The Ring), I am quite willing to add a few pages of ordinary musical criticism, partly to please the amateurs who enjoy that sort of reading, and partly for the guidance of those who wish to obtain some hints to help them through such critical small talk about Wagner and Bayreuth as may be forced upon them at the dinner table or between the acts.

The Old and the New Music

In the old-fashioned opera every separate number involved the composition of a fresh melody; but it is quite a mistake to suppose that this creative effort extended continuously throughout the number from the first to the last bar. When a musician composes according to a set metrical pattern, the selection of the pattern and the composition of the first stave (a stave in music corresponds to a line in verse) generally completes the creative effort. All the rest follows more or less mechanically to fill up the pattern, an air being very like a wall-paper design in this respect. Thus the second stave is usually a perfectly obvious consequence of the first; and the third and fourth an exact or very slightly varied repetition of the first and second. For example, given the first line of Pop Goes the Weasel or Yankee Doodle, any musical cobbler could supply the remaining three. There is very little tune-turning of this kind in The Ring; and it is noteworthy that where it does occur, as in Siegmund's spring song and Mimmy's croon, 'Ein zullendes Kind,'* the effect of the symmetrical staves, recurring as a mere matter of form, is perceptibly poor and platitudinous compared with the free flow of melody which prevails elsewhere.

The other and harder way of composing is to take a strain of free melody, and ring every variety of change of mood upon it as if it were a thought that sometimes brought hope, sometimes melancholy, sometimes exultation, sometimes raging despair and so on. To take several themes of this kind, and weave them together into a rich musical fabric passing panoramically before the ear with a continually varying flow of sentiment, is the highest feat of the musician: it is in this way that we get the fugue of Bach and the symphony of Beethoven. The admittedly inferior musician is the one who, like Auber and Offenbach,* not to mention our purveyors of drawing room ballads, can produce an unlimited quantity of symmetrical tunes, but cannot weave themes symphonically.

When this is taken into account, it will be seen that the fact that there is a great deal of repetition in The Ring does not distinguish it from the old-fashioned operas. The real difference is that in them the repetition was used for the mechanical completion of conventional metric patterns, whereas in The Ring the recurrence of the theme is an intelligent and interesting consequence of the recurrence of the dramatic phenomenon which it denotes. It should be remembered also that the substitution of symphonically treated themes for tunes with symmetrical eight-bar staves and the like, has always been the rule in the highest forms of music. To describe it, or be affected by it, as an abandonment of melody, is to confess oneself an ignoramus conversant only with dance tunes and ballads.

The sort of stuff a purely dramatic musician produces when he hampers himself with metric patterns in composition is not unlike what might have resulted in literature if Carlyle (for example) had been compelled by convention to write his historical stories in rhymed stanzas. That is to say, it limits his fertility to an occasional phrase, and three quarters of the time exercises only his barren ingenuity in fitting rhymes and measures to it. In literature the great masters of the art have long emancipated themselves from metric patterns. Nobody claims that the hierarchy of modern impassioned prose writers, from Bunyan to Ruskin, should be placed below the writers of pretty lyrics, from Herrick to Mr Austin Dobson.* Only in dramatic literature do we find the devastating tradition of blank verse still lingering, giving factitious prestige to the platitudes of dullards, and robbing the dramatic style of the genuine poet of its full natural endowment of variety, force, and simplicity.

This state of things, as we have seen, finds its parallel in musical art, since music can be written in prose themes or in versified tunes; only here nobody dreams of disputing the greater difficulty of the prose forms and the comparative triviality of versification. Yet in dramatic music, as in dramatic literature, the tradition of versification clings with the same pernicious results; and the opera, like the tragedy, is conventionally made like a wall paper. The theatre seems doomed to be in all things the last refuge of the hankering after cheap prettiness in art.

Unfortunately this confusion of the decorative with the dramatic element in both literature and music is maintained by the example of great masters in both arts. Very touching dramatic expression can be combined with decorative symmetry of versification when the artist happens to possess both the decorative and dramatic gifts, and to have cultivated both hand in hand. Shakespear and Shelley, for instance, far from being hampered by the conventional obligation to write their dramas in verse, found it much the easiest and cheapest way of producing them. But if Shakespear had been compelled by custom to write entirely in prose, all his ordinary dialogue might have been as good as the first scene of As You Like It;* and all his lofty passages as fine as 'What a piece of work is Man!';* thus sparing us a great deal of blank verse in which the thought is commonplace, and the expression, though catchingly turned, absurdly pompous. The Cenci* might either have been a serious drama or might never have been written at all if Shelley had not been allowed to carry off its unreality by Elizabethan versification. Still, both poets have achieved many passages in which the decorative and dramatic qualities are not only reconciled, but seem to enhance one another to a pitch otherwise unattainable.

Just so in music. When we find, as in the case of Mozart, a prodigiously gifted and arduously trained musician who is also, by a happy accident, a dramatist comparable to Molière, the obligation to compose operas in versified numbers not only does not embarrass him, but actually saves him trouble and thought. No matter what his dramatic mood may be, he expresses it in exquisite musical verses more easily than a dramatist of ordinary singleness of talent can express it in prose. Accordingly, he too, like Shakespear and Shelley, leaves versified airs, like *Dalla sua pace*, or Gluck's *Che faro senza Euridice*, or Weber's *Leise, leise*,* which are as dramatic from the first note to the last as the untrammelled themes of The Ring. In consequence, it used to be professorially demanded that all dramatic music should present the same double aspect. The demand was unreasonable, since symmetrical versification is no merit in dramatic music: one might as well stipulate that a dinner fork should be constructed so as to serve also as a tablecloth. It was an ignorant demand too, because it is not true that the composers of these exceptional examples were always, or even often, able to combine dramatic expression with symmetrical versification. Side by side with *Dalla sua pace* we have *Il mio tesoro* and *Non mi dir*,* in which exquisitely expressive opening phrases lead to decorative passages which are as grotesque from the dramatic point of view as the music which Alberic sings when he is slipping and sneezing in the Rhine mud is from the decorative point of view. Further, there is to be considered the mass of shapeless 'dry recitative' which separates these symmetrical numbers, and which might have been raised to considerable dramatic and musical importance had it been incorporated into a continuous musical fabric by thematic treatment. Finally, Mozart's most dramatic finales and concerted numbers are more or less in sonata form, like symphonic movements, and must therefore be classed as musical prose. And sonata form dictates repetitions and recapitulations from which the perfectly unconventional form adopted by Wagner is free. On the whole, there is more scope for both repetition and convention in the old form than in the new; and the poorer a composer's musical gift is, the surer he is to resort to the eighteenth century patterns to eke out his invention.

The Nineteenth Century

When Wagner was born in 1813, music had newly become the most astonishing, the most fascinating, the most miraculous art in the world. Mozart's Don Giovanni had made all musical Europe conscious of the enchantments of the modern orchestra and of the perfect adaptability of music to the subtlest needs of the dramatist. Beethoven had shown how those inarticulate mood-poems which surge through men who have, like himself, no exceptional command of words, can be written down in music as symphonies. Not that Mozart and Beethoven invented these applications of their art; but they were the first whose works made it clear that the dramatic and subjective powers of sound were enthralling enough to stand by themselves quite apart from the decorative musical structures of which they had hitherto been a mere feature. After the finales in Figaro* and Don Giovanni, the possibility of the modern music drama lay bare. After the symphonies of Beethoven it was certain that the poetry that lies too deep for words does not lie too deep for music, and that the vicissitudes of the soul, from the roughest fun to the loftiest aspiration, can make symphonies without the aid of dance tunes. As much, perhaps, will be claimed for the preludes and fugues of Bach; but Bach's method was unattainable: his compositions were wonderful webs of exquisitely beautiful Gothic traceries in sound, quite beyond all ordinary human talent. Beethoven's far blunter craft was thoroughly popular and practicable: not to save his soul could he have drawn one long Gothic line in sound as Bach could, much less have woven several of them together with so apt a harmony that even when the composer is unmoved its progressions saturate themselves with the emotion which (as modern critics are a little apt to forget) springs as warmly from our delicately touched admiration as from our sympathies, and sometimes makes us give a composer credit for pathetic intentions which he does not entertain, just as a boy imagines a treasure of tenderness and noble wisdom in the beauty of a woman. Besides, Bach set comic dialogue to music exactly as he set the recitatives of the Passion,* there being for him, apparently, only one recitative possible, and that the musically best. He reserved the expression of his merry mood for the regular set numbers in which he could make one of his wonderful contrapuntal traceries of pure ornament with the requisite gaiety of line and movement. Beethoven bowed to no ideal of beauty: he only sought the expression for his feeling. To him a joke was a joke; and if it sounded funny in music he was satisfied. Until the old habit of judging all music by its decorative symmetry had worn out, musicians were shocked by his symphonies, and, misunderstanding his integrity, openly questioned his sanity. But to those who were not looking for pretty new sound patterns, but were longing for the expression of their moods in music, he achieved a revelation, because, being single in his aim to express his own moods, he anticipated with revolutionary courage and frankness all the moods of the rising generations of the nineteenth century.

The result was inevitable. In the nineteenth century it was no longer necessary to be a born pattern designer in sound to be a composer. One had but to be a dramatist or a poet completely susceptible to the dramatic and descriptive powers of sound. A race of literary and theatrical musicians appeared; and Meyerbeer, the first of them, made an extraordinary impression. The frankly delirious description of his Robert the Devil in Balzac's short story entitled Gambara,* and Goethe astonishingly mistaken notion that he could have composed music for Faust, shew how completely the enchantments of the new dramatic music upset the judgment of artists of eminent discernment. Meyerbeer was, people said (old gentlemen still say so in Paris), the successor of Beethoven: he was, if a less perfect musician than Mozart, a profounder genius. Above all, he was original and daring. Wagner himself raved about the duet in the fourth act of Les Huguenots* as wildly as anyone.

Yet all this effect of originality and profundity was produced by a quite limited talent for turning striking phrases, exploiting certain curious and rather catching rhythms and modulations, and devising suggestive or eccentric instrumentation. On its decorative side, it was the same phenomenon in music as the Baroque school in architecture:* an energetic struggle to enliven organic decay by mechanical oddities and novelties. Meyerbeer was no symphonist. He could not apply the thematic system to his striking phrases, and so had to cobble them into metric patterns in the old style; and as he was no 'absolute musician'* either, he hardly got his metric patterns beyond mere quadrille tunes,*

which were either wholly undistinguished, or else made remarkable by
certain brusqueries which, in the true rococo manner, owed their singularity to their senselessness. He could produce neither a thorough
music drama nor a charming opera. But with all this, and worse,
Meyerbeer had some genuine dramatic energy, and even passion; and
sometimes rose to the occasion in a manner which, whilst the imagination of his contemporaries remained on fire with the novelties of dramatic music, led them to overrate him with an extravagance which
provoked Wagner to conduct a long critical campaign against his
supremacy. In the eighteen-sixties this was inevitably ascribed to the
professional jealousy of a disappointed rival. Nowadays young people
cannot understand how anyone could ever have taken Meyerbeer's
influence seriously. The few who remember the reputation he built on
The Huguenots and The Prophet,* and who now realize what a no-
thoroughfare the path he opened proved to be, even to himself, know
how inevitable and how impersonal Wagner's attack was.

Wagner was the literary musician par excellence. He could not, like
Mozart and Beethoven, produce decorative tone structures independently of any dramatic or poetic subject matter, because, that craft
being no longer necessary for his purpose, he did not cultivate it. As
Shakespear, compared with Tennyson, appears to have an exclusively
dramatic talent, so exactly does Wagner compared with Mendelssohn.
On the other hand, he had not to go to third rate literary hacks for
'librettos' to set to music: he produced his own dramatic poems, thus
giving dramatic integrity to opera, and making symphony articulate.
A Beethoven symphony (except the articulate part of the ninth)
expresses noble feeling, but not thought: it has moods, but no ideas.
Wagner added thought and produced the music drama. Mozart's loftiest opera, his Ring, so to speak, The Magic Flute, has a libretto which,
though none the worse for seeming, like The Rhine Gold, the merest
Christmas tomfoolery to shallow spectators, is the product of a talent
immeasurably inferior to Mozart's own. The libretto of Don Giovanni
is coarse and trivial: its transfiguration by Mozart's music may be
a marvel; but nobody will venture to contend that such transfigur-
ations, however seductive, can be as satisfactory as tone poetry or drama
in which the musician and the poet are at the same level. Here, then, we
have the simple secret of Wagner's pre-eminence as a dramatic musician. He wrote the poems as well as composed the music of his 'stage
festival plays,' as he called them.

Up to a certain point in his career Wagner paid the penalty of undertaking two arts instead of one. Mozart had his trade as a musician at his

fingers' ends when he was twenty, because he had served an arduous apprenticeship to that trade and no other. Wagner was very far from having attained equal mastery at thirty-five: indeed he himself has told us that not until he had passed the age at which Mozart died did he compose with that complete spontaneity of musical expression which can only be attained by winning entire freedom from all preoccupation with the difficulties of technical processes. But when that time came, he was not only a consummate musician, like Mozart, but a dramatic poet and a critical and philosophical essayist, exercising a considerable influence on his century. The sign of this consummation was his ability at last to play with his art, and thus to add to his already famous achievements in sentimental drama that lighthearted art of comedy of which the greatest masters, like Molière and Mozart, are so much rarer than the tragedians and sentimentalists. It was then that he composed the first two acts of Siegfried, and later on The Mastersingers,* a professedly comedic work, and a quite Mozartian garden of melody, hardly credible as the work of the straining artificer of Tannhäuser. Only, as no man ever learns to do one thing by doing something else, however closely allied the two things may be, Wagner still produced no music independently of his poems. The overture to The Mastersingers is delightful when you know what it is all about; but only those to whom it came as a concert piece without any such clue, and who judged its reckless counterpoint by the standard of Bach and of Mozart's Magic Flute overture, can realize how atrocious it used to sound to musicians of the old school. When I first heard it, with the clear march of the polyphony in Bach's B minor Mass fresh in my memory, I confess I thought that the parts had got dislocated, and that some of the band were half a bar behind the others. Perhaps they were; but now that I am familiar with the work, and with Wagner's harmony, I can still quite understand certain passages producing that effect on an admirer of Bach even when performed with perfect accuracy.

The Music of the Future

The ultimate success of Wagner was so prodigious that to his dazzled disciples it seemed that the age of what he called 'absolute' music must be at an end, and the musical future destined to be an exclusively Wagnerian one inaugurated at Bayreuth. All great geniuses produce this illusion. Wagner did not begin a movement: he consummated it. He was the summit of the nineteenth century school of dramatic music in the same sense as Mozart was the summit (the word is Gounod's*) of

the eighteenth century school. All those who attempted to carry on his
Bayreuth tradition have shared the fate of the forgotten purvevors of
second-hand Mozart a hundred years ago. As to the expected supersession of absolute music, Wagner's successors in European rank were
Brahms, Elgar, and Richard Strauss.* The reputation of Brahms rests
on his absolute music alone: such works as his German Requiem endear
themselves to us as being musically great fun; but to take them quite
seriously is to make them oppressively dull. Elgar followed Beethoven
and Schumann: he owes nothing essential to Wagner, and secured his
niche in the temple by his symphonies and his Enigma Variations,
which are as absolutely musical as any modern music can be. Although
Strauss produced works for the musical theatre which maintained it at
the level to which Wagner had raised it, his new departure was a form
of musical drama, comic epic, and soul autobiography in which stage,
singers, and all the rest of the theatrical material of Bayreuth save only
the orchestra are thrown overboard, and the work effected by instrumental music alone, even Beethoven's final innovation of a chorus
being discarded. Just the same thing happened when Elgar took as his
theme Shakespear's Henry IV, with Falstaff as its chief figure. He made
the band do it all, and with such masterful success that one cannot bear
to think of what would have been the result of a mere attempt to turn
the play into an opera.

The Russian composers whose vogue succeeded that of Wagner were
not in the least Wagnerian: they developed from the romantic school,
from Weber and Meyerbeer, from Berlioz and Liszt, much as they
might have done had Wagner never existed except as a propagandist of
the importance of their art. A disparaging attitude towards Wagner
resembling that of Chopin to Beethoven, and a very similar escape from
his influence even in technique, was quite common among the composers whose early lives overlapped the last part of his. In England the
composers who are the juniors of Elgar, but the seniors of (for example)
Bax and Ireland, the most notable of whom are Mr Granville Bantock*
and Mr Rutland Boughton, were heavily Wagnerized in their youth,
and began by Tristanizing and Götterdämmerunging heroically; but
when they found themselves their Wagnerism vanished. The younger
men do not begin with Wagner nor even with Strauss: they are mostly
bent on producing curiosities of absolute music until they settle down
into a serious style of their own. All that can be said for the Wagner
tradition is that it finally killed the confusion between decorative pattern music and dramatic music which muddled Meyerbeer and imposed
absurd repetitions on the heroes and heroines of Handel and Mozart.

Even in absolute music, the post-Wagnerite sonata form has become so much less mechanical and thoughtless that the fact that it still persists in essentials is hardly worth asserting.

Writing before any of these developments had happened, I said in the first edition of this book* that there was no more hope in attempts to out-Wagner Wagner in music drama than there had been in the old attempts to make Handel the starting point of a great school of oratorio. How true this was is now so obvious that my younger readers may wonder why I thought it worth while to say it. But if veterans did not indulge in these day-before-yesterdayisms Music would lose the thread of its history.

BAYREUTH

WHEN the Bayreuth Festival Playhouse was at last completed, and opened in 1876 with the first performance of The Ring, European society was compelled to admit that Wagner was 'a success.' Royal personages, detesting his music, sat out the performances in the row of boxes set apart for princes. They all complimented him on the astonishing 'push' with which, in the teeth of all obstacles, he had turned a fabulous and visionary project into a concrete commercial reality, patronized by the public at a pound a head. It is as well to know that these congratulations had no other effect upon Wagner than to open his eyes to the fact that the Bayreuth experiment, as an attempt to evade the ordinary social and commercial conditions of theatrical enterprise, was a failure. His own account of it contrasts the reality with his intentions in a vein which would be bitter if it were not so humorous. The precautions taken to keep the seats out of the hands of the frivolous public and in the hands of earnest disciples, banded together in little Wagner Societies throughout Europe, had ended in their forestalling by ticket speculators and their sale to just the sort of idle globe-trotting tourists against whom the temple was to have been strictly closed. The money, supposed to be contributed by the faithful, was begged by energetic subscription-hunting ladies from people who must have had the most grotesque misconceptions of the composer's aims: among others, the Khedive of Egypt and the Sultan of Turkey!*

Since then, subscriptions are no longer needed; for the Festival Playhouse pays its own way now, and is commercially on the same footing as any other theatre. The only qualification required from the visitor is money. A Londoner spends twenty pounds on a visit: a native Bayreuther spends one pound. In either case 'the Folk,' on whose behalf Wagner turned out in 1849, are effectually excluded; and the Festival Playhouse must therefore be classed as infinitely less Wagnerian in its character than Hampton Court Palace. Nobody knew this better than Wagner; and nothing can be further off the mark than to chatter about Bayreuth as if it had succeeded in escaping from the conditions of our modern civilization any more than the Grand Opera in Paris or London.

Within these conditions, however, it effected a new departure in that excellent German institution, the summer theatre. Unlike the old opera houses, which are constructed so that the audience may present a splendid pageant to the delighted manager, it was designed to secure an uninterrupted view of the stage, and an undisturbed hearing of the music, to the audience. The dramatic purpose of the performances was taken with entire and elaborate seriousness as the sole purpose of them; and the management was jealous for the reputation of Wagner. The sightseeing globetrotter no longer crowds out the genuine disciple: the audiences are now as genuinely devoted as Wagner could have desired: the disconcerted, bewildered, bored followers of fashion have vanished with the sportsman on a holiday: the atmosphere is the right one for the work. There is, apparently, an effective demand for summer theatres of the highest class. There is no reason why the experiment should not be tried in England. If our enthusiasm for Handel can support Handel Festivals, laughably dull, stupid and anti-Handelian as these choral monstrosities are, as well as annual provincial festivals on the same model, there is no likelihood of a Wagner Festival failing. Suppose, for instance, a Wagner theatre were built at Hampton Court or on Richmond Hill,* not to say Margate pier, so that we could have a delightful summer evening holiday, Bayreuth fashion, passing the hours between the acts in the park or on the river before sunset, is it seriously contended that there would be any lack of visitors? If a little of the money that is wasted on grand stands, Eiffel towers, and dismal Halls by the Sea,* all as much tied to brief annual seasons as Bayreuth, were applied in this way, the profit would be far more certain and the social utility prodigiously greater. Any English enthusiasm for Bayreuth that does not take the form of clamor for a Festival playhouse in England may be set aside as mere pilgrimage mania.

Besides, the early Bayreuth performances were far from delectable. The singing was sometimes tolerable, and sometimes abominable. Some of the singers were mere animated beer casks, too lazy and conceited to practise the self-control and physical training that is expected as a matter of course from an acrobat, a jockey or a pugilist. The women's dresses were prudish and absurd. It is true that after some years Kundry no longer wore an early Victorian ball dress with 'ruchings,' and that Freia was provided with a quaintly modish copy of the flowered gown of Spring in Botticelli's famous picture;* but the mailclad Brynhild still climbed the mountains with her legs carefully hidden in a long white skirt, and looked so exactly like Mrs Leo Hunter* as Minerva that it was quite impossible to feel a ray of illusion whilst looking at her. The ideal of womanly beauty aimed at reminded Englishmen of the barmaids of the seventies, when the craze for golden hair was at its worst. Further, whilst Wagner's stage directions were sometimes disregarded as unintelligently as at the old opera houses, Wagner's quaintly old-fashioned tradition of half rhetorical, half historical-pictorial attitude and gesture prevailed. The most striking moments of the drama were conceived as *tableaux vivants* with posed models, instead of as passages of action, motion, and life.

I need hardly add that the supernatural powers of control attributed by credulous pilgrims to Wagner's widow, and later on to his son, did not exist. Prima donnas and tenors were as unmanageable at Bayreuth as anywhere else. Casts were capriciously changed; stage business was insufficiently rehearsed; the audience was compelled to listen to a Brynhild or Siegfried of fifty when they had carefully arranged to see one of twenty-five, much as in any ordinary opera house. Even the conductors upset the arrangements occasionally. On the other hand, we could always feel assured that in thoroughness of preparation of the chief work of the season, in strenuous artistic pretentiousness, in pious conviction that the work was of such enormous importance as to be worth doing well at all costs, the Bayreuth performances would deserve their reputation. Their example raised the quality of operatic performances throughout the world, even in apparently incorrigible centres of fashion and frivolity.

Bayreuth in England

In 1898 I purposely dwelt on the early shortcomings of Bayreuth to shew that there was no reason in the world why as good and better performances of The Ring should not be given in England, and that neither Wagner's widow nor his son could pretend to handle them with greater authority than any artist who feels the impulse to interpret them. Nobody will ever know what Wagner himself thought of the artists who established the Bayreuth tradition: he was obviously not in a position to criticize them. For instance, had Rubini survived to create Siegmund, Wagner could hardly have written so amusing and vivid a description as he did of his Ottavio* in the old Paris days. Wagner was under great obligations to the heroes and heroines of 1876; and he naturally said nothing to disparage their triumphs; but there is no reason to believe that all or indeed any of them satisfied him as Schnorr of Carolsfeld satisfied him as Tristan, or Schröder Devrient as Fidelio.* It was just as likely that the next Schnorr or Schröder would arise in England. Nowadays it seems odd that anyone should need to be told all this. British and American singers have long since replaced the Bayreuth veterans to considerable advantage.

Wagnerian Singers

No nation need have any difficulty in producing a race of Wagnerian singers. With the single exception of Handel, no composer has written music so well calculated to make its singers vocal athletes as Wagner. Abominably as the Germans sang in Wagner's day, it was astonishing how they throve physically on his leading parts. His secret is the Handelian secret. Instead of specializing his vocal parts after the manner of Verdi and Gounod for shrieking sopranos, goat-bleating tenors, and tremulous baritones with an effective compass of about a fifth at the extreme tiptop of their ranges, and for contraltos with chest registers forced all over their compass in the manner of music hall singers, he employs the entire range of the human voice, demanding from everybody nearly two effective octaves.* The bulk of the work lies easily in the middle of the voice, which is nevertheless well exercised all over, one part of it relieving the other healthily and continually. He uses the highest notes sparingly, and is ingeniously considerate in the matter of instrumental accompaniment. Even when the singer seems to dominate all the thunders of the full orchestra, a glance at the score will shew that he is well heard, not because of a stentorian voice, but because Wagner meant him to be heard. The old lazy Italian style of orchestral accompaniment as we find it in Rossini's Stabat or Verdi's Trovatore,* where the strings play a rum-tum accompaniment whilst the whole wind band blares away, fortissimo, in unison with the singer, is somehow not so brutally opaque in practice as it looks on paper; but Wagner never condescends to it. Even in an ordinary opera house, with the orchestra ranged directly between the singers and the audience, his instrumentation is transparent to the human voice.

On every point, then, a Wagner theatre and Wagner festivals are much more generally practicable than the older and more artificial forms of dramatic music. A presentable performance of The Ring is a big undertaking only in the sense in which the construction of a railway is a big undertaking: that is, it requires plenty of work and plenty of professional skill; but it does not, like the old operas and oratorios, require those extraordinary vocal gifts which only a few individuals scattered here and there throughout Europe are born with. Singers who could never execute the roulades of Semiramis, Assur, and Arsaces in Rossini's Semiramide,* could sing the parts of Brynhild, Wotan, and Erda without missing a note. Any Englishman can understand this if he considers for a moment the difference between a Cathedral service and an Italian opera at Covent Garden. The service is a much more serious

matter than the opera. Yet provincial talent is sufficient for it, if the
requisite industry and devotion are forthcoming. Even at the Opera
I have seen lusty troopers and porters, without art or manners, accepted
by fashion as principal tenors during the long interval between Mario
and Jean de Reszke; and the two most extraordinary dramatic singers of
the twentieth century, Chaliapin and Vladimir Rosing,* are quite independent of the old metropolitan artificialities. Let us remember that
Bayreuth has recruited its Parsifals from the peasantry, and that the
artisans of a village in the Bavarian Alps are capable of a famous and
elaborate Passion Play,* and then consider whether any country is so
poor in talent that its amateurs must journey to the centre of Europe to
witness a Wagner Festival.

Wagnerism with Wagner Left Out

In spite of the fact that my old suggestion of a Festival Playhouse on
Richmond Hill has now been proved perfectly feasible as far as the
availability of the necessary home talent is concerned, only one serious
attempt to establish a Bayreuth in England has come to my knowledge;
and that one, far from concerning itself with Wagner, owes its success
to native British music with some early ultra-classical assistance from
Gluck. Mr Rutland Boughton, who began his career as a composer
when the influence of Wagner was at its height, has attempted to do in
Somerset what Wagner did in Thuringia,* with the very material difference that Wagner had the King of Bavaria at his back, and Mr Boughton
had nothing material at his back at all. He selected Glastonbury as his
Bayreuth; and has established an annual festival there which can already
shew a remarkable record of work done. The very desperation of the
enterprise has been its salvation. Had Mr Boughton been obsessed, as
Wagner was, with the scale to which the Grand Operas of Paris,
London, and Berlin work, he would have had to wait for a king to help
him: that is, he would have waited for ever. Fortunately he remembered
that Wagner was not only the highly professionalized royal conductor
of Dresden, brought up in the belief that the only success that can hall-
mark an opera is a Meyerbeerian success at the Paris Opera: he was also
the author of the saying that music is kept alive, not by the triumphs of
fashionable commercial professionalism, but on the cottage piano of
the amateur. Mr Rutland Boughton began in ordinary village halls in
Somerset, with a piano and his own fingers for orchestra, his wife as
scene painter and costumier, and a fit-up for a stage. The singing and
acting was done by the villagers and by anyone else who would come;

and a surprising number of quite distinguished talents did come. On these terms performances were achieved which in point of atmosphere and intimacy of interest were actually better than the performances at the enormously more pretentious Festival Playhouse in Bayreuth, or its copy the Prince Regent Theatre in Munich.* There were friendly subscribers, not enough to prevent each festival from ruining Mr Boughton for six months or so, but enough to enable him to devote the remaining six months to preparation for another financial catastrophe, encouraged by the fact that the crashes were less and less disastrous as his enterprise became better and better known. His festival is now a yearly event in Avalon,* once an island, now a city in a plain, Glastonbury, steeped in traditions which make it holy ground. But it still has no theatre, no electric light, no convenience for Wagnerian drama that every village does not possess. Yet it is here that the Wagnerist dream has been best realized in England.

That dream, truly interpreted, did not mean that the English soil should bring forth performances of Wagner's music copied from those at Bayreuth. It meant that the English soil should produce English music and English drama, and that English people should perform them in their own way. It is precisely because Mr Boughton has never performed a work of Wagner's, but, with the scholastic exception of an opera or two by Gluck, has composed his own music and had it and other English music sung in English ways, that he can claim to be a Perfect Wagnerite.

By this time there may be other and cognate experiments less known to me. During the twentieth century an important social development has transformed that costly and deleterious bore, the British holiday, into a genuinely recreative change. Under the title of Summer Schools, voluntary associations of artistically minded students of sociology, theosophy, science, history, and what not—shall we say people who take life, or some department of life, seriously, and cannot be happy unless they are using their brains and learning something in the intervals of dancing and singing for pure fun?—now appear every autumn in the prettiest country districts.* These Schools are open to everybody; they afford intimate glimpses of more or less celebrated people who come and lecture to them for the sake of propaganda; and they are very much jollier, as well as substantially cheaper and more genial, than the so-called pleasure resorts in which irritable and overworked professional entertainers hypnotize credulous Britons into believing that they are enjoying themselves when they are only paying through the nose for being worried and pillaged. Where there were formerly only one or two elderly congresses, like the meetings of the British Association, with no activity but that of elderly lecturers all lecturing at the same time in different rooms, there are now dozens of smaller but more youthful and vital gatherings in which, whatever the main subject to be studied may be, Art is continually breaking in in one form or another.

I myself, after a larger experience of professionally and commercially organized art than most men can afford (for I had to earn my living as a critic of such art in my early days), find that it is at such gatherings and from such voluntary enterprises that I can oftenest recapture something of that magic which music and drama had for me in my childhood, and which it is so utterly impossible to preserve under commercial conditions. Commerce in art can save me from many ridiculous blunders and makeshifts that do not matter; but it seldom achieves the things that do matter, never indeed except when they are forced on it in spite of its teeth by some individual artist, mostly one heavily persecuted by it as Wagner was.

Amateur art is discredited art in so far only as the amateur is known as the ape of commercial art. Persons who go to the theatre and opera house only to be smitten with an infatuate ambition to reproduce in their own untrained persons what they see the great professional artists doing there, are mostly foredoomed to failure and ridicule. Here and there one of them succeeds, only to be absorbed by the commercial profession. But the countryside is full of stout characters with no such folly and no such ambition, who will do as much for any really gifted artistic leader as they have done for Mr Boughton and for the organizers of our provincial choirs and brass bands. If Little Bethel has raised the miners of England* in a few generations from troglodyte savagery to pious respectability, Little Bayreuth may as easily raise them from pious respectability to a happy consciousness of and interest in fine art, without which all their piety and respectability will not save their children from resorting to cruel sports and squalid sensualities in their natural need for enjoyment. And so, good luck to Little Bayreuth; and may it be as successful as Little Bethel in demonstrating that the laughter of fools is as the crackling of thorns under a pot!

II

AN OPEN LETTER
AND A PREFACE

THE SANITY OF ART

AN EXPOSURE OF THE CURRENT NONSENSE
ABOUT ARTISTS BEING DEGENERATE

* * *

Impressionism

WHEN I was engaged chiefly in the criticism of pictures, the Impressionist movement was struggling for life in London;* and I supported it vigorously because, being the outcome of heightened attention and quickened consciousness on the part of its disciples, it was evidently destined to improve pictures greatly by substituting a natural, observant, real style for a conventional, taken-for-granted, ideal one. The result has entirely justified my choice of sides. I can remember when Whistler,* bent on forcing the public to observe the qualities he was introducing into pictorial work, had to exhibit a fine drawing of a girl with the head deliberately crossed out with a few rough pencil strokes,* knowing perfectly well that if he left a woman's face discernible the British Philistine would simply look to see whether she was a pretty girl or not, or whether she represented some of his pet characters in fiction, and pass on without having seen any of the qualities of artistic execution which made the drawing valuable. But it was easier for the critics to resent the obliteration of the face as an insolent eccentricity, and to shew their own good manners by writing of Mr Whistler as Jimmy, than to think out what he meant. It took several years of 'propaganda by deed'* before the qualities which the Impressionists insisted on came to be looked for as matters of course in pictures; so that at last the keen picture-gallery frequenter, when he came face to face with Bouguereau's 'Girl in a Cornfield,'* could no longer accept it as a window-glimpse of nature, because he saw at once that the girl is really standing in a studio with what the house agents call a good north light, and that the cornfield is a conventional sham. This advance in the education of our art fanciers was effected by persistently exhibiting pictures which, like Whistler's girl with her head scratched out, were propagandist samples of workmanship rather than complete works of art. But the moment Whistler and his party forced the dealers and the societies of painters to exhibit these studies, and, by doing so, to accustom the public to tolerate what appeared to it at first to be absurdities, the door was necessarily opened to real absurdities. Artists of doubtful or incomplete vocation find it difficult to draw or paint well; but it is easy for them to smudge paper or canvas so as to suggest a picture just as the stains on an old ceiling or the dark spots in a glowing coal-fire do. Plenty of rubbish of this kind was produced, exhibited, and tolerated at the time when people could not see the difference between any daub in which there were aniline shadows and a landscape by Monet.* Not that they thought the daub as good as the Monet: they thought the Monet as ridiculous as the daub; but they were afraid to say so, because they had discovered that people who were good judges did not think Monet ridiculous.

Then, beside the mere impostors, there were certain unaffected and conscientious painters who produced abnormal pictures because they saw abnormally. My own sight happened to be 'normal' in the oculist's sense: that is, I saw things with the naked eye as most people can only be made to see them by the aid of spectacles. Once I had a discussion with an artist who was shewing me a clever picture of his in which the parted lips in a pretty woman's face revealed what seemed to me like a mouthful of virgin snow. The painter lectured me for not consulting my eyes instead of my knowledge of facts. 'You dont see the divisions in a set of teeth when you look at a person's mouth,' he said: 'all you see is a strip of white, or yellow, or pearl, as the case may be. But because you know, as a matter of anatomic fact, that there are divisions there, you want to have them represented by strokes in a drawing. That is just like you art critics, &c., &c.' I do not think he believed me when I told him that when I looked at a row of teeth, I saw, not only the divisions between them, but their exact shape, both in contour and in modelling, just as well as I saw their general color. Some of the most able of the Impressionists evidently did not see forms as definitely as they appreciated color relationship; and, since there is always a great deal of imitation in the arts, we soon had young painters with perfectly good sight looking at landscapes or at their models with their eyes half closed and a little asquint, until what they saw looked to them like one of their favorite master's pictures.

Further, the Impressionist movement led to a busy study of the atmosphere, conventionally supposed to be invisible, but seldom really completely so, and of what were called values: that is, the relation of light and dark between the various objects depicted, on the correctness of which relation truth of effect largely depends. This, though very difficult in full out-door light with the various colors brilliantly visible, was comparatively easy in gloomy rooms where the absence of light reduced all colors to masses of brown or grey of varying depth.

Whistler's portrait of Sarasate,* a masterpiece in its way, would look like a study in monochrome if hung beside a portrait by Holbein;* and the little bouquets of color with which he sometimes decorates his female sitters, exquisite as the best of them are, have the character of enamel, of mosaic, of jewellery: never of primitive nature. His disciples could paint dark interiors, or figures placed apparently in coal cellars, with admirable truth and delicacy of values whilst they were still help- lessly unable to represent a green tree or a blue sky, much less paint an interior with the light and local color as clear as they are in the works of Peter de Hooghe.* Naturally the public eye, with its utilitarian familiar- ity with local color, and its Philistine insensibility to values and atmos- phere, did not at first see what the Impressionists were driving at, and dismissed them as mere perverse, notoriety-hunting cranks.

Here, then, you had a movement wholly beneficial and progressive, and in no sense insane or decadent. Nevertheless it led to the public exhibition of daubs which even the authors themselves would never have presumed to offer for exhibition before; it betrayed aberrations of vision in painters who, on the old academic lines, would have hidden their defects by drawing objects (teeth for instance) as they knew them to exist, and not as they saw them; it set clear-sighted students practis- ing optical distortion, so as to see things myopically and astigmatically; and it substituted canvases which looked like enlargements of under- exposed photographs for the familiar portraits of masters of the hounds in cheerfully unmistakable pink coats, mounted on bright chestnut horses. All of which, and much else, to a man who looked on without any sense of the deficiencies in conventional painting, necessarily sug- gested that the Impressionists and their contemporaries were much less sane than their fathers.

Wagnerism

Again, my duties as a musical critic* compelled me to ascertain very carefully the exact bearings of the controversy which has raged round Wagner's music-dramas since the middle of the century. When you and I last met,* we were basking in the sun between the acts of Parsifal at Bayreuth; but experience has taught me that an American may appear at Bayreuth without being necessarily fonder than most men of a tech- nical discussion on music. Let me therefore put the case to you in a mercifully intelligible way. Music is like drawing, in that it can be purely decorative, or purely dramatic, or anything between the two. A draughtsman may be a pattern-designer like William Morris, or he

may be a delineator of life and character, like Ford Madox Brown.* Or
he may come between these two extremes, and treat scenes of life and
character in a decorative way, like Walter Crane* or Burne-Jones: both
of them consummate pattern-designers, whose subject-pictures and
illustrations are also fundamentally figure-patterns, prettier than
Madox Brown's, but much less convincingly alive. Do you realize that
in music we have these same alternative applications of the art to drama
and decoration? You can compose a graceful, symmetrical sound-
pattern that exists solely for the sake of its own grace and symmetry. Or
you can compose music to heighten the expression of human emotion;
and such music will be intensely affecting in the presence of that emotion, and utter nonsense apart from it. For examples of pure pattern-
designing in music I should have to go back to the old music of the
thirteenth, fourteenth, and fifteenth centuries, before the operatic
movement gained the upper hand; but I am afraid my assertions that
much of this music is very beautiful, and hugely superior to the stuff
our music publishers turn out today, would not be believed in America;
for when I hinted at something of the kind lately in the American
Musical Courier,* and pointed out also the beauty of the instruments
for which this old music was written (viols, virginals, and so on*), one
of your leading musical critics rebuked me with an expatiation on the
superiority (meaning apparently the greater loudness) of the modern
concert grand pianoforte,* and contemptuously ordered the Middle
Ages out from the majestic presence of the nineteenth century.[1] You
must take my word for it that in England alone a long line of composers,
from Henry VIII to Lawes and Purcell,* have left us quantities of
instrumental music which was neither dramatic music nor descriptive
music, but was designed to affect the hearer solely by its beauty of
sound and grace and ingenuity of pattern. This is the art which Wagner
called absolute music. It is represented today by the formal sonata and
symphony; and we are coming back to it in something like its old integrity by a post-Wagnerian reaction led by that greatly gifted absolute
musician and hopelessly commonplace and tedious homilist, Johannes
Brahms.

To understand the present muddle, you must know that modern
dramatic music did not appear as an independent branch of musical
art, but as an adulteration of decorative music. The first modern dramatic composers accepted as binding on them the rules of good

---

[1] Perhaps by this time, however, Mr Arnold Dolmetsch* has educated America in this
matter, as he educated London and educated me.

pattern-designing in sound; and this absurdity was made to appear practicable by the fact that Mozart had such an extraordinary command of his art that his operas contain numbers which, though they seem to follow the dramatic play of emotion and character without reference to any other consideration whatever, are seen, on examining them from the point of view of the absolute musician, to be symmetrical sound-patterns. But these *tours de force* were no real justification for imposing the laws of pattern-designing on other dramatic musicians; and even Mozart himself broke away from them in all directions, and was violently attacked by his contemporaries for doing so, the accusations levelled at him (absence of melody, illegitimate and discordant harmonic progressions, and monstrous abuse of the orchestra) being exactly those with which the opponents of Wagner so often pester ourselves. Wagner, whose leading lay characteristic was his enormous common-sense, completed the emancipation of the dramatic musician from these laws of pattern-designing; and we now have operas, and very good ones too, written by composers like Bruneau,* who are not musicians in the old sense at all: that is, they are not pattern-designers; they do not compose music apart from drama; and when they have to furnish their operas with dances, instrumental intermezzos or the like, they either take themes from the dramatic part of their operas and rhapsodize on them, or else they turn out some perfectly simple song or dance tune, at the cheapness of which Haydn would have laughed, and give it an air of momentousness by orchestral and harmonic fineries.

If I add now that music in the academic, professorial, Conservative, respectable sense always means decorative music, and that students are taught that the laws of pattern-designing are binding on all musicians, and that violations of them are absolutely 'wrong'; and if I mention incidentally that these laws are themselves confused by the survivals from a still older tradition based on the Church art, technically very highly specialized, of writing perfectly smooth and beautiful vocal harmony for unaccompanied voices, worthy to be sung by angelic doctors round the throne of God (this was Palestrina's art),* you will understand why all the professional musicians who could not see beyond the routine they were taught, and all the men and women (and there are many of them) who have little or no sense of drama, but a very keen sense of beauty of sound and prettiness of pattern in music, regarded Wagner as a madman who was reducing music to chaos, perversely introducing ugly and brutal sounds into a region where beauty and grace had reigned alone, and substituting an incoherent, aimless, formless, endless meandering for the old familiar symmetrical tunes like Pop

Goes the Weazel, in which the second and third lines repeat, or nearly repeat, the pattern of the first and second; so that anyone can remember and treasure them like nursery rhymes. It was the unprofessional, 'unmusical' public which caught the dramatic clue, and saw order and power, strength and sanity, in the supposed Wagner chaos; and now, his battle being won and overwon, the professors, to avert the ridicule of their pupils, are compelled to explain (quite truly) that Wagner's technical procedure in music is almost pedantically logical and grammatical; that the Lohengrin and Tristan preludes* are masterpieces of the form proper to their aim; and that his disregard of 'false relations,' and his free use of the most extreme discords without 'preparation,' are straight and sensible instances of that natural development of harmony which has proceeded continuously from the days when common six-four chords were considered 'wrong,' and such free use of unprepared dominant sevenths and minor ninths as had become common in Mozart's time would have seemed the maddest cacophony.[1]

---

[1] As I spent the first twenty years of my life in Ireland I am, for the purposes of this survey of musical art, at least a century and a half old. I can remember the sensation given by the opening chord of Beethoven's youthful Prometheus* overture. It sounded strangely strong and momentous, because the use of the third inversion of the chord of the dominant seventh without preparation was unexpected in those days. As to exploding undiminished chords of the ninth and thirteenth on the unsuspecting ear in the same way (everybody does it nowadays), one might as well have sat down on the keyboard and called it music. The very name of the thirteenth was inconceivable: a discreetly prepared and resolved suspension of 'four to three' was the only form in which that discord was known. I can remember, too, the indignation with which Macfarren,* after correcting his pupils for unintentional consecutive fifths all his life, found himself expected to write an analytic program for the performance at a Philharmonic concert of an overture by a composer (Goetz) who actually wrote consecutive sevenths intentionally because he liked them.

However, I do not insert this note for the sake of my reminiscences, but because, since writing the text above, a composer of the first order (Richard Strauss) has become known in London, and has been attacked, just as Wagner was, by the very men who lived through the huge blunder of anti-Wagnerism. This cannot be accounted for by the superstitions of the age of decorative music. Every critic nowadays is thoroughly inured to descriptive and dramatic music which is not only as independent of the old decorative forms as Strauss's, but a good deal more so; for Strauss lives on the verge of a barcarolle and seldom resists a nursery tune for long. The hostility to him may be partly due to the fact that by his great achievement of rescuing music from the realm of tights and wigs and stage armour in which Wagner, with all his genius, dwelt to the last, and bringing it into direct contact with modern life, he was enabled in his Heldenleben to give an orchestral caricature of his critics which comes much closer home than Wagner's medievally disguised Beckmesser. But Strauss is denounced by men who are quite capable of laughing at themselves, who are sincere advocates of modern realism in other arts, and who are sufficiently good judges to know, for instance, that the greater popularity of Tchaikowsky* is like the greater popularity of Rossini as compared with Beethoven nearly a century ago: that is, the vogue of a musical voluptuary, who, though very pleasant in his lighter vein,

The dramatic development also touched purely instrumental music. Liszt tried hard to extricate himself from pianoforte arabesques, and become a tone poet* like his friend Wagner. He wanted his symphonic poems to express emotions and their development. And he defined the emotion by connecting it with some known story, poem, or even picture: Mazeppa, Victor Hugo's Les Préludes, Kaulbach's Die Hunnenschlacht,* or the like. But the moment you try to make an instrumental composition follow a story, you are forced to abandon the decorative pattern forms, since all patterns consist of some form which is repeated over and over again, and which generally consists in itself of a repetition of two similar halves. For example, if you take a playing-card (say the five of diamonds) as a simple example of a pattern, you find not only that the diamond figure is repeated five times, but that each side of each pip is a reversed duplicate of the other. Now, the established form for a symphony is essentially a pattern form involving just such symmetrical repetitions; and, since a story does not repeat itself, but pursues a continuous chain of fresh incident and correspondingly varied emotions, Liszt had either to find a new musical form for his musical poems, or

very strenuous in his energetic vein, and at least grandiose in his sublime vein, never attains, nor desires to attain, the elevation at which the great modern musicians from Bach to Strauss maintain themselves. Anti-Straussism is therefore accounted for neither by the old anti-Wagnerian confusion nor by the petulance of the critic who is beaten by his job.

I conclude that the disagreeable effect which an unaccustomed discord produces on people who cannot divine its resolution is to blame for most of the nonsense now written about Strauss. Strauss's technical procedure involves a profusion of such shocks. But the disagreeable effect will not last. There is no longer a single discord used by Wagner of which the resolution is not already as much a platitude as the resolution of the simple sevenths of Mozart and Meyerbeer. Strauss not only goes from discord to discord, leaving the implied resolutions to be inferred by people who never heard them before, but actually makes a feature of unresolved discords, just as Wagner made a feature of unprepared ones. Men who were reconciled quite late in life to compositions beginning with dominant thirteenth *fortissimo*, find themselves disquieted now by compositions ending with unresolved tonic sevenths.

I think this phase of protest will soon pass. I think so because I find myself able to follow Strauss's harmonic procedure; to divine the destination of his most discordant passing phrases (it is too late now to talk of mere 'passing notes'); and to tolerate his most offhand ellipses and most unceremonious omissions of final concords, with enjoyment, though my musical endowment is none of the acutest. In twenty years the complaints about his music will be as unintelligible as the similar complaints about Handel, Mozart, Beethoven, and Wagner in the past.

I must apologize for the technical jargon I have had to use in this note. Probably it is all obsolete by this time; but I know nothing newer. Stainer would have understood it thirty years ago. If nobody understands it today, my knowledge will seem all the more profound.

else face the intolerable anomalies and absurdities which spoil the many attempts made by Mendelssohn, Raff,* and others, to handcuff the old form to the new matter. Consequently he invented the symphonic poem, a perfectly simple and fitting commonsense form for his purpose, and one which makes Les Préludes much plainer sailing for the ordinary hearer than Mendelssohn's Melusine overture or Raff's Lenore or Im Walde symphonies,* in both of which the formal repetitions would stamp Raff as a madman if we did not know that they were mere superstitions, which he had not the strength of mind to shake off as Liszt did. But still, to the people who would not read Liszt's explanations and cared nothing for his purpose, who had no taste for symphonic poetry, and consequently insisted on judging the symphonic poems as sound-patterns, Liszt must needs appear, like Wagner, a perverse egotist with something fundamentally disordered in his intellect: in short, a lunatic.

The sequel was the same as in the Impressionist movement. Wagner, Berlioz, and Liszt, in securing tolerance for their own works, secured it for what sounded to many people absurd; and this tolerance necessarily extended to a great deal of stuff which was really absurd, but which the secretly-bewildered critics dared not denounce, lest it, too, should turn out to be great, like the music of Wagner, over which they had made the most ludicrous exhibition of their incompetence. Even at such stupidly conservative concerts as those of the London Philharmonic Society* I have seen ultra-modern composers, supposed to be representatives of the Wagnerian movement, conducting pretentious rubbish in no essential superior to Jullien's British Army Quadrilles.* And then, of course, there are the young imitators, who are corrupted by the desire to make their harmonies sound like those of the masters whose purposes and principles of work they are too young to understand, and who fall between the old forms and the new into simple incoherence.

Here, again, you see, you have a progressive, intelligent, wholesome, and thoroughly sane movement in art, producing plenty of evidence to prove the case of any clever man who does not understand music, but who has a theory which involves the proposition that all the leaders of the art movements of our time are degenerate and, consequently, retrogressive lunatics.

Ibsenism

There is no need for me to go at any great length into the grounds on which any development in our moral views must at first appear insane and blasphemous to people who are satisfied, or more than satisfied, with the current morality. Perhaps you remember the opening chapters of my Quintessence of Ibsenism, in which I shewed why the London press, now abjectly polite to Ibsen, received him four years ago with a shriek of horror. Every step in morals is made by challenging the validity of the existing conception of perfect propriety of conduct; and when a man does that, he must look out for a very different reception from the painter who has ventured to paint a shadow brilliant lilac, or the composer who ends his symphony with an unresolved discord. Heterodoxy in art is at worst rated as eccentricity or folly: heterodoxy in morals is at once rated as scoundrelism, and, what is worse, propagandist scoundrelism, which must, if successful, undermine society and bring us back to barbarism after a period of decadence like that which brought imperial Rome to its downfall. Your function as a philosophic Anarchist in American society is to combat the attempts that are constantly being made to arrest development by using the force of the State to suppress all departures from those habits of the majority which it pretentiously calls its morals. You must find the modern democratic voter a very troublesome person, chicken-heartedly diffident as to the value of his opinions on the technics of art or science, about which he can learn all that there is to be known, but cocksure about right and wrong in morals, politics, and religion, about which he can at best only guess at the depth and danger of his ignorance. Happily, this cocksureness is not confined to the Conservatives. Shelley was as cocksure as the dons who expelled him from Oxford.* It is true that the revolutionist of twenty-five, who sees nothing for it but a clean sweep of all our institutions, finds himself, at forty, accepting and even clinging to them on condition of a few reforms to bring them up to date. But he does not wait patiently for this reconciliation. He expresses his (or her) early dissatisfaction with the wisdom of his elders loudly and irreverently, and formulates his heresy as a faith. He demands the abolition of marriage, of the State, of the Church; he preaches the divinity of love and the heroism of the man who believes in himself and dares do the thing he wills; he contemns the slavery to duty and discipline which has left so many soured old people with nothing but envious regrets for a virtuous youth. He recognizes his gospel in such utterances as that quoted by Nordau from Brandes:* 'To obey one's senses is to have character. He who allows himself to be guided by his passions has individuality.'* For my part, I am not at all afraid of this doctrine, either in Brandes's form or in the older form: 'He that is unjust, let him be unjust still; and he which is filthy, let him be filthy still; and he that is righteous, let him be righteous still; and he that is holy, let him be holy still.'* But Nordau expresses his horror of Brandes with all the epithets he can command: 'debauchery, dissoluteness, depravity disguised as modernity, bestial instincts, *maître de plaisir*,* egomaniacal Anarchist,' and such sentences as the following:—

'It is comprehensible that an educator who turns the school-room into a tavern and a brothel should have success and a crowd of followers. He certainly runs the risk of being slain by the parents if they come to know what he is teaching their children; but the pupils will hardly complain, and will be eager to attend the lessons of so agreeable a teacher. This is the explanation of the influence Brandes gained over the youth of his country, such as his writings, with their emptiness of thought and unending tattle, would certainly never have procured for him.'

To appreciate this spluttering, you must know that it is immediately followed by an attack on Ibsen for the weakness of 'obsession by the doctrine of original sin.' Yet what would the passage I have just quoted be without the doctrine of original sin as a postulate? If 'the heart of man is deceitful above all things, and desperately wicked,' then, truly, the man who allows himself to be guided by his passions must needs be a scoundrel; and his teacher might well be slain by his parents. But how if the youth thrown helpless on his passions found that honesty, that self-respect, that hatred of cruelty and injustice, that the desire for soundness and health and efficiency, were master passions: nay, that their excess is so dangerous to youth that it is part of the wisdom of age to say to the young: 'Be not righteous overmuch: why shouldst thou destroy thyself?' I am sure, my dear Tucker,* your friends have paraphrased that in vernacular American often enough in remonstrating with you for your Anarchism, which defies not only God, but even the wisdom of the United States Congress. On the other hand, the people who profess to renounce and abjure their own passions, and ostentatiously regulate their conduct by the most convenient interpretation of what the Bible means, or, worse still, by their ability to find reasons for it (as if there were not excellent reasons to be found for every conceivable course of conduct, from dynamiting and vivisection to martyrdom), seldom need a warning against being righteous overmuch, their attention, indeed, often needing a rather pressing jog in the opposite direction.

Passion is the steam in the engine of all religious and moral systems. In so far as it is malevolent, the religious are malevolent too, and insist on human sacrifices, on hell, wrath, and vengeance. You cannot read Browning's Caliban upon Setebos* (Natural Theology in The Island) without admitting that all our religions have been made as Caliban made his, and that the difference between Caliban and Prospero is not that Prospero has killed passion in himself whilst Caliban has yielded to it, but that Prospero is mastered by holier passions than Caliban's. Abstract principles of conduct break down in practice because kindness and truth and justice are not duties founded on abstract principles external to man, but human passions, which have, in their time, conflicted with higher passions as well as with lower ones. If a young woman, in a mood of strong reaction against the preaching of duty and self-sacrifice and the rest of it, were to tell me that she was determined not to murder her own instincts and throw away her life in obedience to a mouthful of empty phrases, I should say to her 'By all means do as you propose. Try how wicked you can be: it is precisely the same experiment as trying how good you can be. At worst you will only find out the sort of person you really are. At best you will find that your passions, if you really and honestly let them all loose impartially, will discipline you with a severity which your conventional friends, abandoning themselves to the mechanical routine of fashion, could not stand for a day.' As a matter of fact, we have seen over and over again this comedy of the 'emancipated' young enthusiast flinging duty and religion, convention and parental authority, to the winds, only to find herself, for the first time in her life, plunged into duties, responsibilities, and sacrifices from which she is often glad to retreat, after a few years' wearing down of her enthusiasm, into the comparatively loose life of an ordinary respectable woman of fashion.

Why Law is Indispensable

The truth is, laws, religions, creeds, and systems of ethics, instead of making society better than its best unit, make it worse than its average unit, because they are never up to date. You will ask me: 'Why have them at all?' I will tell you. They are made necessary, though we all secretly detest them, by the fact that the number of people who can think out a line of conduct for themselves even on one point is very small, and the number who can afford the time for it still smaller. Nobody can afford the time to do it on all points. The professional thinker may on occasion make his own morality and philosophy as the cobbler may make his own boots; but the ordinary man of business must buy at the shop, so to speak, and put up with what he finds on sale there, whether it exactly suits him or not, because he can neither make a morality for himself nor do without one.* This typewriter with which I am writing is the best I can get; but it is by no means a perfect instrument; and I have not the smallest doubt that in fifty years' time authors will wonder how men could have put up with so clumsy a contrivance. When a better one is invented I shall buy it: until then, not being myself an inventor, I must make the best of it, just as my Protestant and Roman Catholic and Agnostic friends make the best of their imperfect creeds and systems. Oh, Father Tucker, worshipper of Liberty,* where shall we find a land where the thinking and moralizing can be done without division of labor?

Besides, what have deep thinking and moralizing to do with the most necessary and least questionable side of law? Just consider how much we need law in matters which have absolutely no moral bearing at all. Is there anything more aggravating than to be told, when you are socially promoted, and are not quite sure how to behave yourself in the circles you enter for the first time, that good manners are merely a matter of good sense, and that rank is but the guinea's stamp: the man's the gowd for a' that? Imagine taking the field with an army which knew nothing except that the soldier's duty is to defend his country bravely, and think, not of his own safety, nor of home and beauty, but of ENGLAND! Or of leaving the traffic of Piccadilly or Broadway to proceed on the under-standing that every driver should keep to that side of the road which seemed to him to promote the greatest happiness of the greatest number! Or of stage-managing Hamlet by assuring the Ghost that whether he entered from the right or the left could make no difference to the great-ness of Shakespear's play, and that all he need concern himself about was holding the mirror up to nature! Law is never so necessary as when it has no ethical significance whatever, and is pure law for the sake of law. The law that compels me to keep to the left when driving along Oxford Street* is ethically senseless, as is shewn by the fact that keeping to the right answers equally well in Paris; and it certainly destroys my freedom to choose my side; but by enabling me to count on everyone else keeping to the left also, thus making traffic possible and safe, it enlarges my life and sets my mind free for nobler issues. Most laws, in short, are not the expression of the ethical verdicts of the community, but pure etiquet and nothing else. What they do express is the fact that over most of the field of social life there are wide limits within which it does not matter what people do, though it matters enormously whether under given circum-stances you can depend on their all doing the same thing. The wasp, who can be depended on absolutely to sting you if you squeeze him, is less of a nuisance than the man who tries to do business with you not according to the customs of business, but according to the Sermon on the Mount,* or than the lady who dines with you and refuses, on republican and diet-etic principles, to allow precedence to a duchess or to partake of food which contains uric acid. The ordinary man cannot get through the world without being told what to do at every turn, and basing such calculations as he is capable of on the assumption that everyone else will calculate on the same assumptions. Even your man of genius accepts a hundred rules for every one he challenges; and you may lodge in the same house with an Anarchist for ten years without noticing anything exceptional about him. Martin Luther, the priest, horrified the greater half of Christendom by marrying a nun,* yet was a submissive conformist in countless ways, living orderly as a husband and father, wearing what his bootmaker and tailor made for him, and dwelling in what the builder built for him, although he would have died rather than take his Church from the Pope. And when he got a Church made by himself to his liking, generations of men calling themselves Lutherans took that Church from him just as unquestioningly as he took the fashion of his clothes from his tailor. As the race evolves, many a convention which recommends itself by its obvious utility to everyone passes into an automatic habit, like breathing. Doubtless also an improvement in our nerves and judgment may enlarge the list of emergencies which individuals may be trusted to deal with on the spur of the moment without reference to regulations; but a ready-made code of conduct for general use will always be needed as a matter of overwhelming convenience by all members of communities.

The continual danger to liberty created by law arises, not from the encroachments of Governments, which are always regarded with suspicion, but from the immense utility and consequent popularity of law, and the terrifying danger and obvious inconvenience of anarchy; so that even pirates appoint and obey a captain. Law soon acquires such a good character that people will believe no evil of it; and at this point it becomes possible for priests and rulers to commit the most pernicious crimes in the name of law and order. Creeds and laws come to be regarded as applications to human conduct of eternal and immutable principles of good and evil; and breakers of the law are abhorred as sacrilegious scoundrels to whom nothing is sacred. Now this, I need not tell you, is a very serious error. No law is so independent of circumstances that the time never comes for breaking it, changing it, scrapping it as obsolete, and even making its observance a crime. In a developing civilization nothing can make laws tolerable unless their changes and modifications are kept as closely as possible on the heels of the changes and modifications in social conditions which development involves. Also there is a bad side to the very convenience of law. It deadens the conscience of individuals by relieving them of the ethical responsibility of their own actions. When this relief is made as complete as possible, it reduces a man to a condition in which his very virtues are contemptible. Military discipline, for example, aims at destroying the individuality and initiative of the soldier whilst increasing his mechanical efficiency, until he is simply a weapon with the power of hearing and obeying orders. In him you have legality, duty, obedience, self-denial, submission to external authority, carried as far as it can be carried; and the result is that in England, where military service is voluntary, the common soldier is less respected than any other serviceable worker in the community. The police constable, who is a civilian and has to use his own judgment and act on his own responsibility in innumerable petty emergencies, is by comparison a popular and esteemed citizen. The Roman Catholic peasant who consults his parish priest instead of his conscience, and submits wholly to the authority of his Church, is mastered and governed either by statesmen and cardinals who despise his superstition, or by Protestants who are at least allowed to persuade themselves that they have arrived at their religious opinions through the exercise of their private judgment. The moral evolution of the social individual is from submission and obedience as economizers of effort and responsibility, and safeguards against panic and incontinence, to wilfulness and self-assertion made safe by reason and self-control, just as plainly as his physical growth leads from the perambulator and the nurse's apron-string to the power of walking alone, and from the tutelage of the boy to the responsibility of the man. But it is useless for impatient spirits (you and I, for instance) to call on people to walk before they can stand. Without high gifts of reason and self-control: that is, without strong common-sense, no man dares yet trust himself out of the school of authority. What he does is to claim gradual relaxations of the discipline, so as to have as much liberty as he thinks is good for him, and as much government as he thinks he needs to keep him straight. If he goes too fast he soon finds himself asking helplessly 'What ought I to do?' and so, after running to the doctor, the lawyer, the expert, the old friend, and all the other quacks for advice, he runs back to the law again to save him from all these and from himself. The law may be wrong; but anyhow it spares him the responsibility of choosing, and will either punish those who make him look ridiculous by exposing its folly, or, when the constitution is too democratic for this, at least guarantee that the majority is on his side.

Protestant Anarchism

We see this in the history of British-American Christianity. Man, as the hero of that history, starts by accepting as binding on him the revelation of God's will as interpreted by the Church. Finding his confidence, or rather his intellectual laziness, grossly abused by the Church, he claims a right to exercise his own judgment, which the Reformed Church, competing with the Unreformed for clients,* grants him on condition that he arrive at the same conclusions as itself. Later on he violates this condition in certain particulars, and dissents, flying to America in the Mayflower from the prison of Conformity, but promptly building a new jail, suited to the needs of his sect, in his adopted country. In all these mutinies he finds excellent arguments to prove that he is exchanging a false authority for *the* true one, never daring even to think of brazenly admitting that what he is really doing is substituting his own will, bit by bit, for what he calls the will of God or the laws of Nature. These arguments so accustom the world to submit authority to the test of discussion that he is at last emboldened to claim the right to do anything he can find good arguments for, even to the extent of questioning the scientific accuracy of the Book of Genesis, and the validity of the popular conception of God as an omniscient, omnipotent, and frightfully jealous and vindictive old gentleman sitting on a throne above the clouds. This seems a giant stride towards emancipation; but it leaves our hero, as Rationalist and Materialist, regarding Reason as a creative dynamic motor,* independent of and superior to his erring passions, at which point it is easy for the churches to suggest that if Reason is to decide the matter, perhaps the conclusions of an Ecumenical Council* of learned and skilled churchmen might be more trustworthy than the first crop of cheap syllogisms excogitated by a handful of raw Rationalists in their sects of 'Freethinkers' and 'Secularists' and 'Positivists' or 'Dont Knowists' (Agnostics).

Yet it was not the churches but that very freethinking philosopher Schopenhauer who re-established the old theological doctrine that reason is no motive power; that the true motive power in the world is will (otherwise Life);* and that the setting-up of reason above will is a damnable error. But the theologians could not open their arms to Schopenhauer, because he led gloomily disposed thinkers into the Rationalist-Mercantilist error of valuing life according to its individual profits in pleasure, with its idiotic pessimist conclusion that life is not worth living, and that the will which urges us to live in spite of this is necessarily a malign torturer, or at least a bad hand at business, the desirable end of all things being the cessation of the will and the consequent setting of life's sun 'into the blind cave of eternal night.'* Further, the will of the theologians was the will of a God standing outside man and in authority above him, whereas the Schopenhauerian will is a purely secular force of nature, attaining various degrees of organization, here as a jelly-fish, there as a cabbage, more complexly as an ape or a tiger, and attaining its highest (and sometimes most mischievous) form so far in the human being. As to the Rationalists, they approved of Schopenhauer's secularism and pessimism, but of course could not stomach his metaphysical method nor his dethronement of reason by will. Accordingly, his turn for popularity did not come until after Darwin's, and then mostly through the influence of two great artists, Richard Wagner and Ibsen, whose Tristan and Isolde, and Emperor Or Galilean, shew that Schopenhauer was a true pioneer in the forward march of the human spirit. We can now, as soon as we are strongminded enough, drop the pessimism, the rationalism, the supernatural theology, and all the other subterfuges to which we cling because we are afraid to look life straight in the face and see in it, not the fulfilment of a moral law or of the deductions of reason, but the satisfaction of a passion in us of which we can give no rational account whatever.

It is natural for man to shrink from the terrible responsibility thrown on him by this inexorable fact. All his stock excuses vanish before it: 'The woman tempted me,' 'The serpent tempted me,' 'I was not myself at the time,' 'I meant well,' 'My passion got the better of my reason,' 'It was my duty to do it,' 'The Bible says that we should do it,' 'Everybody does it,' and so on. Nothing is left but the frank avowal: 'I did it because I am built that way.' Every man hates to say that. He wants to believe that his generous actions are characteristic of him, and that his meannesses are aberrations or concessions to the force of circumstances. Our murderers, with the assistance of the jail chaplain, square accounts with the devil and with God, never with themselves. The convict gives every reason for his having stolen something except the reason that he is a thief. Cruel people flog their children for their children's good, or offer the information that a guinea-pig perspires under atrocious torture as an affectionate contribution to science. Lynched negroes are riddled by dozens of superfluous bullets, every one of which is offered as the expression of a sense of outraged justice and chastity in the scamp and libertine who fires it.* And such is the desire of men to keep one another in countenance that they positively demand such excuses from one another as a matter of public decency. An uncle of mine, who made it a rule to offer tramps a job when they begged from him, naturally very soon became familiar with every excuse that human ingenuity can invent for not working. But he lost his temper only once; and that was with a tramp who frankly replied that he was too lazy. This my uncle described with disgust as 'cynicism.' And yet our family arms bear the motto, in Latin, 'Know thyself.'*

As you know, the true trend of this movement has been mistaken by many of its supporters as well as by its opponents. The ingrained habit of thinking of the propensities of which we are ashamed as 'our passions,' and our shame of them and our propensities to noble conduct as a negative and inhibitory department called generally our conscience, leads us to conclude that to accept the guidance of our passions is to plunge recklessly into the insupportable tedium of what is called a life of pleasure. Reactionists against the almost equally insupportable slavery of what is called a life of duty are nevertheless willing to venture on these terms. The revolted daughter, exasperated at being systematically lied to by her parents on every subject of vital importance to an eager and intensely curious young student of life, allies herself with really vicious people and with humorists who like to shock the pious with gay paradoxes, in claiming an impossible licence in personal conduct. No great harm is done beyond the inevitable and temporary excesses produced by all reactions; for, as I have said, the would-be wicked ones find, when they come to the point, that the indispensable qualification for a wicked life is not freedom but wickedness. But the misunderstanding supports the clamor of the opponents of the newest opinions, who naturally shriek as Nordau shrieks in the passages about Brandes, quoted above. Thus you have here again a movement which is thoroughly beneficial and progressive presenting a hideous appearance of moral corruption and decay, not only to our old-fashioned religious folk, but to our comparatively modern scientific Rationalists as well. And here again, because the press and the gossips have found out that this apparent corruption and decay is considered the right thing in some influential quarters, and must be spoken of with respect, and patronized and published and sold and read, we have a certain number of pitiful imitators taking advantage of their tolerance to bring out really silly and vicious stuff, which the reviewers are afraid to expose, lest it, too, should turn out to be the correct thing.

* * *

PREFACE TO THREE PLAYS BY BRIEUX

*   *   *

How the Nineteenth Century found itself out

It is reserved for some great critic to give us a study of the psychology of the nineteenth century. Those of us who as adults saw it face to face in that last moiety of its days when one fierce hand after another—Marx's, Zola's, Ibsen's, Strindberg's, Turgenief's, Tolstoy's*—stripped its masks off and revealed it as, on the whole, perhaps the most villainous page of recorded human history, can also recall the strange confidence with which it regarded itself as the very summit of civilization, and talked of the past as a cruel gloom that had been dispelled for ever by the railway and the electric telegraph. But centuries, like men, begin to find themselves out in middle age. The youthful conceit of the nineteenth had a splendid exponent in Macaulay, and, for a time, a gloriously jolly one during the nonage of Dickens. There was certainly nothing morbid in the air then: Dickens and Macaulay are as free from morbidity as Dumas *père* and Guizot. Even Stendhal and Prosper Merimée, though by no means burgess optimists, are quite sane. When you come to Zola and Maupassant, Flaubert and the Goncourts, to Ibsen and Strindberg, to Aubrey Beardsley and George Moore, to D'Annunzio and Echegaray, you are in a new and morbid atmosphere. French literature up to the middle of the nineteenth century was still all of one piece with Rabelais, Montaigne and Molière. Zola breaks that tradition completely: he is as different as Karl Marx from Turgot or Darwin from Cuvier.*

In this new phase we see the bourgeoisie, after a century and a half of complacent vaunting of its own probity and modest happiness (begun by Daniel Defoe in Robinson Crusoe's praises of 'the middle station of life'), suddenly turning bitterly on itself with accusations of hideous sexual and commercial corruption. Thackeray's campaign against snobbery* and Dickens's against hypocrisy were directed against the vices of respectable men; but now even the respectability was passionately denied: the bourgeois was depicted as a thief, a tyrant, a sweater, a selfish voluptuary whose marriages were simple legalizations of unbridled licentiousness. Sexual irregularities began to be attributed to the sympathetic characters in fiction not as the blackest spots in their portraits, but positively as redeeming humanities in them.

Jack the Ripper*

I am by no means going here either to revive the old outcry against this school of iconoclasts and disillusioners, or to join the new reaction against it. It told the world many truths: it brought romance back to its senses. Its very repudiation of the graces and enchantments of fine art was necessary; for the artistic morbidezza* of Byron and Victor Hugo was too imaginative to allow the Victorian bourgeoisie to accept them as chroniclers of real facts and real people. The justification of Zola's comparative coarseness is that his work could not have been done in any other way. If Zola had had a sense of humor, or a great artist's delight in playing with his ideas, his materials, and his readers, he would have become either as unreadable to the very people he came to wake up as Anatole France* is, or as incredible as Victor Hugo was. He would also have incurred the mistrust and hatred of the majority of Frenchmen, who, like the majority of men of all nations, are not merely incapable of fine art, but resent it furiously. A wit is to them a man who is laughing at them: an artist is a man of loose character who lives by telling lying stories and pandering to the voluptuous passions. What they like to read is the police intelligence, especially the murder cases and divorce cases. The invented murders and divorces of the novelists and playwrights do not satisfy them, because they cannot believe in them; and belief that the horror or scandal actually occurred, that real people are shedding real blood and real tears, is indispensable to their enjoyment. To produce this belief by works of fiction, the writer must disguise and even discard the arts of the man of letters and assume the style of the descriptive reporter of the criminal courts. As an example of how to cater for such readers, we may take Zola's Bête Humaine. It is in all its essentials a simple and touching story, like Prévost's Manon Lescaut.* But into it Zola has violently thrust the greatest police sensation of the nineteenth century: the episode of Jack the Ripper. Jack's hideous neurosis is no more a part of human nature than Cæsar's epilepsy or Gladstone's missing finger. One is tempted to accuse Zola of having borrowed it from the newspapers to please his customers just as Shakespear used to borrow stories of murder and jealousy from the tales and chronicles of his time, and heap them on the head of convivial humorists like Iago and Richard III, or gentle poets like Macbeth and Hamlet. Without such allurements, Shakespear could not have lived by his plays. And if he had been rich enough to disregard this consideration, he would still have had to provide sensation enough to induce people to listen to what he was inspired to say. It is only the man who has no message who is too fastidious to beat the drum at the door of his booth.

Rise of the Scientific Spirit

Still, the Shakesperean murders were romantic murders: the Zolaesque ones were police reports. The old mad heroines, the Ophelias and Lucies of Lammermoor,* were rhapsodists with flowers in their hands: the new ones were clinical studies of mental disease. The new note was as conspicuous in the sensational chapters as in the dull chapters, of which there were many. This was the punishment of the middle class for hypocrisy. It had carried the conspiracy of silence which we call decorum to such lengths that when young men discovered the sup- pressed truths, they felt bound to shout them in the streets. I well remember how when I was a youth in my teens I happened to obtain access to the papers of an Irish crown solicitor through a colleague who had some clerical work to do upon them. The county concerned was not one of the crimeless counties: there was a large camp in it; and the soldier of that day was not the respectable, rather pious, and very low- spirited youth who now makes the King's uniform what the curate's black coat was then. There were not only cases which were tried and not reported: there were cases which could not even be tried, the offenders having secured impunity by pushing their follies to lengths too gro- tesque to be bearable even in a criminal court—also because of the silly ferocity of the law, which punished the negligible indecencies of drunken young soldiers as atrocious crimes. The effect produced by these revelations on my raw youth was a sense of heavy responsibility for conniving at their concealment. I felt that if camp and barrack life involved these things, they ought to be known. I had been caught by the great wave of scientific enthusiasm which was then passing over Europe as a result of the discovery of Natural Selection by Darwin, and of the blow it dealt to the vulgar Bible worship and redemption mon- gering which had hitherto passed among us for religion. I wanted to get at the facts. I was prepared for the facts being unflattering: had I not already faced the fact that instead of being a fallen angel I was first cousin to a monkey? Long afterwards, when I was a well-known writer, I said that what we wanted as the basis of our plays and novels was not romance, but a really scientific natural history. Scientific natural his- tory is not compatible with taboo; and as everything connected with sex was tabooed, I felt the need for mentioning the forbidden subjects, not only because of their own importance, but for the sake of destroying taboo by giving it the most violent possible shocks. The same impulse is unmistakably active in Zola and his contemporaries. He also wanted, not works of literary art, but stories he could believe in as records of things that really happen. He imposed Jack the Ripper on his idyll of the railwayman's wife to make it scientific. To all artists and Platonists he made it thereby very unreal; for to the Platonist all accidents are unreal and negligible;* but to the people he wanted to get at—the anti-artistic people—he made it readable.

The scientific spirit was unintelligible to the Philistines and repulsive to the dilettanti, who said to Zola: 'If you must tell us stories about agricultural laborers, why tell us dirty ones?'* But Zola did not want, like the old romancers, to tell a story. He wanted to tell the world the scientific truth about itself. His view was that if you were going to legislate for agricultural laborers, or deal with them or their business in any way, you had better know what they are really like; and in supplying you with the necessary information he did not tell you what you already knew, which included pretty nearly all that could be decorously mentioned, but what you did not know, which was that part of the truth that was tabooed. For the same reason, when he found a generation whose literary notions of Parisian cocotterie were founded on Marguerite Gauthier, he felt it to be a duty to show them Nana.* And it was a very necessary thing to do. If some Irish writer of the seventies had got himself banished from all decent society, and perhaps convicted of obscene libel, by writing a novel showing the side of camp life that was never mentioned except in the papers of the Crown Solicitor, we should be nearer to a rational military system than we are to-day.

Zolaism as a Superstition

It is, unfortunately, much easier to throw the forces of art into a reaction than to recall them when the reaction has gone far enough. A case which came under my own notice years ago illustrates the difficulty. The wife of an eminent surgeon had some talent for drawing. Her husband wrote a treatise on cancer; and she drew the illustrations. It was the first time she had used her gift for a serious purpose; and she worked hard enough at it to acquire considerable skill in depicting cancerous proliferation. The book being finished and published, she resumed her ordinary practice of sketching for pleasure. But all her work now had an uncanny look. When she drew a landscape, it was like a cancer that accidentally looked like a landscape. She had acquired a cancerous technique; and she could not get rid of it.

This happens as easily in literature as in the other arts. The men who trained themselves as writers by dragging the unmentionable to light, presently found that they could do that so much better than anything else that they gave up dealing with the other subjects. Even their quite mentionable episodes had an unmentionable air. Their imitators assumed that unmentionability was an end in itself—that to be decent was to be out of the movement. Zola and Ibsen could not, of course, be confined to mere reaction against taboo. Ibsen was to the last fascinating and full of a strange moving beauty; and Zola often broke into sentimental romance. But neither Ibsen nor Zola, after they once took in hand the work of unmasking the idols of the bourgeoisie, ever again wrote a happy or pleasant play or novel. Ibsen's suicides and catastrophes at last produced the cry of 'People don't do such things,' which he ridiculed through Judge Brack in Hedda Gabler. This was easy enough: Brack was so far wrong that people do do such things occasionally. But on the whole Brack was right. The tragedy of Hedda in real life is not that she commits suicide but that she continues to live. If such acts of violent rebellion as those of Hedda and Nora and Rebecca and the rest were the inevitable or even the probable consequences of their unfitness to be wives and mothers, or of their contracting repugnant marriages to avoid being left on the shelf, social reform would be very rapid; and we should hear less nonsense as to women like Nora and Hedda being mere figments of Ibsen's imagination. Our real difficulty is the almost boundless docility and submission to social convention which is characteristic of the human race. What balks the social reformer everywhere is that the victims of social evils do not complain, and even strongly resent being treated as victims. The more a dog suffers from being chained the more dangerous it is to release him: he bites savagely at the hand that dares touch his collar. Our Rougon-Macquart families* are usually enormously proud of themselves; and though they have to put up with their share of drunkards and madmen, they do not proliferate into Jack-the-Rippers. Nothing that is admittedly and unmistakably horrible matters very much, because it frightens people into seeking a remedy: the serious horrors are those which seem entirely respectable and normal to respectable and normal men. Now the formula of tragedy had come down to the nineteenth century from days in which this was not recognized, and when life was so thoroughly accepted as a divine institution that in order to make it seem tragic, something dreadful had to happen and somebody had to die. But the tragedy of modern life is that nothing happens, and that the resultant dulness does not kill. Maupassant's Une Vie* is infinitely more tragic than the death of Juliet.

In Ibsen's works we find the old traditions and the new conditions struggling in the same play, like a gudgeon half swallowed by a pike. Almost all the sorrow and the weariness which makes his plays so poignant are the sorrow and weariness of the mean dull life in which nothing happens; but none the less he provides a final catastrophe of the approved fifth-act-blank-verse type.* Hedwig and Hedda shoot themselves: Rosmer and Rebecca throw themselves into the mill-race: Solness and Rubeck are dashed to pieces: Borkman dies of acute stage tragedy without discoverable lesions. I will not again say, as I have said before, that these catastrophes are forced, because a fortunate perform- ance often makes them seem inevitable; but I do submit that the omis- sion of them would leave the play sadder and more convincing.

The Passing of the Tragic Catastrophe and the Happy Ending

Not only is the tradition of the catastrophe unsuitable to modern stud- ies of life: the tradition of an ending, happy or the reverse, is equally unworkable. The moment the dramatist gives up accidents and catastro- phes, and takes 'slices of life' as his material, he finds himself commit- ted to plays that have no endings.* The curtain no longer comes down on a hero slain or married: it comes down when the audience has seen enough of the life presented to it to draw the moral, and must either leave the theatre or miss its last train.

The man who faced France with a drama fulfilling all these condi- tions was Brieux.* He was as scientific, as conscientious, as un- flinching as Zola without being in the least morbid. He was no more dependent on horrors than Molière, and as sane in his temper. He threw over the traditional forced catastrophe uncompromisingly. You do not go away from a Brieux play with the feeling that the affair is finished or the problem solved for you by the dramatist. Still less do you go away in 'that happy, easy, ironically indulgent frame of mind that is the true test of comedy,' as Mr Walkley put it in *The Times* of the 1st October, 1909. You come away with a very disquieting sense that you are involved in the affair, and must find the way out of it for your- self and everybody else if civilization is to be tolerable to your sense of honor.

The Difference between Brieux and Molière or Shakespear

Brieux's task is thus larger than Molière's. Molière destroyed the pres- tige of those conspiracies against society which we call the professions, and which thrive by the exploitation of idolatry. He unmasked the doctor, the philosopher, the fencing master, the priest. He ridiculed their dupes: the hypochondriac, the academician, the devotee, the gentleman in search of accomplishments. He exposed the snob: he showed the gentleman as the butt and creature of his valet, emphasizing thus the inevitable relation between the man who lives by unearned money and the man who lives by weight of service. Beyond bringing this latter point up to a later date Beaumarchais* did nothing. But Molière never indicted society. Burke said that you cannot bring an indictment against a nation; yet within a generation from that utterance men began to draw indictments against whole epochs, especially against the capitalistic epoch. It is true that Molière, like Shakespear, indicted human nature, which would seem to be a broader attack; but such attacks only make thoughtful men melancholy and hopeless, and practical men cynical or murderous. Le Misanthrope, which seems to me, as a foreigner perhaps, to be Molière's dullest and worst play, is like Hamlet in two respects. The first, which is that it would have been much better if it had been written in prose, is merely technical and need not detain us. The second is that the author does not clearly know what he is driving at. Le Festin de Pierre, Molière's best philosophic play, is as brilliant and arresting as Le Misanthrope is neither the one nor the other; but here again there is no positive side: the statue is a hollow creature with nothing to say for himself; and Don Juan* makes no attempt to take advantage of his weakness. The reason why Shakespear and Molière are always well spoken of and recommended to the young is that their quarrel is really a quarrel with God for not making men better. If they had quarrelled with a specified class of persons with incomes of four figures for not doing their work better, or for doing no work at all, they would be denounced as seditious, impious, and profligate corruptors of morality.

Brieux wastes neither ink nor indignation on Providence. The idle despair that shakes its fist impotently at the skies, uttering sublime blasphemies, such as

> 'As flies to wanton boys are we to the gods:
> They kill us for their sport,'*

does not amuse Brieux. His fisticuffs are not aimed heavenward: they fall on human noses for the good of human souls. When he sees human nature in conflict with a political abuse he does not blame human nature, knowing that such blame is the favorite trick of those who wish to perpetuate the abuse without being able to defend it. He does not even blame the abuse: he exposes it, and then leaves human nature to tackle it with its eyes open. And his method of exposure is the dramatic method. He is a born dramatist, differing from the ordinary dramatists only in that he has a large mind and a scientific habit of using it. As a dramatist he must take for his theme a conflict of some sort. As a dramatist of large mind he cannot be satisfied with the trumpery conflicts of the Divorce Court and the Criminal Court: of the husband with the seducer, of the policeman with the murderer. Having the scientific conscience in a higher degree than Zola (he has a better head), he cannot be interested in imaginary conflicts which he himself would have to invent like a child at play. The conflict which inspires his dramatic genius must be a big one and a real one. To ask an audience to spend three hours hanging on the question of which particular man some particular woman shall mate with does not strike him as a reasonable proceeding; and if the audience does not agree with him, why, it can go to some fashionable dramatist of the boulevard* who does agree with it.

Brieux and the Boulevard

This involves Brieux in furious conflict with the boulevard. Up to quite recent times it was impossible for an Englishman to mention Brieux to a Parisian as the only French playwright who really counted in Europe, without being met with astonished assurances that Brieux is not a playwright at all; that his plays are not plays; that he is not (in Sarcey's sense of the phrase) 'du théâtre';* that he is a mere pamphleteer without even literary style. And when you expressed your natural gratification at learning that the general body of Parisian dramatists were so highly gifted that Brieux counted for nothing in Paris—when you respectfully asked for the names of a few of the most prominent of the geniuses who had eclipsed him, you were given three or four of which you had never heard, and one or two known to you as those of cynically commercial manipulators of the *ménage à trois*, the innocent wife discovered at the villain's rooms at midnight (to beg him to spare the virtue of a sister, the character of a son, or the life of a father), the compromising letter, the duel, and all the rest of the claptraps out of which dramatic playthings can be manufactured for the amusement of grown-up children. Not until the Academie Française* elected Brieux did it occur to the boulevardiers that the enormous difference between him and their pet authors was a difference in which the superiority lay with Brieux.

The Pedantry of Paris

Indeed it is difficult for the Englishman to understand how bigotedly the Parisians cling to the claptrap theatre.

The English do not care enough about the theatre to cling to its traditions or persecute anyone for their sake; but the French do. Besides, in fine art, France is a nation of born pedants. The vulgar English painter paints vulgar pictures, and generally sells them. But the vulgar French painter paints classical ones, though whether he sells them or not I do not know: I hope not. The corresponding infatuation in the theatre is for dramas in alexandrines; and alexandrines are far worse than English blank verse, which is saying a good deal. Racine and Corneille, who established the alexandrine tradition, deliberately aimed at classicism, taking the Greek drama as their model. Even a foreigner can hear the music of their verse. Corneille wrote alexandrines as Dryden wrote heroic couplets,*—in a virile, stately, handsome and withal human way; and Racine had tenderness and beauty as well. This drama of Racine and Corneille, with the music of Gluck,* gave the French in the seventeenth and eighteenth centuries a body of art which was very beautiful, very refined, very delightful for cultivated people, and very tedious for the ignorant. When, through the spread of elementary education, the ignorant invaded the theatre in overwhelming numbers, this exquisite body of art became a dead body, and was practised by nobody except the amateurs—the people who love what has been already done in art and loathe the real life out of which living art must continually grow afresh. In their hands it passed from being a commercial failure to being an obsolete nuisance.

Commercially, the classic play was supplanted by a nuisance which was not a failure: to wit, the 'well made play' of Scribe and his school.* The manufacture of well made plays is not an art: it is an industry. It is not at all hard for a literary mechanic to acquire it: the only difficulty is to find a literary mechanic who is not by nature too much of an artist for the job; for nothing spoils a well made play more infallibly than the least alloy of high art or the least qualm of conscience on the part of the writer. 'Art for art's sake' is the formula of the well made play, meaning in practice 'Success for money's sake.' Now great art is never produced for its own sake. It is too difficult to be worth the effort. All the great artists enter into a terrible struggle with the public, often involving bitter poverty and personal humiliation, and always involving calumny and persecution, because they believe they are apostles doing what used to be called the Will of God, and is now called by many prosaic names, of which 'public work' is the least controversial. And when these artists have travailed and brought forth, and at last forced the public to associate keen pleasure and deep interest with their methods and morals, a crowd of smaller men—art confectioners, we may call them—hasten to make pretty entertainments out of scraps and crumbs from the masterpieces. Offenbach laid hands on Beethoven's Seventh Symphony and produced J'aime les militaires,* to the disgust of Schumann,* who was nevertheless doing precisely the same thing in a more pretentious way. And these confectioners are by no means mere plagiarists. They bring all sorts of engaging qualities to their work: love of beauty, desire to give pleasure, tenderness, humor, everything except the high republican conscience, the identification of the artist's purpose with the purpose of the universe, which alone makes an artist great.

But the well made play was not confectionery: it had not even the derived virtue of being borrowed from the great playwrights. Its formula grew up in the days when the spread of elementary schooling produced a huge mass of playgoers sufficiently educated to want plays instead of dog-fights, but not educated enough to enjoy or understand the masterpieces of dramatic art. Besides, education or no education, one cannot live on masterpieces alone, not only because there are not enough of them, but because new plays as well as great plays are needed, and there are not enough Molières and Shakespears in the world to keep the demand for novelty satisfied. Hence it has always been necessary to have some formula by which men of mediocre talent and no conscience can turn out plays for the theatrical market. Such men have written melodramas since the theatre existed. It was in the nineteenth century that the demand for manufactured plays was extended to drawing room plays in which the Forest of Bondy and the Auberge des Adrets, the Red Barn and the Cave at Midnight, had to be replaced by Lord Blank's flat in Whitehall Court and the Great Hall, Chevy Chace.* Playgoers, being by that time mostly poor playgoers, wanted to see how the rich live; wanted to see them actually drinking champagne and wearing real fashionable dresses and trousers with a neatly ironed crease down the knee.

How to Write a Popular Play

The formula for the well made play is so easy that I give it for the benefit of any reader who feels tempted to try his hand at making the fortune that awaits all successful manufacturers in this line. First, you 'have an idea' for a dramatic situation. If it strikes you as a splendidly original idea, whilst it is in fact as old as the hills, so much the better. For instance, the situation of an innocent person convicted by circumstances of a crime may always be depended on. If the person is a woman, she must be convicted of adultery. If a young officer, he must be convicted of selling information to the enemy, though it is really a fascinating female spy who has ensnared him and stolen the incriminating document. If the innocent wife, banished from her home, suffers agonies through her separation from her children, and, when one of them is dying (of any disease the dramatist chooses to inflict), disguises herself as a nurse and attends it through its dying convulsion until the doctor, who should be a serio-comic character, and if possible a faithful old admirer of the lady's, simultaneously announces the recovery of the child and the discovery of the wife's innocence, the success of the play may be regarded as assured if the writer has any sort of knack for his work. Comedy is more difficult, because it requires a sense of humor and a good deal of vivacity; but the process is essentially the same: it is the manufacture of a misunderstanding. Having manufactured it, you place its culmination at the end of the last act but one, which is the point at which the manufacture of the play begins. Then you make your first act out of the necessary introduction of the characters to the audience, after elaborate explanations, mostly conducted by servants, solicitors, and other low life personages (the principals must all be dukes and colonels and millionaires), of how the misunderstanding is going to come about. Your last act consists, of course, of clearing up the misunderstanding, and generally getting the audience out of the theatre as best you can.

Now please do not misunderstand me as pretending that this process is so mechanical that it offers no opportunity for the exercise of talent. On the contrary, it is so mechanical that without very conspicuous talent nobody can make much reputation by doing it, though some can and do make a living at it. And this often leads the cultivated classes to suppose that all plays are written by authors of talent. As a matter of fact the majority of those who in France and England make a living by writing plays are unknown and, as to education, all but illiterate. Their names are not worth putting on the playbill, because their audiences neither know nor care who the author is, and often believe that the actors improvise the whole piece, just as they in fact do sometimes improvise the dialogue. To rise out of this obscurity you must be a Scribe or a Sardou,* doing essentially the same thing, it is true, but doing it wittily and ingeniously, at moments almost poetically, and giving the persons of the drama some touches of real observed character.

Why the Critics are always Wrong

Now it is these strokes of talent that set the critics wrong. For the talent, being all expended on the formula, at least consecrates the formula in the eyes of the critics. Nay, they become so accustomed to the formula that at last they cannot relish or understand a play that has grown naturally, just as they cannot admire the Venus of Milo* because she has neither a corset nor high heeled shoes. They are like the peasants who are so accustomed to food reeking with garlic that when food is served to them without it they declare that it has no taste and is not food at all.

This is the explanation of the refusal of the critics of all nations to accept great original dramatists like Ibsen and Brieux as real dramatists, or their plays as real plays. No writer of the first order needs the formula any more than a sound man needs a crutch. In his simplest mood, when he is only seeking to amuse, he does not manufacture a plot: he tells a story. He finds no difficulty in setting people on the stage to talk and act in an amusing, exciting or touching way. His characters have adventures and ideas which are interesting in themselves, and need not be fitted into the Chinese puzzle of a plot.

The Interpreter of Life

But the great dramatist has something better to do than to amuse either himself or his audience. He has to interpret life.* This sounds a mere pious phrase of literary criticism; but a moment's consideration will discover its meaning and its exactitude. Life as it appears to us in our daily experience is an unintelligible chaos of happenings. You pass Othello in the bazaar in Aleppo, Iago on the jetty in Cyprus, and Desdemona in the nave of St Mark's in Venice* without the slightest clue to their relations to one another. The man you see stepping into a chemist's shop to buy the means of committing murder or suicide, may, for all you know, want nothing but a liver pill or a toothbrush. The statesman who has no other object than to make you vote for his party at the next election, may be starting you on an incline at the foot of which lies war, or revolution, or a smallpox epidemic, or five years off your lifetime. The horrible murder of a whole family by the father who finishes by killing himself, or the driving of a young girl on to the streets, may be the result of your discharging an employee in a fit of temper a month before. To attempt to understand life from merely looking on at it as it happens in the streets is as hopeless as trying to understand public questions by studying snapshots of public demonstrations. If we possessed a series of cinematographs* of all the executions during the Reign of Terror, they might be exhibited a thousand times without enlightening the audiences in the least as to the meaning of the Revolution: Robespierre would perish as 'un monsieur' and Marie Antoinette* as 'une femme.' Life as it occurs is senseless: a policeman may watch it and work in it for thirty years in the streets and courts of Paris without learning as much of it or from it as a child or a nun may learn from a single play by Brieux. For it is the business of Brieux to pick out the significant incidents from the chaos of daily happenings, and arrange them so that their relation to one another becomes significant, thus changing us from bewildered spectators of a monstrous confusion to men intelligently conscious of the world and its destinies. This is the highest function that man can perform—the greatest work he can set his hand to; and this is why the great dramatists of the world, from Euripides and Aristophanes to Shakespear and Molière, and from them to Ibsen and Brieux, take that majestic and pontifical rank which seems so strangely above all the reasonable pretensions of mere strolling actors and theatrical authors.

How the Great Dramatists torture the Public

Now if the critics are wrong in supposing that the formula of the well made play is not only an indispensable factor in playwriting, but is actually the essence of the play itself—if their delusion is rebuked and confuted by the practice of every great dramatist, even when he is only amusing himself by story telling, what must happen to their poor formula when it impertinently offers its services to a playwright who has taken on his supreme function as the Interpreter of Life? Not only has he no use for it, but he must attack and destroy it; for one of the very first lessons he has to teach to a play-ridden public is that the romantic conventions on which the formula proceeds are all false, and are doing incalculable harm in these days when everybody reads romances and goes to the theatre. Just as the historian can teach no real history until he has cured his readers of the romantic delusion that the greatness of a queen consists in her being a pretty woman and having her head cut off, so the playwright of the first order can do nothing with his audiences until he has cured them of looking at the stage through the keyhole, and sniffing round the theatre as prurient people sniff round the divorce court. The cure is not a popular one. The public suffers from it exactly as a drunkard or a snuff taker suffers from an attempt to conquer the habit. The critics especially, who are forced by their profession to indulge immoderately in plays adulterated with falsehood and vice, suffer so acutely when deprived of them for a whole evening that they hurl disparagements and even abuse and insult at the merciless dramatist who is torturing them. To a bad play of the kind they are accustomed to they can be cruel through superciliousness, irony, impatience, contempt, or even a Rochefoucauldian pleasure in a friend's misfortune.* But the hatred provoked by deliberately inflicted pain, the frantic denials as of a prisoner at the bar accused of a disgraceful crime, the clamor for vengeance thinly disguised as artistic justice, the suspicion that the dramatist is using private information and making a personal attack: all these are to be found only when the playwright is no mere *marchand de plaisir*,* but, like Brieux, a ruthless revealer of hidden truth and a mighty destroyer of idols.

* * *

PARKNASILLA AND AYOT ST LAWRENCE.   G.B.S.
1909.

III

SHORTER ESSAYS AND REVIEWS

PLEASANT it is to see Mr Gilbert and Sir Arthur Sullivan working together again full brotherly. They should be on the best of terms; for henceforth Sir Arthur can always say, 'Any other librettist would do just as well: look at Haddon Hall'; whilst Mr Gilbert can retort, 'Any other musician would do just as well: look at The Mountebanks.'* Thus have the years of divorce cemented the happy reunion at which we all assisted last Saturday. The twain still excite the expectations of the public as much as ever. How Trial by Jury and The Sorcerer surprised the public, and how Pinafore, The Pirates, and Patience* kept the sensation fresh, can be guessed by the youngest man from the fact that the announcement of a new Savoy opera* always throws the middle-aged playgoer into the attitude of expecting a surprise. As for me, I avoid this attitude, if only because it is a middle-aged one. Still, I expect a good deal that I could not have hoped for when I first made the acquaintance of comic opera.

Those who are old enough to compare the Savoy performances with those of the dark ages, taking into account the pictorial treatment of the fabrics and colors on the stage, the cultivation and intelligence of the choristers, the quality of the orchestra, and the degree of artistic good breeding, so to speak, expected from the principals, best know how great an advance has been made by Mr D'Oyly Carte* in organizing and harmonizing that complex co-operation of artists of all kinds which goes to make up a satisfactory operatic performance. Long before the run of a successful Savoy opera is over Sir Arthur's melodies are dinned into our ears by every promenade band and street piano, and Mr Gilbert's sallies are quoted threadbare by conversationalists and journalists; but the whole work as presented to eye and ear on the Savoy stage remains unhackneyed.

Further, no theatre in London is more independent of those executants whose personal popularity enables them to demand ruinous salaries; and this is not the least advantageous of the differences between opera as the work of a combination of manager, poet, and musician, all three making the most of one another in their concerted striving for the common object of a completely successful representation, and opera as the result of a speculator picking up a libretto, getting somebody with a name to set it to music, ordering a few tradesmen to 'mount' it, and then, with a stage manager hired here, an acting manager hired there, and a popular prima donna, comedian, and serpentine dancer stuck in at reckless salaries like almonds into an underdone dumpling, engaging some empty theatre on the chance of the affair 'catching on.'

If any capitalist wants to succeed with comic opera, I can assure him that he can do so with tolerable security if he only possesses the requisite managerial ability. There is no lack of artistic material for him to set to work on: London is overstocked with artistic talent ready to the hand of anyone who can recognize it and select from it. The difficulty is to find the man with this power of recognition and selection. The effect of the finer artistic temperaments and talents on the ordinary speculator is not merely nil (for in that case he might give them an engagement by accident), but antipathetic. People sometimes complain of the indifference of the public and the managers to the highest elements in fine art. There never was a greater mistake. The Philistine is not indifferent to fine art: he *hates* it.

The relevance of these observations will be apparent when I say that, though I enjoyed the score of Utopia more than that of any of the previous Savoy operas, I am quite prepared to hear that it is not as palatable to the majority of the human race—otherwise the mob—as it was to me. It is written with an artistic absorption and enjoyment of which Sir Arthur Sullivan always had moments, but which seem to have become constant with him only since he was knighted, though I do not suggest that the two things stand in the relation of cause and effect. The orchestral work is charmingly humorous; and as I happen to mean by this only what I say, perhaps I had better warn my readers not to infer that Utopia is full of buffooneries with the bassoon and piccolo, or of patter and tum-tum.

Whoever can listen to such caressing wind parts—zephyr parts, in fact—as those in the trio for the King and the two Judges in the first act, without being coaxed to feel pleased and amused, is not fit even for treasons, stratagems, and spoils;* whilst anyone whose ears are capable of taking in more than one thing at a time must be tickled by the sudden busyness of the orchestra as the city man takes up the parable. I also confidently recommend those who go into solemn academic raptures over themes 'in diminution' to go and hear how prettily the chorus of the Christy Minstrel* song (borrowed from the plantation dance Johnnie, get a gun*) is used, very much in diminution, to make an exquisite mock-banjo accompaniment. In these examples we are on the plane, not of the bones and tambourine, but of Mozart's accompaniments to Soave sia il vento in Cosi fan tutte* and the entry of the gardener in Le Nozze di Figaro.* Of course these things are as much thrown away on people who are not musicians as a copy of Fliegende Blätter* on people who do not read German, whereas anyone can understand mere horseplay with the instruments.

But people who are not musicians should not intrude into opera-houses: indeed, it is to me an open question whether they ought to be allowed to exist at all. As to the score generally, I have only one fault to find with Sir Arthur's luxurious ingenuity in finding pretty timbres of all sorts, and that is that it still leads him to abuse the human voice most unmercifully. I will say nothing about the part he has written for the unfortunate soprano, who might as well leave her lower octave at home for all the relief she gets from the use of her upper one. But take the case of Mr Scott Fishe, one of Mr Carte's most promising discoveries, who did so much to make the ill-fated Jane Annie* endurable.

What made Mr Fishe's voice so welcome was that it was neither the eternal callow baritone nor the growling bass: it rang like a genuine 'singing bass'; and one felt that here at last was a chance of an English dramatic *basso cantante*, able to 'sing both high and low,' and to contrast his high D with an equally fine one an octave below. Unfortunately, the upper fifth of Mr Fishe's voice, being flexible and of excellent quality, gives him easy command (on occasion) of high passages; and Sir Arthur has ruthlessly seized on this to write for him an excessively specialized baritone part, in which we get not one of those deep, ringing tones which relieved the Jane Annie music so attractively. I have in my time heard so many singers reduced by parts of this sort, in the operas of Verdi and Gounod, to a condition in which they could bawl F sharps *ad lib.* at high pressure, but could neither place a note accurately nor produce any tolerable tone from B flat downwards, that I always protest against vocal parts, no matter what voice they are written for, if they do not employ the voice all over its range, though lying mainly where the singer can sing continuously without fatigue.

A composer who uses up young voices by harping on the prettiest notes in them is an ogreish voluptuary; and if Sir Arthur does not wish posterity either to see the stage whitened with the bones of his victims or else to hear his music transposed wholesale, as Lassalle transposes Rigoletto,* he should make up his mind whether he means to write for a tenor or a baritone, and place the part accordingly. Considering that since Santley retired from the stage and Jean de Reszke turned tenor all the big reputations have been made by *bassi cantanti* like Edouard de Reszke* and Lassalle, and that all the great Wagner parts in which reputations of the same calibre will be made for some time to come are impossible to completely specialized baritones, I venture, as a critic

who greatly enjoys Mr Fishe's performance, to recommend him to ask
the composer politely not to treat him worse than Mozart treated Don
Giovanni, than Wagner treated Wolfram, or than Sir Arthur himself
would treat a clarinet. Miss Nancy McIntosh, who was introduced to
us, it will be remembered, by Mr Henschel at the London Symphony
Concerts, where she sang in a selection from Die Meistersinger and in
the Choral Symphony, came through the trials of a most inconsiderate
vocal part very cleverly, evading the worst of the strain by a treatment
which, if a little flimsy, was always pretty. She spoke her part admirably,
and, by dint of natural tact, managed to make a positive advantage of
her stage inexperience, so that she won over the audience in no time.
As to Miss Brandram, Mr Barrington (who by means of a remarkable
pair of eyebrows transformed himself into a surprising compound of
Mr Goschen and the late Sir William Cusins), Messrs Denny, Kenningham,
Le Hay, Gridley, and the rest, everybody knows what they can do; and
I need only particularize as to Miss Owen and Miss Florence Perry,*
who gave us some excellent pantomime in the very amusing lecture
scene, contrived by Mr Gilbert, and set to perfection by Sir Arthur, in
the first act.

The book has Mr Gilbert's lighter qualities without his faults. Its main
idea, the Anglicization of Utopia by a people boundlessly credulous as
to the superiority of the English race, is as certain of popularity as that
reference to England by the Gravedigger in Hamlet,* which never yet
failed to make the house laugh. There is, happily, no plot; and the stage
business is fresh and well invented—for instance, the lecture already
alluded to, the adoration of the troopers by the female Utopians, the
Cabinet Council 'as held at the Court of St James's Hall,' and the quadrille,
are capital strokes. As to the 'Drawing Room,' with *débutantes*, cards,
trains, and presentations all complete, and the little innovation of a cup
of tea and a plate of cheap biscuits, I cannot vouch for its verisimilitude,
as I have never, strange as it may appear, been present at a Drawing
Room; but that is exactly why I enjoyed it, and why the majority of the
Savoyards will share my appreciation of it.

WHEN I ran across to Bayreuth the other day I was fully aware that the cost of my trip would have been better spent in bringing a German critic to England. And I greatly regret that this article is not written in German, and for a German paper, since it is now evident that, as far as any musical awakening and impulse can come from one country to another, it must come for the present from England to Bayreuth, and not from Bayreuth to England.

First, as to the wonderful Bayreuth orchestra, to the glories of which we have been taught to look with envious despair. I beg to observe here, in the most uncompromising manner, that the Bayreuth orchestra, judged by London standards, is not a first-rate orchestra, but a very carefully worked up second-rate one. The results of the careful working up are admirable: the smoothness, the perfect *sostenuto*,* the unbroken flow of tone testify to an almost perfect orchestral execution in passages which lend themselves to such treatment. But there are two factors in the effect produced by an orchestra: the quality of the execution, and the quality of the instruments on which the execution is done. How much this may vary may be judged by the wide range of prices for musical instruments, even leaving out of account the scarcity values reached by certain exceptionally desirable old fiddles and bassoons.

Take, for example, the cheapest and most popular wind instrument in the orchestra—the cornet. Heaven knows how low the prices of the vilest specimens of cornet may run! but between the cheapest orchestrally presentable cornet and a first-rate one by Courtois* or a good English maker the variation in price, without counting anything for electroplating or decoration of any sort, is from about thirty-five shillings to eight or ten pounds. Fiddles range from a few shillings to the largest sums any orchestral player can afford to give for them; and the scale of prices for wood-wind instruments varies from one to three figures.

Now, if there were such a thing as an international musical parliament, I should certainly agitate for a return of the prices of the instruments used in the Bayreuth and Crystal Palace* orchestras respectively; and I should be surprised if the German total came to as much as half the English one. In the brass especially, the peculiar dull rattle of inferior thin metal at once strikes an ear accustomed to the smooth, firm tone of the more expensive instruments used in England. There is a difference in brightness too; but that I leave out of the question, as possibly due to the difference between Continental and English pitch, a difference which is all to the bad for us.

In judging the wood-wind I am on less certain ground, since the tone is so greatly affected by the way in which the reed is cut. I have heard in the street what I supposed to be an execrable cracked cornet, and on coming round the corner have found an old man playing a clarinet with an old slack reed as easy for his feeble jaws as the reed one cuts for a child in a cornfield. The tone produced by such ancient men and that produced by Lazarus in his best days (which was, I think, purer, if less rich, than Mühlfeld's)* mark the two poles of my experience of clarinet-playing; and I have always found that in German orchestras the standard tone leans more to the man in the street than to Lazarus.

Unfortunately, I am not expert enough to discriminate confidently between the difference due to the cutting of the reed and that due to the quality of the instrument; but except in the case of unusually fine players, who generally take the first chance of coming to England and settling here, the German wood-wind player is content with a cheaper tone than the English one; and Bayreuth is no exception to this rule. The oboe there is as reedy as the *cor anglais* is here. The strings, as compared with ours, are deficient in power and richness; and even in the case of the horns, which we somehow or other cannot play, whilst the Germans can, the tone is much rougher and more nearly allied to that of the Alpine cowhorn than what may be called the standard tone here.

I rather harp on the word standard, because the facts that so many of our best orchestral players are Germans, and that Mr August Manns,* the conductor whose band, in the wind section, puts the Germans most completely to shame in point of fineness of tone, is himself not merely a German, but a Prussian,* conclusively prove that the inferiority of the German orchestra to the English is not an inferiority in natural capacity, but an inferiority in the current national standard of musical beauty—that is, an inferiority in the higher physical culture, and consequently in the quality of the demand to which the orchestral supply is a response.

That this inferiority is no new thing, and was well weighed by Wagner himself, is clear from the stress which he laid on the superiority of the instruments used by our Philharmonic band, and also by the fact that he always cited the Conservatoire concerts in Paris* as the source of what he had learned from actual experience as to fineness of orchestral execution. All the other points he so strenuously urged on conductors have been mastered at Bayreuth; and the superficialities of the Mendelssohnian system have disappeared.

But the material of it all—the brute physical sound of the instruments which are so ably handled—still remains comparatively cheap and ugly; and the worst of it is that no German seems to care. As far as I can make out, the payment of an extra five pounds to an instrument-maker for the sake of a finer tone would strike both conductor and player as an unreasonable waste of money.

And yet this German indifference to the final degrees of excellence in instrumental tone is conscientiousness itself compared to their atrocious insensibility to the beauty of the human voice and the graces of a fine vocal touch. The opening performance of Parsifal this season was, from the purely musical point of view, as far as the principal singers were concerned, simply an abomination. The bass howled, the tenor bawled, the baritone sang flat, and the soprano, when she condescended to sing at all, and did not merely shout her words, screamed, except in the one unscreamable song of Herzeleide's death, in which she subsided into commonplaceness.

The bass, who was rather flustered, perhaps from nervousness, was especially brutal in his treatment of the music of Gurnemanz;* and it struck me that if he had been a trombone-player in the band, instead of a singer, the conductor, Levi* of Munich, would have remonstrated. Indeed, I presently heard a trombone-player, who was helping with the fanfares outside the theatre between the acts, pulled up by the sub-conductor for being 'a little too strong.' Accordingly, having the opportunity of exchanging a few words with Levi afterwards, I expressed my opinion about the bass in question. Levi appeared surprised, and, declaring that the singer had the best bass voice in Germany, challenged me to find him anyone who would sing the part better, to which I could only respond with sufficient emphasis by offering to sing it better myself, upon which he gave me up as a lunatic.

It had to be explained to him that I was accustomed to the 'smooth' singing popular in England. That settled the question for the Bayreuth conductor. Good singing there is merely 'glatt,'* obviously an effeminate, silly, superficial quality, unsuited to the utterances of primeval heroes. The notion that this particular sort of smoothness is one of the consequences of aiming at beauty of tone and singing in tune is apparently as strange in Germany as the notion that it is more truly virile to sing like a man than like a bullock.

If I had passed the whole season listening to Alvary, Klafsky, and Wiegand at Drury Lane, no doubt I should not have noticed any great deficiency in Grengg or Rosa Sucher.* Even as it was, after the first three performances my ear became so corrupted that the second performance of Parsifal did not infuriate me as the first one did. I had become accustomed to second-rate intonation, especially after Tannhäuser, in which from beginning to end there was not a vocal note placed, I will not say as Melba or Miss Eames or the De Reszkes* would have placed it, but as any tolerable English concert singer would have placed it.

This inveterate carelessness of intonation is only partly due to bad method. It is true that German singers at Bayreuth do not know how to sing: they shout; and you can see them make a vigorous stoop and lift with their shoulders, like coalheavers, when they have a difficult note to tackle, a *pianissimo* on any note above the stave being impossible to them.

But this system is nothing like so injurious to them as that of many of the operatic singers to whom we are accustomed. Their voices, it is true, get stale and rough; but they last astonishingly in that condition; the singers themselves are as robust as dray horses; and sixty appears to be about the prime of their shouting life. The thin, worn, shattered voice, with its goat-bleat or tremolo, and its sound as if it had taken to drink and wrecked its nerves and constitution, all shockingly common here, even among quite young singers, is not to be heard, as a rule, at Bayreuth. Singing there, in fact, is exactly like public speaking in England—not a fine art, but a means of placing certain ideas intelligibly and emphatically before the public without any preoccupation as to beauty of voice or grace of manner.

The music-dramas are, so to speak, effectively debated; and the exposition of the poetic theme has all the qualities of a good Budget speech; but there is just about as much charm of voice and style as there is at a conference of the National Liberal Federation. The English political speaker learns his business by practice, and has neither the vices of the artificial elocutionist nor the fascinations of the cultivated artist. Nobody will listen to his voice for its own sake; but he does not break it: it lasts him until he is old enough to retire; and his general health is improved by the vigorous exercise of his lungs.

And that is just exactly the case of the German singer. Unfortunately, this disqualifies him from presenting the works of Wagner as completely as Sir William Harcourt* is disqualified from playing Hamlet—a matter which will appear more fully when I come to describe the fate of Parsifal and Tannhäuser in the hands of German singers as compared with that of Lohengrin as performed by Belgian, Roumanian,

American, and English singers. For I shall require more than one article
to make myself sufficiently unpleasant to help those German lovers of
music who are in revolt against the coarseness and laxity of German
taste in this matter, and who are struggling to awaken the national conscience to the impossibility of a school of art in which the first lesson is
one of callous indifference to beauty.

SITTING, as I am today, in a Surrey farmhouse with the sky overcast, and a big fire burning to keep me from shivering, it seems to me that it must be at least four or five months since I was breathing balmy airs in the scented pine-woods on the hills round Bayreuth. If I could only see the sun for five minutes I could better recall what I have to write about. As it is, I seem to have left it all far behind with the other vanities of the season. I no longer feel any impulse to describe Lohengrin and Tannhäuser as I promised, or to draw morals for Frau Wagner on the one hand, or Sir Augustus Harris* on the other. For months I have held the whole subject of musical art in an intense grip, which never slackened even when I was asleep; but now the natural periodicity of my function asserts itself, and compels me to drop the subject in August and September, just as hens moult in November (so they tell me here in the farmhouse).

What I feel bound to record concerning the Bayreuth Lohengrin—remember that this is the first time the work has been done there, and probably the first time it has ever been thoroughly done at all, if we except the earliest attempt under Liszt at Weimar—is that its stage framework is immensely more entertaining, convincing, and natural than it has ever seemed before. This is mainly because the stage management is so good, especially with regard to the chorus. In Lohengrin there are only two comparatively short scenes in which the chorus is not present and in constant action.

The opera therefore suffers fearfully on ordinary occasions from the surprising power of the average Italian chorister to destroy all stage illusion the moment he shambles on the scene with his blue jaws, his reach-me-down costume, his foolish single gesture, his embarrassed eye on the prompter, and his general air of being in an opera chorus because he is fit for nothing better. At Covent Garden he is, in addition, generally an old acquaintance: it is not only that he is destroying the illusion of the opera you are looking at, but that he has destroyed the illusion of nearly all the operas you have ever seen; so that the conflict of his claim upon you as one of 'the old familiar faces' with the claims of the art which he outrages finally weakens your mind and disturbs your conscience until you lose the power of making any serious effort to get rid of him. As to the ladies of our opera chorus, they have to be led by competent, sensible women; and as women at present can only

acquire these qualities by a long experience as mothers of large families, our front row hardly helps the romance of the thing more than the
men do.

Now I am not going to pretend that at Bayreuth the choristers produce an overwhelming impression of beauty and chivalry, or even to
conceal the fact that the economic, social, and personal conditions
which make the Covent Garden chorus what it is in spite of the earnest
desire of everybody concerned that it should be something quite different, dominate Frau Wagner just as they dominate Sir Augustus Harris,
and compel her to allot to Elsa a bevy of maidens, and to Henry the
Fowler a band of warriors, about whose charms and prowess a good deal
of make-believe is necessary. The stouter build of the men, the prevalence of a Teutonic cast among them, and their reinforcement by
a physically and artistically superior class of singers who regard it as an
honor to sing at Bayreuth, even in the chorus, certainly help the illusion as far as the Saxon and Brabantine* warriors in Lohengrin are
concerned; but this difference in raw material is as nothing compared
with the difference made by the intelligent activity of the stage-manager.

One example of this will suffice. Those who know the score of
Lohengrin are aware that in the finale to the first act there is a section,
usually omitted in performance, in which the whole movement is
somewhat unexpectedly repeated in a strongly contrasted key, the
modulation being unaccountable from the point of view of the absolute
musician, as it is not at all needed as a relief to the principal key. At
Bayreuth its purpose is made clear. After the combat with Telramund
and the solo for Elsa which serves musically as the exposition of the
theme of the finale, the men, greatly excited and enthusiastic over the
victory of the strange knight, range themselves in a sort of wheel formation, of which Lohengrin is the centre, and march round him as they
take up the finale from Elsa in the principal key. When the modulation
comes, the women, in their white robes, break into this triumphal
circle, displace the men, and march round Elsa in the same way, the
striking change of key being thus accompanied by a correspondingly
striking change on the stage, one of the incidents of which is a particularly remarkable kaleidoscoping of the scheme of color produced by
the dresses.

Here you have a piece of stage management of the true Wagnerian
kind, combining into one stroke a dramatic effect, a scenic effect, and
a musical effect, the total result being a popular effect the value of which
was proved by the roar of excitement which burst forth as the curtains
closed in. A more complex example of the same combination was

afforded by the last act of Tannhäuser, which produced the same outburst from the audience, and which was all the more conclusive because
none of the enthusiasm could be credited to the principal artists, who
had, in the first two acts, effectually cleared themselves of all suspicion
of being able to produce any effect except one of portentous boredom.

Here, then, we have the point at which Bayreuth beats Drury Lane
and Covent Garden in staging Wagner and every other composer
whose works have been for some years in our repertory. I have over and
over again pointed out the way in which the heroic expenditure of
Sir Augustus Harris gets wasted for want of a stage-manager who not
only studies the stage picture as it is studied, for instance, at the Savoy
Theatre, or at any of our music-halls where ballets form part of the
entertainment, but who studies the score as well, and orders the stage
so that the spectator's eye, ear, and dramatic sense shall be appealed to
simultaneously.

I have sometimes had to point out, in the case of old stock operas,
that there is often reason to suspect that the stage-manager either does
not even know the story of the opera he has in hand, or has become cynically convinced that an opera is in itself such a piece of nonsense that
an extra absurdity or two cannot matter much. This is of course quite
a tenable view argumentatively; but it is not the understanding upon
which the public pays for its seats. The moment you take a guinea, or
half-a-crown,* or whatever it may be, from an individual for a performance of an opera, you are bound to treat the performance as a serious
matter, whatever your private philosophic convictions may be.

At Bayreuth they do take the performance seriously in all its details:
the heroine does not die in the middle of the street on a lodging-house
sofa, nor does the tenor step out of a window with a rope ladder attached
to it, and openly walk off at the level of the chamber floor. The rank and
file are carefully instructed as to what they are supposed to be doing;
and nobody dreams of taking any liberties with the work or with the
public. It is quite a mistake to suppose that the makeshifts which circumstances force upon Covent Garden are unknown at Bayreuth, or that
the stock works are as well rehearsed and prepared as the new works;
but there is, at any rate, always the habit of discipline; and though things
may be left undone for want of time or ill done for want of rehearsal,
nothing is let slide on the assumption that it is not worth doing. I have
been tortured there by bad singing, and bored by solemnly prosaic
acting; but I have never been offended by wanton trifling.

I have sufficiently explained in my last article how Bayreuth's scrupulous artistic morality is heavily counterbalanced by the callousness

of its musical sensibility. The cure for this, however, is not the writing
of homilies about it, but the cultivation of the German ear by actual
experience of something better than the singing they are accustomed to
tolerate. Already the popularity of Van Dyck,* a Belgian singer with
none of the German bluntness about him, whose charm of voice and
style was sufficient, when he appeared as Des Grieux* at Covent
Garden, to produce on Jean de Reszke, who was at that time taking his
supremacy for granted somewhat too lazily, the effect popularly known
as 'making him sit up,' is rendering the Bayreuth stage more accessible
to foreigners, who will finally, if the Germans do not realize their own
deficiencies, make it difficult for a German singer to get an engagement
there. This year we have Nordica and Miss Brema* as well as Van Dyck;
and it is probable that Frau Wagner will look for more help in the same
direction—across the frontier, that is—on future occasions.

I am not quite done with the subject even yet; but as this farmhouse
is beyond the sphere of the Post Office, I must conclude, in order to
allow three or four days for the journey of thirty miles or so which my
communication must make before it reaches London.

POSTSCRIPT 1931.—As it happened I *was* done with the subject. I had
already resigned my post as musical critic to The World on the death
of its editor Edmund Yates* on the 19th May 1894. But his successor
pleaded that it would seem a personal slight to himself if I did not go on
under his editorship until the end of the season; and this, to save
appearances, I consented to do. After the autumn recess my vacant
place was filled by Mr Robert Smythe Hichens,* who had trained
himself as a musician, not knowing that he was destined to be a famous
novelist.

I never again undertook regular duties as a critic of music.

THE CASE FOR THE CRITIC-DRAMATIST

A DISCUSSION has arisen recently as to whether a dramatic critic can also be a dramatic author without injury to his integrity and impartiality. The feebleness with which the point has been debated may be guessed from the fact that the favorite opinion seems to be that a critic is either an honest man or he is not. If honest, then dramatic authorship can make no difference to him. If not, he will be dishonest whether he writes plays or not. This childish evasion cannot, for the honor of the craft, be allowed to stand. If I wanted to ascertain the melting-point of a certain metal, and how far it would be altered by an alloy of some other metal, and an expert were to tell me that a metal is either fusible or it is not—that if not, no temperature will melt it; and if so, it will melt anyhow—I am afraid I should ask that expert whether he was a fool himself or took me for one. Absolute honesty is as absurd an abstraction as absolute temperature or absolute value. A dramatic critic who would die rather than read an American pirated edition of a copyright English book might be considered an absolutely honest man for all practical purposes on that particular subject—I say on that one, because very few men have more than one point of honor; but as far as I am aware, no such dramatic critic exists. If he did, I should regard him as a highly dangerous monomaniac. That honesty varies inversely with temptation is proved by the fact that every additional penny on the income-tax yields a less return than the penny before it, shewing that men state their incomes less honestly for the purposes of taxation at sevenpence in the pound than sixpence. The matter may be tested by a simple experiment. Go to one of the gentlemen whose theory is that a man is either honest or he is not, and obtain from him the loan of half a crown on some plausible pretext of a lost purse or some such petty emergency. He will not ask you for a written acknowledgment of the debt. Return next day and ask for a loan of £500 without a promissory note, on the ground that you are either honest or not honest, and that a man who will pay back half a crown without compulsion will also pay back £500. You will find that the theory of absolute honesty will collapse at once.

Are we then to believe that the critic-dramatist who stands to make anything from five hundred to ten thousand pounds by persuading a manager to produce his plays, will be prevented by his honesty from writing about that manager otherwise than he would if he had never written a play and were quite certain that he never should write one? I can only say that people who believe such a thing would believe anything. I am myself a particularly flagrant example of the critic-dramatist. It is not with me a mere case of an adaptation or two raked up against me as incidents in my past. I have written half a dozen 'original' plays, four of which have never been performed;* and I shall presently write half a dozen more. The production of one of them, even if it attained the merest success of esteem, would be more remunerative to me than a couple of years of criticism. Clearly, since I am no honester than other people, I should be the most corrupt flatterer in London if there were nothing but honesty to restrain me. How is it, then, that the most severe criticisms of managers come from me and from my fellow critic-dramatists, and that the most servile puffery comes from writers whose every sentence proves that they have nothing to hope or fear from any manager? There are a good many answers to this question, one of the most obvious being that as the respect inspired by a good criticism is permanent, whilst the irritation it causes is temporary, and as, on the other hand, the pleasure given by a venal criticism is temporary and the contempt it inspires permanent, no man really secures his advancement as a dramatist by making himself despised as a critic. The thing has been tried extensively during the last twenty years; and it has failed. For example, the late Frank Marshall,* a dramatist and an extravagantly enthusiastic admirer of Sir Henry Irving's genius,* followed a fashion which at one time made the Lyceum Theatre a sort of court formed by a retinue of literary gentlemen. I need not question either their sincerity or the superiority of Canute to their idolatry; for Canute never produced their plays: Robert Emmett* and the rest of their masterpieces remain unacted to this day. It may be said that this brings us back to honesty as the best policy; but honesty has nothing to do with it: plenty of the men who know that they can get along faster fighting than crawling, are no more honest than the first Napoleon was. No virtue, least of all courage, implies any other virtue. The cardinal guarantee for a critic's integrity is simply the force of the critical instinct itself. To try to prevent me from criticizing by pointing out to me the superior pecuniary advantages of puffing is like trying to keep a young Irving from going on the stage by pointing out the superior pecuniary advantages of stockbroking. If my own father were an actor-manager, and his life depended on his getting favorable notices of his performance, I should orphan myself without an instant's hesitation if he acted badly. I am by no means the willing victim of this instinct. I am keenly susceptible to contrary influences—to flattery, which

I swallow greedily if the quality is sufficiently good; to the need of money, to private friendship or even acquaintanceship, to the pleasure of giving pleasure and the pain of giving pain, to consideration for people's circumstances and prospects, to personal likes and dislikes, to sentimentality, pity, chivalry, pugnacity and mischief, laziness and cowardice, and a dozen other human conditions which make the critic vulnerable; but the critical instinct gets the better of them all. I spare no effort to mitigate its inhumanity, trying to detect and strike out of my articles anything that would give pain without doing any good. Those who think the things I say severe, or even malicious, should just see the things I do *not* say. I do my best to be partial, to hit out at remediable abuses rather than at accidental shortcomings, and at strong and responsible people rather than weak and helpless ones. And yet all my efforts do not alter the result very much. So stubborn is the critic within me, that with every disposition to be as goodnatured and as popular an authority as the worst enemy of art could desire, I am to all intents and purposes incorruptible. And that is how the dramatist-critic, if only he is critic enough, 'slates' the actor-manager in defiance of the interest he has in conciliating him. He cannot help himself, any more than the ancient mariner could help telling his story. And the actor-manager can no more help listening than the wedding guest could.* In short, the better formula would have been, that a man is either a critic or not a critic; that to the extent to which he is one he will criticize the man-agers in spite of heaven or earth; and that to the extent to which he is not, he will flatter them anyhow, to save himself trouble.

The advantage of having a play criticized by a critic who is also a playwright is as obvious as the advantage of having a ship criticized by a critic who is also a master shipwright. Pray observe that I do not speak of the criticism of dramas and ships by dramatists and shipwrights who are not also critics; for that would be no more convincing than the criticism of acting by actors. Dramatic authorship no more constitutes a man a critic than actorship constitutes him a dramatic author; but a dramatic critic learns as much from having been a dramatic author as Shakespear or Mr Pinero* from having been actors. The average London critic, for want of practical experience, has no real confidence in himself: he is always searching for an imaginary 'right' opinion, with which he never dares to identify his own. Consequently every public man finds that as far as the press is concerned his career divides itself into two parts: the first, during which the critics are afraid to praise him; and the second, during which they are afraid to do anything else. In the first, the critic is uncomfortably trying to find faults enough to make out a case for his timid coldness: in the second, he is eagerly picking out excellences to justify his eulogies. And of course he blunders equally in both phases. The faults he finds are either inessential or are positive reforms, or he blames the wrong people for them: the triumphs of acting which he announces are stage tricks that any old hand could play. In criticizing actresses he is an open and shameless voluptuary. If a woman is pretty, well dressed, and self-satisfied enough to be at her ease on the stage, he is delighted; and if she is a walking monument of handsome incompetence, so much the better, as your voluptuary rarely likes a woman to be cleverer than himself, or to force him to feel deeply and think energetically when he only wants to wallow in her good looks. Confront him with an actress who will not condescend to attack him on this side—who takes her work with thorough seriousness and self-respect—and his resentment, his humiliation, his sense of being snubbed, break out ludicrously in his writing, even when he dare not write otherwise than favorably. A great deal of this nonsense would be taken out of him if he could only write a play and have it produced. No dramatist begins by writing plays merely as excuses for the exhibition of pretty women on the stage. He comes to that ultimately perhaps; but at first he does his best to create real characters and make them pass through three acts of real experiences. Bring a critic who has done this face to face with the practical question of selecting an actress for his heroine, and he suddenly realizes for the first time that there is not such a galaxy of talent on the London stage as he thought, and that the handsome walking ladies whom he always thought good enough for other people's plays are not good enough for his own. That is already an immense step in his education. There are other steps, too, which he will have taken before the curtain falls on the first public representation of his play; but they may be summed up in the fact that the author of a play is the only person who really wants to have it well done in every respect, and who therefore has every drawback brought fully home to him. The man who has had that awakening about one play will thenceforth have his eyes open at all other plays; and there you have at once the first moral with the first technical qualification of the critic—the determination to have every play as well done as possible, and the knowledge of what is standing in the way of that consummation. Those of our critics who, either as original dramatists or adapters and translators, have superintended the production of plays with paternal anxiety, are never guilty of the wittily disguised indifference of clever critics who have never seen a drama through from its first beginnings behind the scenes. Compare the genuine excitement of Mr Clement Scott, or the almost Calvinistic seriousness of Mr William Archer, with the gaily easy what-does-it-matterness of Mr Walkley, and you see at once how the two critic-dramatists* influence the drama, whilst the critic-playgoer only makes it a pretext for entertaining his readers. On the whole there is only as much validity in the theory that a critic should not be a dramatist, as in the theory that a judge should not be a lawyer nor a general a soldier. You cannot have qualifications without experience; and you cannot have experience without personal interest and bias. That may not be an ideal arrangement; but it is the way the world is built; and we must make the best of it.

* * *

THE LATE CENSOR

MR E. F. SMYTH PIGOTT, for twenty years examiner of stage plays to the Lord Chamberlain's department, has joined the majority. It is a great pity that the Censorship cannot be abolished* before the appointment of a successor to Mr Pigott creates a fresh vested interest in one of the most mischievous of our institutions.

The justification of the Censorship is to be found in the assumption, repeatedly and explicitly advanced by the late holder of the office, that, if the stage were freed, managers would immediately produce licentious plays; actresses would leave off clothing themselves decently; and the public would sit nightly wallowing in the obscenity which the Censor now sternly withholds from them. This assumption evidently involves the further one, that the Examiner of Plays is so much better than his neighbors, as to be untainted by their assumed love of filth. This is where the theory of the Censorship breaks down in practice. The Lord Chamberlain's reader is not selected by examination either in literature or morals. His emoluments, estimated at about £800 a year, will fetch nothing more in the market than well connected mediocrity. Therefore it is necessary to give him absolute power, so that there may be no appeal from his blunders. If he vetoes serious plays and licenses nasty ones, which is exactly what the late Mr Pigott did, there is no remedy. He is the Tsar of the theatres, able to do things that no prime minister dare do. And he has the great advantage that in ninety-eight out of every hundred plays submitted to him (this is an official estimate), no question of morals is raised. He has nothing to do but read the play, pocket his two guineas, license the performance, and leave the manager and the author under the impression that he is a very agreeable, unobjectionable person, whose licence is cheap at the price since it relieves every one of responsibility* and makes things pleasant all round. It is not until the two per cent of plays in which received opinions and hardened prejudices are called in question, and offered for testing under the searching rays of the footlights—in other words, the plays on which the whole growth and continued vitality of the theatre depend—that the Censor has his opportunity of shewing how much better he is than the public by saying, 'You should listen to these plays, however much they may shock you. I have read them, and can certify that they will interest really cultivated people and help to set everybody thinking.' But as the Censor never is any better than the average public, he does exactly the reverse of this. He shares its ignorant intolerance and its petulance under criticism, and uses his official authority to forbid the performance of the exceptional plays. The late Mr Pigott is declared on all hands to have been the best reader of plays we have ever had; and yet he was a walking compendium of vulgar insular prejudice, who, after wallowing all his life in the cheapest theatrical sentiment (he was a confirmed playgoer), had at last brought himself to a pitch of incompetence which, outside the circle of those unfortunate persons who have had to try and reason with him personally, can only be measured by reading his evidence before the Commission of 1892,* and the various letters of his which are just now finding their way into print. He had French immorality on the brain; he had American indecency on the brain; he had the womanly woman on the brain; he had the Divorce Court on the brain; he had 'not before a mixed audience' on the brain; his official career in relation to the higher drama was one long folly and panic, in which the only thing definitely discernible in a welter of intellectual confusion was his conception of the English people rushing towards an abyss of national degeneration in morals and manners, and only held back on the edge of the precipice by the grasp of his strong hand.

In the Daily Telegraph of Monday last there was an obituary notice of Mr Pigott from the sympathetic pen of Mr Clement Scott, who is far too kind-hearted to tell the truth on so sad an occasion, and who, I am afraid, will characterize my remarks, in his very ownest style, as 'a cowardly attack on a dead man.' Mr Scott tells us of Mr Pigott's 'difficult and delicate duties,' of his 'admirable discretion,' his 'determination to persist in the path that seemed right to him,' his conscientiousness, zeal, efficiency, tact, and so on. I do not question Mr Pigott's personal character: I have no doubt he was as excellent a man for all private purposes as Charles I.* But when Mr Scott's benevolence to Mr Pigott leads him to discredit my protests against the Censorship as 'allegations that are as coarse as they are untrue,' I must open Mr Scott's eyes a little. Not that I deny the coarseness. To accuse anyone of encouraging lewd farce at the expense of fine drama is to bring a coarse charge against him; but Mr Scott will admit that the policeman must not be put out of court because he has a coarse charge to prefer. The question is, Is the charge true? Mr Scott says no. I produce my evidence, and leave the public to judge.

Not very many seasons ago, in the exercise of my duties as a musical critic, I went to an opera at a certain West End theatre.* (Mr Scott, not having enjoyed the advantage of a training as musical critic, misses these things.) There were two heroines, one a princess. The hero had to marry the princess, though he loved the other heroine. In the second act, the stage represented an antechamber in the palace of the bride's father on the night of the wedding. The door of the nuptial chamber appeared on the stage. It was guarded by an elderly duenna. The reluctant bridegroom arrived on his way to join his bride. The duenna presented him with the golden key of the chamber. Suddenly it occurred to him that if he were to criminally assault this lady, who was renowned at court for her austerity, her screams would rouse the court, and he would be consigned by the outraged monarch to a dungeon, thereby escaping his conjugal obligations. On proceeding to carry out this stratagem, he was taken aback by finding the old lady, far from raising an alarm, receive his advances with the utmost ardour. In desperation he threw her to the ground, and was about to escape when she, making no effort to rise, said, with archly affectionate reproach, 'Dont you see where youve left me, duckie?' On this he fled; and presently a young man and a young woman entered and flirted until they were interrupted by the king. He, overhearing a kiss, supposed it to proceed from the bridal chamber of his daughter. He immediately went to the door; listened at the keyhole; and, hearing another kiss, remarked with an ecstatic shiver that it made him feel young again. If that scene had not been presented to the public under the authority of the Lord Chamberlain, it would be impossible for me to describe it in these columns. The sole justification for the Censorship is that, without its restraining hand, the scene would have been worse than it was. Pray how much worse could it have been?

Take another instance, this time of a well-known farcical comedy which Mr Scott must have witnessed. I spare the details: suffice it to say that the piece contained three or four 'laughs' which could not possibly have been explained or described at a dinner party, which is, if I mistake not, Mr Scott's test of propriety. I did not see the piece until, finding myself at Northampton* on the eve of a political meeting in which I had to take part, I went into the theatre, and found this comedy 'on tour' there. Now Northampton is not like London: it is not large enough to support one theatre where improper jests are permitted, and another guaranteed safe for clergymen and their daughters. What was the result? The Censorship of public opinion—of that Monsieur Tout le Monde who is admitted to be wiser than everyone except the Lord Chamberlain—acted spontaneously. The questionable points were either omitted or slurred over in such a way that nobody could possibly catch their intention. Everything that Mr Pigott might have done, and did not do, to make the play decent was done without compulsion by the management in order to avoid offending that section of the public which does not relish smoking-room facetiousness.

These two typical cases, which, as Mr Scott knows better than any-one else, I can easily multiply if he puts me to it, will, I hope, convince him that my statement that the Censorship does not withhold its approval from blackguardism on the stage is much better considered than his counter-statement that I have simply said the thing that is not. But if he demands equally direct proof of my statement that the Censorship suppresses fine work, he has me at a disadvantage; for I nat-urally cannot produce the plays that the Censorship has prevented from existing. And yet this is the very statement I chiefly desire to establish; for I do not in the least object to the licensing of plays which disgust me, if there are people who are entertained by them: what I object to is the suppression, because they disgust other people, of plays that entertain me. All I can do is to offer to produce a staggering list of authors who have not written for the stage since the evil day when Walpole established the Censorship to prevent Fielding from exposing the corruption of Parliament on the stage.* Fielding never wrote another play; and from his time to that of Dickens, who was once very fond of the stage, a comparison of our literature with our drama shews a rela-tive poverty and inferiority on the part of the latter not to be paralleled in any of the countries where the Censor only interferes on political grounds. May I ask Mr Scott whether he thinks that Mr Grant Allen's The Woman who Did would have been licensed by Mr Pigott if it had been a play, or whether The Heavenly Twins could have been written under the thumb of a Censor? Or, to come to actual plays, would Ibsen's Ghosts have been licensed had Mr Grein risked subjecting himself to a £50 penalty by making the attempt? Is Tolstoi's Dominion of Darkness likely to be produced here as it has been elsewhere? Would Die Walküre* be licensed as a spoken play? Would Shakespear, or the great Greek dramatists, have stood a chance with Mr Pigott? Mr Scott may reply that Mr Pigott actually did license Ibsen's plays. Fortunately, I am in a position to give both Mr Pigott's opinion of Ibsen's plays and his reason for licensing them. Here are his own words, uttered on one of the most responsible occasions of his official career:

'I have studied Ibsen's plays pretty carefully; and all the characters in Ibsen's plays appear to me morally deranged. All the heroines are dissatisfied spinsters who look on marriage as a monopoly, or dissatis-fied married women in a chronic state of rebellion against not only the conditions which nature has imposed on their sex, but against all the duties and obligations of mothers and wives. As for the men, they are all rascals or imbeciles.'

Not unnaturally, Mr Woodall* asked Mr Pigott on this why he did not think the plays sufficiently injurious to public morals to be suppressed. Mr Pigott replied that they were too absurd to do any harm. Thus the one great writer who has escaped what Mr Scott has called 'the kindly blue pencil,' was let pass, not because he was a great writer, but because Mr Pigott was so stupendously incompetent as to think him beneath contempt. I have suggested that Shakespear would have been vetoed by him; but he has anticipated that misgiving in the following remarkable utterance: 'Shakespear himself was a member, I believe, at one time, of the Lord Chamberlain's company; but that did not prevent his plays being written.' Imagine Mr Pigott, who refused to license The Cenci,* confronted with the relationship between the king and queen in Hamlet, or with the closet scene in that play.

Let me add a few more touches to the sketch of Mr Pigott's mind. First, as to his notion of morality in an audience, of vice and virtue, of fine sentiment:

'The further east you go, the more moral your audience is. You may get a gallery full of roughs in which every other boy is a pickpocket, and yet their collective sympathy is in favor of self-sacrifice; collectively they have a horror of vice and a love of virtue. A boy might pick your pocket as you left the theatre, but have his reserve of fine sentiment in his heart.'

This is immoral balderdash, nothing more and nothing less; and yet poor Mr Pigott believed it as firmly as he believed that Browning and George Meredith and James Russell Lowell,* in attending the Shelley Society's unlicensed performance of The Cenci, were indulging a vicious taste for immoral exhibitions.

Mr Pigott's highly praised tact, both as a critic and a controversialist, may be judged from the following *obiter dicta*:*

'Managers' backers are in most cases men who do not care to keep a theatre—I will not say for the elevation of dramatic art, or for the public edification—but for purposes which can be openly avowed.'

'Absolute free trade in theatres and theatrical representation may be left to the advocacy of disciples of Jack Cade,* whose political economy is a sort of Benthamism burlesqued. These purveyors of theatrical scandals are equally in favor of absolute free trade in disorderly houses and houses of ill-fame.'

I must say I wish Mr Scott had not trifled so outrageously as he has with this great public question. It is a frightful thing to see the greatest

thinkers, poets, and authors of modern Europe—men like Ibsen, Wagner,
Tolstoi, and the leaders of our own literature—delivered helpless into
the vulgar hands of such a noodle as this amiable old gentleman—this
despised and incapable old official—most notoriously was. And just
such a man as he was his successor is likely to be too, because a capable
man means a known man; and a known man means one whose faults
have become as public as his qualities. The appointment of Mr Archer,
for instance, would awaken Mr Scott to the infamy of the Censorship
as effectually as the appointment of Mr Scott himself would fortify
Mr Archer's case against the institution. Yet the Lord Chamberlain cannot possibly find a better man than either one or other of these gentlemen. He will therefore have to appoint a nobody whose qualifications,
being unknown, can be imagined by foolish people to be infinite. Is this,
then, the time for Mr Scott to announce that 'the dramatic world is well
content with the control now vested in the Lord Chamberlain and his
staff?' Who constitute the dramatic world?! take the first handful of
names that comes to hand. Do Messrs Oscar Wilde, Sydney Grundy,
Robert Buchanan, Henry Arthur Jones belong to it? Do Mr Hermann
Vezin, Mr Lewis Waller, Mr Charles Charrington, Miss Alma Murray,
Mrs Theodore Wright, Miss Janet Achurch, Miss Elizabeth Robins*
belong to it? Does Mr Scott himself belong to it? and, if so, do I?—does
Mr Archer?—does Mr Walkley?—do the numerous critics who never
refer to the Censorship except in terms of impatient contempt at such
an anomaly? Would one of the managers who pay the Lord Chamberlain
compliments now that they are in his power, waste a word on him if
they were out of it? No: the dramatic world, Mr Scott may depend
on it, wants the same freedom that exists in America and—oddly
enough—in Ireland. Not, mind, a stage controlled by the County
Council or any such seventy-seven times worse evil than the present,
but a stage free as the Press is free and as speech is free. When Mr Scott
has dropped his tear over the lost friend whom he has forced me to
handle so roughly, I shall thank him to come back to his own side and
fight for that freedom. Abominations like the Censorship have quite
enough flatterers without him.

CHURCH AND STAGE

A LITTLE squall of controversy has been raised by the church scene in Michael and his Lost Angel at the Lyceum.* It is contended by gentlemen who get their living by going to the theatre and reporting or criticizing performances there, that Church ritual, and indeed anything of a sacred character, is out of place on the stage, and its dramatic representation a breach of good taste and an offence against public decency. Let us see exactly what this means.

Of all the vile places on earth that are not absolutely contrary to law, the vilest is a convict prison. The vilest thing in the prison is the gallows; and the vilest thing done there is an execution. Yet the prison has its chaplain; and his prayers are an indispensable part of the disgusting business of hanging a man. The most heathenish and wasteful, not to say bestial civic celebration now tolerated is a City* dinner. Men go there with the intention of eating too much and drinking too much; and many of them exceed their intention. But the proceedings always commence with the ritual called 'grace before meat.'* For wrath and violence, terror and ferocity, on a scale of the most frightful magnitude, nothing can compare with a battle, especially when the victims are poor men tempted by a shilling a day to fight for the glorification of blood-thirsty fools and cowards who sit at home at ease and gloat over sensational 'special correspondence.' Yet no victory is complete without the 'Te Deum'* by which Christian combatants assume that their God is an accomplice in their crime, and praise Him for it. But, if you please, there is one lawful place worse than the gallows and the battlefield, one tolerated pursuit filthier than gluttony and more damnable than whole-sale murder. That place is the theatre; that pursuit, playgoing. We may drag the symbols of our religion through seas of blood, waste, riot, and rapine, if only we spare it the final outrage of mentioning it on the stage of the Lyceum. If I am to accept this as good sense—if actors are infamous wretches prostituting themselves to the desire of the audience to indulge a detestable vice, then pray what am I, the critic, who sell myself to advertize such abomination by writing seductive descriptions and eulogies of the plays with which I am especially pleased? And what are those still more abandoned colleagues of mine who lard the managers with flatteries which even Mr Wilson Barrett's Nero* might find a trifle hyperbolical? Clearly we are baser than Molière, to whom Christian burial was refused in France, baser than the ballet dancer to whom the Bishop of London refused the Sacrament* (though this certainly occurred a few years before the knighting of Sir Henry Irving) by as much as the pandar is baser than his employer.

Let us look at the case from another point of view. It is said that 'some things' are too sacred to be represented on the stage. The phrase 'some things' is highly characteristic: it recalls the intelligent member of Parliament who supported the attempt to exclude the late Charles Bradlaugh from the House of Commons on the ground that 'a man ought to believe in something or another.' But since it is just as well not to be frivolously vague in speaking of sacred things, let us replace 'some things' by the mysteries of religion, which is what the objectors would mean if, on this subject, they were earnest enough to mean anything at all. Pray what are the mysteries of religion? Are they faith, hope, love, heroism, life, creation; or are they pews and pulpits, prayer-books and Sunday bonnets, copes and stoles and dalmatics? Even that large section of the population of these islands whose religion is the merest idolatry of material symbols will not deny that the former are the realities of religion. Then I ask the gentlemen who think that the pews and prayer-books are too sacred to be represented on the stage, why it is that they have never protested against the fact that all our dramas deal with faith, hope, love, and the rest of the essentials? The most sacred feelings and the holiest names are never long out of the mouths of our stage heroes and heroines. In the last Adelphi melodrama* but two the heroine recited the service for the dead on the stage, whilst her father danced round her in a frenzy, trying to make up his mind to shoot her before the Indians took the place by storm. The critics who are protesting against the procession in the fourth act of Michael and his Lost Angel did not protest against that. Of course it is possible that they did not recognize it because Miss Millward* did not wear a surplice during the passage, just as they mistook a homily of Mr Wilson Barrett's the other day for the Sermon on the Mount because the actor stood on a hill in a long gown, and gave it out like a clergyman reading the lessons. But I could easily find instances for which that unpresentable excuse cannot be alleged. The real objection to Mr Jones's play is the objection to Michael's treatment of religion as co-extensive with life: that is, as genuinely catholic. To the man who regards it as only a watertight Sunday compartment of social observance, such a view is not only inconvenient but positively terrifying. I am sorry for him; but I can assure him that the British drama is annexing steadily the territory on which he feels so uncomfortable. And whoever tries to obstruct that advance will be inevitably ground into the mud. When I want to exhibit the might of criticism,

I may throw an express train off the line; but you do not catch me trying to stop the imperceptibly slow march of a glacier.

Yet another point of view. It is argued that a stage representation is only a pretence, a mockery, a sham, a thing made to simulate something that it is not by tricks of light and paint and feats of mimicry. Granted; but what, then, is to be said of the pictures in the National Gallery,* in which canvas and colored clay are made to simulate, not only churches and priests, but the very persons of the Trinity themselves? Is a crucifix an offence against the sacredness of what it represents? Are religious fictions, such as Barabbas and The Sorrows of Satan* at one extreme, and Goethe's Faust at the other, to be suppressed? The Cromwellian Puritans would have said 'Yes' to all this. Those of them who believed, like the Reverend Michael, that life and religion are coextensive, were for destroying, not only theatres, but images, pictures, statues, symbols, and simulations of all kinds. Those who held the more convenient watertight-compartment theory, thus dividing life into the sacred and profane, encouraged and rejoiced in profane art, but would not have sacred art on any terms. They would have family portraits, but no pictures of saints and virgins: they were musicians, but would not have music in church. They would have sacked the National Gallery, and burnt its most precious treasures in Trafalgar Square; and they actually did enter cathedrals, smash everything they could get at that was in the nature of statuary, pulled the organs to pieces, and tore up the music-books. In short, though they were too fond of art to want to exterminate it, they excommunicated it. Are our watertight-compartment critics willing to take the same line? Are they prepared to excommunicate art altogether, or do they wish to excommunicate the theatre only, leaving the cathedral, the picture gallery, the library, untouched? If so, this also involves them in the conclusion that some quite peculiar infamy and disgrace attaches to the theatre; and I am again compelled to submit that, since they have voluntarily chosen theatregoing as a means of livelihood, they fall under their own condemnation as infamous and disgraceful persons, unworthy as such to lead public opinion on this or any other matter. Having no such unfriendly opinion of them, I had rather coax them to retreat from their position than see them impale themselves on either horn of so inhuman a dilemma. For what alternative is left to them, except, perhaps, to follow the example of Sheridan Knowles* by abandoning their profession and spending the rest of their lives in warning others against it?

The public, consisting as it does of many who do not go to the theatre, is in no way bound, as a critic is, to be loyal to it or else leave it.

But the playgoing, art-supporting public may reasonably be called on to make up its mind whether religion is to be denied the services of art or not. Something may be learnt from past follies on this subject. Music, for instance, has always been highly privileged in the popular imagination. No other art has ever been conceived as practised in Heaven. Prophets may have been inspired to write books on earth; and St Luke is supposed to have painted a portrait of the Virgin; but who ever dreamt of easels and inkbottles, or typewriters, in Heaven? Yet what would Heaven be without its harps, and trumpets, and choir of angels? It was owing to this association of ideas that Handel met with no opposition when he popularized the oratorio. He gave us, in the concert-room, Samson and Delilah, and Manoah, and the rest of the persons in the Bible story; and no one was scandalized. But when Salvini came over here, a hundred and thirty years later, he found that Samson was out of the question in a theatre.* The playgoing public was perfectly willing—and, indeed, highly curious—to see him walk off with the gates of Gaza, throw his father across his shoulder with one hand and carry him away, and finally perish between the pillars under a shower of dummy Philistines. But the people who never go to the theatre might have been offended; and so Samson had to be reserved for a much more Puritan country—America. Even music itself has had to make absurd concessions to pietistic prudery. Beethoven composed an oratorio called The Mount of Olives; and immediately the question arose whether the Handelian privilege extended to the New Testament. After about thirty years consideration we made up our minds the wrong way, and turned The Mount of Olives into Engedi, with David for the principal figure.* Thirty years more, and the original work was performed at the Leeds Festival,* with such complete impunity that it was evident the Engedification had been an act of gratuitous folly. We were kept for a long time out of one of the world's great possessions, Bach's St Matthew Passion, on the same grounds. If it had been an acre of blue dirt, with a few handfuls of trumpery diamonds in it, we should have gone to war about it. Let nobody suppose that our ultimate emancipation from these silly restrictions was the result of any growth or change in public opinion on the matter. There was no such growth and no such change. On the contrary, the sort of people who were supposed to object to The Mount of Olives when it was first performed as a Lenten oratorio at Drury Lane in 1814 are much more numerous at present than they were then. And they are just as free to stay away from performances they disapprove of as they were then. The restrictions are always the work of half a dozen busybodies, actuated less by cowardice than by a desire to make an officious display of the undesirable quality they call 'good taste.'

Goethe's taste being even worse than that displayed by Mr Henry Arthur Jones in the fourth act of Michael and his Lost Angel, he placed the scene of the prologue to his best known drama, not in Cleveheddon church, but in Heaven itself, with the Almighty conversing with Satan on easy terms, as in the Book of Job.* Some of our dramatic critics (especially those who are not suspected of reading Goethe, and who see no difference between the literary styles of St Matthew and Mr Wilson Barrett) will be shocked at this, and will exult in the fact that no attempt was made, or could have been made, to introduce the prologue on the English stage when the Lyceum Faust provided the opportunity. But I, having graduated as a musical critic, can assure my colleagues that I have seen this prologue repeatedly on no less English a stage than that of Covent Garden, under no less respectable a manager than Sir Augustus Harris.* And nothing could have been more English than the manner in which the scene was represented. There was a front cloth with clouds painted on it. In the right-hand top corner (from the spectator's point of view) there was a large hole irradiated with white light, and in the left-hand bottom corner a similar hole, glowing with red light. Satan appeared bodily in the red hole and sang his speeches. Nothing but the white glory could be seen through the higher rift in the clouds; and the speeches were sung by the chorus, as in the case of the words 'Saul, why persecutest thou me?' in Mendelssohn's oratorio.* This has occurred as often as Boïto's Mefistofele* has been performed; and I have not heard up to the present that any grave social consequences have ensued, or that any person has been shocked, hurt, injured, demoralized, or other than edified and delighted—except, perhaps, when the chorus sang flat, as choruses behind the scenes are apt to do.

When there is anything artistic to be done in England, all that is necessary is to do it as a matter of course without saying anything about it. If you raise the question whether it is permissible, there will be an outcry against it as impossibly scandalous, especially if it is something that has been done over and over again for hundreds of years. If the proprietors of the French Gallery had asked the leave of the British press and public before they exhibited Van Uhde's picture of Christ sitting in a room speaking to people in tall hats and frock coats,* a horror-stricken prohibition would have been voiced by writers who would have tried their utmost to get a private peep at the picture. The proprietors of the French Gallery wisely said nothing. They exhibited the picture; and all the genuinely religious visitors were greatly touched and pleased by it. If any sculptor were to ask public permission to exhibit a figure of a lady or gentleman with nothing on at Burlington House,* that permission would be sternly refused. But the thing is done every year without permission, and nobody is any the worse. The man who submits a moral syllabus of a work of art to the public is a fool. Submit the work of art itself, and then the public can judge. Of course, if they dislike it they will beat it with any stick they can lay hold of. If the drama of Michael had pleased the critics who imagined they were scandalized by the fourth act, Mr Jones might have introduced not only a consecration, but a baptism, a confirmation, a marriage, and a communion, as safely as the Adelphi authors introduced the service for the dead.

I do not lay down the law on this subject according to any canon of taste or theory of permissibility. I take things as I find them. I have seen not only Michael and his Lost Angel, but Parsifal at Bayreuth, and the Passion Play at Ober Ammergau. I found them good, and should be glad to see them brought within the reach of English playgoers. I have also seen Gentleman Joe;* and I have no doubt that some of my colleagues whom Mr Jones has shocked would be glad to see that piece brought within the reach of Bavarian playgoers. And with this reminder that you cannot attack the freedom of the plays you do not like without equally endangering the freedom of those you like, and that it is better to tolerate the catholicly religious people who are claiming for the theatre its share in the common spiritual heritage than to put a weapon into the hands of the sectarianly religious people who would make an end of the theatre altogether if they could, I leave the subject until the next week in which there happens to be nothing else to write about.

NIETZSCHE IN ENGLISH

IT is with a most opportune consideration for my Easter holiday that Messrs Henry & Co. have just issued the first volume of their translation of the works of Friedrich Nietzsche.* And such a volume, too! containing everything that he wrote just before he reached the point at which Germany made up its mind that he was mad, and shut him up, both figuratively and actually. Whilst I am still at large I may as well explain that Nietzsche is a philosopher—that is to say, something unintelligible to an Englishman. To make my readers realize what a philosopher is, I can only say that *I* am a philosopher. If you ask incredulously, 'How, then, are your articles so interesting?' I reply that there is nothing so interesting as philosophy, provided its materials are not spurious. For instance, take my own materials—humanity and the fine arts. Any studious, timorously ambitious bookworm can run away from the world with a few shelvesful of history, essays, descriptions, and criticisms, and, having pieced an illusory humanity and art out of the effects produced by his library on his imagination, build some silly systematization of his worthless ideas over the abyss of his own nescience. Such a philosopher is as dull and dry as you please: it is he who brings his profession into disrepute, especially when he talks much about art, and so persuades people to read him. Without having looked at more than fifty pictures in his life, or made up his mind on the smallest point about one of the fifty, he will audaciously take it upon himself to explain the development of painting from Zeuxis and Apelles to Raphael and Michael Angelo.* As to the way he will go on about music, of which he always has an awe-stricken conceit, it spoils my temper to think of it, especially when one remembers that musical composition is taught (a monstrous pretension) in this country by people who *read* scores, and never by any chance listen to performances. Now, the right way to go to work—strange as it may appear—is to look at pictures until you have acquired the power of seeing them. If you look at several thousand good pictures every year, and form some sort of practical judgment about every one of them—were it only that it is not worth troubling over—then at the end of five years or so you will, if you have a wise eye, be able to see what is actually in a picture, and not what you think is in it. Similarly, if you listen critically to music every day for a number of years, you will, if you have a wise ear, acquire the power of hearing music. And so on with all the arts. When we come to humanity it is still the same: only by intercourse with men and women can we learn anything about it. This involves an active life, not a contemplative one; for unless you do something in the world, you can have no real business to transact with men; and unless you love and are loved, you can have no intimate relations with them. And you must transact business, wirepull politics, discuss religion, give and receive hate, love, and friendship with all sorts of people before you can acquire the sense of humanity. If you are to acquire the sense sufficiently to be a philosopher, you must do all these things unconditionally. You must not say that you will be a gentleman and limit your intercourse to this class or that class; or that you will be a virtuous person and generalize about the affections from a single instance—unless, indeed, you have the rare happiness to stumble at first upon an all-enlightening instance. You must have no convictions, because, as Nietzsche puts it, 'convictions are prisons.'* Thus, I blush to add, you cannot be a philosopher and a good man, though you may be a philosopher and a great one. You will say, perhaps, that if this be so, there should be no philosophers; and perhaps you are right; but though I make you this handsome concession, I do not defer to you to the extent of ceasing to exist. If you insist on the hangman, whose pursuits are far from elevating, you may very well tolerate the philosopher, even if philosophy involve philandering; or, to put it another way, if, in spite of your hangman, you tolerate murder within the sphere of war, it may be necessary to tolerate comparatively venial irregularities within the sphere of philosophy. It is the price of progress; and, after all, it is the philosopher, and not you, who will burn for it.

These are shocking sentiments, I know; but I assure you you will think them mere Sunday School commonplaces when you have read a little of Nietzsche. Nietzsche is worse than shocking, he is simply awful: his epigrams are written with phosphorus on brimstone. The only excuse for reading them is that before long you must be prepared either to talk about Nietzsche or else retire from society, especially from aristocratically minded society (not the same thing, by the way, as aristocratic society), since Nietzsche is the champion of privilege, of power, and of inequality. Famous as Nietzsche has become—he has had a great *succès de scandale* to advertise his penetrating wit—I never heard of him until a few years ago,* when, on the occasion of my contributing to the literature of philosophy a minute treatise entitled The Quintessence of Ibsenism, I was asked whether I had not been inspired by a book called Out at the other side of Good and Evil, by Nietzsche. The title seemed to me promising; and in fact Nietzsche's criticism of morality and idealism is essentially that demonstrated in my book as at the bottom of

Ibsen's plays. His pungency; his power of putting the merest platitudes of his position in rousing, startling paradoxes; his way of getting underneath moral precepts which are so unquestionable to us that common decency seems to compel unhesitating assent to them, and upsetting them with a scornful laugh: all this is easy to a witty man who has once well learnt Schopenhauer's lesson, that the intellect by itself is a dead piece of brain machinery, and our ethical and moral systems merely the pierced cards you stick into it to make it play a certain tune. So far I am on common ground with Nietzsche. But not for a moment will I suffer anyone to compare me to him as a critic. Never was there a deafer, blinder, socially and politically inepter academician. He has fancies concerning different periods of history, idealizing the Romans and the Renascence, and deducing from his idealization no end of excellences in their works. When have I ever been guilty of such professorial folly? I simply go and look at their works, and after that you may talk to me until you go black in the face about their being such wonderful fellows: I know by my senses that they were as bad artists, and as arrant intellect-mongers, as need be. And what can you say to a man who, after pitting his philosophy against Wagner's with refreshing ingenuity and force, proceeds to hold up as the masterpiece of modern dramatic music, blazing with the merits which the Wagnerian music dramas lack—guess what! Don Giovanni, perhaps, or Orfeo, or Fidelio? Not at all: Carmen, no less. Yes, as I live by bread, as I made that bread for many a year by listening to music, Georges Bizet's Carmen.* After this one is not surprised to find Nietzsche blundering over politics and social organization and administration in a way that would be impossible to a man who had ever served on a genuine working committee long enough—say ten minutes—to find out how very little attention the exigencies of practical action can be made to pay to our theories when we have to get things done, one way or another. To him modern Democracy, Pauline Christianity, Socialism, and so on are deliberate plots hatched by malignant philosophers to frustrate the evolution of the human race and mass the stupidity and brute force of the many weak against the beneficial tyranny of the few strong. This is not even a point of view: it is an absolutely fictitious hypothesis: it would not be worth reading were it not that there is almost as much evidence for it as if it were true, and that it leads Nietzsche to produce some new and very striking and suggestive combinations of ideas. In short, his sallies, petulant and impossible as some of them are, are the work of a rare spirit and are pregnant with its vitality. It is notable that Nietzsche does not write in chapters or treatises: he writes leading articles, leaderettes, occasional notes, and epigrams. He recognizes that humanity, having tasted the art of the journalist, will no longer suffer men to inflict books on it. And he simplifies matters, quite in the manner of the leading article writer, by ignoring things as they are, and dealing with things as it is easiest, with our prejudices and training, to think they are, except that he supplies the training and instils the prejudices himself as he goes along, instead of picking up those that lie about the street as one does in writing leaders for the daily press.

* * *

MADOX BROWN, WATTS, AND IBSEN

It has not yet been noticed, I think, that the picture galleries in London are more than usually interesting just now to those lovers of the theatre who fully understand the saying 'There is only one art.' At the Grafton Gallery we have the life-work of the most dramatic of all painters, Ford Madox Brown, who was a realist; at the New Gallery that of Mr G. F. Watts, who is an idealist; and at the Academy that of Leighton,* who was a mere gentleman draughtsman.

I call Madox Brown a realist because he had vitality enough to find intense enjoyment and inexhaustible interest in the world as it really is, unbeautified, unidealized, untitivated in any way for artistic consumption. This love of life and knowledge of its worth is a rare thing—whole Alps and Andes above the common market demand for prettiness, fashionableness, refinement, elegance of style, delicacy of sentiment, charm of character, sympathetic philosophy (the philosophy of the happy ending), decorative moral systems contrasting roseate and rapturous vice with lilied and languorous virtue, and making 'Love' face both ways as the universal softener and redeemer, the whole being worshipped as beauty or virtue, and set in the place of life to narrow and condition it instead of enlarging and fulfilling it. To such self-indulgence most artists are mere pandars; for the sense of beauty needed to make a man an artist is so strong that the sense of life in him must needs be quite prodigious to overpower it. It must always be a mystery to the ordinary beauty-fancying, life-shirking amateur how the realist in art can bring his unbeautified, remorseless celebrations of common life in among so many pretty, pleasant, sweet, noble, touching fictions, and yet take his place there among the highest, although the railing, the derision, the protest, the positive disgust, are almost universal at first. Among painters the examples most familiar to us are Madox Brown and Rembrandt. But Madox Brown is more of a realist than Rembrandt;* for Rembrandt idealized his color; he would draw life with perfect integrity, but would paint it always in a golden glow—as if he cared less for the direct light of the sun than for its reflection in a pot of treacle—and would sacrifice real color to that stage glow without remorse. Not so Madox Brown. You can all but breathe his open air, warm yourself in his sun, and smell 'the green mantle of the standing pool'* in his Dalton picture. Again, Rembrandt would have died rather than paint a cabbage unconditionally green, or meddle with those piercing aniline discords of color which

modern ingenuity has extracted from soot and other unpromising
materials. Madox Brown took to Paisley shawls and magenta ribbons
and genuine greengrocer's cabbages as kindly as Wagner took to 'false
relations' in harmony. But turn over a collection of Rembrandt's etchings, especially those innumerable little studies which are free from the
hobby of the chiaroscurist; and at once you see the uncompromising
realist. Examine him at the most vulnerable point of the ordinary male
painter—his studies of women. Women begin to be socially tolerable at
thirty, and improve until the deepening of their consciousness is
checked by the decay of their faculties. But they begin to be pretty
much earlier than thirty, and are indeed sometimes at their best in that
respect long before their chattering is, apart from the illusions of sex,
to be preferred in serious moments to the silent sympathy of an intelligent pet animal. Take the young lady painted by Ingres as La Source,*
for example. Imagine having to make conversation for her for a couple
of hours. Ingres is not merely indifferent to this: he is determined to
make you understand that he values her solely for her grace of form,
and is too much the classic to be affected by any more cordial consideration. Among Rembrandt's etchings, on the other hand, you will find
plenty of women of all sorts; and you will be astonished and even scandalized at the catholicity of his interest and tolerance. He makes no
conditions, classical or moral, with his heroines: Venus may be seventy,
and Chloe* in her least presentable predicament: no matter: he draws
her for her own sake with enormous interest, neither as a joke, nor
a moral lesson, nor a model of grace, but simply because he thinks her
worth drawing as she is. You find the same thing in Madox Brown.
Nature itself is not more unbiassed as between a pretty woman and
a plain one, a young woman and an old one, than he. Compare the
comely wife of John of Gaunt in the Wycliffe picture with the wife of
Foscari,* who has no shop-window good looks to give an agreeable turn
to the pitifulness of her action as she lifts the elbow of the broken
wretch whose maimed hands cannot embrace her without help. A *bonne
bouche** of prettiness here would be an insult to our humanity; but in
the case of Mrs John of Gaunt, the good looks of the wife as she leans
over and grabs at the mantle of John, who, in the capacity of the politically excited Englishman, is duly making a fool of himself in public,
give the final touch to the humor and reality of the situation. Nowhere
do you catch the mature Madox Brown at false pathos or picturesque
attitudinizing. Think of all the attitudes in which we have seen
Francesca da Rimini and her lover; and then look at the Grafton Gallery
picture of that deplorable, ridiculous pair, sprawling in a death agony of

piteous surprise and discomfiture where the brutish husband has just struck them down with his uncouthly murderous weapon. You ask disgustedly where is the noble lover, the beautiful woman, the Cain-like avenger? You exclaim at the ineptitude of the man who could omit all this, and simply make you feel as if the incident had really happened and you had seen it—giving you, not your notion of the beauty and poetry of it, but the life and death of it. I remember once, when I was an 'art critic,' and when Madox Brown's work was only known to me by a few drawings, treating Mr Frederick Shields* to a critical demonstration of Madox Brown's deficiencies, pointing out in one of the drawings the lack of 'beauty' in some pair of elbows that had more of the wash tub than of The Toilet of Venus about them. Mr Shields contrived without any breach of good manners to make it quite clear to me that he considered Madox Brown a great painter and me a fool. I respected both convictions at the time; and now I share them. Only, I plead in extenuation of my folly that I had become so accustomed to take it for granted that what every English painter was driving at was the sexual beautification and moral idealization of life into something as unlike itself as possible, that it did not at first occur to me that a painter could draw a plain woman for any other reason than that he could not draw a pretty one.

Now turn to Mr Watts, and you are instantly in a visionary world, in which life fades into mist, and the imaginings of nobility and beauty with which we invest life become embodied and visible. The gallery is one great transfiguration: life, death, love and mankind are no longer themselves: they are glorified, sublimified, lovelified: the very draperies are either rippling lakes of color harmony, or splendid banners like the flying cloak of Titian's Bacchus in the National Gallery.* To pretend that the world is like this is to live the heavenly life. It is to lose the whole world and gain one's own soul. Until you have reached the point of realizing what an astonishingly bad bargain that is you cannot doubt the sufficiency of Mr Watts's art, provided only your eyes are fine enough to understand its language of line and color.

Now if you want to emulate my asinine achievements as a critic on the occasion mentioned above in connection with Mr Shields, you cannot do better than criticize either painter on the assumption that the other's art is the right art. This will lead you by the shortest cut to the conclusion either that Mr Watts's big picture of the drayman and his horses is the only great work he ever achieved, or that there is nothing endurable in Madox Brown's work except the embroidery and furniture, a few passages of open-air painting, and such technical *tours de force* as his combination of the virtuosities of the portrait styles of Holbein, Antonio Moro, and Rembrandt in the imaginary portrait of Shakespear.* In which event I can only wish you sense enough to see that your con- clusion is not a proof of the futility of Watts or Madox Brown but a *reductio ad absurdum** of your own critical method.

And now, what has all this to do with the drama? Even if it had noth- ing to do with it, reader, the question would be but a poor return for the pains I am taking to improve your mind; but let that pass. Have you never been struck with the similarity between the familiar paroxysms of Anti-Ibsenism and the abuse, the derision, the angry distaste, the invincible misunderstanding provoked by Madox Brown? Does it not occur to you that the same effect has been produced by the same cause—that what Ibsen has done is to take for his theme, not youth, beauty, morality, gentility, and propriety as conceived by Mr Smith of Brixton and Bayswater,* but real life taken as it is, with no more regard for poor Smith's dreams and hypocrisies than the weather has for his shiny silk hat when he forgets his umbrella? Have you forgotten that Ibsen was once an Idealist like Mr Watts, and that you can read The Vikings, or The Pretenders, or Brand, or Emperor and Galilean in the New Gallery as suitably as you can hang Madox Brown's Parisina or Death of Harold* in the Diploma Gallery at the Royal Academy? Or have you not noticed how the idealists who are full of loathing for Ibsen's realistic plays will declare that these idealistic ones are beauti- ful, and that the man who drew Solveig the Sweet* could never have descended to Hedda Gabler unless his mind had given way.

I had intended to pursue this matter much further; but I am checked, partly by want of space, partly because I simply dare not go on to Leighton, and make the application of his case to the theatre. Madox Brown was a man; Watts is at least an artist and poet; Leighton was only a gentleman. I doubt if it was ever worth while being a gentleman, even before the thing had become the pet fashion of the lower-middle class; but today, happily, it is no longer tolerated among capable people, except from a few old Palmerstonians* who do not take it too seriously. And yet you cannot cure the younger actor-managers of it. Sir Henry Irving stands on the Watts plane as an artist and idealist, cut off from Ibsen and reality by the deplorable limitations of that state, but at least not a snob, and only a knight on public grounds and by his own per- emptory demand,* which no mere gentleman would have dared to make lest he should have offended the court and made himself ridicu- lous. But the others!—the knights expectant. Well, let me not be too highminded at their expense. If they are Leightonian, they might easily be worse. There are less handsome things in the world than that collection of pictures at the Academy, with its leading men who are all gentlemen, its extra ladies whose Liberty silk robes follow in their flow the Callipygean curves beneath without a suggestion of coarseness, its refined resolution to take the smooth without the rough, Mayfair without Hoxton, Melbury Road without Saffron Hill.* All very nice, gentlemen and ladies; but much too negative for a principle of dramatic art. To suppress instead of to express, to avoid instead of to conquer, to ignore instead of to heal: all this, on the stage, ends in turning a man into a stick for fear of creasing his tailor's handiwork, and a woman into a hairdresser's window image lest she should be too actressy to be invited to a fashionable garden-party.

*   *   *

THE BOARD SCHOOL

THE electioneering farce on which the curtain fell at nine o'clock the day before yesterday, must not pass without a word of dramatic criticism. Its bearing on the theatre needs no renewed explanation in this column. I have pointed out, only too often, how the theatre has stooped to meet the rising flood of popular literateness. Hitherto I have not complained; for it is better that the theatre should stoop to raise the millions above sing-songs and cock-fights, than soar for the benefit of a handful of experts above the level of Shakespear and Molière.

But behind this magnanimous preference for the interests of the many there has always lurked in me an implacable contempt for the process of literation, commonly and most erroneously called education, conducted in the popular school. I make no distinction between Board school and Voluntary school, or, for the matter of that, between the workhouse school and Harrow or Eton.* They all turn out barbarians. I grant that the taste of the barbarian is the opportunity of the dauber in all the arts; but I understand the importance of the artist's function in society far too well to accept this result with complacency. We all quote the gentleman who professed the most complete indifference as to who made the laws of his country so long as he was allowed to write its songs; yet how many of us, I wonder, feel any real force in that epigram, even in England, the nation of all others most governed by artists? We are so susceptible to artistic fiction, rhetoric, and oratory, that we will not receive them as art, but rather as clear matter of fact or divinely revealed truth. Let me explain myself gently, coming to my dangerous point by degrees.

Some twenty years or so ago I found myself in the Isle of Wight, lodging in the house of an intelligent London & South-Western railway guard, who placed his library at my disposal. Its principal attraction happened to be Robinson Crusoe, which I then read through for the first time since my childhood. My host's wife, noticing this, informed me that it was her husband's favorite book. Thereupon I made some conventional remark about it. The conventional remark unhappily implied that I regarded Robinson as a creature of Defoe's invention. She at once begged me not to betray any such scepticism in her husband's presence, he being absolutely convinced, on the internal evidence of the narrative, that it was no vain product of a romancer's fancy, but a veracious record of a seaman's experience. She confessed that she herself leaned towards my view of the matter; but she thought it best, for the sake of her home and her affections, to conform to her husband's faith. He was, she explained, a man of a prosaic turn, hating idle stories, and loving gravity and verity in all things: in short, precisely the sort of man to be fiction-ridden all his life without suspecting it. Now please observe that to read Robinson Crusoe and believe it literally, is to become the dupe of an imposture and the champion of a lie. On the other hand, to read it as a work of art—that is, to surrender oneself voluntarily to the illusion it creates, without for a moment compromising the integrity of our relations with the real world—is to learn a good deal from it, both of life and art, to say nothing of our enjoyment of the story.

Let us now suppose, merely to amuse ourselves, that my friend the railway guard were a member of the Isle of Wight School Board, if such a body exists. He would no doubt propose Robinson Crusoe as a standard reading-book for the school curriculum; and so excellent a proposal could hardly be rejected on its merits. But somebody would be sure to question his view that it should be presented to the children as history, not as parable. If he found any considerable support on the Board, or among the ratepayers, the result would probably be a compromise. Robinson Crusoe would be read; but the children would be left to draw their own conclusions, or to consult their parents or other advisers out of school.

The pious will now perceive the cloven hoof. The School Board election this week turned on a compromise concerning, not merely a book, but actually a whole literature; though, to be sure, the average English citizen thinks it a book, because it is all bound into one cover, and because he never reads it, not being literary in his tastes. If he does not actually regard it as an amulet, and believe that if a soldier carries it into battle it will magically attract and stop the Lee-Metford bullet,* he may be regarded as an exceptionally enlightened person. But, numerically strong as he is, the very existence of the nation depends on the force of character with which those who know better overrule, in the public work of education, a superstition which would have horrified the Fathers of the Church, and which arose a few hundred years ago as an ephemeral effect of early Protestantism on minds not yet strong enough for so heroic a doctrine. In other departments of Government it may be expedient to fool your democratic voter to the top of his bent; but when he clamors to be allowed to perpetuate his folly by forcing educated people to teach what they do not believe, then it is for those educated people to refuse to do anything of the sort; to support one another resolutely in that refusal; and to invite the average North Sea Islander to do without them if he can.

Like all highly developed literatures, the Bible contains a great deal of sensational fiction, imagined with intense vividness, appealing to the most susceptible passions, and narrated with a force which the ordinary man is no more able to resist than my friend the railway guard was able to resist the force of Defoe. Perhaps only an expert can thoroughly appreciate the power with which a story well told, or an assertion well made, takes possession of a mind not specially trained to criticize it. Try to imagine all that is most powerful in English literature bound into one volume, and offered to a comparatively barbarous race as an instrument of civilization invested with supernatural authority! Indeed, let us leave what we call barbarous races out of the question, and suppose it offered to the English nation on the same assumptions as to its nature and authority which the children in our popular schools are led to make today concerning the Bible under the School Board compromise! How much resistance would there be to the illusion created by the art of our great storytellers? Who would dare to affirm that the men and women created by Chaucer, Shakespear, Bunyan, Fielding, Goldsmith, Scott, and Dickens had never existed? Who could resist the force of conviction carried by the tremendous assertive power of Cobbett, the gorgeous special-pleading of Ruskin, or the cogency of Sir Thomas More, or even Matthew Arnold? Above all, who could stand up against the inspiration and moral grandeur of our prophets and poets, from Langland to Blake and Shelley?* The power of Scripture has not waned with the ages. We have no right to trick a child's instinctive sense of revelation and inspiration by such a surpassingly blasphemous pessimistic lie as that both have become extinct, and that the wretched world, like its dead moon, is living out its old age on a scanty remnant of spiritual energy, hoarded from thousands of years ago. And yet the whole question at stake in the School Board election was whether this lie should be told as a black lie or a white one. The stupid part of the business is that it is quite unnecessary to tell any lies at all. Why not teach children the realities of inspiration and revelation as they work daily through scribes and lawgivers? It would, at all events, make better journalists and parish councillors of them.

Until some such conception of the dignity and importance of art as the sole possible method of revelation for the forecasts of the spirit reaches our Board School population, the theatre will remain pretty much at its present level, in spite of such superficial improvements as the ordinary march of progress involves. In the meantime, however, man will not submit to spiritual starvation. I have over and over again pointed out that whilst the theatre has done hardly anything to adapt itself to modern demands, the Church has been waking up in all directions to its opportunities. I believe that many of the playgoers who are sufficiently conscious of the social importance of art to care to read these columns, never dream of going to church, and have no idea that they would find anything there but boredom, hypocrisy, and superstition. Let me beg them to try the experiment. Let them spend a fortnight in going to the best London churches, and a fortnight in going to the best London theatres. If they find one-tenth as much boredom, hypocrisy, superstition, humbug, snobbery, stupidity, vulgarity, foul air, bad music, draughts, late hours, stuffy smells, and unhappy and disagreeable people in the auditorium, not to mention professional incompetence on the part of the performers, in the churches as they will in the theatres, I will eat this number of the Saturday Review unbuttered.

* * *

HENRY IRVING AND ELLEN TERRY

* * *

SIR HENRY IRVING, who has just died suddenly after an evening spent in the only way he cared to spend an evening: that is, on the stage, was 68 years old, and had been for thirty years the foremost actor in London. His death, like his life and his art, is an event of personal interest only. He was an extraordinarily interesting actor, enthusiastically admired by some, violently disliked by others, but never ignored, never insignificant, always able to force the world to accept him as a public dignitary standing quite alone in his eminence. The crowning event of his life was his admission to the order of knighthood. He was the first English actor whose social status was ever officially confirmed in this way; and, what is still more remarkable, he actually compelled the Court to knight him by publicly and explicitly demanding that he, as the head of the London stage, should be treated as the peer of the President of the Royal Academy of Arts, who is always knighted in England as a matter of course. The demand was made at a lecture which Irving delivered at the Royal Institution on the 1st February 1895, ostensibly on some dramatic subject, but really on the claims of his profession and of himself to official recognition. Any other actor would have been laughed at. Irving was knighted with apologies for the delay, and with gratitude for his condescension in accepting a title which he never afterwards deigned to print on a playbill.

There is nothing more to be said about him. When I was asked, the day after his death, to pay a tribute to his memory, I wrote: 'He did nothing for the living drama; and he mutilated the remains of the dying Shakespear; but he won his lifelong fight to have the actor recognized as the peer of all other artists; and this was enough for one man to accomplish. *Requiescat in pace.*'* The truth is that Irving took no interest in anything except himself; and he was not interested even in himself except as an imaginary figure in an imaginary setting. He lived in a dream which he was so loth to have disturbed that when an actor told him once that he was being scandalously robbed, he thanked him and begged him not to tell him anything of the kind again. His scholarship and his connoisseurship in art and literature were equally imaginary. He was willing to have a retinue of writers, with Lord Tennyson, the Poet Laureate, at the head, and the journalists who helped him to write his lectures and speeches at the tail; but he had no literary sense, and was quite outside the intellectual life of his time. He was ignorant even of the theatre, having seen nothing of it since about thirty years ago, when he became master in his own playhouse, and shut the world out. He murdered Shakespear's Lear so horribly in cutting it down that he made it unintelligible; and he allowed one of his retainers to turn Goethe's Faust into so cheap a spectacular melodrama that it was repeated every night for a year. He played Macaire, the Corsican Brothers, Richelieu, Claude Melnotte, and all the old repertory of Charles Kean* without a thought that they could be in the least old-fashioned. In the case of Macaire the new version by Robert Louis Stevenson,* a masterpiece of literature, lay ready to his hand; but he used the old traditional version which is still played in booths and barns. Many persons were indignant at his supposed pretensions to be a thinker, a scholar, a connoisseur; but though such pretensions were undoubtedly made for him, he never made them himself. The truth is, his bearing was so dignified that the world made all possible pretences for him. When they saw him as Becket, they could not doubt that he was a great statesman and church-man; when they saw him as the Vicar of Wakefield, they recognized the scholar and the divine in every silver hair in his wig; when they saw him as Charles I,* they felt that the patron of Van Dyck could not be ignorant of painting.

And yet this artist, who could produce every illusion about himself off the stage by the mere force and singularity of his personality, was prevented by just this force and singularity from producing any great range of illusion on it. He had really only one part; and that part was the part of Irving. His Hamlet was not Shakespear's Hamlet, nor his Lear Shakespear's Lear: they were both avatars of the imaginary Irving in whom he was so absorbingly interested. His huge and enduring success as Shylock was due to his absolutely refusing to allow Shylock to be the discomfited villain of the piece. The Merchant of Venice became the Martyrdom of Irving, which was, it must be confessed, far finer than the Tricking of Shylock. His Iachimo, a very fine performance, was better than Shakespear's Iachimo, and not a bit like him. On the other hand, his Lear was an impertinent intrusion of a quite silly con-ceit of his own into a great play. His Romeo, though a very clever piece of acting, wonderfully stage-managed in the scene where Romeo dragged the body of Paris down a horrible staircase into the tomb of the Capulets, was an absurdity, because it was impossible to accept Irving as Romeo, and he had no power of adapting himself to an author's conception: his creations were all his own; and they were all Irvings.

Technically he became very skilful. He was too much interested in himself not to cultivate himself to the utmost possible degree; and he was both imaginative and industrious in devising and executing stage effects, and what is called on the English stage 'business.' His Vanderdecken was a stage effect from first to last, and a most weirdly and beautifully effective one. His Mathias in The Bells* and his Charles I were elaborated to the most extreme degree. They were such miracles of finished execution that they raised a melodrama of no importance and a surpassingly bad historical play into dramatic masterpieces. Just as Paganini* fascinated the world with trumpery music by his own skill and strangeness, so Irving fascinated London with trumpery plays. But he had some serious physical defects and peculiarities; and though he succeeded in making the peculiarities interesting and characteristic, the defects limited him to the last. His voice was so poor that it would have prevented him from attaining any success at all had he not had a large and cavernous nose. By throwing his voice forward into it he gave it an impressive resonance which sometimes produced a strikingly beautiful effect in spite of its nasal tone. But this was only practicable when he could deliver a speech slowly. In rapid, violent, energetic passages, his nasal method produced a hysterical whinnying which was ridiculous; and for many years after he began playing heavy tragic parts he was the butt of every mimic and the object of continual ridicule from vulgar people who could see his obvious physical defects but could not appreciate his artistic qualities. It was not until he abandoned all pretence of robust acting that the laughter stopped. He was thus driven into a very slow method; and the more subtly he elaborated it, the worse became the performances at his theatre; for though he himself was always effective, those who were on the stage with him had to wait so long for his replies, and were so hurried in the vain attempt to make up for the time he was losing (if they had all played as slowly as he the play would never have ended), that they soon gave up all attempt to act, and simply gave him his cues as he wanted them. Under our English actor-manager system they could not remonstrate. They were his employees, completely in his power, and he simply could not get his effects in any other way.

In judging Irving, Austrians must remember that he had to assume a very high position without having had the training and culture that can be given only by a great national theatre with a highly trained audience and an established artistic tradition. There is nothing of the sort in England. Imagine a lad with his head full of nothing but romances, pitchforked into a city office, and leaving it to go on the stage as a member of the stock company in provincial cities where the theatre was abhorred as the gate of hell, and playing a piano on Sunday considered an unpardonable crime, by many of the most respectable citizens! Imagine him, after picking up his profession technically in this way, being enabled, by a private subvention from a charitable lady, to lease a metropolitan theatre and become its absolute and sole director, and you will get some idea of Irving's position in London. It would carry me too far to go into the whole question of the deplorable intellectual and artistic condition of the English theatre in Irving's time. Suffice it to say that the environment and tradition which an actor can obtain in Vienna cannot be obtained in England, and that Irving had to do his best to supply them out of his own romantic imagination, without much schooling and virtually without any general artistic culture. His success under such disadvantages was extraordinary; but in the end he had to give up his theatre and take to the provinces to live on his reputation. A theatre without a living drama is in the long run impossible; and when Irving had exhausted the old plays in which his personality was effective, he was—to be quite frank—too ignorant and old-fashioned to know how to choose fresh material. His greatest achievement was his social achievement, the redemption of his profession from Bohemianism, the imposing himself on the nation as one of the most eminent men in it, and the official acknowledgment of that estimate by the accolade.

* * *

ELLEN TERRY, apart from her professional accomplishments as an actress, is so remarkable a woman that it is very difficult to describe her to the Austrian public without writing her private rather than her public history.

The part she has played in the life of her time will never be known until some day—perhaps fifty years hence—when her correspondence will be collected and published in twenty or thirty volumes.* It will then, I believe, be discovered that every famous man of the last quarter of the nineteenth century—provided he were a playgoer—has been in love with Ellen Terry, and that many of them have found in her friendship the utmost consolation one can hope for from a wise, witty, and beautiful woman whose love is already engaged elsewhere, and whose heart has withstood a thousand attempts to capture it. To me—for I am one of the unsuccessful lovers—Ellen Terry's skill as an actress is the least interesting thing about her. Unlike Irving, to whom his art was everything and his life nothing, she found life more interesting than art; and when she became associated with him in his long and famous management of the Lyceum Theatre, she—the most modern of modern women, the most vital of modern personalities—set to work, more in the spirit of a thrifty intelligent housekeeper than of a self-obsessed artist, to fill up the leading feminine rôles in the old-fashioned plays he delighted in. Fortunately these plays included the handful of Shakespearean comedies and tragedies which still keep the stage in England as stalking horses for ambitious actors. We therefore had at the Lyceum Theatre Ellen Terry as Portia, as Beatrice, as Juliet, as Imogen, as Ophelia, though never as Rosalind in As You Like It, which she would certainly have insisted on playing if she had cared as much for her own professional renown as for helping Irving.

Probably there were never two eminent members of the same profession so unlike one another as Ellen Terry and Henry Irving. They both had beautiful and interesting faces; but faces like Irving's have looked at the world for hundreds of years past from portraits of churchmen, statesmen, princes, and saints, whilst Ellen's face had never been seen in the world before. She actually invented her own beauty; for her portraits as a girl have hardly anything in them of the wonderful woman who, after leaving the stage for seven years, reappeared in 1875 and took London by storm. The much abused word 'unique' was literally true of Ellen Terry. If Shakespear had met Irving in the street, he would have recognized a distinguished but familiar type. Had he met Ellen Terry, he would have stared as at a new and irresistibly attractive species of womankind. Her portrait as Lady Macbeth, by Sargent,* will stand out among all the portraits of famous women as that of a woman who was like nobody else. Again, Irving was simple, reserved, and slow. Ellen Terry is quick, restless, clever, and can get on the most unembarrassed and familiar terms in an instant with even the shyest strangers. Irving did not like writing: his correspondence was carried on by the late L. F. Austin, Bram Stoker,* and perhaps others of his retinue: the few letters he really wrote himself owing their charm to their unaffected and unskilled lack of literary pretence and the handwriting not remarkable. Ellen Terry, on the other hand, is one of the greatest letter writers that ever lived. She can flash her thought down on paper in a handwriting that is as characteristic and as unforgettable as her face. When you find a letter from her among your morning's correspondence, you see the woman as vividly as you see the handwriting; and you open that letter first and feel that the day is a fortunate one. Her few published writings give no idea of her real literary power. All her letters are too intimate, too direct, too penetrating to be given to anyone but those to whom they are addressed. And here we come to another difference from Irving. Irving was sentimental and affectionate, and like most sentimental and affectionate people was limited and concentrated in his interests. He never understood others, and indeed never understood himself. Ellen Terry is not sentimental and not affectionate; but she is easily interested in anybody or anything remarkable or attractive: she is intelligent: she understands: she sympathizes because she understands and is naturally benevolent; but she has been interested oftener than deeply touched, and has pitied and helped oftener than loved. With all her ready sacrifice of her stage talent and skill, first to domestic ties, and then, on her return to the stage, to the Lyceum enterprise, she has never really sacrificed her inner self. In sacrificing her art she only sacrificed a part of herself. Irving's art was the whole of himself; and that was why he sacrificed himself—and everybody and everything else—to his art. It is a curious piece of artistic psychology, this, and will be misunderstood by stupid people and Philistines; but one does not write about artists of genius for people who know nothing about genius.

I have never, either in public or private, made any secret of my opinion that the Lyceum enterprise, famous as it became, was on the purely dramatic side of theatrical art a deplorable waste of two of the most remarkable talents of the last quarter of a century. In a former article I described how Irving used the plays of Shakespear as settings for figures which were the creations of his own fancy—how his Shylock was not Shakespear's Shylock, his Iachimo not Shakespear's Iachimo, his Lear not Shakespear's Lear. I may now add that if circumstances had forced Irving into the living drama of his own time—if he had gone forward from his early successes as Digby Grant in Albery's Two Roses* to Ibsen's Master Builder and John Gabriel Borkman—if he had played Bishop Nicolas instead of Shakespear's Wolsey and Tennyson's Becket and Sardou's Dante—he would have carried the English theatre forward into line with the Scandinavian and German-speaking theatre instead of being, as he actually was, the most conspicuous obstacle to its development. Now in precisely the same way as he wasted his own talent on obsolete reactionary or Shakespearean drama, so also he wasted Ellen Terry's. He did so, of course, quite unconsciously: if anyone had accused him of it, he would have pointed to The Lady of Lyons, The Amber Heart, Wills's Faust, Olivia (an adaptation of Goldsmith's Vicar of Wakefield), the Shakespearean repertory, and finally, as a daring concession to the ultra-modern spirit made expressly for Ellen Terry's sake, Madame Sans Gêne.* He would have asked whether anyone but a madman could say that a talent which had triumphed in all these masterpieces had been wasted. What more could any actress desire? Was not Shakespear the greatest of all dramatic poets, past, present, or future? Was not Goethe, though a foreigner, at least worthy to be 'adapted' by Wills? Was not Lord Tennyson the Poet Laureate? Were obscure, eccentric, and immoral Norwegians and Germans— Ibsens, Hauptmanns, Sudermanns,* and their English imitators—to be accepted at the Lyceum Theatre merely because literary cliques talked about them, and because Duse, Réjane,* and English actresses poor enough to play for such private subscription enterprises as the Independent Theatre and the Stage Society occasionally played a new and objectionable sort of stage heroine like Nora Helmer, Magda, Hedda Gabler, etc., etc.?

All this seemed, and even still seems, sound common sense to the bulk of our English playgoers and their critical bellwethers. In Germany and Austria the position of Ellen Terry at the Lyceum Theatre will be more intelligible. It meant that she was completely cut off from the modern drama and all its intensely interesting heroines. And her opportunities in the older drama were much less satisfying than Irving's, because she understood Shakespear and played Beatrice, Juliet, Portia, Imogen, etc., intelligently and charmingly just as Shakespear planned them, whereas Irving, as Benedick, Romeo, Shylock, or Iachimo, was embodying some fancy of his own, the irrelevance of which only made it more enigmatic and consequently more Irvingesque and fascinating. It was inevitable that she should at last break loose from the Lyceum and practise her art under her own management.

But the question remains, why did she stay so long? The answer to that is that the Lyceum, whilst it starved her dramatically, gave great scope to her wonderful sense of pictorial art. Ellen Terry has always been adored by painters. She was married almost in her childhood to one of the greatest painters of her time.*

Now whatever the Lyceum productions may have lacked in intellectual modernity, they never failed as stage pictures. If Ellen could not collaborate with Ibsen to explain the revolt of Nora Helmer, she could collaborate with Burne-Jones and Alma Tadema to make living pictures of Guinevere and Imogen. I quite forget what Tennyson's first play at the Lyceum Theatre was about; but I shall never forget Ellen Terry as Camma.* I can recall picture after picture in which she and Irving posed as no other artists of that time could pose. Her incomparable beauty and his incomparable distinction: there lay the Lyceum magic: that was the spell that blinded everyone to the fact that the converts of the grim old gentleman in Norway were biding their time, and that

when the enchantment of youth was no longer added to the enchantment of beauty, the Lyceum would come down like the walls of Jericho.*

I escaped the illusion solely because I was a dramatist, and wanted
Ellen Terry for my own plays. When her son, Mr Gordon Craig,*
became a father she said that nobody would write plays for a grandmother. I immediately wrote Captain Brassbound's Conversion* to
prove the contrary. I had already tried to tempt her by writing into my
play called The Man of Destiny a description of the heroine which is
simply a description of Ellen Terry:* a very faint one, by the way; for
who can describe the indescribable? But Irving checkmated me on that
occasion by announcing his desire to perform the play; and it was
impossible for me to evade the compliment, though, of course, nothing
came of it. In the case of Captain Brassbound's Conversion, it was
impossible for Irving to persuade himself even momentarily that he
could produce it. Yet it was clear that it was in plays of this modern
kind, with parts for women which were intellectually interesting and of
commanding importance, that Ellen Terry's future business lay. Of this
she said nothing; but she could not be restrained from telling the world
that she was born in 1848 and that her apparent youthfulness was an
illusion: in short, that the day had gone by for the Lady of Lyons,
Gretchen, and Juliet. Her withdrawal from Sir Henry Irving's company at last became inevitable, though she postponed it long after it had
become urgently advisable in her own interest if not in his.

Even then her first step shewed all her old indifference to her own
career. She produced Ibsen's Vikings in Helgeland solely to enable
Mr Gordon Craig to make an expensive experiment in his peculiar methods
of stage presentation. It was a most unnecessary maternal extravagance;
for Mr Gordon Craig's new development of the art of the theatre had
already been convincingly demonstrated in London. No doubt his pro-
cessions of Vikings coming up the cliffs from the sea in the moonlight,
with their spears used as cunningly for decorative purposes as the
spears in Velasquez's Surrender at Breda, or in the pictures of Paolo di
Uccello*, were very striking, and very instructive as to the possibility of
doing away with the eternal flat wooden floor and footlight illumination
which are so destructive of stage illusion; but they could not enable
Ellen Terry to contradict her own nature by playing the fierce Hiordis
of Ibsen convincingly. The public wanted Ellen Terry in an Ellen Terry
part, and was too Philistine to see the beauty or care about the importance of Mr Gordon Craig's art. So Mr Gordon Craig shook the dust of
London off his feet, and went to Germany. And Ellen Terry at last did
what she should have done many years before—devoted herself to

a modern play written for her by a modern playwright. She made a decisive success in creating Sir James Barrie's Alice Sit by the Fire;* and she will follow that up next March [1905] by at last appearing as Lady Cicely in Captain Brassbound's Conversion, which has waited seven years for her. And here for the present I must leave her; for her saga is not yet ended.

P.S. 1930. Her saga as an actress ended with her impersonation of Lady Cicely, which she played on her final tour through America as her farewell to the stage. But she lived to be eighty and Dame Grand Cross of The British Empire. To the generation that grew up with the Great War, to which horror she never deigned to hold a candle, she had become a legend. She was born in 1848 and died in 1928.

EDGAR ALLAN POE

THERE was a time when America, the Land of the Free, and the birth-place of Washington, seemed a natural fatherland for Edgar Allan Poe. Nowadays the thing has become inconceivable: no young man can read Poe's works without asking incredulously what the devil he is doing in *that* galley. America has been found out; and Poe has not; that is the situation. How did he live there, this finest of fine artists, this born aristocrat of letters? Alas! he did not live there: he died there, and was duly explained away as a drunkard and a failure, though it remains an open question whether he really drank as much in his whole lifetime as a modern successful American drinks, without comment, in six months.

If the Judgment Day were fixed for the centenary of Poe's birth, there are among the dead only two men born since the Declaration of Independence whose plea for mercy could avert a prompt sentence of damnation on the entire nation; and it is extremely doubtful whether those two could be persuaded to pervert eternal justice by uttering it. The two are, of course, Poe and Whitman;* and there is between them the remarkable difference that Whitman is still credibly an American, whereas even the Americans themselves, though rather short of men of genius, omit Poe's name from their Pantheon, either from a sense that it is hopeless for them to claim so foreign a figure, or from simple Monroeism.* One asks, has the America of Poe's day passed away, or did it ever exist?

Probably it never existed. It was an illusion, like the respectable Whig* Victorian England of Macaulay. Karl Marx stripped the white-wash from that sepulchre; and we have ever since been struggling with a conviction of social sin which makes every country in which industrial capitalism is rampant a hell to us. For let no American fear that America, on that hypothetic Judgment Day, would perish alone. America would be damned in very good European company, and would feel proud and happy, and contemptuous of, the saved. She would not even plead the influence of the mother from whom she has inherited all her worst vices. If the American stands today in scandalous pre-eminence as an anarchist and a ruffian, a liar and a braggart, an idolater and a sensual-ist, that is only because he has thrown off the disguises of Catholicism and feudalism which still give Europe an air of decency, and sins openly, impudently, and consciously, instead of furtively, hypocritically, and muddle-headedly, as we do. Not until he acquires European manners does the American anarchist become the gentleman who assures you that people cannot be made moral by Act of Parliament (the truth being that it is only by Acts of Parliament that men in large communities can be made moral, even when they want to); or the American ruffian hand over his revolver and bowie knife to be used for him by a policeman or soldier; or the American liar and braggart adopt the tone of the newspaper, the pulpit, and the platform; or the American idolater write authorized biographies of millionaires; or the American sensualist secure the patronage of all the Muses* for his pornography.

Howbeit, Poe remains homeless. There is nothing at all like him in America: nothing, at all events, visible across the Atlantic. At that distance we can see Whistler plainly enough, and Mark Twain.* But Whistler was very American in some ways: so American that nobody but another American could possibly have written his adventures and gloried in them without reserve. Mark Twain, resembling Dickens in his combination of public spirit and irresistible literary power with a congenital incapacity for lying and bragging, and a congenital hatred of waste and cruelty, remains American by the local color of his stories. There is a further difference. Both Mark Twain and Whistler are as Philistine as Dickens and Thackeray. The appalling thing about Dickens, the greatest of the Victorians, is that in his novels there is nothing personal to live for except eating, drinking, and pretending to be happily married. For him the great synthetic ideals do not exist, any more than the great preludes and toccatas of Bach, the symphonies of Beethoven, the paintings of Giotto and Mantegna,* Velasquez and Rembrandt. Instead of being heir to all the ages, he came into a comparatively small and smutty literary property bequeathed by Smollett* and Fielding. His criticism of Fechter's Hamlet,* and his use of a speech of Macbeth's to illustrate the character of Mrs. Macstinger, shew how little Shakespear meant to him. Thackeray is even worse: the notions of painting he picked up at Heatherley's school were further from the mark than Dickens's ignorance; he is equally in the dark as to music; and though he did not, when he wished to be enormously pleasant and jolly, begin, like Dickens, to describe the gorgings and guzzlings which make Christmas our annual national disgrace, that is rather because he never does want to be enormously pleasant and jolly than because he has any higher notions of personal enjoyment. The truth is that neither Dickens nor Thackeray would be tolerable were it not that life is an end in itself and a means to nothing but its own perfection; consequently any man who describes life vividly will entertain us, however uncultivated the life he describes may be. Mark Twain has lived long enough to become a much better philosopher than either Dickens or Thackeray: for instance, when he immortalized General Funston by scalping him,* he did it scientifically, knowing exactly what he meant right down to the foundation in the natural history of human character. Also, he got from the Mississippi something that Dickens could not get from Chatham and Pentonville.* But he wrote A Yankee at the Court of King Arthur just as Dickens wrote A Child's History of England.* For the ideal of Catholic chivalry he had nothing but derision; and he exhibited it, not in conflict with reality, as Cervantes did, but in conflict with the prejudices of a Philistine compared to whom Sancho Panza is an Admirable Crichton,* an Abelard, even a Plato. Also, he described Lohengrin as 'a shivaree,' though he liked the wedding chorus; and this shews that Mark, like Dickens, was not properly educated; for Wagner would have been just the man for him if he had been trained to understand and use music as Mr Rockefeller* was trained to understand and use money. America did not teach him the language of the great ideals, just as England did not teach it to Dickens and Thackeray. Consequently, though nobody can suspect Dickens or Mark Twain of lacking the qualities and impulses that are the soul of such grotesque makeshift bodies as Church and State, Chivalry, Classicism, Art, Gentility, and the Holy Roman Empire; and nobody blames them for seeing that these bodies were mostly so decomposed as to have become intolerable nuisances, you have only to compare them with Carlyle and Ruskin, or with Euripides and Aristophanes, to see how, for want of a language of art and a body of philosophy, they were so much more interested in the fun and pathos of personal adventure than in the comedy and tragedy of human destiny.

Whistler was a Philistine, too. Outside the corner of art in which he was a virtuoso and a propagandist, he was a Man of Derision. Important as his propaganda was, and admired as his work was, no society could assimilate him. He could not even induce a British jury to award him substantial damages against a rich critic who had 'done him out of his job'; and this is certainly the climax of social failure in England.

Edgar Allan Poe was not in the least a Philistine. He wrote always as if his native Boston was Athens, his Charlottesville University* Plato's Academy, and his cottage the crown of the heights of Fiesole.* He was the greatest journalistic critic of his time, placing good European work at sight when the European critics were waiting for somebody to tell them what to say. His poetry is so exquisitely refined that posterity will refuse to believe that it belongs to the same civilization as the glory of Mrs Julia Ward Howe's lilies or the honest doggerel of Whittier.*

Tennyson, who was nothing if not a virtuoso, never produced a success that will bear reading after Poe's failures. Poe constantly and inevitably produced magic where his greatest contemporaries produced only beauty. Tennyson's popular pieces, The May Queen and The Charge of the Six Hundred, cannot stand hackneying: they become positively nauseous after a time. The Raven; The Bells, and Annabel Lee* are as fascinating at the thousandth repetition as at the first.

* * *

But Poe, for all his virtuosity, is always a poet, and never a mere virtuoso. Poe put forward his Eureka, the formulation of his philosophy, as the most important thing he had done. His poems always have the universe as their background. So have the figures in his stories. Even in his tales of humor, which we shake our heads at as mistakes, they have this elemental quality. Toby Dammit* himself, though his very name turns up the nose of the cultured critic, is more impressive and his end more tragic than the serious inventions of most story-tellers. The shortsighted gentleman who married his grandmother is no common butt of a common purveyor of the facetious: the grandmother has the elegance and free mind of Ninon de l'Enclos,* the grandson the *tenue** of a marquis. This story was sent by Poe to Horne,* whose Orion he had reviewed as poetry ought to be reviewed, with a request that it might be sold to an English magazine. The English magazine regretted that the deplorable immorality of the story made it for ever impossible in England!

In his stories of mystery and imagination Poe created a world-record for the English language: perhaps for all the languages. The story of the Lady Ligeia* is not merely one of the wonders of literature: it is unparalleled and unapproached. There is really nothing to be said about it: we others simply take off our hats and let Mr Poe go first. It is interesting to compare Poe's stories with William Morris's. Both are not merely stories: they are complete works of art, like prayer carpets; and they are, in Poe's phrase, stories of imagination. They are masterpieces of style: what people call Macaulay's style is by comparison a mere method. But they are more different than it seems possible for two art works in the same kind to be. Morris will have nothing to do with mystery. 'Ghost stories,' he used to say, 'have all the same explanation: the people are telling lies.'* His Sigurd* has the beauty of mystery as it has every other sort of beauty, being, as it is, incomparably the greatest English epic; but his stories are in the open from end to end, whilst in Poe's stories the sun never shines.

Poe's limitation was his aloofness from the common people. Grotesques, negroes, madmen with delirium tremens, even gorillas,* take the place of ordinary peasants and courtiers, citizens and soldiers, in his theatre. His houses are haunted houses, his woods enchanted woods; and he makes them so real that reality itself cannot sustain the comparison. His kingdom is not of this world.

Above all, Poe is great because he is independent of cheap attractions, independent of sex, of patriotism, of fighting, of sentimentality, snobbery, gluttony, and all the rest of the vulgar stock-in-trade of his profession. This is what gives him his superb distinction. One vulgarized thing, the pathos of dying children, he touched in Annabel Lee, and devulgarized it at once. He could not even amuse himself with detective stories without purifying the atmosphere of them until they became more edifying than most of Hymns, Ancient and Modern. His verse sometimes alarms and puzzles the reader by fainting with its own beauty; but the beauty is never the beauty of the flesh. You never say to him as you have to say uneasily to so many modern artists: 'Yes, my friend, but these are things that men and women should *live* and not write about. Literature is not a keyhole for people with starved affections to peep through at the banquets of the body.' It never became one in Poe's hands. Life cannot give you what he gives you except through fine art; and it was his instinctive observance of this distinction, and the fact that it did not beggar him, as it would beggar most writers, that makes him the most legitimate, the most classical, of modern writers.

It also explains why America does not care much for him, and why he has hardly been mentioned in England these many years. America and England are wallowing in the sensuality which their immense increase of riches has placed within their reach. I do not blame them: sensuality is a very necessary and healthy and educative element in life. Unfortunately, it is ill distributed; and our reading masses are looking on at it and thinking about it and longing for it, and having precarious little holiday treats of it, instead of sharing it temperately and continuously, and ceasing to be preoccupied with it. When the distribution is better adjusted and the preoccupation ceases, there will be a noble reaction in favor of the great writers like Poe, who begin just where the world, the flesh, and the devil leave off.

RODIN

In the year 1906 it was proposed to furnish the world with an authentic portrait-bust of me before I had left the prime of life too far behind. The question then arose: Could Rodin be induced to undertake the work?* On no other condition would I sit, because it was clear to me that Rodin was not only the greatest sculptor then living, but the greatest sculptor of his epoch: one of those extraordinary persons who, like Michael Angelo, or Phidias, or Praxiteles,* dominate whole ages as fashionable favorites dominate a single London season. I saw, therefore, that any man who, being a contemporary of Rodin, deliberately allowed his bust to be made by anybody else, must go down to posterity (if he went down at all) as a stupendous nincompoop.

Also, I wanted a portrait of myself by an artist capable of seeing me. Many clever portraits of my reputation were in existence; but I have never been taken in by my reputation, having manufactured it myself. A reputation is a mask which a man has to wear just as he has to wear a coat and trousers: it is a disguise we insist on as a point of decency. The result is that we have hardly any portraits of men and women. We have no portraits of their legs and shoulders; only of their skirts and trousers and blouses and coats. Nobody knows what Dickens was like, or what Queen Victoria was like, though their wardrobes are on record. Many people fancy they know their faces; but they are deceived: we know only the fashionable mask of the distinguished novelist and of the queen. And the mask defies the camera. When Mr Alvin Langdon Coburn wanted to exhibit a full-length photographic portrait of me,* I secured a faithful representation up to the neck by the trite expedient of sitting to him one morning as I got out of my bath. The portrait was duly hung before a stupefied public as a first step towards the realization of Carlyle's antidote to political idolatry: a naked parliament. But though the body was my body, the face was the face of my reputation. So much so, in fact, that the critics concluded that Mr Coburn had faked his photograph, and stuck my head on somebody else's shoulders. For, as I have said, the mask cannot be penetrated by the camera. It is transparent only to the eye of a veritably god-like artist.

Rodin tells us that his wonderful portrait-busts seldom please the sitters. I can go further, and say that they often puzzle and disappoint the sitters' friends. The busts are of real men, not of the reputations of celebrated persons. Look at my bust, and you will not find it a bit like that brilliant fiction known as G. B. S. or Bernard Shaw. But it is most frightfully like me. It is what is really there, not what you think is there. The same with Puvis de Chavannes* and the rest of them. Puvis de Chavannes protested, as one gathers—pointed to his mirror and to his photographs to prove that he was not like his bust. But I am convinced that he was not only like his bust, but that the bust actually was himself as distinct from his collars and his public manners. Puvis, though an artist of great merit, could not see himself. Rodin could. He saw me. Nobody else has done that yet.

Troubetskoi once made a most fascinating Shavian bust of me.* He did it in about five hours, in Sargent's studio. It was a delightful and wonderful performance. He worked convulsively, giving birth to the thing in agonies, hurling lumps of clay about with groans, and making strange, dumb movements with his tongue, like a wordless prophet. He covered himself with plaster. He covered Sargent's carpets and curtains and pictures with plaster. He covered me with plaster. And, finally, he covered the block he was working on with plaster to such purpose that, at the end of the second sitting, lo! there stood Sargent's studio in ruins, buried like Pompeii* under the scoriæ of a volcano, and in the midst a spirited bust of one of my reputations, a little idealized (quite the gentleman, in fact) but recognizable a mile off as the sardonic author of Man and Superman, with a dash of Offenbach, a touch of Mephistopheles, and a certain aristocratic delicacy and distinction that came from Troubetskoi himself, he being a prince. I should like to have that bust; but the truth is, my wife cannot stand Offenbach-Mephistopheles; and I was not allowed to have the bust any more than I was allowed to have that other witty jibe at my poses, Neville Lytton's portrait of me as Velasquez's Pope Innocent.*

Rodin worked very differently. He plodded along exactly as if he were a river-god doing a job of wall-building in a garden for three or four francs a day. When he was in doubt he measured me with an old iron dividers, and then measured the bust. If the bust's nose was too long, he sliced a bit out of it, and jammed the tip of it up to close the gap, with no more emotion or affectation than a glazier putting in a window pane. If the ear was in the wrong place, he cut it off and slapped it into its right place, excusing these ruthless mutilations to my wife (who half expected to see the already terribly animated clay bleed) by remarking that it was shorter than to make a new ear. Yet a succession of miracles took place as he worked. In the first fifteen minutes, in merely giving a suggestion of human shape to the lump of clay, he produced so spirited a thumbnail bust of me that I wanted to take it away and relieve him from further labor. It reminded me of a highly finished bust by Sarah Bernhardt,* who is very clever with her fingers. But that phase vanished like a summer cloud as the bust evolved. I say evolved advisedly; for it passed through every stage in the evolution of art before my eyes in the course of a month. After that first fifteen minutes it sobered down into a careful representation of my features in their exact living dimensions. Then this representation mysteriously went back to the cradle of Christian art, at which point I again wanted to say: 'For Heaven's sake, stop and give me that: it is a Byzantine masterpiece.' Then it began to look as if Bernini had meddled with it. Then, to my horror, it smoothed out into a plausible, rather elegant piece of eighteenth-century work, almost as if Houdon had touched up a head by Canova or Thorwaldsen,* or as if Leighton had tried his hand at eclecticism in bust-making. At this point Troubetskoi would have broken it with a hammer, or given it up with a wail of despair. Rodin contemplated it with an air of callous patience, and went on with his job, more like a river-god turned plasterer than ever. Then another century passed in a single night; and the bust became a Rodin bust, and was the living head of which I carried the model on my shoulders. It was a process for the embryologist to study, not the æsthete. Rodin's hand worked, not as a sculptor's hand works, but as the Life Force works. What is more, I found that he was aware of it, quite simply. I no more think of Rodin as a celebrated sculptor than I think of Elijah as a well-known *littérateur* and forcible after-dinner speaker. His 'Main de Dieu'* is his own hand. That is why all the stuff written about him by professional art-critics is such ludicrous cackle and piffle. I have been a professional art-critic myself, and perhaps not much of one at that (though I fully admit that I touched nothing I did not adorn), but at least I knew how to take off my hat and hold my tongue when my cacklings and pifflings would have been impertinences.

Rodin took the conceit out of me most horribly. Once he shewed me a torso of a female figure; an antique. It was a beauty; and I swallowed it whole. He waited rather wistfully for a moment, to see whether I really knew chalk from cheese, and then pointed out to me that the upper half of the figure was curiously inferior to the lower half, as if the sculptor had taught himself as he went along. The difference, which I had been blind to a moment before, was so obvious when he pointed it out, that I have despised myself ever since for not seeing it. There never was such an eye for carved stone as Rodin's. To the average critic or connoisseur half the treasures he collects seem nothing but a heap of old paving-stones. But they all have somewhere a scrap of modelled surface, perhaps half the size of a postage stamp, that makes gems of them. In his own work he shews a strong feeling for the beauty of marble. He gave me three busts of myself: one in bronze, one in plaster, one in marble. The bronze is me (growing younger now). The plaster is me. But the marble has quite another sort of life: it glows; and light flows over it. It does not look solid: it looks luminous; and this curious glowing and flowing keeps people's fingers off it; for you feel as if you could not catch hold of it. People say that all modern sculpture is done by the Italian artizans who mechanically reproduce the sculptor's plaster model in the stone. Rodin himself says so. But the peculiar qualities that Rodin gets in his marbles are not in the clay models. What is more, other sculptors can hire artizans, including those who have worked for Rodin. Yet no other sculptor produces such marbles as Rodin. One day Rodin told me that all modern sculpture is imposture; that neither he nor any of the others can use a chisel. A few days later he let slip the remark: 'Handling the chisel is very interesting.' Yet when he models a portrait-bust, his method is neither that of Michael Angelo with his chisel nor of a modeller in the round, but that of a draughtsman outlining in clay the thousand profiles which your head would present if it were sliced a thousand times through the centre at different angles.

Rodin, like all great workmen who can express themselves in words, was very straight and simple, and disposed to be useful to those who listened to him, and not to waste their time. He knew what is important and what is not, and what can be taught and what cannot. After all, apart from the acquired skill of his hands, which he shared with any stone-mason, he had only two qualifications to make him the divinest workman of his day. One was a profounder and more accurate vision than anyone else's. The other was an incorruptible veracity. That was all, ladies and gentlemen. Now I have told you his secret, you can all become great sculptors. It is as easy as any other sort of manual labor, and much pleasanter—if you can pick up those two simple qualifications.

MR ARNOLD BENNETT THINKS PLAY-WRITING EASIER THAN NOVEL WRITING

THE AUTHOR'S CRAFT. BY ARNOLD BENNETT.
(HODDER & STOUGHTON.)

I DID not at first understand why the Editor of The Nation sent me
Mr Bennett's book as one which I might like to review. Mr Bennett
talks shop and debits harmless tosh about technique for the entertainment of literary amateurs in a very agreeable and suggestive manner, as
he has every right to do, being so distinguished a master of the craft.
But why on earth should I join in the conversation and snatch a professional job from some young reviewer whose week's board and lodging it
would provide?

I found the solution of the enigma on page 76, which begins with the
words, 'One reason why a play is easier to write than a novel.' That
fetched me. I did not want to know 'one reason' for so outrageous
a stroke of novelist's bluff. But the impetus of my reading carried me
on, in spite of the shock; and so I learnt that this one reason is 'that
a play is shorter than a novel.' It is; and so is the Bible shorter than the
London Directory. 'Excuse the length of my letter,' said Pascal: 'I had
no time to write a short one.'*

Now, I am not going to argue. I never do. I will simply take one of the
shortest, most intense, and most famous scenes in English dramatic
literature, and rewrite it as a chapter in a novel in the style of my friends
Bennett and Galsworthy* when they are too lazy to write plays:

MACBETH

A PLAY. By William Shakespear. *Act V. Scene* 8
The precinct of Macbeth's Castle on Dunsinane Hill
Enter Macbeth

MACB. Why should I play the Roman fool, and die
On mine own sword? Whiles I see lives, the gashes
Do better upon *them.*
Enter Macduff

MACD. Turn, hell-hound, turn.

MACB. Of all men else I have avoided thee;
But get thee back: my soul is too much charg'd
With blood of thine already.

MACD. I have no words,
       My voice is in my sword, thou bloodier villain
       Than terms can give thee out! (*They fight.*)

MACB. Thou losest labor.
       As easy may'st thou the intrenchment air
       With thy keen sword impress, as make me bleed.
       Let fall thy blade on vulnerable crests:
       I bear a charmed life, which must not yield
       To one of woman born.

MACD. Despair thy charm;
       And let the angel whom thou still hast serv'd
       Tell thee, Macduff was from his mother's womb
       Untimely ripp'd.

MACB. Accursèd be that tongue that tells me so;
       For it hath cow'd my better part of man.
       And be these juggling fiends no more believ'd
       That palter with us in a double sense;
       That keep the word of promise to our ear,
       And break it to our hope. I'll not fight with thee.

MACD. Then yield thee, coward;
       And live to be the show and gaze o' the time.
       We'll have thee, as our rarer monsters are,
       Painted upon a pole; and, underwrit,
       'Here may you see the tyrant.'

MACB. I'll not yield,
       To kiss the ground before young Malcolm's feet,
       And to be baited with the rabble's curse.
       Though Birnam wood *be* come to Dunsinane,
       And thou oppos'd, being of no woman born,
       Yet I will try the last: before my body
       I throw my warlike shield. Lay on, Macduff;
       And damn'd be him that first cries, 'Hold! Enough!'
                                          (*Exeunt fighting.*)

MACBETH

A NOVEL. By Arnold Bennett, John Galsworthy, or Anybody.
The Last Chapter

He was to fail, after all, then. The day was going against him. His men were not really fighting. They had conveyed to Old Siward that they were open to an offer of quarter; and the hint had not been lost on that ancient campaigner, whose son he had just slain.

What was the use of killing? Duncan, Banquo, the Macduff people: he had waded through their blood; and how much better would it not be if it were all a dream and they were alive and kind to him?

How the martins were singing! Banquo, always a bit of a fool, had been sentimental about the martins. Gruach, the dear dead wife whom the southrons persisted in calling Lady Macbeth, had argued with Banquo about them, telling him that their habits were insanitary, and that they were infested with small bugs which got into the castle, already too rich in insect life. But Duncan had agreed with Banquo; and when Gruach became queen she would not let the martins' nests be broken down, being anxious to copy Duncan's tastes in every way, lest anyone should say that the Macbeths did not know how kings lived. And so the martins were singing, singing, always singing when they were not fly-catching.

It came to him, with a twist at the heart, that he had never told Gruach the truth about Banquo. He had left her to believe that he had killed him because the witches had foretold that his posterity should be kings. But the real reason was that Banquo had given himself moral airs. That is hard to bear at any time; but when you are within ten minutes of committing a murder, it is insufferable. Morality is easy for a man who does not intend to do anything; but a man of action cannot stand on scruples. These idle thanes who sat down on their little patrimonies and had no ambition: they had invented this moral twaddle to excuse their laziness.

What an exquisite morning it was! Was there anything so blue as a blue sky, anything so white a white cloud, any gold so golden as the gold of the gorse? From the summit of Dunsinane he could see almost to the Roman wall on the south and to the Forth Bridge on the north. The wind had backed a little to the north: perhaps it would rain later. But no such foreboding troubled the wood pigeon that now called to him, 'Tak two coos, Taffy: tak two coos, Taffy.' He smiled grimly. He had taken from first to last not less than a thousand coos; and this funny bird kept on exhorting him to take two. And yet he did not throw a stone at it as he once would have done. It seemed all so useless. You strove and strove, and killed and killed, and made journeys to consult witches; and at the end of it all the wood pigeon had no more to say to you than before; and the sky was no bluer, the cloud no whiter, the whins no yellower. Curse the sky! Curse the whins! Doubly damn the wood pigeon! Why not make an end of it, like the Roman fool at Philippi? He stood his claymore on its hilt on the flags and bent over the point. Just to lean on it, and let it go through him: then the wood pigeon might coo itself black in the face: Macbeth would beat rest with Duncan. Where had he heard about Philippi? It seemed unlikely that he could have learned Roman history; and yet he found that he did know. Do men know everything before death? He shuddered. Strange, that he, who rather enjoyed killing other people, should feel an intense repugnance to kill himself! Yet there was one canny thing about killing yourself: it relieved you of all concern for the future. You could kill as many other people as you liked first without considering the consequences. He would, please God, spit a few more of his enemies on that sword before his own turn came. He tossed it into the air by the point, and caught the hilt as it came down. He no longer heard the wood pigeon.

And yet, what was that? Had the wood pigeon called him a hellhound? He turned, and saw Macduff there, between him and the sun, glaring at him. If the sun had been in his eyes, he could not have glared. It was clever of him to come that way and get the advantage of the sun.

Macduff! Yes, Macduff: the man of whom the spirit called up by the witches had bade him beware. The man whose wife and child he had slaughtered. Could he blame him for glaring? Would not any man glare after such an experience? Banquo had glared even after his death, but with no speculation in his eyes. There was speculation enough in Macduff's: he was speculating on the sun being in the eyes of his adversary.

How the martins were singing! How fresh the air tasted! How good life was! How many pleasant paths there were on those hillsides, paths that had led his feet and Macduff's to this one spot of all spots in the world! Well, if Macduff had not come by one path he would have come by another. That was life, always inscrutable, sometimes a little ironical. The wind dropped: the banner had ceased to flap, and hung inert. A number of birds and crickets, no longer scared into silence by its flapping, joined the concert of the martins. Again came the wood pigeon's incitement, 'Tak two coos, Taffy: tak——' What was that? A sharp, rasping sound called Macbeth from the landscape. He looked again at the man against whom he had been warned.

Macduff had stooped to sharpen his claymore on the flags. He was squatting down in an attitude which brought his boney knees into prominence just below his kilt, and drawing his blade to and fro with a harsh, rhythmical grating on the granite. By the mere instinct of imitation, Macbeth did the same. His knees were fleshier; and it was harder for him to stoop; but he did it. It is never easy for a king to stoop; but Fate will have it so sometimes. Now there were two blades scraping. The birds stopped singing, and listened in astonished suspicious silence. Only a jay laughed.

Macbeth heard it. Something stirred in him, and distorted his lips into a grin. It seemed to him that he suddenly opened a book that had always been sealed to him. When Gruach was dying he had asked the doctor for some physic for the mind; and the doctor had failed him. Then he had asked the porter, because he had noticed that the porter, alone among all the men of his acquaintance, was light-hearted, and would laugh, even when nobody was being hurt or ridiculed, and seemed to despise ambition. And the porter had told him that life is not so bad if you can see the fun of it. Old Siward had nailed the porter to the door that morning because he refused to open it to the enemy. Did he see the fun of that, Macbeth wondered? Yet here, as he squatted before Macduff, and they both sharpened their blades on the flags, a dim sense of something laughable in the situation touched him, though, God knows, there was nothing to laugh at if the warning of the witches were trustworthy. The spirits had said that no man born of woman should harm Macbeth. That seemed pretty conclusive. But they had also said that he would not be vanquished until Birnam Wood came to Dunsinane. That also seemed conclusive; yet the thing had happened: he had seen the wood walking.

He decided to give Macduff a chance. He was tired of killing people named Macduff. He said so. He advised Macduff to go away.

Macduff tried to speak; gulped; and came on. His voice was in his sword.

Macbeth was not afraid, though he knew he was not the man he had been. He had drunk heavily since he seized the throne: the Scots expected that from a king. But he could fight as well as ever for forty-five seconds; and then he could clinch, and try to get in his dirk somewhere. After all, Macduff was no teetotaller, if one might judge by his nose, which was red and swollen. Only, the doubt came: was the redness and the swelling from drink, or from weeping over his slaughtered family? With that thought came Macduff's first blow: a feint, followed by a vicious thrust at the groin.

Macbeth was quick enough to drop his targe and stop the thrust, even while he guarded the blow that did not come. That reassured him, and took some of the bounce out of Macduff. He was equally successful the next time, and the next. He became elated. At last his pride in his charmed life got the better of his prudence. He told Macduff that he was losing his labor, and told him why.

The effect was exactly the contrary of what he had anticipated. A gleam of savage delight came into Macduff's eyes.

What did it mean?

Macbeth was not left long in doubt. He stood petrified, whilst a tale poured from Macduff's lips such as had never before blasted the ears of mortal man. It cannot be repeated here: there is such a thing as the library censorship. Let it suffice that it was a tale of the rude but efficient obstetric surgery of those ancient times, and that it established beyond all question the fact that Macduff had never been born.

After that, Macbeth felt that he simply could not fight with him. It was not that he was afraid, even now. Nor was it that he was utterly disgusted at the way the witches had let him down again. He just could not bring himself to hack at a man who was not natural. It was like trying to eat a cat. He flatly refused further combat.

Of course, Macduff called him Coward. He did not mind that so much; for he had given his proofs, and nobody would believe Macduff; nor, indeed, would any reasonable Scot expect him to fight an unborn adversary. But Macduff hinted at unbearable things: at defeat, disgrace, the pillory even.

There was a lark singing now. Far down the hillside, where the rugged road wound up to the barbican, the last of Birnam Wood was still on the march. A hawk hovered motionless over a walking oak: he could see the glint of the sun on its brown back. The oak's legs must be those of an old soldier, he thought, who had cunningly taken the heaviest tree so that he might be late for the fighting. But, old or young, the soldier was now anxious lest he should be late for the plunder and the other sequels to the sack of a castle; for the oak was coming up at a rattling pace. There were nests in it, too. Curious, to wonder how those nesting pairs took their moving!

A surge of wrath went through Macbeth. He was, above all things, a country gentleman; and that another country gentleman should move his timber without acquiring any rights infuriated him. He became reckless. Birnam Wood—*his* wood—had been taken to Dunsinane: was that a thing he could be expected to stand? What though Macduff had not been properly born: was it not all the more likely that he had a weak constitution and could not stick it out if he were pressed hard in the fight? Anyhow, Macbeth would try. He braced himself; grasped his claymore powerfully; thrust his shield under the chin of his adversary; and cried, 'Lay on, Macduff.'

He could not have chosen a more unfortunate form of defiance. When the news had come to Macduff of the slaughter of his wife and boy, he had astonished the messenger by exclaiming, 'What! All my pretty chickens and their dam at one fell swoop!' Accustomed from his earliest youth to deal with horses, he knew hardly anything of poultry, which was a woman's business. When he applied the word dam, properly applicable only to a mare, to a hen, Malcolm, though deeply moved by his distress, had a narrow escape of a fit of hysterics; for the innocent blunder gave him an impulse of untimely laughter. The story had been repeated; and something of it had come to Macduff's ears. He was a highly-strung man, exquisitely sensitive to ridicule. Since that time the slightest allusion to chickens had driven him to transports of fury. At the words 'Lay on,' he saw red. Macbeth, from the instant those fatal words passed his lips, had not a dog's chance.

In any case, he would not have been ready to meet a sudden attack. All his life he had been subject to a strange discursiveness which sent his mind wandering to the landscape, and to the fauna and flora of the district, at the most exciting crises of his fate. When he meant to tell Gruach that he had arranged to have Banquo killed, he had said to her, instead, 'Light thickens; and the crow makes wing to the rooky wood.' His attention had already strayed to the wood pigeon when Macduff's yell of fury split his ears; and at the same moment he felt his foe's teeth snap through his nose and his foe's dirk drive through his ribs.

When Malcolm arrived, there was little left of Macbeth but a pile of mince. Macduff was panting. 'That will teach him,' he said, and stopped, exsufflicate.

They laid Macbeth beside Gruach in God's quiet acre in the little churchyard of Dunsinane. Malcolm erected a stately tomb there, for the credit of the institution of kingship; and the epitaph, all things considered, was not unhandsome. There was no reproach in it, no vain bitterness. It said that Macbeth had 'succeeded Duncan.'

The birds are still singing on Dunsinane. The wood pigeon still coos about the coos; and Malcolm takes them frankly and generously. It is not for us to judge him, or to judge Macbeth. Macbeth was born before his time. Men call him a villain; but had the press existed in his day, a very trifling pecuniary sacrifice on his part would have made a hero of him. And, to do him justice, he was never stingy.

Well! Well!

THE END

There! that is what is called novel writing. I raise no idle question as to whether it is easy or not. Fine art of any sort is either easy or impossible.* But that sort of thing I can write by the hundred thousand words on my head. I believe that if I turned my attention to mechanics for a month or two, I could make a typewriter attachment that would do it, like the

calculating attachment that has lately come into use.* The odd thing is
that people seem to like it. They swallow it in doses of three hundred
pages at a time; and they are not at all keen on Shakespear. Decidedly,
when my faculties decay a little further, I shall go back to novel writing.
And Arnold Bennett can fall back on writing plays.

OSCAR WILDE

My Dear Harris:—*

Why was Wilde so good a subject for a biography that none of the previous attempts which you have just wiped out are bad? Just because his stupendous laziness simplified his life almost as if he knew instinctively that there must be no episodes to spoil the great situation at the end of the last act but one. It was a well-made life in the Scribe sense. It was as simple as the life of Des Grieux, Manon Lescaut's lover;* and it beat that by omitting Manon and making Des Grieux his own lover and his own hero.

Des Grieux was a worthless rascal by all conventional standards; and we forgive him everything. We think we forgive him because he was unselfish and loved greatly. Oscar seems to have said: 'I will love nobody: I will be utterly selfish; and I will be not merely a rascal but a monster; and you shall forgive me everything. In other words, I will reduce your standards to absurdity, not by writing them down, though I could do that so well—in fact, *have* done it—but by actually living them down and dying them down.'

However, I mustnt start writing a book to you about Wilde: I must just tumble a few things together and tell you them. To take things in the order of your book, I can remember only one occasion on which I saw Sir William Wilde,* who, by the way, operated on my father to correct a squint, and overdid the correction so much that my father squinted the other way all the rest of his life. To this day I never notice a squint: it is as normal to me as a nose or a tall hat.

I was a boy at a concert in the Antient Concert Rooms in Brunswick Street in Dublin. Everybody was in evening dress; and—unless I am mixing up this concert with another (in which case I doubt if the Wildes would have been present)—the Lord-Lieutenant* was there with his courtiers in blue facings. Wilde was dressed in snuffy brown; and as he had the sort of skin that never looks clean, he produced a dramatic effect beside Lady Wilde* (in full fig) of being, like Frederick the Great,* Beyond Soap and Water, as his Nietzschean son was beyond Good and Evil. He was currently reported to have a family in every farmhouse; and the wonder was that Lady Wilde didnt mind—evidently a tradition from the Travers case,* which I did not know about until I read your account, as I was only eight in 1864.

Lady Wilde was nice to me in London during the desperate days between my arrival in 1876 and my first earning of an income by my pen in 1885, or rather until, a few years earlier, I threw myself into Socialism and cut myself contemptuously loose from everything of which her at-homes—themselves desperate affairs enough, as you saw for yourself—were part. I was at two or three of them; and I once dined with her in company with an ex-tragedy queen named Miss Glynn,* who, having no visible external ears, reared a head like a turnip. Lady Wilde talked about Schopenhauer; and Miss Glynn told me that Gladstone formed his oratorical style on Charles Kean.

I ask myself where and how I came across Lady Wilde; for we had no social relations in the Dublin days. The explanation must be that my sister,* then a very attractive girl who sang beautifully, had met and made some sort of innocent conquest of both Oscar and Willie.* I met Oscar once at one of the at-homes; and he came and spoke to me with an evident intention of being specially kind to me. We put each other out frightfully; and this odd difficulty persisted between us to the very last, even when we were no longer mere boyish novices and had become men of the world with plenty of skill in social intercourse. I saw him very seldom, as I avoided literary and artistic coteries like the plague, and refused the few invitations I received to go into society with burlesque ferocity, so as to keep out of it without offending people past their willingness to indulge me as a privileged lunatic.

The last time I saw him was at that tragic luncheon of yours at the Café Royal;* and I am quite sure our total of meetings from first to last did not exceed twelve, and may not have exceeded six.

I definitely recollect six: (1) At the at-home aforesaid. (2) At Macmurdo's* house in Fitzroy Street in the days of the Century Guild and its paper The Hobby Horse.* (3) At a meeting somewhere in Westminster at which I delivered an address on Socialism, and at which Oscar turned up and spoke. Robert Ross* surprised me greatly by telling me, long after Oscar's death, that it was this address of mine that moved Oscar to try his hand at a similar feat by writing The Soul of Man Under Socialism.* (4) A chance meeting near the stage door of the Haymarket Theatre, at which our queer shyness of one another made our resolutely cordial and appreciative conversation so difficult that our final laugh and shakehands was almost a reciprocal confession. (5) A really pleasant afternoon we spent together on catching one another in a place where our presence was an absurdity. It was some exhibition in Chelsea: a naval commemoration, where there was a replica of Nelson's Victory and a set of P. & O. cabins* which made one seasick by mere association of ideas. I dont know why I went or why Wilde went; but we did; and the question what the devil we were doing in that galley tickled us both. It was my sole experience of Oscar's wonderful gift as a raconteur. I remember particularly an amazingly elaborate story which you have no doubt heard from him: an example of the cumulation of a single effect, as in Mark Twain's story* of the man who was persuaded to put lightning conductor after lightning conductor at every possible point on his roof until a thunderstorm came and all the lightning in the heavens went for his house and wiped it out.

Oscar's much more carefully and elegantly worked out story was of a young man who invented a theatre stall which economized space by ingenious contrivances which were all described. A friend of his invited twenty millionaires to meet him at dinner so that he might interest them in the invention. The young man convinced them completely by his demonstration of the saving in a theatre holding, in ordinary seats, six hundred people, leaving them eager and ready to make his fortune. Unfortunately he went on to calculate the annual saving in all the theatres of the world; then in all the churches of the world; then in all the legislatures; estimating finally the incidental and moral and religious effects of the invention until at the end of an hour he had estimated a profit of several thousand millions: the climax of course being that the millionaires folded their tents and silently stole away, leaving the ruined inventor a marked man for life.

Wilde and I got on extraordinarily well on this occasion. I had not to talk myself, but to listen to a man telling me stories better than I could have told them. We did not refer to Art, about which, excluding literature from the definition, he knew only what could be picked up by reading about it. He was in a tweed suit and low hat like myself, and had been detected and had detected me in the act of clandestinely spending a happy day at Rosherville Gardens* instead of pontificating in his frock-coat and so forth. And he had an audience on whom not one of his subtlest effects was lost. And so for once our meeting was a success; and I understood why Morris, when he was dying slowly, enjoyed a visit from Wilde more than from anybody else, as I understand why you say in your book that you would rather have Wilde back than any friend you have ever talked to, even though he was incapable of friendship, though not of the most touching kindness on occasion.

Our sixth meeting, the only other one I can remember, was the one at the Café Royal. On that occasion he was not too preoccupied with his danger to be disgusted with me because I, who had praised his first plays, handsomely, had turned traitor over The Importance of Being

Earnest.* Clever as it was, it was his first really heartless play. In the others the chivalry of the eighteenth-century Irishman and the romance of the disciple of Théophile Gautier* (Oscar was old-fashioned in the Irish way, except as a critic of morals) not only gave a certain kindness and gallantry to the serious passages and to the handling of the women, but provided that proximity of emotion without which laughter, however irresistible, is destructive and sinister. In The Importance of Being Earnest this had vanished; and the play, though extremely funny, was essentially hateful. I had no idea that Oscar was going to the dogs, and that this represented a real degeneracy produced by his debaucheries. I thought he was still developing; and I hazarded the unhappy guess that The Importance of Being Earnest was in idea a young work written or projected long before under the influence of Gilbert and furbished up for Alexander as a potboiler. At the Café Royal that day I calmly asked him whether I was not right. He indignantly repudiated my guess, and said loftily (the only time he ever tried on me the attitude he took to John Gray* and his more abject disciples) that he was disappointed in me. I suppose I said, 'Then what on earth has happened to you?' but I recollect nothing more on that subject except that we did not quarrel over it.

When he was sentenced I spent a railway journey on a Socialist lecturing excursion to the North drafting a petition for his release. After that I met Willie Wilde at a theatre which I think must have been the Duke of York's, because I connect it vaguely with St Martin's Lane. I spoke to him about the petition, asking him whether anything of the sort was being done, and warning him that though I and Stewart Headlam would sign it,* that would be no use, as we were two notorious cranks, and our names would by themselves reduce the petition to absurdity and do Oscar more harm than good. Willie cordially agreed, and added, with maudlin pathos and an inconceivable want of tact: 'Oscar was NOT a man of bad character: you could have trusted him with a woman anywhere.' He convinced me, as you discovered later, that signatures would not be obtainable; so the petition project dropped; and I dont know what became of my draft.

When Wilde was in Paris during his last phase I made a point of sending him inscribed copies of all my books as they came out; and he did the same to me.*

In writing about Wilde and Whistler, in the days when they were treated as witty triflers, and called Oscar and Jimmy in print, I always made a point of taking them seriously and with scrupulous good manners. Wilde on his part also made a point of recognizing me as a man of distinction by his manner, and repudiating the current estimate of me as a mere jester. This was not the usual reciprocal-admiration trick: I believe he was sincere, and felt indignant at what he thought was a vulgar underestimate of me; and I had the same feeling about him. My impulse to rally to him in his misfortune, and my disgust at 'the man Wilde' scurrilities of the newspapers, was irresistible: I dont quite know why; for my charity to his perversion, and my recognition of the fact that it does not imply any general depravity or coarseness of character, came to me through reading and observation, not through sympathy. I have all the normal violent repugnance to homosexuality— if it be really normal, which nowadays one is sometimes provoked to doubt.

Also, I was in no way predisposed to like him: he was my fellow-townsman, and a very prime specimen of the sort of fellow-townsman I most loathed: to wit, the Dublin snob. His Irish charm, potent with Englishmen, did not exist for me; and on the whole it may be claimed for him that he got no regard from me that he did not earn.

What first established a friendly feeling in me was, unexpectedly enough, the affair of the Chicago anarchists,* whose Homer* you constituted yourself by your story called The Bomb,* I tried to get some literary men in London, all heroic rebels and sceptics on paper, to sign a memorial asking for the reprieve of these unfortunate men. The only signature I got was Oscar's. It was a completely disinterested act on his part; and it secured my distinguished consideration for him for the rest of his life.

To return for a moment to Lady Wilde. You know that there is a disease called giantism, caused by 'a certain morbid process in the sphenoid bone of the skull—viz., an excessive development of the anterior lobe of the pituitary body' (this is from the nearest encyclopedia). 'When this condition does not become active until after the age of twenty-five, by which time the long bones are consolidated, the result is acromegaly, which chiefly manifests itself in an enlargement of the hands and feet.' I never saw Lady Wilde's feet; but her hands were enormous, and never went straight to their aim when they grasped anything, but minced about, feeling for it. And the gigantic splaying of her palm was reproduced in her lumbar region.

Now Oscar was an overgrown man, with something not quite normal about his bigness: something that made Lady Colin Campbell,* who hated him, describe him as 'that great white caterpillar.' You yourself describe the disagreeable impression he made on you physically, in spite of his fine eyes and style. Well, I have always maintained that

Oscar was a giant in the pathological sense, and that this explains a good deal of his weakness.

I think you have affectionately underrated his snobbery, mentioning only the pardonable and indeed justifiable side of it; the love of fine names and distinguished associations and luxury and good manners. You say repeatedly, and *on certain planes*, truly, that he was not bitter and did not use his tongue to wound people. But this is not true on the snobbish plane. On one occasion he wrote about T. P. O'Connor* with deliberate, studied, wounding insolence, with his Merrion Square* Protestant pretentiousness in full cry against the Catholic.* He repeatedly declaimed against the vulgarity of the British journalist, not as you or I might, but as an expression of the odious class feeling that is itself the vilest vulgarity. He made the mistake of not knowing his place. He objected to be addressed as Wilde, declaring that he was Oscar to his intimates and Mr Wilde to others, quite unconscious of the fact that he was imposing on the men with whom, as a critic and journalist, he had to live and work, the alternative of granting him an intimacy he had no right to ask or a deference to which he had no claim. The vulgar hated him for snubbing them; and the valiant men damned his impudence and cut him. Thus he was left with a band of devoted satellites on the one hand, and a dining-out connection on the other, with here and there a man of talent and personality enough to command his respect, but utterly without that fortifying body of acquaintance among plain men in which a man must move as himself a plain man, and be Smith and Jones and Wilde and Shaw and Harris instead of Bosie and Robbie* and Oscar and Mister. This is the sort of folly that does not last forever in a man of Wilde's ability; but it lasted long enough to prevent Oscar laying any solid social foundations.

Another difficulty I have already hinted at. Wilde started as an apostle of Art; and in that capacity he was a humbug. The notion that a Portora boy, passed on to T.C.D.* and thence to Oxford and spending his vacations in Dublin, could without special circumstances have any genuine intimacy with music and painting, is to me ridiculous. When Wilde was at Portora, I was at home in a house where important musical works, including several typical masterpieces, were being rehearsed from the point of blank amateur ignorance up to fitness for public performance. I could whistle them from the first bar to the last as a butcher's boy whistles music-hall songs, before I was twelve. The toleration of popular music—Strauss's waltzes, for instance—was to me positively a painful acquirement, a sort of republican duty.

I was so fascinated by painting that I haunted the National Gallery, which Doyle* had made perhaps the finest collection of its size in the world; and I longed for money to buy painting materials with. This afterwards saved me from starving: it was as a critic of music and painting in The World that I won through my ten years of journalism before I finished up with you on The Saturday Review. I could make deaf stockbrokers read my two pages on music, the alleged joke being that I knew nothing about it. The real joke was that I knew all about it.

Now it was quite evident to me, as it was to Whistler and Beardsley, that Oscar knew no more about pictures than anyone of his general culture and with his opportunities can pick up as he goes along. He could be witty about Art, as I could be witty about engineering; but that is no use when you have to seize and hold the attention and interest of people who really love music and painting. Therefore, Oscar was handicapped by a false start, and got a reputation for shallowness and insincerity which he never retrieved until too late.

Comedy: the criticism of morals and manners *viva voce*,* was his real forte. When he settled down to that he was great. But, as you found when you approached Meredith about him, his initial mistake had produced that 'rather low opinion of Wilde's capacities,' that 'deep-rooted contempt for the showman in him,' which persisted as a first impression and will persist until the last man who remembers his æsthetic period has perished. The world has been in some ways so unjust to him that one must be careful not to be unjust to the world.

In the preface on education, called Parents and Children, to my volume of plays beginning with Misalliance,* there is a section headed Artist Idolatry, which is really about Wilde. Dealing with 'the powers enjoyed by brilliant persons who are also connoisseurs in art,' I say, 'the influence they can exercise on young people who have been brought up in the darkness and wretchedness of a home without art, and in whom a natural bent towards art has always been baffled and snubbed, is incredible to those who have not witnessed and understood it. He (or she) who reveals the world of art to them opens heaven to them. They become satellites, disciples, worshippers of the apostle. Now the apostle may be a voluptuary without much conscience. Nature may have given him enough virtue to suffice in a reasonable environment. But this allowance may not be enough to defend him against the temptation and demoralization of finding himself a little god on the strength of what ought to be a quite ordinary culture. He may find adorers in all directions in our uncultivated society among people of stronger character than himself, not one of whom, if they had been artistically educated, would have had anything to learn from him, or regarded him as in any way extraordinary apart from his actual achievements as an artist. Tartufe* is not always a priest. Indeed, he is not always a rascal: he is often a weak man absurdly credited with omniscience and perfection, and taking unfair advantages only because they are offered to him and he is too weak to refuse. Give everyone his culture, and no one will offer him more than his due.'

That paragraph was the outcome of a walk and talk I had one afternoon at Chartres* with Robert Ross.

You reveal Wilde as a weaker man than I thought him: I still believe that his fierce Irish pride had something to do with his refusal to run away from the trial. But in the main your evidence is conclusive. It was part of his tragedy that people asked more moral strength from him than he could bear the burden of, because they made the very common mistake—of which actors get the benefit—of regarding style as evidence of strength, just as in the case of women they are apt to regard paint as evidence of beauty. Now Wilde was so in love with style that he never realized the danger of biting off more than he could chew: in other words, of putting up more style than his matter would carry. Wise kings wear shabby clothes, and leave the gold lace to the drum major.

I was at your Saturday Review lunch at the Café Royal when Wilde came in just before the trial. He said he had come to ask you to go into the witness box next day and testify that Dorian Gray* was a highly moral work. Your answer was something like this: 'For God's sake, man, put everything on that plane out of your head. You dont realize what is going to happen to you. It is not going to be a matter of clever talk about your books. They are going to bring up a string of witnesses that will put art and literature out of the question. Clarke* will throw up his brief. He will carry the case to a certain point; and then, when he sees the avalanche coming, he will back out and leave you in the dock. What you have to do is to cross to France tonight. Leave a letter saying that you cannot face the squalor and horror of a law case; that you are an artist and unfitted for such things. Dont stay here clutching at straws like testimonials to Dorian Gray. *I tell you I know*. I know what is going to happen. I know Clarke's sort. I know what evidence they have got. You must go.'

It was no use. Wilde was in a curious double temper. He made no pretence either of innocence or of questioning the folly of his proceedings against Queensberry. But he had an infatuate haughtiness as to the impossibility of his retreating, and as to his right to dictate your course. Oscar finally rose with a mixture of impatience and his grand air, and walked out with the remark that he had now found out who were his real friends.

What your book needs to complete it is a portrait of yourself as good as your portrait of Wilde. Oscar was not combative, though he was supercilious in his early pose. When his snobbery was not in action, he liked to make people devoted to him and to flatter them exquisitely with that end. Mrs Calvert,* whose great final period as a stage old woman began with her appearance in my Arms and the Man, told me one day, when apologizing for being, as she thought, a bad rehearser, that no author had ever been so nice to her except Mr Wilde.

Pugnacious people, if they did not actually terrify Oscar, were at least the sort of people he could not control, and whom he feared as possibly able to coerce him. You suggest that the Queensberry pugnacity was something that Oscar could not deal with successfully. But how in that case could Oscar have felt quite safe with you? You were more pugnacious than six Queensberrys rolled into one. When people asked, 'What has Frank Harris been?' the usual reply was, 'Obviously a pirate from the Spanish Main.'*

Oscar, from the moment he gained your attachment, could never have been afraid of what you might do to him, as he was sufficient of a connoisseur in Blut Bruderschaft* to appreciate yours; but he must always have been mortally afraid of what you might do or say to his friends.

You had quite an infernal scorn for nineteen out of twenty of the men and women you met in the circles he most wished to propitiate; and nothing could induce you to keep your knife in its sheath when they jarred on you. The Spanish Main itself would have blushed rosy red at your language when classical invective did not suffice to express your feelings.

It may be that if, say, Edmund Gosse* had come to Oscar when he was out on bail, with a couple of first-class tickets in his pocket, and gently suggested a mild trip to Folkestone, or the Channel Islands, Oscar might have let himself be coaxed away. But to be called on to gallop *ventre à terre* to Erith—it might have been Deal—and hoist the Jolly Roger on board your lugger,* was like casting a light comedian and first lover for Richard III.* Oscar could not see himself in the part.

I must not press the point too far; but it illustrates, I think, what does not come out at all in your book: that you were a very different person from the submissive and sympathetic disciples to whom he was accustomed. There are things more terrifying to a soul like Oscar's than an as yet unrealized possibility of a sentence of hard labor. A voyage with Captain Kidd* may have been one of them. Wilde was a conventional man: his unconventionality was the very pedantry of convention: never was there a man less an outlaw than he. You were a born outlaw, and will never be anything else.

That is why, in his relations with you, he appears as a man always shirking action—more of a coward (all men are cowards more or less) than so proud a man can have been. Still this does not affect the truth and power of your portrait. Wilde's memory will have to stand or fall by it.

You will be blamed, I imagine, because you have not written a lying epitaph instead of a faithful chronicle and study of him; but you will not lose your sleep over that. As a matter of fact, you could not have carried kindness further without sentimental folly. I should have made a far sterner summing up. I am sure Oscar has not found the gates of heaven shut against him: he is too good company to be excluded; but he can hardly have been greeted as 'Thou good and faithful servant.' The first thing we ask a servant for is a testimonial to honesty, sobriety, and industry; for we soon find out that these are the scarce things, and that geniuses and clever people are as common as rats. Well, Oscar was not sober, not honest, not industrious. Society praised him for being idle, and persecuted him savagely for an aberration which it had better have left unadvertized, thereby making a hero of him; for it is in the nature of people to worship those who have been made to suffer horribly: indeed I have often said that if the Crucifixion could be proved a myth, and Jesus convicted of dying of old age in comfortable circumstances, Christianity would lose ninety-nine per cent of its devotees.

We must try to imagine what judgment we should have passed on Oscar if he had been a normal man, and had dug his grave with his teeth in the ordinary respectable fashion, as his brother Willie did. This brother, by the way, gives us some cue; for Willie, who had exactly the same education and the same chances, must be ruthlessly set aside by literary history as a vulgar journalist of no account. Well, suppose Oscar and Willie had both died the day before Queensberry left that card at the Club!* Oscar would still have been remembered as a wit and a dandy, and would have had a niche beside Congreve* in the drama. A volume of his aphorisms* would have stood creditably on the library shelf with La Rochefoucauld's Maxims. We should have missed the Ballad of Reading Gaol and De Profundis;* but he would still have cut a considerable figure in the Dictionary of National Biography, and been read and quoted outside the British Museum reading room.

As to the Ballad and De Profundis, I think it is greatly to Oscar's credit that, whilst he was sincere and deeply moved when he was protesting against the cruelty of our present system to children and to prisoners generally, he could not write about his own individual share in that suffering with any conviction or sympathy. Except for the passage where he describes his exposure at Clapham Junction,* there is hardly a line in De Profundis that he might not have written as a literary feat five years earlier. But in the Ballad, even in borrowing form and melody from Coleridge, he shews that he could pity others when he could not seriously pity himself. And this, I think, may be pleaded against the reproach that he was selfish. Externally, in the ordinary action of life as distinguished from the literary action proper to his genius, he was no doubt sluggish and weak because of his giantism. He ended as an unproductive drunkard and swindler; for his repeated sales of the Daventry plot,* in so far as they imposed on the buyers and were not transparent excuses for begging, were undeniably swindles. For all that, he does not appear in his writings a selfish or base-minded man. He is at his worst and weakest in the suppressed part of De Profundis; but in my opinion it had better be published, for several reasons. It explains some of his personal weakness by the stifling narrowness of his daily round, ruinous to a man whose proper place was in a large public life. And its concealment is mischievous because, first, it leads people to imagine all sorts of horrors in a document which contains nothing worse than any record of the squabbles of two touchy men on a holiday; and, second, it is clearly a monstrous thing that one of them should have a torpedo launched at him and timed to explode after his death.

Now that you have written the best life of Oscar Wilde, let us have the best life of Frank Harris. Otherwise the man behind your works will go down to posterity as the hero of my very inadequate preface to The Dark Lady of the Sonnets.*

RUSKIN'S POLITICS

* * *

I THINK Ruskin was more misunderstood as a politician than in any other department of his activity. People complained that he was unintelligible. I do not think he was unintelligible. If you read his political utterances, the one thing that you cannot say of them is that they were unintelligible. You would imagine that no human being could ever have been under the slightest delusion as to what Ruskin meant and was driving at. But what really puzzled his readers—and incidentally saved his life, because he certainly would have been hanged if they had grasped what he was driving at, and believed that he believed it—was that he was incredible. You see, he appealed to the educated, cultivated, and discontented. It is true that he addressed himself to the working-classes generally; and you can find among the working-classes, just as Mr Charles Rowley has found in the Ancoats quarter of Manchester,* a certain proportion of working-men who have intellectual tastes and artistic interests. But in all classes his disciples were the few who were at war with commercial civilization. I have met in my lifetime some extremely revolutionary characters; and quite a large number of them, when I have asked, 'Who put you on to this revolutionary line? Was it Karl Marx?' have answered, 'No, it was Ruskin'. Generally the Ruskinite is the most thoroughgoing of the opponents of our existing state of society.

Now the reason why the educated and cultured classes in this country found Ruskin incredible was that they could not bring themselves to believe that he meant what he was saying, and indeed shouting. He was even shouting in such terms that if I were to describe it merely as abusive I should underdo the description. Think of the way in which his readers were brought up! They were educated at our public schools and universities; they moved in a society which fitted in with those public schools and universities; they had been brought up from their earliest childhood as above everything respectable people; taught that what respectable people did was the right and proper thing to do, was good form and also high culture; that such people were the salt of the earth; that everything that existed in the way of artistic culture depended on their cultured and leisured existence. When you have people saturated from their childhood with views of that kind, and they are suddenly confronted with a violently contrary view, they are unable to take it in.

For instance, to put it quite simply, they knew that there were the Ten Commandments, and that the Ten Commandments were all right; and they argued from this that as respectable people were all right in everything they did they must be living according to the Ten Commandments. Therefore their consciences were entirely untroubled.

I have here a volume of Ruskin which I took up this morning, intending to read it, but had not time. I opened it at random, and happened on a page on which Ruskin gave the Ten Commandments according to which in his conception our polite and cultured society really lives. This is the only passage I shall read today, though I feel, of course, the temptation that every lecturer on Ruskin feels to get out of his job by reading, because anything he reads is likely to be better than anything he can say of his own. Ruskin says:*

'Generally the ten commandments are now: Thou shalt have any other god but me. Thou shalt worship every bestial imagination on earth and under it. Thou shalt take the name of the Lord in vain to mock the poor; for the Lord will hold him guiltless who rebukes and gives not; thou shalt remember the sabbath day to keep it profane; thou shalt dishonour thy father and thy mother; thou shalt kill, and kill by the million, with all thy might and mind and wealth spent in machinery for multifold killing; thou shalt look on every woman to lust after her; thou shalt steal, and steal from morning till evening; the evil from the good, and the rich from the poor; thou shalt live by continual lying in million-fold sheets of lies; and covet thy neighbour's house, and country, and wealth and fame, and everything that is his. And finally, by word of the Devil, in short summary, through Adam Smith,* a new commandment give I unto you: that ye hate one another.'

If anybody is going to tell me, here or elsewhere, that this is unintelligible, I do not know what to think of that person's brains. Nothing could well be clearer. But, as I have said, and repeat, it was profoundly incredible to those to whom it was addressed.

Ruskin's political message to the cultured society of his day, the class to which he himself belonged, began and ended in this simple judgement: 'You are a parcel of thieves.' That is what it came to. He never went away from that; and he enforced it with a very extraordinary power of invective. Ruskin was a master of invective. Compare him, for instance, with Cobbett. Cobbett had immense literary style; and when he hated a thing, he hated it very thoroughly indeed. Think of Cobbett's writing about the funding system—think of his writing about the spoliation of the Church by Henry VIII*—think of his writing about the barrenness of Surrey, which cultured society likes so much and which Cobbett loathed as a barren place—think of what he said about 'barbarous, bestial Malthus'—think of Cobbett at the height of his vituperation. Then go on to Karl Marx. Karl Marx was a Jew who had, like Jeremiah, a great power of invective. Think of the suppression of the Paris Commune of 1871, and then of that terrific screed that Marx wrote,* exposing the Empire, denouncing the Versaillese generals, execrating the whole order of things which destroyed the Commune so remorselessly. There you have a masterpiece of invective, a thing which, although it was not reproduced in any of the newspapers, or popular literary issues of the day, nevertheless did leave such an effect that when, thirty years after, a proposal was made in the French Chamber to put Gallifet into a public position of some credit,* the governing classes having forgotten that a word had ever been said against him, suddenly that terrible denunciation of Marx rose up against him and struck him absolutely out of public life. Yet when you read these invectives of Marx and Cobbett, and read Ruskin's invectives afterwards, somehow or other you feel that Ruskin beats them hollow. Perhaps the reason was that they hated their enemy so thoroughly. Ruskin does it without hatred, and therefore he does it with a magnificent thoroughness. You may say that his strength in invective is as the strength of ten because his heart is pure. And the only consequence of his denunciation of society was that people said, 'Well, he can't possibly be talking about us, the respectable people'; and so they did not take any notice of it.

I must now go on to Ruskin's specific contribution to economics and sociology, because that, as you know, to-day means a contribution to politics. In Ruskin's own time this was not so clear. People did not understand then that your base in politics must be an economic base and a sociological base. We all know it to-day, and know it to our cost; and will know it to our still greater cost unless we find a way out, which, it seems, lies not very far from Ruskin's way. Ruskin took up the treatises of our classic political economy, the books by which our Manchester Capitalism sought to justify its existence. In this he did what Karl Marx had done before; and, like Marx, he did it in a way which I do not like exactly to describe as a corrupt way, because you cannot think of corruption in connexion with Ruskin: nevertheless, he did not take it up as a man with a disinterested academic enthusiasm for abstract political economy. I think we must admit that, like Marx, he took it up because he was clever enough to see that it was a very good stick to beat the Capitalist dog with. Marx took up the theory of value which had been begun by Adam Smith, and developed by Malthus,* and, seeing that he could turn it against Capitalism, tried to re-establish it on a basis of his own. Thus we got his celebrated theory of value, which is now a cele-brated blunder. What Ruskin did was this. He held up to us the defin-ition of value given by the economists, and said: 'These gentlemen define value as value in exchange. Therefore', he said, 'a thing that you cannot exchange has no value: a thing that you can exchange has value. Very well. When on my way to Venice I go through Paris, I can buy there for two francs fifty an obscene lithograph, produced by the French to sell to English tourists. When I reach Venice, I go to the Scuola di San Rocco and look at the ceiling painted there by Tintoretto,* because it is one of the treasures of the world. But that ceiling cannot be sold in the market. It has no exchange value. Therefore, according to John Stuart Mill, the obscene lithograph has a higher value than the ceiling, which in fact has no value at all. After that, I have no further use for your political economy. If that is the way you begin, I hesitate to go on to the end; for I know where your journey must land you—in hell. You may be under the impression that after all hell is a thing you can think of later on; but you are mistaken: you are already at your destin-ation: the condition in which you are living is virtually hell.' Then he gave his version of your Ten Commandments. If you had said to him, 'We may be in hell; but we feel extremely comfortable', Ruskin, being a genuinely religious man, would have replied, 'That simply shows that you are dammed to the uttermost depths of damnation, because not only are you in hell, but you like being in hell'.

Ruskin got no farther than that in political economy. It was really a pregnant contribution; but he did not go on. Having knocked the spurious law of value into a cocked hat, he did not go on to discover a scientific law of value; and he took no interest in and never reached that other very revolutionary law, the law of economic rent. I see no sign in his writings that he ever discovered it.

When Karl Marx (let me make this contrast) demonstrated that, in his phrase, the working-man was being exploited by the Capitalist—and Karl Marx took a great deal of trouble to establish what he called the rate of surplus value: that is to say, the rate at which the Capitalist was robbing the working-man—he made a pretence of doing the thing mathematically. He was not a mathematician; but he had a weakness for posing as a mathematician and using algebraic symbols. He tried to determine the quantitative aspect of exploitation. That sort of thing did not interest Ruskin. Ruskin said to the Capitalist, 'You are either a thief or an honest man. I have discovered that you are a thief. It does not matter to me whether you are a fifty per cent. thief or a seventy per cent. thief. That may be interesting to men of business who are interested in figures. I am not. Sufficient to me that you are a thief. Having found out that you are a thief, I can now tell you what your taste in art will be. And as I do not like a thievish taste in art I suggest you should become an honest man.' And I dare say the Capitalists who read it said: 'Aha! that serves Jones right!' I doubt if they ever applied it to themselves.

* * *

I think I can give you a simpler illustration of the importance of the economic basis, and why it was that Ruskin, beginning as an artist with an interest in art—exactly as I did myself, by the way—was inevitably driven back to economics, and to the conviction that your art would never come right whilst your economics were wrong.

The illustration I will give you is this. Here am I addressing you, a cultivated audience. I wish to keep before you the most elevated view of all the questions Ruskin dealt with. I am straining all my mental faculties and drawing on all my knowledge. Now suppose you were to chain me to this table and invite me to go on and on. What would happen? Well, after some hours a change would take place in the relative importance of the things presenting themselves to my mind. At first, I should be thinking of Ruskin, and attending to my business here as a lecturer on Ruskin. But at last my attention would shift from the audience in front of me to that corner of the room behind me, because that is where the refreshment room is. I should in fact be thinking of nothing but my next meal. I should finally reach a point at which, though I am a vegetarian, I should be looking at the chubbiest person in the audience, and wishing I could eat that chubby person.

That is the real soundness of Marxism and of Ruskin's change of ground from art to economics. You may aim at making a man cultured and religious; but you must feed him first; and you must feed him to the point at which he is reasonably happy, because if you feed him only to the point at which you can make a bare drudge of him and not make him happy, then in his need for a certain degree of happiness he will go and buy artificial happiness at the public-house and other places. Working-men do that at the present day: indeed we all do it to a certain extent, because all our lives are made more or less unhappy by our economic slavery, whether we are slaves or masters. Economics are fundamental in politics: you must begin with the feeding of the individual. Unless you build on that, all your superstructure will be rotten.

There you have the condition postulated by Marx and every sensible man. That is why Ruskin, when he was twenty, gave you *Modern*

Painters, and at thirty, *The Stones of Venice*, also about art, but very largely about the happiness of working-men who made the art; for the beauty of Venice is a reflection of the happiness of the men who made Venice. When he was forty he wrote *Unto this Last*, and there took you very far away from art and very close to politics. At fifty he gave us the *Inaugural Lectures*, and, finally, *Fors Clavigera*,* in which you find his most tremendous invectives against modern society.

Now since Ruskin's contemporaries neglected him politically because they found the plain meaning of his words incredible, I put the question whether in the course of time there has developed any living political activity on behalf of which you might enlist Ruskin if he were living at the present time. It goes without saying, of course, that he was a Communist. He was quite clear as to that. But now comes the question, What was his attitude towards Democracy? Well, it was another example of the law that no really great man is ever a democrat in the vulgar sense, by which I mean that sense in which Democracy is identified with our modern electoral system and our system of voting. Ruskin never gave one moment's quarter to all that. He set no store by it whatever, any more than his famous contemporary, Charles Dickens—in his own particular department the most gifted English writer since Shakespeare, and resembling Ruskin in being dominated by a social conscience. Dickens was supposed to be an extremely popular person, always on the side of the people against the ruling class; whereas Ruskin might, as a comparatively rich University man, have been expected to be on the other side. Yet Dickens gives no more quarter to Democracy than Ruskin. He begins by unmasking mere superficial abuses like the Court of Chancery* and imprisonment for debt, imagining them to be fundamental abuses. Then, suddenly discovering that it is the whole framework of society that is wrong, he writes *Hard Times*, and after that becomes a prophet as well as a storyteller. You must not imagine that prophets are a dead race, who died with Habakkuk and Joel.* The prophets are always with us. We have [*indicating Dr Inge, the Dean of St Paul's**] some of them in this room at the present time. But Dickens the prophet is never Dickens the Democrat. Take any book of his in which he plays his peculiar trick of putting before you some shameful social abuse, and then asking what is to be done about it! Does he in any single instance say: 'You working-men who have the majority of votes: what are you going to do about it?' He never does. He always appeals to the aristocracy. He says: 'Your Majesty, my lords and gentlemen, right honourables and wrong honourables of every degree: what have you to say to this?' When he introduces a working-man, he may make that working-man complain bitterly that society is all wrong; but when the plutocrats turn round on that man and say to him, 'Oh, you think yourself very clever. What would you do? You complain about everything. What would you do to set things right?' he makes the working-man say, 'It is not for the like of me to say. It is the business of people who have the power and the knowledge to understand these things, and take it on themselves to right them.' That is the attitude of Dickens, and the attitude of Ruskin; and that really is my attitude as well. The people at large are occupied with their own special jobs; and the reconstruction of society is a very special job indeed. To tell the people to make their own laws is to mock them just as I should mock you if I said, 'Gentlemen: you are the people: write your own plays'. The people are the judges of the laws and of plays; but they can never be the makers of them.

Thus Ruskin, like Dickens, understood that the reconstruction of society must be the work of an energetic and conscientious minority. Both of them knew that the government of a country is always the work of a minority, energetic, possibly conscientious, possibly the reverse, too often a merely predatory minority which produces an illusion of conscientiousness by setting up a convention that what they want for their own advantage is for the good of society. They pay very clever people to prove it; and the clever people argue themselves into believing it. The Manchester or anti-Ruskin school had plenty of sincere and able apologists. If you read Austin's lectures on jurisprudence,* for instance, you will find a more complete acknowledgement of the horrors inevitable under Capitalism than in most Socialist writers, because Austin had convinced himself that they are the price of liberty and of progress. But then nobody in his day conceived Socialism as a practical alternative: indeed it was not then practicable. Austin's argument, or rather his choice of evils, is no longer forced on us; so we need not concern ourselves about it except as a demonstration that Ruskin's scepticism as to government by the people as distinguished from government of the people for the people is shared by his most extreme and logical opponents as well as by his kindred spirits.

Is there, then, any existing political system in operation in Europe at this moment which combines Communism with a belief in government by an energetic and enlightened minority, and whose leaders openly say, 'There is no use talking about Democracy. If reforms are to wait until a majority of the people are converted to an intelligent belief in them, no reforms will ever be made at all. If we, whose intentions are honest, wait for such an impossible conversion, the only result of our sitting down and doing nothing will be that another energetic majority, whose intentions are evil, will seize the lead and govern in our stead. Democracy in that sense would be merely an excuse to enable us to go on talking, without ever being called upon to take the responsibility of doing anything. Moreover, our opponents would kill us'?

* * *

So it comes to this, that when we look for a party which could logically claim Ruskin to-day as one of its prophets, we find it in the Bolshevist party.* (Laughter.) You laugh at this. You feel it to be absurd. But I have given you a demonstration; and I want you now to pick a hole in the demonstration if you can. You got out of the difficulty in Ruskin's own time by saying that he was a Tory. He said so himself. But then you did not quite grasp the fact that all Socialists are Tories in that sense. The Tory is a man who believes that those who are qualified by nature and training for public work, and who are naturally a minority, have to govern the mass of the people. That is Toryism. That is also Bolshevism. The Russian masses elected a National Assembly: Lenin and the Bolshevists ruthlessly shoved it out of the way, and indeed shot it out of the way as far as it refused to be shoved.

Some of you, in view of the shooting, repudiate Bolshevism as a blood-stained tyranny, and revolt against the connexion of Ruskin's name with it. But if you are never going to follow any prophet in whose name Governments have been guilty of killing those who resist them, you will have to repudiate your country, your religion, and your humanity. Let us be humble. There is no use in throwing these terms at one another. You cannot repudiate religion because it has been connected with the atrocities of the wars of religion. You cannot, for instance, ask any Roman Catholic to repudiate his Church because of the things that were done in the Inquisition, or any Protestant to admit that Luther must stand or fall by the acts of the soldiers of Gustavus Adolphus.* All you can do is to deplore the atrocities. Lenin said the other day, 'Yes: there have been atrocities; and they have not all been inevitable'. I wish every other statesman in Europe had the same candour. Look at all that has been done not only by Bolshevists, but by anti-Bolshevists, by ourselves, and by all the belligerents! There is only one thing that it becomes us to say; and that is, 'God forgive us all'.

KEATS

It is very difficult to say anything about Keats except that he was a poet. His merits are a matter of taste. Anyone who can read his best lines without being enchanted by them is verse-deaf. But whether the enchantment works or fails there is nothing more to be said. Other poets have other strings to their bows. Macaulay could have written a very interesting essay on Shelley without liking or even mentioning a line of his verse. He did write a very interesting essay on Byron,* which would have been equally readable had Byron been an amateur like Count D'Orsay.* Societies have been established to discuss Browning; and they would not have held a meeting the less if Browning had been a revivalist preacher who had never penned a rhyme in his life. But out of Keats Macaulay could not have made two pages; and a Keats Society would be gravelled for lack of matter half-way through its first sitting unless it resolved itself into a Fanny Brawne Society,* when it might conceivably make good for a few evenings of gossip. Being at this moment asked to write about Keats, a thing I should never have dreamt of doing on my own initiative, I find myself with nothing to say except that you cannot write about Keats.

Another way of putting this is to say that he was the most literary of all the major poets: literary to the verge of being but the greatest of the minor poets; only, if you go over that verge you achieve a *reductio ad absurdum*; for the strength of a poet is the strength of his strongest lines; and Keats's strongest lines are so lovely, and there are so many of them, that to think of him as a minor poet is impossible. Even his worst lines: for example,

> A bunch of blooming plums
> Ready to melt between an infant's gums,*

have nothing minor about them; they are not poor would-be lines: they are brazenly infamous, like Shakespear's

> In a most hideous and dreadful manner,*

which I once accused Ellen Terry of having improvised to cover a lapse of memory, so incredible it seemed that Shakespear should have perpetrated it.

What I mean by a literary poet is one who writes poetry for the sake of writing poetry; who lisps in numbers because he prefers that method of utterance; who wants to be a poet as if that were an end in itself. Such a one will force the forms and graces of poetry on the most prosaic subject matter, and turn a page of prose into a thousand lines of epic. Poe, a master of both prose and verse, complained that epics are not really homogeneous poems, but patches of poetry embroidered on long stretches of prosaic fabric disguised as poetry by the arts of versification. Even Milton did this, though no man knew better than he that prose has a music of its own, and that many pensters write verses because their ears are not good enough to enable them to write readable prose, and because, though nobody will give them any credit for calling a window a window, lots of people will take them for poets if they call it a casement.

Now Keats was the sort of youth who calls a window a casement. That was why the reviewers told him to go back to his gallipots.* Critics who are only waiting for a chance to make themselves disagreeable trip themselves by jumping at the chance, when it comes, without looking before they leap. If an apothecary's apprentice happens to be born a poet, one of the first symptoms of his destiny will be a tendency to call windows casements (on paper). The fact that if he is born a poetaster the symptoms will be just the same, may mislead a bad critic, but not a good one, unless the good one (as often happens) is such a snob that when he has to review the poems of a shopman the critic in him is killed by the snob. If Keats had ever described a process so remote from Parnassus* as the taking down and putting up of the shop shutters, he would have described them in terms of a radiant sunrise and a voluptuous sunset, with the red and green bottles as heavenly bodies and the medicines as Arabian Balsams.* What a good critic would have said to him was not 'Go back to your gallipots,'* but 'If you can call a window a casement with such magical effect, for heaven's sake leave your gallipots and do nothing but write poetry all your life.'

The other sort of poet is the one for whom poetry is only a means to an end, the end being to deliver a message which clamors to be revealed through him. So he secures a hearing for it by clothing it with word-garments of such beauty, authority, and eternal memorableness, that the world must needs listen to it. These are prophets rather than poets; and for the sake of being poets alone would not take the trouble to rhyme love and dove or bliss and kiss.

It often happens that a prophet-poet begins as a literary poet, the prophet instinctively training himself by literary exercises for his future work. Thus you have Morris exercising himself in his youth by re-writing all the old stories in very lovely verses, but conscientiously stating at the beginning that he is only 'the idle singer of an empty day.' Later on he finds his destiny as propagandist and prophet, the busy singer of a bursting day. Now if Morris had lived no longer than Keats, he would have been an even more exclusively literary poet, because Keats achieved the very curious feat of writing one poem of which it may be said that if Karl Marx can be imagined as writing a poem instead of a treatise on Capital, he would have written Isabella.* The immense indictment of the profiteers and exploiters with which Marx has shaken capitalistic civilization to its foundations, even to its overthrow in Russia, is epitomized in

> With her two brothers this fair lady dwelt
>   Enrichéd from ancestral merchandise;
> And for them many a weary hand did swelt
>   In torchéd mines and noisy factories;
> And many once proud-quivered loins did melt
>   In blood from stinging whip: with hollow eyes
> Many all day in dashing river stood
> To take the rich-ored driftings of the flood.
>
> For them the Ceylon diver held his breath,
>   And went all naked to the hungry shark:
> For them his ears gushed blood: for them in death
>   The seal on the cold ice with piteous bark
> Lay full of darts: for them alone did seethe
>   A thousand men in troubles wide and dark.
> Half ignorant, they turned an easy wheel
> That set sharp racks at work to pinch and peel.
>
> Why were they proud? Because their marble founts
>   Gush'd with more pride than do a wretch's tears?
> Why were they proud? Because fair orange-mounts
>   Were of more soft ascent than lazar stairs?
> Why were they proud? Because red-lin'd accounts
>   Were richer than the songs of Grecian years?
> Why were they proud? Again we ask aloud,
> Why in the name of Glory were they proud?*

Everything that the Bolshevik stigmatizes when he uses the epithet 'bourgeois' is expressed forcibly, completely, and beautifully in those three stanzas, written half a century before the huge tide of middle-class commercial optimism and complacency began to ebb in the wake of the planet Marx. Nothing could well be more literary than the wording: it is positively euphuistic. But it contains all the Factory Commission Reports that Marx read, and that Keats did not read because they were not yet written in his time. And so Keats is among the prophets with

Shelley, and, had he lived, would no doubt have come down from Hyperions and Endymions* to tin tacks as a very full-blooded modern revolutionist. Karl Marx is more euphuistic in calling the profiteers *bourgeoisie* than Keats with his 'these same ledger-men.'* Ledger-men is at least better English than bourgeois: there would be some hope for it yet if it had not been supplanted by profiteer.

Keats also anticipated Erewhon Butler's gospel of Laodicea* in the lines beginning (Shakespeareanly) with

> How fever'd is the man who cannot look
> Upon his mortal days with temperate blood!*

triumphantly driving home the nail at the end with (Words-worthily)

> Why then should Man, teasing the world for grace,
> Spoil his salvation for a fierce miscreed?

On the whole, in spite of the two idle epics, voluptuously literary, and the holiday globe-trotting 'from silken Samarcand to cedar'd Lebanon,'* Keats manages to affirm himself as a man as well as a poet, and to win a place among the great poets in virtue of a future he never lived to see, and of poems he never lived to write. And he contributed a needed element to that august Communion of Saints: the element of geniality, rarely associated with lyrical genius of the first order. Dante is not notably genial. Milton can do a stunt of geniality, as in L'Allegro;* but one does not see him exuberantly fighting the butcher, as Keats is said to have done. Wordsworth,* cheerful at times as a pious duty, is not genial. Cowper's John Gilpin is a turnpike tragedy. Even the thought of Shelley kills geniality. Chesterton's resolute conviviality is about as genial as an *auto da fé** of teetotallers. Byron's joy is derision. When Moore is merry he ceases to be a poet so utterly that we are tempted to ask when did he begin. Landor and Browning are capable of Olympian joviality: their notion of geniality is shying thunderbolts. Mr Pecksniff, saying 'Let us be merry' and taking a captain's biscuit, is as successful as most of them. If Swinburne* had attempted to be genial he would have become a mere blackguard; and Tennyson would have been like a jeweller trying to make golliwogs. Keats alone remains for us not only a poet, but a merry soul, a jolly fellow, who could not only carry his splendid burthen of genius, but swing it round, toss it up and catch it again, and whistle a tune as he strode along.

But there is no end to talking about poets; and it often prevents people reading them; so enough.

TOLSTOY: TRAGEDIAN OR COMEDIAN?

WAS Tolstoy tragedian or comedian? The popular definition of tragedy is heavy drama in which everyone is killed in the last act, comedy being light drama in which everyone is married in the last act. The classical definition is, of tragedy, drama that purges the soul by pity and terror, and, of comedy, drama that chastens morals by ridicule. These classical definitions, illustrated by Eschylus-Sophocles-Euripides *versus* Aristophanes* in the ancient Greek theatre, and Corneille-Racine *versus* Molière in the French theatre, are still much the best the critic can work with. But the British school has always scandalized classic scholarship and French taste by defying them: nothing will prevent the English playwright from mixing comedy, and even tomfoolery, with tragedy. Lear may pass for pure tragedy; for even the fool in Lear is tragic; but Shakespear could not keep the porter out of Macbeth nor the clown out of Antony and Cleopatra. We are incorrigible in this respect, and may as well make a merit of it.

We must therefore recognize and examine a third variety of drama. It begins as tragedy with scraps of fun in it, like Macbeth, and ends as comedy without mirth in it, the place of mirth being taken by a more or less bitter and critical irony. We do not call the result melodrama, because that term has come to mean drama in which crude emotions are helped to expression by musical accompaniment. Besides, there is at first no true new species: the incongruous elements do not combine: there is simply frank juxtaposition of fun with terror in tragedy and of gravity with levity in comedy. You have Macbeth; and you have Le Misanthrope, Le Festin de Pierre, All's Well That Ends Well, Troilus and Cressida: all of them, from the Aristotelian and Voltairean point of view,* neither fish, fowl, nor good red herring.

When the censorship killed serious drama in England, and the dramatists had to express themselves in novels,* the mixture became more lawless than ever: it was practised by Fielding and culminated in Dickens, whose extravagances would have been severely curbed if he had had to submit his Micawbers and Mrs Wilfers* to the test of representation on the stage, when it would have been discovered at once that their parts are mere repetitions of the same joke, and have none of that faculty of developing and advancing matters which constitutes stage action

* * *

After Dickens, Comedy completed its development into the new species, which has been called tragi-comedy when any attempt has been made to define it. Tragedy itself never developed: it was simple, sublime, and overwhelming from the first: it either failed and was not tragedy at all or else it got there so utterly that no need was felt for going any further. The only need felt was for relief; and therefore, though tragedy remains unchanged from Eschylus to Richard Wagner (Europe's last great tragic poet), the reaction to a moment of fun which we associate with Shakespear got the upper hand even of Eschylus, and produced his comic sentinels who, afraid to go to the rescue of Agamemnon, pretend that nothing is happening, just as it got the better of Victor Hugo, with his Don Cæsar de Bazan tumbling down the chimney, and his Rustighello playing Wamba to the Duke of Ferrara's Cedric the Saxon.* But in the main Tragedy remained on its summit, simple, unmixed, and heroic, from Sophocles to Verdi.

Not so Comedy. When the Merry Wives of Windsor gave way to Marriage à la Mode, Romeo to Hamlet, Punch to Don Juan, Petruchio to Almaviva,* and, generally, horseplay and fun for fun's sake to serious chastening of morals less and less by ridicule and more and more by irony, the comic poet becoming less and less a fellow of infinite jest and more and more a satirical rogue and a discloser of essentially tragic ironies, the road was open to a sort of comedy as much more tragic than a catastrophic tragedy as an unhappy marriage, or even a happy one, is more tragic than a railway accident. Shakespear's bitter play with a bitter title, All's Well That Ends Well, anticipates Ibsen: the happy ending at which the title sneers is less comforting than the end of Romeo and Juliet. And Ibsen was the dramatic poet who firmly established tragi-comedy as a much deeper and grimmer entertainment than tragedy. His heroes dying without hope or honor, his dead, forgotten, superseded men walking and talking with the ghosts of the past, are all heroes of comedy: their existence and their downfall are not soul-purifying convulsions of pity and horror, but reproaches, challenges, criticisms addressed to society and to the spectator as a voting constituent of society. They are miserable and yet not hopeless; for they are mostly criticisms of false intellectual positions which, being intellectual, are remediable by better thinking.

Thus Comedy has become the higher form. The element of accident in Tragedy has always been its weak spot;* for though an accident may be sensational, nothing can make it interesting or save it from being irritating. Othello is spoilt by a handkerchief, as Shakespear found out afterwards when he wrote A Winter's Tale. The curtain falls on The School for Scandal* just when the relations between the dishonorable Joseph Surface and the much more dishonorable Lady Teazle have become interesting for the first moment in the play. In its tragedy and comedy alike, the modern tragi-comedy begins where the old tragedies and comedies left off; and we have actually had plays made and produced dealing with what happened to Ibsen's *dramatis personae* before the first act began.

Tolstoy is now easily classed as a tragi-comedian, pending the invention of a better term. Of all the dramatic poets he has the most withering touch when he wants to destroy. His novels shew this over and over again. A man enters a house where someone lies dead.* There is no moralizing, no overt irony: Tolstoy, with the simplicity he affects so well, just tells you that the undertaker has left the coffin lid propped against the wall in the entrance hall, and that the visitor goes into the drawing room and sits down on a *pouf*. Instantly the mockery and folly of our funeral pomps and cemetery sentimentalities laugh in our faces. A judge goes into court to set himself up as divine justice and send his fellow-creatures to the gallows. Tolstoy does not improve the occasion or allow his brow to contract or his eye to twinkle; but he mentions that before the judge leaves his room he goes through a few gymnastic exercises. Instantly that judge is in the mud with his ermine and scarlet making him and all judges unspeakably ridiculous. Dickens makes us laugh by describing how the handle of the Orfling's corkscrew comes off and hits her on the chin.* We applaud the wanton humorist; but the Orfling is none the worse five minutes later. Tolstoy could slay a soul with a corkscrew without letting you know either that he was a humorist or that you are laughing.

This terrible but essentially comedic method is the method of all Tolstoy's plays except the first, The Powers of Darkness, which is, on the whole, a true tragedy. His Fruits of Culture, coming long before Granville-Barker's Marrying of Ann Leete or the plays of Tchekov, is the first of the Heartbreak Houses,* and the most blighting. He touches with his pen the drawing room, the kitchen, the doormat in the entrance hall, and the toilet tables upstairs. They wither like the garden of Klingsor at the sign of Parsifal. The Living Corpse* is as alive as most fine gentlemen are. But gentry as an institution crumble to dust at his casual remark that unless a gentleman gets a berth under Government as soldier or diplomatist, there is nothing left for him to do but to kill himself with wine and women. It is a case of 'God damn you, merry gentlemen: let all things you dismay.'*

But Tolstoy's masterpiece is his Light Shining Through Darkness.*
In it he turns his deadly touch suicidally on himself. The blight falls on
him ruthlessly. That the hero of Sevastopol* becomes a second-rate
dug-out is nothing. That the Levine of Anna Karenina* becomes
a common domestic quarreller is hardly noticed. It is the transfiguration of the great prophet into a clumsy mischievous cruel fool that
makes the tragi-comedy. Mr Aylmer Maude, in his biography of Tolstoy,*
holds the scales very fairly between husband and wife, and gives no
quarter to the notion that a great man can do no wrong; but where he is
respectfully critical Tolstoy himself is derisively merciless. He does not
even pay himself the compliment of finishing the play. He left the last
act unwritten, but with precise instructions as to how he was to be shot
in it like a mad dog by the mother of the young man he had ruined by
his teaching as he ruined everyone else who listened to him.

Nevertheless Tolstoy does not really give the verdict against himself:
he only shews that he was quite aware of the disastrousness of his
negative anarchistic doctrine, and was prepared to face that disastrousness sooner than accept and support robbery and violence merely
because the robbers and militarists had acquired political power enough
to legalize them. It must be assumed that if everyone refused compli-
ance, the necessities of the case would compel social reconstruction on
honest and peaceful lines. His own notions of such reconstruction did
not go apparently beyond an uncritical acceptance of Henry George's
demonstration of the need for land nationalization;* and he does not
seem to have foreseen that any reconstruction whatever must involve
more State compulsion of the individual than the present system,
which relies for its unofficial but omnipresent compulsion on the pressure of circumstances brought about by the destitution of the proletariat. Tolstoy, like the rather spoiled aristocrat, natural and artificial, that
he was, could not stand compulsion, and instinctively refused to give
his mind to the practical problem of social reconstruction on his principles: that is, how to organize the equitable sharing among us of the
burden of that irreducible minimum of exertion without which we must
perish: a matter involving, as Lenin has discovered, a considerable
shooting up of the recalcitrant.* Like many other prophets, he preached
the will without finding the way. Therefore his influence was extremely
dangerous to individual fools (he included himself among the number
in Light Shining Through Darkness); but he is a great Social Solvent,
revealing to us, as a master of tragi-comic drama, the misery and
absurdity of the idle proud life for which we sacrifice our own honor
and the happiness of our neighbors.

BEETHOVEN'S CENTENARY

A HUNDRED years ago a crusty old bachelor of fifty-seven, so deaf that he could not hear his own music played by a full orchestra, yet still able to hear thunder, shook his fist at the roaring heavens for the last time, and died as he had lived, challenging God and defying the universe. He was Defiance Incarnate: he could not even meet a Grand Duke and his court in the street without jamming his hat tight down on his head and striding through the very middle of them. He had the manners of a disobliging steamroller (most steamrollers are abjectly obliging and conciliatory); and he was rather less particular about his dress than a scarecrow: in fact he was once arrested as a tramp because the police refused to believe that such a tatterdemalion could be a famous composer, much less a temple of the most turbulent spirit that ever found expression in pure sound. It was indeed a mighty spirit; but if I had written the mightiest, which would mean mightier than the spirit of Handel, Beethoven himself would have rebuked me; and what mortal man could pretend to a spirit mightier than Bach's? But that Beethoven's spirit was the most turbulent is beyond all question. The impetuous fury of his strength, which he could quite easily contain and control, but often would not, and the uproariousness of his fun, go beyond anything of the kind to be found in the works of other composers. Greenhorns write of syncopation now as if it were a new way of giving the utmost impetus to a musical measure; but the rowdiest jazz sounds like The Maiden's Prayer* after Beethoven's third Leonora overture; and certainly no negro corobbery* that I ever heard could inspire the blackest dancer with such *diable au corps** as the last movement of the Seventh Symphony. And no other composer has ever melted his hearers into complete sentimentality by the tender beauty of his music, and then suddenly turned on them and mocked them with derisive trumpet blasts for being such fools. Nobody but Beethoven could govern Beethoven; and when, as happened when the fit was on him, he deliberately refused to govern himself, he was ungovernable.

It was this turbulence, this deliberate disorder, this mockery, this reckless and triumphant disregard of conventional manners, that set Beethoven apart from the musical geniuses of the ceremonious seventeenth and eighteenth centuries. He was a giant wave in that storm of the human spirit which produced the French Revolution. He called no man master. Mozart, his greatest predecessor in his own department, had from his childhood been washed, combed, splendidly dressed, and beautifully behaved in the presence of royal personages and peers. His childish outburst at the Pompadour, 'Who is this woman who does not kiss me? The Queen kisses me,'* would be incredible of Beethoven, who was still an unlicked cub even when he had grown into a very grizzly bear. Mozart had the refinement of convention and society as well as the refinement of nature and of the solitudes of the soul. Mozart and Gluck are refined as the court of Louis XIV* was refined: Haydn is refined as the most cultivated country gentlemen of his day were refined: compared to them socially Beethoven was an obstreperous Bohemian: a man of the people. Haydn, so superior to envy that he declared his junior, Mozart, to be the greatest composer that ever lived, could not stand Beethoven: Mozart, more farseeing, listened to his playing, and said 'You will hear of him some day'; but the two would never have hit it off together had Mozart lived long enough to try. Beethoven had a moral horror of Mozart, who in Don Giovanni had thrown a halo of enchantment round an aristocratic blackguard, and then, with the unscrupulous moral versatility of a born dramatist, turned round to cast a halo of divinity round Sarastro, setting his words to the only music yet written that would not sound out of place in the mouth of God.

Beethoven was no dramatist: moral versatility was to him revolting cynicism. Mozart was still to him the master of masters (this is not an empty eulogistic superlative: it means literally that Mozart is a composer's composer much more than he has ever been a really popular composer); but he was a court flunkey in breeches whilst Beethoven was a Sansculotte;* and Haydn also was a flunkey in the old livery: the Revolution stood between them as it stood between the eighteenth and nineteenth centuries. But to Beethoven Mozart was worse than Haydn because he trifled with morality by setting vice to music as magically as virtue. The Puritan who is in every true Sansculotte rose up against him in Beethoven, though Mozart had shewn him all the possibilities of nineteenth-century music. So Beethoven cast back for a hero to Handel, another crusty old bachelor of his own kidney, who despised Mozart's hero Gluck, though the pastoral symphony in The Messiah* is the nearest thing in music to the scenes in which Gluck, in his Orfeo, opened to us the plains of Heaven.

Thanks to broadcasting, millions of musical novices will hear the music of Beethoven this anniversary year* for the first time with their expectations raised to an extraordinary pitch by hundreds of newspaper articles piling up all the conventional eulogies that are applied indiscriminately to all the great composers. And like his contemporaries they will be puzzled by getting from him not merely a music that they did not expect, but often an orchestral hurlyburly that they may not recognize as what they call music at all, though they can appreciate Gluck and Haydn and Mozart quite well. The explanation is simple enough. The music of the eighteenth century is all dance music. A dance is a symmetrical pattern of steps that are pleasant to move to; and its music is a symmetrical pattern of sound that is pleasant to listen to even when you are not dancing to it. Consequently the sound patterns, though they begin by being as simple as chessboards, get lengthened and elaborated and enriched with harmonies until they are more like Persian carpets; and the composers who design these patterns no longer expect people to dance to them. Only a whirling Dervish* could dance a Mozart symphony: indeed, I have reduced two young and practised dancers to exhaustion by making them dance a Mozart overture. The very names of the dances are dropped: instead of suites consisting of sarabands, pavanes, gavottes, and jigs, the designs are presented as sonatas and symphonies consisting of sections called simply movements, and labelled according to their speed (in Italian) as allegros, adagios, scherzos, and prestos. But all the time, from Bach's preludes to Mozart's Jupiter Symphony,* the music makes a symmetrical sound pattern, and gives us the dancer's pleasure always as the form and foundation of the piece.

Music, however, can do more than make beautiful sound patterns. It can express emotion. You can look at a Persian carpet and listen to a Bach prelude with a delicious admiration that goes no further than itself; but you cannot listen to the overture to Don Giovanni without being thrown into a complicated mood which prepares you for a tragedy of some terrible doom overshadowing an exquisite but Satanic gaiety. If you listen to the last movement of Mozart's Jupiter Symphony, you hear that it is as much a riotous corobbery as the last movement of Beethoven's Seventh Symphony: it is an orgy of ranting drumming tow-row-row, made poignant by an opening strain of strange and painful beauty which is woven through the pattern all through. And yet the movement is a masterpiece of pattern designing all the time.

Now what Beethoven did, and what made some of his greatest contemporaries give him up as a madman with lucid intervals of clowning and bad taste, was that he used music altogether as a means of expressing moods, and completely threw over pattern designing as an end in itself. It is true that he used the old patterns all his life with dogged conservatism (another Sansculotte characteristic, by the way); but he imposed on them such an overwhelming charge of human energy and passion, including that highest passion which accompanies thought, and reduces the passion of the physical appetites to mere animalism, that he not only played Old Harry with their symmetry but often made it impossible to notice that there was any pattern at all beneath the storm of emotion. The Eroica Symphony* begins by a pattern (borrowed from an overture which Mozart wrote when he was a boy), followed by a couple more very pretty patterns; but they are tremendously energized, and in the middle of the movement the patterns are torn up savagely; and Beethoven, from the point of view of the mere pattern musician, goes raving mad, hurling out terrible chords in which all the notes of the scale are sounded simultaneously, just because he feels like that, and wants you to feel like it.

And there you have the whole secret of Beethoven. He could design patterns with the best of them; he could write music whose beauty will last you all your life; he could take the driest sticks of themes and work them up so interestingly that you find something new in them at the hundredth hearing: in short, you can say of him all that you can say of the greatest pattern composers; but his diagnostic, the thing that marks him out from all the others, is his disturbing quality, his power of unsettling us and imposing his giant moods on us. Berlioz was very angry with an old French composer who expressed the discomfort Beethoven gave him by saying '*J'aime la musique qui me berce*,'* 'I like music that lulls me.' Beethoven's is music that wakes you up; and the one mood in which you shrink from it is the mood in which you want to be let alone.

When you understand this you will advance beyond the eighteenth century and the old-fashioned dance band (jazz, by the way, is the old dance band Beethovenized),* and understand not only Beethoven's music, but what is deepest in post-Beethoven music as well.

MY FIRST TALKIE

To the uninitiated general patrons of the Talkies the little film entitled How He Lied to Her Husband is a talkie like any other talkie.* To those behind the scenes it is an experiment. Like all playwrights, I have had many proposals from the great film corporations for the screening of my plays, some of them tempting enough commercially. In the days of the Movies the objection to these proposals was that my plays were made to be spoken and could be of no use as silent plays,* no matter how ingeniously they were patched by scraps of printed dialogue thrown on the screen as 'sub-titles.' When the Talkies arrived the situation was changed. It became possible for the screen not only to shew my plays, but to speak them. The rejected proposals were renewed.*

But when we came down to the tacks, I found that the film corporations were nearly as far as ever from real play screening. The only business they had mastered was the Movie business; and their notion of a screened play was really only a Movie with spoken sub-titles. The only use they had for a play was to re-arrange it as a Movie in which the actors were occasionally heard as well as seen; and the movie stars, instead of putting drama into their voices, put it, as they were accustomed to, into their facial expression and gesture, and then repeated the words by rote, unmeaningly and often very discordantly. Though they had acquired to perfection the special art of moving for the lens, they had no idea of the equally special art of speaking for the microphone.

In this phase the talkie art was quite useless to me. My plays do not consist of occasional remarks to illustrate pictures, but of verbal fencing matches between protagonists and antagonists, whose thrusts and ripostes, parries and passados, follow one another much more closely than thunder follows lightning. The first rule for their producers is that there must never be a moment of silence from the rise of the curtain to its fall. Hollywood would not hear of such a condition: it was, they said, impossible. To cut out half my dialogue, in order to insert dozens of changing pictures between the lines of what was left, seemed to them quite indispensable. So we parted with reciprocal assurances of the highest consideration, but—nothing doing.

It was, I think, the great success of the talking films in which Mr George Arliss* appeared that first shook the Hollywood superstition. Mr Arliss's performances proved that a good play could be a good play, and good acting good acting, on the screen exactly as on the stage. British

International Pictures resolved to try an experiment in the new manner; and I placed How He Lied to Her Husband at their disposal for the purpose. Mr Cecil Lewis,* a playwright and stage producer, keen on developing the talkie dramatically, and free from Hollywood superstitions, undertook the direction.

The result can be seen and heard at the Malvern Picture House* during the Festival. The points for connoisseurs are (*a*) that the dialogue is continuous from end to end, except when Mr Gwenn* purposely makes a silence more dramatic than words could be, and (*b*) that as the entire action takes place in the same room, the usual changes from New York to the Rocky Mountains, from Marseilles to the Sahara, from Mayfair to Monte Carlo, are replaced by changes from the piano to the sideboard, from the window to the door, from the hearth rug to the carpet. When the husband arrives he is not shewn paying his taxi, taking out his latchkey, hanging up his hat, and mounting the stairs. There is no time for that sort of baby padding when the action of a real play is hastening to its climax. Yet I do not think anyone will miss it. It will seem incredible that only the other day Hollywood declared that such things are the life and soul of the films.

When How He Lied was produced in London the young film fans complained that the conversation of my characters was such as had never been heard except in old-fashioned nineteenth century super-literary books. The poor fellows had never read anything but a Hollywood subtitle. They could not be persuaded that English people really talk like that. My Malvern patrons will know better.

August, 1931.   G.B.S.

AM I AN EDUCATED PERSON?

I CANNOT too often repeat that though I have no academic qualifications I am in fact much more highly educated than most university scholars. My home was a musical one; and the music was the 'learned' music that began for me with Handel, and the dramatic music that began with Gluck and Mozart, the two constituting a body of modern cultural art to which the literature of the dead languages can make no pretension except in the great translations of Gilbert Murray,* which are as English and as modern as any original works in our tongue, and remind us that Shakespear also was a translator and transfigurer of old stories and not their first inventor. My family, though kindly, might be called loveless; but what did that matter to a child who could sing *A te O cara* and *Suone la tromba intrepida** before he was perfect in the Church Catechism. In these there was sentiment and chivalry enough for any child.

This education has never ceased. It has gone on from Rossini, Meyerbeer, and Verdi to Wagner, from Beethoven to Sibelius, from British dilutions of Handel and Mendelssohn to the genuine English music of Elgar and Vaughan Williams and from the wholetone mode of Debussy and the chromatic mode of Schonberg to the experiments of Cyril Scott* in the technical chaos which ensued when the forbidden consecutives and unprepared unresolved discords and 'false relations' of the old textbooks became the latest fashion. Much of it has proved the soundness of Oscar Wilde's precept 'Avoid the latest fashion or you will be hopelessly out of date in six months.'* When Wagner trumpeted unprepared major ninths at us in Tannhauser, we stopped our ears. He went on to do the same with thirteenths. They startle nobody nowadays; but they certainly startled me, who could remember being impressed as by something tremendous when I first heard Beethoven's youthful Prometheus Overture open with an unprepared diminished seventh with the seventh in the bass.

How is this for textbook jargon? Can any university graduate who has had Virgil and Homer, Horace and Juvenal,* rubbed mercilessly into him at Eton, Harrow, Winchester, or Rugby,* beat it? Is the involution of the pattern verse of John Gilpin and The Ancient Mariner into the unmeasured wamblings now printed to look like poetry more educative than the evolution from decorative dance music to the mood-expressing music of Beethoven, bridged by Mozart's miraculous gift for combining the two?

I shall be reminded that there are university musicians: Doctors of Music like Stanford and Parry.* But the effect of such degrees is to make their holders believe that they are composing when they are only covering music paper with imitations of outmoded composers, disparaging meanwhile masters like Bach and Elgar, neither of whom ever had a lesson in thoroughbass. My governess taught me my alphabet; but nobody taught me to write my plays, which were denounced as no plays until they made so much money that the fashion changed, and I was hailed successor to Shakespear.

Personal experience of contemporary developments in art is far more instructive than any study of ancient documents can be. No memorizing examinee can feel the development from Aeschylus to Euripides and its *dégringolade** to Menander as I felt the development from Donizetti to Wagner, from Bouguereau to Gauguin, from Leader to Wilson Steer and Monet, from Canova to Rodin, from Scribe and Sardou to Ibsen, from Barry Sullivan to Irving, from Colenso to Inge, from Tennyson to Browning, from Macaulay to Marx, from Max Weismann to Herbert Dingle, from Tyndall to Clerk-Maxwell, Planck, and Einstein, and from Kingdom Clifford to Hardy:* in short, from adoring rehearings of the masterpieces of the dead to the pressures on my living self of startling departures that were new to me.

Academic educational tests are better than none. Whoever has studied the steps from Aristotle to Lucretius, from Plato-cum-Socrates to Plotinus, Thucydides to Gibbon, Ptolemy to Copernicus, Saint Peter to Robert Owen, Aquinas to Hus and Luther, Erasmus* to Voltaire, can at least find out what was done last time and give certificates to those who can do it again. But without living experiences no person is educated. With nothing but academic degrees, even when overloaded by a smattering of dead languages and twopennorth of algebra, the most erudite graduates may be noodles and ignoramuses. The vital difference between reading and experience is not measurable by examination marks. On the strength of that difference I claim arrogantly to be one of the best educated men in the world, and on occasion have dismissed 95 per cent. of the academic celebrities, with all due respect for the specific talents enjoyed by a few of them, as nitwits.

It was this equipment that saved me from being starved out of literature. When William Archer delegated to me a job as a critic of painting which had been pushed on him, and for which he was quite unqualified, I rose like a rocket. My weekly feuilletons on all the fine arts in succession are still readable after sixty years. All that the exhibitions and performances that London could provide were open freely to me throughout the decade that followed my unanimous rebuffs as novelist. The better my novels the more they revolted the publishers' professional readers; but as a critic I came to the top irresistibly, whilst contemporary well-schooled literary beginners, brought up in artless British homes, could make no such mark.

These years of criticism advanced my mental education by compelling me to deliver carefully considered judgments, and to discriminate between the brilliant talents and technical accomplishments of the fashionable celebrities whose vogue ended with their deaths or sooner, and the genius that is not for an age but for all time. I heard beginners who, fresh from their teachers' coaching, gave the most promising displays. But not knowing the value of what they had been taught, they collapsed into commonplace when they escaped from tutelage. Only from such experiences can a critic become skilled in analysis, and learn that the critic who cannot analyze is easily duped.

I am still learning in my ninetysecond year.

As to languages and mathematics, my qualifications are negligible. I can read French as familiarly as English; and in Italy and Spain I can gather the news from the local papers. I know enough German to guess my way through most of the letters I receive in that language. As a linguist in conversation I am hopeless. As to mathematics I have the arithmetic (now very fallible) of an ex-cashier; but higher mathematics I can only comprehend and imagine without the smallest expertness. Technically I am a duffer; but in my day, measured by its yardsticks, I seemed an Admirable Crichton.

Great as is my debt to famous books, great pictures, and noble music for my education I should be even more ignorant than I am but for my removal at the age of ten from the street in which I was born, half of it faced with a very unpicturesque field which was soon obscured by a hoarding plastered with advertisements, to Torca Cottage, high on Dalkey Hill, commanding views of Dublin Bay from Dalkey Island to Howth Head and of Killiney Bay from the island to Bray Head, with a vast and ever changing expanse of sea and sky far below and far above.

Happiness is never my aim. Like Einstein I am not happy and do not want to be happy: I have neither time nor taste for such comas, attainable at the price of a pipeful of opium or a glass of whiskey, though I have experienced a very superior quality of it two or three times in dreams. But I had one moment of ecstatic happiness in my childhood when my mother told me that we were going to live in Dalkey. I had only to open my eyes there to see such pictures as no painter could make for me. I could not believe that such skies existed anywhere else in the world until I read Shakespear's 'this majestical roof fretted with golden fire,'* and wondered where he could have seen it if not from Torca Cottage.

The joy of it has remained with me all my life.

AYOT SAINT LAWRENCE,
3rd August 1947

THE PLAY OF IDEAS

I READ Mr Rattigan's article on this subject, and was not surprised when my friend Bridie* promptly wiped the floor with him, and subsequent contributors made hay of what was left. Let me say a word in his defence.

He is, of course, vulnerable as a reasoner; but he is not a reasoner, nor does he profess to be one. The difference between his practice and mine is that I reason out every sentence I write to the utmost of my capacity before I commit it to print, whereas he slams down everything that comes into his head without reasoning about it at all. This of course leads him into all sorts of Jack o' Lantern contradictions, dead ends, and even delusions; but as his head is a bright one and the things that come into it, reasonable or not, are all entertaining, and often penetrating and true, his practice is pleasing, whilst my reasoned-out syllogisms amuse my readers by seeming the first things that would come into a fool's head and only my fun, provoking hasty contradictions and reactions instead of stimulating thought and conviction.

Now there are ideas at the back of my plays; and Mr Rattigan does not like my plays because they are not exactly like his own, and no doubt bore him; so he instantly declares that plays that have any ideas in them are bad plays, and indeed not plays at all, but platform speeches, pamphlets, and leading articles. This is an old story! It used to take the form of complaints that my plays are all talk. Now it is quite true that my plays are all talk, just as Raphael's pictures are all paint, Michael Angelo's statues all marble, Beethoven's symphonies all noise. Mr Rattigan, not being a born fool, does not complain of this, but, being an irrational genius, does let himself in for the more absurd complaint that, though plays must be all talk, the talk should have no ideas behind it, though he knows as well as I do when, if ever, he thinks for a moment, that without a stock of ideas, mind cannot operate and plays cannot exist. The quality of a play is the quality of its ideas.

What, then, is the function of the playwright? If he only 'holds a mirror up to nature'* his vision of life will be that of a policeman on point duty. Crowds of people pass him; but why they pass him, who they are, whither they are going and why, what they will do when they pass on and what they have done before they came into his field of vision, whether they are married or single or engaged, which of them is a criminal and which a philanthropist, he cannot tell, though he knows that there are all sorts in every thousand of them.

The policeman, however, is not always on point duty. He has a home. He is a son, a brother, a husband, a father, has cousins and aunts and in-laws, has been an infant, a boy, an adolescent, has friends, male and female. He has likes and dislikes, lovings and loathings, lusts and appetites, jealousies, antipathies, propensities, tastes and talents, all the virtues, all the vices, all the common needs and all the senses in some degree. He keeps a dog or cat or parrot: perhaps all three. He has been to the seaside, and has seen trees and flowers if he has not actually cultivated them. Thus, though the passing crowd means nothing to him, there is a cross-section of it, including himself, under his daily observation that gives him as much knowledge of human nature as his mind will hold.

Everybody, being thus provided with a sample cross-section of the crowd and a faculty of observation, reasoning, and introspection, has the data for at least some biological hypotheses, however crude. But now the mysterious activity I call the Life Force, and pious people call Providence, steps in, with its trials and successes and errors, its miracles and games and caprices, its blessings and blunders and botherations. It not only varies human capacity to such a degree that what is child's play to a Napoleon, an Einstein, or a Nuffield,* is beyond the comprehension of common men, but specializes them in the most fantastic manner, notably for what children call pretending. And even their pretending is specialized. One pretender will have an irresistible propensity to figure as a King, a High Priest, a Conquering Hero. Another must make people laugh at him by pretending to be a liar, a coward, a drunkard, kicked, fooled, and degraded in every possible comic way. Now, as tragedians and clowns alike must have fictitious stories and plots invented for them, another specialization produces a class of professional liars who make no pretence that their tales are true. Here is where your playwright comes in.

But here also the differences in mental capacity come in. One playwright is capable of nothing deeper than short-lived fictitious police and divorce court cases of murder and adultery. Another can rise to the masterpieces of Æschylus, Euripides, and Aristophanes, to Hamlet, Faust, Peer Gynt, and—well, no matter: all these having to be not only entertaining, but intensely didactic (what Mr Rattigan calls plays with ideas), and long-lived enough to be hyperbolically called immortal.

And there are many gradations between these extremes: tragedy and melodrama, high and low comedy, farce and filth.

Why this occurs I do not know. If I did, I should be the supreme god among all biologists, philosophers, and dramatists. I should have solved the riddle of the universe, as every criticaster complains I have never done. Of course not. Nobody knows. Only Simple Simons ask.

Theatre technique begins with the circus clown and ringmaster and the Greek tribune, which is a glorified development of the pitch from which the poet of the market place declaims his verses, and, like Dickens's Sloppy or a modern playwright reading his play to the players, reads all the parts 'in different voices.'* On any fine Sunday in Ceylon* the street poet may still be seen declaiming his works and taking round his hat: I have seen him do it.

But you need not go so far as Ceylon to see this primitive performance. Wherever there is a queue waiting for the doors of a theatre to open you may see some vagabond artist trying to entertain it in one way or another; and that vagabond may be an incipient Shakespear or Garrick.* Nor need you go to the doors of a theatre to witness this parturition of pavement art. In Hyde Park I have seen an elderly man, dressed in black (his best, but old and seedy), step aside to the grass and address the empty air with the exordium 'Ah, fahst EEbrews is very campfitn.'* Presently people stopped to listen to him; and he had a congregation. I myself have done the same on Clapham Common, and collected sixteen shillings in my hat at the end for the Socialist cause. I have stopped on the Thames Embankment; set my back to the river wall; and had a crowd listening to me in no time. A friend of mine who happened to pass described the scene to Henry James,* who could not believe that such a thing was possible for a man of letters. He asked me at our next meeting was the tale true? I said it was. In his most impressive manner (he was always impressive) he said: 'I could not do that. I *could* not.' And from that day his affectionate regard for me was tinged with wonder and even veneration.

Now I, the roofless pavement orator, ended in the largest halls in the country with overcrowds that filled two streets. I harangued an audience of millionaires in the Metropolitan Opera House in New York.* I was specially proud of a speech in the Usher Hall in Edinburgh,* where 8,640 pennies were collected at the end.

Why do I tell this tale? Because it illustrates the development of the theatre from the pavement to the tribune and the cathedral, and the promotion of its outcasts to palaces, parliaments, and peerages. On the tribune there was no changeable picture scenery; but there were structures to represent houses, temple gates, or the like. When the tribune developed into a stage for the religious Mystery and Passion plays of the Middle Ages,* these structures were multiplied until Pilate's pretorium, Herod's palace, the mouth of hell, the Blessed Virgin's throne in heaven, the Mount of Olives, the Hill of Calvary, and the court of Caiaphas were on the stage* all through the play as now at Oberammergau, the players moving from one to the other as the action required.

Then came the Elizabethan stage (Shakespear's), with neither structures nor scenery but with a balcony above, an inner stage made with curtains called traverses, an apron stage projecting into the auditorium (relic of the innyard), and placards describing where the action was supposed to be taking place. The traverses distinguished indoor scenes from outdoor. The balcony distinguished castle ramparts from the plain below. But still there was no movable changeable scenery.

Suddenly Italian Opera came along and was tolerated and encouraged by Cromwell, who ranked the theatre as the gate of hell, but loved music. With it came changeable pictorial scenery, side wings, flats, and perspective. Still more sensational, women came on the stage as sopranos, mezzo-sopranos, and contraltos, replacing epicene boys, and founding the tradition that every actress is, or must pretend to be, sexually immoral. Opera taught me to shape my plays into recitatives, arias, duets, trios, ensemble finales, and bravura pieces to display the technical accomplishments of the executants, with the quaint result that all the critics, friendly and hostile, took my plays to be so new, so extraordinary, so revolutionary, that the Times critic declared they were not plays at all as plays had been defined for all time by Aristotle. The truth was that I was going back atavistically to Aristotle, to the tribune stage, to the circus, to the didactic Mysteries, to the word music of Shakespear, to the forms of my idol Mozart, and to the stage business of the great players whom I had actually seen acting, from Barry Sullivan, Salvini, and Ristori to Coquelin* and Chaliapin. I was, and still am, the most old-fashioned playwright outside China and Japan. But I know my business both historically and by practice as playwright and producer; and I am writing all this to show that without knowing it historically and studying critically the survivals of it that are still in practice—for instance the Westminster School performances of the ancient Latin drama, where the women's parts are played by boys as Shakespear's women's parts were, and are so effective that Shakespear must have been as strongly against having them played by women as any Holy

Willie*—no playwright can be fully qualified, nor any theatre critic know what he is pontificating about.

And so I close, I hope, this series of essays started by Mr Rattigan,* all of them entertaining in their way, but containing no convincing evidence that the writers have ever seen, written or produced a play.

EXPLANATORY NOTES

QUINTESSENCE OF IBSENISM

3 *not less than fifteen millions*: printed in 1922, the third edition followed the First World War by just four years. The second edition was published in 1913, only a year before the start of the conflict and twenty-two years after the book first appeared in 1891.

spiritual high explosive: note the allusion to Shaw's own *Major Barbara* (1905), which likewise draws a potent comparison between armaments and ideologies in pre-war Europe.

a bomb thrown at Serajevo . . . to blow the centre out of Europe: Shaw is here referencing the assassination of Archduke Franz Ferdinand (1863–1914) on 28 June 1914 by Bosnian and Serbian nationalists bent on breaking away from the Austro-Hungarian Empire, an event which led directly to the start of the First World War when Austria-Hungary invaded Serbia in response to the assassination.

reculer pour mieux sauter: (Fr.) literally, 'to retreat so as to better jump forward', conveying the idea of pulling back and regrouping to make a more aggressive move later.

4 *old prophets . . . importance of their message*: compare to Andrew Undershaft's inverse pronouncement in *Major Barbara*: 'Well, you have made for yourself something that you call a morality or a religion or what not. It doesn't fit the facts. Well, scrap it. Scrap it and get one that does fit . . . If your old religion broke down yesterday, get a newer and a better one for tomorrow' (*The Bodley Head Bernard Shaw: Collected Plays with their Prefaces*, ed. Dan H. Laurence (London: Bodley Head, 1970–4), v. 171).

5 *I have never admitted the right of an elderly author . . . former self*: Shaw would significantly revise his opinion on such matters later in life. His 1939 edition of *Pygmalion* altered the ending of the play, previously published in 1914; and his 1941 edition of *Pygmalion* integrates scenes from the 1938 screenplay. He also revised his play *Geneva* (1938) as geopolitical conditions changed. On the changes to *Pygmalion*, see Derek McGovern, 'From Stage Play to Hybrid: Shaw's Three Editions of *Pygmalion*', *SHAW* 31/1 (2011), 9–30.

What I have written I have written: Shaw is here quoting from John 19:22, wherein Pilate refuses to change the sign fastened to Jesus's cross reading 'Jesus of Nazareth, the King of the Jews' over the protests of those who want him to change it to state that Jesus merely claimed to be king of the Jews.

when he was in the pillory: when Shaw published the first edition of *The Quintessence*, Ibsen was still very much an active and, in England, controversial playwright—his play *Hedda Gabler* (1891), later considered by many to be his masterpiece, was published only a year before Shaw's book appeared and had its stage premiere in the same year as *The Quintessence*'s publication in 1891. Though Ibsen's works produced much debate (and sometimes wide condemnation) in the English press and elsewhere, he was also more of an established figure by this time than Shaw lets on. Already in 1873, the distinguished playwright was named a 'Knight of St Olaf' by the new king of Norway upon his coronation.

6 *shillings*: a unit of currency then in use in the United Kingdom. At the time, a shilling coin was worth twelve pence, and twenty shillings was worth a pound sterling. Those values changed in 1971, when a shilling became worth five pence. The shilling was removed from circulation in the UK in 1990.

le mieux est l'ennemi du bien: (Fr.) literally, 'the best is the enemy of the good'.

brass lectern eagles and the new reredos: typical ornamentation of a Christian church, the brass lectern eagle referring to the decoration on a church pulpit and the reredos being a screen or other decoration placed behind the altar.

the prostitution of Piccadilly Circus: Piccadilly Circus is a prominent road junction between Regent Street and Piccadilly in London. While prostitutes commonly worked in the area during the 1950s, Shaw is also referring to the prominent focus on commerce and public entertainment in the area, with several popular theatres being located nearby.

7 *Votes for Women*: popular slogan of the suffragette movement in Britain, which advocated for women's suffrage throughout the later nineteenth century and early twentieth. Women did not receive the right to vote in the UK until the passage of the Representation of the People Act in 1918.

The Madras House: play of 1909 by British playwright Harley Granville-Barker (1877–1946), which premiered in repertory with Shaw's *Misalliance* at the Duke of York's Theatre in London in the spring of 1910.

8 *Gorki . . . Tchekov . . . Strindberg . . . Brieux's Les Hannetons*: Shaw refers to several contemporary and near-contemporary playwrights: Russian dramatists Maxim Gorky (1868–1936) and Anton Chekhov (1860–1904), Swedish playwright (and arch-critic of Ibsen) August Strindberg (1849–1912), and French playwright Eugène Brieux (1858–1932), whose play *Les Hannetons* (*The Beetles*) (1906) he mentions. Of these, Gorky and Brieux were strongly associated with realist trends in European modern drama, as was Ibsen. Chekhov and Strindberg were associated with the development of naturalism both as a staging practice and a mode of dramaturgy.

filled three columns of The Times with a wild Strindbergian letter: the article 'Letter on Militant Hysteria' by Sir Almroth Wright (1861–1947) appeared in *The Times* on 28 March 1912. Wright was a prominent immunologist at St Mary's Hospital in Paddington, London, and an outspoken opponent of women's suffrage.

a performance of a play by myself: The Philanderer, written in 1893 but not performed until 1902.

Sardou and Tom Taylor: Victorien Sardou (1831–1908) and Tom Taylor (1817–80) were prominent playwrights of the nineteenth century, French and English respectively. Sardou was associated with the movement of bourgeois domestic drama known as the 'well-made play', while Taylor was known for writing extravaganzas and melodramas, all forms of popular dramaturgy to which Ibsen's more philosophical and socially conscious work was opposed.

9 *Tchekov's Cherry Orchard, Galsworthy's Silver Box, and Granville-Barker's Anne Leete*: all plays that premiered in London in the early 1900s. Shaw was instrumental in arranging the first English-language performance of *The Cherry Orchard* by the Stage Society for two nights in 1911. John Galworthy's (1867–1933) *Silver Box* premiered at the Royal Court Theatre in 1906 and Harvey Granville-Barker's (1877–1946) *The Marrying of Ann Leete* at Wyndham's Theatre in 1902.

Malthus: Thomas Robert Malthus (1766–1834) was an influential English economist whose book *An Essay on the Principle of Population* (1798) cautioned against unchecked population growth that could outstrip a nation's food supply. Malthus was also a curate in the Church of England, hence Shaw's reference to him as a 'churchman'.

10 *Fabian Society*: a society of British socialists founded in London in 1884, of which Shaw was a prominent and active member. The Fabians were committed to the promotion of socialist principles in England through a gradual process of discussion and influence rather than through revolutionary means.

The Fabian Essayists . . . general stock of information on Socialism in Contemporary Literature: of the aforementioned contributors to this Fabian enterprise, Sydney Olivier (1859–1943) was a civil servant and colonial secretary to the government of British Honduras; Hubert Bland (1855–1914) was a journalist and one of the founders of the Fabian Society; William Morris (1834–96) was a prominent writer, designer, and artist; Sergius Stepniak (1851–95) was a Ukrainian revolutionary and militant; and Annie Besant (1847–1933), mentioned below, was a prominent women's rights advocate also known for her support of home-rule movements in the then-British colonies of Ireland and India.

pièce d'occasion: (Fr.) an artistic work commissioned or created for a special event.

the production of Rosmersholm . . . a performance of Ghosts . . . the experiment . . . with Hedda Gabler: three seminal Ibsen productions took place in London in quick succession in the months before the publication of *The Quintessence*. Each was the play's English-language premiere. The production of *Rosmersholm*, directed by and starring Florence Farr (1860–1917), took place in March 1891 at the Vaudeville Theatre, the production of *Ghosts* at the Independent Theatre Society that same month. The production of

Hedda Gabler took place in April 1891 at the Vaudeville Theatre. J. T. Grein (1862–1935) was a Dutch-British theatre impresario who founded the Independent Theatre Society in 1891; Elizabeth Robins (1862–1952) an English actress, writer, and suffragette; and Marion Lea (1864–1944) an English actress. *The Quintessence* was first published in September 1891, just after these productions.

12 *Shelley*: Percy Bysshe Shelley (1792–1822), English Romantic poet and political radical.

tables of Consanguinity: a table or chart used to map blood relations across generations.

Herbert Spencer . . . Westermarck: Spencer (1820–1903) was an English biologist and sociologist best known today for his connection to the idea of social Darwinism and his coinage of the term 'survival of the fittest' in *Principles of Biology* in 1864. Edvard Westermarck (1862–1939) was a Finnish sociologist who studied the incest taboo and published *The History of Human Marriage* in 1891.

Laon and Cythna, Siegmund and Sieglinda: the incestuous brother-and-sister pairs in Shelley's *Laon and Cythna; or, The Revolution of the Golden City: A Vision of the Nineteenth Century* (1817) and *Die Walküre* (1870) by Richard Wagner (1813–83).

It is not wrong to take your sister as your wife: Shaw is here referencing Shelley's *Laon and Cythna* (see note above).

13 *'Any possible move . . . wrong direction'*: a famous line from *Bleak House* (1853) by Charles Dickens (1812–70), which in part involves a murder investigation.

The Quarterly Review used to attack Shelley: reference to a nineteenth-century periodical of literature and politics which frequently attacked Shelley for his radical views. See Kim Wheatley, 'Paranoid Politics: Shelley and the Quarterly Review', *Romantic Circles Praxis* (July 1997), https://romantic-circles.org/praxis/conspiracy/wheatley/kim2.html.

Clement Scott: Scott (1841–1904) was a playwright and theatre critic, best known for his work for the *Daily Telegraph*. In addition to pioneering many of the norms of later theatre criticism, including essay-style reviews written after attending an opening-night performance, Scott was notable for his moralistic attacks on Shaw, Ibsen, and contemporary actresses.

the plays of Robertson: the topical 'problem plays' of the 1860s English dramatist Thomas William Robertson (1829–71) were a strong influence on Shaw.

14 *Mr Alfred Watson*: Watson (1849–1922) was the music and drama critic for the Conservative daily paper *The Standard* for over thirty years.

Lord Campbell's Act: popular name for the Obscene Publications Act of 1857 which made possible the prosecution of several obscene acts or the sale of obscene material, which had previously been classified as misdemeanours.

Sir Edwin Arnold: Arnold (1832–1904) was the editor-in-chief of the *Daily Telegraph*, at which he worked in various capacities for over forty years.

15 *the case of Proudhon*: Pierre-Joseph Proudhon (1809–65) was an influential French anarchist who declared property to be theft in *What is Property? Or, an Inquiry into the Principle of Right and Government* (1840).

Married Women's Property Act . . . practitioners: Shaw refers to an 1882 Act of Parliament that allowed married women to own and control property in their own names, to the right of women to vote in local elections conferred by the Municipal Franchise Act of 1869, and to the Medical Act of 1876, which allowed for women to be licensed as medical practitioners.

16 *Luther . . . Cromwell . . . Mary Wollstonecraft*: for Martin Luther, see note to p. 36; Oliver Cromwell (1599–1658) led the deposition of Charles I (1600–49, r. 1625–49) during the English Civil War (1642–51) and served as Lord Protector of the Commonwealth of England from 1653 until his death; Mary Wollstonecraft (1759–97) was an influential feminist philosopher of the eighteenth century (and mother of Mary Shelley (1797–1851)), author of *Frankenstein*).

the late Charles Bradlaugh: Bradlaugh (1833–91) was a friend of Shaw's and a prominent atheist who served as a Liberal MP and founded the National Secular Society in 1866.

Voltaire and Tom Paine: the French philosopher François-Marie Arouet, known as Voltaire (1694–1778), and the English-American philosopher and revolutionary Thomas Paine (1737–1809) were both well known for their criticisms of organized religion—although, as Shaw points out below, Voltaire commissioned a church building at Ferney, where he lived for the last twenty years of his life.

saves the rationalist: Shaw's use of the term 'rationalist' was quixotic and malleable, acquiring numerous different valances across his career. Here, he means to refer to those who rely unquestioningly on intellectual reason for their decision-making. For a detailed consideration of Shaw's use of the term across his career in light of its general usage in the Victorian and Edwardian eras, see John von B. Rodenbeck, 'Shaw's Revolt Against Rationalism', *Victorian Studies*, 15/4 (June 1972), 409–37.

Contagious Diseases Acts: the various Contagious Diseases Acts passed by Parliament between 1864 and 1869 allowed for the arrest and confinement of prostitutes in the name of halting the spread of venereal disease.

Dagon, Moloch, and Jehovah: deities mentioned in the Old Testament of the Bible, including Dagon and Moloch, both Canaanite gods (the latter identified with child sacrifice), and Jehovah, the God of Israel.

17 *Herbert Spencer's Data of Ethics*: 1879 treatise by the English philosopher and sociologist which espouses an individualist moral philosophy; for Spencer, see note to p. 12.

'One must live.' 'I don't see the necessity,' replied Voltaire: Shaw is referring to an exchange recounted in 1760 by Voltaire between the Abbé des Fontaines

and the Comte d'Argental, censor of books, when the former was accused of publishing libels. The exchange can be found in Voltaire, *Œuvres complètes*, vol. xlviii, ed. René Pomeau (Oxford: Voltaire Foundation, 1980), 99.

17 *the Father of Lies*: the Devil (John 8:44).

Schopenhauer: see note to p. 200.

the Hegelian dialectic: the system of argumentation associated with the German philosopher Georg Wilhelm Friedrich Hegel (1770–1831), which involves the joining of a thesis and antithesis to form a synthesis and which is explored in his *Phenomenology of Spirit* (1807) and other works.

18 *pessimism of Koheleth . . . Dryden, and Swift*: Koheleth (also spelled Kohelet or Qoheleth) was the name given to the anonymous author of the Book of Ecclesiastes, in the Old Testament of the Bible; John Dryden (1631–1700) was a seventeenth-century English poet and playwright; Jonathan Swift (1667–1745), an eighteenth-century Anglo-Irish writer and satirist.

Young, Helmholtz, Darwin, Haeckel . . . Tyndall and Huxley: aside from the English naturalist Charles Darwin (1809–82), Shaw references a number of prominent scientists of the eighteenth and nineteenth centuries who made contributions across various fields. The British physician Thomas Young (1773–1829), whose discoveries ranged from optics to Egyptology; Hermann von Helmholtz (1821–94), a German physician and philosopher whose work ranged from optics and acoustics to thermodynamics; Ernst Haeckel (1834–1919), a German naturalist influential in spreading Darwin's work; the Irish physicist John Tyndall (1820–93), who wrote a number of popular science books from the 1860s to the 1880s; and English biologist Thomas Henry Huxley (1825–95) (grandfather of Aldous Huxley (1894–1963), author of *Brave New World* (1932)), who was one of Darwin's most vocal advocates.

The Child's Guide to Knowledge: a popular children's primer of the nineteenth century by Fanny Umphelby (1788–1852), first published in 1825.

19 *Rationalism isolated the great mystery of the will to live*: although Shaw earlier claims that his references to rationalism and rationalists are meant in the colloquial sense of individuals who ascribe to decision-making based on reason over feelings, he here shifts his meaning to use the terms rationalism and materialism in their philosophical forms. Rationalism, also known as Idealism, broadly describes a tradition of philosophical thought that holds that reason offers unique access to truths that lie beyond the purely material realm; prominent philosophers in this tradition include René Descartes (1596–1650) and Immanuel Kant (1724–1804). Materialism, sometimes seen as overlapping with empiricism, holds that all of reality is composed of material substrates such that sensory perception must take precedence in our understanding of the world over abstract thinking; prominent philosophers in this tradition include John Locke (1632–1704) and David Hume (1711–76). Shaw's reference below to having 'escaped forever from the cloudy region of metaphysics' alludes to a long-standing

debate between rationalism's focus on metaphysics, or the philosophical conceptualization of reality, and materialism's more scientific rejection of the same.

Ferdinand Lassalle: nineteenth-century German socialist (1825–64) famous for coining the phrase 'iron law of wages', based on the ideas of economist David Ricardo (1772–1823), which argues that wages in a capitalist society will always trend towards the lowest possible subsistence level.

20 *Man's duty to himself, assessed by himself?*: Shaw is here echoing a strong individualist strain in nineteenth-century radical thought, one that saw its intellectual genesis in such diverse figures as Ralph Waldo Emerson (1803–82), Friedrich Nietzsche (1844–1900), and the early anarchist movement. Not long after the publication of *The Quintessence*, Shaw for a brief time in 1898 became a frequent contributor to a small journal of such radical individualist thought run out of Edinburgh called *The Eagle and the Serpent*, which was designed to promote discussion of Emerson, Thoreau, and Nietzsche and described itself as 'A Journal for Free Spirits and for Spirits Struggling to be Free'.

21 *the Infallible Pope*: dogma of the Catholic Church, formally adopted at the First Vatican Council of 1869–70, holding that the Pope is incapable of error when speaking *ex cathedra* (from his chair) on matters of doctrine.

22 *to be more and more a realist*: in contrast to the discussions of realism and Idealism in the previous chapter 'The Two Pioneers', Shaw is here introducing a new usage of the terms, one that will persist for most of the remainder of the book. In Shaw's own idiosyncratic coinages, which he describes in further detail in the passages below, an idealist refers to one who views life through the lens of preformed ideals and comforting ideologies, whereas a realist refers to one who sees life 'as it is' without preconception or prejudice, moral or otherwise. Throughout, Shaw typically renders the realist an iconoclast and the idealist a figure of tradition. Shaw's usage should not be confused with the different usages of these terms in philosophy, art, or other disciplines.

Sandwich islanders' masks in the British Museum: the British Museum holds a collection of traditional ceremonial masks of native Hawaiian peoples, the Sandwich Islands being the name originally given to the Hawaiian Islands by the explorer James Cook (1728–79).

23 *he also insists that the sloes he can get are sweet*: Shaw's arguments here are markedly in tune with aspects of those put forward by Friedrich Nietzsche in *On the Genealogy of Morals* (1887):

> The problem of the *other* origin of 'good', of good as thought up by the man of *resentiment*, demands its solution.—There is nothing strange about the fact that lambs bear a grudge towards large birds of prey: but that is no reason to blame the large birds of prey for carrying off the little lambs. And if the lambs say to each other, 'These birds of prey are evil; and whoever is least like a bird of prey and most like its opposite,

a lamb,—is good, isn't he?', then there is no reason to raise objections to this setting-up of an ideal beyond the fact that the birds of prey will view it somewhat derisively, and will perhaps say: 'We don't bear any grudge at all towards these good lambs, in fact we love them, nothing is tastier than a tender lamb' (Nietzsche, *On the Genealogy of Morality and Other Writings*, ed. Keith Ansell-Pearson, trans. Carol Diethe (Cambridge: Cambridge University Press, 1994), 25–6).

24 *Mandeville and Larochefoucauld*: the Anglo-Dutch philosopher Bernard Mandeville (1670–1733), most famous for *The Fable of the Bees* (1714), which argued against public instruction in morality and for the necessity of vices like greed, and the French aristocrat and essayist François de La Rochefoucauld (1613–80), whose *Maximes* (1664) likewise criticized traditional morality.

25 *Tennyson and Longfellow*: the nineteenth-century British poet Alfred, Lord Tennyson (1809–92), and his American contemporary Henry Wadsworth Longfellow (1807–82), among the most popular and celebrated poets of their era.

Henry Salt: Henry Stephens Salt (1851–1939) was an English literary critic and social activist who wrote extensively on Shelley.

26 *Zola and Maupassant . . . Plato*: the nineteenth-century French novelist and playwright Émile Zola (1840–1902) was associated early in his career with Romantic idealism; his contemporary, the short-story writer Guy de Maupassant (1850–93), was known for his highly polished form. Plato (*c*.428–*c*.348 BCE) was a classical philosopher whose theory of forms posited that material reality was derived from a realm of pure ideals. Though Shaw frequently criticized Plato's thought, he was in his own day frequently compared to him (as well as to his iconoclastic mentor Socrates). For a detailed study of these contemporary comparisons and the intellectual linkages behind them, see Sidney P. Albert, *Shaw, Plato, and Euripides: Classical Currents in 'Major Barbara'* (Gainesville, FL: University Press of Florida, 2012).

William Blake . . . Owen . . . Ruskin: the eighteenth-century Romantic poet and visionary William Blake (1757–1827); the early nineteenth-century utopian socialist Robert Owen (1771–1858); and Shaw's contemporary, the art critic and essayist John Ruskin (1819–1900), who wrote widely across many academic and political topics.

Ibsen was 'a Zola with a wooden leg': a quote from critic Robert Buchanan (1841–1901), who published an article on *A Doll's House* titled 'Is Ibsen "A Zola With a Wooden Leg"?' in the *Pall Mall Gazette* on 11 June 1889. Two days later, Shaw wrote a response, also in the *Pall Mall Gazette*, titled 'Is Mr Buchanan a Critic with a Wooden Head?'

Wagner the inferior of Mendelssohn and Meyerbeer: the German composer and opera innovator Richard Wagner (1813–83), discussed at length in *The Perfect Wagnerite* and elsewhere in this volume, and his fellow German contemporaries, the Romantic composer Felix Mendelssohn (1809–47) and opera composer Giacomo Meyerbeer (1791–1864). It is important to note that Mendelssohn and Meyerbeer were both Jewish by heritage (although Mendelssohn was a practising Christian), whereas Wagner was an avowed anti-Semite who directly attacked both composers in the essay 'Judaism in Music' (1869). Shaw's echoing of Wagner's attacks on these two composers foreshadows his later intellectual flirtations with various authoritarian movements.

Burne Jones: Sir Edward Burne-Jones (1833–98) was a British painter and designer associated with the Pre-Raphaelite movement of the mid-to-late nineteenth century, which took the detail and complex compositions of Italian painting before Raphael (1483–1520) as its inspiration. As Shaw notes, Burne-Jones had a tempestuous relationship with the Royal Academy of Arts, a prominent arts institution and exhibition space in London founded in 1768: though an associate of the Royal Academy, Burne-Jones exhibited there only once and resigned his membership after only eight years.

28 *the Diary of Marie Bashkirtseff*: the Ukrainian painter and sculptor Marie Bashkirtseff (1858–84) published her personal diary (started when she was 13) in France in 1887, followed by an English translation in 1889 that was received to great acclaim.

William Stead: William Thomas Stead (1849–1912) was a prominent British newspaper editor and social activist, best known as the editor of the Liberal *Pall Mall Gazette*. As Shaw notes below, Stead wrote an infamous exposé of child prostitution in which he arranged for the purchase of an underage girl, for which he was later imprisoned. The incident had a particularly strong effect on Shaw and became, in part, the basis for his play *Pygmalion*.

'Of the distinctively womanly . . . antithesis of a true woman': Shaw is quoting, here and below, from a polemic against *The Diary of Marie Bashkirtseff* written by William Stead (1849–1912) in *Review of Reviews* in June 1890.

29 *suttee is abolished in India*: the Indian practice of sati (*suttee*), or widow-burning (whose actual incidence was likely quite rare), was a topic of great public interest and discussion in England during the eighteenth and early nineteenth centuries and was eventually outlawed by the British Governor-General of India in 1829. For a detailed history, see Norbert Schürer, 'The Impartial Spectator of Sati, 1757–1784', *Eighteenth-Century Studies* 42/1 (Fall 2008), 19–44.

That was the first I ever heard of Nietzsche: Shaw would repeatedly deny having ever read or heard of Nietzsche before writing *The Quintessence*, including in this note added to *The Quintessence* in 1912, in the preface to *Major Barbara* (1907), and in his essay 'Nietzsche in English' (1896) (pp. 291–4). However, in an untitled article published in *The Eagle and the Serpent* on 1 November 1898, he described first encountering Nietzsche's thought in 1889, placing the encounter before writing *The Quintessence*, although he does not specify which if any of the philosopher's works he read in that year, none of which had yet appeared in English translation. Specifically, he wrote that it was in '1889, when Ibsen and Nietzsche began to make themselves felt' among the London intelligentsia (77). The 'German lady' mentioned in the note here and described in greater detail in the preface to *Major Barbara* was most likely Rosa Borchardt (1843–1911), née Oppenheim, the wife of Carl Borchardt (1817–80), a prominent German mathematician of the era.

31 *Dante loved Beatrice*: Shaw is referring to the well-known affection of the Italian poet Dante Alighieri (1265–1321) for Beatrice di Folco Portinari (1265–90), the basis for the figure Beatrice who appears in the *Divine Comedy* (1320). Although both Dante and Beatrice were married to others, Dante wrote numerous poems in praise of her.

Tannhäuser may die in the conviction: Shaw is here referring to legends associated with the German medieval troubadour Tannhäuser. Tannhäuser's story is told in Wagner's 1845 opera of the same name, in which the princess Elisabeth (based on St Elizabeth of Hungary, 1207–31) holds a platonic love for him and ultimately redeems him from sin through her untimely death.

When Blake told men . . . learn moderation: Shaw is referring to lines in William Blakes's *The Marriage of Heaven and Hell* (1793).

through the Venusberg: in the Tannhäuser (see note to p. 31), the Venusberg is the realm of the underworld associated with the goddess Venus.

de convenance: (Fr.) a marriage arranged for expediency or convenience instead of love.

32 *Belfort Bax*: Ernest Belfort Bax (1854–1926) was an English journalist and political activist who was particularly known for his anti-feminist writings and advocacy of the legal rights of men in works like *The Legal Subjection of Men* (1896).

33 *it would have been extremely hard to induce her to get married at all*: Shaw's discussion of marriage foreshadows aspects of *Pygmalion* (1913), wherein Eliza asserts that she prefers to marry someone who will love her and show her kindness while Higgins insists she marry within her new station and seek out 'somebody who wants a deputy-queen' (Bernard Shaw, *Pygmalion*, in *Androcles and the Lion, Overruled, Pygmalion* (New York: Brentano's, 1916), 207).

34 *as easy as playing the piano is to Paderewski*: Ignacy Jan Paderewski (1860–1941) was a virtuosic Polish pianist (and later statesman), who first performed in London to sensational acclaim in 1890.

35 '*the old beauty is no longer beautiful, the new truth no longer true*': compare to Shaw's statement in the Epistle Dedicatory to *Man and Superman* (1903), 'All the assertions get disproved sooner or later, and so we find the world full of magnificent debris of artistic fossils, with the matter-of-fact credibility gone clean out of them' ('Epistle Dedicatory to Arthur Bingham

Walkley', in *The Bodley Head Bernard Shaw: Collected Plays with their Prefaces*, ed. Laurence, ii. 527).

36 *Drury Lane type*: a reference to the Theatre Royal at Drury Lane, a prominent West End playhouse known in Shaw's day for its emotional melodramas and spectacular extravaganzas rather than sophisticated dramas.

it is his seventh: in fact, Ibsen had written ten previous plays, making *Brand* his eleventh. Shaw does not count Ibsen's earliest works (his first play appearing in print when the playwright was only 22) and includes only the five plays Ibsen wrote while working at Det norske Theater in Bergen, Norway, starting in 1855. The ten plays Ibsen wrote before *Brand* were *Catiline* (1850), *The Burial Mound* (1850), *Norma* (1851), *St John's Eve* (1852), *Lady Inger of Oestraat* (1854), *The Feast at Solhaug* (1855), *Olaf Liljekrans* (1856), *The Vikings at Helgeland* (1857), *Love's Comedy* (1862), and *The Pretenders* (1863).

like another Luther . . . Temple of Morality: Martin Luther (1483–1546), the priest and monk whose criticisms of the Roman Catholic Church (to which he belonged) in his *Ninety-five Theses* (1517)—which according to legend he nailed to the door of All Saints' church in Wittenberg, Germany—were instrumental in beginning the Protestant Reformation.

37 *killed by an avalanche*: the fact that Ibsen never intended *Brand* (1865) to be performed on stage helps account for the extremity of its conclusion. Yet the premiere at the Nya Teatern in Stockholm in 1867 proved its viability on stage, and such elaborate visuals would become a feature of certain later Ibsen plays. His final play, *When We Dead Awaken* (1899), for instance, calls for another avalanche that carries two characters to their deaths. A 1902 production at the Moscow Art Theatre used cotton batting for the effect, according to an account from the poet Valery Bryusov. See No. 99, 'A critical attack on superfluous realism', in Claude Schumacher (ed.), *Naturalism and Symbolism in European Theatre* (Cambridge: Cambridge University Press, 1996), 219–20.

38 *thaumaturgy*: the practice of working miracles.

the Trold king's daughter: a section of Ibsen's play in which Peer Gynt encounters mythical trolls who offer him the chance to wed their king's daughter, which he declines. The sequence is the basis for the well-known melody 'In the Hall of the Mountain King' from the *Peer Gynt, Suite No. 1*, Op. 46 (1875) by Norwegian composer Edvard Grieg (1843–1907).

39 *accepted on its account as the Messiah by an Arab tribe*: the scholar Nehad Selaiha attributes the North African portions of *Peer Gynt* to 'the distorting, stereotyping lens of romantic orientalism'. See Nehad Selaiha, '*Peer Gynt* by the Pyramids in Giza', in Erika Fischer-Lichte, Barbara Gronau, and Christel Weiler (eds), *Global Ibsen: Performing Multiple Modernities* (London: Routledge, 2012), 127.

the Eternal-Feminine of Goethe: the concept of *das Ewig-Weibliche*, which figures prominently at the conclusion of *Faust* (1831) by Johann Wolfgang von Goethe (1749–1832) when the protagonist is spiritually saved by his love Gretchen. Ibsen's character alludes to the play here and elsewhere throughout the drama. For the deep connections between Ibsen's play and Goethe's, see, for instance, Patricia Merivale, '*Peer Gynt:* Ibsen's *Faustiad*', *Comparative Literature*, 35/2 (Spring 1983), 126–39.

39 *the Sphinx is itself*: in recognition of the central role that the Egyptian Sphinx plays in Ibsen's play, and of the play's place in the history of modern drama, Norwegian and Egyptian artists collaborated in a landmark production of the play in Giza in 2006, staged in the very shadow of the Sphinx, as the culmination to the Norwegian government's 'Ibsen Year' in 2006, marking the 100th anniversary of the playwright's death.

40 *Miss Pagan*: Isabelle M. Pagan (1867–1960) was an early translator of Ibsen, who in 1909 published *The Fantasy of Peer Gynt: Being Selections from the Dramatic Poem 'Peer Gynt'*.

41 *Don Quixote acts . . . farm wenches*: in *Don Quixote de la Mancha* (1605–15) by Miguel de Cervantes (1547–1622), the nobleman Don Quixote imagines himself to be a medieval knight instead of acknowledging his quotidian reality.

the tower of Babel: Shaw is referring to the story told in Genesis 11:1–9 wherein the world's populations are punished with speaking different languages for trying to build a tower tall enough to reach the heavens.

Nelson: English Admiral Horatio Nelson (1758–1805), who served during the Napoleonic Wars and was regarded as a hero by many Britons. Nelson was killed during the Battle of Trafalgar in 1805, despite being victorious in the battle.

a Philistine like Sancho: Shaw is referring to Don Quixote's companion (see note to p. 41), the simple, uncultured farmer Sancho Panza, who regards Quixote's exploits sceptically.

42 *Shakespear, in Hamlet . . . Henry V . . . Troilus and Cressida*: Shaw is here referring to three plays by William Shakespeare (1564–1616), believed to be written in close proximity: *Henry V* (*c*.1599), *Hamlet* (*c*.1600), and *Troilus and Cressida* (*c*.1602). He contrasts the optimism of the first with the existential questioning of the second and general cynicism of the last.

apostasy of the Emperor Julian: Julian, Roman emperor from 361 to 363 CE, was most remembered for his rejection of Christianity.

Cain, who slew because he willed: in the story of Cain and Abel in Genesis 4:1–18, Cain murders his brother out of jealousy and is forever cursed.

Weismann: German evolutionary biologist August Weismann (1834–1914), an influential figure in the early development of genetics.

Judas asks . . . foreknowingly: the question appears in Matthew 26:25.

Strauss's Leben Jesu: *Das Leben Jesu* (*The Life of Jesus*) (1835), by German theologian David Strauss (1808–74), was an influential account of Jesus's life from a historical rather than religious perspective.

43 *George Eliot's novels, vainly protested against by Ruskin*: reference to John Ruskin's intensive criticism of English novelist George Eliot (Mary Ann Evans, 1819–80), whom he called 'a common rail-road station novelist' in his 1880 essay 'Fiction Fair and Foul'.

Mill's favourite dialectical weapon: the philosopher and economist John Stuart Mill (1806–73) argued in *Nature* (1874) that 'If the maker of the world can all that he will, he wills misery, and there is no escape from the conclusion.' See *Nature, The Utility of Religion, and Theism* (1885), 388.

as our Samuel Butler did: socialist novelist Samuel Butler (1835–1902), best known for his satirical novel *Erewhon* (1872). Like Shaw, Butler rejected natural selection as the mechanism by which evolution occurred, as famously argued by Charles Darwin, and expressed those criticisms in *Evolution, Old and New* (1879). Butler's ideas would prove influential on Shaw's theory of Creative Evolution and the Life Force (see note below).

overrating of Natural Selection: Shaw proved notoriously sceptical of natural selection, the process used by Charles Darwin in *On the Origin of Species* (1859) to explain the operations of evolution wherein natural variation produces differences in species development due to changes in environmental conditions. For Shaw, natural selection was disturbingly lacking in agency on the part of the organisms themselves, and he adhered instead to the notion of 'Creative Evolution', which allowed for the willed development of adaptive traits. For more, see Piers Hale, 'The Search for Purpose in a Post-Darwinian Universe: George Bernard Shaw, "Creative Evolution," and Shavian Eugenics: "The Dark Side of the Force"', *History and Philosophy of the Life Sciences*, 28/2 (1 January 2006), 191–213.

'the Almighty Fiend' of Shelley: the quotation, a negative reference to God, is from Shelley's 'Queen Mab: Part VI'.

44 *play Greatheart and reduce it*: in *Pilgrim's Progress* (1678) by John Bunyan (1628–88), a character called Greatheart slays a monster known as Giant Despair. The book had a substantial influence on Shaw, and he returns to it often in his writings.

45 *after Kant . . . the equal liberty of others, etc. etc*: three different philosophical systems of morality—the idea of a categorical imperative developed by Immanuel Kant (1724–1804) in his *Grounding for the Metaphysics of Morals* (1785), the idea of a utilitarian calculus as developed by Jeremy Bentham (1747–1832) and John Stuart Mill in the eighteenth and nineteenth centuries, and the ideas of natural law and natural rights as developed by John Locke in the seventeenth century.

imperial purple: a metonymic reference to secular authority, specifically to the colour 'Tyrian purple' used by Romans in ceremonial robes.

46 *'Lead us not into temptation . . . and the glory'*: Shaw is quoting from the Lord's Prayer, a common prayer across Christian denominations recounted in Matthew 6:9 and Luke 11:2.

47 *The seer of Nazareth*: Jesus Christ of Nazareth.

Logos in Pan, Pan in Logos: the phrase also appears verbatim in the biblical-themed play *Lazarus Laughed* (1927) by Eugene O'Neill (1888–1953) and refers to the synthesis of pagan and classical thought represented by the turn to Christianity.

He is self-begotten in the man who wills: Ibsen's thought—and Shaw's—here runs especially close to the philosophy of Friedrich Nietzsche, particularly the passage in *The Gay Science* (1882) where he writes that 'we . . . want to *become who we are*—human beings who are new, unique, incomparable, who who give themselves laws, who create themselves!' (189). Ibsen's play, written in 1873 though not first performed until 1896, predates Nietzsche's statement by nearly ten years, though Ibsen would have been writing the play around the time that Nietzsche's *The Birth of Tragedy* was first published in 1872. Whether Ibsen ever read Nietzsche remains open to debate—we know that Nietzsche in fact read Ibsen, disapprovingly, from references to him in *Ecce Homo* (1888). As Shaw states earlier in *The Quintessence*, questions of genealogies were less important to him than the fact of a new modern world-view coming into being: 'I attach great importance to the evidence that the movement voiced by Schopenhauer, Wagner, Ibsen, Nietzsche, and Strindberg, was a world movement' (p. 29, note 2).

48 *clinging, like Macbeth, to an ambiguous oracle*: the character Macbeth in Shakespeare's play of the same name (1606) bases his actions on the vague proclamations of the three witches.

give Cæsar what is Cæsar's: from Matthew 22:21, referring to the injunction to separate religious and secular affairs and to follow established secular political authority.

50 *long after the current 'Crosstianity'*: Shaw offers a definition of this coinage in his Preface to *Major Barbara* (1907), where he writes: 'By example and precept the law and public opinion teach him to impose his will on others by anger, violence, and cruelty, and to wipe off the moral score by punishment. That is sound Crosstianity' (*The Bodley Head Bernard Shaw: Collected Plays with Their Prefaces*, ed. Laurence v. 44).

51 *in Relling, in Lövborg, in Ellida's stranger from the sea*: antagonist characters in various Ibsen plays: Dr Relling from *The Wild Duck* (1884), Eilert Løvborg from *Hedda Gabler* (1891), and a character known as The Stranger who has a past history with the character Ellida Wangel in *The Lady from the Sea* (1889).

art for art's sake: the famous slogan of the aesthetic movement in nineteenth-century Britain, promoted by figures including William Morris and Oscar Wilde (1854–1900) and first popularized by the French writer Théophile Gautier (1811–72) in the preface to his book *Mademoiselle de Maupin* (1835).

52 *the school of Scribe*: the work of the prominent nineteenth-century French dramatist Eugène Scribe (1791–1861) was synonymous with the genre of

the 'well-made play' (though he in fact worked across numerous genres and modes, including opera libretti) and had a profound influence on other popular dramatists of the era.

54 *as well as by Labiche*: nineteenth-century French dramatist Eugène Labiche (1815–88), best known for his farces.

in the famous Doll's House: though Shaw refers to *A Doll's House* as already being famous, the play was still quite new to the London stage when *The Quintessence* was first published in 1891. It originally appeared in 1884 in a loose adaptation by Henry Arthur Jones (1851–1929) and Henry Herman (1832–94) called *Breaking a Butterfly* (based on an English translation of the German translation of the original play). The first performance in England of an accurate translation of the play occurred two years later, when the writer and scientist Edward Aveling (1849–98) and the political activist Eleanor Marx (1855–98), daughter of Karl Marx (1818–83), organized a private reading of the play at their London home, with Eleanor Marx playing Nora and Shaw himself playing Krogstad while Aveling played Torvald. The first public performance occurred in 1889 at London's Novelty Theatre, just two years before the appearance of *The Quintessence*.

55 *induced her father to endorse the promissory note*: as women were not granted full legal personhood at the time, a male guardian (typically a father or husband) was usually required to endorse any legal or financial document to which a woman was party. Nora's illicit circumvention of this requirement becomes a key plot point in *A Doll's House*, as Shaw explains.

56 *wonder whether . . . come to pass between them*: Shaw's description belies the real finality of the play's ending, in which, as rendered in the translation by William Archer (1856–1924) that premiered in 1889, Torvald has a moment of hope that Nora will return, declaring 'Ah! The miracle of miracles—?!', followed by the stage direction 'From below is heard the reverberation of a heavy door closing.' See Henrik Ibsen, *A Doll's House*, trans. William Archer (London: Fisher Unwin, 1889), 123.

58 *Sir Walter Besant intended his own sequel*: here and in his own footnote below Shaw is referencing the following works written in response to *A Doll's House*: Walter Besant's 'The Doll's House and After', published in *English Illustrated Magazine* (January 1890); his own 'Still After The Doll's House', published in *Time* (February 1890); and Israel Zangwill and Eleanor Marx (as Eleanor Marx Aveling), '*A Doll's House* Repaired', published in *Time* (March 1891). For a detailed consideration of these texts, especially the last, see Bernard F. Dukore, 'Karl Marx's Youngest Daughter and *A Doll's House*', *Theatre Journal*, 42/3 (October 1990), 308–21.

59 *the Wagner Schimpf-Lexicon*: the compendium of anti-Wagnerian insults and invectives compiled by music critic Wilhelm Tappert (1830–1907) and published in 1877 as *Ein Wagner-Lexikon*. The term *schimpf-lexikon* literally means 'insult dictionary'.

60 *nookshotten*: a largely obsolete English word meaning 'jutting out at multiple angles'.

In petto: (It.) meaning 'in private'.

the Lock Hospital: a specialized hospital that treated venereal diseases in Britain.

The Lord Chamberlain: the Lord Chamberlain's Office, a royal office tasked with theatre censorship in 1737 until the role was abolished with the Theatres Act of 1968.

61 *cry raised in New York in 1905 . . . Mrs Warren's Profession*: the run of *Mrs Warren's Profession* at the Garrick Theater in New York on 28 October 1905 was closed by the authorities after one performance and led to many of those involved in the production being arrested for obscenity. For an account of the history of censorship associated with the play, see L. W. Conolly, ' "Mrs. Warren's Profession" and The Lord Chamberlain', *SHAW* 24 (2004), 46–95.

62 *fainéants*: (Fr.) an idle person or layabout.

Ratepayers' Association: local political organization designed to represent the interests of landlords and property owners, i.e. those who pay property taxes (or rates).

Monsieur Tout-le-monde: (Fr.) literally 'Mr Everybody', roughly analogous to the idea of the 'common man'. Shaw's reference to Voltaire invokes the philosopher's criticisms of democracy as leading inevitably to mob rule.

63 *there is urgent need for the guillotine*: Shaw here foreshadows his later statements in support of violent political purgation towards the end of his career. For an extended consideration of this theme, see Matthew Yde, *Bernard Shaw and Totalitarianism: Longing for Utopia* (London: Palgrave-Macmillan, 2013).

as far as Maximus the Mystic's Third Empire is concerned: the character Maximus the Mystic in Ibsen's *Emperor and Galilean* (1896) prophesied a 'third empire' to succeed both Rome and Christianity.

69 *the first performance of Rosmersholm in England*: see note to p. 10. Shaw in fact assisted with the production and wrote much of his analysis of the play for *The Quintessence* during that period.

71 *Ulric Brendel*: one of the characters in *Rosmersholm* (1886), the childhood tutor of Rosmer.

Hedda Gabler, 1890: at the time *The Quintessence* was first published, *Hedda Gabler* was the latest of Ibsen's plays. It was first published in Copenhagen in December 1890 and saw its world premiere in Munich at the Königliches Residenz-Theater in January 1891. See also note to p. 10.

72 *faute de mieux*: (Fr.) literally 'lack of better', meaning for lack of a better alternative.

74 *an arrant poseur and male coquet*: a *poseur*, from the French, is a person who pretends to be what they are not, while a *coquet(te)* is a flirtatious individual.

a shunter's: a low-level railway worker who helps move train cars into position.

his life as a man of genius: Shaw returned to the idea of the 'man of genius' throughout his career, later supplementing his terminology with the idea of a 'woman of genius'. He offers the following definition of the former in the 'Epistle Dedicatory' to *Man and Superman*: 'But ordinary men cannot produce really impressive art-works. Those who can are men of genius: that is, men selected by Nature to carry on the work of building up an intellectual consciousness of her own instinctive purpose' (*The Bodley Head Bernard Shaw: Collected Plays with Their Prefaces*, ed. Laurence, ii. 509). Though the man of genius might conceivably stand alone and apart from women (but did not have to), Shaw inevitably viewed the 'woman of genius' in terms of her supposedly rapacious pursuit of and attempt to control men, as in the 'Epistle Dedicatory': 'When it is complicated by the genius being a woman, then the game is one for a king of critics: your George Sand becomes a mother to gain experience for the novelist and to develop her, and gobbles up men of genius, Chopins, Mussets and the like, as mere hors d'oeuvres' (509). George Sand (Amantine Lucile Aurore Dupin, 1804–76) was a renowned French novelist; Fryderyk Chopin (1810–49) was a Polish composer and piano virtuoso, who maintained a tempestuous relationship with Sand; Alfred de Musset (1810–57) was a French poet, playwright, and novelist who also had a love affair with Sand.

75 *and so the story ends*: in fact, the play ends not with Hedda's suicide but with the reaction to Hedda's suicide, its famous last line being Judge Brack's exclamation 'Good God!—people don't do such things' upon hearing the news. This return to questions of social reception and social opprobrium is in fact central to Shaw's evaluation of Ibsen's importance, yet his decision to focus on the end of *Hedda Gabler* only in terms of Hedda's own actions centres her agency within the play.

76 THE LAST FOUR PLAYS: this section was added with the 1913 edition.

Solness: Halvard Solness, protagonist of *The Master Builder* (1892), as Shaw explains below.

77 *and adolescent girls idolize elderly gentlemen*: though Shaw wrote these words for the 1913 edition, they would become part of his own life by the time of the 1922 edition. In 1921, at the age of 65, the playwright began a correspondence with the American actress Molly Tompkins (1898–1960), then 24, which continued for nearly thirty years and may have included an extramarital affair. His caution to Tompkins in one letter bears a marked similarity to his language from *The Quintessence*: 'We are an old man and a young thing, and to exhibit ourselves in any other relation would be ridiculous and most unbecoming' (quoted in Michiko Kakutani, 'G. B. Shaw and the Women in His Life', *New York Times*, 27 September 1981). For a study of Shaw's relationship with Tompkins, see Charles A. Berst, 'Passion at Lake Maggiore: Shaw, Molly Tompkins, and Italy, 1921–1950', *SHAW* 5 (1985), 81–114.

77 *Bettina and Goethe*: the German writers Johann Wolfgang von Goethe (1749–1832) and Bettina von Arnim (1785–1859) struck up a correspondence when Bettina was in her youth and continued their platonic friendship until Bettina had a falling-out with Goethe's wife in 1811.

80 *Reign of Terror*: a period during the French Revolution from 1793 to 1794 marked by frequent public executions of those deemed to have committed political crimes against the Revolution, totalling more than 17,000 deaths.

our millions of private Neros . . . Semiramises: the Roman emperor Nero (37–68 CE); Tomás de Torquemada (1420–98), Grand Inquisitor of the Spanish Inquisition; John Calvin (1509–64), the French Protestant theologian; Mary Tudor (1516–58, r. 1553–8); Cleopatra Philopator (69–*c.*10 BCE), the last Ptolemaic ruler of Egypt; and Semiramis (ninth century BCE), queen of the Assyrians. All were known for brutality of one form or another, especially towards religious outsiders.

81 *'a fellow almost damned in a fair wife'*: from *Othello* I.i.22, when Iago describes Michael Cassio.

82 *seraglio*: from Italian, a reference to the female living spaces in a sultan's court. Shaw's use builds on his reference above to Rita as a sultana, or female sultan.

83 *'There stood your champagne and you tasted it not'*: from the poem 'Republikanerne' (1839) by the Norwegian writer Johan Sebastian Welhaven (1807–73).

84 *'Inasmuch . . . have done it unto me'*: Matthew 25:40.

85 *the sham political economy that took in Mr Gradgrind*: Thomas Gradgrind, the hard-nosed school board superintendent in Charles Dickens's novel *Hard Times* (1854), is at one point an adherent of Utilitarian political philosophy, which argues for a mechanistic pursuit of maximum well-being.

James Mill: noted Scottish historian, economist, and philosopher (1773–1836) of the eighteenth century, who personally oversaw the education of his son John Stuart Mill at home, leading, as Shaw notes below, to the adoption by Mill *fils* of political positions that anticipated later socialism. Shaw's claim that John Stuart Mill was a socialist, while in line with Mill's own descriptions, is complicated by Mill's advocacy of certain economic positions that would later be seen as antithetical to modern socialism. See Raimund Ottow, 'Why John Stuart Mill Called Himself a Socialist', *History of European Ideas* 17/4 (July 1993), 479–83.

Herbert Spencer lived to write despairing pamphlets . . . ablest pupils: the English sociologist Herbert Spencer (1820–1903) wrote numerous tracts against socialism, such as 'The Coming Slavery' (1884) and the introduction to *A Plea for Liberty* (1891). On the idea that his own students became socialists themselves, see Charles Zueblin's statement, in 1897, that 'Perhaps it will suffice to illustrate this estimate of Spencer by saying that the most intellectual woman among the collectivists was a personal student of Spencer for years'. See Charles Zueblin, 'A Sketch of Socialistic

Thought in England: For Students of Social Philosophy', *American Journal of Sociology*, 2/5 (March 1897), 643–61, at 654.

86 *sovereign*: a British coin worth one pound sterling, used from 1817 to 1914.

87 *Plato . . . Sir Thomas More . . . a necessary qualification for aristocracy*: book 5 of Plato's *Laws* proposes prohibiting any individual from owning gold or silver and instead requiring the use of currency for all transactions. Sir Thomas Moore's *Utopia* (1516) likewise eliminates the use of precious metals.

89 *leaves the dead to bury their dead*: an allusion to Matthew 8:22, wherein Jesus uses the phrase 'let the dead bury their dead' in commanding a disciple to leave his family and his dying father in pursuit of a spiritual calling, an ironic parallel to how Erhart leaves his family for the pretty lady.

90 *the Militant Suffrage Movement*: the arm of the British suffrage movement committed to direct action, including acts of violence. Though its origins can be traced to the 1860s, the movement had grown more prominent by the 1910s when Shaw wrote this section of *The Quintessence*. For a history of the movement, see Laura E. Nym Mayhall, *The Militant Suffrage Movement: Citizenship and Resistance in Britain, 1860–1930* (Oxford: Oxford University Press, 2003).

91 *Dumas*: Alexandre Dumas *père* (1802–70), the French novelist and author of *The Count of Monte Cristo* (1844), about a man who plots and executes his revenge over a lifetime.

92 *Dickens was inspired to make Pecksniff*: Seth Pecksniff was an architect and one of the villains in Charles Dickens's *Martin Chuzzlewit* (1844).

a Hyperion or a Hercules: figures of Greek mythology, the Titan Hyperion and the demigod Hercules, both known for their power and strength.

Defoe: Daniel Defoe (1660–1731), author of *Robinson Crusoe* (1719).

the virtues of 'the middle station of life': the praise expressed in *Robinson Crusoe* for a stable, middle-class life, against the adventure sought by Crusoe by journeying to sea.

93 *Dr Johnson*: the eighteenth-century essayist and literary critic Dr Samuel Johnson (1709–84).

what they really are: the Scottish essayist Thomas Carylyle (1795–1881) proposed that the House of Lords hold their proceedings in the nude in his comic novel *Sartor Resartus* (1833).

94 *modern kinematographs*: an early form of projected film, the name being derived from the French *cinématographe*, one of the world's first motion picture cameras, invented by Auguste and Louis Lumière (1862–1954 and 1864–1948) in the 1890s.

before crowds in Variety Theatres in living pictures: the *tableaux vivant* was a form of music hall performance popular in the 1890s in which women recreated or imitated classical paintings and statues on stage, including nude works in some cases. For a detailed discussion, see Brenda Assael,

'Art or Indecency? *Tableaux Vivants* on the London Stage and the Failure of Late Victorian Moral Reform', *Journal of British Studies*, 45/4 (2006), 744–58.

95 *what the Italian Futurist painters of today are calling them*: Shaw is likely thinking here of the 'Founding and Manifesto of Futurism' (1909) by Filippo Tomaso Marinetti (1876–1944), in which he likens museums to cemeteries and slaughterhouses and proclaims the need for new art forms focused on conveying and celebrating the modern world of industry and technology.

97 *Jeanie Deans*: the heroine of Walter Scott's (1771–1832) novel *The Heart of Midlothian* (1818), known especially for her honesty and religiosity.

the deus ex machina expedient . . . agreeable: (Lat.) literally 'god from the machine', *deus ex machina* refers to a god appearing from a machine on the stage near the end of a Greek tragedy to facilitate an unlikely ending, and metaphorically to any unlikely change of events that allows the hero of a story to triumph. In *The Heart of Midlothian*, a major character is saved from execution at the last minute when the novel's protagonist, Jeanie, facilitates his escape.

Many years ago I witnessed a performance . . . this story: Shaw is most likely referring to the play *The Trial of Effie Deans* by Dion Boucicault (1820–90), produced at the Westminster Theatre in London in 1863.

98 *The Sophoclean or Shakespearean good man persecuted by Destiny*: the most obvious examples would be Oedipus and Hamlet respectively.

99 *the Paris Commune . . . La Vendée . . . the Boyne or Culloden*: revolutionary and counter-revolutionary movements. The Paris Commune was a radical socialist government that ruled Paris for a brief period following the chaos after defeat in the Franco-Prussian War in 1871. During the French Revolution, there were counter-revolutionary uprisings in the Vendée in western France in 1793–6. The Boyne and Culloden were pivotal battles in the struggle to maintain the Stuart monarchy over the ascension of King William and Queen Mary and later the Hanoverians, the Battle of the Boyne being part of the Williamite War that ran from 1689 to 1691 in Ireland and Culloden being the site of the final battle of the Jacobite Uprising of 1746 in Scotland.

Gladstone . . . Cardinal Newman: political figures of the era whose politics differed greatly from Bradlaugh's. The Liberal William Ewart Gladstone (1809–98, prime minister four times between 1868 and 1894), journalist and Liberal MP John Morley (1838–1923), newspaper editor and investigative journalist William Thomas Stead (1849–1912), Italian general and nationalist Giuseppe Garibaldi (1807–82), and religious reformer John Henry Newman (1801–90), who was part of the Oxford Movement which argued for a return of certain Catholic practices and tenets to the Church of England, and who eventually became a Catholic priest and cardinal.

Wat Tyler . . . Archbishop of Canterbury: a diverse array of political figures. Walter Tyler (1341–81), leader of the 1381 Peasants' Revolt; Jack Cade (*c*.1420–50), who led a rebellion against the English government in 1450; Whig MP Richard Penn (1735–1811); William Wilberforce (1759–1833), an Independent MP and devout Christian who was instrumental in helping to abolish the slave trade; Arthur Wellesley, Duke of Wellington (1769–1852), who defeated Napoleon at Waterloo and subsequently served as Tory prime minister (1828–30 and November–December 1834); anarchist Pierre-Joseph Proudhon (1809–65); and the Archbishop of Canterbury, the spiritual leader of the Church of England.

100 *Lucretia*: a figure of Roman legend whose virtuous suicide following rape helped inspire the founding of the Roman Republic.

as the dramatic critic of Piccadilly did defend it: Edmund Gosse (1849–1928), theatre critic for the *Fortnightly Review*, published two articles in defence of Ibsen in 1891, 'Ibsen's New Drama' (vol. 55, Jan. 1891) and 'The Free Stage and the New Drama' (vol. 56, Jan. 1891). The offices of the *Fortnightly Review* were at 193 Piccadilly.

the town of Morality . . . the City of Destruction: locations and characters from John Bunyan's *Pilgrim's Progress* (1678).

101 *garotted*: archaic word for strangled.

102 *the catechism*: a statement of faith, phrased in question-and-answer format, used in many Christian denominations.

the Pharisee: specifically a sect of Judaism of the first century CE but more generally a strictly observant religious adherent who believes their literalist approach to religious practice is superior to other forms of spirituality.

latest spiritual heiress of Nell Gwynne: Nell Gwynne (1650–87) was an immensely popular stage actress of the seventeenth century and one of the earliest celebrity figures in theatre history. She was also known as Charles II's mistress; Shaw later depicted her in his 1939 play *In Good King Charles's Golden Days*.

103 *Catherine of Russia*: Catherine II 'the Great' (1729–96, r. 1762–96) of Russia was rumoured to have a large sexual appetite; Shaw depicted her in this manner in his 1913 playlet *Great Catherine*.

Mrs Proudie: an upright and controlling wife in the novel *Barchester Towers* (1857) by Anthony Trollope (1815–82).

Dumas musketeers: the free-wheeling heroes of Alexandre Dumas *père*'s *The Three Musketeers* (1844).

105 WHAT IS THE NEW ELEMENT IN THE NORWEGIAN SCHOOL?: this section was added in the 1913 edition.

were asked by the shepherds what their religion was: compare to Act III of *Man and Superman* (1903), where Jack Tanner is waylaid in the Spanish countryside by brigands who speak to him extensively about religion, particularly in the 'Don Juan in Hell' dream sequence.

106 *hidalgo*: a Spanish aristocratic title.

106 *Paul Bert*: Paul Bert (1833–86) was a French scientist, anticlericalist, atheist, and left-wing politician.

'*There's a divinity . . . rough hew them how we will*': from *Hamlet* V.ii.10–11.

from the novels of Smollett to Tom Cringle's Log: references to the eighteenth-century Scottish novel-writer Tobias Smollett (1721–71), who influenced Dickens, and the seafaring novel *Tom Cringle's Log* by Michael Scott (1789–1835), which was serialized in *Blackwood's Magazine* in 1829.

Humphrey Clinker: *The Expedition of Humphry Clinker* (1771), by Tobias Smollett.

107 *Shakespear's Falstaff*: impoverished and mercurial knight Sir John Falstaff first appeared as a major supporting character in Shakespeare's *Henry IV Part 1* (*c.*1597) and *Henry IV Part 2* (*c.*1599) (and is mentioned in *Henry V* (*c.*1599)) but grew so popular he was made the protagonist of his own play, *The Merry Wives of Windsor* (*c.*1602).

the raisonneur of the piece: (Fr.) literally the 'reasoner' or 'arguer' but more generally meaning the character of a play who most represents the author's point of view.

'*Old do I wax . . . from my weary limbs honor is cudgelled*': from *Henry V*, V.i.76–7.

'*a half-pennyworth of bread . . . deal of sack*': from *Henry IV Part 1*, II.iv.543.

Falstaff and Sir Toby Belch: two of Shakespeare's most notoriously intoxicated characters. Falstaff (see note to p. 107), and Sir Toby Belch from *Twelfth Night* (*c.*1601).

Zola's L'Assommoir: Zola's 1877 novel, focusing on alcoholism and poverty.

Cassio: Michael Cassio, from *Othello* (*c.*1603).

108 *The Taming of the Shrew . . . modern Feminist demonstration in the theatre*: ironically, Shaw himself once issued such a call against the play, which controversially concerns the 'taming' of an unwilling romantic partner through deception and control. Seemingly in jest, on 8 June 1888 he wrote a letter to the editor of the *Pall Mall Gazette* under the assumed name of Horatia Ribbonson, in which he asked that 'all men and women who respect one another will boycott *The Taming of the Shrew* until it is driven off the boards'.

Mary Wollstonecraft . . . Mrs Fawcett and Mrs Pankhurst: prominent feminists of the eighteenth and nineteenth centuries. Mary Wollstonecraft (1759–97), author of *A Vindication of the Rights of Woman* (1792); Dame Millicent Fawcett (1847–1929), a famous political activist and campaigner for women's suffrage; and Emmeline Pankhurst (1858–1928), a militant suffragette and one of the founders of the British suffragette movement.

Katharine and Petruchio: the main characters of *The Taming of the Shrew* (*c.*1592).

Mrs Raddle and Mrs Macstinger and Mrs Jo Gargery: three characters from Dickens's novels: Mrs Raddle from *The Pickwick Papers* (1836), Mrs MacStinger from *Dombey and Son* (1848), and Mrs Jo Gargery from *Great Expectations* (1861).

George Gissing: English novelist (1857–1903) of the later nineteenth century, most famous for *New Grub Street* (1891) about the London literary scene. His observations on Dickens are found primarily in his book *Charles Dickens: A Critical Study* (1898).

'Woman, lovely woman': title of a popular song written by Felix McGlennon (1856–1943) in 1881. The phrase is also the opening of a long ode to women in the opening scene of *Venice Preserv'd* (1682) by Thomas Otway (1652–85).

Betsy Trotwood . . . Miss Havisham . . . perversion of her humanity: Betsy Trotwood is a character in Dickens's *David Copperfield* (1850) and Miss Havisham a character in his *Great Expectations* (1861). Shaw's reference to the idea of a 'Chinese monster' is an allusion to Empress Dowager Cixi (1835–1908), a palace concubine who came to rule China as a regent for nearly fifty years from 1861 to 1908 and who was widely known for her ruthlessness.

109 *The nurse in his play who . . . slips a strait waistcoat on him revolts us*: reference to August Strindberg's play *The Father* (1887).

Sairey Gamp: Sarah, or Sairey, Gamp is a nurse in Dickens's novel *Martin Chuzzlewit* (1844).

Punch and Judy showman: in the 'Punch and Judy' puppet shows, the two main characters, a husband and wife, relentlessly attack one another for children's amusement.

'but for the grace of God': a common paraphrase of 1 Corinthians 15:10, commonly attributed to the sixteenth-century English clergyman John Bradford (1510–55).

Mrs Wilfer is treated with less levity than Mrs Nickleby: Mrs Wilfer in Charles Dickens's *Our Mutual Friend* (1865) is marked by her discontent and ill will, while the obtuseness of Mrs Nickleby in Dickens's *Nicholas Nickleby* (1839) is a source of comedy in the novel.

Micawber and Chivery: Wilkins Micawber from Dickens's *David Copperfield* (1850) and John Chivery from his *Little Dorrit* (1857).

110 *Dick Swiveller and Ulrik Brendel*: Dick Swiveller from Dickens's *The Old Curiosity Shop* (1840) and Ulrick Brendel from Ibsen's *Rosmersholm*.

the old lady who was edified by the word Mesopotamia: Shaw is referencing a common story of the time, used aphoristically and likely apocryphal, of a devout churchgoer who tells her pastor that she takes comfort in the word 'Mesopotamia', thinking it a word of spiritual importance rather than a geographic designation.

Samuel Butler's Chowbock . . . the prayer for Queen Adelaide: an incident in Samuel Butler's novel *Erewhon* (1872); Chowbok is a native of the fictional country of Erewhon.

110 *the late Clement Scott*: Clement Scott (1841–1904), the conservative theatre critic for the *Daily Telegraph* in the 1880s and 1890s.

Hard Times . . . Bleak House: Shaw is comparing the heavy subject matter in Dickens's later novels—including industrial labour in *Hard Times* (1854), debtors' prison in *Little Dorrit* (1857), and illness and death in *Our Mutual Friend* (1865)—to the lighter subjects of his earlier works, including picaresque adventures in *The Pickwick Papers* (1836) and legal satire in *Bleak House* (1853).

Charles Lever: Irish writer (1806–72) of the nineteenth century known for his youthful picaresque novels.

All the Year Round: weekly literary magazine founded and edited by Charles Dickens and published between 1859 and 1895.

A Day's Ride: A Life's Romance: 1861 comedic novel by Charles Lever about the failed adventures of a young man. The novel was unpopular at the time (leading to a marked decline in circulation of the periodical in which it was serialized, *All the Year Round*), but it had a notable impact on Shaw, who described it as his first brush with 'modern ideas'. See Stanley Weintraub, 'Bernard Shaw, Charles Lever, and *Immaturity*', *Bulletin of the Shaw Society of America* 2/1 (January 1957), 11–15, at 11.

111 *Bob Acres and Mr Winkle*: Bob Acres in the play *The Rivals* (1775) by Richard Sheridan (1751–1816), and Nathaniel Winkle in Dickens's novel *The Pickwick Papers* (1836).

Turgenieff: while the others in Shaw's list have been mentioned elsewhere in *The Quintessence*, this reference is to the nineteenth-century Russian playwright and novelist Ivan Turgenev (1818–83), best known for his novel *Fathers and Sons* (1862).

full of Charles O'Malley and Mickey Free: two characters, a soldier and his faithful servant, in Charles Lever's comic adventure novel *Charles O'Malley, The Irish Dragoon* (1841).

the death of Little Nell: the tragic death of the child Little Nell in Dickens's *The Old Curiosity Shop* (1840) was one of the most famous death scenes in nineteenth-century literature.

Swiveller . . . Trabbs's boy: characters in Dickens's *The Old Curiosity Shop* (1841) and *Great Expectations* (1861) respectively.

Mr Badman: John Bunyan's *The Life and Death of Mr. Badman* (1680).

Sheridan: Anglo-Irish comic playwright Richard Sheridan (1751–1816).

'Rightly to be great . . . straw': from Hamlet IV.iv.52–4, describing the necessity of fighting for honour even when the stakes are small.

112 *the sort of laughter . . . an animal trapped and wounded*: Shaw's idea of the supposed connection between laughter and pain in the outlooks and practices of African peoples was a common one among intellectuals of his era, derived from the accounts of British adventurers. Compare Shaw's comments to those of the British anthropologists William Scoresby Routledge

(1859–1939) and Katherine Routledge (1866–1935) in *With a Prehistoric People: The Akikuyu of British East Africa* (London: Edward Arnold, 1910), published just three years before the second edition of *The Quintessence*: 'In disposition the Akikuyu are naturally cheerful, merry, loquacious, and laughter-loving, soon forgetting their troubles and lacking the spirit of vindictiveness; they have a great sense of justice, and endorse the infliction of the severest punishment if they know they are in the wrong' (23).

113 *THE TECHNICAL NOVELTY IN IBSEN'S PLAYS*: this section was added in the 1913 edition.

the Newgate Calendar: a popular compendium of true crime stories related to the execution of prisoners from Newgate Prison. First published in 1773, it was reprinted in four volumes between 1824 and 1826 and had a strong moralizing component.

114 *any attempt to Chadbandize*: an original coinage of Shaw's, referring to the Evangelical preacher Chadband in Dickens's *Bleak House* (1853).

Milton's phrase, 'moral babble': from the play (technically a masque) *Comus* (1634) by John Milton (1608–74).

dramatis personae: (Lat.) the characters in a play.

Grimaldi . . . Sothern, Jefferson, and Henry Irving: famous actors of the eighteenth and nineteenth centuries: English comic actors Joseph Grimaldi (1778–1837) and Edward Askew Sothern (1826–81), American comic actor Joseph Jefferson (1829–1905), and English actor-manager Henry Irving (1838–1905).

115 *the variety theatres*: theatres of the nineteenth and early twentieth centuries, as in vaudeville theatres in the United States and music hall theatres in the UK, which offered a programme of entertainment composed of multiple short performances, ranging from comedy to acrobatics to musical acts, rather than long-form dramatic works.

turned into a very ordinary French drama by the excision of a few lines: Shaw refers here to the well-made plays popularized by such French dramatists as Scribe and Sardou.

116 *Within twenty years women were writing better plays than men*: Shaw refers to a vanguard of female dramatists that would become known as the 'New Woman playwrights' of the 1890s and early 1900s, including figures such as Janet Achurch (1864–1916) and Constance Fletcher (1886–1960). For a further history, see Katherine Newey's *Women's Theatre Writing in Victorian Britain* (London: Palgrave-Macmillan, 2005), which covers the period from 1820 to 1918.

as to which no moral question is raised: here and below Shaw articulates his vision for the 'drama of ideas', the form of intellectual play-craft he helped to popularize and with which he is most associated. Compare to his statement in the 'Author's Apology' to *Mrs Warren's Profession* (1902) that 'there is, flatly, no future now for any drama without music except the drama of thought' (Bernard Shaw, *Mrs Warren's Profession* (London: Constable, 1905), p. xxii).

118 *a simple Moorish soldier . . . a 'supersubtle' Venetian lady of fashion*: Shaw is
referring to the characters of Othello and Desdemona in Shakespeare's
Othello, although in fact Othello was not 'a simple Moorish soldier' in the
play but a renowned general.

out-Heroded Herod: from *Hamlet*, III.ii.14, originally referring to the tendency of actors to overact villainous parts and used here to refer to early
modern dramatists' tendency to include increasingly sensational and lurid
elements in their plays. The phrase refers more to the performance of
Herod as a villain character in medieval drama than to the original biblical
figure who ruled Judaea at the time of Jesus's birth and according to the
Bible ordered the murder of all infants in Bethlehem, as in Matthew 2:16.

in common with Webster: English playwright John Webster (1580–1632),
known for his especially bloody tragedies like The Duchess of Malfi
(1614).

Stratford: Stratford-upon-Avon, the provincial Warwickshire town that
was Shakespeare's birthplace and childhood home and to which he retired.

119 *the fat boy . . . ('I wants to make your flesh creep')*: reference to a character
in Dickens's *Pickwick Papers* (actually known as 'the fat boy') who wants to
sensationalize stories for their shock effect.

John Shakespear's mutton: John Shakespeare (*c*.1531–1601), a provincial
glovemaker, was William Shakespeare's father. Shaw is referring to the
elder Shakespeare's simplicity, mutton being a rougher and less expensive
form of sheep's meat than the more delicate and refined lamb.

Tchekov's Cherry Orchard: the last play by Anton Chekhov (1860–1904),
written in 1903, which inspired Shaw's own play *Heartbreak House:
A Fantasia in the Russian Manner on English Themes* (1919).

Granville-Barker's plays . . . the waste which was the subject of the play:
here Shaw describes the play *Waste* (1906) by Harvey Granville-Barker
(1877–1946), based loosely on the real-life MPs Charles Stewart Parnell
and Charles Wentworth Dilke.

dénouement: (Fr.) the falling action of a story after its climax.

to cut the Gordian knot as Alexander did with a stroke of the sword: the classical legend that Alexander the Great (356–323 BCE), when confronted
with an intractable knot in the palace at Gordium, a part of the Persian
Empire, fulfilled the prophecy of a conqueror one day untying the knot by
simply cutting it with his sword.

Judge Brack . . . such things: Brack says this at the end of Ibsen's *Hedda
Gabler* (1891), when Hedda commits suicide.

120 *the deaths of Little Nell and Paul Dombey*: two of Dickens's most famous
death scenes, that of Little Nell (see note to p. 111) and that of Paul
Dombey in *Dombey and Son* (1848).

When at a loss, kill a child: John Ruskin, in his essay 'Fiction—Fair and
Foul' (1880), writes that 'Nell, in the *Old Curiosity Shop*, was simply killed

for the market, as a butcher kills a lamb'. See John Ruskin, *The Ethics of the Dust, Fiction Fair and Foul, and The Elements of Drawing* (New York: Bryan, Taylor, & Company, 1894), 161.

Phaeton's fall from the chariot of the sun: in the Greek myth, Phaeton, son of the sun-god Apollo Helios, wishes to drive his father's chariot through the sky but cannot control it and is struck down by Zeus.

Shakespear killed Juliet: Shaw is referring to Shakespeare's decision to have his character Juliet kill herself at the end of *Romeo and Juliet* (*c*.1595) after discovering Romeo dead.

Horatio . . . Fortinbras: in Shakespeare's *Hamlet*, Horatio is the only major character still alive by the end of the play; Shaw quips that in Ibsen's hands, Horatio's minimal importance to the plot would have been cause to have him killed by Fortinbras, the Norwegian prince who in Shakespeare's version inherits the Danish throne.

Lady Inger: the main character of Ibsen's third performed play, *Lady Inger of Ostat* (1854), about the unsuccessful struggle for Norwegian independence against Danish rule in the early sixteenth century.

Our uncles . . . cannot legally marry our mothers: this was true at the time of Shaw's writing, as consanguinity laws governing prohibited incestuous relations restricted relationships across marital affinity (i.e., between in-laws). The prohibitions against affinity relationships in the UK were later lifted under the Marriage Act of 1986.

121 *the Angel of the Annunciation*: the angel Gabriel, who in the New Testament announces to the Virgin Mary that she is to carry God's child (Luke 1:26–38).

Mr A. B. Walkley in the prologue of Fanny's First Play: theatre critic Arthur Bingham Walkley (1855–1926) worked with Shaw at *The Star* before becoming critic for *The Times*. Shaw's 1911 play *Fanny's First Play* (which was originally produced anonymously to help increase publicity) contains a play-within-a-play (much like *Hamlet*) and lampoons several theatre critics of the day.

122 *'guilty creatures sitting at a play'*: from *Hamlet* II.ii.551.

123 NEEDED: AN IBSEN THEATRE: this section was added in the 1913 edition.

Swedenborg: Swedish mystic Emanuel Swedenborg (1688–1772).

the formula 'Also sprach Zarathustra': the common refrain in Friedrich Nietzsche's *Thus Spake Zarathustra* (1883), which was intended in part to supplant the Bible as a source of moral and metaphysical teachings.

124 *the story of the wise and foolish virgins*: as recounted in Matthew 25:1–13, ten virgins (likely bridesmaids) await the coming of the bridegroom to a wedding but only five have brought enough oil for their lamps for the duration so the other five are excluded from the wedding when their lamps no longer shine. The story is generally taken as a parable about preparing for the Day of Judgement.

124 *I myself wrote a play for the Salvation Army*: Major Barbara (1905).

no better than Ananias: in Acts 5:1–6, Ananias is a figure who gives only part of his wealth to the apostle Peter and secretly holds back the rest. He is confronted for lying to God and dies from the encounter.

The Second Mrs Tanqueray: the title character of *The Second Mrs Tanqueray* (1892) by Arthur Wing Pinero (1855–1934), who hides the truth about her past. Shaw's *Mrs Warren's Profession* (1893) was in large part a response to Pinero's play.

sciolists: people who pretend to be well informed.

Jeremiah: book of the Old Testament of the Bible, based on the teachings of the prophet Jeremiah and primarily concerning the idea of the Jewish people's exile in Babylon as punishment for paganistic practices.

125 *For this sort of enterprise an endowment is necessary*: Shaw's advocacy for a national theatre was part of various ongoing efforts to establish such a theatre in the United Kingdom since at least 1848, when several London luminaries put forth a proposal for a National Theatre. In 1908, Shaw joined a committee advocating for such a theatre, then called the Shakespeare Memorial National Theatre. In 1913, when this section was added to *The Quintessence*, a bill was brought before the House of Commons to establish a National Theatre, but the effort failed. The drive for a National Theatre did not achieve success until 1949, when the National Theatre Bill passed through Parliament, though the theatre would not actually open until 1963.

THE PERFECT WAGNERITE

127 *since this book was first published twenty-four years ago*: the first edition of *The Perfect Wagnerite* appeared in 1898 and the fourth in 1923.

Handel . . . Bach . . . Mozart . . . Beethoven: leading composers. George Frideric Handel (1685–1759), English composer (of German origin) of the Baroque period; Johann Sebastian Bach (1685–1750), German composer of the Baroque period and most important member of his family of musicians; Wolfgang Amadeus Mozart (1756–91), Austrian composer of the Classical period; Ludwig van Beethoven (1770–1827), German composer widely considered to be the dominant musical figure of the age.

draw the bow of Ulysses: allusion to *The Odyssey* wherein Penelope announces that she will marry the suitor who is strong enough to bend Odysseus' bow, the only one strong enough to do so being Odysseus himself.

tone poem: similar to symphonic poem, a genre of orchestral music that seeks to evoke particular imagery or emotions rather than conform to pre-set musical forms.

'false relations' in the score of Tristan: in classical music, a false (or non-harmonic) relation is 'a chromatic contradiction between two notes sounded together or in different parts of adjacent chords' (Grove Music

Online). The score of Richard Wagner's *Tristan und Isolde* (1859) was marked by use of this device.

Bax . . . Howells: the English composers Arnold Bax (1883–1953), John Ireland (1879–1962), Cyril Scott (1879–1970), Gustav Holst (1874–1934), Eugene Goossens (1845–1906), Ralph Vaughan Williams (1872–1958), Frank Bridge (1879–1941), Rutland Boughton (1878–1960), Joseph Holbrooke (1878–1958), and Herbert Howells (1892–1983).

Haydn: Franz Joseph Haydn (1732–1809), leading Austrian composer during the Classical period.

Elgar: Sir Edward Elgar (1857–1934), leading English composer of the late Romantic period who enjoyed a strong reputation in Europe.

128 *no question of going to Bayreuth . . . when we wish to hear The Ring or Parsifal*: reference to the Bayreuth Festspielhaus in Bayreuth, Germany, the theatre constructed to Wagner's exact specifications for the performances of his operas and opened in 1876.

the Old Vic: leading London theatre, formally the Royal Victoria Hall, first founded as the Royal Coburg Theatre in 1818 (later the Royal Victoria Theatre in 1833), and known in Shaw's lifetime for its traditionalism, largely producing melodramas throughout much of the nineteenth century before becoming known for its Shakespeare repertory in the early twentieth century.

Black-Eyed Susan: comic play of 1829 by Douglas Jerrold (1803–57).

the monarchy and the theatre were restored . . . on the accession of Charles II: the restoration of King Charles II to the throne of England, Scotland, and Ireland in 1660 was followed by the restoration of the theatre: plays had been banned during the Interregnum of 1649–60.

the representation . . . made impossible: Shaw is referring to the change in British stage design from the thrust stages of the Elizabethan and Jacobean periods, during which Shakespeare wrote, to the rise of proscenium-style stages, based on French and Italian models during the period of the Restoration in the late seventeenth century. For more on this revolution in English scenography and theatre design, see David Kornhaber, 'Restoration and Eighteenth-Century England', in Arnold Aronson (ed.), *The Routledge Companion to Scenography* (London: Routledge, 2017), 338–43.

fill up the time by smoking cigarets and drinking: Shaw's descriptions are accurate to much of nineteenth-century theatre, wherein elaborate changes were required between scenes or acts, a condition that Wagner sought to change.

129 *to ask the Théâtre Français to scrap the Molière tradition*: the Théâtre Français, or Comédie-Française, founded in 1680, is a state theatre in Paris, France, and the oldest active theatre company in the world. Its original acting company was composed of members of the theatre troupe led by the playwright and actor Molière (né Jean-Baptiste Poquelin, 1622–73). Although

the theatre was not founded until after Molière's death, it is popularly known as 'La Maison de Molière' (The House of Molière).

129 *Mr William Poel*: English actor (1852–1934) and manager of the Royal Victoria Hall from 1881 to 1883, known especially for his Shakespearean performances.

the Shakespear Memorial Theatre at Stratford-on-Avon: theatre founded in Shakespeare's birthplace and home town in 1879 for the performance of Shakespeare's plays. It was destroyed by fire in 1926, reopened under a new design in 1932, and renamed the Royal Shakespeare Theatre (home of the Royal Shakespeare Company) in 1961.

the play of Coriolanus: Shaw is most likely referring to a 1919 production of *Coriolanus* at the Shakespeare Memorial theatre directed by and starring F. R. (Francis Roberts, or Frank) Benson (1858–1939), presented in abridged form alongside *The Merry Wives of Windsor*.

Mr Bridges Adams: William Bridges-Adams (1889–1965), an English director and designer who worked with the Shakespeare Memorial Theatre from 1919 to 1934.

Mr Atkins: Robert Atkins (1886–1972), director of productions at the Old Vic Theatre from 1921 to 1926.

130 *Herr Reinhardt*: eminent Austrian theatre director Max Reinhardt (1873–1944).

Mr Gordon Craig: Edward Gordon Craig (1872–1966), eminent English scenic designer, one of the foremost practitioners of modernist stage design.

from the revolutions of 1848 . . . to the Imperialist climax of 1871: Shaw is referring to that period of German history running from the unsuccessful left-wing uprisings of 1848 to the unification of the modern German nation state in 1871.

Royal William: Kaiser Wilhelm I (1797–1888), the king of Prussia who became the first German emperor and ruled from 1871 to 1888.

William had to seek safety in Holland: Kaiser Wilhelm II (1859–1941, r. 1888–1918) fled Germany after its defeat in the First World War and sought refuge in the Netherlands, where he lived until his death.

Rhine maidens . . . marking the ruins of empires: aspects of Europe in the years after the First World War. In order, these are: courtship between German women and British soldiers, or Tommies; the French decision to post sentries from their regiments of Senegalese tirailleurs outside Goethe's home in Frankfurt when they occupied the city in 1920; the Bolshevik Revolution in Russia and the execution of the Romanov Tsar Nicholas II and his family; the end of the Habsburg and Hohenzollern dynasties in Austria and Germany respectively.

the Stuarts and Bourbons: the Stuart dynasty ruled Scotland, England, and Ireland in various combinations from 1371 to 1714; the Bourbon dynasty ruled France, Spain, Luxembourg, Sicily, Parma, and Portugal in various combinations from 1272 to 1861.

Götterdämmerung: (Ger.) literally 'the downfall of the gods'; name of the 1848 opera by Wagner, the last episode in the Ring Cycle, sometimes rendered in English by Shaw as 'Night Falls on the Gods'.

131 *Siegfried Trebitsch*: Austrian playwright (1868–1956) and Shaw's German translator. Their letters are collected in *Bernard Shaw's Letters to Siegfried Trebitsch*, ed. Samuel E. Weiss (Stanford, CA: Stanford University Press, 1986).

132 *crotchets and quavers*: notes in musical notation, a quaver being half the value of a crotchet: in US usage, a crotchet is a quarter note, a quaver is an eighth note.

133 *Engels's Condition of the Laboring Classes in England*: influential treatise *The Condition of the Working Class in England* (1845) by Friedrich Engels (1820–95), first published in English in 1885.

the most exclusive Dresden circles: Wagner lived in Dresden from 1842 to 1849, during a critical moment in his career when he served as the Hofkapellmeister (court conductor). His operas *Rienzi* (1840), *The Flying Dutchman* (1843), and *Tannhäuser* (1845) were all staged in the city.

grand opera: genre of opera prevalent in the nineteenth century, marked by large casts, long narratives covering multiple acts, and elaborate stage spectacle.

serious music-drama: Wagner's works are often described as music drama rather than opera to differentiate the predominance of dramatic narrative and the use of music in the service of such storytelling. He himself preferred the term *Gesamtkunstwerk* (total artwork). See in particular his 1851 treatise on the topic, *Opera and Drama*.

popular . . . As You Like It . . . true . . . Measure for Measure: Shaw is here drawing a distinction between the more light-hearted Shakespeare comedies such as *As You Like It* and those darker comedies like *Measure for Measure* that would become known as his 'problem plays', as first designated by F. S. Boas in *Shakespeare and His Predecessors* (1896).

134 *Die Feen is a first essay in romantic opera*: *Die Feen* (1834) was Wagner's first opera and remained unperformed in his lifetime.

an attempt to revive the barricades of Dresden in the Temple of the Grail: references to the uprising in Dresden, Germany, in May 1849, in which Wagner was involved, and to a key location in his opera *Parsifal* (1882).

135 *the dilemma of Wotan*: one of the central dramatic events in *Die Walküre* (1856) wherein Wotan, king of the gods, finds himself in irreconcilable conflicts with both his wife and daughter.

political mugwumps: political centrists, referring specifically to American politicians and activists of the Republican Party who supported Democratic presidential candidate Grover Cleveland (1837–1908) in 1884 in protest over financial corruption.

135 *an eminent addition to our literature*: Shaw refers to William Ashton Ellis's *Richard Wagner's Prose Works* (London: Kegan Paul, Trench, Trübner & Co., 1892).

having learnt more about music than about anything else in my youth: Shaw came from a very musical household which included the prominent Dublin music instructor George John Vandaleur Lee (1830–86), who lived with the Shaws through much of the playwright's youth. Both his mother Lucinda Elizabeth Shaw, née Gurly (1830–1913) and his sister Lucinda Frances Shaw (1853–1920) were singers.

136 *Christmas pantomimes*: spectacular Christmas-themed extravaganzas that have been popular with British and Irish audiences since the eighteenth century; the Theatre Royal at Drury Lane was especially known for its Christmas pantomimes.

137 *giving musical expression to the drama*: here Shaw recapitulates one of the defining distinctions between bel canto opera and Wagner's music dramas.

In classical music . . . there are first subjects . . . hypodiapente: Shaw employs various musical terms here. In a movement in sonata form, the two principal thematic ideas are designated first and second 'subject'; a 'fantasia' is a composition that deliberately follows no set structure; a 'recapitulation' is the third and final section of a movement in sonata form that returns to the composition's principal thematic ideas introduced in the first; a 'coda' is the last part, literally 'tail', of a musical composition. A 'fugue' (from Lat. *fuga*, flight) is 'a piece of music based on canonic imitation (one voice 'chasing' another), with imitative counterpoint as the single unifying feature'. Within a fugue: the 'counter-subject' is thematic material within the fugue which appears as counterpoint to the subject; a 'stretto' is a section of overlapping voices offering different portions of a subject or counter-subject; a 'pedal point' is 'a long sustained note held through many bars while movement continues in other parts of the piece'. A 'ground bass' is 'a melody, usually in the bass, recurring many times in succession, accompanied by continuous variation in the upper parts'; a set of these variations, usually in triple meter, is often called a passacaglia. A 'canon' is a composition in which one voice begins a melody which is then imitated precisely in another voice, beginning a few beats later at the same or different interval; in a 'canon ad hypodiapente' the second voice begins a fifth below. (Quoted definitions from Grove Music online.)

sonnets, triolets: poetical forms, the sonnet following a fourteen-line structure and one of several standard rhyme schemes, the triolet following an eight-line structure with a standard rhyme scheme.

aria . . . recitative . . . cabaletta . . . full close: operatic terms. 'Aria' and 'recitative' are the two main vocal forms in traditional opera, the 'aria' being a primarily lyrical piece written for a solo voice with full orchestral accompaniment and the 'recitative' being text recited with less rich accompaniment, the main vehicle for dialogue and action. The 'cabaletta' is the second movement of a double aria in nineteenth-century Italian opera, typically faster and more animated than the first, and often with opportunities for virtuosic display. A 'full close' (or perfect cadence) is a harmonic progression consisting of a dominant chord followed by a tonic chord which is usually used at the end of an aria.

138 *at Klondyke five years ago*: during the Klondike Gold Rush of 1896–9 over 100,000 prospectors descended on the Yukon region of Canada in search of gold.

found the Plutonic empire: turning one's focus to base things, both of the earth and sinister, derived from Pluto, the Roman god of the underworld.

139 *the Rhine*: major European river that runs from Switzerland through Germany into the North Sea. Long the subject of literary and artistic reflection, the river became an especially important symbol of German identity during the nineteenth century in the lead-up to the formation of the German state in 1871.

barcarolles . . . about the Lorely and her fated lovers: a barcarolle is a piece imitating or suggesting 'songs sung by Venetian gondoliers as they propel their boats through the water' (Grove Music online). The legendary maiden Loreley lured boats along the Rhine to destruction with her siren song and beauty.

141 *it is called Godhead*: Shaw's descriptions in this paragraph strongly evoke the theory of Creative Evolution and the Life Force that he put forward in plays like *Man and Superman* (1905), *Back to Methuselah* (1922), and elsewhere, holding that an overriding organic will gave direction and purpose to human evolution. Shaw was strongly influenced in these beliefs by his contemporary Samuel Butler (1835–1902), particularly Butler's book *Evolution, Old and New* (1879). For a detailed consideration, see Carl Henry Mills, 'Shaw's Theory of Creative Evolution', *Shaw Review*, 16/3 (September 1973), 123–32.

143 *a European Power, as Lassalle said*: German radical thinker Ferdinand Lassale (1825–64) wrote on the function of lies in European civil society and their role in suppressing radical change. Speaking of the press, he condemned 'daily new lies: lies by means of pure fact alone, lies by means of invented facts, lies by means of facts distorted into their opposites—such were the weapons with which we were fought!' ('The Press', *Speeches of Ferdinand Lassalle*, ed. Jakob Altmaier (New York: International Publishers, 1927), 28).

145 *Thou mak'st me . . . Thine only care*: untitled hymn composed in 1680 by English poet and MP Benjamin Rudyerd (1572–1658). See *Memoirs of Sir Benjamin Rudyerd*, ed. James Alexander Manning (London: T&W Boone, 1861), 255.

146 *'Hab' Acht!'*: (Ger.) 'Pay attention!'

147 *seized on the Jew and drained him as a Christian duty*: here, as elsewhere, Shaw recapitulates anti-Semitic tropes common to Wagner's work and thought. On this aspect of Wagner's legacy and Shaw's relationship to it,

Explanatory Notes

see Marc A. Weiner, *Richard Wagner and the Anti-Semitic Imagination* (Lincoln, NE: University of Nebraska Press, 1997).

148 *rob the Church . . . as in France and Italy for instance*: Shaw's implicit statement on the corruption of the Roman Catholic Church, the dominant religious force in both France and Italy, was part of widespread expressions of anti-Catholic sentiment in England in the nineteenth and early twentieth centuries. For more, see Christopher Clark and Wolfram Kaiser (eds), *Culture Wars: Secular–Catholic Conflict in Nineteenth-Century Europe* (Cambridge: Cambridge University Press, 2003).

151 *Bishop took in the English Reform agitation . . . Sterndale Bennett in the . . . Free Trade movements*: English composers Sir Henry Rowley Bishop (1787–1856) and Sterndale Bennett (1816–75). Neither participated in the major political upheavals during their lifetimes, the English Reform Act of 1832, which changed the British electoral system, and the further reforms called by the working-class Chartist movement of the mid-nineteenth century.

August Roeckel: German composer (1814–76) and friend of Wagner as well as of Mikhail Bakunin (see note below). Wagner's letters to Roeckel, mentioned here by Shaw, were written while Roeckel was serving a long prison sentence for his involvement in the uprisings of 1848 and are a primary source for understanding Wagner's revolutionary intention in writing the Ring Cycle. See *Richard Wagner's Letters to August Roeckel*, trans. Eleonor C. Sellar (Bristol: Arrowsmith, n.d.).

Michael Bakoonin, afterwards a famous apostle of revolutionary Anarchism: Shaw's idiosyncratic spelling makes it somewhat unclear that he is referring to Mikhail Bakunin (1814–76), the influential Russian anarchist.

153 *Stonehenge and the cromlechs and round towers*: the famous Neolithic stone monument in Wiltshire, England; a series of megalithic stone tombs found in Wales and elsewhere; and early medieval stone towers found primarily in Ireland.

a Fellow of the Royal Society: a member of the Royal Society of London for Improving Natural Knowledge, an esteemed learned society founded in 1660 by King Charles II.

thrusting towards higher and higher organization as it has hitherto done: decades later, Shaw would come to dramatize much of this vision in *Back to Methuselah*, in which artists and thinkers dominate the distant future.

Bishop Colenso's criticism of the Pentateuch: Shaw is referring to *The Pentateuch and the Book of Joshua Critically Examined* (1862) by Bishop J. W. Colenso (1814–83), an Anglican cleric, who argued that portions of the Bible should not be taken as literally true. The Pentateuch refers to the first five books of the Old Testament of the Bible, while the Book of Joshua is the sixth book.

Bakoonin . . . find its own way: Bakunin's ideas were communicated in a great number of articles, pamphlets, and books, but the most comprehensive and influential account was probably that which he offered in *Statism and Anarchy* (1873).

156 *'Was keinemn . . . red' ich zu dir'*: (Ger.) translated by Andrew Porter as 'These thoughts that I have never uttered, though I may think them, still they're unspoken; I think aloud, then, speaking to you' (Richard Wagner, *Die Walküre*, trans. Andrew Porter (London: Overture, 2011), 77). Shaw's rendition of Wagner's libretto is missing the word *denn* (because) prior to the word *ewig* (forever).

160 *Joshua told the sun to stand still*: in Joshua 10:1–15, God holds the sun in place to allow Joshua to defeat his enemies in battle.

a whale's throat . . . swallow Jonah: in Jonah 1:17, Jonah is described as being swallowed by a 'great fish' and remains in its stomach for three days and three nights. Contra Shaw's point, a sperm whale is physically capable of swallowing a human whole and there are accounts by whalers of this very occurrence. See Rose Eveleth, 'Could a Whale Accidentally Swallow You? It Is Possible', *Smithsonian Magazine*, 25 February 2013.

161 *repeal our monstrous laws against 'blasphemy'*: in fact, such laws were not repealed in England until 2008, more than a century after Shaw wrote these words.

162 *an anticipation of the 'overman' of Nietzsche*: Shaw's comparison of Wagner's Siegfried to the idea of the Übermensch, or overman, developed by Friedrich Nietzsche, was a common one at the time. In 1901, the German music critic Alfred Lorenz-Gotha (1868–1939) put forward this argument directly in an article titled 'Parsifal as Übermensch' (*Die Musik*, 1 (1901–2), 1876–82). Nietzsche himself, who was at one time close to Wagner, famously broke with him years before he developed his concept of the Übermensch in *Thus Spake Zarathustra* and would lay out his criticisms of the composer in one of his last works, *Nietzsche contra Wagner* (1889). Whether or not Nietzsche's Übermensch can be connected to Wagner, the figure would have a profound influence on Shaw, particularly in his play *Man and Superman*. On the similarities and differences between the Nietzschean Übermensch and Shavian superman, see Mills, 'Shaw's Theory of Creative Evolution'.

the eyeless fish of the American caverns: Shaw is referring to obligate cavefish, many of which are marked by an evolutionary regression of the eyes. While there are over 200 species found across the world, cavefish are common to the American West.

168 *the allied sovereigns*: those European monarchs allied with England for the defeat of Napoleon Bonaparte in 1814, most notably the tsar of Russia and the king of Prussia.

170 *cadenza . . . high C for the soprano all complete*: a 'cadenza' is a highly ornamented passage sung by a soloist; *allegro a capella* (correctly *a cappella*) is a musical indication combining a tempo marking, 'allegro', meaning lively, and 'a capella', meaning 'in chapel or choir style', typically

singing unaccompanied; 'triplets' are 'a group of three notes to be played in the time of two of the same kind' (Grove), in this case semiquavers (sixteenth notes in US usage). *Don Giovanni* (1787) is one of the most famous operas by Wolfgang Amadeus Mozart with libretto by Da Ponte; for 'coda', see note to p. 137; the Leonore overture discussed here is Beethoven's Leonore, Overture No. 3 from his opera *Fidelio* (rev. 1806). 'Contrapuntal' refers to two simultaneous but independent melody lines within a work of music; *points d'orgue* (Fr.) literally 'organ points', refers to several harmonies carried over a sustained note; a 'high C' is the highest C note of the soprano vocal range.

170 *La Favorita or 'Per te immenso giubilo' in Lucia*: *La Favorita* (1840) is a grand opera by Gaetano Donizetti (1797–1848), while 'Per te d'immenso giubilo' is a chorus with solo interlude in his earlier opera *Lucia di Lammermoor* (1835).

Verdi: Italian opera composer Giuseppe Verdi (1813–1901).

pezzi d' insieme: (It.) lit. 'pieces together', meaning ensemble pieces for the singers.

171 *Covent Garden*: name commonly used to designate the Royal Opera House, from its location in Covent Garden, London. *Lohengrin* had its English premiere there on 8 May 1875.

flute obbligato ... prima donna: in this context, 'obbligato' refers to a prominent instrumental part, here for flute, in an aria; 'prima donna' (first lady) is the leading female role in an opera.

Ibsen's Vikings in Helgeland: *The Vikings at Helgeland* (1858), Henrik Ibsen's seventh play.

172 *Punch and Don Juan ... the pantomime clown*: Punch, the violent husband character from the tradition of 'Punch and Judy' puppet shows in England; Don Juan, the legendary Spanish libertine (who would also serve as inspiration for Jack Tanner in Shaw's own *Man and Superman*); Robert Maccaire, an amoral swindler who first appeared in the play *L'Auberge des Adrets* (1823) by Benjamin Antier (1787–1870), Jean-Armand Lacoste (known as Saint-Amand) (1797–1885), and Alexandre Chaponnier (known as Polyanthe) (1793–1852); Jeremy Diddler, a swindler character who originally appeared in the play *Raising the Wind* (1803) by James Kenney (1780–1849); 'pantomime clown' is a comic stage figure who appeared in British Christmas pantomimes and other popular comic forms, of the sort that would later be adapted by Charlie Chaplin (himself a former music-hall performer) into his character of The Tramp.

the late Lord Lytton, in his Strange Story: the novel *A Strange Story* (1845) was written by Edward Bulwer-Lytton (1803–73).

173 *'indirect taxation'*: taxes levied on goods and services rather than individuals, such as sales tax.

174 *The majority of men at present in Europe have no business to be alive*: Shaw would make such dark and extremely dangerous proclamations throughout

his career, as in his play *The Simpleton of the Unexpected Isles* (1935), where an angel determines who will live and who will die on the basis of 'whether you are worth your salt or not' (*The Bodley Head Bernard Shaw: Collected Plays with their Prefaces*, ed. Laurence, vi. 822). On this aspect of Shaw's thought, see Arnold Silver, *Bernard Shaw: The Darker Side* (Stanford, CA: Stanford University Press, 1982).

until we address ourselves earnestly and scientifically to the task of producing trustworthy human material for society: Shaw would develop these ideas further in *Man and Superman*. Compare to the celebration voiced by Don Juan/Jack Tanner in Act III of that play for 'the great central purpose of breeding the race, ay, breeding it to heights now deemed superhuman'. See George Bernard Shaw, *Man and Superman*, in *The Bodley Head Bernard Shaw: Collected Plays with their Prefaces*, vol. 2 (London: The Bodley Head, 1971), 637. For the connections between Shaw's views and the history of the eugenics movement, see Piers J. Hale, 'The Search for Purpose in a Post-Darwinian Universe: George Bernard Shaw, "Creative Evolution," and Shavian Eugenics: "The Dark Side of the Force"', *History and Philosophy of the Life Sciences*, 28/2 (2006), 191–213.

the Freewiller of Necessity: compare to Friedrich Nietzsche's statements on the connection between necessity and the 'free spirits' for whom his philosophy is intended in *Human, All Too Human* (1878): 'The sun of a new gospel is casting its first beam on the topmost summits in the soul of every individual . . . Everything is necessity—thus says the new knowledge; and this knowledge itself is necessity' (Nietzsche, *Human, All Too Human: A Book for Free Spirits*, trans. R. J. Hollingdale (Cambridge: Cambridge University Press, 1986), 58).

175 *the austerity of the Commonwealth . . . the licence of the Restoration*: the Commonwealth period in England, which lasted from the execution of Charles I in 1649 to the restoration of Charles II in 1660, was marked by great social austerity in line with Puritan religious beliefs, whereas the Restoration period of the 1660s to the 1680s was marked by greater social freedom under the libertine rule of Charles II, sometimes known as 'the Merry Monarch'.

some permanently practical . . . the correction of its excesses by the next reaction: Shaw's dispiriting view of democracy and social progress will come to a head in late plays like *On the Rocks* (1933), in which the Prime Minister of England imagines being able to 'take both the people and the spoilers and oppressors by the scruff of their silly necks and just sling them into the way they should go with as many kicks as may be needful to make a thorough job of it' (*The Bodley Head Bernard Shaw: Collected Plays with their Prefaces*, ed. Laurence, vi. 719).

primo tenore robusto: one of the subcategories of leading tenors, connoting one with an emotive and powerful voice. Despite Shaw's categorization, the character of Siegfried is typically considered a *Heldentenor*, a subcategory that is similar to the *tenore robusto* but with a deeper, baritonal quality.

176 *as the scene of the Ghost in Hamlet, or the statue in Don Giovanni*: in Shakespeare's *Hamlet*, the character of Hamlet must confront the ghost of his father, whereas in Mozart's opera *Don Giovanni*, the title character is confronted with a statue of the Commendatore, whom he killed, who comes to life and warns him to repent his libertine ways.

Prometheus Unbound: 1820 verse drama by Shelley about the trials of Prometheus, the Greek mythological figure who brought fire to humans, and the overthrow of the Graeco-Roman god Jupiter.

177 *Dr Johnson kicking the stone to confute Berkeley*: in a famous passage in the *Life of Samuel Johnson* (1791) by James Boswell (1740–95), Johnson humorously refutes the philosopher George Berkeley (known as Bishop Berkeley) (1685–1753) regarding the non-existence of matter by kicking a stone.

178 *Browning's David . . . 'All's Love; yet all's Law'*: quotation from the poem 'Saul' (1855) by Robert Browning (1812–89). David is Browning's version of King David, the biblical king of Israel, who succeeded Saul.

Tristan and Isolde: 1865 opera by Richard Wagner based on the Celtic legend of star-crossed lovers who would rather perish than live without one another.

179 *Das ewig Weibliche*: see note to p. 39.

180 *will share the fate of China*: Shaw refers to the encroachments of European imperialism in China, which by the end of the nineteenth century led to much of the country's territory and many of its most important cities being under the official or de facto control of various European powers.

published by the Fabian Society and entitled The Impossibilities of Anarchism: this was published in London in 1893.

183 *Ruy Gomez and Ernani, or Othello and Iago*: in the play *Hernani* (1830) by French author Victor Hugo (1802–85), the character of Don Ruy Gomes de Silva convinces the young lover Hernani to kill himself in vengeance for his marriage to Gomes's niece and fiancée. In Shakespeare's *Othello*, Iago drives Othello to murder by convincing him, falsely, of his wife's infidelity.

the Richter concerts: a series of six concerts of Wagner's work given in London in 1877 by the Hungarian conductor Hans Richter (1843–1916) at Wagner's behest, followed by further concerts across Britain through the end of the nineteenth century where Richter introduced audiences to leading European composers of the day.

185 *Rossini*: Gioachino Antonio Rossini (1792–1868), prominent Italian opera composer.

186 *Un Ballo in Maschera*: 1859 opera by Giuseppe Verdi. It originally concerned the 1792 assassination of the King of Sweden at a masked ball and is usually heard in that form today, but in order to pass the censor the setting was moved to Boston during the colonial period which is likely the version which Shaw would have heard.

the Hiordis of Ibsen: character in Ibsen's *The Vikings at Helgeland* (1857).

187 *The Daily Telegraph . . . The Daily Chronicle*: while Shaw does not provide enough context to determine the specific articles to which he is referring, the occasion for the debate he describes was most likely the publication by Edward Arnold in London in 1896 of *Wagner's Heroines* by Constance Elizabeth Maud (1857–1929), which was widely reviewed and discussed at the time.

188 *Wagner's most eminent English interpreter*: William Ashton Ellis (1852–1919), who published the first authoritative English translations of Wagner's prose works beginning in 1892.

189 *as unconsciously as Julius Cæsar disclosed it long ago*: in Shakespeare's *Julius Caesar* Caesar declares: 'Cowards die many times before their deaths. | The valiant never taste of death but once. | Of all the wonders that I yet have heard, | It seems to me most strange that men should fear, | Seeing that death, a necessary end, | Will come when it will come' (II.ii.33–8).

Trauermarsch: (Ger.) funeral march. Siegfried's funeral march, in Act III of *Götterdämmerung* (1876), is among Wagner's most famous compositions.

190 *The situation of Cleopatra and Antony*: the doomed lovers beset by enemies in Shakespeare's *Antony and Cleopatra*.

192 *the crash of 1849 at Dresden*: see note to p. 134.

the first Bayreuth festival in 1876: this was held at the Bayreuth Festspielhaus in Bayreuth, Germany, which continues to this day to showcase Wagner's works.

Why He Changed His Mind: this section was added beginning with the 1907 (third) edition.

the history of Germany from 1849 to 1876: the timeline between the May Uprising in Dresden in 1849, the year after Wagner began composing the Ring cycle, to the opening of the Bayreuth Festspielhaus in 1876, the year in which he completed his opera.

Bismarck: Otto von Bismarck (1815–98), the powerful Prussian politician who masterminded the unification of Germany in 1871 and served as its chancellor until 1890.

The International . . . Karl Marx: the dissolution of the International Workingmen's Association (IWA), known as the First International, which operated from 1864 to 1876. Mikhail Bakunin joined the First International in 1868 and was later expelled by Karl Marx at the fifth congress of the IWA in 1872.

193 *The suppression of the Paris Commune*: the violent conclusion to the rule of the Paris Commune, the socialist revolutionary body that briefly governed Paris in March–May 1871 following the chaos of the Franco-Prussian War, until it was dislodged by the French army after a week of street battles.

193 *Thiers . . . Delescluze*: important French figures. Adolphe Thiers (1797–
1877) was a former revolutionary who played leading roles in the July
Revolution of 1830, which ended the Bourbon monarchy, and the
Revolution of 1848, which established the Second French Republic. He
later ordered the suppression of the Paris Commune following the end of
the Franco-Prussian war, and served as president of the Third Republic
from 1871 to 1873. For Galliffet, see note to p. 343. The novelist Victor
Hugo (1802–85) left France when Louis-Napoleon (later Napoleon III)
came to power in 1851 and criticized the new ruler from his home on
Jersey, one of the British Channel Islands; Félix Pyat (1810–89), a radical
journalist, was one of the leaders of the Paris Commune; Louis Charles
Delescluze (1809–71), another radical journalist, served as military leader
of the Paris Commune.

New Caledonia: French overseas protectorate in the South Pacific that
partly served as a penal colony during the late nineteenth century.

194 *celebrated the event with his Kaisermarsch*: march composed by Wagner in
1871 celebrating the German victory in the Franco-Prussian War and the
coronation of Kaiser Wilhelm I as the new emperor of a united Germany.

Marseillaise or the Carmagnole: 'La Marseillaise' is the national anthem of
France, composed in 1792 by Claude Joseph Rouget de Lisle (1760–1836);
'La Carmagnole' was a popular song during the French Revolution. Both
songs were frequently sung by French soldiers during the Revolutionary
wars.

Hôtel de Ville: seat of city government in Paris, which was burned during
the final days of the Paris Commune.

Arc de Triomphe . . . the Champs Elysées: monumental arch commissioned
by Napoleon Bonaparte in 1806 and finished in 1836 by King Louis
Philippe (1773–1850, r. 1830–48), who also expanded the Avenue des
Champs-Élysées at the end of which the arch stands, turning the street
into a major thoroughfare of the city.

195 *pelf*: money, with a negative connotation implying it was obtained dis-
honestly.

exoterically a model philanthropic employer and esoterically a financier: here
and below Shaw foreshadows the development of his own character of
Andrew Undershaft in *Major Barbara*, who is also 'a model philanthropic
employer' and, after a sort, a proponent of social change.

The Press, which manufactures public opinion on his side: Shaw's descriptions
here anticipate the ideas of fellow radical thinker Noam Chomsky (1928–),
co-author with Edward S. Herman of *Manufacturing Consent: The Political
Economy of the Mass Media* (New York: Pantheon Books, 1988).

196 *ci-devant*: (Fr.) 'from before', meaning out-of-date or obsolete.

ten years reading in the library of the British Museum: Karl Marx spent
many years researching and writing in the reading rooms of the British
Museum (now the British Library), where he wrote *Das Kapital*. Ironically,

Shaw too began his career in London by also reading and writing at the British Museum before securing his first journalism post.

197 *mitrailleuses*: small mounted artillery pieces that were forerunners to the machine gun, firing multiple rounds of ammunition at once or in succession.

Eine Kapitulation: unperformed script by Wagner, written in 1871, which satirizes the events of the Paris Commune; though intended as a libretto, it was never set to music.

doggerel . . . Overture to William Tell: Shaw is saying that the famous tune of Rossini's Overture to his opera *William Tell* (1829) was mocked by Wagner in the rhythm of 'Republik, Republik, Republik-lik-lik' in his libretto *Eine Kapitulation*.

volte-face: (Fr.) 'about face', or to turn around suddenly.

the Tannhäuser fiasco: the disastrous run at the Paris Opéra in 1861 of Wagner's opera *Tannhäuser*, which closed after only three performances.

the realities of political power . . . and train their guns: compare to *Major Barbara*, where Undershaft declares 'Your pious mob fills up ballot papers and imagines it is governing its masters; but the ballot paper that really governs is the paper that has a bullet wrapped up in it' (*The Bodley Head Bernard Shaw: Collected Plays with Their Prefaces*, ed. Laurence, v. 174).

199 *Henry the Eighth*: per Shaw's description, Henry VIII (1491–1509, r. 1509–47) showed a keen interest in medical matters and founded the Royal College of Physicians in 1518.

Harvey: English physician William Harvey (1578–1657) was among the first to determine the working of the human circulatory system.

Home Office: department of the British government responsible for immigration, security, and law enforcement. Shaw uses the term metaphorically to refer to ideas that were basic and obvious to Wagner.

200 *Schopenhauer's famous treatise 'The World as Will and Representation'*: seminal work of metaphysics *The World as Will and Representation*, first published in 1818 and subsequently revised and expanded in 1844 and 1859, by German philosopher Arthur Schopenhauer (1788–1860), whose work had a profound influence on Shaw. For more on Shaw's philosophical debt, see Arthur H. Nethercot, 'Bernard Shaw, Philosopher', *PMLA* 69/1 (Mar. 1954), 57–75.

'seldom has there . . . reasonably formed ideas': from a letter Wagner wrote to Roeckel on 23 August 1856. See *Richard Wagner's Letters to August Roeckel*, 147.

peace, annihilation and Nirvana: the Buddhist concept of Nirvana, as it is adopted within Schopenhauer's philosophy, refers to the idea of spiritual enlightenment attained through intellectual detachment from the world—a process that Schopenhauer came to believe was necessary to escape from the inevitability of human disappointment and despair.

200 *Meliorist*: one who believes that progress can be achieved through human action.

201 *'had taken form at a time . . . existence free from pain'*: the passage comes from a letter Wagner wrote to Roeckel on 23 August 1856. See *Richard Wagner's Letters to August Roeckel*, 149.

'*Hellenic*': for Wagner, the Greek, or Hellenic, spirit was defined by what he called 'the ordinary enjoyment of life', as he described in a letter to Roeckel on 12 September 1856. This view is partly derived from Schopenhauer, who describes 'Greek paganism' as 'wholly optimistic'. See *Richard Wagner's Letters to August Roeckel*, 60; and Arthur Schopenhauer, *The World as Will and Representation*, trans. E. F. J. Payne (New York: Dover, 1966), ii. 605.

the Jew having at that time become for him the whipping boy for all modern humanity: here again Shaw acknowledges, but does not challenge, Wagner's virulent anti-Semitism. On Shaw's relationship to Wagner's anti-Semitism, see Marc A. Weiner, *Richard Wagner and the Anti-Semitic Imagination* (Lincoln, NE: University of Nebraska Press, 1997).

203 *Beethoven's adagios could be quoted against his scherzos . . . as to whether he was a melancholy man or a merry one*: Shaw is saying that Beethoven wrote both slow sombre adagios and livelier scherzos, so that two fools, quoting him against himself, might dispute as to whether he was melancholy or merry, whereas such judgements are simplistic and ill-informed.

204 *God Save the Queen*: the national anthem of the United Kingdom.

Leitmotifs: first reference in Shaw's treatise to Wagner's famous system of leitmotifs, the recurring musical themes by which different characters or situations were known and one of the most influential aspects of his musical system.

Haydn's Creation: Haydn's oratorio *The Creation* (1799).

206 *the chord of the minor ninth, ci-devant diminished seventh*: a chord of a minor ninth is one that reaches one semitone above an octave; a diminished seventh chord is the same chord with the root omitted. Both chords are tonally unstable.

Weber's Freischütz or Meyerbeer's Robert the Devil: the operas *Der Freischütz* (1821) by Carl Maria von Weber (1786–1826) and *Robert le Diable* (1831) by Meyerbeer.

207 *distinguished by the character of their music . . . Don Giovanni from Leporello . . . Sarastro from Papagena*: the distinctions between the musical characterizations of the aristocratic Don Giovanni and his servant Leporello in Mozart's *Don Giovanni* (1787), and between Sarastro, high priest, and Papagena, who becomes the bird-catcher's wife, in Mozart's *The Magic Flute* (1791).

209 '*Ein zullendes Kind*': (Ger.) literally 'a crying child', the name of one of the arias from *Siegfried*.

Auber and Offenbach: French composers Daniel Auber (1782–1871) and Jacques Offenbach (1819–80).

210 *Bunyan . . . Austin Dobson*: English writers, the author John Bunyan (1628–88), art critic and essayist John Ruskin (1819–1900), and poets Robert Herrick (1591–1674) and Henry Austin Dobson (1840–1921).

211 *all his ordinary dialogue . . . As You Like It*: *As You Like It* is unique among Shakespeare's plays in that the majority of the text is written in prose rather than verse. Shaw praises this aspect of the play elsewhere, as in his review of an 1896 production of the play, where he writes that the play 'has the overwhelming advantage of being written for the most part in prose instead of in blank verse . . . And such prose! The first scene alone . . . is worth ten acts of the ordinary Elizabethan sing-song.' See Bernard Shaw, *Dramatic Opinions and Essays* (New York: Bretano's, 1906), ii. 119.

'*What a piece of work is Man!*': title character's line in *Hamlet*, II.ii.306.

The Cenci: see note to p. 283.

Dalla sua pace . . . Leise, leise: Shaw refers to three arias, 'Dalla sua pace' (From her Peace) from Mozart's *Don Giovanni* (1787); 'Che farò senza Euridice' (What shall I do without Eurydice?) from Gluck's *Orfeo ed Euridice* (1762); and 'Leise, Leise' (Softly, Softly) from Weber's *Der Freischütz*.

Il mio tesoro and Non mi dir: two arias ('My treasure' and 'Tell me not') from Mozart's *Don Giovanni*.

212 *Figaro*: *The Marriage of Figaro* (1786), an opera buffa, or comic opera, with music by Mozart and libretto by Lorenzo Da Ponte (1749–1838).

213 *Bach set comic dialogue . . . as he set the recitatives of the Passion*: the Passion refers to the final events of Jesus's life, including his arrest, crucifixion, and resurrection. Two of Bach's Passions survive, the St John (1723) and St Matthew (1727), in which soloists, chorus, and orchestra tell the story of the Passion according to the accounts in those Gospels. Shaw is saying that Bach does not distinguish between secular and sacred music in terms of the music he writes for his recitatives.

Balzac's short story entitled Gambara: a short story of 1837.

Les Huguenots: opera of 1836 by Meyerbeer.

the Baroque school in architecture: an ornate form of architecture prevalent in Italy and elsewhere from the seventeenth century to the mid-eighteenth century.

'*absolute musician*': absolute music was a German expression first appearing in Romantic writings and suggesting an ideal of musical purity, instrumental and without words.

quadrille tunes: simple music composed of five or six melodic parts to accompany quadrille folk dances in the eighteenth and nineteenth centuries.

214 *The Prophet*: the 1849 opera *Le Prophète* by Meyerbeer.

215 *The Mastersingers*: Wagner's *Die Meistersinger von Nürnberg* (1876).

Gounod: French composer Charles-François Gounod (1818–93). The quotation on Mozart as a 'summit', made specifically in reference to *Don Giovanni*, appears in the 'Mozart Supplement' in *Musical Times*, 1 December 1894, 28.

216 *Wagner's successors in European rank were Brahms, Elgar, and Richard Strauss*: Shaw says that Wagner was at the summit of a movement rather than its beginning and in fact the most important composers who came after him did not follow in his footsteps. Shaw claims that the reputation of Johannes Brahms (1833–97) rests on absolute music and not on works like the choral *German Requiem* (1865–8). Elgar's importance is said to derive from his symphonies and *Enigma Variations* (1899); when using Shakespeare as a theme, he writes *Falstaff* (1913) as a symphonic study not an opera. Similarly in the work of Richard Strauss (1864–1949), the work is 'effected by instrumental music alone'.

Berlioz . . . Bantock: French composer Louis-Hector Berlioz (1803–69), Hungarian composer Franz Liszt (1811–86), English composer Sir Granville Bantock (1868–1946).

217 *I said in the first edition of this book*: while this section, 'The Music of the Future', had existed since the first edition of the book in 1898, Shaw revised and expanded it for the fourth edition in 1922.

218 *the Khedive of Egypt and the Sultan of Turkey*: the ruler of the Khedivate of Egypt, a subsidiary state of the Ottoman Empire, who was at the time Ismail Pasha (1830–95, r. 1863–79), and the ruler of the Ottoman Empire, who was at the time Sultan Abdulaziz (1830–76, r. 1861–76).

219 *Hampton Court Palace . . . Richmond Hill*: Hampton Court is a royal palace, now in Greater London and accessible from the river, originally built for Cardinal Wolsey, then 'gifted' to Henry VIII, and rebuilt under William and Mary. Richmond Hill is a hillside and park in London near the site of the former Richmond Palace.

Margate Pier . . . Halls by the Sea: Margate Pier is the jetty (since destroyed) in the British seaside town of Margate, in south-east England; Halls by the Sea was a restaurant and dance hall in Margate, later the site of an amusement park.

Kundry . . . Botticelli's famous picture: Kundry is a 'wild woman' character in Wagner's opera *Parsifal* (1882) and Freia is the goddess of love in Wagner's Ring Cycle; Shaw is referring to the gown worn by Primavera (Spring) in the painting, (tempera on panel), of the same name by Sandro Botticelli (1445–1510) from the 1470s or 1480s.

Mrs Leo Hunter: character from Dickens's *The Pickwick Papers*.

220 *Rubini . . . Ottavio*: Italian tenor Giovanni Battista Rubini (1794–1854) sang the part of Don Ottavio in Mozart's *Don Giovanni* many times in his career.

Schnorr of Carolsfeld satisfied him as Tristan, or Schröder Devrient as Fidelio: Ludwig Schnorr von Carolsfeld (1836–65) was a German tenor who created the role of Tristan in Wagner's *Tristan und Isolde*. Wilhelmine Schröder-Devrient (1804–60) was a German soprano who performed in many of Wagner's operas during his lifetime and also famously as Leonore in Beethoven's *Fidelio* numerous times earlier in her career; Wagner claimed to have seen one such performance in 1829 when he was 16.

221 *he employs the entire range of the human voice, demanding from everybody nearly two effective octaves*: Shaw claims that Wagner's operas demand a much wider vocal range than those of more traditional opera composers. In fact, there is an entire vocal classification known as the 'Wagnerian Soprano' that describes a female singer with a vocal range covering more than two octaves. Although in truth this aspect is not unique to Wagner's music; many bel canto roles require much more than two octaves.

Rossini's Stabat or Verdi's Trovatore: *Stabat Mater* (1842) by Rossini and *Il Trovatore* (1853) by Verdi.

Semiramide: Rossini's opera of 1823.

222 *Mario . . . Vladimir Rosing*: the Italian tenor Cavaliere Giovanni Matteo de Candia, known as Mario (1810–83); the Polish tenor Jean de Reszke (1850–1925); and the Russian singers Feodor Chaliapin (1873–1938) and Vladimir Rosing (1890–1963).

the artisans of a village . . . Passion Play: the famous Oberammergau Passion Play has been performed every ten years by the residents of the town of Oberammergau in Bavaria since the year 1633.

Mr Rutland Boughton . . . has attempted to do in Somerset what Wagner did in Thuringia: Boughton established a 'Glastonbury Festival' in Glastonbury, Somerset, modelled on the Bayreuth Festivals that ran from 1914 to 1926.

223 *Prince Regent Theatre in Munich*: the Prinzregententheater, an opera house designed specifically for Wagner's work and opened in Munich in 1901.

Avalon: ancient name for the area now occupied by Glastonbury, site of the 'Glastonbury Festival' from 1914 to 1926 (see note to p. 222).

Under the title of Summer Schools . . . prettiest country districts: Shaw regularly participated in the Fabian Summer School, which ran yearly from 1907 to the 1940s at Pen-yr-allt, a large house and former school near the village of Llanbedr in Wales.

224 *If Little Bethel has raised the miners of England*: a reference to the various small church-run education societies that dotted England in the eighteenth and nineteenth centuries and played a role in spreading both academic and religious education among the working classes.

THE SANITY OF ART

227 *the Impressionist movement was struggling for life in London*: Shaw served as a professional art critic from 1886 to 1891, first for *The World* and then additionally for *The Star* and *Truth*. The impressionist movement, which

broke with the tradition of historical and mythological painting by focusing on scenes from nature and contemporary life using evocative brushstrokes and bold colours, began in France in the 1860s. Artists working in the impressionist style were present in England from the beginning, but the movement coalesced with the exhibition *London Impressionists* at London's Goupil Gallery in 1889, during Shaw's tenure as an art critic.

227 *Whistler*: American painter James McNeil Whistler (1834–1903), who settled in London in 1859.

fine drawing of a girl with the head deliberately crossed out with a few rough pencil strokes: although Shaw's subject is not entirely clear, this is most likely a reference to Whistler's *The Blue Girl*, first exhibited in 1874, in which the subject's face is indistinguishable.

'propaganda by deed': political action meant to serve as an example to others, often associated with anarchist violence of the nineteenth century.

Bouguereau's 'Girl in a Cornfield': there is no painting with this title by the French painter William-Adolphe Bouguereau (1825–1905). Shaw is most likely referring to Bouguereau's *Moissoneuse* (Reaper), from 1868, which is as he describes.

228 *Monet*: French painter Claude Monet (1840–1926), one of the founders of impressionism. His painting *Impression: Soleil Levant* (1874) gave the movement its name.

229 *Whistler's portrait of Sarasate*: Whistler's 1884 painting *Arrangement in Black: Portrait of Señor Pablo de Sarasate*.

Holbein: German painter Hans Holbein the Younger (1497–1543), who spent important portions of his career working in England.

Peter de Hooghe: Dutch Golden Age painter Pieter de Hooch (1629–84).

my duties as a musical critic: Shaw served as a professional music critic from 1888 to 1894, first for *The Star* and subsequently for *The World*.

When you and I last met: Shaw is addressing American anarchist Benjamin Tucker (1854–1939); *The Sanity of Art* was originally written as an open letter to Tucker and first published in his journal *Liberty*.

230 *Ford Madox Brown*: English painter (1821–93), often associated with the Pre-Raphaelite movement.

Walter Crane: English illustrator (1845–1915).

when I hinted . . . in the American Musical Courier: Shaw is referring to his article 'The Musical Revolution' in the *Musical Courier* (September 1894).

viols, virginals, and so on: instruments of the Renaissance and Baroque periods. Viols were a family of bowed stringed instruments with frets, played upright and held between the legs; virginals were small keyboard instruments related to the harpsichord.

the modern concert grand pianoforte: a large instrument used in concert halls, capable of producing a wide range of volume; a typical Steinway concert grand is almost 9 feet in length.

Mr Arnold Dolmetsch: French-English instrument maker (1858–1940) who was a leading figure in the revival of interest in early music of the Renaissance and Baroque periods.

from Henry VIII to Lawes and Purcell: the Tudor king Henry VIII, William Lawes (1602–45), and Henry Purcell (1659–95).

231 *Bruneau*: French opera composer Alfred Bruneau (1857–1934).

vocal harmony for unaccompanied voices . . . Palestrina's art: the Italian Giovanni Pierluigi da Palestrina (*c.*1525–94) is primarily noted as a composer of masses and motets.

232 *the Lohengrin and Tristan preludes*: the preludes to Wagner's operas *Lohengrin* (1850) and *Tristan und Isolde* (1859).

Prometheus: *The Creatures of Prometheus* (1801), a ballet composed by Beethoven.

Macfarren: Sir George Alexander Macfarren (1813–87), English composer and music scholar.

Tchaikowsky: Shaw's spelling of the Russian composer Pyotr Ilich Tchaikovsky (1840–93).

233 *Liszt . . . arabesques . . . tone poet*: Shaw refers here to Liszt's compositions for piano known as arabesques, or highly ornamented instrumental arrangements, and his later symphonic tone poems, single movements of orchestral music meant to evoke a particular image or theme.

Mazeppa, Victor Hugo's Les Préludes, Kaulbach's Die Hunnenschlacht: three of Liszt's symphonic poems. *Mazeppa* (1851), written after the 1819 Lord Byron poem of the same name; *Les Préludes* (1848), written after the 1823 book of the same name by Alphonse de Lamartine (1790–1869) (which Shaw here misattributes to Victor Hugo); and *Hunnenschlacht* (1857), written after the 1837 painting of the same name by Wilhelm von Kaulbach (1805–74).

234 *Mendelssohn, Raff*: German Romantic composers Felix Mendelssohn (1809–47) and (Joseph) Joachim Raff (1822–82).

Mendelssohn's Melusine overture . . . Raff's Lenore or Im Walde symphonies: Mendelssohn's Overture 'Die schöne Melusine' (1834); Raff's Symphony No. 5 in E major ('Lenore') (1872) and Symphony No. 3 in F major ('Im Walde') (In the Forest) (1869).

London Philharmonic Society: the Royal Philharmonic Society, an influential British music society formed in 1813 to arrange concerts at a time when there was no permanent orchestra in the city.

Jullien's British Army Quadrilles: an 1846 work of patriotic popular music by the French-born London composer Louis Jullien (1812–60).

235 *Shelley was as cocksure as the dons who expelled him from Oxford*: the English Romantic poet Shelley was expelled from Oxford in 1811 over his authorship of a pamphlet in support of atheism.

235 *Nordau from Brandes*: Max Nordau (1849–1923), whose book *Degeneration* (1892) Shaw is responding to in *The Sanity of Art*, and the influential Danish literary critic Georg Brandes (1842–1927).

'To obey one's senses . . . individuality': Nordau parroting what he believes to be Brandes's philosophy in *Degeneration*. See Max Nordau, *Degeneration* (New York: D. Appleton & Company, 1895), 356.

'He that is unjust . . . let him be holy still': an Angel of God says this to John in Revelation 22:11.

236 *maître de plaisir*: (Fr.) master of pleasure.

my dear Tucker: see note to p. 229.

Browning's Caliban upon Setebos: Robert Browning's poem 'Caliban upon Setebos' (1864), based upon the characters from Shakespeare's *The Tempest*, primarily Prospero, the overthrown sorcerer and Duke of Milan who rules over a desert island, and his slave Caliban, depicted as a half-human monster.

237 *because he can neither make a morality for himself nor do without one*: Shaw's argument here, which is also developed further below, about great thinkers fashioning new moralities for themselves even as they accept ready-made clothing from cobblers and tailors, anticipates a particular line of criticism levelled at Shaw later in his career, when it was claimed that much of what he put forward as his own original thought was actually borrowed second-hand from other thinkers. Witness in particular the editorial cartoon by the English illustrator Max Beerbohm (1872–1956) entitled 'George Bernard Shaw at the Tailor' (1914), where the caption conveys the following dialogue between Shaw and Georg Brandes, the latter working as a tailor and the former trying to sell him a pile of clothing labelled 'Life-Force, Woman-Set-Free, Superman, etc.':

GEORG BRANDES: 'What'll you take for the lot?'

SHAW: 'Immortality.'

BRANDES: 'Come, I've handled these same goods before! Coat, Mr Schopenhauer's; waistcoat, Mr Ibsen's; trousers Mr Nietzsche's.'

SHAW: 'Oh, but look at the patches!'

238 *Father Tucker . . . Liberty*: see note to p. 229.

Oxford Street: prominent thoroughfare in London.

the Sermon on the Mount: the teachings of Jesus as recounted in Matthew 5–7, which includes several injunctions against usury, debt, and other financial matters.

239 *Martin Luther . . . marrying a nun*: Martin Luther (see note to p. 36) married the former nun Katharina von Bora (1499–1552) on 13 June 1525.

241 *the Reformed Church, competing with the Unreformed for clients*: Shaw's terminology here, which is common in English religious writing, uses the

demarcation 'Reformed Church' for Protestantism in general and the Church of England in particular and 'Unreformed Church' for the Roman Catholic Church.

regarding Reason as a creative dynamic motor: Shaw's reflections here on the limitations of rational thought echo those put forward in *The Quintessence of Ibsenism* in the section 'The Two Pioneers'.

Ecumenical Council: in the Christian tradition, a gathering of religious leaders to determine questions of doctrine, dating back to the First Council of Nicaea, held in 325 CE.

that the true motive power in the world is will (otherwise Life): while the idea of a 'life force' behind Shaw's notion of 'creative evolution' is often taken as a derivation from the idea of will as it appears in Nietzsche's philosophy, this is one of the clearest articulations in Shaw's writing that his concept of will is derived more directly from Schopenhauer's work than from Nietzsche's.

'into the blind cave of eternal night': from Shakespeare's *Richard III* (V.iii.62).

242 *Lynched negroes . . . who fires it*: Shaw is condemning the deplorable practice of lynching that victimized and terrorized African-Americans across the United States in the nineteenth and twentieth centuries. As Shaw notes, such actions were often undertaken under false pretences of enacting justice and protecting the chastity of white women. A 'scamp' is a wicked and worthless person; a 'libertine' is someone without morals in general and with loose sexual morals in particular.

'Know thyself': the first of the Delphic maxims inscribed in the Temple of Apollo at Delphi, frequently invoked by Socrates in several of Plato's dialogues.

PREFACE TO THREE PLAYS BY BRIEUX

244 *Marx's, Zola's, Ibsen's, Strindberg's, Turgenief's, Tolstoy's*: eminent figures of the nineteenth century. German philosopher and radical Karl Marx, French novelist and playwright Émile Zola, Norwegian playwright Henrik Ibsen, Swedish playwright August Strindberg, and the Russian novelists Ivan Turgenev and Leo Tolstoy.

Macaulay . . . Cuvier: British historian and politician Thomas Babington Macaulay (1800–59), English novelist Charles Dickens, French novelist Alexandre Dumas *père*, French historian François Guizot (1787–1874), French novelist Stendhal (Marie-Henri Beyle) (1783–1842), French short-story writers Prosper Merimée (1803–70) and Guy de Maupassant (1850–93), French novelist Gustave Flaubert (1821–80), the French writers and brothers Édmond (1822–96) and Jules de Goncourt (1830–70), English illustrator Aubrey Beardsley (1872–98), Irish novelist George Moore (1852–1933), Italian poet Gabriele D'Annunzio (1863–1938), Spanish dramatist José Echegaray (1832–1916), French Renaissance writers François Rabelais (1483–1553) and Michel de Montaigne (1533–92), French playwright Molière (Jean-Baptiste Poquelin) (1622–73), French economist Anne Robert Jacques Turgot (1727–81), and French naturalist Georges Cuvier (1769–1832).

244 *Thackeray's campaign against snobbery*: English novelist William Makepeace Thackeray (1811–63) frequently satirized the behaviour of the upper classes in England.

245 *Jack the Ripper*: the infamous serial killer, uncaught and unidentified, who committed at least five murders in impoverished districts in London in 1888 and captured national and international media attention. Shaw wrote on the subject on several occasions and was critical of the press for only focusing their attention on the conditions of London's slums on account of these sensational murders. For more, see Nelson O'Ceallaigh Ritschel, 'Shaw, Murder, and the Modern Metropolis', *SHAW* 32/1 (2012), 102–16.

morbidezza: (It.) delicacy and softness, used of artistic representations.

Anatole France: esteemed French poet and novelist (1844–1924).

Zola's Bête Humaine . . . Prévost's Manon Lescaut: Zola's 1890 novel *La Bête humaine* (*The Human Beast*, or *The Beast Within*) and the 1731 novel *Manon Lescaut* by Antoine François Prévost (1697–1763).

246 *the Ophelias and Lucies of Lammermoor*: the characters of Ophelia from Shakespeare's *Hamlet* and Lucy from Walter Scott's novel *The Bride of Lammermoor* (1819).

247 *for to the Platonist all accidents are unreal and negligible*: Shaw is here referring to the distinction between essence and accident in Greek philosophy. Although Plato touches on this in his *Phaedo*, the argument against accident that Shaw is alluding to here is more typically associated with Aristotle, who puts forth such distinctions in his *Categories* and *Physics*.

'If you must tell us stories about agricultural laborers, why tell us dirty ones?': Shaw is here referring to Émile Zola's 1887 novel *La Terre* (*The Earth*), which concerns the suffering of agricultural labourers in central France. Compare Shaw's phrasing of an apocryphal criticism of Zola to that offered by Ernest Alfred Vizetelly five years earlier: 'For more than twenty years the critics had constantly said to him: "If you must show the vileness of life, you should at least point the moral."' See Ernest Alfred Vizetelly, *Émile Zola: Novelist and Reformer, an Account of His Work* (London: Bodley Head, 1904), 406.

Marguerite Gauthier . . . Nana: the character Marguerite Gauthier in the romantic novel *La Dame aux Camélias* (1848) by Alexandre Dumas *fils* (1824–95), adapted into a play by the author in 1852; and the eponymous character in Zola's naturalist novel *Nana* (1880).

248 *Rougon-Macquart families*: the families at the centre of Zola's twenty-novel cycle *Les Rougon-Macquart*, published between 1871 and 1893.

Maupassant's Une Vie: Guy de Maupassant's novel *Une vie* (*A Life*) (1883).

249 *the approved fifth-act-blank-verse type*: the inevitably bloody endings in the fifth and final act of Elizabethan and Jacobean-era tragedies, typically written in blank verse.

'slices of life' . . . *plays that have no endings*: though now in common usage, Shaw's use of a 'slice of life' is specifically a reference to the coinage of that phrase by the French dramatist and critic Jean Jullien (1854–1919) in his book *The Living Theatre* (1892), where he used it as a means to describe the new naturalist dramas prevalent in France in the later nineteenth century, particularly at the famed Théâtre Libre in Paris. Shaw's reflections on the absence of a final ending in much modern drama and literature echo Jullien's own observations in that work.

Brieux: French playwright Eugène Brieux (1858–1932), whose social message plays were the occasion for Shaw's Preface.

250 *Beaumarchais*: French playwright Pierre-Augustin Caron de Beaumarchais (1732–99).

Le Misanthrope . . . *Don Juan*: Molière's plays *The Misanthrope* (1666) and *Dom Juan or The Feast with the Statue* (1683), the latter of which would influence Shaw's own *Man and Superman*.

'As flies . . . *sport'*: from Shakespeare's *King Lear* (IV.i.37–8).

251 *dramatist of the boulevard*: the tradition of Parisian 'boulevard theatre', or popular drama, was offered in the theatres located around the Boulevard du Temple from the nineteenth century onwards, especially frivolous comedies, melodramas, and well-made plays.

Sarcey's . . . *'du théâtre'*: French drama critic Francisque Sarcey (1827–99); *du théâtre* (Fr.) 'of the theatre'.

the Academie Française: the eminent learned council, founded in 1635, that oversees and advises on matters of language and the literary arts more generally in France.

252 *alexandrines* . . . *English blank verse* . . . *heroic couplets*: an alexandrine is the dominant metrical structure of French verse drama, a twelve-syllable poetic meter commonly used in eighteenth-century France. By contrast, the English tradition is to write verse drama in blank (unrhymed metered) verse, typically in iambic pentameter. A heroic couplet is a common form of English meter involving rhyming lines in iambic pentameter.

Racine and Corneille . . . *Dryden* . . . *Gluck*: French dramatists Jean Racine (1639–99) and Pierre Corneille (1606–84), English poet and playwright John Dryden (1631–1700), and Bohemian-Austrian opera composer Christoph Willibald Gluck (1714–87).

the 'well made play' of Scribe and his school: the tradition of 'well made plays', practised and popularized by French dramatist Eugène Scribe, centred on the formulaic construction of narratives often involving domestic secrets and multiple plot twists.

253 *Offenbach* . . . *J'aime les militaires*: 'Ah, que j'aime les militaires' (Ah, how I love soldiers) is an air from the comic opera *La Grande-Duchesse de Gérolstein* (1867) by the German-French opera composer Jacques Offenbach. The rhythm and melody of the opening words recall the theme of the final movement of Beethoven's Symphony No. 7.

253 *Schumann*: German Romantic composer Robert Schumann (1810–56).

Forest of Bondy . . . the Great Hall, Chevy Chace: the Forest of Bondy is a location in the 1814 French melodrama *The Dog of Montargis* by René Charles Guilbert de Pixérécourt (1773–1844); the Auberge des Adrets, an estate featured in the 1823 melodrama of the same name by French dramatist Benjamin Antier (1787–1870); the Red Barn, the location of a famous murder in England in 1827 and the subject of numerous popular retellings; the Cave at Midnight, a stereotypically melodramatic location as in English genre painter Charles Robert Leslie's (1794–1859) popular painting *Murder* (1813); and two posh aristocratic locations, Whitehall Court in London and Great Hall, Chevy Chase in Cornwall.

254 *a Scribe or a Sardou*: see note to p. 8.

255 *the Venus of Milo*: perhaps the most famous work of ancient Greek statuary, an image of the goddess Aphrodite sculpted by Alexandros of Antioch around 100 BCE. It has been on permanent display at the Louvre Museum in Paris since 1821.

He has to interpret life: Shaw's arguments here and below about the purpose of playwriting are notably similar to those he would put forward years later in the preface to his playlet *The Six of Calais* (1934).

Othello . . . Venice: Shaw refers here to various characters and locations featured or mentioned in Shakespeare's *Othello*.

256 *cinematographs*: a now-antiquated word for films, based on the name of the early motion-picture camera and projector invented by the brothers Auguste and Louis Lumière (1862–1954 and 1894–1948).

Robespierre . . . Marie Antoinette: Maximilien Robespierre (1758–94) was a French Revolutionary associated with the Reign of Terror who was eventually guillotined in 1794. Marie Antoinette (1755–93), archduchess of Austria, was the wife of Louis XVI, becoming queen of France in 1774; she was executed the year before Robespierre in 1793.

257 *Rochefoucauldian pleasure in a friend's misfortune*: French author François VI, duc de La Rochefoucauld (1613–80). Shaw is referring to Maxim 235 of his *Reflections, or Sentences and Moral Maxims* (1678), which reads 'We are easily consoled at the misfortunes of our friends when they enable us to prove our tenderness for them.'

marchand de plaisir: (Fr.) literally merchant of pleasure.

11 OCTOBER 1893

This article originally ran in *The World* on the date stated and was reprinted in *Music in London, 1890–1894* in 1932. Shaw's review is of Gilbert and Sullivan's *Utopia, Limited*, which premiered at the Savoy Theatre in London on 7 October 1893. It was the second-to-last of their collaborations and the first in four years, after *The Gondoliers* in 1889 and a subsequent legal dispute also involving the management of the Savoy Theatre.

261 *Haddon Hall . . . The Mountebanks*: *Haddon Hall* (1892), operetta by Arthur Sullivan (1842–1900) with libretticist Sydney Grundy (1848–1914), and *The Mountebanks* (1892), operetta by W. S. Gilbert (1836–1911) with composers Alfred Cellier (1844–91) and Ivan Caryll (1861–1921).

Trial by Jury . . . Patience: Gilbert and Sullivan's operettas *Trial by Jury* (1875), *The Sorcerer* (1877), *HMS Pinafore* (1878), *The Pirates of Penzance* (1879), and *Patience* (1881).

a new Savoy opera: Gilbert and Sullivan's style of comic opera, or operetta, became known as Savoy opera for its association with the Savoy Theatre in London where many of their works premiered.

Mr D'Oyly Carte: London theatre producer Richard D'Oyly Carte (1844–1901), who fostered the collaboration between Gilbert and Sullivan and built the Savoy Theatre to premiere their works.

262 *not fit even for treasons, stratagems, or spoils*: a reference to Shakespeare's *Merchant of Venice*, V.i.81–3: 'The man that hath no music in himself, | Nor is not moved with concord of sweet sounds, | Is fit for treasons, stratagems, and spoils.'

Christy Minstrel: or Christy's Minstrels, a group of white singers who performed in blackface, founded by Edwin Pearce Christy in Buffalo, New York, in 1843; the group proved instrumental in the development and standardization of the racist tradition of blackface minstrel performance in the United States and abroad. Given the date of the song that he connects to the group (see note below), Shaw is most likely referring not to the original Christy's Minstrels but to a successor group that used the same name, claimed to include members of the original troupe, and performed at London's St James's Hall from 1865 until 1904. For more on the troubling history of the English reception of blackface minstrel performance, see Derek B. Scott, 'Blackface Minstrels, Black Minstrels, and their Reception in England', in Julian Rushton (ed.), *Europe, Empire, and Spectacle in Nineteenth-Century British Music* (London: Routledge, 2006), 265–80.

Johnnie, get a gun: the minstrel song 'Johnny, Get Your Gun', written by the Jewish American songwriter Monroe Rosenfeld (1861–1918) in 1886 under the name F. Belasco. The fact that Shaw credits the song as a 'plantation dance', referring to a form of folk dance practised in American slave communities, reveals his ignorance of American popular music (Rosenfeld being a professional songwriter associated with the American popular music industry known as 'Tin Pan Alley'), of authentic African-American music and dance traditions, and of the hateful legacy of minstrel shows like those of Christy's Minstrels, which put forward a derogatory vision of impersonated racial performance for the consumption of white audiences.

Soave sia il vento . . . Cosi fan tutte: the trio 'Soave sia il vento' (May the wind be gentle) from Mozart's opera *Cosi fan tutte* (1790).

262 *Le Nozze di Figaro*: Mozart's opera *The Marriage of Figaro* (1786).

263 *Fliegende Blätter*: a German humour magazine published out of Munich.

    Mr Scott Fishe . . . Jane Annie: R. Scott Fishe (1871–98) was a British actor and singer who appeared in the comic opera *Jane Annie* (1839), which featured a libretto by J. M. Barrie (1860) and Arthur Conan Doyle (1859–1930) (of Peter Pan and Sherlock Holmes fame respectively) and music by Ernest Ford (1858–1919). It premiered at the Savoy Theatre in May 1893.

    as Lassalle transposes Rigoletto: the French baritone Jean Lassalle (1847–1909) appeared in the title role of Giuseppe Verdi's opera *Rigoletto* (1851).

    Santley . . . de Reszke: English baritone Charles Santley (1834–1922), the Polish tenor Jean de Reszke (1850–1925) and his brother, bass Édouard de Reszke (1853–1917).

264 *Miss Nancy McIntosh . . . Miss Florence Perry*: the American singer and actress Miss Nancy McIntosh (1866–1954), who performed primarily in London; the German-born British singer, conductor, and composer Sir George Henschel (1850–1934); the London Symphony Orchestra, founded in 1904; the English opera singer and actress Rosina Brandram (1845–1907); the English singer and comedian Rutland Barrington (1853–1922); the English politician George Goschen (1831–1907); the English pianist and conductor William Cusins (1833–93); English singer and actor W. H. Denny (1853–1915); English opera singer Charles Kenningham (1860–1925); English singer and actor John Le Hay (John Mackway Healy) (1854–1926); English actor and singer Lawrence Gridley (1859–1901); English actress and singer Emmie Owen (1871–1905); and English actress Florence Perry (1869–1949).

    that reference to England by the Gravedigger in Hamlet: the Gravedigger (technically, the First Clown) in *Hamlet* replies to a question as to why the prince was sent to England for being mad by stating that "Twill, a not be seen in him there; there the men | are as mad as he' (V.i.154–5).

1 AUGUST 1894

This article originally ran in *The World* on the date stated and was reprinted in *Music in London, 1890–1894* in 1932.

265 *sostenuto*: (It.) literally 'sustained', musical term for a long, sustained passage, frequently found in Wagner's music.

    Courtois: prominent Parisian brass instrument-makers Antoine Courtois & Mille.

    Crystal Palace: in London, an enormous festival complex that included space for a 4,000-piece grand orchestra and chorus and that was used, beginning in 1852, for a triennial Handel Festival.

266 *Lazarus . . . Mühlfeld's*: English clarinet virtuoso Henry Lazarus (1815–95) and German clarinettist Richard Mühlfeld (1856–1907).

August Manns: German-born British conductor (1825–1907), who served as long-time director of music at London's Crystal Palace.

not merely a German, but a Prussian: Prussia was the most powerful of the German states. It was instrumental in the formation of a unified Germany in 1871 and remained a state within Germany until 1947.

the Conservatoire concerts in Paris: concerts held at the famed Conservatoire de Paris, the French college of music and dance founded in 1795.

267 *Gurnemanz*: a Knight of the Grail in Wagner's *Parsifal*.

Levi: Hermann Levi (1839–1900), a German Jewish conductor who, despite Wagner's virulent anti-Semitism, was closely associated with the composer and conducted the first performance of *Parsifal* at Bayreuth in 1882.

'glatt': (Ger.) smooth.

268 *Alvary . . . Rosa Sucher*: Wagner singers Max Alvary (1856–98), Katharina Klafsky (1855–96), and Heinrich Wiegand (1855–1909), all of whom appeared at Drury Lane Theatre in London, as well as the Austrian opera singer Karl Grengg (1851–1914) and the German opera singer Rosa Sucher (1849–1927).

Melba or Miss Eames or the De Reszke: Australian opera singer Nellie Melba (1861–1931), American opera singer Emma Eames (1865–1952), and the Polish De Reszke (see note to p. 222).

Sir William Harcourt: William Harcourt (1827–1904) was a British politician, not an actor.

8 AUGUST 1894

This article originally ran in *The World* on the date stated and was reprinted in *Music in London, 1890–1894* in 1932.

270 *Frau Wagner . . . Sir Augustus Harris*: Cosima Wagner (1837–1930), the composer's wife who ran the Bayreuth Festival from 1886 to 1906, and Augustus Harris (1852–96), playwright and manager of the Drury Lane Theatre in London, which premiered many of Wagner's operas in London.

271 *Teutonic . . . Saxon . . . Brabantine*: by Teutonic, Shaw is referring to the Germans, who are descended from the Teutons; Saxons refers to Germans from the north-west region of the country formerly known as Saxony (not to be confused with the modern German state of Saxony or the Anglo-Saxons of Britain); Brabantine refers to people from Brabant, part of the modern-day Netherlands.

272 *guinea, or half-a-crown*: a guinea was a gold coin in British currency worth one pound and one shilling, or twenty-one shillings. Although the coin was retired in 1816, the term continued to be used in reference to the same currency amount; a half-a-crown, or half-crown, was a coin worth two

shillings and sixpence, or one-eighth of a pound, and which remained in circulation until 1970.

273 *Van Dyck*: Belgian tenor Ernest van Dyck (1861–1923).

Des Grieux: leading male character in the opera *Manon Lescaut* (1893) by Giacomo Puccini (1858–1924).

Nordica and Miss Brema: American soprano Lillian Nordica (1857–1914) and British mezzo-soprano Marie Brema (1856–1925).

Edmund Yates: Edmund Yates (1831–94) was a British journalist and editor of *The World* from 1874 to 1894.

Mr Robert Smythe Hichens: English journalist, music critic, and novelist Robert Smythe Hitchens (1864–1950).

THE CASE FOR THE CRITIC-DRAMATIST

This article originally ran in the *Saturday Review* on 16 November 1895 and was reprinted *Our Theatres in the Nineties* in 1932.

275 *I have written half a dozen 'original' plays, four of which have never been performed*: at this point in his career, Shaw had written the plays *Widowers' Houses* (1892), *The Philanderer* (1893), *Mrs Warren's Profession* (1893), *Arms and the Man* (1894), *Candida* (1894), and *The Man of Destiny* (1895). Of these, only *Widowers' Houses* and *Arms and the Man* had yet been performed, in 1893 and 1894 respectively.

Frank Marshall: English playwright Frank Marshall (1840–89).

Sir Henry Irving's genius: English actor-manager Henry Irving (1838–1905), who ran the Lyceum Theatre in London from 1878 to 1899. Irving was the first British actor to receive a knighthood.

Canute . . . Robert Emmett: Canute was the ancient king of England, Denmark, and Norway (r. 1016–35), who rebuffed his fawning courtiers. *Robert Emmet* (1884) was a play about the Irish martyr rebel Robert Emmet (1778–1803) by Francis Marshall (1840–89), originally commissioned by Henry Irving but ultimately not performed by him.

276 *the ancient mariner . . . the wedding guest could*: the poem *The Rime of the Ancient Mariner* (1798) by Samuel Taylor Coleridge (1772–1834), in which a character known as the ancient mariner stops a guest at a wedding to tell him his pitiful tale.

Mr Pinero: English playwright Arthur Wing Pinero (1885–1934), who began his career as an actor.

278 *Mr Clement Scott . . . two critics-dramatists*: Clement Scott (1841–1904), the theatre critic for the *Daily Telegraph* and also a playwright; William Archer (1856–1924), the Scottish theatre critic for *The World* in London; and Arthur Bingham Walkley (1855–1926), the theatre critic for *The Star* and *The Times*. Shaw's reference to 'the two critic-dramatists' is to Scott and Archer, the former an active playwright and the latter an attempted

playwright (he collaborated with Shaw on the material that would ultimately become Shaw's own *Widowers' Houses*) also involved in translations of foreign plays for the English stage and vice versa.

THE LATE CENSOR

This article originally ran in the *Saturday Review* on 2 March 1895 and was reprinted in *Our Theatres in the Nineties* in 1932.

279 *It is a great pity that the Censorship cannot be abolished*: Shaw refers to the Lord Chamberlain's Office, a royal office tasked with theatre censorship since 1737 until the role was abolished with the Theatres Act of 1968. Edward Frederick Smyth Pigott (1824–95) served in the position of Deputy Licensership of Plays, the role within the Lord Chamberlain's Office that controlled censorship and play licences, from 1874 to 1895.

since it relieves every one of responsibility: plays that received a licence from the Lord Chamberlain's Office could not be sued or prosecuted for obscenity.

280 *reading his evidence before the Commission of 1892*: the hearings of Parliament's Select Committee on Theatres and Places of Entertainment, 1892, examined the licensing practices of the Lord Chamberlain's Office.

Charles I: Charles I (1600–49), king of England, Scotland, and Ireland from 1625 until his execution in 1649, was known for his personal probity.

I went to an opera at a certain West End theatre: Shaw's details do not allow for the particular opera to be identified, though it is worth noting that this anecdote by Shaw circulated in arguments regarding the inadequacies of the Lord Chamberlain's licensing for several years after it was first printed, including being quoted at length in the influential tome *Censorship in England* (1913) by Frank Fowell (1883–1965).

281 *Northampton*: town in the East Midlands of England.

282 *the evil day . . . corruption of Parliament on the stage*: Shaw refers to the passage of the Licensing Act of 1737, pushed through by Robert Walpole (1676–1745; prime minister 1721–42) in part to limit the satirical broadsides of Henry Fielding (1707–54), who was up to that point one of the most popular playwrights of the era and who subsequently ceased writing plays.

Grant Allen's . . . Die Walküre: the 1895 novel *The Woman Who Did* by Grant Allen (1848–99); the 1893 novel *The Heavenly Twins* by Sarah Grand (1854–1943); Jacob Thomas Grein (1862–1935), the British theatre producer who produced the first English staging of Ibsen's *Ghosts* in 1891 in a 'subscription performance' that did not require licensing; Russian novelist Leo Tolstoy's 1886 play *The Dominion of Darkness*; and Richard Wagner's 1870 opera *Die Walküre*.

283 *Mr Woodall*: William Woodall (1832–1901), Liberal MP from 1880 to 1900.

283 *The Cenci*: Shelley's play of 1819, which was produced in a private performance in London in 1886, much to Pigott's consternation. Shaw was in charge of publicity of the performance, which was produced by the Shelley Society, of which he was an active member.

Browning and George Meredith and James Russell Lowell: English poet Robert Browning (1812–89); English novelist George Meredith (1828–1909); and American poet James Russell Lowell (1819–91).

obiter dicta: (Lat.) literally 'by the way'; in legal parlance meaning a judge's incidental remarks.

Jack Cade: see note to p. 99.

284 *Oscar Wilde . . . Elizabeth Robins*: prominent dramatists (Wilde to Jones) and actors (Vezin to Robins). Specifically, they are Oscar Wilde (1854–1900), Sydney Grundy (1848–1914), Robert Buchanan (1841–1901), Henry Arthur Jones (1851–1929), Hermann Vezin (1829–1910), Lewis Waller (1860–1915), Charles Charrington (1854–1926), Alma Murray (1854–1945), Theodore Wright (1883–1914), Janet Achurch (1864–1916), and Elizabeth Robins (1862–1952).

CHURCH AND STAGE

This article originally ran in the *Saturday Review* on 25 January 1896 and was reprinted in *Our Theatres in the Nineties* in 1932.

285 *Michael and his Lost Angel at the Lyceum*: the 1896 play by Henry Arthur Jones (1851–1929), which premiered at London's Lyceum Theatre.

City: usually 'the City', the central business district of London.

'grace before meat': the tradition in certain Protestant sects, such as the Presbyterian Church, of offering a prayer before eating meat (versus other Christian denominations, where prayer is offered before any meal).

'Te Deum': a short offering of blessing or thanks based on the Christian hymn *Te Deum*, written in 387 CE.

Mr Wilson Barrett's Nero: the 1895 play *The Sign of the Cross*, written and produced by Wilson Barrett (1846–1904). Barrett himself does not play Nero but the Roman patrician Marcus Superbus.

286 *Molière . . . refused the Sacrament*: the beloved French actor and playwright Molière (Jean-Baptiste Poquelin, 1622–73) was initially refused Christian burial on account of his being an actor, though he was later interred at Père Lachaise Cemetery in Paris. Shaw's second reference is most likely to Mademoiselle Parisot (*c.*1775–*c.*1837), a French ballet dancer whose revealing costumes and provocative dancing at the King's Theatre in London brought her into conflict with numerous English clerics, including the bishop of London who in 1805 sought to enforce an early closure of the King's Theatre to curtail Parisot's performances.

Adelphi melodrama: a melodrama performed at the Adelphi Theatre in London, which was known for the genre in the nineteenth century.

Miss Millward: the English actress Jessie Millward (1861–1932).

287 *the National Gallery*: large and historic art museum founded in 1824 and located in Trafalgar Square in central London.

Barabbas and The Sorrows of Satan: novels of 1893 and 1895 respectively by the extremely popular English novelist Marie Corelli (1855–1924).

Sheridan Knowles: Irish playwright and actor James Sheridan Knowles (1784–1862), who ultimately retired from the stage to become a Baptist preacher.

288 *Salvini . . . Samson was out of the question in a theatre*: the play *Samson* by Ippolito d'Aste (1809–66) was performed in Italy and internationally by the Italian actor Tommaso Salvini (1829–1915) in 1889.

turned The Mount of Olives . . . the principal figure: this passage refers to *Christ on the Mount of Olives*, Op. 85 (1803) by Ludwig von Beethoven, later adapted to the piece *Engedi* (1840) by Henry Hudson (1798–1889), who replaced the libretto but left Beethoven's music intact. As Shaw notes, Hudson objected to Christ being the central figure of Beethoven's work and replaced him with the Old Testament figure of David, the king of Israel.

the Leeds Festival: classical music festival in Leeds, England, from 1858 to 1985.

289 *Book of Job*: book of the Old Testament of the Bible in which God and Satan converse over the fate of the righteous man Job, who endures great suffering at Satan's hands in order to prove his devotion to God.

Lyceum Faust . . . Sir Augustus Harris: the opera *Faust* by Charles Gounod (1818–93), based on Goethe's play, which played numerous times at Drury Lane Theatre in Covent Garden under the directorship of Augustus Harris (1852–96).

in Mendelssohn's oratorio: *St Paul*, Op. 36 (1836) by Felix Mendelssohn.

Boïto's Mefistofele: the opera *Mefistofele* (1868) by Arrigo Boito (1842–1918).

Van Ude's . . . frock coats: the painting *Let the Little Children Come to Me* (1883) by the German religious painter Fritz von Uhde (1848–1911), which was displayed at the French Gallery in London in 1890.

290 *at Burlington House*: in London, frequent site of art exhibitions from the Royal Academy.

I have also seen Gentleman Joe: the musical comedy *Gentleman Joe, The Hansom Cabbie* by Walter Slaughter (1860–1908) and Basil Hood (1864–1917), which premiered in London in 1895.

NIETZSCHE IN ENGLISH

This article originally ran in the *Saturday Review* on 11 April 1896 and was reprinted in *Our Theatres in the Nineties* in 1932.

291 *the first volume of their translation of the works of Friedrich Nietzsche*: the
     1896 publication of the first volume of Thomas Common's translations of
     Nietzsche's works, which included *The Case of Wagner* (1888), *The Twilight
     of the Idols* (1889), *Nietzsche Contra Wagner* (1889), and *The Anti-Christ*
     (1895).

     Zeuxis . . . Michael Angelo: Zeuxis (*c.*5th century BCE) and Apelles of Kos
     (*c.*4th century BCE) were prominent Greek painters; Raphael (1483–1520)
     and Michelangelo (1475–1564) prominent painters (and in Michelangelo's
     case, also sculptor) of the Italian Renaissance.

292 *'convictions are prisons'*: a quote from section 54 of Nietzsche's *The Anti-
     Christ*.

     I never heard of him until a few years ago: Shaw's claims of ignorance
     regarding Nietzsche's work are belied by his own writings elsewhere. See
     note to p. 29.

293 *Don Giovanni . . . Carmen*: Mozart's opera *Don Giovanni* (1787), Claudio
     Monteverdi's opera *L'Orfeo* (1607), Ludwig van Beethoven's opera *Fidelio*
     (1805), and Georges Bizet's *Carmen* (1875), which Nietzsche praises at
     length in *The Case of Wagner* and elsewhere.

MADOX BROWN, WATTS, AND IBSEN

This article originally ran in the *Saturday Review* on 13 March 1897 and was
reprinted in *Our Theatres in the Nineties* in 1932.

295 *Madox Brown . . . Leighton*: English painters Ford Madox Brown (1821–
     93), G. F. Watts (1817–1904), and Frederic Leighton (1830–96).

     Rembrandt: prominent and influential Dutch painter Rembrandt van Rijn
     (1606–69).

     'the green mantle of the standing pool': from Shakespeare's *King Lear* (III.
     iv.120).

296 *the young lady painted by Ingres as La Source*: the neoclassical nude paint-
     ing *The Source* (1856) by the French artist Jean Auguste Dominique Ingres
     (1780–1867).

     Venus . . . Chloe: Venus was the Roman goddess of love, while Chloe was
     a young female shepherdess and the subject of *Daphnis and Chloe* (date
     unknown) by Longus (*c.* second century CE).

     *the comely wife of John of Gaunt in the Wycliffe picture with the wife of
     Foscari*: Madox Brown's painting *John Wycliffe reading his translation of the
     bible to John of Gaunt* (1861). John Wycliffe (1320–84) was an English theo-
     logian and philosopher; John of Gaunt (1340–99) was a wealthy and power-
     ful English prince, father of Henry IV. The 'wife of Foscari' was Marina
     Nani (1400–73), who played an active role in Venetian politics during the
     reign of her husband, Francesco Foscari (1373–1457) as doge (1423–57).

     bonne bouche: (Fr.) tasty bite.

297 *Frederick Shields*: British painter and decorative artist (1833–1911) associated with the Pre-Raphaelite movement.

   Titian's Bacchus in the National Gallery: *Bacchus and Ariadne* (1522–3) by the Italian painter Titian (*c.*1488–1576), which hangs in the National Gallery in London.

298 *Antonio Moro . . . the imaginary portrait of Shakespear*: Netherlandish painter Antonio Moro (1517–77) and Madox Brown's painting *Portrait of William Shakespeare* (1849).

   reductio ad absurdum: (Lat.) literally, reduction to absurdity, referring to a rhetorical move to discredit an argument by showing how it leads to an absurdity.

   Mr Smith of Brixton and Bayswater: Shaw's formulation of an everyman figure, similar to the American 'John Doe'.

   Madox Brown's Parisina or Death of Harold: *Parisina's Sleep—Study for Head of Parisina* (1842) and *The Body of Harold Brought Before William the Conqueror* (1844) by Ford Madox Brown (1821–93).

   Solveig the Sweet: the character Solveig, a young girl, in Ibsen's *Peer Gynt* (1867).

   old Palmerstonians: the era of Henry John Temple (1784–1865), 3rd Viscount Palmerston, who served as prime minister from 1859 to 1865.

   a knight on public grounds and by his own peremptory demand: Shaw refers to the 1895 knighting of Sir Henry Irving, the first actor to ever be granted that honour.

299 *Mayfair without Hoxton, Melbury Road without Saffron Hill*: here Shaw contrasts upper-class (the first of each pair) and working-class sections (the second of each pair) of London.

THE BOARD SCHOOL

This article originally ran in the *Saturday Review* on 27 November 1897 and was reprinted in *Our Theatres in the Nineties* in 1932.

300 *Board school . . . Harrow or Eton*: the major forms of education available in England in the nineteenth century, board schools being government-funded schools available to all, voluntary schools being religiously affiliated schools that predated the formation of the board schools, workhouse schools designed to educate the children of impoverished families subsiding in government-run workhouses, and public schools like Harrow School and Eton College, although originally founded or endowed for public use, developing into private elite boarding schools serving the upper classes.

301 *Lee-Metford bullet*: bullet fired by the Lee-Metford British army service rifle.

302 *Chaucer . . . Shelley*: throughout this section Shaw refers to various luminary figures of British arts and letters; in addition to those discussed

above, these include the English novelist Henry Fielding, the Irish novelist Oliver Goldsmith, the Scottish novelist Walter Scott, the English journalist and pamphleteer William Cobbett, and the medieval English writer William Langland.

HENRY IRVING AND ELLEN TERRY

The essay as follows was published in *Pen Portraits and Reviews* in 1932 but draws from two prior sources. The first is an obituary that Shaw wrote for Sir Henry Irving that was first published in German in *Die Neue Freie Presse* on 20 October 1905 and in English in the *Morning Post* on 5 December 1905. The second is an article on Ellen Terry that ran in German in *Die Neue Freie Presse* on 24 December 1905 and in English in the *Boston Transcript* on 20 January 1906. Sir Henry Irving (1838–1905) was a prominent English stage actor and manager of the Lyceum Theatre, with whom Shaw had a tempestuous relationship; Dame Alice Ellen Terry (1847–1928) was a prominent English actress who frequently performed with Irving and also regularly appeared in Shaw's plays.

304 *'He did nothing for the living drama ... Requiescat in pace'*: Shaw is referring to the original English draft of his article for *Die Neue Freie Presse*. Mistranslations of that draft resulted in a scandal surrounding Shaw's supposed disrespect for Irving's memory, prompting the publication of the English-language version in the *Morning Post* (see headnote above). *Requiescat in pace*: (Lat.) 'rest in peace'.

305 *Macaire ... Charles Kean*: Shaw refers here to various parts played by Irving, including the character Robert Macaire, who first appeared in Benjamin Antier's (1787–1870) *L'Auberge des Adrets* (1823); the characters known as the Corsican Brothers who first appeared in a novella of the same name by Alexandre Dumas *père* in 1844; the historical Cardinal Richelieu (1585–1642), who appears as a fictional character in numerous works, including famously in Dumas *père*'s *The Three Musketeers* (1844); and the character Claude Melnotte from the melodrama *The Lady of Lyons* (1838) by Edward Bulwer-Lytton (1803–73). Charles Kean (1811–68) was a prominent Anglo-Irish actor of the early and mid-nineteenth century.

the new version by Robert Louis Stevenson: *Macaire: A Melodramatic Farce* (1885) by William Ernest Henly (1849–1903) and Robert Louis Stevenson (1850–94).

Becket ... Charles I: Shaw refers to several of Irving's most famous roles, including as Archbishop of Canterbury Thomas Becket in Alfred, Lord Tennyson's play *Becket* (1884); as the Vicar of Wakefield in W. G. Wills's play *Olivia* (1885), adapted from Oliver Goldsmith's novel *The Vicar of Wakefield* (1766); and as the title character in *Charles I* (1872) by William Gorman Wills (1828–91).

306 *His Vanderdecken ... The Bells*: Shaw is referring to two roles played by Irving, Vanderdecken in *Vanderdecken* (1878) by Percy Fitzgerald

(1834–1925) and William Gorman Wills (1828–91), and Mathias in *The Bells* (1871) by Leopold David Lewis (1828–90), one of Irving's most famous parts.

Paganini: virtuoso Italian violinist Niccolò Paganini (1782–1840).

307 *her correspondence will be collected and published in twenty or thirty volumes*: Shaw's correspondence with Terry was published in 1932 in *Ellen Terry and Bernard Shaw: A Correspondence* (London: G. P. Putnam's Sons, 1932).

308 *Her portrait as Lady Macbeth, by Sargent*: Ellen Terry as Lady Macbeth (1889) by John Singer Sargent (1856–1925), which hangs at the Tate Britain in London.

L. F. Austin, Bram Stoker: Louis Frederic Austin (*c.*1852–1905) was a journalist and theatre critic in addition to being Irving's secretary; Abraham 'Bram' Stoker (1847–1912) was the business manager of the Lyceum Theatre in addition to being Irving's secretary but is better known today as the author of *Dracula* (1897).

309 *Albery's Two Roses*: *Two Roses: A Comedy in Three Acts* (1870) by James Albery (1838–89).

The Lady of Lyons . . . Madame Sans Gêne: Shaw refers to various plays that Irving and Terry staged at the Lyceum Theatre, Bulwer-Lytton's *The Lady of Lyons* (1838); *The Amber Heart* (1887) by Alfred Calmour (1857–1912); Wills's English adaptation of Goethe's *Faust* and his *Olivia* (both 1885); and *Madame Sans Gêne* (1893) by Victorien Sardou and Émile Moreau (1852–1922).

310 *Hauptmanns, Sudermanns*: German dramatists Gerhart Hauptmann (1862–1946) and Hermann Sudermann (1857–1928).

Duse, Réjane: Italian actress Eleonora Duse (1858–1924) and French actress Gabrielle Réjane (1856–1920).

She was married almost in her childhood to one of the greatest painters of her time: Shaw is referring to Terry's one-year marriage to the British painter George Frederic Watts (1817–1904) when she was 16 and he 46.

Ellen Terry as Camma: Terry's role in Tennyson's play *The Cup* (1881).

311 *the walls of Jericho*: in the Book of Joshua, the Israelites conquer the city of Jericho by making its fortified walls collapse.

Gordon Craig: Edward Gordon Craig (1872–1966) was the son of Ellen Terry and one of the most acclaimed and influential scenic designers of the modern period.

Captain Brassbound's Conversion: Shaw's play *Captain Brassbound's Conversion* was written in 1900 and first performed in that year; Terry appeared in the play in 1906. (Below, Shaw mistakenly places the date as 1905.)

The Man of Destiny . . . Ellen Terry: Shaw's *The Man of Destiny* was written and first premiered in 1897, with Florence West in the role written for Terry. He had written the titular role of Napoleon for Irving, who never played the part.

311 *Velasquez's Surrender at Breda, or in the pictures of Paolo di Uccello*: *The Surrender of Breda* (1634–5) by Diego Velázquez (1599–1660), which hangs at the Museo del Prado in Madrid, Spain; the Florentine Paolo Uccello (1397–1475) painted scenes such as *The Battle of San Romano* (*c.*1435–40).

312 *Sir James Barrie's Alice Sit by the Fire*: *Alice Sit-by-the-Fire* (1905) by J. M. Barrie (1860–1937).

EDGAR ALLAN POE

This article originally ran in *The Nation* on 16 January 1909 and was reprinted in *Pen Portraits and Reviews* in 1932. Edgar Allan Poe (1809–49) was an American poet and short-story writer.

313 *Whitman*: American poet Walt Whitman (1819–12).

Monroeism: Shaw refers to the 'Monroe Doctrine' formulated during the administration of President James Monroe (1758–1831; president 1817–25), which warned European powers to stay out of the affairs of nations in the Western Hemisphere, where the United States sought to exert influence.

Whig: British political party of the seventeenth to mid-nineteenth centuries, which in its nineteenth-century manifestation was associated with centre-left political positions including free trade, abolition, and the expansion of suffrage rights.

314 *the Muses*: the nine ancient Greek goddesses of inspiration.

Mark Twain: pen name of prominent American writer and humorist Samuel Langhorne Clements (1835–1910).

Giotto and Mantegna: Italian painters Giotto di Bondone (1267–1337) and Andrea Mantegna (1431–1506).

Smollett: Scottish novelist Tobias Smollett (1721–71).

Fechter's Hamlet: the 1861 London production of *Hamlet* at the Princess's Theatre starring Anglo-French actor Charles Fechter (1824–79) caused a sensation in London society and was actively championed by Dickens.

315 *when he immortalized General Funston by scalping him*: Twain's satirical essay 'A Defense of General Funston' (1902) criticizes the American general and expansionist Frederick Funston (1865–1917).

Mississippi . . . Pentonville: the Mississippi River is one of the primary waterways of North America, in and around which Twain set many of his works; Chatham is a town in south-east England where Dickens spent his childhood and which features in several of his works, while Pentonville is a section of London north of the city centre that features in Dickens's novel *Oliver Twist* (1838).

A Yankee . . . A Child's History of England: the novel *A Connecticut Yankee in King Arthur's Court* (1889) by Mark Twain and the history book *A Child's History of England* (1851–3) by Charles Dickens.

Admirable Crichton: the learned and capable protagonist of the play *The Admirable Crichton* (1902) by J. M. Barrie.

Mr Rockefeller: American businessman John D. Rockefeller (1839–1937), one of the wealthiest individuals in modern history.

Charlottesville University: University of Virginia, located in Charlottesville, Virginia.

Fiesole: hillside town overlooking Florence, Italy.

Julia Ward Howe's lilies . . . Whittier: the poetry book *Passion-Flowers* (1853) by Julia Ward Howe (1819–1910) and American poet John Greenleaf Whittier (1807–92).

316 *The Raven; The Bells, and Annabel Lee*: Poe's poems 'The Raven' (1845), 'The Bells' (1849), and 'Annabel Lee' (1849).

Toby Dammit: the character Toby Dammit from Poe's short story 'Never Bet the Devil Your Head' (1841).

Ninon de l'Enclos: French author and courtesan (1620–1705) known for her wit and beauty.

tenue: (Fr.) manner or bearing.

This story was sent by Poe to Horne: English poet and newspaper editor Richard Henry Horne (1802–84). As Shaw alludes below, Poe had previously reviewed Horne's poem *Orion* in *Graham's Magazine*, March 1844.

The story of the Lady Ligeia: the short story 'Ligeia' (1838) by Poe.

'Ghost stories . . . telling lies': the comment Shaw attributes to British artist and writer William Morris (1834–96) does not appear to have been previously published. Morris's distrust of the supernatural, however, was well known. One early biography recounts, ' "Such nonsense!" Morris would mutter in impatient disgust, when told a ghost story by a more impressionable friend. "Such awful nonsense!" ' See Arthur Compton-Rickett, *William Morris: A Study in Personality* (New York: EP Dutton and Company, 1913), 81.

His Sigurd: *The Story of Sigurd the Volsung and the Fall of the Niblungs* (1876), an epic poem by William Morris.

Grotesques . . . gorillas: Shaw is referring to Poe's tendency to focus on marginalized figures in his stories. The inclusion of gorillas refers to Poe's story 'Hop-Frog' (1849), in which a court jester with dwarfism takes revenge on the king and his court by setting them on fire while they are dressed as orang-utans for a court masquerade.

RODIN

This article originally ran serially in *The Nation* on 9 November 1912 and 24 November 1917 and was reprinted in *Pen Portraits and Reviews* in 1932. Auguste Rodin (1840–1917) was an influential French sculptor.

318 *Could Rodin be induced to undertake the work?*: Shaw did indeed sit for a bust with Rodin in Paris in 1906. It is now part of the permanent collection at Shaw's Corner, Hertfordshire, part of the UK's National Trust. Rodin made several copies, including others that are now in Dublin and the Rodin Museum in Paris.

Phidias, or Praxiteles: Phidias (480–430 BCE) was the Greek sculptor responsible for the Statue of Zeus at Olympia, one of the Seven Wonders of the Ancient World, and the statue of the goddess Athena inside the Parthenon in Athens; Praxiteles (*c.* fourth century BCE) was another renowned sculptor of the ancient world.

Mr Alvin Langdon Coburn . . . portrait of me: British photographer Alvin Langdon Coburn (1882–1966) famously took a nude photograph of Shaw in the pose of Rodin's *The Thinker* shortly after the two attended the 1906 unveiling of the famous sculpture. The photograph is now in the permanent collection of the Musée Rodin in Paris.

319 *Puvis de Chavannes*: French painter Pierre Puvis de Chavannes (1824–98).

Troubetskoi once made a most fascinating Shavian bust of me: Italian-Russian sculptor Prince Paolo Petrovich Troubetzkoy (1866–1938) created multiple busts and statues of Shaw between 1908 and 1926.

Pompeii: ancient Roman city near present-day Naples buried under volcanic ash after the eruption of Mount Vesuvius in 79 CE.

Neville Lytton's portrait of me as Velasquez's Pope Innocent: Shaw refers to the portrait painted by British artist Neville Lytton (1879–1951) which features Shaw in papal robes and crafted in imitation of Diego Velázquez's (1599–1660) portrait of Pope Innocent X (1574–1655; pope 1644–55).

320 *Sarah Bernhardt*: famed French actress Sarah Bernhardt (1844–1923) was the subject of numerous portraits and busts in her lifetime, including one by Louise Abbema (1853–1927) in 1878 and another by Jean-Léon Gérôme (1824–1904) in 1895. Bernhardt became a sculptor herself later in her career, creating more than fifty works, including a famed high-relief plaque titled *The Death of Ophelia* (1880).

Bernini . . . Houdon . . . Canova . . . Thorwaldsen: Italian Baroque sculptor Gian Lorenzo Bernini (1598–1680), French neoclassical sculptor Jean-Antoine Houdon (1741–1828), Italian sculptor Antonio Canova (1757–1822), and Danish sculptor Bertel Thorvaldsen (1770–1844).

'Main de Dieu': (Fr.) Hand of God.

MR ARNOLD BENNETT THINKS PLAY-WRITING EASIER THAN NOVEL WRITING

This article originally ran in *The Nation* on 11 March 1916 and was reprinted in *Pen Portraits and Reviews* in 1932. *The Author's Craft* was a non-fiction book on the process of writing published by the popular English novelist Arnold Bennett (1867–1931) in 1914.

322 '*I had no time to write a short one*': a famous quip by French philosopher and mathematician Blaise Pascal (1623–62).

Galsworthy: English novelist John Galsworthy (1867–1933).

328 *Fine art of any sort is either easy or impossible*: Shaw echoes a comment often attributed to Victor Hugo (1802–85), including in several references of the 1890s that predate Shaw's usage here and elsewhere. See, for instance, the American minister Joseph Parker's memoir *Might Have Been: Some Life Notes* (1896), 53, or the self-improvement journal *Youth's Companion*, 64 (1891), 585.

329 *I could make a typewriter . . . lately come into use*: Shaw essentially anticipates here the computer algorithm and the idea of creative writing via artificial intelligence.

OSCAR WILDE

This essay (which began as a letter to Frank Harris, see note to p. 330) was first published as 'My Memories of Oscar Wilde' and included as an appendix to the second, 1918 edition of Frank Harris's *Oscar Wilde: His Life and Confessions* (first published in 1916). The version here comes from Shaw's *Pen Portraits and Reviews* in 1932. Oscar Wilde (1854–1900) was a prominent and influential Anglo-Irish poet and playwright and renowned wit, who was famously put on trial in 1895 for crimes of 'gross indecency', i.e. homosexual relationships with men, and sentenced to two years' hard labour from 1895 to 1897. For more on the relationship between Wilde and Shaw, see Stanley Weintraub, 'The Hibernian School: Oscar Wilde and Bernard Shaw', *SHAW* 13 (1993), 25–49.

330 *My Dear Harris*: Shaw's essay began as a letter to his friend and former editor Frank Harris (1855–1931), who wrote an important early biography of Oscar Wilde, *Oscar Wilde: His Life and Confessions* (1916), and who had asked Shaw for his recollections of Wilde. Harris later published a biography of Shaw, titled *Bernard Shaw: An Unauthorized Biography based on First-Hand Information* (1931), but passed away before final revisions on the manuscript were complete; Shaw undertook them himself to benefit Harris's estate, affecting the content of the volume.

Des Grieux, Manon Lescaut's lover: in the novel *Manon Lescaut* (1731) by Antoine François Prévost.

Sir William Wilde: Oscar's father, William (1815–76), was a prominent eye and ear surgeon in Dublin, where both Wilde and Shaw spent their youth.

The Lord-Lieutenant: one of several personal representatives of the British monarch within the United Kingdom, each assigned to a specific lieutenancy area (roughly equivalent to established counties).

Lady Wilde: Jane Wilde (1821–96), avowed Irish nationalist, was the mother of Oscar Wilde and a poet under the pen name 'Speranza' (Hope).

Frederick the Great: Frederick II (1712–86), king of Prussia from 1740 to 1786.

330 *the Travers case*: in 1864, Mary Travers (b. 1835) brought a libel against
Wilde's mother stemming from a letter that she had written to her father
impugning her former friend's behaviour after Travers accused Sir
William, Wilde's father, of sexually assaulting her while she was his
patient. For more, see Matthew Sturgis, *Oscar: A Life* (London: Apollo,
2019), xvii–xxii.

331 *Miss Glynn*: Shaw is most likely referring to Jenny Lind (1820–87),
a Swedish opera singer who rose to great prominence touring England and
the United States and who was rumoured to have no ears on account of
her distinctive hairstyle, which completely covered both sides of her head.

   my sister: Lucinda Frances Shaw (1853–1920), who sang musical comedy
   and light opera. Shaw also had another sister, Elinor Agnes Shaw
   (1855–76).

   Willie: journalist and poet Willie Wilde (1852–99), Oscar's older brother.

   that tragic luncheon of yours at the Café Royal: on 24 March 1895, Harris
   met with Wilde at the Café Royal in London and advised him to drop his
   charges of libel against the Marquess of Queensberry (1844–1900), who
   had accused Wilde of homosexual activity and whose claims later became
   the basis for the gross indecency charges against Wilde.

   Macmurdo's: Arthur Heygate Mackmurdo (1851–1942), influential English
   architect and designer.

   the Century Guild and its paper The Hobby Horse: English group of artists
   founded by Arthur Heygate Mackmurdo and active between 1883 and
   1892. The group published a quarterly magazine called *The Century Guild
   Hobby Horse* (later *The Hobby Horse*) from 1884 to 1894.

   Robert Ross: Robert Baldwin Ross (1869–1918), known as Robbie Ross, an
   influential art critic and intimate of Wilde's who later served as his literary
   executor.

   The Soul of Man Under Socialism: an 1891 essay by Oscar Wilde.

   Nelson's Victory and a set of P. & O. cabins: HMS *Victory*, the flagship of
   Vice-Admiral Horatio Nelson (1758–1805) at the Battle of Trafalgar in
   1805; P & O cabins were cabins of the ships of the Peninsular and Oriental
   Steam Navigation Company, founded in 1837 to carry mail by sea.

332 *Mark Twain's story*: the story comes from the September 1870 installation
of Mark Twain's regular column 'Memoranda' in *The Galaxy*.

   Rosherville Gardens: a public pleasure garden in Kent, England.

333 *turned traitor over The Importance of Being Earnest*: Shaw's negative review
of Wilde's 1895 play ran in the *Saturday Review*, 23 February 1895, 249–
50, and is reprinted in *Our Theatres in the Nineties* (London: Constable,
1932), ii. 41–4.

   Théophile Gautier: French poet and dramatist (1811–72).

   John Gray: English poet and later Catholic priest (1866–1934), a close
   associate of Wilde's.

I and Stewart Headlam would sign it: radical Anglican priest Stewart Headlam (1847–1924), a proponent of Christian socialism and associate of Shaw's in the Fabian Society, provided bail for Wilde during his trials for gross indecency. The petition referenced here is one that Shaw drafted and at one point intended to submit to the Home Secretary for Wilde's early release, though the effort was eventually dropped.

and he did the same to me: in fact, Wilde wrote to Shaw complimenting him on the publication of *The Quintessence of Ibsenism* and included a copy of *Salomé* with his note: '[Y]our little book on Ibsenism and Ibsen is such a delight to me that I constantly take it up, and always find it stimulating and refreshing: England is the land of intellectual fogs but you have done much to clear the air.' See Merlin Holland and Rupert Hart-Davis (eds), *The Complete Letters of Oscar Wilde*, edited by Merlin Holland and Rupert Hart-Davis (New York: Henry Holt, 2000), 554.

334 *the affair of the Chicago anarchists*: the Haymarket Riots in Chicago in May 1886, which resulted after the detonation of a bomb at a labour demonstration in support of striking workers. As noted below, Shaw crafted a petition in 1887 asking that those involved in the riots be granted a reprieve.

Homer: ancient author, possibly apocryphal, of *The Iliad* and *The Odyssey*.

The Bomb: anarchist novel of 1908 by Frank Harris.

Lady Colin Campbell: Gertrude Elizabeth Blood (1857–1911), Anglo-Irish journalist and playwright and a relation, by marriage, of Queen Victoria (1819–1901, r. 1837–1901).

335 *T. P. O'Connor*: Irish nationalist, journalist, and politician Thomas Power O'Connor (1848–1929).

Merrion Square: an exclusive neighbourhood south of Dublin's city centre. Wilde's childhood home was at No. 1 Merrion Square.

against the Catholic: Though he was from a largely secular Protestant background, Wilde's relationship to Catholicism was a complicated one. He expressed an interest in the Catholic Church at various points in his life and formally converted to Catholicism two days before his death in 1900.

Bosie and Robbie: Lord Alfred 'Bosie' Douglas (1870–1945), Wilde's lover, whose father, the Marquess of Queensberry, accused Wilde of homosexuality, instigating Wilde's suit for libel and his later trial for gross indecency. For Robert Baldwin 'Robbie' Ross, see note to p. 331.

a Portora boy, passed on to T.C.D.: the Portora Royal School in Enniskillen, Northern Ireland, and Trinity College Dublin, where Wilde was educated before heading to Magdalen College, Oxford.

336 *Doyle*: director of the National Gallery of Ireland Henry Doyle (1827–93). Upon his death, Shaw bequeathed the National Gallery one-third of the royalties from his estate.

viva voce: (Lat.) literally 'with living voice', meaning by word of mouth.

336 *to my volume of plays beginning with Misalliance*: the 1914 first edition of *Misalliance* published by Constable and Company in London, which also included *The Dark Lady of the Sonnets, Fanny's First Play*, and his 'Treatise on Parents and Children', mentioned here.

337 *Tartufe*: the hypocritical and conniving religious figure who is the title character in *Tartuffe, or The Imposter* (1664) by Molière.

Chartres: town in central France famous for its cathedral.

Dorian Gray: the novel *The Picture of Dorian Gray* (1890) by Oscar Wilde.

Clarke: Sir Edward George Clarke (1841–1931), barrister who represented Wilde in his libel suit against the Marquess of Queensberry.

338 *Mrs Calvert*: British playwright and actress Adelaide Calvert (1836–1921), who appeared in the premiere of *Arms and the Man* at London's Avenue Theatre in 1894.

the Spanish Main: the mainland portions of the Spanish Empire in North and South America from the sixteenth to the nineteenth centuries, a frequent target of pirates.

Blut Bruderschaft: (Ger.) blood brotherhood.

Edmund Gosse: English poet and critic (1849–1928).

ventre à terre: (Fr.) literally 'belly to the ground', meaning at full speed.

the Jolly Roger on board your lugger: the Jolly Roger was a traditional flag of piracy, while a lugger is a small two- or three-masted sailing vessel.

casting a light comedian and first lover for Richard III: casting an actor who typically plays comic or romantic parts for a tragic role such as the lead in Shakespeare's *Richard III* (*c.*1593).

Captain Kidd: William Kidd (1655–1701), Scottish sailor tried and executed for piracy.

339 *Queensberry left that card at the Club!*: Wilde's libel suit against Queensberry was instigated when, in 1895, the Marquess left a card at Wilde's social club reading 'For Oscar Wilde, posing Somdomite', accusing him of homosexuality, which was then illegal.

Congreve: English playwright William Congreve (1670–1729).

A volume of his aphorisms: in fact, Wilde did publish three aphoristic texts in his lifetime: the preface to *The Picture of Dorian Gray* (1890), 'A Few Maxims for the Instruction of the Over-Educated' in the *Saturday Review* (17 November 1894), and 'Phrases and Philosophies for the Use of the Young' in *The Chameleon* (December 1894), an Oxford student magazine.

the Ballad of Reading Gaol and De Profundis: Wilde's last two works, *De Profundis* (written in 1897, published in 1905), a long letter written during his last year in prison, and *The Ballad of Reading Gaol* (1898), a poem on prison life.

340 *his exposure at Clapham Junction*: on 20 November 1895, Wilde was forced to stand for half an hour at the busy Clapham Junction train station during

a prison transfer and endure abuse and ridicule from the public. In 2019, a rainbow plaque was placed at the station to commemorate Wilde's homophobic ordeal.

his repeated sales of the Daventry plot: late in his life, Wilde attempted to raise funds by selling the rights to a scenario for a planned play about an adulterous couple, named the Daventrys, claiming to multiple parties that when he finished the play they would have the right to stage it. Separately, he also convinced Frank Harris to write a version of the play. When Harris premiered *Mr and Mrs Daventry* in 1900, he was forced to make payments to various stakeholders in the play from Wilde's previous arrangements. For more, see Joseph Bristow, 'Oscar Wilde's Unfinished Society Plays: *Mr and Mrs Daventry*, *A Wife's Tragedy*, and *Love is Law*', in Michael Y. Bennett (ed.), *Oscar Wilde's Society Plays* (London: Palgrave-Macmillan, 2015), 51–74.

the hero of my very inadequate preface to The Dark Lady of the Sonnets: in the preface to his 1910 short play *The Dark Lady of the Sonnets*, Shaw intimates that Shakespeare bore a literary resemblance to a deceased friend of his, presumably Wilde. For more, see Reiko Oya, ' "Talk to Him": Wilde, his Friends, and Shakespeare's *Sonnets*', *Critical Survey* 21/3 (2009), 22–40.

RUSKIN'S POLITICS

This text was first delivered as a speech to the Royal Academy in 1919 and subsequently published as a stand-alone volume in 1921.

341 *Mr Charles Rowley . . . Manchester*: Charles Rowley (1839–1933), the socialist councillor of Ancoats, Manchester, known for supporting public exhibitions and concerts in his district.

342 *Ruskin says*: the quotation can be found in 'Letter 78 (June 1877)' in *The Works of John Ruskin*, xxix, ed. E. T. Cook and Alexander Wedderburn (London: George Allen, 1907), 124–45.

Adam Smith: influential Scottish economist and philosopher (1723–90), whose book *The Wealth of Nations* (1776) helped explain and lay the foundations of modern capitalism.

the spoliation of the Church by Henry VIII: Henry VIII broke from the Roman Catholic Church over questions of divorce between 1532 and 1534, founding the Church of England in its stead.

343 *that terrific screed that Marx wrote*: the pamphlet *The Civil War in France* published 13 June 1871.

a proposal . . . some credit: Gaston Alexandre August, Marquis de Galliffet (1830–1909), was a French general who was instrumental in the defeat and dismantling of the Paris Commune in 1871 and who later served briefly as war minister (1899–1900), suffering sharp criticism and quickly retiring.

343 *Marx . . . Malthus*: Shaw is correct to note that Adam Smith, Thomas Malthus, and Karl Marx all adopted and developed a similar theory of economic value based heavily or primarily on costs of labour.

344 *Scuola di San Rocco . . . Tintoretto*: the Scuola Grande di San Rocco is the headquarters of a local fraternity in Venice, Italy, that houses some of the most acclaimed paintings by the Italian painter Tintoretto (1518–94).

346 *Fors Clavigera*: letters by Ruskin addressed generally to British workers and published in 1871. The title is his own derivation, indicating the striking of a nail (*clavus* in Latin) or turning of a key (*clavis* in Latin) with the right combination of force, fortitude, and fortune to effect social change.

the Court of Chancery: specialized court in England and Wales dealing with trusts, land, and guardianship and dissolved in 1875.

Habakkuk and Joel: Hebrew prophets (*c*.600 BCE and 900 BCE respectively) who each have dedicated books in the Bible but are considered 'minor prophets'.

Dr Inge, the Dean of St Paul's: Anglican priest William Inge (1860–1954), a prolific English author and dean of St Paul's Cathedral.

347 *Austin's lectures on jurisprudence*: English legal theorist John Austin (1790–1859), author of *The Province of Jurisprudence Determined* (1832).

348 *the Bolshevist party*: Marxist political party founded in 1912 by Vladimir Lenin (1870–1924) and others, which took power in Russia in 1917, initiating the foundation of the Soviet Union, which Lenin ruled from 1917 to 1924. Though Shaw's ostensible subject is Ruskin, the final portion of his essay is as much an admission of his own growing interest in totalitarian systems. For an extended consideration of this theme in Shaw's later work, see Matthew Yde, *Bernard Shaw and Totalitarianism: Longing for Utopia* (London: Palgrave-Macmillan, 2013).

Gustavus Adolphus: Gustavus Adolphus (1594–1632), king of Sweden (1611–32), led his country's Protestant soldiers to victory in the Thirty Years War.

KEATS

This article originally appeared in the *John Keats Memorial Volume*, ed. G. C. Williamson, issued on 23 February 1921 by the Keats House Committee. The version here comes from Shaw's *Pen Portraits and Reviews*, from 1932. John Keats (1795–1821) was a prominent English Romantic poet.

349 *He did write a very interesting essay on Byron*: British historian and Whig politician Thomas Babington Macaulay (1800–59) wrote an essay on Byron, titled simply 'Lord Byron', published in 1856.

Count D'Orsay: French aristocrat and amateur artist Alfred d'Orsay (1801–52).

Fanny Brawne Society: Keats's fiancée and muse Frances Brawne (1800–65).

A bunch . . . infant's gums: from Keats's poem *Endymion* (1818).

In a most hideous and dreadful manner: from Shakespeare's *The Merry Wives of Windsor* (IV.iv.36).

350 *gallipots*: small pots used by pharmacists to hold medicine. As Shaw alludes to below, Keats served as an apprentice to an apothecary in his youth from 1810 to 1813.

Parnassus: a mountain in Greece believed to be the home of the Muses, the goddesses of inspiration.

Arabian Balsams: trees native to Saudi Arabia renowned for their fragrance and medicinal properties.

'Go back to your gallipots': Shaw is alluding to an infamous negative review by John Wilson Croker (1780–1857) of Keats's *Endymion* (1818) that ran in the *Quarterly Review* in April 1818 and which had a profound effect on Keats.

351 *he would have written Isabella*: the narrative poem *Isabella, or the Pot of Basil* (1818) by John Keats.

With her . . . proud: the quotation is from Keats's *Isabella* (1818).

352 *Hyperions and Endymions*: figures of Greek mythology, a Titan and a shepherd respectively.

'these same ledger-men': another quotation from Keats's *Isabella* (1818).

Erewhon Butler's gospel of Laodicea: Shaw is referring to the satirical novel *Erewhon: or, Over the Range* (1872) by Samuel Butler (1835–1902) and alluding to the church of Laodicea, which is called to repent in the Book of Revelation and which Butler discusses in his novel *The Way of All Flesh* (1903).

How fever'd . . . temperate blood!: here and below Shaw quotes from the first of Keats's 'Two Sonnets on Fame' (1819).

'from silken Samarcand to cedar'd Lebanon': from Keats's poem 'The Eve of St Agnes' (1819).

L'Allegro: pastoral poem (1645) by John Milton.

Wordsworth: prominent English Romantic poet William Wordsworth (1770–1850).

auto da fé: this phrase, from Portuguese, means literally an 'act of faith' but refers to the burning of heretics under the ecclesiastical authority of the Spanish Inquisition (1478–1834).

Cowper . . . Swinburne: William Cowper (1731–1800), author of *The Diverting History of John Gilpin* (1782), English author G. K. Chesterton (1874–1936), Irish poet Thomas Moore (1779–1852), English poet Walter Landor (1775–1864), and English poet Algernon Charles Swinburne (1837–1909).

TOLSTOY: TRAGEDIAN OR COMEDIAN?

This article first appeared in the *London Mercury*, 4/19 (May 1921). The version here comes from Shaw's *Pen Portraits and Reviews* from 1932.

353 *Eschylus-Sophocles-Euripides versus Aristophanes*: Shaw is referring to the major dramatic figures of ancient Greece, the tragedians Aeschylus (*c*.525–*c*.456 BCE), Sophocles (*c*.497–*c*.406 BCE), and Euripides (*c*.480–*c*.406 BCE), and the comic writer Aristophanes (*c*.446–386 BCE).

from the Aristotelian and Voltairean point of view: both the Greek philosopher Aristotle (384–322 BCE), in his *Poetics* (*c*.335 BCE), and the French writer and philosopher Voltaire (1694–1778), in his tragedies written along Aristotelian principles, promoted a strict view of tragic form that did not allow for the inclusion of comic material.

When the censorship . . . in novels: the Licensing Act of 1737 led several prominent playwrights of the period, including Henry Fielding, to turn to novel-writing instead.

Micawbers and Mrs Wilfers: characters in Charles Dickens's novels *David Copperfield* (1850) and *Our Mutual Friend* (1865) respectively.

354 *Victor Hugo . . . Cedric the Saxon*: characters from the plays of French novelist and dramatist Victor Hugo (1802–85), including Don César de Bazan in *Ruy Blas* (1838) and Rustighello and the Duke of Ferrara in *Lucrezia Borgia* (1833), the latter being compared to the characters of Wamba and Cedric the Saxon in *Ivanhoe* (1820) by Sir Walter Scott (1771–1832).

Petruchio to Almaviva: Shaw is drawing a comparison between the character of Petruchio in Shakespeare's *Taming of the Shrew* (*c*.1594) and Count Almaviva in Mozart's *The Marriage of Figaro* (1786).

The element of accident in Tragedy has always been its weak spot: Shaw refers here to prominent English tragedies, as he describes below, but it is worth noting that in remarking on the accidental element of tragedy he is contradicting one of Aristotle's foremost dictums in his *Poetics*, namely that the tragic effect 'is heightened when . . . they follow as cause and effect. The tragic wonder will then be greater than if they happened of themselves or by accident' (pt IX).

355 *The School for Scandal*: comedy (1777) by Richard Brinsley Sheridan (1751–1816).

A man enters a house where someone lies dead: Shaw is referring to Tolstoy's novella *The Death of Ivan Illyich* (1886).

Dickens makes us laugh . . . hits her on the chin: in *David Copperfield* (1850).

Powers of Darkness . . . Heartbreak Houses: Tolstoy's plays *The Dominion of Darkness* (1886) and *The Fruits of Enlightenment* (1891), Harvey Granville-Barker's *The Marry of Ann Leete* (1909), and Shaw's *Heartbreak House* (1920), the last modelled on the work of Chekhov and other Russian writers.

The Living Corpse: Tolstoy's play *The Living Corpse* (written 1900; premiered 1911).

'God damn you . . . dismay': parody of the opening lines of the English Christmas carol 'God Rest You Merry, Gentlemen', which dates to the sixteenth century and was first printed in 1760.

356 *Light Shining Through Darkness*: Tolstoy's play *The Light Shines in Darkness* (1890).

Sevastopol: title of Tolstoy's collection of stories (1855).

Anna Karenina: Tolstoy's novel of 1878.

Mr Aylmer Maude, in his biography of Tolstoy: *The Life of Tolstoy: First Fifty Years* (1908) and *The Life of Tolstoy: Later Years* (1911), by Aylmer Maude (1858–1938).

Henry George's demonstration of the need for land nationalization: American political economist Henry George (1839–97), who had a profound influence on the development of Shaw's socialism, was the author of the popular *Progress and Poverty* (1879), which argues for land nationalization.

a considerable shooting up of the recalcitrant: Shaw's casual acceptance of political execution echoes his positions in the play *The Simpleton of the Unexpected Isles* (1935), where an angel appears to carry out the Day of Judgement as a kind of worldwide version of the Soviet Cheka commissions, charged with determining who will live and who will die on the basis of 'whether you are worth your salt or not'. For more on Shaw's flirtations with totalitarian systems and political violence towards the end of his career, see Matthew Yde, *Bernard Shaw and Totalitarianism: Longing for Utopia* (London: Palgrave-Macmillan, 2013).

BEETHOVEN'S CENTENARY

This article first appeared in the *Radio Times* on 18 March 1927. The version here comes from Shaw's *Pen Portraits and Reviews*, from 1932.

357 *The Maiden's Prayer*: sentimental composition of 1859 by Polish composer Tekla Bądarzewska-Baranowska (*c*.1829–61).

negro corobbery: Shaw is referring to the Corroboree, a form of dance practised by the Australian Aboriginal peoples involving rhythmic singing and movement by specially painted dancers, sometimes numbering in the hundreds.

diable au corps: (Fr.) devil in the flesh.

358 *the Pompadour . . . The Queen kisses me*: incident recounted in biographies of Mozart where the young composer is introduced to Madame de Pompadour (1721–64) in the court of Louis XV (1710–74, r. 1715–74) and recoils when she would not kiss him, as he had previously been kissed by the Empress Maria Theresa of Austria (1717–80, r. 1745–65). See, for instance, *Life of Mozart* by Otto Jahn, trans. Pauline D. Townsend (London: Novello, Ewer, & Co., 1882), 35.

Louis XIV: powerful and influential king of France (1638–1715, r. 1643–1715).

Sansculotte: nickname for lower-class radical republicans of the French Revolution. They were called *sans-culottes* (Fr., 'without knee-breeches') to refer to their poor dress.

358 *The Messiah*: oratorio (1741) by Handel.

Beethoven this anniversary year: as Shaw indicates, the 100th anniversary of Beethoven's death in 1927 involved numerous commemorations around the world, including an entire week set aside for heavy programming of Beethoven's music in the United States from 20 to 26 March. See 'Beethoven Memorial Planned for Radio', *New York Times*, 30 January 1927, 17.

359 *whirling Dervish*: members of a Sufi religious order in Islam who use whirling as a form of worship.

Jupiter Symphony: Mozart's Symphony No. 41 in C major (1788).

360 *The Eroica Symphony*: Beethoven's Symphony No. 3 in E flat major (1805).

'*J'aime la musique qui me berce*': attributed to the French composer Adolphe Adam (1803–56).

jazz, by the way, is the old dance band Beethovenized: it is important to note that Shaw is not making a claim that Beethoven was responsible for jazz or that he proved directly influential to it. Rather, he is observing a musical similarity between aspects of Beethoven's compositions and those that would become dominant in the development of jazz by Black musicians in the United States. Others have also noted certain musical similarities, particularly in Beethoven's use of syncopation. For more, see Michael Broyles, *Beethoven in America* (Bloomington: Indiana University Press, 2011).

MY FIRST TALKIE

This essay first appeared in the Malvern Festival Programme in August 1931. This was an annual theatre festival in Malvern, England, held from 1929 to 1939 and focused especially on Shaw's plays. Several of Shaw's later plays had their English or world premieres at the festival, including *The Apple Cart* (1928), *Geneva* (1938), and *In Good King Charles's Golden Days* (1939).

361 *the little film . . . any other talkie*: Shaw refers to the 1931 film adaptation of his one-act play *How He Lied to Her Husband* (1904), directed by Cecil Arthur Lewis (see note to p. 361). It should be noted that the 'talkies', or films featuring synchronized sound, were still relatively new at this point. Though they were first introduced in 1927 and had almost entirely replaced silent film in the United States by 1929, the transition to sound film continued to unfold across Europe and elsewhere around the world throughout the early to mid-1930s.

my plays . . . silent plays: in fact, Shaw's work had appeared on the silent screen, after a sort. Alexander Korda's 1924 silent film *Everybody's Woman* was loosely based on Shaw's *Pygmalion*. Korda (1893–1956), born in Hungary, would go on to become one of the leading producers in the British film industry after emigrating to London in 1930.

The rejected proposals were renewed: arguably the most successful of these film ventures was the 1938 film adaptation of *Pygmalion*, directed by

Anthony Asquith (1902–68) and Leslie Howard (1893–1943), which won for Shaw an Academy Award for Best Screenplay. Other notable film adaptations in Shaw's lifetime include *Arms and the Man* (1932), *Major Barbara* (1941), *Caesar and Cleopatra* (1945), and, shortly after his death, *Androcles and the Lion* (1952), all of them produced or directed by the enigmatic Hungarian film-maker Gabriel Pascal (1894–1954).

George Arliss: British dramatist and actor (1868–1946), who starred in numerous British and American films during both the silent and talkie periods, from the early 1920s to the late 1930s.

362 *Cecil Lewis*: British writer and broadcaster (1898–1997) who was one of the founding executives of the British Broadcasting Company, precursor to the British Broadcasting Corporation (BBC).

Malvern Picture House: local cinema in Malvern, England, opened in 1923.

Mr Gwenn: English stage and film actor Edmund Gwenn (1877–1959), who played the lead in the film version of Shaw's *How He Lied to Her Husband* and is best known for his performance as Kris Kringle in *Miracle on 34th Street* (1947).

AM I AN EDUCATED PERSON?

This essay was written in August 1947 and first appeared in *Sixteen Self Sketches* in 1949.

363 *the great translations of Gilbert Murray*: Oxford professor Gilbert Murray (1866–1957) was a prominent classicist on whom the character of Adolphous Cusins in *Major Barbara* is based.

A te O cara and Suone la tromba intrepida: arias (the second correctly *Suoni la tromba, e intrepido*) from *I Puritani* by Vincenzo Bellini (1801–35).

Sibelius . . . Debussy . . . Schonberg . . . Cyril Scott: Finnish composer Jean Sibelius (1865–1957); French composer Claude Debussy (1862–1918); Austrian composer Arnold Schoenberg (1874–1951); and English composer Cyril Scott (1879–1970).

'Avoid the latest fashion . . . six months': Wilde seems to have made no such statement. Shaw is most likely thinking of Wilde's statement 'And, after all, what is a fashion? From the artistic point of view, it is usually a form of ugliness so intolerable that we have to alter it every six months', in 'Literary and Other Notes', *The Woman's World*, ed. Oscar Wilde (London: Cassell & Company, 1888), 40.

Virgil and Homer, Horace and Juvenal: the ancient Roman poets Virgil (70–19 BCE), Horace (65–8 BCE), and Juvenal (first–second centuries CE); and ancient Greek poet Homer (dates unknown).

Eton, Harrow, Winchester, or Rugby: exclusive English boarding schools located in the towns that share their names.

364 *Stanford and Parry*: Irish composer Charles Villiers Stanford (1852–1924) and English composer Charles Hubert Hastings Parry (1848–1918).

364 *dégringolade*: (Fr.) literally 'tumbling down', meaning a decline or deterioration.

Menander . . . Hardy: Shaw alludes to a plethora of artists and thinkers. In addition to those noted elsewhere, these are the ancient Greek dramatist Menander (*c.*342–*c.*290 BCE), associated with Athenian New Comedy; French post-impressionist painter Paul Gauguin (1848–1903); English landscape painter Benjamin Williams Leader (1831–1923); British landscape painter Philp Wilson Steer (1860–1942); the Italian neoclassical sculptor Antonio Canova (1757–1822); Irish stage actor Barry Sullivan (1821–91); British theologian John William Colenso (1814–83); American playwright William Inge (1913–73); German biologist August Weismann (here listed as Max Weismann) (1834–1914); British physicist Herbert Dingle (1890–1978); Irish physicist John Tyndall (1820–93); Scottish scientist James Clerk-Maxwell (1831–79); German theoretical physicist Max Planck (1858–1947); British mathematician William Kingdon Clifford (1845–79); and British mathematician G. H. Hardy (1877–1947).

Lucretius . . . Erasmus: Shaw again alludes to numerous writers and thinkers. In addition to those noted elsewhere, these are the Roman poet and philosopher Lucretius (*c.*99–*c.*55 BCE); the Roman philosopher Plotinus (*c.*204–70 CE); the ancient Greek historian Thucydides (*c.*460–*c.*400 BCE); the English historian Edward Gibbon (1737–94); the Roman astrologer Ptolemy (*c.*100–*c.*170 CE); the Polish astronomer Nicolaus Copernicus (1473–1543), who promoted the heliocentric model of the solar system; the apostle and leader of the early Christian Church Saint Peter (1st century CE); Welsh utopian socialist Robert Owen (1771–1858); medieval Czech theologian Jan Hus (1372–1415); Dutch philosopher Erasmus (1466–1536).

366 *'this majestical roof fretted with golden fire'*: from Shakespeare's *Hamlet* (II.ii.293).

THE PLAY OF IDEAS

This essay first appeared in the *New Statesman and Nation* 39, 6 May 1950. Shaw's article was a response to criticism of his playcraft by the playwright Terence Rattigan (1911–77), one of the most popular mid-century English dramatists, whose work drew from the tradition of the well-made play that Shaw opposed. See Terence Rattigan, 'Concerning the Play of Ideas', *New Statesman and Nation*, 4 March 1950. For more on the debate between Shaw and Rattigan, see Susan Ruskino, 'Rattigan Versus Shaw: The "Drama of Ideas" Debate', *SHAW* 2 (1982), 171–8.

367 *Bridie*: Scottish playwright James Bridie (Osborne Henry Mavor, 1888–1951), who responded to Rattigan's initial article on Shaw with his own article in the pages of the *New Statesman and Nation*. Others who contributed articles to the debate were playwright and Labour MP Benn Levy (1900–73), English actor Sir Peter Ustinov (1921–2004), Irish playwright Sean O'Casey (1880–1964), British playwright Edward Henry Willis

(1914–92), and English playwright Christopher Fry (1907–2005). For more, see Ruskino, 'Rattigan Versus Shaw'.

'holds a mirror up to nature': Shaw is alluding to Hamlet's advice to the Players 'to hold, as 'twere, the mirror up to nature' (*Hamlet* III.ii.22–3).

368 *Nuffield*: English industrialist and philanthropist William Morris (1877–1963), 1st Viscount Nuffield, not to be confused with the artist and designer of the same name.

369 *Dickens's Sloppy . . . 'in different voices'*: from Dickens's novel *Our Mutual Friend* (1864).

Ceylon: the nation of Sri Lanka, which adopted its current name in 1972.

Garrick: acclaimed English actor David Garrick (1717–79).

'Ah, fahst EEbrews is very campfitn': 'Oh, 1st Hebrews [Epistle to the Hebrews 1 in the New Testament] is very comforting', rendered in Shaw's version of the cockney dialect of east London.

Henry James: American-born novelist (1843–1916), who lived and worked primarily in England.

I harangued an audience of millionaires in the Metropolitan Opera House in New York: Shaw refers to his speech at New York's Metropolitan Opera House on 11 April 1933, which drew a crowd of 3,500 people.

Usher Hall in Edinburgh: concert hall built in 1914.

370 *religious Mystery and Passion plays of the Middle Ages*: amateur theatricals depicting events from the Bible in general or the events of the Passion, i.e. the final days of the life of Jesus Christ, specifically, which were common across Europe during the Middle Ages.

Pilate's pretorium . . . on the stage: common features of medieval mystery and passion plays, including the residence of Pontius Pilate (r. 26–36 CE), who condemned Jesus Christ to crucifixion; the palace of Herod I (73–4 BCE), king of Judaea and a frequent villain in such plays who orders the massacre of infants in Bethlehem; the entrance to hell known as the 'hell mouth'; the heavenly throne of the Virgin Mary, mother of Jesus; the Mount of Olives in Jerusalem where several key events of the Passion take place; the Hill of Calvary where Jesus was crucified; and the court where the Jewish high priest Caiaphas presided over the trial of Jesus.

Salvini . . . Coquelin: the Italians Sandro Salvini (1890–1955) and Adelaide Ristori (1822–1906), the Frenchman Benoît-Constant Coquelin (1841–1909) were all notable actors.

371 *Holy Willie*: reference to the satirical poem 'Holy Willie's Prayers' (1789) by Robert Burns (1759–96).

this series of essays started by Mr Rattigan: see note to p. 367 regarding the various literary figures who contributed essays in response to Rattigan's initial article on Shaw.

The Oxford World's Classics Website

www.worldsclassics.co.uk

- Browse the full range of Oxford World's Classics online

- Sign up for our monthly e-alert to receive information on new titles

- Read extracts from the Introductions

- Listen to our editors and translators talk about the world's greatest literature with our Oxford World's Classics audio guides

- Join the conversation, follow us on Twitter at OWC_Oxford

- Teachers and lecturers can order inspection copies quickly and simply via our website

www.worldsclassics.co.uk

American Literature

British and Irish Literature

Children's Literature

Classics and Ancient Literature

Colonial Literature

Eastern Literature

European Literature

Gothic Literature

History

Medieval Literature

Oxford English Drama

Philosophy

Poetry

Politics

Religion

The Oxford Shakespeare

A complete list of Oxford World's Classics, including Authors in Context, Oxford English Drama, and the Oxford Shakespeare, is available in the UK from the Marketing Services Department, Oxford University Press, Great Clarendon Street, Oxford OX2 6DP, or visit the website at www.oup.com/uk/worldsclassics.

In the USA, visit www.oup.com/us/owc for a complete title list.

Oxford World's Classics are available from all good bookshops. In case of difficulty, customers in the UK should contact Oxford University Press Bookshop, 116 High Street, Oxford OX1 4BR.

	Late Victorian Gothic Tales
	Literature and Science in the
	Nineteenth Century
JANE AUSTEN	Emma
	Mansfield Park
	Persuasion
	Pride and Prejudice
	Selected Letters
	Sense and Sensibility
MRS BEETON	Book of Household Management
MARY ELIZABETH BRADDON	Lady Audley's Secret
ANNE BRONTË	The Tenant of Wildfell Hall
CHARLOTTE BRONTË	Jane Eyre
	Shirley
	Villette
EMILY BRONTË	Wuthering Heights
ROBERT BROWNING	The Major Works
JOHN CLARE	The Major Works
SAMUEL TAYLOR COLERIDGE	The Major Works
WILKIE COLLINS	The Moonstone
	No Name
	The Woman in White
CHARLES DARWIN	The Origin of Species
THOMAS DE QUINCEY	The Confessions of an English
	Opium-Eater
	On Murder
CHARLES DICKENS	The Adventures of Oliver Twist
	Barnaby Rudge
	Bleak House
	David Copperfield
	Great Expectations
	Nicholas Nickleby

CHARLES DICKENS	**The Old Curiosity Shop**
	Our Mutual Friend
	The Pickwick Papers
GEORGE DU MAURIER	**Trilby**
MARIA EDGEWORTH	**Castle Rackrent**
GEORGE ELIOT	**Daniel Deronda**
	The Lifted Veil and Brother Jacob
	Middlemarch
	The Mill on the Floss
	Silas Marner
EDWARD FITZGERALD	**The Rubáiyát of Omar Khayyám**
ELIZABETH GASKELL	**Cranford**
	The Life of Charlotte Brontë
	Mary Barton
	North and South
	Wives and Daughters
GEORGE GISSING	**New Grub Street**
	The Nether World
	The Odd Women
EDMUND GOSSE	**Father and Son**
THOMAS HARDY	**Far from the Madding Crowd**
	Jude the Obscure
	The Mayor of Casterbridge
	The Return of the Native
	Tess of the d'Urbervilles
	The Woodlanders
JAMES HOGG	**The Private Memoirs and Confessions of a Justified Sinner**
JOHN KEATS	**The Major Works**
	Selected Letters
CHARLES MATURIN	**Melmoth the Wanderer**
HENRY MAYHEW	**London Labour and the London Poor**

A SELECTION OF   **OXFORD WORLD'S CLASSICS**

WILLIAM MORRIS   News from Nowhere
JOHN RUSKIN   Praeterita
                        Selected Writings

WALTER SCOTT   Ivanhoe
                        Rob Roy
                        Waverley

MARY SHELLEY   Frankenstein
                        The Last Man

ROBERT LOUIS STEVENSON Strange Case of Dr Jekyll and Mr Hyde
                            and Other Tales
                        Treasure Island

BRAM STOKER   Dracula

W. M. THACKERAY   Vanity Fair

FRANCES TROLLOPE   Domestic Manners of the Americans

OSCAR WILDE   The Importance of Being Earnest
                            and Other Plays
                        The Major Works
                        The Picture of Dorian Gray

ELLEN WOOD   East Lynne

DOROTHY WORDSWORTH   The Grasmere and Alfoxden Journals

WILLIAM WORDSWORTH   The Major Works

WORDSWORTH and   Lyrical Ballads
COLERIDGE

ANTHONY TROLLOPE

The American Senator
An Autobiography
Barchester Towers
Can You Forgive Her?
Cousin Henry
Doctor Thorne
The Duke's Children
The Eustace Diamonds
Framley Parsonage
He Knew He Was Right
Lady Anna
The Last Chronicle of Barset
Orley Farm
Phineas Finn
Phineas Redux
The Prime Minister
Rachel Ray
The Small House at Allington
The Warden
The Way We Live Now

A SELECTION OF   **OXFORD WORLD'S CLASSICS**

HANS CHRISTIAN ANDERSEN	**Fairy Tales**
J. M. BARRIE	**Peter Pan in Kensington Gardens and Peter and Wendy**
L. FRANK BAUM	**The Wonderful Wizard of Oz**
FRANCES HODGSON BURNETT	**The Secret Garden**
LEWIS CARROLL	**Alice's Adventures in Wonderland and Through the Looking-Glass**
CARLO COLLODI	**The Adventures of Pinocchio**
KENNETH GRAHAME	**The Wind in the Willows**
ANTHONY HOPE	**The Prisoner of Zenda**
THOMAS HUGHES	**Tom Brown's Schooldays**
CHARLES PERRAULT	**The Complete Fairy Tales**
ANNA SEWELL	**Black Beauty**
ROBERT LOUIS STEVENSON	**Kidnapped** **Treasure Island**

A SELECTION OF   OXFORD WORLD'S CLASSICS

ANTON CHEKHOV   About Love and Other Stories
                       Early Stories
                       Five Plays
                       The Princess and Other Stories
                       The Russian Master and Other Stories
                       The Steppe and Other Stories
                       Twelve Plays
                       Ward Number Six and Other Stories

FYODOR DOSTOEVSKY   Crime and Punishment
                       Devils
                       A Gentle Creature and Other Stories
                       The Idiot
                       The Karamazov Brothers
                       Memoirs from the House of the Dead
                       Notes from the Underground and
                            The Gambler

NIKOLAI GOGOL   Dead Souls
                       Plays and Petersburg Tales

MIKHAIL LERMONTOV   A Hero of Our Time

ALEXANDER PUSHKIN   Boris Godunov
                       Eugene Onegin
                       The Queen of Spades and Other Stories

LEO TOLSTOY   Anna Karenina
                       The Kreutzer Sonata and Other Stories
                       The Raid and Other Stories
                       Resurrection
                       War and Peace

IVAN TURGENEV   Fathers and Sons
                       First Love and Other Stories
                       A Month in the Country

	French Decadent Tales
	Six French Poets of the Nineteenth Century
HONORÉ DE BALZAC	Cousin Bette
	Eugénie Grandet
	Père Goriot
	The Wild Ass's Skin
CHARLES BAUDELAIRE	The Flowers of Evil
	The Prose Poems and Fanfarlo
DENIS DIDEROT	Jacques the Fatalist
	The Nun
ALEXANDRE DUMAS (PÈRE)	The Black Tulip
	The Count of Monte Cristo
	Louise de la Vallière
	The Man in the Iron Mask
	La Reine Margot
	The Three Musketeers
	Twenty Years After
	The Vicomte de Bragelonne
ALEXANDRE DUMAS (FILS)	La Dame aux Camélias
GUSTAVE FLAUBERT	Madame Bovary
	A Sentimental Education
	Three Tales
VICTOR HUGO	Notre-Dame de Paris
J.-K. HUYSMANS	Against Nature
PIERRE CHODERLOS DE LACLOS	Les Liaisons dangereuses
MME DE LAFAYETTE	The Princesse de Clèves
GUILLAUME DU LORRIS and JEAN DE MEUN	The Romance of the Rose

A SELECTION OF   **OXFORD WORLD'S CLASSICS**

GUY DE MAUPASSANT	A Day in the Country and Other Stories
	A Life
	Bel-Ami
PROSPER MÉRIMÉE	Carmen and Other Stories
MOLIÈRE	Don Juan and Other Plays
	The Misanthrope, Tartuffe, and Other Plays
BLAISE PASCAL	Pensées and Other Writings
ABBÉ PRÉVOST	Manon Lescaut
JEAN RACINE	Britannicus, Phaedra, and Athaliah
ARTHUR RIMBAUD	Collected Poems
EDMOND ROSTAND	Cyrano de Bergerac
MARQUIS DE SADE	The Crimes of Love
	Justine
	The Misfortunes of Virtue and Other Early Tales
GEORGE SAND	Indiana
MME DE STAËL	Corinne
STENDHAL	The Red and the Black
	The Charterhouse of Parma
PAUL VERLAINE	Selected Poems
JULES VERNE	Around the World in Eighty Days
	Journey to the Centre of the Earth
	Twenty Thousand Leagues under the Seas
VOLTAIRE	Candide and Other Stories
	Letters concerning the English Nation
	A Pocket Philosophical Dictionary

           L'Assommoir
           The Belly of Paris
           La Bête humaine
           The Conquest of Plassans
           The Fortune of the Rougons
           Germinal
           The Kill
           The Ladies' Paradise
           The Masterpiece
           Money
           Nana
           Pot Luck
           Thérèse Raquin

A SELECTION OF   **OXFORD WORLD'S CLASSICS**

THOMAS AQUINAS	Selected Philosophical Writings
FRANCIS BACON	The Major Works
WALTER BAGEHOT	The English Constitution
GEORGE BERKELEY	Principles of Human Knowledge and Three Dialogues
EDMUND BURKE	A Philosophical Enquiry into the Sublime and Beautiful Reflections on the Revolution in France
CONFUCIUS	The Analects
RENÉ DESCARTES	A Discourse on the Method Meditations on First Philosophy
ÉMILE DURKHEIM	The Elementary Forms of Religious Life
FRIEDRICH ENGELS	The Condition of the Working Class in England
JAMES GEORGE FRAZER	The Golden Bough
SIGMUND FREUD	The Interpretation of Dreams
G. W. E. HEGEL	Outlines of the Philosophy of Right
THOMAS HOBBES	Human Nature and De Corpore Politico Leviathan
DAVID HUME	An Enquiry concerning Human Understanding Selected Essays
IMMANUEL KANT	Critique of Judgement
SØREN KIERKEGAARD	Repetition and Philosophical Crumbs
JOHN LOCKE	An Essay concerning Human Understanding

A SELECTION OF   **OXFORD WORLD'S CLASSICS**

NICCOLÒ MACHIAVELLI	**The Prince**
THOMAS MALTHUS	**An Essay on the Principle of Population**
KARL MARX	**Capital** **The Communist Manifesto**
J. S. MILL	**On Liberty and Other Essays** **Principles of Political Economy and Chapters on Socialism**
FRIEDRICH NIETZSCHE	**Beyond Good and Evil** **The Birth of Tragedy** **On the Genealogy of Morals** **Thus Spoke Zarathustra** **Twilight of the Idols**
THOMAS PAINE	**Rights of Man, Common Sense, and Other Political Writings**
JEAN-JACQUES ROUSSEAU	**The Social Contract** **Discourse on the Origin of Inequality**
ARTHUR SCHOPENHAUER	**The Two Fundamental Problems of Ethics**
ADAM SMITH	**An Inquiry into the Nature and Causes of the Wealth of Nations**
MARY WOLLSTONECRAFT	**A Vindication of the Rights of Woman**

A SELECTION OF   **OXFORD WORLD'S CLASSICS**

JOHN BUCHAN

Greenmantle
Huntingtower
The Thirty-Nine Steps

JOSEPH CONRAD

Chance
Heart of Darkness and Other Tales
Lord Jim
Nostromo
An Outcast of the Islands
The Secret Agent
Typhoon and Other Tales
Under Western Eyes

ARTHUR CONAN DOYLE

The Adventures of Sherlock Holmes
The Case-Book of Sherlock Holmes
The Hound of the Baskervilles
The Lost World
The Memoirs of Sherlock Holmes
Sherlock Holmes: Selected Stories
A Study in Scarlet

FORD MADOX FORD

The Good Soldier

JOHN GALSWORTHY

The Forsyte Saga

JEROME K. JEROME

Three Men in a Boat

JAMES JOYCE

A Portrait of the Artist as a Young Man
Dubliners
Occasional, Critical, and Political Writing
Ulysses

RUDYARD KIPLING

Captains Courageous
The Complete Stalky & Co
The Jungle Books
Just So Stories
Kim
The Man Who Would Be King

A SELECTION OF   **OXFORD WORLD'S CLASSICS**

RUDYARD KIPLING   **Plain Tales from the Hills**
                      War Stories and Poems

D. H. LAWRENCE   **The Rainbow**
                      Sons and Lovers
                      Women in Love

WYNDHAM LEWIS   **Tarr**

KATHERINE MANSFIELD   **Selected Stories**

ROBERT FALCON SCOTT   **Journals**

ROBERT TRESSELL   **The Ragged Trousered Philanthropists**

VIRGINIA WOOLF   **Between the Acts**
                      Flush
                      Jacob's Room
                      Mrs Dalloway
                      The Mark on the Wall and Other Short Fiction
                      Night and Day
                      Orlando: A Biography
                      A Room of One's Own and Three Guineas
                      To the Lighthouse
                      The Voyage Out
                      The Waves
                      The Years

W. B. YEATS   **The Major Works**